New Zealand's South Island

Brett Atkinson

Sarah Bennett, Scott Kennedy

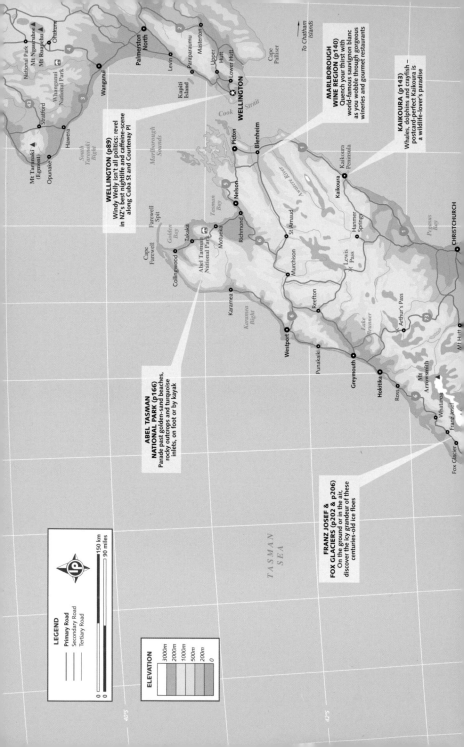

LEGEND

Primary Road
Secondary Road
Tertiary Road

0   150 km
0   90 miles

ELEVATION

3000m
2000m
1000m
500m
200m
0

WELLINGTON (p89)
Windy Welly isn't all politics: revel in NZ's best nightlife and caffeine-scene along Cuba St and Courtenay Pl

MARLBOROUGH WINE REGION (p140)
Quench your thirst with world-famous sauvignon blanc as you wobble through gorgeous wineries and gourmet restaurants

KAIKOURA (p143)
Whales, dolphins and crayfish – postcard-perfect Kaikoura is a wildlife-lover's paradise

ABEL TASMAN NATIONAL PARK (p166)
Parade past golden-sand beaches, rocky outcrops and turquoise inlets, on foot or by kayak

FRANZ JOSEF & FOX GLACIERS (p202 & p206)
On the ground or in the air, discover the icy grandeur of these centuries-old ice floes

National Park
Mt Ngauruhoe
Mt Ruapehu
Ohakune
Whanganui National Park
Stratford
Mt Taranaki (Egmont)
Opunake
Hawera
Wanganui
Palmerston North
Levin
Masterton
Paraparaumu
Kapiti Island
Upper Hutt
Lower Hutt
Cape Palliser
WELLINGTON
Cook Strait
To Chatham Islands

South Taranaki Bight

Marlborough Sounds

Picton
Blenheim
Farewell Spit
Cape Farewell
Golden Bay
Takaka
Collingwood
Tasman Bay
Abel Tasman National Park
Motueka
Richmond
Nelson
St Arnaud
Awatere River
Kaikoura
Kaikoura Peninsula
Hanmer Springs
Lewis Pass
Murchison
Reefton
Karamea
Karamea Bight
Westport
Punakaiki
Greymouth
Hokitika
Ross
Lake Brunner
Arthur's Pass
Mt Hutt
Pegasus Bay
CHRISTCHURCH
Mt Arrowsmith
Whataroa
Franz Josef
Fox Glacier

TASMAN SEA

40°S
42°S

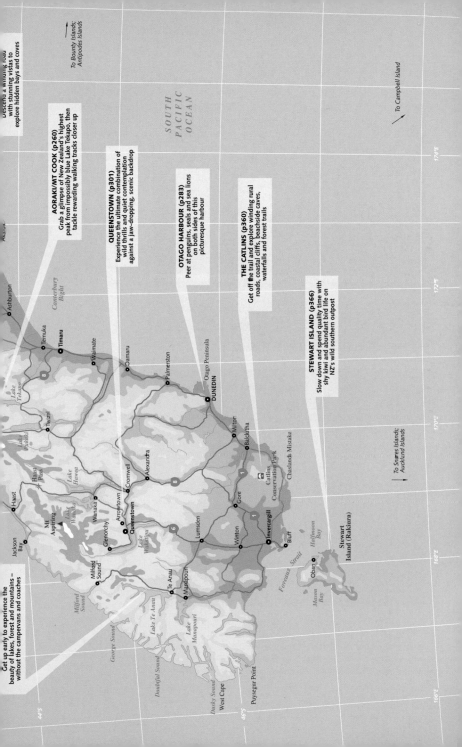

Descend a winding road with stunning vistas to explore hidden bays and coves

To Bounty Islands;
Antipodes Islands

SOUTH
PACIFIC
OCEAN

174°E

AORAKI/MT COOK (p260)
Grab a glimpse of New Zealand's highest peak from impossibly blue Lake Tekapo, then tackle rewarding walking tracks closer up

QUEENSTOWN (p301)
Experience the ultimate combination of wild thrills and quiet contemplation against a jaw-dropping, scenic backdrop

OTAGO HARBOUR (p283)
Peer at penguins, seals and sea lions on both sides of this picturesque harbour

THE CATLINS (p360)
Get off the trail and explore winding rural roads, coastal cliffs, beachside caves, waterfalls and forest trails

STEWART ISLAND (p366)
Slow down and spend quality time with shy kiwi and abundant bird life on NZ's wild southern outpost

To Campbell Island

Get up early to experience the beauty of lakes, forest and mountains – without the campervans and coaches

Ashburton

Canterbury
Bight

Temuka
Timaru
Waimate
Oamaru

Lake
Tekapo

8

Lake
Pukaki

Twizel

Palmerston

Otago Peninsula

DUNEDIN

Hasst
Pass

Lake
Hawea

Cromwell
Alexandra

Lake
Wanaka

Wanaka

8

Milton
Balclutha

Mt
Aspiring

Arrowtown

Gore

Catlins
Conservation Park

Chaslands Mistake

Jackson
Bay

Glenorchy
Queenstown

Lake
Wakatipu

6

Lumsden
Winton
1

1
Invercargill
Bluff

Milford
Sound

Te Anau
Manapouri

Lake Te Anau

George Sound

Lake
Manapouri

Foveaux
Strait

Mason
Bay

Oban

Stewart
Island (Rakiura)

Halfmoon
Bay

To Snares Islands;
Auckland Islands

Doubtful Sound

Dusky Sound

West Cape

Puysegur Point

166°E
168°E
170°E
172°E

44°S
46°S

On the Road

BRETT ATKINSON
Coordinating Author
I didn't spy any whales during my time in the Catlins, but this wind-up cetacean at the Lost Gypsy Gallery (p362) was definitely the next best thing. It's bigger than most of Blair Sommerville's other kinetic sculptures, and loads of fun. Later, I did increase my marine mammal tally, and spied a sea lion chilling on the beach at nearby Nugget Point.

SCOTT KENNEDY You can't come to Queenstown (p301), the Adventure Capital of the World, and not scare yourself – *right*? In a town where all things *fear* and *beer* intermingle, I found myself hanging over the edge of a cliff wondering what the hell I was doing. No turning back, all there was to do was lean back and enjoy the ride.

SARAH BENNETT Tipped off by members of the local mountain-bike club, I needed little encouragement to check out the new Canaan Downs loop track (p170). Despite a few tricky bits and the odd sheep hazard, I managed to stay in the saddle most of the time. I also got a little air – woo hoo!

For full author biographies see p415

SOUTH ISLAND INTENSIVE

There may only be a million people on the South Island (under a quarter of New Zealand's population), but *Te Wai Pounamu* punches well above its weight when it comes to wilderness and outdoor action. Whatever floats your boat – skiing, bungy jumping, sea kayaking, mountain biking, tramping or surfing – there's pretty much nothing you can't do here! And while you're down south you can engage with Maori culture and lore, immerse yourself in the healing heat of a geothermal hot spring, and wonder where the hell everyone else is while you're on an isolated beach, island or lagoon.

JOHN ELK III

Action Stations

Forget your briefcase, your Blackberry, your business suit...the South Island delivers more adrenaline-charged outdoor options than you could squeeze into a year. Bungy yourself silly, take a skydive, try paragliding or rampage along a country trail on a mountain bike.

❶ Skiing Treble Cone
A short hop from Wanaka, Treble Cone (p80) is the biggest and loftiest of the southern lakes snow zones. The slopes here are *steep* (intermediate to advanced skiers will carve them up), plus there are half-pipes and a terrain park for snowboarders.

❷ Queenstown Bungy
Queenstown has built a reputation as *the* place to hurl yourself off a perfectly good bridge/canyon/highwire into empty space. Take the 43m Kawarau Bridge, the 134m Nevis Highwire, or the world's highest rope swing at Shotover Canyon (p305).

❸ Whitewater Rafting on Buller Gorge
Not far from Murchison, Buller Gorge (p179) coughs up Grade III and IV rapids to test your nerve. You can also take a jetboat ride, a riverbank horse trek or a quad-bike tour.

❹ Surfing Dunedin
Dunedin is home to one of NZ's most reliable breaks – suburban St Clair Beach (p272). Expect consistently good left-handers (and chilly water). If it's not pumping, try nearby St Kilda or Blackhead, or Aramoana on Otago Harbour's north shore.

❺ Otago Central Rail Trail
The Otago Central Rail Trail (p286) attracts thousands of trampers and mountain-bikers: a magnificent trail taking you over viaducts, through tunnels, across farmland, and to wee country pubs where people call you 'mate' and ask you where you're from.

❻ Paragliding & Kiteboarding in Nelson
With long sunny days and warm water, Nelson is the place to try paragliding and kiteboarding (p153). Strap yourself into a harness and let the wind blow the travelling cobwebs away.

❼ Milford Sound Scuba Diving
In Fiordland, Milford Sound has amazingly dark tannin-stained waters – dark enough to harbour deep-water coral species within a few scuba-accessible metres of the surface. If you're not an underwater fan, you can snorkel across the surface instead (p348).

❽ Skydive Abel Tasman
If you don't have time to hike or kayak through the bays, inlets and turquoise waters of Abel Tasman National Park, take a 13,000ft tandem skydive with Skydive Abel Tasman (p161) in Motueka – the views are mind-blowing.

❾ Nile River Caves
Go underground near Westport with Norwest Adventures (p180), which runs cave-rafting and abseiling adventures into the Nile River Caves. Glowworms light the way as you take the 30m drop into Te Tahi *tomo* (hole) – unforgettable.

❿ West Coast Glaciers
Take a scenic flight or helicopter ride above the gargantuan fractures of Franz Josef Glacier (p202) and Fox Glacier (p206) on the West Coast. Want to get closer? Try a helihike or guided walk around the stupendous floes.

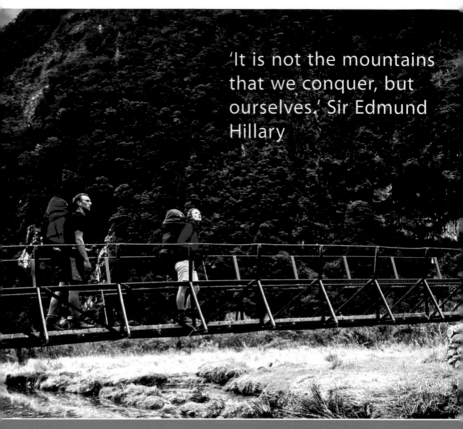

'It is not the mountains that we conquer, but ourselves.' Sir Edmund Hillary

Tramping Down South

Let's not beat around the bush: if you've got two feet and even the slightest fondness for wild country, tramping on New Zealand's South Island is an absolute must. You can tackle six of the nine NZ Great Walks here, or a shorter hike if you're short on time.

① Heaphy Track

The 78km Heaphy Track (p174) remains one of the most popular tramps in NZ, but there's plenty of wild, abandoned coastline and craggy mountain terrain (it's almost entirely within Kahurangi National Park) to ensure you get your dose of solitude.

② Abel Tasman Coast Track

Many travellers kayak around the coast rather than walk the three- to five-day, 51km Abel Tasman Coast Track (p166). Either way, you're in for a treat: sheltered beaches, craggy cliffs, islands and aquamarine inlets await.

③ Milford Track

One of the world's finest walks, the four-day, 54km Milford Track (p345) runs from the top of Lake Te Anau to the heads of Milford Sound. Expect stunningly beautiful rainforest surrounded by towering mountains, sculpted canyons and valley vistas.

④ Banks Peninsula Track

The Banks Peninsula Track (p238) is a two- or four-day self-guided amble across private farmland, skirting around the perforated, jellyfish-like Banks Peninsula coastline south of Christchurch.

⑤ Nelson Lakes National Park

Take a day-trip to the lesser-known Nelson Lakes National Park (p158) for a slew of magical alpine walks, ranging from 15 minutes to seven hours in length. Expect mountain slopes, beech forest, trout-filled glacial lakes and bountiful birdlife.

⑥ Tunnel Beach Walkway

The short-but-sweet Tunnel Beach Walkway (p272) near Dunedin crosses farmland then scales sea cliffs down to Tunnel Beach, where arches, sea stacks and weird rock shapes have been eroded by the Pacific Ocean's hurly-burly.

⑦ Kaikoura Peninsula Walkway

The brilliant, three- to four-hour Kaikoura Peninsula Walkway (p145) kicks of in Kaikoura then trundles around the cliffs to South Bay and back to town. Along the way you'll pass red-billed seagull and mutton bird colonies and stinky fur seals.

⑧ Queen Charlotte Track

Darting through the Marlborough Sounds is the fabulous three- to five-day, 71km Queen Charlotte Track (p132), which can be tackled on foot or by mountain bike. Camp at isolated inlets, traverse forested ridges and dip your toe in dolphin-infested waters.

⑨ Rakiura Track

Stewart Island's 29km, three-day Rakiura Track (p370) is another of NZ's Great Walks. Extensively boardwalked, it's a well-maintained, easy loop starting and ending at Oban, with plenty of birds, beaches and bush along the way.

⑩ Kepler Track

The 60km, four-day Kepler Track (p340) meanders through the amazing Fiordland National Park, part of the Te Wahipounamu South West New Zealand World Heritage Area. The tempo is easy-going, the scenery astounding.

'*Waiho ma te tangata e mihi* – Let someone else acknowledge your virtues.'
Maori proverb

Maoritanga

Opportunities to explore the past and present of Maori culture are booming across Aotearoa. On the South Island, you can take a Maori-run cultural tour, learn how to craft your own bone carving and immerse yourself in centuries-old or contemporary Maori art.

1 Otago Museum
Atmospheric and stylish, the Tangata Whenua Gallery at Otago Museum (p269) in Dunedin was put together in collaboration with the local Ngai Tahu iwi (tribe), and includes wonderfully ancient and worn carvings from around Aotearoa.

2 Maori Tours
If you're swinging through Kaikoura, take an engaging half-day tour with Maori Tours (p146). Visit ancient sites, hear local legends and learn about the indigenous uses of trees and plants.

3 Hokitika Pounamu
The streets of Hokitika (p194) are paved with *pounamu* (greenstone or jade), sought and carved by South Island Maori for generations. There are myriad shops here selling gorgeous carvings – pick up a souvenir from an authentic Maori dealer.

4 Maori & Colonial Museum
Just a short stroll from one of Banks Peninsula's loveliest beaches, the Maori & Colonial Museum (p238) at Okains Bay presents one of the country's best private collections of indigenous Maori art

5 Te Hikoi Southern Journey
Te Hikoi Southern Journey (p353) is a modern museum and gallery in the small town of Riverton, celebrating the journey that all people – Maori, Pakeha and others – have made in reaching this farthest point of Maui's canoe.

6 Maori Rock Art
The history of Maori civilisation in the South Island comes to life at various natural alfresco galleries around Timaru (p251) in South Canterbury, and Oamaru (p291) in North Otago.

7 Bone Carving
Book yourself in for an engrossing session of traditional Maori bone carving with Bonz 'N' Stonz (p196) in Hokitika. See also Nelson Bonecarving (p154) in Nelson and the Bone Dude (p222) in Christchurch.

8 Myths & Legends Eco-tours
Head out onto the photogenic Marlborough Sounds from Picton with Myths & Legends Eco-tours (p130), run by a local Maori family. Expect plenty of environmental insights and local lore.

9 Ulva's Guided Walks
Descended from the first Maori inhabitants of Stewart Island, Ulva Goodwillie runs walking tours (p371) crammed with the history and cultural background of local Maori. Most popular is her tour of bird-rich Ulva Island.

10 Arts Centre, Christchurch
Explore the hallowed Gothic architecture at Christchurch's Arts Centre (p219), and discover contemporary Maori art and design at the Visually Maori and Te Toi Mana galleries.

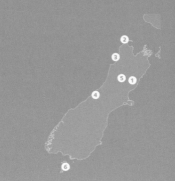

1 & 2 DAVID WALL

Relax & Unwind

Any old thrill-seeker can dive out of a plane or rubber-band off a bridge, but a true holiday connoisseur might prefer to slip into a steaming geothermal spring, meditate on an empty beach, or track down a remote natural wonder and *really* relax!

① Hanmer Springs

Let it all hang out at Hanmer Springs (p242), a subalpine resort where you can dial up the indulgence with a 'Because I'm worth it' session at the newly completed luxury spa complex.

② Wharariki Beach

Hike out to tumultuous, isolated Wharariki Beach (p174) on the West Coast's northern end, with cresting dunes, rocky crags and a grunting seal colony. You get the feeling nothing much has changed here in a looong time...

③ Gentle Annie Beach

Broken surf surges up the beach and the sea wind whips through the palms at Gentle Annie Beach (p183), north of Westport – the perfect place to forget about whatever's been bugging you.

④ Okarito Lagoon

Teeming with birdlife, Okarito Lagoon (p200) on the West Coast is a huge pristine wetland – a bio-rich environment of tidal flats encircled by rainforest. Watch your reflection ripple as you canoe slowly across the surface.

⑤ Maruia Springs

A resort complex in North Canterbury, Maruia Springs (p245) features a traditional sex-segregated Japanese bathhouse and outdoor thermal rock pools. Book in for a massage.

⑥ Stewart Island

Veer off the trampled tourist path with a detour to Stewart Island (p366), across Foveaux Strait from Invercargill. It's the perfect place to chill out: ramble along a few trails, admire the aurora australis, take a cold-water swim or spot a kiwi.

Contents

Regional Map Contents

Wellington Region
p89

Marlborough
& Nelson
p124

The West Coast
p177

Christchurch &
Canterbury
p212

Queenstown
& Wanaka
p301

Dunedin
& Otago
p267

Fiordland &
Southland
p337

Stewart Island
p367

Destination South Island

Locked in an age-old struggle with the North Island for travellers' hearts and minds, New Zealand's South Island wins hands down when it comes to the great outdoors. Remote, rainy and thinly populated – maybe so – but *Te Wai Pounamu* (The Waters of Greenstone – the Maori name for the South Island) delivers more than its fair share of eye-popping panoramas and heart-pumping outdoor activities, not to mention festivals, Maori culture and stellar food and wine. Even a concise week-long hop across the Tasman will provide plenty of opportunity to explore NZ's rugged and photogenic southern jewel.

Kick things off in Christchurch – a cultured, east-coast hub with pumping cafes, good shopping and nightlife, and around 350,000 Kiwis. Further south, Dunedin is smaller but has almost as many coffeeshops and bars as University of Otago students. Equal parts Edinburgh and Seattle, 'Dunners' has no problem at all with the 'second city' tag and revels in its gourmet status. Under the eternal sunshine of the island's north coast, Nelson is a hip, hippie city brimming with bookshops, classy eateries and gorgeous Victorian architecture. Way down south, Queenstown is a hotspot for skiing, white-water rafting, skydiving and bungy jumping. If accelerating your heart rate and overdosing on adrenalin doesn't appeal, slow right down in sleepy, scenic Glenorchy, or the heritage streets of Arrowtown.

But what many travellers come to the South Island for lies beyond the city limits. With less than a quarter of NZ's population spread over 56% of its land mass, this is a place where the phrase 'Get lost!' regularly assumes literal connotations. Truly wild places are rare in today's world, but the South Island delivers them in droves: fiords, sounds, glaciers, cloud-topping mountain ranges, remote islands, raggedy peninsulas and wide river plains.

And when you come in from the wild, you'll find the table is laid: Kaikoura crayfish, Central Otago pinot noir, Motueka kiwifruit and the gloriously hoppy microbrews of Marlborough. Add a side order of artisan cheeses and gourmet chocolates, and any preconceptions of the South Island as a culinary desert are deliciously dismissed.

The country is slowly shrugging off the global economic gloom that had pushed the economy into recession and sent unemployment soaring. It's a challenge faced by the National Party, NZ's first centre-right government for several years. It was elected in late 2008 following nine years under Helen Clark's centre-left Labour Party; Clark went on to accept the third-highest job at the United Nations as Head of the UN Development Program. At the time of writing, prime minister John Keys was surfing a wave of popularity due in large part to his image as a thoroughly likeable Kiwi bloke. He's the guy pictured, beer in hand, hosting a barbecue for NZ's future king, Prince William. He's the guy doing an awkward dance with a couple of drag queens at a gay and lesbian festival in Auckland. He's the goofy guy slipping down the stairs and breaking his arm at a Chinese New Year celebration. Sure, he's a self-made millionaire after years working as a currency trader in London and New York, but his easy-going and likeable manner continues to strike a chord with Kiwis, especially after Helen Clark's sometimes severe and intellectual demeanour.

FAST FACTS

Population: NZ 4.4 million; South Island 1 million

Area: NZ 268,680 sq km; South Island 151,215 sq km

NZ GDP growth: -1% (2009)

NZ inflation: 2%

NZ unemployment: 6.5%

NZ life expectancy: men 78, women 82, tuatara (native lizards) 100+, kauri trees 2000+

Number of international visitors to NZ: 2.4 million in 2009

Number of South Island glaciers over 100m long: 3155

Number of South Island microbreweries: 26, give or take a couple

Height of Aoraki/Mt Cook: 3754m (12,316ft)

Interestingly, both the Maori and Greens parties increased their House of Representatives holdings in the 2008 election, gaining one and three seats respectively. Green issues are often front-page news across NZ, and when they're not talking politics, South Islanders love to talk environment. Lean into a local conversation and you'll likely hear about the Department of Conservation (DOC) using 1080 poison to control possums, rats and stoats on the West Coast, or the proposal by John Key's government to allow mining in areas of the country currently under DOC protection. Sometimes it's possible to sit in a South Island pub and hear opposing views in each ear. Tourism operators will be against any increase in mining, but for other locals the promise of steady employment is a compelling argument.

Also causing consternation is *Didymosphenia geminata*, aka didymo or 'rock snot'. First detected in 2004 in Southland's Waiau River (the River Anduin in the *Lord of the Rings* movies), didymo is a fast-spreading algae that is ravaging freshwater ecosystems. The entire South Island has been branded a 'Controlled Area' – if you knowingly spread rock snot you'll get five years in the clink or a NZ$100,000 hole in your wallet. Ask at local visitor information centres – normally dubbed 'i-SITES' – about how you can do your bit to stop the spread, especially if you're travelling by campervan and staying in remote campsites.

Tourists' love affair for the wilderness of the South Island is also impacting in other ways. Campers' shampoo occasionally bubbles away in Catlins' creeks, the skies above Franz Josef Glacier drone with aeroplanes and some locals simply avoid entire chunks of the South Island because of the tourist hordes. Feeling the pinch, the tourism industry is embracing all things 'eco', while the DOC has implemented a booking system for its nine Great Walks (six of which are on the South Island) to combat overcrowding and environmental damage. Organic farmers markets and cafes proliferate, while the 100-mile diet and 'locavore' concepts are gaining converts.

Beyond politics and the environment, most Kiwis are also interested in the rugby. In September and October 2011, NZ will host the Rugby World Cup and chances are, whether you travel before, during or after the tournament, you'll be thoroughly sick of hearing about rugby by the end of your stay.

Rugby plays a special part in the nation's consciousness, partly because it was one of the first things in which NZ truly excelled. The All Blacks are the most successful rugby team in history (with a 74% winning record) but they've only snagged the Cup once. After yet another dazzling failure in France in 2007, the All Blacks are determined to redeem themselves on home soil. With NZ's next general election scheduled for November 2011, the tournament finale at Auckland's Eden Park on October 23 promises to be more than just a rugby match. More than one political pundit has opined – and not entirely in jest – that an All Blacks victory or defeat could influence the decision-making of voters on election day. Watch this space.

Green issues are often front-page news across NZ, and when they're not talking politics, South Islanders love to talk environment.

Getting Started

By world standards, New Zealand is an easy, accessible place to visit. Amiable locals, a moderate climate, good personal security, brilliant roads, well-organised activities and the fantastic i-SITE visitor information centre network (see p390) make travelling here a breeze! There's also a network of around 30 Department of Conservation (DOC) visitor centres around NZ – a handy resource for planning activities in parks, and for natural and cultural features. There are accommodation and eating options for all budgets, from a felafel and a dorm bunk to a crayfish dinner and a spa suite.

If you're scuttling between cities pursuing urban virtues, you won't need to do much forward planning, but if you're tramping into the wilderness or devising a cycling epic, do some research on equipment, accommodation, track and hut passes, and weather, and book what you need to well in advance.

There's a multitude of things to see and do here; consider your priorities and allow enough time to achieve them. Don't forget to factor some time into your itinerary for those random, serendipitous moments to happen – they can really make your trip.

See Climate Charts (p380) for more information.

WHEN TO GO

The warmer high-season months (November to April) are ripe for outdoor exploration. Summer (December to February) is also when Kiwis crank up the food and wine festivals, concerts and sports events. December in the far north can be rainy, however. If you're a snow bunny, visit when the powder is thickest – June to August is skiing high season. Remember, though, that in winter, warm-weather beach towns might be half asleep.

If you want a *real* holiday, staying and eating in your venues of choice, avoid school holidays (particularly late December to early February) and public holidays (p384). Most places are packed to the gills with campervans, tourists, highly strung parents and inexhaustible children in the post-Christmas weeks. In the less touristed 'shoulder' period from late February to April, the weather is at its best (less chance of rain), the kids are back at school, and the ocean is still warm(ish) – a much better time to travel.

NZ is smack-bang in the middle of the Roaring Forties; these prevailing west-to-east winds buffet the country year-round, ranging from gentle breezes to tempestuous gales. On both islands it's drier in the east than in the west, where mountain ranges snare moisture-laden winds from the Tasman Sea. It's usually a few degrees cooler on the South Island than the

---

DON'T LEAVE HOME WITHOUT...

- Double-checking the visa situation (see p391)
- A travel-insurance policy covering you for high-risk activities (see p384)
- Insect repellent to keep the sandflies off your ass (see p382)
- The ability to get excited over a game of rugby (p41)
- Your driver's licence – the best way to see NZ's nooks and crannies is at your own speed (p400)
- A bottomless appetite for Kiwi food and wine (p57)
- A mobile phone (p389) for booking restaurants and accommodation on the hop
- An open ear and a notepad to jot down the NZ bands you're going to download when you get home (see www.amplifier.co.nz)

North Island. Wherever you are, remember that NZ has a maritime climate – the weather changes rapidly. Anyone tramping at any time of year needs to be well prepared for all weather conditions. The **New Zealand Mountain Safety Council** (☎ 04-385 7162; www.mountainsafety.org.nz) has the information you need – available from DOC visitor centres nationwide.

COSTS & MONEY

In recent years the NZ dollar has gained ground against international currencies, and burgeoning tourism has seen prices rise with demand. However, if you're visiting from Europe or North America, it's still a fairly economical destination, unless you're jumping out of a plane or jetboating every day. Activities like these generally top expense lists – think carefully about what you'll spend your money on. Action-addicts should consider cheaper accommodation to help finance their exertions, while sedentary types who'd rather dangle a fork in some pasta than themselves at the end of a bungy should curtail the activities.

Gastronomes will find food to be surprisingly pricey – cooked breakfasts at snazzy cafes average around $16, while main courses at top-end restaurants cost $30 and beyond. Food in remote areas also costs more, without necessarily being of better quality.

If you do some sightseeing, eat out once or twice a day and stay in cheap motels or B&Bs, budget on at least $150 per day (per person, travelling as a pair), not including car hire or activities. Packing kids into your suitcases obviously means greater expense, but museums, cinemas, and tour and activity organisers usually offer discounts for young'uns, and there are plenty of open-air attractions available for free! At the low-cost end, if you camp or stay in hostels, cook your own meals, repress the urge to drink beer, tackle attractions independently and travel on a bus pass, you could probably eke out an existence on $80 per day. But if you want to enjoy the occasional restaurant meal and glass of wine, then $100 per day is more realistic.

TRAVELLING RESPONSIBLY

Since our inception in 1973, Lonely Planet has encouraged readers to tread lightly, travel responsibly and enjoy the magic independent travel affords. International travel is growing at a jaw-dropping rate, and we still firmly believe in the benefits it can bring – but, as always, we encourage you to consider the impact your visit will have on both the global environment and the local economies, cultures and ecosystems.

It's not hard to make your NZ trip ecosavvy. For starters, check out our GreenDex (p434), which lists ecofriendly operators. Volunteer some of your time to a local environmental program. Consider carbon-offsetting your flights to/from NZ. Taking a tour? Ask about the company's environmental

HOW MUCH?

Cup of decent coffee $4

Movie ticket $14

Dorm bed $25-35

Motel room $100-160

Magnificent scenery $0

See also the Lonely Planet Index, inside front cover

DIY NZ

At Lonely Planet we love travel (no kidding...), and we reckon part of the adventure is to fly by the seat of your pants. We're dedicated to bringing you comprehensive in-depth destination coverage, but we also encourage you to ditch your guidebook. Really! Go AWOL for a day or a week and explore NZ beyond the pages of a book.

Low population density = empty spaces – it's easy to get off the beaten track. Buy a detailed road map, pick a little town down a little road and go for it – you can't really lose when the scenery is so great. Scan the bulletin boards at local cafes for performances that night; swap a yarn or two with locals at a country pub. Kiwis are famously friendly – ask them about their favourite places to eat, hang out or blow off steam.

After your trip, drop us a line and tell us what you discovered: www.lonelyplanet.com/contact.

TOP 10

MANDATORY MOVIES

Spending an evening or three watching classic NZ movies makes a great intro to the country's much-publicised scenery, and will help you get under the national skin. Captured on celluloid, wry humour and an often-bleak mysticism await. See p44 for reviews of these and other locally produced films.

1 *Once Were Warriors* (1994) Director: Lee Tamahori

2 *The Lord of the Rings* trilogy (2001–03) Director: Peter Jackson

3 *Whale Rider* (2002) Director: Niki Caro

4 *An Angel at My Table* (1990) Director: Jane Campion

5 *The Piano* (1993) Director: Jane Campion

6 *In My Father's Den* (2004) Director: Brad McGann

7 *Kaikohe Demolition* (2004) Director: Florian Harbicht

8 *Avatar* (2009) Director: James Cameron

9 *Out of the Blue* (2006) Director: Robert Sarkies

10 *Sione's Wedding* (2006) Director: Chris Graham

BRILLIANT BOOKS

Escapist plots, multilayered fiction, reinvented realities and character-driven social commentary: Kiwi literature presents an opportunity to learn much about the country, drawing on NZ's unsettled history, burgeoning cultural awareness and the physical power of the landscape. See p44 for more on NZ literature.

1 *The Bone People* (1988) Keri Hulme

2 *Mister Pip* (2007) Lloyd Jones

3 *The Carpathians* (1988) Janet Frame

4 *Potiki* (1986) Patricia Grace

5 *Bulibasha: King of the Gypsies* (1994) Witi Ihimaera

6 *Live Bodies* (1998) Maurice Gee

7 *The 10pm Question* (2009) Kate de Goldi

8 *The Vintner's Luck* (2000) Elizabeth Knox

9 *Opportunity* (2007) Charlotte Grimshaw

10 *Hibiscus Coast* (2005) Paula Morris

FESTIVAL FRENZY

Kiwis love to party, and many travellers plan their journeys around food, wine and arts fiestas. Following are some of our favourite excuses to get festive. For events in the South Island and further suggestions, see the Directory (p383) and the Festivals & Events sections in destination chapters.

1 **World Buskers Festival** (www.worldbuskers festival.com) Christchurch, January (p225)

2 **Rippon Festival** (www.ripponfestival.com) Wanaka, February (p330)

3 **Marlborough Wine Festival** (www.wine -marlborough-festival.co.nz) February (p138)

4 **Fringe NZ** (www.fringe.org.nz) Wellington, February/March (p100)

5 **Wildfoods Festival** (www.wildfoods.co.nz) Hokitika, March (p196)

6 **New Zealand Gold Guitar Awards** (www. goldguitars.co.nz) Gore, June (p360)

7 **Queenstown Winter Festival** (www.winter festival.co.nz) Queenstown, June/July (p312)

8 **Nelson Arts Festival** (www.nelsonartsfestival. co.nz) Nelson, October (p154)

9 **Seafest** (www.seafest.co.nz) Kaikoura, October (p146)

10 **NZ Cup & Show Week** (www.nzcupandshow. co.nz) Christchurch, November (p225)

policies: are they NZ-owned? Sensitive to indigenous culture? How do they dispose of rubbish? Support NZ businesses rather than multinational chains. Eat at local restaurants and buy from farmers markets that sell locally sourced produce. Instead of car hire, consider car-pooling to travel from town to town; check hostel noticeboards to find a ride. Stay at hotels and hostels that actively engage in recycling and waste reduction. If you're tramping into the forests or along the coast, carry out your rubbish, travel in small groups, camp on durable surfaces, and don't wash in or near water sources.

For more tips online:

Department of Conservation (www.doc.govt.nz/getting-involved) Conservation events and programs that visitors can engage with.

Leave No Trace (www.lnt.org) Low-impact camping and tramping tips.

Lonely Planet (www.lonelyplanet.com/responsibletravel) Tips on sustainable travel.

Organic Explorer (www.organicexplorer.co.nz) Comprehensive guide to ecofriendly places to eat, stay and explore throughout NZ.

TRAVEL LITERATURE

Given NZ's starring role on the world tourism stage, the current bloom in dedicated NZ travel literature isn't surprising.

Bob Moore, a Wellington-based Englishman, traversed every kilometre of State Hwy 1 (NZ's national drag) then wrote *The 1 Thing: A Small Epic Journey Down New Zealand's Mother Road* (2006). Lyttelton-based Joe Bennett, another Englishman-in-NZ, wrote *A Land of Two Halves* (2004), a tale of hitchhiking around the country.

If you're into cycling, pick up *Long Cloud Ride* by Josie Dew (2007). Dew – a roaming Brit cyclist – chronicles her nine-month, 10,000km NZ journey. Through wind and rain, she gets close to the Kiwi psyche.

Liberal-minded travellers who don't mind the odd tree-hug will love *Slipping into Paradise: Why I Live in New Zealand* by Jeffrey Moussaieff Masson (2004), a gushing sonnet to NZ from a relative newcomer to the country.

How to Watch a Game of Rugby by Spiro Zavos (2004) is a brilliant insight into the national preoccupation by a respected sports journalist, and will ensure you don't ask stupid questions when you're watching the All Blacks at the pub. In the same series, astronomer Richard Hall helps you find the Southern Cross in *How to Gaze at the Southern Stars* (2005).

They're not technically travel lit, but fans of Kiwi films will enjoy Hamish McDouall's *100 Essential New Zealand Films* (2009), and history buffs will be engrossed by the *Penguin History of New Zealand* (2003) by Michael King.

INTERNET RESOURCES

100% Pure New Zealand (www.newzealand.com) NZ's official tourism site, with comprehensive visitor info.

Department of Conservation (www.doc.govt.nz) Indispensable DOC parks, recreation and conservation info across NZ.

Destination New Zealand (www.destination-nz.com) Excellent website listings.

DineOut (www.dineout.co.nz) Restaurant reviews and info across the nation.

Living Landscapes (www.livinglandscapes.co.nz) Maori tourism operators across NZ.

Lonely Planet (www.lonelyplanet.com) Get started with NZ summaries and travellers trading info on the Thorn Tree.

Muzic.net (www.muzic.net.nz) Gigs, reviews, bios, charts — Wellington rock to Dunedin dub.

New Zealand Tourism Online (www.tourism.net.nz) Commercial site with 10,000-plus listings and plenty of useful info.

Stuff (www.stuff.co.nz, www.stuff.co.nz/blogs) NZ news (sourced from Fairfax New Zealand publications) and an array of blogs.

Te Ara (www.teara.govt.nz) An online encyclopaedia of NZ.

Itineraries
SHORT BREAK

CHRISTCHURCH EXPLORER

Four to Seven Days /
Christchurch to Christchurch

Winging in to Christchurch with a week up your sleeve, there'll be plenty to keep you entertained, both wild and urbane.

Hit the city running with a kick-arse coffee on **High St** (p229), then assess the lay of the land on the city's juddery **tramway** (p219). Jump off at the **Arts Centre** (p219) and have a sticky-beak around the local galleries. Other 'ChCh' essentials include the **Canterbury Museum** (p219), the **Christchurch Art Gallery** (p219), punting on the Avon River in the **Botanic Gardens** (p218) and shopping on **High St** (p232). Don't miss an evening session in the kooky bars in **Lyttelton** (p234) and restaurants in **Sumner** (p228).

Beyond the city, spend a few nights on the rambling road: drive out to Francophile **Akaroa** (p236) on the Banks Peninsula, or head north for some whale-watching and crayfishing in **Kaikoura** (p143). Wander west to **Lake Tekapo** (p255) and the snowy heights of **Aoraki/Mt Cook** (p260), or south to check out the zany boulders at **Moeraki** (p298); don't miss dinner at **Fleur's Place** (p298), before heading back to Christchurch.

Christchurch has that unusual mix of urban civility and wild abandon just beyond the doorstep. Spend a few days pinballing between downtown bars, shops, museums and galleries, then hit the road (Jack) and chase down some mountains, whales, lakes and forests on this 650–750km trail.

TRAVEL FURTHER

CLASSIC SOUTH ISLAND   10 to 14 Days / Picton to Christchurch

You'll have to move fast to experience the best of the south in two weeks! Kick things off in picturesque port-town **Picton** (p125), then disappear into the **Marlborough Sounds** (p130) for a day. Sip yourself silly in the **Marlborough Wine Region** (p140) around Blenheim, then truck west for some paragliding, kiteboarding and hang gliding (and good coffee!) in hippie-city **Nelson** (p150). Sea kayaking through **Abel Tasman National Park** (p166) is an unforgettable experience.

Backtrack through Blenheim and jump on a boat/plane/helicopter for a close encounter with a massive marine mammal in **Kaikoura** (p143). Further south, manicured **Christchurch** (p213) awaits – shop, drink, eat and soak up the arts. Further south the coast road rolls into Timaru, from where SH8 veers inland to cloud-piercing **Aoraki/Mt Cook** (p260). Back on the coast, the wildlife-rich **Otago Peninsula** (p279) juts abstractly away from the Victorian facades of student-filled **Dunedin** (p268). Try to catch some live music while you're in town!

Head inland to bungy-obsessed **Queenstown** (p301), then mix and match highways to Te Anau for the side road to **Milford Sound** (p347). Backtrack to Haast Pass, from where you'll wind down to **Jackson Bay** (p210) on the rain-soaked West Coast. Further north come face-to-face with the **Fox Glacier** (p206) and **Franz Josef Glacier** (p202), then check out some *pounamu* (jade or greenstone) in **Hokitika** (p194). Wet your whistle at Greymouth's **Monteith's Brewing Co** (p190), then get your camera ready for the **Punakaiki rocks** (p186). Heading east on SH7, cross Lewis Pass and head back to cathedral-hearted **Christchurch** (p213).

On good roads with little traffic (well, mostly...), this 3500km South Island lap – taking in the classic sights, cities and scenery – is a glorious drive. Prepare yourself for urban virtues, magnificent mountains and the world's best sauvignon blanc. And if you've never seen a glacier before, now's your chance!

ROADS LESS TRAVELLED   Two Weeks / Christchurch to Christchurch

Journey to the ends of the South Island and experience places far removed from civilisation's clash and humdrum.

It doesn't take long to clear the **Christchurch** (p213) suburbs in any direction: head north along the coast and you'll soon leave the traffic behind. **Kaikoura** (p143) is pretty touristy these days, but it's a low-key place to chill for a day or two. Continue north to Blenheim then detour inland on SH65 to alpine **Nelson Lakes National Park** (p158) – a little slice of Fiordland sans the crowds.

From Picton, it's easy to lose your way for a day in the watery embrace of the **Marlborough Sounds** (p130). Continue west past artsy Nelson to eco-friendly, chilled-out **Golden Bay** (p169) and gargantuan **Kahurangi National Park** (p174). End-of-the-line **Farewell Spit** (p173) is perfectly desolate.

Travel southwest on SH6 to Westport, from where a memorable road trundles north up to the caverns of **Oparara Basin** (p183). Southbound on SH6, divert inland on SH73 to the extremities of **Arthur's Pass National Park** (p246), then continue south to the mirror-surfaced **Okarito Lagoon** (p200), bypassing Queenstown for a voyage on isolated **Doubtful Sound** (p350).

Cross over to Invercargill from where you can ferry yourself out to southerly **Stewart Island** (p366), then kick back in the overgrown **Catlins** (p360) for a couple of days.

Heading north on SH8 through Central Otago, you'll pass through goldrush-era towns en route to mountain-biking **Alexandra** (p287) and hang-glider-hung **Omarama** (p296). Trek back to the east coast via the **Waitaki Valley** (p296) on SH83, then hop south to mellow, underrated **Oamaru** (p297) before a big-city reality check back in **Christchurch** (p213).

If there's anywhere in NZ you can still find paths less travelled, the South Island is it! You'll be flat out covering 3200 far-flung kilometres over two weeks, but if your timing's good, you may feel like you've carved off a slice of heaven all for yourself.

TAILORED TRIPS

PLANES, TRAINS & AUTOMOBILES

With eye-popping panoramas out every South Island window, getting from A to B is half the fun.

For a bird's-eye view of the south, take a glider trip over **Omarama** (p296), a scenic flight above **Milford Sound** (p311), a chopper ride over **Aoraki/Mt Cook** (p263) or the **West Coast glaciers** (p204 & p206), or a knee-trembling hang-glide above **Nelson** (p153) or **Queenstown** (p308).

Train-spotting romantics should book a seat on the **Taieri Gorge Railway** (p279) or the **TranzAlpine** (p193) route from Christchurch to Greymouth over Arthur's Pass. Spend a few days in Greymouth, or chug back over the pass an hour later.

If you're arriving in Picton from the north island by boat, bobbing around on the **Wellington–Picton ferry** (p110) is a perfect Marlborough Sounds snapshot (keep an eye out for dolphins!). Other waterborne southern highlights include a kayak trip through the bays and inlets of **Abel Tasman National Park** (p168), **Doubtful Sound** (p351) or **Okarito Lagoon** (p200), a cruisy jetboat safari up the **Haast River** (p209), or a white-knuckle thrill-ride in **Queenstown** (p306) or **Buller Gorge** (p179).

The best stretches of windy South Island tarmac include State Highway 6 (SH6) down the West Coast (especially around Punakaiki and from Haast to Queenstown), SH73 from Christchurch to Greymouth across Arthur's Pass, and SH60 over Takaka Hill west of Motueka. Enjoy the ride!

FOODIE SOUTH ISLAND

Forget porridge and meat-and-two-veg: contemporary Kiwi cuisine is a gourmet delight, highlighted by fab festivals, boutique wineries, locally sourced produce and traditional Maori fare.

Highlights of the South Island food festival calendar include the **Hokitika Wildfoods Festival** (p196) in March, **Bluff Oyster & Southland Seafood Festival** (p359) in May, Kaikoura's **Seafest** (p146) in October, and the **Marlborough Wine Festival** (p138) around Blenheim in February. Beervana for hopheads is Nelson's **Marchfest** (p154), held in, er, April.

Organic produce floods the region. Stock up at the **Organic Greengrocer** (p157) in Nelson. Regional farmers markets across the island embrace the 100-mile diet and 'locavore' culture: try **Lyttelton Farmers Market** (p236) near Christchurch, **Dunedin Farmers Market** (p276) or the weekly market at the **Founders Brewery & Cafe** (p152) in Nelson.

For a *hangi* (Maori feast) visit the **Tamaki Maori Village** (p220) in Christchurch. It's set in a re-created Maori village and includes cultural performances that bring to life interaction between Maori and early settlers.

History James Belich

One of NZ's foremost modern historians, James Belich has written a number of books on NZ history and hosted the TV documentary series *NZ Wars*.

New Zealand's history is not long, but it is fast. In less than a thousand years these islands have produced two new peoples: the Polynesian Maori and European New Zealanders. The latter are often known by their Maori name, 'Pakeha' (though not all like the term). NZ shares some of its history with the rest of Polynesia, and with other European settler societies, but has unique features as well. It is the similarities that make the differences so interesting, and vice versa.

MAKING MAORI

Despite persistent myths (see the boxed text, p30), there is no doubt that the first settlers of NZ were the Polynesian forebears of today's Maori. Beyond that, there are a lot of question marks. Exactly where in east Polynesia did they come from – the Cook Islands, Tahiti, the Marquesas? When did they arrive? Did the first settlers come in one group or several? Some evidence, such as the diverse DNA of the Polynesian rats that accompanied the first settlers, suggests multiple founding voyages. On the other hand, only rats and dogs brought by the founders have survived, not the more valuable pigs and chickens. The survival of these cherished animals would have had high priority, and their failure to be successfully introduced suggests fewer voyages.

For more about Maui and other mythological figures, Maori tribal structure and performing arts, see Maori Culture, p50.

NZ seems small compared to Australia, but it is bigger than Britain, and very much bigger than other Polynesian islands. Its regions vary wildly in environment and climate. Prime sites for first settlement were warm coastal gardens for the food plants brought from Polynesia (kumara or sweet potato, gourd, yam and taro); sources of workable stone for knives and adzes; and areas with abundant big game. NZ has no native land mammals apart from a few species of bat, but 'big game' is no exaggeration: the islands were home to a dozen species of moa (a large flightless bird), the largest of which weighed up to 240kg, about twice the size of an ostrich. There were also other species of flightless bird and large sea mammals such as fur seals, all unaccustomed to being hunted. For people from small Pacific islands, this was like hitting the jackpot. The first settlers spread far and fast, from the top of the North Island to the bottom of the South Island within the first 100 years. High-protein diets are likely to have boosted population growth.

Similarities in language between Maori and Tahitian indicate close contact in historical times. Maori is about as similar to Tahitian as Spanish is to French, despite the 4294km separating these island groups.

By about 1400, however, with big-game supply dwindling, Maori economics turned from big game to small game – forest birds and rats – and from hunting to gardening and fishing. A good living could still be made, but it required detailed local knowledge, steady effort and complex communal organisation, hence the rise of the Maori tribes. Competition for resources increased, conflict did likewise, and this led to the building of increasingly

TIMELINE

AD 1000–1200	1642	1769
Possible date of the arrival of Maori in NZ. Solid archaeological evidence points to about AD 1200, but much earlier dates have been suggested for the first human impact on the environment.	First European contact: Abel Tasman arrives on an expedition from the Dutch East Indies (Indonesia) to find the 'Great South Land'. The party leaves without landing after a sea skirmish with Maori, but its legacy remains in the country's name.	European contact recommences with visits by James Cook and Jean de Surville. Despite some violence, both managed to communicate with Maori, and this time NZ's link with the outside world proved permanent.

THE MORIORI & THEIR MYTH

One of NZ's most persistent legends is that Maori found mainland NZ already occupied by a more peaceful and racially distinct Melanesian people, known as the Moriori, whom they exterminated. This myth has been regularly debunked by scholars since the 1920s, but somehow hangs on.

To complicate matters, there were real 'Moriori', and Maori did treat them badly. The real Moriori were the people of the Chatham Islands, a windswept group about 900km east of the mainland. They were, however, fully Polynesian, and descended from Maori – 'Moriori' was their version of the same word. Mainland Maori arrived in the Chathams in 1835, as a spin-off of the Musket Wars, killing some Moriori and enslaving the rest. But they did not exterminate them. The mainland Moriori remain a myth.

sophisticated fortifications, known as *pa*. Vestiges of *pa* earthworks can still be seen around the country, on the hilltops of Auckland for example.

The Maori had no metals and no written language (and no alcoholic drinks or drugs). But their culture and spiritual life was rich and distinctive. Below Ranginui (sky father) and Papatuanuku (earth mother) were various gods of land, forest and sea, joined by deified ancestors over time. The mischievous demigod Maui was particularly important. In legend, he vanquished the sun and fished up the North Island before meeting his death between the thighs of the goddess Hine-nui-te-po in an attempt to conquer the human mortality embodied in her. Maori traditional performance art, the group singing and dancing known as *kapa haka*, has real power, even for modern audiences. Visual art, notably woodcarving, is something special – 'like nothing but itself', in the words of 18th-century explorer-scientist Joseph Banks.

ENTER EUROPE

NZ became an official British colony in 1840, but the first authenticated contact between Maori and the outside world took place almost two centuries earlier in 1642, in Golden Bay at the top of the South Island. Two Dutch ships sailed from Indonesia, to search for southern land and anything valuable it might contain. The commander, Abel Tasman, was instructed to pretend to any natives he might meet 'that you are by no means eager for precious metals, so as to leave them ignorant of the value of the same'.

When Tasman's ships anchored in the bay, local Maori came out in their canoes to make the traditional challenge: friends or foes? Misunderstanding this, the Dutch challenged back, by blowing trumpets. When a boat was lowered to take a party between the two ships, it was attacked. Four crewmen were killed. Tasman sailed away and did not come back; nor did any other European for 127 years. But the Dutch did leave a name: 'Nieuw Zeeland' or 'New Sealand'.

Contact between Maori and Europeans was renewed in 1769, when English and French explorers arrived, under James Cook (see the boxed text, p29)

Abel Tasman named NZ Statenland, assuming it was connected to Staten Island near Argentina. It was subsequently named after the province of Zeeland in Tasman's Holland.

1790s	1818–36	1840
Whaling ships and sealing gangs arrive in the country. Relations are established with Maori, with Europeans depending on the contact for essentials such as food, water and protection.	Intertribal Maori 'Musket Wars' take place: tribes acquire muskets and win bloody victories against tribes without them. The war tapers off in 1836, probably as a result of the equal distribution of weapons.	On 6 February, the Treaty of Waitangi is signed by 40 chiefs in a sovereignty settlement presented by William Hobson. Copies of the treaty are circulated countrywide to collect signatures. NZ becomes a nominal British colony.

Rumours of late survivals of the giant moa bird abound, but none have been authenticated. So if you see a moa in your travels, photograph it – you have just made the greatest zoological discovery of the last 100 years.

Scottish influence can still be felt in NZ, particularly in the south of the South Island. NZ has more Scottish pipe bands per capita than Scotland itself.

For a thorough overview of NZ history from Gondwanaland to today, visit http://history-nz.org.

and Jean de Surville. Relations were more sympathetic, and exploration continued, motivated by science, profit and great power rivalry. Cook made two more visits between 1773 and 1777, and there were further French expeditions.

Unofficial visits, by whaling ships in the north and sealing gangs in the south, began in the 1790s. The first mission station was founded in 1814, in the Bay of Islands, and was followed by dozens of others: Anglican, Methodist and Catholic. Trade in flax and timber generated small European-Maori settlements by the 1820s. Surprisingly, the most numerous category of European visitor was probably American. New England whaling ships favoured the Bay of Islands for rest and recreation; 271 called there between 1833 and 1839 alone. To whalers, 'rest and recreation' meant sex and drink. Their favourite haunt, the little town of Kororareka (now Russell) was known to the missionaries as 'the hellhole of the Pacific'. New England visitors today might well have distant relatives among the local Maori.

One or two dozen bloody clashes dot the history of Maori-European contact before 1840 but, given the number of visits, inter-racial conflict was modest. Europeans needed Maori protection, food and labour, and Maori came to need European articles, especially muskets. Whaling stations and mission stations were linked to local Maori groups by intermarriage, which helped keep the peace. Most warfare was between Maori and Maori: the terrible intertribal 'Musket Wars' of 1818–36. Because Northland had the majority of early contact with Europe, its Ngapuhi tribe acquired muskets first. Under their great general Hongi Hika, Ngapuhi then raided south, winning bloody victories against tribes without muskets. Once they acquired muskets, these tribes saw off Ngapuhi, but also raided further south in their turn. The domino effect continued to the far south of the South Island in 1836. The missionaries claimed that the Musket Wars then tapered off through their influence, but the restoration of the balance of power through the equal distribution of muskets was probably more important.

Europe brought such things as pigs (at last) and potatoes, which benefited Maori, while muskets and diseases had the opposite effect. The negative effects have been exaggerated, however. Europeans expected peoples like the Maori to simply fade away at contact, and some early estimates of Maori population were overly high – up to one million. Current estimates are between 85,000 and 110,000 for 1769. The Musket Wars killed perhaps 20,000, and new diseases did considerable damage too (although NZ had the natural quarantine of distance: infected Europeans usually recovered or died during the long voyage, and smallpox, for example, which devastated native Americans, did not make it here). By 1840, the Maori had been reduced to about 70,000, a decline of at least 20%. Maori bent under the weight of European contact, but they certainly did not break.

1844	1853–56	1860–61
Young Ngapuhi chief, Hone Heke, challenges British sovereignty, first by cutting down the British flag at Russell, and then by sacking the town itself. The ensuing Northland War continues till 1846.	Provincial and central elected governments established. In 1853 the first elections are held for the New Zealand parliament; votes are restricted to adult, male, British subjects, and Maori votes are limited due to property-right rules.	First Taranaki war. Starting with the controversial swindling of Maori land by the government at Waitara, the war involves many military participants from the Waikato tribes (despite being traditional enemies of the Taranaki Maori).

CAPTAIN JAMES COOK Tony Horwitz

If aliens ever visit earth, they may wonder what to make of the countless obelisks, faded plaques and graffiti-covered statues of a stiff, wigged figure gazing out to sea from Alaska to Australia, from NZ to North Yorkshire, from Siberia to the South Pacific. James Cook (1728–79) explored more of the earth's surface than anyone in history, and it's impossible to travel the Pacific without encountering the captain's image and his controversial legacy in the lands he opened to the West.

For a man who travelled so widely, and rose to such fame, Cook came from an extremely pinched and provincial background. The son of a day labourer in rural Yorkshire, he was born in a mud cottage, had little schooling, and seemed destined for farm work – and for his family's grave plot in a village churchyard. Instead, Cook went to sea as a teenager, worked his way up from coal-ship servant to naval officer, and attracted notice for his exceptional charts of Canada. But Cook remained a little-known second lieutenant until, in 1768, the Royal Navy chose him to command a daring voyage to the South Seas.

In a converted coal ship called *Endeavour*, Cook sailed to Tahiti, and then became the first European to land at NZ and the east coast of Australia. Though the ship almost sank after striking the Great Barrier Reef, and 40% of the crew died from disease and accidents, the *Endeavour* limped home in 1771. On a return voyage (1772–75), Cook became the first navigator to pierce the Antarctic Circle and circled the globe near its southernmost latitude, demolishing the ancient myth that a vast, populous and fertile continent surrounded the South Pole. Cook also crisscrossed the Pacific from Easter Island to Melanesia, charting dozens of islands between. Though Maori killed and cooked 10 sailors, the captain remained strikingly sympathetic to islanders. 'Notwithstanding they are cannibals,' he wrote, 'they are naturally of a good disposition'.

On Cook's final voyage (1776–79), in search of a northwest passage between the Atlantic and Pacific, he became the first European to visit Hawaii, and coasted America from Oregon to Alaska. Forced back by Arctic pack ice, Cook returned to Hawaii, where he was killed during a skirmish with islanders who had initially greeted him as a Polynesian god. In a single decade of discovery, Cook had filled in the map of the Pacific and, as one French navigator put it, 'left his successors with little to do but admire his exploits'.

But Cook's travels also spurred colonisation of the Pacific, and within a few decades of his death, missionaries, whalers, traders and settlers began transforming (and often devastating) island cultures. As a result, many Indigenous people now revile Cook as an imperialist villain who introduced disease, dispossession and other ills to the Pacific (hence the frequent vandalising of Cook monuments). However, as islanders revive traditional crafts and practices, from tattooing to *tapa*, they have turned to the art and writing of Cook and his men as a resource for cultural renewal. For good and ill, a Yorkshire farm boy remains the single most significant figure in the shaping of the modern Pacific.

Tony Horwitz is a Pulitzer-winning reporter and nonfiction author. In researching Blue Latitudes (or Into the Blue), Tony travelled the Pacific – 'boldly going where Captain Cook has gone before'.

1861	1868–72	1882
Gold discovered in Otago by Gabriel Read, an Australian prospector. As a result, the population of Otago climbs from less than 13,000 to over 30,000 in six months.	East Coast war. Te Kooti, having led an escape from his prison on the Chatham Islands, leads a holy guerrilla war in the Urewera region. He finally retreats to establish the Ringatu Church.	First refrigerated cargo to Britain. Exports to Britain had been dominated by the wool trade, but this development allows diversification into meat and dairy, and establishes NZ's early lead in the industry.

MAKING PAKEHA

By 1840, Maori tribes described local Europeans as 'their Pakeha', and valued the profit and prestige they brought. Maori wanted more of both, and concluded that accepting nominal British authority was the way to get them. At the same time, the British government was overcoming its reluctance to undertake potentially expensive intervention in NZ. It too was influenced by profit and prestige, but also by humanitarian considerations. It believed, wrongly but sincerely, that Maori could not handle the increasing scale of unofficial European contact. In 1840, the two peoples struck a deal, symbolised by the treaty first signed at Waitangi on 6 February that year. The Treaty of Waitangi now has a standing not dissimilar to that of the Constitution in the US, but is even more contested. The original problem was a discrepancy between British and Maori understandings of it. The English version promised Maori full equality as British subjects in return for complete rights of government. The Maori version also promised that Maori would retain their chieftainship, which implied local rights of government. The problem was not great at first, because the Maori version applied outside the small European settlements. But as those settlements grew, conflict brewed.

In 1840, there were only about 2000 Europeans in NZ, with the shanty town of Kororareka (now Russell) as the capital and biggest settlement. By 1850, six new settlements had been formed with 22,000 settlers between them. About half of these had arrived under the auspices of the New Zealand Company and its associates. The company was the brainchild of Edward Gibbon Wakefield, who also influenced the settlement of South Australia. Wakefield hoped to short-circuit the barbarous frontier phase of settlement with 'instant civilisation', but his success was limited. From the 1850s, his settlers, who included a high proportion of upper-middle-class gentlefolk, were swamped by succeeding waves of immigrants that continued to wash in until the 1880s. These people were part of the great British and Irish diaspora that also populated Australia and much of North America, but the NZ mix was distinctive. Lowland Scots settlers were more prominent in NZ than elsewhere, for example, with the possible exception of parts of Canada. NZ's Irish, even the Catholics, tended to come from the north of Ireland. NZ's English tended to come from the counties close to London. Small groups of Germans, Scandinavians and Chinese made their way in, though the last faced increasing racial prejudice from the 1880s, when the Pakeha population reached half a million.

Much of the mass immigration from the 1850s to the 1870s was assisted by the provincial and central governments, which also mounted large-scale public works schemes, especially in the 1870s under Julius Vogel. In 1876, Vogel abolished the provinces on the grounds that they were hampering his development efforts. The last imperial governor with substantial power was the talented but Machiavellian George Grey, who ended his second

1890–1912	1893	1914–18
The Liberal government is in power over an economy recovering from depression. Their major leader is Richard John Seddon, 'King Dick, as I am usually known'.	Votes for women granted, following a campaign led by Kate Sheppard, who had been petitioning the government for years. NZ becomes the first country in the world to grant the vote to women.	NZ's contribution to WWI is quite staggering for a country of just over one million people: about 100,000 NZ men serve overseas, and close on 60,000 became casualties, mostly on the Western Front in France.

governorship in 1868. Thereafter, the governors (governors-general from 1917) were largely just nominal heads of state; the head of government, the premier or prime minister, had more power. The central government, originally weaker than the provincial governments, the imperial governor and the Maori tribes, eventually exceeded the power of all three.

The Maori tribes did not go down without a fight, however. Indeed, their resistance was one of the most formidable ever mounted against European expansion, comparable to that of the Sioux and Seminole in the US. The first clash took place in 1843 in the Wairau Valley, now a wine-growing district. A posse of settlers set out to enforce the myth of British control, but encountered the reality of Maori control. Twenty-two settlers were killed, including Wakefield's brother, Arthur, along with about six Maori. In 1845, more serious fighting broke out in the Bay of Islands, when Hone Heke sacked a British settlement. Heke and his ally Kawiti baffled three British punitive expeditions, using a modern variant of the traditional *pa* fortification. Vestiges of these innovative earthworks can still be seen at Ruapekapeka (south of Kawakawa). Governor Grey claimed victory in the north, but few were convinced at the time. Grey had more success in the south, where he arrested the formidable Ngati Toa chief Te Rauparaha, who until then wielded great influence on both sides of Cook Strait. Pakeha were able to swamp the few Maori living in the South Island, but the fighting of the 1840s confirmed that the North Island at that time comprised a European fringe around an independent Maori heartland.

In the 1850s, settler population and aspirations grew, and fighting broke out again in 1860. The wars burned on sporadically until 1872 over much of the North Island. In the early years, a Maori nationalist organisation, the King Movement, was the backbone of resistance. In later years, some remarkable prophet-generals, notably Titokowaru and Te Kooti, took over. Most wars were small-scale, but the Waikato War of 1863–64 was not. This conflict, fought at the same time as the American Civil War, involved armoured steamships, ultramodern heavy artillery, telegraph and 10 proud British regular regiments. Despite the odds, the Maori won several battles, such as that at Gate Pa, near Tauranga, in 1864. But in the end they were ground down by European numbers and resources. Maori political, though not cultural, independence ebbed away in the last decades of the 19th century. It finally expired when police invaded its last sanctuary, the Urewera Mountains, in 1916.

Maurice Shadbolt's *Season of the Jew* (1987) is a semifictionalised story of bloody campaigns led by warrior Te Kooti against the British in Poverty Bay in the 1860s. Te Kooti and his followers compared themselves to the Israelites who were cast out of Egypt.

WELFARE & WARFARE

From the 1850s to the 1880s, despite conflict with Maori, the Pakeha economy boomed on the back of wool exports, gold rushes and massive overseas borrowing for development. The crash came in the 1880s, when NZ experienced its Long Depression. In 1890, the Liberals came to power, and stayed there until 1912, helped by a recovering economy. The Liberals were NZ's first

'Kaore e mau te rongo – ake, ake!' (Peace never shall be made – never, never!) War chief Rewi Maniapoto in response to government troops at the battle of Orakau, 1864

1935–49	1939–45	1974
First Labour government in power, under Michael Savage. This government creates NZ's pioneering version of the welfare state, and also takes some independent initiatives in foreign policy.	NZ troops back Britain and the Allied war effort during WWII, while a hundred thousand or so Americans arrive from 1942 to protect NZ from the Japanese.	Pacific Island migrants who have outstayed visas (dubbed 'overstayers') subjected to Dawn Raids (crackdowns by immigration police) under Robert Muldoon and the National government. These raids continue till the early 1980s.

organised political party, and the first of several governments to give NZ a reputation as 'the world's social laboratory'. NZ became the first country in the world to give women the vote in 1893, and introduced old-age pensions in 1898. The Liberals also introduced a long-lasting system of industrial arbitration, but this was not enough to prevent bitter industrial unrest in 1912–13. This happened under the conservative 'Reform' government, which had replaced the Liberals in 1912. Reform remained in power until 1928, and later transformed itself into the National Party. Renewed depression struck in 1929, and the NZ experience of it was as grim as any. The derelict little farmhouses still seen in rural areas often date from this era.

To find out more about the New Zealand Wars, visit www.newzealandwars.co.nz.

In 1935, a second reforming government took office: the First Labour government, led by Michael Joseph Savage, easily NZ's favourite Australian. For a time, the Labour government was considered the most socialist government outside Soviet Russia. But, when the chips were down in Europe in 1939, Labour had little hesitation in backing Britain.

NZ had also backed Britain in the Boer War (1899–1902) and WWI (1914–18), with dramatic losses in WWI in particular. You can count the cost

---

LAND WARS *Errol Hunt*

Five separate major conflicts made up what are now collectively known as the New Zealand Wars (also referred to as the Land Wars or Maori Wars). Starting in Northland and moving throughout the North Island, the wars had many complex causes, but *whenua* (land) was the one common factor. In all five wars, Maori fought both for and against the government, on whose side stood the Imperial British Army, Australians and NZ's own Armed Constabulary. Land confiscations imposed on the Maori as punishment for involvement in these wars are still the source of conflict today, with the government struggling to finance compensation for what are now acknowledged to have been illegal seizures.

Northland war (1844–46) 'Hone Heke's War' began with the famous chopping of the flagpole at Kororareka (now Russell) and 'ended' at Ruapekapeka (south of Kawakawa). In many ways, this was almost a civil war between rival Ngapuhi factions, with the government taking one side against the other.

First Taranaki war (1860–61) Starting in Waitara, the first Taranaki war inflamed the passions of Maori across the North Island.

Waikato war (1863–64) The largest of the five wars. Predominantly involving Kingitanga, the Waikato war was caused in part by what the government saw as a challenge to sovereignty. However, it was land, again, that was the real reason for friction. Following defeats such as Rangiriri, the Waikato people were pushed entirely from their own lands, south into what became known as the King Country.

Second Taranaki war (1865–69) Caused by Maori resistance to land confiscations stemming from the first Taranaki war, this was perhaps the war in which the Maori came closest to victory, under the brilliant, one-eyed prophet-general Titokowaru. However, once he lost the respect of his warriors (probably through an indiscretion with the wife of one of his warriors), the war too was lost.

East Coast war (1868–72) Te Kooti's holy guerrilla war.

1975	1981	1984
Waitangi Tribunal set up to investigate grievances of Maori people in relation to the Treaty of Waitangi. The tribunal's power is later extended to allow investigations of Crown confiscations as far back as 1840.	Springbok rugby tour divides the nation. Many New Zealanders show a strong anti-apartheid stance by protesting the games. Other Kiwis feel that sport and politics should not mix, and support the South African tour going ahead.	Fourth Labour government elected, adopting an anti-nuclear foreign policy, and a more-market economic policy. Social restrictions are removed almost as fast as economic ones – the pubs still close at six, but am, not pm.

in almost any little NZ town. A central square or park will contain a memorial lined with names – more for WWI than WWII. Even in WWII, however, NZ did its share of fighting: a hundred thousand or so New Zealanders fought in Europe and the Middle East. NZ, a peaceful-seeming country, has spent much of its history at war. In the 19th century it fought at home; in the 20th, overseas.

BETTER BRITONS?

British visitors have long found NZ hauntingly familiar. This is not simply a matter of the British and Irish origin of most Pakeha. It also stems from the tightening of NZ links with Britain from 1882, when refrigerated cargoes of food were first shipped to London. By the 1930s, giant ships carried frozen meat, cheese and butter, as well as wool, on regular voyages taking about five weeks one way. The NZ economy adapted to the feeding of London, and cultural links were also enhanced. NZ children studied British history and literature, not their own. NZ's leading scientists and writers, such as Ernest Rutherford and Katherine Mansfield (see the boxed text, p98), gravitated to Britain. This tight relationship has been described as 'recolonial', but it is a mistake to see NZ as an exploited colony. Average living standards in NZ were normally better than in Britain, as were the welfare and lower-level education systems. New Zealanders had access to British markets and culture, and they contributed their share to the latter as equals. The list of 'British' writers, academics, scientists, military leaders, publishers and the like who were actually New Zealanders is long. Indeed, New Zealanders, especially in war and sport, sometimes saw themselves as a superior version of the British – the Better Britons of the south. The NZ-London relationship was rather like that of the American Midwest and New York.

'Recolonial' NZ prided itself, with some justice, on its affluence, equality and social harmony. But it was also conformist, even puritanical. Until the 1950s, it was technically illegal for farmers to allow their cattle to mate in fields fronting public roads, for moral reasons. The 1953 American movie, *The Wild One*, was banned until 1977. Sunday newspapers were illegal until 1969, and full Sunday trading was not allowed until 1989. Licensed restaurants hardly existed in 1960, nor did supermarkets or TV. Notoriously, from 1917 to 1967, pubs were obliged to shut at 6pm. Yet the puritanical society of Better Britons was never the whole story. Opposition to Sunday trading stemmed, not so much from belief in the sanctity of the Sabbath, but from the belief that workers should have weekends too. Six o'clock closing was a standing joke in rural areas, notably the marvellously idiosyncratic region of South Island's west coast. There was always something of a Kiwi counterculture, even before imported countercultures took root from the 1960s.

There were also developments in cultural nationalism, beginning in the 1930s but really flowering from the 1970s. Writers, artists and film-makers were by no means the only people who 'came out' in that era.

'God's own country, but the devil's own mess.' Prime Minister Richard (King Dick) Seddon, speaking on the source of NZ's self-proclaimed nickname 'Godzone'.

Wellington-born Nancy Wake (codenamed 'The White Mouse') led a guerrilla attack against the Nazis with a 7000-strong army. She had the multiple honours of being the Gestapo's most-wanted person and being the most decorated Allied servicewoman of WWII.

1985	**1987**	**1992**
Rainbow Warrior sunk in Auckland Harbour by French government agents to prevent the Greenpeace protest ship from making its intended voyage to Moruroa, where the French government is conducting a nuclear-testing program.	The international stock market crash known as 'Black Monday' hits the NZ economy particularly hard, following optimistic financial investment in the free-market atmosphere. The economy takes years to recover.	Government begins reparations for land confiscated in the Land Wars, and confirms Maori fishing rights in the 'Sealord deal'. Major settlements of historical confiscation follow including, in 1995, reparations for the Waikato land confiscations.

COMING IN, COMING OUT

The 'recolonial' system was shaken several times after 1935, but managed to survive until 1973, when Mother England ran off and joined the Franco-German commune now known as the EU. NZ was beginning to develop alternative markets to Britain, and alternative exports to wool, meat and dairy products. Wide-bodied jet aircraft were allowing the world and NZ to visit each other on an increasing scale. NZ had only 36,000 tourists in 1960, compared with more than two million a year now. Women were beginning to penetrate first the upper reaches of the workforce and then the political sphere. Gay people came out of the closet, despite vigorous efforts by moral conservatives to push them back in. University-educated youths were becoming more numerous and more assertive.

From 1945, Maori experienced both a population explosion and massive urbanisation. In 1936, Maori were 17% urban and 83% rural. Fifty years later, these proportions had reversed. The immigration gates, which until 1960 were pretty much labelled 'whites only', widened, first to allow in Pacific Islanders for their labour, and then to allow in (East) Asians for their money. These transitions would have generated major socioeconomic change whatever happened in politics. But most New Zealanders associate the country's recent 'Big Shift' with the politics of 1984.

In 1984, NZ's third great reforming government was elected – the Fourth Labour government, led nominally by David Lange and in fact by Roger Douglas, the Minister of Finance. This government adopted an antinuclear foreign policy, delighting the left, and a more-market economic policy, delighting the right. NZ's numerous economic controls were dismantled with breakneck speed. Middle NZ was uneasy about the antinuclear policy, which threatened NZ's ANZUS alliance with Australia and the US. But in 1985, French spies sank the antinuclear protest ship *Rainbow Warrior* in Auckland Harbour, killing one crewman. The lukewarm American condemnation of the French act brought middle NZ in behind the antinuclear policy, which became associated with national independence. Other New Zealanders were uneasy about the more-market economic policy, but failed to come up with a convincing alternative. Revelling in their new freedom, NZ investors engaged in a frenzy of speculation, and suffered even more than the rest of the world from the economic crash of 1987.

The early 21st century is an interesting time for NZ. Like NZ food and wine, film and literature are flowering as never before, and the new ethnic mix is creating something very special in popular music. There are continuities, however – the pub, the sportsground, the quarter-acre section, the bush, the beach and the bach – and they too are part of the reason people like to come here. Realising that NZ has a great culture, and an intriguing history, as well as a great natural environment, will double the bang for your buck.

The Ministry for Culture & Heritage's history website (www.nzhistory.net.nz) is an excellent source of info on NZ history.

The Six o'clock Swill referred to the frantic after-work drinking at pubs when men tried to drink as much as possible from 5.05pm until strict closing time at 6pm.

NZ's staunch antinuclear stance earned it the nickname 'The Mouse that Roared'.

1996	2004	2008
NZ changes from a two-party 'first past the post' (FPP) electoral system to Mixed Member Proportional (MMP) representation, allowing minority parties such as the Greens to take a representative role in government.	Maori TV begins broadcasting – for the first time, a channel committed to NZ content and the revitalisation of Maori language and culture hits the small screen.	An election replaces nine-year Labour prime minister Helen Clark with a National (conservative) government under John Key.

The Culture   Peter Dragicevich

THE NATIONAL PSYCHE

New Zealand is like that little guy at school when they're picking rugby teams – quietly waiting to be noticed, desperately wanting to be liked. Then, when he does get the nod, his sheer determination to prove himself propels him to score a completely unexpected try. When his team-mates come to congratulate him he stares at the ground and mumbles, 'It was nothing, ay'.

While a proud little nation, Kiwis traditionally don't have time for show-offs. Jingoistic flag-waving is generally frowned upon. People who make an impression on the international stage are respected and admired, but flashy tall poppies have traditionally had their heads lopped off. This is perhaps a legacy of NZ's early egalitarian ideals – the ones that sought to avoid the worst injustices of the 'mother country' (Britain) by breaking up large land holdings and enthusiastically adopting a 'cradle to grave' welfare state. 'Just because someone's got a bigger car than me, or bigger guns, doesn't make them better' is the general Kiwi attitude.

NZ has rarely let its size get in the way of making a point on the international stage. A founding member of the League of Nations (the precursor to the UN), it ruffled feathers between the world wars by failing to blindly follow Britain's position. It was in the 1980s, however, that things got really interesting.

Modern Kiwi culture pivots on that decade. Firstly, the unquestioned primacy of rugby union as a source of social cohesion (which rivalled the country's commitment to the two world wars as a foundation of nation-building) was stripped away when tens of thousands of New Zealanders took to the streets to protest a tour by the South African rugby side in 1981. They held that the politics of apartheid not only had a place in sport, they trumped it. The country was starkly divided; there were riots in paradise. The scar is still strong enough that most New Zealanders over 35 will recognise the simple phrase 'The Tour' as referring to those events.

The tour protests both harnessed and nourished a political and cultural renaissance among Maori which had already been rolling for a decade. Three years later, that renaissance found its mark when a reforming Labour government gave statutory teeth to the Waitangi Tribunal, an agency that has since guided a process of land return, compensation for past wrongs and interpretation of the Treaty of Waitangi – the 1840 pact between Maori and the Crown – as a living document.

At the same time antinuclear protests that had been rumbling for years gained momentum, with mass blockades of visiting US naval ships. In 1984 Prime Minister David Lange barred nuclear-powered or armed ships from entering NZ waters. The mouse had roared. As a result the US threw NZ out of ANZUS, the country's main strategic military alliance, which also included Australia, declaring NZ 'a friend but not an ally'.

The following year an event happened that would completely change the way NZ related to the world when French government agents launched an attack in Auckland Harbour, sinking Greenpeace's antinuclear flagship *Rainbow Warrior* and killing one of its crew. Being bombed by a country that NZ had fought two world wars with and the muted or nonexistent condemnation by other allies left an indelible mark. It strengthened NZ's resolve to follow its own conscience in foreign policy and in 1987 the NZ Nuclear Free Zone, Disarmament & Arms Control Act became law.

For many, Sir Edmund Hillary, the first person to climb Mt Everest, was the consummate New Zealander: humble, practical and concerned for social justice. A public outpouring of grief followed his death in 2008.

Ironically, the person responsible for the nuclear age was a New Zealander. In 1917 Ernest Rutherford was the first to split the nucleus of an atom. His face appears on the $100 note.

From the Boer to the Vietnam War, NZ had blithely trotted off at the behest of the UK or US. Not anymore, as is demonstrated by its lack of involvement in the invasion of Iraq. That's not to say that the country shirks its international obligations. NZ troops continue to be deployed in peacekeeping capacities throughout the world and are currently active in Afghanistan.

'...a sordid act of international state-backed
terrorism...' – Prime
Minister David Lange,
describing the bombing
of the *Rainbow Warrior*
(1986)

If that wasn't enough upheaval for one decade, 1986 saw another bitter battle split the community – this time over the decriminalisation of homosexuality. The debate was particularly rancorous, but the law that previously incarcerated consenting gay adults was repealed – paving the way for the generally accepting society that NZ is today. Just 13 years later Georgina Beyer, an openly transsexual former prostitute, would win a once safe rural seat off a conservative incumbent – an unthinkable achievement in most of the world.

Yet while the 1980s saw the country jump to the left on social issues, simultaneously economic reforms were carried out that were an extreme step to the right (to paraphrase one-time Hamiltonian Richard O'Brien's song *The Time Warp*). The bloated public sector was slashed, any state assets that weren't bolted to the floor were sold off, regulation was removed from many sectors, trade barriers dismantled and the power of the unions greatly diminished.

If there is broad agreement that the economy had to be restructured, the reforms carried a heavy price. The old social guarantees are not as sure. New Zealanders work long hours for lower wages than their Australian cousins would ever tolerate. Compared with other Organisation for Economic Cooperation and Development (OECD) nations, family incomes are low, child poverty rates are high and the gap between rich and poor is widening.

Yet there is a dynamism about NZ that was rare in the 'golden weather' years before the reforms. NZ farmers take on the world without the massive subsidies of yore, and Wellington's inner city – once virtually closed after dark by oppressive licensing laws – now thrives with great bars and restaurants.

As with the economic reforms, the 'Treaty process' of redress and reconciliation with Maori makes some New Zealanders uneasy, more in their uncertainty about its extent than that it has happened at all. A court decision suggesting that some Maori might have unforeseen rights to stretches of the country's seabed and foreshore (not the beaches themselves, but the area from the high tide outwards) hit a raw nerve among some. The assumption had long been that access to the beach was a NZ birthright, although its basis in law proved to be shaky. The conservative National Party, then ailing in opposition, tapped into public unease over this new and unexpected dimension to the Treaty process, claiming the country was moving towards 'separatism' – and shot up in the opinion polls. The Labour government, spooked by the public response, passed a law that confirmed the seabed and foreshore in Crown (public) ownership but offered Maori groups the chance to explore their 'customary rights' to places they had traditionally used.

Many Maori, feeling they had been denied due process, were angry, and a *hikoi* (march) of 15,000 protested at parliament, amid speculation that political allegiances were being re-drawn. The speculation was well founded: the momentum generated by the *hikoi* led directly to the formation of the Maori Party, which now holds five of the seven electorates reserved for Maori (unseating a Labour MP in each). The Maori Party currently has a 'confidence and supply' agreement with the National-led government and, at the time of research, it seems likely that they will win some concessions on the foreshore and seabed issue from their former foes.

For the younger generation, for whom the 1980s are prehistory, political apathy is the norm. Perhaps it's because a decade of progressive government has given them little to kick against – unlike those politicised by the anti–Iraq War movements in the UK, US and Australia. Ironically, as NZ has finally achieved its own interesting, independent cultural sensibility, the country's youth seem more obsessed by US culture than ever.

This is particularly true within the hip-hop scene where a farcical identification with American gangsta culture has developed into a worrying youth gang problem. Even more ridiculous is the epidemic of boy racers, pulling burnouts and street-racing in souped-up V8s.

Despite all the change, key elements of the NZ identity are an unbroken thread, and fortune is still a matter of economics rather than class. If you are well served in a restaurant or shop, it will be out of politeness or pride in the job, rather than servility.

In country areas and on bush walks don't be surprised if you're given a cheery greeting from passers-by, especially in the South Island. In a legacy of the British past, politeness is generally regarded as one of the highest virtues. A 'please' and 'thank you' will get you a long way. The three great exceptions to this rule are: a) on the road, where genteel Dr Jekylls become raging Mr Hydes, especially if you have the misfortune of needing to change lanes; b) if you don't speak English very well; and c) if you are Australian.

The latter two traits are the product of insularity and a smallness of world view that tends to disappear among Kiwis who have travelled (and luckily many do). The NZ/Australian rivalry is taken much more seriously on this side of the Tasman Sea. Although it's very unlikely that Kiwis will be rude outright, visiting Aussies must get pretty sick of the constant ribbing, much of it surprisingly ill-humoured. It's a sad truth that while most Australians would cheer on a NZ sports team if they were playing anyone other than their own, the opposite is true in NZ.

You might on your travels hear the phrase 'number-eight wire' and wonder what on earth it means. It's a catchphrase New Zealanders still repeat to themselves to encapsulate a national myth: that NZ's isolation and its pioneer stock created a culture in which ingenuity allowed problems to be solved and tools to be built from scratch. A NZ farmer, it was said, could solve pretty much any problem with a piece of number-eight wire (the gauge used for fencing on farms).

It's actually largely true – NZ farms are full of NZ inventions. One reason big offshore film and TV producers bring their projects here – apart from the low wages and huge variety of locations – is that they like the can-do attitude and ability to work to a goal of NZ technical crews. Many more New Zealanders have worked as managers, roadies or chefs for famous recording artists (everyone from Led Zeppelin and U2 to Madonna) than have enjoyed the spotlight themselves. Which just goes to show that New Zealanders operate best at the intersection of practicality and creativity, with an endearing (and sometimes infuriating) humility to boot.

> In 2009 NZ topped the Global Peace Index earning the distinction of being rated the world's most peaceful country.

> NZ is defined as a state in the Australian constitution. At the time of Australia's federation into one country it was hoped that NZ would join. On this side of the Tasman that idea proved as unpopular then as it does now.

> Kiwi inventions include the disposable syringe, nonshortable electric fence, Navman GPS and the child-proof top for pill bottles.

LIFESTYLE

Living on an island has its perks, especially in summer. By the middle of the week your average Kiwi office worker is keeping a nervous watch on the weather, praying that the rain will hold off for the weekend so that they can head to the beach, maybe start working on the garden or at least get the kids out of the house for a few hours. Of course, the more gung-ho are already making the most of the long summer evenings – there's Carmen the teacher taking the kayak out fishing after school; and Steven the quantity surveyor with the surfboard in the car, itching to hit the breaks during the last few hours of daylight.

For all the stereotypes of the active healthy Kiwi, other clichés are just as real. Susan's working late at the office. Again. (New Zealanders have among the longest working hours in the developed world.) She'll probably grab some fast food on her way home and, yes, she does want fries with that. (A quarter of NZ adults are obese.) Then there's Dean, hanging around on the street with his other teenage mates, trying to look staunch while sweating into his hoodie. The fact is, there is no one NZ lifestyle.

No matter where you are in NZ, you're never more than 128km from the sea.

Most Kiwis (except perhaps the farmers) would probably wish it rained a little less and they got paid a little more, but it sometimes takes a few years travelling on their 'Big OE' (Overseas Experience – a traditional right of passage) before they realise how good they've got it. In a 2009 study of the quality of life in the world's major cities, Auckland was rated fourth-equal and Wellington 12th.

For most of its history, NZ's small population and plentiful land has seen its people live in stand-alone houses on large, green sections. And while that's still the norm, for a number of reasons it has started to change.

In Auckland, concern about suburban sprawl and poor public transport, and the gentrification of once-poor inner-city suburbs, has seen a boom in

---

'SO, WHAT DO YOU THINK OF NEW ZEALAND?' *Russell Brown*

That, by tradition, is the question that visitors, especially important ones, are asked within an hour of disembarking in NZ. Sometimes they might be granted an entire day's research before being asked to pronounce, but asked they are. The question – composed equally of great pride and creeping doubt – is symbolic of the national consciousness.

When George Bernard Shaw visited for four weeks in 1934, he was deluged with what-do-you-think-of questions from newspaper reporters the length of the country. Although he never saw fit to write a word about NZ, his answers to those newspaper questions were collected and reprinted as *What I Saw in New Zealand: the Newspaper Utterances of George Bernard Shaw in New Zealand*. Yes, people really were that keen for vindication.

Other visitors were willing to pronounce in print, including the British Liberal MP, David Goldblatt, who came to NZ to convalesce from a heart attack in 1955, became fascinated with the place and wrote an intriguing and prescient little book called *Democracy At Ease: a New Zealand Profile*.

Goldblatt found New Zealanders a blithe people; kind, prosperous, fond of machines, frequently devoid of theory. In 'a land in which the practice of neighbourliness is most strongly developed' no one went wanting, yet few seemed to aspire. He admired the country's education system and its newspapers, despaired of its tariffs and barriers and wondered at laws that amounted to 'the complete control of the individual by the government'.

He was far from the first visitor to muse about NZ's contradictions – the American academic Leslie Lipson, who weathered the WWII years at Wellington's Victoria University, admired NZ's 'passion for social justice' but fretted about its 'restraint on talent' and 'lack of cultural achievement'.

For the *bon vivant* Goldblatt, the attitude towards food and drink was all too telling. Apart from one visit to a clandestine European-style restaurant in Auckland, where the bottles were hidden under tables, he found only 'the plain fare and even plainer fetch and carry of the normal feeding machine of this country' and shops catering 'in the same pedestrian fashion for a people never fastidious – the same again is the order of the day'.

Thus, a people with access to some of the best fresh ingredients on earth tended to boil everything to death. A nation strewn almost its entire length with excellent microclimates for viticulture produced only fortified plonk. Material comfort was valued, but was a plain thing indeed.

It took New Zealanders a quarter of a century more to shuck 'the same dull sandwiches', and embrace a national awareness – and, as Goldblatt correctly anticipated, it took 'hazards and misfortunes' to spur the 'divine discontent' for change.

But when it did happen, it *really* happened.

Russell Brown is a journalist and manager of the popular Public Address blog site (www.publicaddress.net).

terraced housing and apartments, either in the central city or on its fringes. As immigration-fuelled population growth continues to put pressure on space and prices, more Auckland citizens are learning to do without the birthright of owning their own home – let alone one with a backyard.

Wellington's inner-city boom is slightly different. As the public service has shrunk and large companies have moved their head offices away, old office buildings and warehouses have been converted for apartment living.

At the same time, a parallel trend has seen a rush to the coastlines, and to beautiful areas such as Nelson, at the top of the South Island, where property values have rocketed and orchards have been ploughed under to make way for more housing. In the process, an icon of the Kiwi lifestyle, the bach (pronounced 'batch') – a rough beach house, often passed down through families – has begun to disappear. Many New Zealanders feel this as a loss, especially when the land goes to foreign buyers, and the fear that coastal land is getting beyond the reach of ordinary families is a significant political issue.

The growth in economic inequality in recent decades is a serious problem. In a few poor urban areas such as South Auckland, two or three families may share a single house, with attendant public health problems. A partial return to the public housing policies that created a chunk of the country's current housing stock aims to address this problem.

Family trends, meanwhile, are similar to those in other Western countries: New Zealanders are marrying later (the median age for marriage has increased from just over 20 to over 30 years of age in the last 20 years) or not marrying at all. For those under 25 years of age, de facto unions are now more common than formal marriage, and about a third of all people between the ages of 15 and 44 who are living in partnerships are not legally married. About 21,000 couples still get married every year, and half that many get divorced.

The law extends matrimonial property principles to unmarried couples, including same-sex couples. Despite the obligatory outrage from conservatives, civil unions were introduced in 2005 – creating a new category of union similar to but separate from marriage – with the support of the majority of the population.

ECONOMY

NZ may be a long way away from just about everywhere but it is not immune to the vagaries of the global economy. In the quarter to June 2009 it just edged out of its worst recession in 30 years, following six quarters of negative growth. At the time of research it was uncertain as to whether the recovery would hold.

NZ escaped the worst of the global financial crisis due in part to the strength of its banking sector, which was never exposed to the subprime mortgage crisis that triggered the problem. NZ's Gross Domestic Product (GDP) currently stands at around $128 billion per annum. Unemployment has risen to 6.5% – a nine-year high.

The median annual income is $24,400, and wealth is far less evenly spread than it was 25 years ago – 18% earn more than double that, while 43% survive on less than $20,000. The wealthiest region is Wellington, where one in 20 adults reaps more than $100,000 per annum.

With regards to wealth, NZ sits 22nd among the 30 OECD countries on a measure of GDP per head in terms of 'purchasing power parity', indicating that its people are nearly a quarter less affluent than those of Australia, or roughly as wealthy as the average South Korean.

Back in the heady post-WWII days, NZ was towards the top of the list, buoyed by strong demand for wool, meat and dairy products. Things changed for the worse in 1973 when the country's preferential arrangements with

'How do you feel about your life as a whole?' In 2009, 86% responded 'satisfied' or 'very satisfied' to a Statistics NZ poll.

According to a 2009 survey, the happiest women in the country live in the Bay of Plenty, while the happiest men live in Nelson/Marlborough. Wellingtonians were the least happy.

NZ now has the sixth worst gap between rich and poor in the developed world, according to a 2009 UN report.

Britain ceased after the UK joined the European Economic Community (later the European Union). NZ was forced to find new markets, and now it exports mainly to Australia, the US, Japan and China. The main commodities exported (in order of value) are dairy products, meat, wood, fish and machinery. The country imports a great deal more than it exports (especially consumer and other manufactured goods) leading to a problematic balance of payments.

POPULATION & MULTICULTURALISM

There are an estimated 4.4 million resident New Zealanders, and almost one in three of them live in the largest city, Auckland, where growth has been fuelled both by a long-term drift north and more recent waves of immigration. The general drift to the cities means that urban areas now account for about 86% of the population.

The Maori population was somewhere between 100,000 and 200,000 at the time of first European contact 200 years ago. Disease and warfare subsequently brought the population near to collapse, but a high birth rate now sees about 15% of New Zealanders (565,000 people) identify as Maori, and that proportion is likely to grow.

NZ's population would hit 11 million if it were to take in all the people that wanted to settle there, according to Gallup, who rated it third in its 2009 Potential Net Migration Index.

The implication of the Treaty of Waitangi is one of partnership between Maori and the Crown (representing the New Zealanders who are 'Pakeha', or of British heritage), together forging a bicultural nation. After decades of attempted cultural assimilation it's now accepted in most quarters that the indigenous culture has a special and separate status within the country's ethnic mix. For example, Maori is an official language and there is a separate electoral role granting Maori guaranteed parliamentary seats.

Yet room has had to be found for the many New Zealanders of neither British nor Maori heritage. In each new wave of immigration there has been an unfortunate tendency to demonise before gradually accepting and celebrating what the new cultures have to offer. This happened with the Chinese in the mid-19th century, Croatians at the beginning of the 20th, Pacific Islanders in the 1970s and most recently the Chinese again in the 1990s. That said, NZ society is more integrated and accepting than most. People of all races are represented in all levels of society and race isn't an obstacle to achievement.

Auckland has been the prime destination for ethnic Chinese since immigration rules were relaxed in 1987. While many Asian immigrants have chosen to cluster in Auckland's eastern suburbs, visitors are often surprised by the 'Asianisation' of its central city, where thousands of East Asian students reside, either studying at Auckland University, learning English, or both.

People born in other countries make up 23% of NZ residents. Of these, the main regions of origin are the UK and Ireland (29%), the Pacific Islands (15%), Northeast Asia (15%) and Australia (7%).

Occasional incidents involving Asians – including some high-profile Asian-on-Asian crimes – have added to disquiet about Asian immigration in some parts of society. But opinion polls indicate that most Aucklanders tend to value the contribution of new migrants. Today, 13% of Aucklanders are of Asian extraction and it's estimated that numbers will reach 400,000 within seven years.

About 20% of Auckland Chinese were born in NZ, but considerable attention has been focused on the so-called '1.5 generation': young Chinese born overseas but socialised (and sometimes educated) in NZ. The traditionally quiescent culture of Chinese New Zealanders has been challenged in recent years, and a dynamic group of young ethnic Asians is emerging into leadership roles not only within their own community, but in wider NZ society.

Auckland is easily the most multicultural centre in NZ, with only slightly over half of the population of European descent (as opposed to around 80% in most of the South Island). It is effectively the capital of the South Pacific, with nearly 177,000 people of Pacific Island heritage living there. Pacific Islanders make up about 7% of the nation's population but 14% of Auckland's.

NZ never had an official 'white' immigration policy as Australia did, but for decades it tended to regard itself as an outpost of Britain. Now it is other influences – NZ's role in the Pacific, its burgeoning economic links to Asia, its offering of sanctuary to refugees – that will continue to shape what it is to be a New Zealander.

In percentage terms, Auckland is the seventh largest city for people of Chinese origin outside of China.

SPORT

The arena where Kiwis have most sated their desperation for recognition on the world stage is sport. For most of the 20th century, NZ's All Blacks dominated international rugby union, with one squad even dubbed 'The Invincibles'. Taking over this pastime of the British upper class did wonders for national identity and the game is now interwoven with NZ's history and culture. So when the All Blacks dip out of the Rugby World Cup at semifinal stage (as they have done no fewer than four times in recent tournaments), there is national mourning. Few seem to take solace in (or barely notice) the success of the NZ women's team, the Black Ferns, who have won the last three Women's Rugby World Cups. Below top international level, the Super 14 competition (with teams from Australia and South Africa) offers the world's best rugby, although local purists still prefer the National Provincial Championship (NPC).

For all rugby's influence on the culture, don't go to a game expecting to be caught up in an orgy of noise and cheering. Rugby crowds at Auckland's Eden Park are as restrained as their teams are cavalier, but they get noisier as you head south. Fans at Canterbury's excellent AMI Stadium (p232) are reputed to be the most one-eyed in the land.

In contrast, a home game for the NZ Warriors rugby league team at Auckland's Mt Smart Stadium is a thrilling spectacle, especially when the Polynesian drummers kick in. The Warriors are the only NZ team in the Australian NRL (National Rugby League) competition. Rugby League has traditionally been considered the working-class sport and support is strongest from Auckland's Maori, Polynesian and other immigrant communities.

RUGBY WORLD CUP 2011

On September 9, 2011 a burly bunch of men in black jerseys will start slapping their meaty thighs, rolling their eyes back in their heads, poking out their tongues and hurtling a blood-thirsty chant at their opposition. Such is NZ's rugby tradition. An overwhelming majority of the crowd packed into Auckland's Eden Park for the match against Tonga that marks the start of the 7th Rugby World Cup will be hoping and praying that the same ritual will be repeated here on October 23 at the final.

In the interim, 20 teams (divided into four pools of five) will be competing in games held all over the country, from Whangarei in the north to Invercargill in the south. The quarter finals are scheduled for the weekend of October 8 and 9 (in Wellington and Christchurch), with the semifinals in Auckland the following weekend. Expect accommodation to be scarce at these times.

Tickets go on sale to the public in late 2010, with a ballot for tickets for the finals held in early 2011 (see www.rugbyworldcup.com for details). Prices range from as little as $30 (children $15), for pool games featuring the minnows, up to $450 for top seats at All Blacks pool matches. Quarter finals tickets start at $190 and finals from $390.

If you can't nab (or can't afford) a ticket, the main centres are planning public events with big screens to follow the proceedings, particularly Auckland which is considering turning Princes Wharf into 'party central' for the duration. Whether you find yourself cheering on Namibia at a match or you watch all the action from a small-town pub, it's guaranteed to be a fascinating time to visit.

NZ are the current rugby league world champions, taking the trophy from Australia (in Australia) in 2008. Defeating the neighbours in their favourite game brought a smile to the faces of even the strongest supporters of the rival rugby code.

By the time this book is published the All Whites, NZ's national soccer (football) squad will have competed in the 2010 FIFA World Cup, qualifying for the second time in history. Nobody expects them to do as well as the rugby league boys but getting there is a huge achievement for such a rugby-mad nation. Scoring a few goals or (gasp!) winning a game would be the icing on the cake.

Netball is the leading sport for women and the one in which the national team, the Silver Ferns, perpetually vies for world supremacy with the Australians – one or other of the countries has taken the world championship at every contest (except for a tie in 1979). The rivalry has intensified since 2008 when both countries disbanded their national club leagues to start a new trans-Tasman competition featuring five teams from each country.

Cricket is the established summer team sport, and the State Shield (one-day) and State Championship provincial competitions take place alongside international matches involving the national side, the Black Caps, through the summer months. Wellington's Basin Reserve is the last sole-use test cricket venue in the main centres (and only a few minutes' walk from the bars and restaurants of Courtenay Pl) while New Plymouth's Pukekura Park is simply one of the prettiest cricket grounds in the world.

Other sports in which NZ pushes above its weight include sailing, rowing, canoeing, equestrian and triathlon. The most Olympic medals NZ has won have been in athletics, particularly in track and field events.

New Zealanders not only watch sport, they play it. Many workplaces have social teams or groups of mates get together for a friendly match. The most popular sports for men to participate in are (in order) golf, cricket, tennis, touch football and rugby union. For women it's netball, tennis, golf, touch football and skiing. Other popular active pursuits include kayaking, mountain biking, walking and running.

> The first referee in the world to use a whistle to halt a game was William Atack of Christchurch. He thought of this now seemingly obvious and ubiquitous refereeing tool in 1884.

MEDIA

Almost all NZ cities have their own morning newspapers, sometimes coexisting with the Auckland-based *New Zealand Herald* (www.nzherald.co.nz).

The magazine market is more varied, and dominated by independent publishers. The *Listener* (like the *Herald*, owned by Australian company APN) is published weekly and offers TV and radio listings. Auckland's own magazine, *Metro,* is a good-looking guide to the style of the city. *Cuisine* is a sleek, popular and authoritative guide to food and wine.

Free-to-air TV is dominated by the two publicly owned TV New Zealand channels (TV One and TV2), versus the Australian-owned TV3 and its sibling music channel C4. Maori TV is a great source of locally produced programming as well as screening some interesting foreign documentaries and films. Much of it is broadcast in Maori, although subtitles are often added.

Radio Sport carries one of the sounds of the NZ summer: cricket commentaries. The public broadcaster, Radio New Zealand, is based in Wellington: its flagship, National Radio, offers strong news and feature programming and is available nationwide. The network of student stations, the bNet, offers an engaging and adventurous alternative (they're also the best place to hear about local gigs), and the most sophisticated of the stations, Auckland's 95bFM, is influential in its advocacy of new alternative music.

There is also a nationwide network of *iwi* (tribal) stations, some of which, including Waikato's Radio Tainui, offer welcome respite from the commercial networks – others, such as Auckland's Mai FM, take on the commercial broadcasters at their own game. Also worth noting are the national Pacific Island station Niu FM and the dance station George FM, which started from a bedroom in Auckland's Grey Lynn and can now be heard in 16 towns.

For interesting analysis of the issues of the day and the buzz on the streets check out the excellent *Public Address* blog site (www.publicaddress.net). Wellington is well serviced by the *Wellingtonista* (www.wellingtonista.com), which serves up 'random stuff about NZ's capital city'.

RELIGION

Although the national anthem, 'God Defend New Zealand', is an appeal to the Almighty, and parliament begins every day with prayers, New Zealanders are not a particularly pious people – far less so, according to polls, than Australians. A New Zealander is more likely to be spiritually fulfilled in the outdoors than in church. The land and sea were spiritual constants in pre-European Maori culture and they are scarcely less so today.

NZ is predominantly a Christian country (56%), although over a third of the population claim no religious affiliation at all. The number of people identifying as Christian has been falling – by 5% between the 2001 and 2006 censuses – although religion remains strong in the Pacific Island community, where 80% are members of that faith.

Reflecting its English heritage, NZ is nominally Anglican; where religion has a place in public affairs it will be of that flavour. Yet the Catholic Church is gaining ground, increasing its numbers by 5% in recent years. Catholicism now has 508,000 adherents to Anglicanism's 555,000.

Maori spirituality has been fused with Christianity since colonisation in movements such as Ratana and Ringatu, but is increasingly expressed in its own right.

Immigrants have brought their faiths with them, but religions such as Islam, Hinduism, Sikhism, Judaism and Buddhism in total account for less than 4% of the population.

WOMEN IN NEW ZEALAND

NZ is justifiably proud of being the first country in the world to give women the vote (in 1893). Kate Sheppard, the hero of the women's suffrage movement, even features on the $10 bill.

Despite that early achievement, the real role for women in public life was modest for many years. That can hardly be said now. The country has had two female prime ministers and for a time in 2000 every key constitutional position was held by a woman, including the attorney general, chief justice, governor general and head of state – although New Zealanders can't take credit for choosing Betty Windsor for that role. At the same time a Maori queen headed the Kingitanga and a woman led NZ's biggest listed corporation.

Yet, even with the presence of a Ministry of Women's Affairs, some benefits have been slow to come to ordinary NZ women: paid parental leave was only instituted in 2002, for example. As in most other countries, women's wages tend to be lower than men's, although the gap is closing. Women are nearly twice as likely to work more than one job and there are three times more men in the top earnings decile (over $67,000 per annum) than women.

When NZ women complain that there aren't enough decent men to go around, they've got a point: there are 104 women for every 100 men. The man shortage is particularly acute for straight women in their 30s, an age at which Kiwi blokes are more likely to be living overseas than their

Glamorous Rotorua-born Jean Batten, known as Hine-o-te-Rangi (Daughter of the Skies), was a famous pilot and the most famous New Zealander of the 1930s. During a glittering career, she broke several records for long-distance solo flights.

countrywomen. If they do snag a keeper, chances are he'll be older – the median age for brides is 30, while its 33 for bridegrooms.

On the plus side, women live longer: the average life expectancy for women is 82, as opposed to 78 for men.

NZ has shamefully high rates of domestic and child abuse. A 2007 study suggested that as many as a quarter of NZ women had suffered some form of sexual abuse by the time they were 15. The figures were higher for rural women.

In 1989 when Penny Jamieson was consecrated as the Bishop of Dunedin she became the world's second ever female Anglican bishop and the first to lead a diocese in her own right.

ARTS
Literature

A nationalist movement arose in literature in the 1930s, challenging the notion of NZ being an annex of the 'mother country' and striving for an independent identity. Some writers who appeared then – especially the poets Allen Curnow, Denis Glover, ARD Fairburn and RAK Mason – became commanding figures in the definition of a new culture, and were still around in the 1950s to be part of what prominent historian Keith Sinclair (himself a poet) called the time 'when the NZ intellect and imagination came alive'.

Katherine Mansfield's work began a NZ tradition in short fiction, and for years the standard was carried by novelist Janet Frame, whose dramatic life was depicted in Jane Campion's film of her autobiography, *An Angel at My Table*. Her novel *The Carpathians* (1989) won the Commonwealth Writers' Prize. A new era of international recognition began in 1985 when Keri Hulme's haunting *The Bone People* won the Booker Prize (the world is still waiting for the follow-up, *Bait*).

It wasn't until 2007 that another Kiwi looked likely to snag the Booker. Lloyd Jones' *Mister Pip* was pipped at the post, but the nomination rocketed his book up literature charts the world over.

Less recognised internationally, Maurice 'gee-I've-won-a-lot-of-awards' Gee has gained the nation's annual top fiction gong for *Blindsight* (2005), *Live Bodies* (1998), *Going West* (1992), *The Burning Boy* (1990), *Plumb* (1978) and *A Glorious Morning Comrade* (1975). His much-loved children's novel *Under The Mountain* (1979) was made into a seminal NZ TV series in 1981 and then a major motion picture in 2009. In 2004 the adaptation of another of his novels, *In My Father's Den* (1972), won major awards at international film festivals and is one of the country's highest grossing films. His latest novel is *Access Road* (2009).

Some of the most interesting and enjoyable NZ fiction voices belong to Maori writers. Witi Ihimaera's novels give a wonderful insight into small-town Maori life on the East Coast – especially *Bulibasha* (1994) and *The Whale Rider* (1987), which was made into an acclaimed film – while *Nights In The Gardens Of Spain* (1996) casts a similar light on Auckland's gay scene. His most recent novel is *The Trowenna Sea* (2009). Patricia Grace's work is similarly filled with exquisitely told stories of rural *marae*-centred life: try *Mutuwhenua* (1978), *Potiki* (1986) or *Tu* (2004).

Also worth checking out are Elizabeth Knox (*The Vintner's Luck*, 1998; *The Angel's Cut*, 2009), Charlotte Grimshaw (*Opportunity*, 2007) and Emily Perkins (*Novel About My Wife*, 2008).

Witi Ihimaera wrote his novel *The Whale Rider* in a three-week burst in 1987, inspired by his daughters' complaints that he took them to movies with only male heroes.

Cinema & TV

If you first got interested in NZ by watching it on the silver screen, you're in good company. Peter Jackson's NZ-made *Lord of the Rings* (*LOTR*) trilogy was the best thing to happen to NZ tourism since Captain Cook.

Yet NZ cinema is hardly ever easy-going. In his BBC-funded documentary, *Cinema of Unease*, NZ actor Sam Neill described the country's film industry

NEW ZEALAND'S LORD OF THE REELS *Errol Hunt*

Peter Jackson was already a hero to NZ's small film industry before he directed his career-defining *Lord of the Rings* (*LOTR*) trilogy. From his very first film, *Bad Taste* (vomit-eating aliens and exploding sheep; 1987), it was obvious that he was a unique talent. It was followed by *Meet the Feebles* (muppets on acid; 1989) and an even gorier zombie movie, *Braindead* ('I kick ass for the Lord'; 1992). Two slightly-less-bloodstained films – *Heavenly Creatures* (1994) and *The Frighteners* (1996) – preceded the *LOTR* films, while *King Kong* (2005) and *The Lovely Bones* (2009) have followed in the tiny hobbits' giant footsteps.

The effect of the three *LOTR* films on NZ was unparalleled: the country embraced Jackson and his trilogy with a passion. Wellington was renamed Middle-earth for the week of the first film's release in late 2001, a Minister for the *LOTR* was named in the NZ government and Jackson was made a Companion of the New Zealand Order of Merit for his services in the film industry. The frenzy only increased for the second and third films, especially when the world premiere (*world* premiere!) of *The Return of the King* was held in Wellington in December 2003, and of course went on to win a record 11 Oscars.

For rainy-weekend viewing, hit the Jackson DVD back-catalogue and look for the man himself. He stars as both the chainsaw-wielding Derek and Robert the Alien in *Bad Taste,* and has cameos as the undertaker's assistant in *Braindead,* a hobo outside a cinema in *Heavenly Creatures* and a clumsy, chain-wearing biker in *The Frighteners.* In the *LOTR* films, Jackson appears as a belching hobbit outside a pub in *The Fellowship of the Ring,* a stone-throwing Helms Deep defender in *The Two Towers* and a captain of the Corsairs in *The Return of the King.* In *King Kong,* a slimmed-down Jackson plays a biplane machine gunner, while in *The Lovely Bones* he's a customer in the camera store.

---

as 'uniquely strange and dark', producing bleak, haunted work. One need only watch Lee Tamahore's harrowing *Once Were Warriors* (1994) to see what he means.

The *Listener*'s film critic, Philip Matthews, makes a slightly more upbeat observation: 'Between (Niki Caro's) *Whale Rider,* (Christine Jeffs') *Rain* and *Lord of the Rings,* you can extract the qualities that our best films possess. Beyond slick technical accomplishment, all share a kind of land-mysticism, an innately supernatural sensibility'.

You could add to this list Jane Campion's *The Piano* (1993), Brad McGann's *In My Father's Den* (2004), James Napier-Roberston's *I'm Not Harry Jenson* (2009) and Jackson's *Heavenly Creatures* (1994) – all of which use magically lush scenery to couch disturbing violence. It's a land-mysticism constantly bordering on the creepy.

Even when Kiwis do humour it's as resolutely black as their rugby jerseys. Check out Jackson's early splatter-fests (see the boxed text, above), Taika Cohen's oddball loser-palooza *Eagle vs Shark* (2007) and Jonathan King's sickly hilarious *Black Sheep* (2006) – 'get ready for the violence of the lambs'. Exporting NZ comedy hasn't been easy, yet the HBO-produced TV musical parody *Flight of the Conchords* – featuring a mumbling, bumbling Kiwi folk-singing duo trying to get a break in New York – has found surprising international success, particularly in the supposed irony-free zone that is the US.

New Zealanders have gone from never seeing themselves in international cinema to having whole cloned armies of Temuera Morrisons invading the universe in *Star Wars*. Familiar faces such as Cliff Curtis and Karl Urban seem to constantly pop up playing Mexican or Russian gangsters in action movies. Many of them got their start in long-running soap opera *Shortland St* (7pm weekdays, TV2).

Other local shows worth catching are *Outrageous Fortune,* a rough-edged comedy-drama set in West Auckland, and *bro'Town,* a better-drawn

Other than 2003's winner *Return of the King, The Piano* is the only NZ movie to be nominated for a Best Picture Oscar. Jane Campion was the first Kiwi nominated as Best Director and Peter Jackson the first to win it.

The only Kiwi actors to have won an Oscar are Anna Paquin (for *The Piano*) and Russell Crowe (for *Gladiator*). Paquin was born in Canada but moved to NZ when she was four, while Crowe moved from NZ to Australia at the same age.

Polynesian version of *South Park*. It's the Polynesian giggle-factor that seems likeliest to break down the bleak house of NZ cinema. The *bro'Town* boys (who also do stand-up comedy as the Naked Samoans) hit the big screen with the feel-good-through-and-through *Sione's Wedding* in 2006 – with the second-biggest local takings of any NZ film.

While another *LOTR*-style blockbuster has proved illusive, the NZ film industry has quietly continued producing well-crafted, affecting movies such as *Dean Spanley* (2008), *The Strength Of Water* (2009), *The Topp Twins: Untouchable Girls* (people's choice documentary winner at the Toronto and Melbourne film festivals, 2009) and *The Lovely Bones* (2009).

Music   Gareth Shute

New Zealand music began with the early forms of *waiata* (singing) developed by Maori following their arrival in the country. The main musical instruments were wind instruments made of bone or wood, the most well-known of which is the *nguru* (commonly known as the 'nose flute'), while percussion was provided by chest- and thigh-slapping. These days, the liveliest place to see Maori music being performed is at Kapa Haka competitions, in which groups compete with their own routines of traditional song and dance. In a similar vein is the Pasifika Festival in Auckland, which has sections that represent each of the Pacific Islands. It is a great place to see both traditional and modern forms of Polynesian music, whether that means modern hip-hop beats or throbbing Cook Island drums, or island-style guitar, ukulele, and slide guitar.

European music first arrived in New Zealand with immigrants from Europe, and steadily developed local variants over the early 1900s. In the 1950s Douglas Lilburn became one of the first internationally recognised NZ classical composers. More recently the country has produced a number of world-renowned musicians in this field, including opera singer Dame Kiri Te Kanawa, million-selling pop diva Hayley Westenra, composer John Psathas (who composed music for the 2004 Olympic Games) and composer/percussionist Gareth Farr (who also performs in drag under the name, Lilith). Each of the main universities in New Zealand runs its own music school and these often have free concerts which visitors can attend. More large scale performances are held at various venues within the Edge conglomerate of venues in Auckland, the Town Hall/Michael Fowler Centre in Wellington (p108), and the Town Hall in Christchurch (p231).

New Zealand also has a strong rock music scene, its most acclaimed exports being the revered indie label Flying Nun and the music of the Finn Brothers (p47). In 1981 Flying Nun was started by Christchurch record store owner, Roger Shepherd. Many of the early groups came from Dunedin, where local

---

Gareth Shute is the author of four books, including *Hip Hop Music In Aotearoa* and *NZ Rock 1987–2007*. He is also a musician and has toured the UK, Europe, and Australia as a member of The Ruby Suns and The Brunettes. He now plays in The Conjurors and The Cosbys.

A wide range of cultural events are listed on www.nzlive.com – this is a good place to find out about Kapa Haka performances.

MIDDLE-EARTH TOURISM

If you are one of those travellers inspired to come down under by the scenery of the *LOTR* movies, you won't be disappointed. Jackson's decision to film in NZ wasn't mere patriotism. Nowhere else on earth will you find such wildly varied, unspoiled landscapes.

You will doubtless recognise some places from the films. For example, Hobbiton (near Matamata; , Mt Doom (instantly recognisable as towering Ngauruhoe; or the Misty Mountains (the South Island's Southern Alps). The visitor information centres in Wellington, Twizel or Queenstown should be able to direct you to local *LOTR* sites of interest. If you're serious about finding the exact spots where scenes were filmed, buy a copy of Ian Brodie's nerdtastic *The Lord of the Rings: Location Guidebook*, which includes instructions, and even GPS coordinates, for finding all the important scenes.

musicians took the do-it-yourself attitude of punk but used it to produce a lo-fi indie-pop which received rave reviews from the likes of *NME* in the UK and *Rolling Stone* magazine in the US. *Billboard* even claimed in 1989: 'There doesn't seem to be anything on Flying Nun Records that is less than excellent.' Many of the musicians from the Flying Nun scene still perform live to this day, including David Kilgour (from The Clean), Martin Phillipps (from The Chills), and Shayne Carter (from the Straitjacket Fits, now fronting Dimmer). Chick's Hotel (p278) in Port Chalmers (near Dunedin) and the Dux De Lux (p230) in Christchurch (and during the winter, its sister bar in Queenstown – see p317) continue to be home to a flourishing indie-rock scene. Also recommended is Wunderbar (p236) in Lyttelton (near Christchurch) which is a rustic venue with a fantastic hillside view of the harbour below.

Flying Nun was recently bought back by its original owner, Roger Shepherd, and continues to release exciting new acts such as The Mint Chicks. Other young indie labels have also sprung up in the meantime including Lil Chief Records and Arch Hill Recordings. For more adventurous listeners, Bruce Russell continues to play in influential underground group The Dead C, and releases music through his Corpus Hermeticum label.

Since the new millennium, the NZ music scene has developed a new vitality after the government convinced commercial radio stations in the country to adopt a voluntary quota of 20% local music. This has enabled the more commercially orientated musicians to have solid careers. Rock groups such as Shihad, The Feelers, and Op-shop have thrived in this environment, as have a set of soulful female solo artists (who all happen to have Maori heritage): Bic Runga, Anika Moa, and Brooke Fraser (daughter of All Black, Bernie Fraser).

However, the genres of music that have been adopted most enthusiastically by Maori and Polynesian New Zealanders have been reggae (in the 1970s) and hip hop (in 1980s), which has led to distinct local variants of these musical styles. In Wellington, a thriving jazz scene took on a reggae influence to create a host of groups that blend dub, roots, and funky jazz – most notably Fat Freddy's Drop. Most of the venues for this music can be found

Concerts and classical music recitals can be found at www.event finder.co.nz. For more specific information on the NZ classical music scene, see: www.sounz .org.nz.

One of the most complete listings of NZ bands that have existed over the last couple of decades is available at www .muzic.net.nz. A thriving community of bloggers also discuss local music at www.nzmusic.com.

THE BROTHERS FINN

There are certain tunes that all Kiwis can sing along to, given a beer and the opportunity. The music of Tim and Neil Finn makes up a good proportion of these, and many of their songs have gone on to be international hits.

Tim Finn first came to prominence in late-70s group, Split Enz. When their original guitarist quit, Neil flew over to join the band in the UK despite being only 15 at the time. Split Enz amassed a solid following in Australia, New Zealand, and Canada before disbanding in 1985. Neil then formed Crowded House with two Australian musicians (Paul Hester and Nick Seymour) and one of their early singles, 'Don't Dream It's Over' went on to hit number two on the US charts. Tim later did a brief spell in the band, during which the brothers wrote 'Weather With You' – a song which reached number seven on the UK charts, pushing their album *Woodface* to gold sales. The original line-up of Crowded House played their final show in 1996, in front of 100,000 people on the steps of the Sydney Opera House (though Finn and Seymour reformed the group briefly in 2007 and continue to tour and record occasionally). Tim and Neil have both released a number of solo albums, as well as combining for the occasional album as the Finn Brothers.

More recently, Tim's solo career was reinvigorated when one of his songs was picked up for the movie *The Chronicles of Narnia: The Lion, the Witch & the Wardrobe*. Neil has also remained busy, organising a set of shows/releases under the name Seven Worlds Collide, which is a collaboration with well-known overseas musicians, including Jeff Tweedy (Wilco), Johnny Marr (The Smiths), and members of Radiohead. Both Tim and Neil were born in the small town of Te Awamutu and the local museum has a collection that documents their work.

ICONIC NEW ZEALAND SONGS

Listed below are 20 songs that any self-respecting Kiwi is bound to know. If you'd like a local soundtrack for your NZ visit, then you might consider downloading the following 20 songs (legally of course) to your MP3 player either via i-Tunes or through www.amplifier.co.nz, which specialises in NZ music downloads. Alternatively, you may wish to search out the collection, *The Great New Zealand Songbook*, or the series of *Nature's Best* compilations.

Bic Runga (1997) Sway	**Hello Sailor** (1977) Blue Lady
Che Fu and DLT (1996) Chains	**John Rowles** (1970) Cheryl Moana Marie
The Chills (1991) Heavenly Pop Hit	**Kiri Te Kanawa** (this version, 1999) Pokarekare Ana
Chris Knox (1990) Not Given Lightly	**Ladyhawke** (2009) Magic
The Clean (1981) Tally Ho	**Savage** (2008) Swing
Crowded House (1986) Don't Dream it's Over	**Scribe** (2003) Not Many
David Dobbyn with Herbs (1986) Slice of Heaven	**Shihad** (1997) Home Again
Dragon (1978) April Sun in Cuba	**Split Enz** (1982) Six Months in a Leaky Boat
The Exponents (1991) Why Does Love Do This to Me?	**Straitjacket Fits** (1987) She Speeds
Fourmyula (1969) Nature	**The Swingers** (1981) Counting the Beat

---

along Courtenay Place or between the shops on Cuba Mall (see p107). The national public holiday, Waitangi Day, on February 6th also happens to fall on the birthday of Bob Marley and yearly reggae concerts are held on this day in Auckland and Wellington.

The local hip-hop scene has its heart in the suburbs of South Auckland, which have a high concentration of Maori and Pacific Island residents. This area is home to one of New Zealand's foremost hip-hop labels, Dawn Raid, which takes its name from the infamous early-morning house raids of the 1970s that police performed on Pacific Islanders who outstayed their visas. Dawn Raid's most successful artist is Savage, who sold a million copies of his single 'Swing' after it was featured in the movie, *Knocked Up*. Within New Zealand, the most well-known hip-hop acts are Scribe, Che Fu, and Smashproof (who broke the record for the longest running single at number one). Hip-hop shows in Auckland are held at a wide range of venues, though popular favourites are 4:20 and Rising Sun and funk-fuelled club, Khuja Lounge.

Early in the new millennium, New Zealand became known as a home for garage rock after the international rise of two local acts: the Datsuns and the D4. In Auckland the main venues for rock music are the Kings Arms and Cassette Number Nine, though two joint venues in St Kevins Arcade (off Karangahape Rd) are also popular – the Wine Cellar/Whammy Bar. Wellington is also rife with live music venues from Mighty Mighty (p106), to the San Francisco Bath House (p108), to Bodega (p108).

Dance music had its strongest following in Christchurch in the 1990s, when it gave rise to the popular dub/electronica outfit, Salmonella Dub. Drum 'n' bass remains popular locally and has spawned internationally successful acts such as Concord Dawn and Shapeshifter.

In summer, many of the beachfront towns throughout the country are visited by touring bands (winery shows are also popular). One venue of note in this respect is the Leigh Sawmill Café in Leigh (85km from Auckland), which also offers accommodation and is located near the popular scuba-diving/snorkelling spot at Goat Island.

A number of festivals also take place over the summer months, including the local leg of the Big Day Out, new year's celebration Rhythm & Vines, and the Christian-rock festival, Parachute (www.parachutemusic.com), in January

An up-to-date list of gigs in the main centres is listed at www.groove guide.co.nz. For those interested in indie rock, a great source of information is www.cheese ontoast.co.nz, which lists gigs and has interviews/photographs of bands (both local and international).

The TV show, *Popstars*, originated in New Zealand though the resulting group, True Bliss, was short-lived. The series concept was then picked up in Australia, the UK, and the US, before inspiring the *Idol* series.

(held near Wellington). Also recommended is the underground festival held early each year by A Low Hum (www.alowhum.com). Lovers of world music may enjoy the local version of Womad, which is held in New Plymouth and features both local and overseas acts that draw from traditional music forms.

Visual Arts

The NZ 'can do' attitude extends to the visual arts. If you're visiting a local's home don't be surprised to find one of the owner's paintings on the wall or one of their mate's sculptures in the back garden, pieced together out of bits of shell, driftwood and a length of the magical 'number-eight wire'.

This is symptomatic of a flourishing local art and crafts scene cultivated by lively tertiary courses churning out traditional carvers and weavers, jewellery makers, multimedia boffins, and moulders of metal and glass. The larger cities have excellent dealer galleries representing interesting local artists working across all mediums.

Not all the best galleries are in Auckland or Wellington. The energetic Govett-Brewster Art Gallery – home to the legacy of sculptor and film-maker Len Lye – is worth a visit to New Plymouth in itself, and Gore's Eastern Southland Gallery (p360) has an important and growing collection of works by Ralph Hotere, Rita Angus and others.

Traditional Maori art has a distinctive visual style with well-developed motifs that have been embraced by NZ artists of every race. In the painting medium, these include the cool modernism of the work of Gordon Walters and the more controversial pop-art approach of Dick Frizzell's *Tiki* series. Likewise, Pacific Island themes are common, particularly in Auckland. An example is the work of Niuean-born Auckland-raised John Pule, who is also a poet and novelist.

It should not be surprising that in a nation so defined by its natural environment, landscape painting constituted the first post-European body of art. John Gully and Petrus van der Velden were among those to arrive and paint memorable (if sometimes overdramatised) depictions of the land.

A little later, Charles Frederick Goldie painted a series of compelling, realist portraits of Maori, who were feared to be a dying race. Debate over the political propriety of Goldie's work raged for years, but its value is widely accepted now: not least because Maori themselves generally acknowledge and value them as ancestral representations.

From the 1930s NZ art took a more modern direction and produced some of the country's most celebrated artists including Rita Angus, Toss Woollaston and Colin McCahon. McCahon is widely regarded to have been the country's most important artist. His paintings might seem inscrutable, even forbidding, but, even where McCahon lurched into Catholic mysticism or quoted screeds from the Bible, his spirituality was rooted in geography. His bleak, brooding landscapes evoke the sheer power of NZ's terrain. The influence of his dramatic, simple canvasses can be seen in the work of celebrated current artists, such as Ralph Hotere and Shane Cotton.

How Bizarre was a massive hit in Europe, the UK, the US, and Australia during 1996. The song was by OMC – an acronym for 'Otara Millionaire's Club', which made light of OMC's poverty-stricken home suburb of Otara.

Rita Angus' 1936 work *Cass* was voted the country's greatest painting in a 2006 poll. It hangs at the Christchurch Art Gallery.

Maori Culture John Huria

John Huria (Ngai Tahu, Muaupoko) has an editorial, research and writing background with a focus on Maori writing and culture. He was senior editor for Maori publishing company Huia (NZ) and now runs an editorial and publishing services company, Ahi Text Solutions Ltd (www. ahitextsolutions.co.nz).

'Maori' once just meant 'common' or 'everyday', but now it means…let's just begin this chapter by saying that there is a lot of 'then' and a lot of 'now' in the Maori world. Sometimes the cultural present follows on from the past quite seamlessly; sometimes things have changed hugely; sometimes we just want to look to the future.

Maori today are a diverse people. Some are engaged with traditional cultural networks and pursuits; others are occupied with adapting tradition and placing it into a dialogue with globalising culture. The Maori concept of *whanaungatanga* – family relationships – is important to the culture. And families spread out from the *whanau* (extended family) to the *hapu* (subtribe) and *iwi* (tribe) and even, in a sense, beyond the human world and into the natural and spiritual worlds.

Maori are New Zealand's *tangata whenua* (people of the land), and the Maori relationship with the land has developed over hundreds of years of occupation. Once a predominantly rural people, many Maori now live in urban centres, away from their traditional home base. But it's still common practice in formal settings to introduce oneself by referring to home: an ancestral mountain, river, sea or lake, or an ancestor. There's no place like home, but it's good to be away as well.

If you're looking for a Maori experience in NZ you'll find it – in performance, in conversation, in an art gallery, on a tour…

MAORI THEN

Some three millennia ago people began moving eastwards into the Pacific, sailing against the prevailing winds and currents (hard to go out, easier to return safely). Some stopped at Tonga and Samoa, and others settled the small central East Polynesian tropical islands.

The Maori colonisation of Aotearoa began from an original homeland known to Maori as Hawaiki. Skilled navigators and sailors travelled across the Pacific, using many navigational tools – currents, winds, stars, birds and wave patterns – to guide their large, double-hulled ocean-going craft to a new land. The first of many was the great navigator Kupe who arrived, the story goes, chasing an octopus named Muturangi. But the distinction of giving NZ its well-known Maori name – Aotearoa – goes to his wife, Kuramarotini, who cried out, '*He ao, he ao tea, he ao tea roa!*' (A cloud, a white cloud, a long white cloud!).

Kupe and his crew journeyed around the land, and many places around Cook Strait (between the North and South Islands) and the Hokianga in Northland still bear the names that they gave them and the marks of his passage. Kupe returned to Hawaiki, leaving from (and naming) Northland's Hokianga. He gave other seafarers valuable navigational information. And then the great *waka* (ocean-going craft) began to arrive.

The *waka* that the first setters arrived on, and their landing places, are immortalised in tribal histories. Well-known *waka* include *Takitimu, Kurahaupo, Te Arawa, Mataatua, Tainui, Aotea* and *Tokomaru*. There are many others. Maori trace their genealogies back to those who arrived on the *waka* (and further back as well).

What would it have been like making the transition from small tropical islands to a much larger, cooler land mass? Goodbye breadfruit, coconuts, paper mulberry; hello moa, fernroot, flax – and immense space (relatively speaking). NZ has over 15,000km of coastline. Rarotonga, by way of contrast, has a little over 30. There was land, lots of it, and a flora and fauna that had developed more or less separately from the rest of the world for 80 million years. There was an untouched, massive fishery. There were great seaside mammalian convenience stores – seals and sea lions – as well as a fabulous array of birds.

The early settlers went on the move, pulled by love, by trade opportunities and greater resources; pushed by disputes and threats to security. When they settled, Maori established *mana whenua* (regional authority), whether by military campaigns, or by the peaceful methods of intermarriage and diplomacy. Looking over tribal history it's possible to see the many alliances, absorptions and extinctions that went on.

Histories were carried by the voice, in stories, songs and chants. Great stress was placed on accurate learning – after all, in an oral culture where people are the libraries, the past is always a generation or two away from oblivion.

Maori lived in *kainga*, small villages, which often had associated gardens. Housing was quite cosy by modern standards – often it was hard to stand upright while inside. From time to time people would leave their home base and go to harvest seasonal foods. When peaceful life was interrupted by conflict, the people would withdraw to *pa*, fortified dwelling places.

And then Europeans began to arrive (see p27).

Maori legends are all around you as you tour NZ: Maui's *waka* became today's Southern Alps; a *taniwha* formed Lake Waikaremoana in its death throes; and a rejected Mt Taranaki walked into exile from the central North Island mountain group, carving the Whanganui River.

MAORI TODAY

Today's culture is marked by new developments in the arts, business, sport and politics. Many historical grievances still stand, but some *iwi* (Ngai Tahu and Tainui, for example) have settled historical grievances and are major forces in the NZ economy. Maori have also addressed the decline in Maori language use by establishing *kohanga reo, kura kaupapa Maori* and *wananga* (Maori-medium preschools, schools and universities). There is now a generation of people who speak Maori as a first language. There is a network of Maori radio stations, and Maori TV is attracting a committed viewership. A recently

---

HOW THE WORLD BEGAN

In the Maori story of creation, first there was the void, then the night, then Rangi-nui and Papa-tu-a-nuku (sky father and earth mother) came into being, embracing with their children nurtured between them. But nurturing became something else. Their children were stifled in the darkness of their embrace. Unable to stretch out to their full dimensions and struggling to see clearly in the darkness, their children tried to separate them. Tawhiri-matea, the god of winds, raged against them; Tu-mata-uenga, the god of war, assaulted them. Each god child in turn tried to separate them, but still Rangi and Papa pressed against each other. And then Tane-mahuta, god of the great forests and of humanity, placed his feet against his father and his back against his mother and slowly, inexorably, began to move them apart. Then came the world of light, of demigods and humanity.

In this world of light Maui, the demigod ancestor, was cast out to sea at birth and was found floating in his mother's topknot. He was a shape-shifter, becoming a pigeon or a dog or an eel if it suited his purposes. He stole fire from the gods. Using his grandmother's jawbone, he bashed the sun so that it could only limp slowly across the sky, so that people would have enough time during the day to get things done (if only he would do it again!). Using the South Island as a canoe, he used the jawbone as a hook to fish up Te Ika a Maui (the fish of Maui) – the North Island. And, finally, he met his end trying to defeat death itself. The goddess of death, Hine Nui Te Po, had obsidian teeth in her vagina (obsidian is a volcanic glass that takes a razor edge when chipped). Maui attempted to reverse birth (and hence defeat death) by crawling into her birth canal to reach her heart as she slept. A small bird – a fantail – laughed at the absurd sight. Hine Nui Te Po awoke, and crushed Maui between her thighs. Death one, humanity nil.

revived Maori event is becoming more and more prominent – Matariki, or Maori New Year. The constellation Matariki is also known as the Pleiades. It begins to rise above the horizon in late May or early June and its appearance traditionally signals a time for learning, planning and preparing as well as singing, dancing and celebrating. Watch out for talks and lectures, concerts, dinners, and even formal balls.

RELIGION

You can check out a map that shows *iwi* distribution and a good list of *iwi* websites on Wikipedia (www.wikipedia.org).

Christian churches and denominations are important in the Maori world: televangelists, mainstream churches for regular and occasional worship, and two major Maori churches (Ringatu and Ratana) – we've got it all.

But in the (non-Judaeo Christian) beginning there were the *atua Maori*, the Maori gods, and for many Maori the gods are a vital and relevant force still. It is common to greet the earth mother and sky father when speaking formally at a *marae*. The gods are represented in art and carving, sung of in *waiata* (songs), invoked through *karakia* (prayer and incantation) when a meeting house is opened, when a *waka* is launched, even (more simply) when a meal is served. They are spoken of on the *marae* and in wider Maori contexts. The traditional Maori creation story is well known and widely celebrated (see the boxed text, opposite).

THE ARTS

There are many collections of Maori *taonga* (treasures) around the country. Some of the largest and most comprehensive are at Wellington's Te Papa Museum (p97) and the Auckland Museum. Canterbury Museum (p219) in Christchurch also has a good collection, and Hokitika's West Coast Historical Museum (p194) has an exhibition showing the story of *pounamu* (nephrite jade, or greenstone).

Depending on area, the *powhiri* has gender roles: women *karanga* (call), men *whaikorero* (orate); women lead the way on to the *marae*, men sit on the *paepae* (the speakers' bench at the front). In a modern context, the debate around these roles continues.

You can stay up to date with what is happening in the Maori arts by reading *Mana* magazine (available from most newsagents), listening to *iwi* stations (www.irirangi.net) or weekly podcasts from Radio New Zealand (www.radionz.co.nz/genre/maori,pacific). Maori TV also has regular features on the Maori arts – check out www.maoritelevision.com.

Maori TV went to air in 2004, an emotional time for many Maori who could at last see their culture, their concerns and their language in a mass medium. Over 90% of content is NZ made, and programs are in both Maori and English: they're subtitled and accessible to everyone. If you want to really get a feel for the rhythm and metre of spoken Maori from the comfort of your own chair, switch to Te Reo, a Maori-language-only channel.

Ta Moko

Ta moko is the Maori art of tattoo, traditionally worn by men on their faces, thighs and buttocks, and by women on their chins and lips. *Moko* were permanent grooves tapped into the skin using pigment (made from burnt caterpillar or kauri gum soot), and bone chisels: fine, sharp combs for broad work, and straight blades for detailed work. Museums in the major centres – Auckland, Wellington and Christchurch – all display traditional implements for *ta moko*.

See Ngahuia Te Awekotuku's *Mau Moko: The World of Maori Tattoo* (2007) for the big picture, with powerful, beautiful images and an incisive commentary.

The modern tattooist's gun is common now, but bone chisels are coming back into use for Maori who want to reconnect with tradition. Since the general renaissance in Maori culture in the 1960s, many artists have taken up *ta moko* and now many Maori wear *moko* with quiet pride and humility.

Can visitors get involved, or even get some work done? The term *kirituhi* (skin inscriptions) has arisen to describe Maori motif-inspired modern tattoos that non-Maori can wear. If you'd like to experience *ta moko*, or even get *kirituhi,* your first stop is www.tamoko.org.nz. This website has articles, galleries and links to artists within NZ.

Carving

Traditional Maori carving, with its intricate detailing and curved lines, can transport the viewer. It's quite amazing to consider that it was done with stone tools, themselves painstakingly made, until the advent of iron (nails suddenly became very popular).

Some major traditional forms are *waka* (canoes), *pataka* (storage buildings), and *wharenui* (meeting houses). You can see sublime examples of traditional carving at Te Papa (p97) in Wellington.

The apex of carving today is the *whare whakairo* (carved meeting house). A commissioning group relates its history and ancestral stories to a carver, who then draws (sometimes quite loosely) on traditional motifs to interpret or embody the stories and ancestors in wood or composite fibreboard.

Rongomaraeroa Marae, by artist Cliff Whiting, at Te Papa in Wellington is a colourful example of a contemporary re-imagining of a traditional art form. The biggest change in carving (as with most traditional arts) has been in the use of new mediums and tools. Rangi Kipa uses a synthetic polymer called Corian to make his *hei tiki,* the same stuff that is used to make kitchen benchtops. You can check out his gallery at www.rangikipa.com.

Weaving

Weaving was an essential art that provided clothing, nets and cordage, footwear for rough country travel, mats to cover earthen floors, and *kete* (bags) to carry stuff in. Many woven items are beautiful as well as practical. Some were major works – *korowai* (cloaks) could take years to finish. Woven predominantly with flax and bird feathers, they are worn now on ceremonial occasions, a stunning sight.

Working with natural materials for the greater good of the people involved getting things right by maintaining the supply of raw material and ensuring that it worked as it was meant to. Protocols were necessary, and women were dedicated to weaving under the aegis of the gods. Today, tradition is greatly respected, but not all traditions are necessarily followed.

Flax was (and still is) the preferred medium for weaving. To get a strong fibre from flax leaves, weavers scraped away the leaves' flesh with a mussel shell, then pounded until it was soft, dyed it, then dried it. But contemporary weavers are using everything in their work: raffia, copper wire, rubber – even polar fleece and garden hoses!

The best place to experience weaving is to contact one of the many weavers running workshops. By learning the art, you'll appreciate the examples of weaving in museums even more. And if you want your own? Woven *kete* and backpacks have become fashion accessories and are on sale in most cities. Weaving is also found in dealer art galleries around the country.

For information on Maori arts today, check out Toi Maori www.maoriart.org.nz.

Haka

Experiencing *haka* can get the adrenaline flowing, as it did for one Pakeha observer in 1929 who thought of dark Satanic mills: 'They looked like fiends

---

CONNECTION WITH THE LAND

The best way to learn about the relationship between the land and the *tangata whenua* is to get out there and start talking with Maori. See the Maori New Zealand boxed texts in individual chapters for recommendations on Maori experiences in each area.

from hell wound up by machinery'. *Haka* can be awe-inspiring; it can also be uplifting. The *haka* is not only a war dance – it is used to welcome visitors, honour achievement, express identity or to put forth very strong opinions.

Haka involves chanted words, vigorous body movements, and *pukana* (when performers distort their faces, eyes bulging with the whites showing, perhaps with tongue extended).

The well-known *haka* 'Ka Mate', performed by the All Blacks before rugby test matches, is credited to the cunning fighting chief Te Rauparaha. It celebrates his escape from death. Chased by enemies, he hid himself in a food pit. After they had left, a friendly chief named Te Whareangi (the 'hairy man' referred to in the *haka*), let him out; he climbed out into the sunshine and performed 'Ka Mate'.

You can experience *haka* at various cultural performances including at Mitai Maori Village, Tamaki Maori Village, Te Puia and Whakarewarewa Thermal Village in Rotorua; Katoro Waka Heritage Tours (p221) and Ko Tane (p220) in Christchurch; Maori Tours (p146) in Kaikoura; and Myths & Legends Eco-tours (p130) in Picton.

But the best displays of *haka* are at the national Te Matatini National Kapa Haka Festival (www.tematatini.org.nz), when NZ's top groups compete. It is held every two years, with the next festival in February 2011 in Gisborne.

Before you go touring NZ, pick up a Manaaki Card. This little beauty of a card will get you discounts at most Maori-operated tourist attractions. It also doubles as a phone card. See www.manaaki.co.nz.

Contemporary Visual Art

A distinctive feature of Maori visual art is the tension between traditional Maori ideas and modern artistic mediums and trends. Shane Cotton produced a series of works that conversed with 19th-century painted meeting houses, which themselves departed from Maori carved houses. Kelcy Taratoa uses toys, superheroes and pop urban imagery alongside weaving and carving design.

Of course not all Maori artists use Maori motifs. Ralph Hotere is a major NZ artist who 'happens to be Maori' (his words), and his career-long exploration of black speaks more to modernism than the traditional *marae* context.

Contemporary Maori art is by no means only about painting. Many other artists use installations as the preferred medium – look out for work by Jacqueline Fraser and Peter Robinson.

See Hirini Moko Mead's *Tikanga Maori*, Pat and Hiwi Tauroa's *Visiting a Marae*, and Anne Salmond's *Hui* for detailed information on Maori customs.

There are some great permanent exhibitions of Maori visual arts in the major centres. Both the Auckland and Christchurch Art Galleries hold strong collections, as does Wellington's Te Papa.

Contemporary Theatre

The 1970s saw the emergence of many Maori playwrights and plays, and theatre is a strong area of the Maori arts today. Maori theatre drew heavily on the traditions of the *marae*. Instead of dimming the lights and immediately beginning the performance, many Maori theatre groups began with a stylised *powhiri* (see above), had space for audience members to respond to the play, and ended with a *karakia* (blessing or prayer) or a farewell.

Taki Rua is an independent producer of Maori work for both children and adults and has been in existence for over 25 years. As well as staging its shows in the major centres, it also tours most of its work – check out its website (www.takirua.co.nz) for the current offerings. Maori drama is also often showcased at the professional theatres in the main centres as well as the biennial New Zealand International Festival. Hone Kouka and Briar Grace-Smith (both have published playscripts available) have toured their works around NZ and to festivals in the UK.

Contemporary Dance

Contemporary Maori dance often takes its inspiration from *kapa haka* and traditional Maori imagery. The exploration of pre-European life also provides inspiration. For example a Maori choreographer, Moss Patterson, used *kokowai* (a body-adorning paste made from reddish clay and shark oil) as the basis of his most recent piece of the same name.

NZ's leading specifically Maori dance company is the Atamira Dance Collective (www.atamiradance.co.nz). They have been producing critically acclaimed, beautiful and challenging work since 2000. If that sounds too earnest, another choreographer to watch out for is Mika Torotoro, who

---

VISITING MARAE

As you travel around NZ, you will see many *marae* complexes. Often *marae* are owned by a descent group. They are also owned by urban Maori groups, schools, universities and church groups, and they should only be visited by arrangement with the owners. Some *marae* that may be visited include: Huria Marae in Tauranga; Koriniti Marae on the Whanganui River Rd; Pipitea Marae in Wellington (p93); and Te Papa Museum Marae in Wellington (p97).

Marae complexes include a *wharenui* (meeting house), which often embodies an ancestor. Its ridge is the backbone, the rafters are ribs, and it shelters the descendants. There is a clear space in front of the *wharenui* (ie the *marae atea*). Sometimes there are other buildings: a *wharekai* (dining hall); a toilet and shower block; perhaps even classrooms, play equipment and the like.

Hui (gatherings) are held at *marae*. Issues are discussed, classes conducted, milestones celebrated and the dead farewelled. Te reo Maori (the Maori language) is prominent, sometimes exclusively so.

Visitors sleep in the meeting house if a *hui* goes on for longer than a day. Mattresses are placed on the floor, someone may bring a guitar, and stories and jokes always go down well as the evening stretches out…

The Powhiri

If you visit a *marae* as part of an organised group, you'll be welcomed in a *powhiri*. The more common ones are outlined here.

There may be a *wero* (challenge). Using *taiaha* (quarter-staff) moves a warrior will approach the visitors and place a baton on the ground for a visitor to pick up.

There is a *karanga* (ceremonial call). A woman from the host group calls to the visitors and a woman from the visitors responds. Their long, high, falling calls begin to overlap and interweave and the visiting group walks on to the *marae atea*. It is then time for *whaikorero* (speechmaking). The hosts welcome the visitors, the visitors respond. Speeches are capped off by a *waiata* (song), and the visitors' speaker places *koha* (gift, usually an envelope of cash) on the *marae*. The hosts then invite the visitors to *hariru* (shake hands) and *hongi* (see below). Visitors and hosts are now united and will share light refreshments or a meal.

The Hongi

Press forehead and nose together firmly, shake hands, and perhaps offer a greeting such as 'Kia ora' or 'Tena koe'. Some prefer one press (for two or three seconds, or longer), others prefer two shorter (press, release, press). Men and women sometimes kiss on one cheek. Some people mistakenly think the *hongi* is a pressing of noses only (awkward to aim!) or the rubbing of noses (even more awkward).

Tapu

Tapu (spiritual restrictions) and *mana* (power and prestige) are taken seriously in the Maori world. Sit on chairs or seating provided (never on tables), and walk around people, not over them. The *powhiri* is *tapu*, and mixing food and *tapu* is right up there on the offence-o-meter. Do eat and drink when invited to do so by your hosts. You needn't worry about starvation: an important Maori value is *manaakitanga* (kindness).

happily blends *kapa haka,* drag, opera, ballet and disco into his work. You can check out clips of his work at www.mika.co.nz.

Maori Film-making

Although there had already been successful Maori documentaries (*Patu!* and the *Tangata Whenua* series are brilliant, and available from some urban video stores), it wasn't until 1987 that NZ had its first fiction feature-length movie by a Maori director with Barry Barclay's *Ngati*. Mereta Mita was the first Maori woman to direct a fiction feature with *Mauri* (1988). Both Mita and Barclay had highly political aims and ways of working, which involved a lengthy pre-production phase, during which they would consult with and seek direction from their *kaumatua* (elders). Films with significant Maori participation or control include the harrowing *Once Were Warriors* and the uplifting *Whale Rider*. Oscar-shortlisted Taika Waititi, of Te Whanau-a-Apanui descent, wrote and directed *Eagle vs Shark*.

The New Zealand Film Archive (www.filmarchive.org.nz) is a great place to experience Maori film, with most showings being either free or relatively inexpensive. It has offices in Auckland and Wellington (p94).

Maori Writing

There are many novels and collections of short stories by Maori writers, and personal taste will govern your choices. How about approaching Maori writing regionally? Read Patricia Grace (*Potiki, Cousins, Dogside Story, Tu*) around Wellington, and maybe Witi Ihimaera (*Pounamu, Pounamu, The Matriarch, Bulibasha, The Whale Rider*) on the North Island's East Coast. Keri Hulme (*The Bone People, Stonefish*) and the South Island go together like a mass of whitebait bound in a frying pan by a single egg (ie very well). Read Alan Duff (*Once Were Warriors*) anywhere, but only if you want to be saddened, even shocked. Definitely take James George (*Hummingbird, Ocean Roads*) with you to Auckland's West Coast beaches and Northland's Ninety Mile Beach. Paula Morris (*Queen of Beauty, Hibiscus Coast, Trendy but Casual*) and Kelly Ana Morey (*Bloom, Grace is Gone*) – hmm, Auckland and beyond? If poetry appeals you can't go past the giant of Maori poetry in English, the late, lamented Hone Tuwhare (*Deep River Talk: Collected Poems*). Famously sounding like he's at church and in the pub at the same time, you *can* take him anywhere.

Music plays an importa role in traditional and contemporary Maori culture: see p46 for mo details.

The first NZ hip-hop son to become a hit was Dalvanius Prime's 'Poi E which was sung entirel in Maori by the Patea Maori Club. It was the highest-selling single of 1984 in NZ, outselling a international artists.

Food & Drink <small>Lauraine Jacobs</small>

New Zealand's international reputation as a clean, green producer of food products is well earned: its temperate climate, fertile soil and balance of sunshine and rainfall allows farmers to grow an abundance of produce for local and export markets; and there is an emphasis throughout the country on fresh, natural production.

With good advice on where to eat, and regional and seasonal specialities and the local wines to match them with, travelling in NZ can be a culinary adventure not to be missed.

FROM THE HANGI TO INTERNATIONAL-FUSION CUISINE

Before European settlement, Maori people ate a diet predominantly made up of fish, bird and root vegetables such as kumara (sweet potatoes brought from Polynesia and cultivated in NZ). They often cooked their food in an underground pit known as a *hangi*.

The first European settlers (most of whom were British) introduced beef, sheep and pigs to the country, and for more than a century thereafter the Kiwi diet was a stolid fare similar to the prewar food served up throughout the UK. There was lots of bread and potatoes, and plain cooking – with roasting and boiling as the predominant culinary techniques. Bland meat (mutton and beef) with three vegetables was served up throughout the nation each night for dinner.

For some, that style of cooking continues today, often supplemented by the international fast-food brands found throughout the country. However, over the past 30 years there has been a massive shift towards a more varied, internationally inspired diet. NZ has embraced Asia and the Pacific Islands, and immigration from those regions has brought new flavours and cooking styles to NZ kitchens. At the same time, young New Zealanders have set off on overseas experiences and returned home with a keen appetite for lighter, fresher fare and a fusion of the culinary delights experienced in the Mediterranean and the East, or the 'new' British cuisine they have learnt about working in kitchens and pubs in the UK. The main style of cuisine now found in NZ cafes and restaurants is best described as Pacific Rim fusion, incorporating elements and ingredients from the countries of Southeast Asia, India and the Pacific.

Some farmers have also moved to diversify from traditional pastoral farming and ventured into vines, olives and kiwifruit. Wine and kiwifruit

Lauraine Jacobs is an award-winning food writer, and food editor of *Cuisine* magazine. Passionate about NZ's wine and food, she travels the country extensively seeking out the best culinary experiences and new and exciting wines and food products.

For an authoritative guide to food and wine, visit www.cuisine.co.nz.

ORGANIC NEW ZEALAND

No one is more aware of the importance of sustainability of the land than the farmers of NZ. With the country's economy, past and future, dependent on agricultural and pastoral industries, maintaining clean, unpolluted soil, water and air is a constant consideration.

Organic production and awareness is growing rapidly – many New Zealanders embrace the idea of organic food, convinced of the health benefits, and actively seek certified organic produce – and organic stores can be found in every major city throughout the country. In farmers markets and supermarkets organically grown and produced food will be proudly displayed and labelled as such.

However, in a country that produces more food than it could possibly consume, many food products are still imported. To really taste the goodness of NZ it is necessary to check that the meat, poultry, vegetables and fruit on menus and in stores has been grown in NZ.

TOP NZ EATING EXPERIENCES

Just as the climate changes from south to north, so do the local speciality foods of each region. In more upmarket restaurants, menus often reflect pride in the regional produce. Chefs carefully seek the very best, and celebrate fresh locally grown fruit, vegetables, olive oils and meat and locally caught fish, and often credit their suppliers on their menus. Cafes also occasionally pay homage to local producers.

Some specialities to look for on menus in the far north and the Auckland region are avocados, nuts, citrus fruits and Asian vegetables, as the subtropical climate allows them to flourish. North Island fish differ from the catch of more southern fishermen: fresh snapper, hapuku, tarakihi and flounder are common in the north; in the colder south there's more emphasis on groper, sole, brill, blue cod and turbot.

High-quality local lamb and beef can be found in Hawke's Bay, Taranaki, Wairarapa, Canterbury and Southland, and cervena venison (a low-fat, healthy red meat) is mostly raised in these regions.

A variety of fruits thrive in most of NZ's grape-growing districts, and travellers will also find some great local food matches with the speciality wines of each region. Farmers market stall holders will willingly point travellers in the direction of restaurants and cafes that champion and use local produce.

Our authors' favourite NZ eating experiences:

- Mt Maunganui's shiny new food haven, **Providores Urban Food Store**, maintains a beachy, raffish charm while delivering a serious dose of culinary quality. Surf videos flickered across the walls as I tried to choose between buttery fresh-baked pastries, home-smoked meats and cheeses, sticky organic jams and killer coffee (…or all of the above). Further east around the Bay of Plenty, lonesome Maketu has seen better days, but it's worth a detour if only to visit legendary **Maketu Pies**. I snaffled a mint-and-lamb special from the factory-shop pie warmer and wolfed it down on the foreshore, pastry flakes flying on the salty breeze. *Charles Rawlings-Way*

- It's not often that you get to sample every single item on a menu, but a friend's hen's party lunch at **Clooney** gave me just that opportunity (I was the bridesman – it was a very modern wedding). Every single dish was a winner – interesting, deftly executed and delicious. One wit quipped, 'Great, the strippers have arrived', just as two well-known middle-aged

---

particularly – industries hardly dreamed of 35 years ago – have grown from boutique operations to huge export earners.

STAPLES & SPECIALITIES
Meat

The Wildfoods Festival is held in Hokitika in March, with gastronomically challenging treats such as deep-fried huhu grubs (a fat, nutritious larvae) or fish eyes and marinated duck tongues.

One of the joys of NZ fare is grass-fed meat. Cattle, sheep and venison munch on lush pastures year-round, enjoying the freedom of the outdoors and producing meat that's lean, tasty and sustainably grown.

Lamb is a must for any meat-eating visitor, whether it's taken as marinated chops sizzling on the barbecue, a roast leg with traditional mint sauce enjoyed around the farm table or a stylish dish in a top restaurant. The perfect accompaniments are roasted potatoes, chunks of kumara and fresh green vegies.

New Zealanders also love their steak, and restaurants often list at least one fine-grained beef dish. Following hard on the heels of the sauvignon-blanc phenomenon, local red wines have garnered international attention, and both pinot noir and syrah varietals make a fine accompaniment to any red-meat meal.

Seafood

With more than 19,000km of pristine coastline and the largest fishing grounds of any country on earth, seafood is also a must-try on any culinary tour of NZ. Shellfish abound in coastal waters; the highly rated Bluff

conservative politicians sat down at the next table. It's that kind of place. **Mangonui Fish Shop** is a very different kind of place. A stingray swam past while I was polishing off my fish and chips. Magic! *Peter Dragicevich*

- It's official: Stewart Island's **Kai Kart** (p373) is NZ's southernmost eatery, and I reckon you could travel the length of the country without finding better fish and chips. The wee caravan turns out incredibly fresh blue cod and delicious battered mussels or oysters. Order up large, wrap up warm, and eat alfresco with the southern ocean winds whipping up in your face. Don't forget to grab a bottle of satay sauce to go with the mussels. In the Catlins, I may have been slightly underwhelmed by NZ's own, more subtle version of Niagara Falls, but the nearby **Niagara Falls Café** (p364) left me with no feelings of disappointment. Housed in a restored 19th-century schoolhouse, the cafe and art gallery is definitely worth a stop. My first visit was for South Island's best coffee and cheesecake, and I returned a few days later with my wife and enjoyed wonderful parmesan-baked blue cod. Beers from the Invercargill Brewery, and Central Otago wines, are also pretty compelling reasons to drop by. *Brett Atkinson*

- Nowhere on my travels did I find the Kiwi home-baking tradition in finer fettle than at the **Wakamarinian Café** (p136) in Havelock. To quote the owner of the Havelock Garden Motel, 'If you don't love the raspberry-and-white-chocolate shortcake, there must be something wrong with you'. Too true! But there's more to life than pastry. There's paua ravioli, signature dish of **Logan-Brown** (p105). Housed in a grand 1920s banking chamber on groovy Cuba St, this is Wellington's – and NZ's – best. *Sarah Bennett*

- Eating in Queenstown is an under-rated pleasure. If you're in the mood for some quick eats you can't go past **Fergburger** (p316). This perennial favourite has become an essential Queenstown experience. Ferg's so sewn into the collective dining fabric that it has become a must for all Queenie visitors – backpacker or billionaire. Rightfully so – the burgers are *that* good. Those wanting to eat indoors, or at least without thumping drum 'n' bass, should look no further then around the corner at **Solero Vino** (p315). This fine-dining French restaurant is the bee's knees for the cultured culinary crowd. Delicate flavours, amazing wine and awesome service – *bon appetit! Scott Kennedy*

oysters are first choice with locals. It's rare, however, to find an oyster freshly shucked to order in NZ. Fish shops, supermarkets and markets sell fresh oysters, sometimes in the shell, but most often already shucked and packed in sea water in small plastic containers.

Seafood specialities include Greenshell mussels (which are tasty and often far larger than those served in other parts of the world), cockles, clams and scallops. Crayfish (a rock lobster) is rich and sweet, but expensive. Whitebait are much prized tiny threadlike fish that are most commonly served in fritters, and can be tracked down on the west coasts of both islands during the months of September through December. Getting takeaway fish and chips, a popular meal that is good value and in plentiful supply throughout NZ, is a common Friday-night family ritual.

Apart from large-scale salmon, oyster and mussel farming, NZ's aquaculture industry is still in its infancy. Keen fishermen will find plenty of places to catch their own rainbow or brown trout in the many lakes and rivers of NZ, and will be the only visitors to enjoy these treats as trout cannot be sold lawfully.

Fresh Produce

Fresh local produce can be found everywhere from farmers markets to local supermarkets, specialty food stores and road-side stalls. In the North, look

The furry-skinned kiwifruit with an emerald green, vitamin C–rich interior has become the champion of pastry chefs worldwide. Its sister, known as Gold, has a smoother skin and pale yellow interior that's even higher in vitamin C.

POLYNESIAN SPECIALITIES

Some foods are highly prized by the Maori and Pacific Island population, but won't be found on many menus.

Mutton bird is not for everyone, as it is very fatty and has a fishy taste, but is a must for travellers who venture to Stewart Island. Equally fatty is *palusami*, traditionally a favourite with Pacific Islanders. Taro leaves or spinach are slow-cooked with coconut and corned beef to make this rich tasty meal.

Puha (prickly sow thistle) is a popular feature of Maori cooking, found growing wild in backyards and farms across the country. These leafy greens are boiled up with pork, mussels or mutton bones.

Kina and paua (abalone) are two types of shellfish to seek out. Kina is a sea urchin found among rocks on the coastline, with roe that is eaten raw from within the spiny shell. Paua has dark black meat and can be grilled or minced for fritters; it's very expensive and has a meaty savoury flavour.

Recently chefs have become interested in a range of local herbs and spices, which they add to meat and fish dishes. Peppery horopito (a bush pepper), scented kawakawa (bush basil) and kelp salt (from the seaweed plant) can be found on menus and in packets in speciality food stores.

for citrus fruit at farm stands around Kerikeri, avocados and kiwifruit near Tauranga and apples and stone fruit in Hawke's Bay. In the South, there are fruit and vegetable stalls throughout Nelson and Marlborough; freshly dug potatoes can be bought directly from farmers near Oamaru; and some excellent dried fruit can be sampled at several stops around Cromwell in Central Otago.

Sweets & Desserts

Visitors should also look for uniquely NZ foods such as pavlova (an indulgent cream-and-fruit-topped meringue cake) and hokey pokey ice cream (a vanilla ice cream filled with nuggets of crunchy golden toffee). Those with a sweet tooth will fall in love with the range of varietal honeys with the aromas of the specific vegetation of the region in which they are made – especially Manuka honey, which has extraordinary healthful and healing properties.

The Dairy

Owner-operated stores, known locally as the 'dairy', are ubiquitous in small towns and city suburbs. All manner of food items, from ice creams rolled to order, bread and milk to newspapers and almost every staple need are stocked.

For years only recognised for high-quality cheddar cheese, many small producers are now making artisan cheeses from cow's, sheep and goat's milk. All NZ cheese is made (by law) from pasteurised milk.

DRINKS

After work, around the barbecue, at the beach and in cafes up and down the country, beer, wine and cocktails are part of the social culture.

The zingy Marlborough sauvignon blanc – with fresh, fruity, almost herbal aromas that leap out of the glass – holds a unique position in the wine world, and is sought after all over the globe. Walk into any restaurant, and almost every table will be graced with a bottle or two of opened wine to accompany the meal. All supermarkets sell local wines, often at bargain prices, but the very best NZ wines are mainly sold in specialist wine stores or found on the wine lists of the better restaurants.

Beer, too, has long been part of the Kiwi culture, and boutique hand-crafted beers abound. Nelson – the region where hops, an essential ingredient in beer, are grown – has become a treasure trove of boutique beers and visitors can call in to several operations to pick up 'a dozen' or two to take to the beach.

Another speciality drink to look for is the internationally acclaimed 42Below vodka, a great example of Kiwi ingenuity. Innovator Geoff Ross produced uniquely NZ flavoured vodkas (kiwifruit, Manuka honey, feijoa and more), presented them in elegant bottles and then sold his company to Bacardi for many millions. He's been retained by Bacardi to oversee and guard the standards.

Coffee drinking has also become an important part of NZ culture, coinciding with the rise and rise of the cafe. To find the best coffee, follow the tried and tested rule of joining the crowd at the busiest spot in town.

CELEBRATIONS

During the harvest period in late summer (February to April) wine and food is celebrated in many of the wine regions with local festivals. Wine flows freely, there's no shortage of food stalls with local specialities, and it's all terrific fun, especially as the day lengthens and the wine kicks in.

Some visitors may be fortunate enough to attend a Maori *hangi*, a feature of almost any gathering, occasion or funeral at the *marae* (Maori meeting house). A pit is dug, a fire lit and stones placed in it. When the set-up is finally deemed hot enough, chicken, lamb, pork, kumara, potatoes, corn, pumpkin and other vegetables are covered with sacks and placed over the hot stones. The pit is covered with earth and the food steamed for an hour or two before being lifted out and carried to the table. The flavour of the food, which is usually not seasoned with spices or herbs, is earthy and tender. A great deal of associated drinking, chatter and comradeship are very much part of a *hangi*.

As NZ has evolved into a more multicultural society, many different ethnic groups have introduced their own celebrations. Pasifika, a festival celebrating Polynesian culture, takes place in Auckland over a weekend in February. It's two days of eating Island foods such as Pacific fruits and vegetables, sticky coconut buns, suckling pig, baked spinach or taro leaves with coconut and much more. Island sports, singing and cultural dancing take place.

> Smoking is banned in the workplace and any public place where food or drink is served, and it is considered very bad manners to smoke indoors or without requesting permission.

WINE TOURING

Visitors to NZ who have a real passion for food and wine can follow a wine trail right through the country from north to south, rather than following traditional tourist routes. Tour options include cycling or guided tours in minivans, organised by wine experts. Where good wines are created, there's usually good local food too.

Within each wine region there are numerous wineries that welcome visits at the cellar door, and many have good restaurants with food matched to the wines grown and produced on the estate.

As most international visitors arrive through the airport of Auckland, a great place to start is with a day visit to Matakana for its pinot gris, or to Waiheke Island, a 45-minute ferry ride from Auckland's downtown, to taste the island's intense red wines and local chardonnays.

To take in the major wine-making areas, first head south from Auckland to Hawke's Bay for chardonnays and syrahs. This is a vast area so careful planning of a trail is essential to avoid endless criss-crossing. Next it's off through extensive sheep country to the Wairarapa to try the renowned pinot noirs of Martinborough (p117). From there an exhilarating drive over the Rimutaka hills will get you to Wellington, from where you can cross Cook Strait to Marlborough by ferry or air.

Marlborough's sauvignon blancs have made their mark internationally and firmly established NZ's credibility in the world of wine. (A side trip to experience the aromatic white wines of Nelson is also suggested.)

The wine tourist can then hit the trail through Waipara and North Canterbury (p242) for rieslings and pinot noirs, and finish in the scenic Central Otago region (p283) where wine tourism is a popular addition to the area's famous adventure tourism. The pinot noirs of Otago exhibit all the characteristics of the wild thyme- and heather-clad hills throughout the region.

The Diwali celebration of the Indian community has also become part of the Auckland calendar and many tiny food stalls are set up near the harbour in October for a weekend celebration. Spicy aromas waft through the air, and the vast array of savoury snacks and jewel-like sweets are irresistible.

In rural areas, agricultural and pastoral associations host annual showcases of farming practices and animal displays at local showgrounds. These fun days are full of competitions and events; food tends to be hearty, but hardly gourmet, including basic pies, hamburgers, barbecued sausages and hot dogs.

WHERE TO EAT & DRINK

The main cities are remarkably well served with a range of eating choices, from restaurants where the food is stylish and imaginative to small places where the ambience is simple, but the food authentic and prepared with love. Cafes are found everywhere, particularly in towns along the main touring routes, and usually serve hearty country fare. Many cafes open at 7am but close around 4pm or 5pm and don't serve dinner. For pub and restaurant opening hours see p379.

B&Bs in the more remote regions will often cook dinner, but usually only by request well ahead of arrival. Country-style pubs can be found in most places, and although very few offer a 'gastro' experience, they serve up a basic menu to accompany a frothy cold beer.

Farmers markets are generally held on Saturday or Sunday mornings, and all are great places to explore local food culture, meet local food producers and taste some terrific fresh food. Most have a mobile coffee stand, and usually there will be an entrepreneur serving a 'breakfast roll' bun stuffed with fried eggs and bacon.

The restaurant industry is NZ's largest private-sector employer, with nearly 4% of the total workforce.

TOP 10 NZ MICROBREWERIES

New Zealanders sure can brew up a storm! Here are our picks for the best Kiwi microbreweries you're likely to find:

Brew Moon Brewery (p242) The roadside Brew Moon Brewery in Amberley lures visitors in with three different beers on tap and an excellent cafe. Try the chocolatey Brew Moon Dark Side Stout. Amberley is just before the Waipara Valley wine region in North Canterbury.

Croucher Brewing Co (www.croucherbrewing.co.nz) Croucher's crafty pale ale and pilsner rule the roost at Rotorua's boozy Underground Bar.

Emerson's Brewery (p276; www.emersons.co.nz) Dunedin is full of students, and students like beer – and how blessed they are to drink Emerson's! Wheat beers, pilsners, porters, and bitter ales heavy on the malt and spice.

Founders Brewery (p152; www.biobrew.co.nz) NZ's first certified organic brewery is in Nelson. Take a behind-the-scenes tour and sip the immaculate product.

Hallertau (www.hallertau.co.nz) Auckland beer boffins are big fans of this microbrewery, where sexy packaging and barrel-aged beers collide (its 'Porter Noir' does time in old pinot barrels!). The pale ale is hoppy heaven.

Moa Beer (p143; www.moabeer.co.nz) Winemaker's son Josh Scott produces a range of excellent bottle-fermented beers at his tasting room–bar in the thick of Marlborough's vineyards.

Renaissance Brewing Co (p143; www.renaissancebrewing.co.nz) Seriously good ales with the medals to prove it. A fantastic use for a former ice-cream factory in Blenheim.

Three Boys Brewery (www.threeboysbrewery.co.nz) Three Boys IPA is available at discerning bars and restaurants in Christchurch. Packed with hops, it's an authentic version of the Indian Pale Ales originally crafted to last the long sea journey to colonial India.

Wanaka Beerworks (p327; www.wanakabeerworks.co.nz) Look for this brewery's beers in restaurants around Queenstown and Wanaka. The Brewski pilsner is packed with floral, hoppy flavours and is an excellent rendition of a Czech-style lager.

White Cliffs Organic Brewery (www.organicbeer.co.nz) White Cliffs enjoys a reputation far beyond Taranaki, particularly for Mike's Mild – an amber ale with notes of fruit and roasted nuts: a real connoisseur's drop.

TO MARKET, TO MARKET

Farmers markets are a relatively new introduction to the shopping options in NZ. In the past five years there has been extraordinary growth and from one market in 2001 (at Whangarei, in the north), the number has steadily increased each year to more than 50 throughout the country.

Most are held on weekend mornings and are happy local affairs where visitors will meet local producers and find fresh produce. It's a great way to find out just what food is the speciality of the region. Mobile coffee carts are usually present, and tastings are often offered by enterprising and innovative stall holders selling value-added food products.

Always take a bag to carry purchases in as many of the sustainable-minded markets ban the use of plastic bags. Arrive as early as possible – the best produce always sells out very quickly.

Look at www.farmersmarkets.org.nz to find dates and times of farmers markets throughout NZ.

VEGETARIANS & VEGANS

Vegetarians need not worry that they will not find suitable food around NZ. There isn't a great range of vegetarian restaurants, but almost all restaurants and cafes offer vegetarian choices on their menus (although sometimes only one or two). Many cafes also provide gluten-free and vegan options. Always check that the stocks and sauces are vegetarian, as chefs who have not traditionally cooked for those with strict vegetarian diets tend to think of vegetarian cooking as simply omitting the main serving of meat or fish from a meal.

It always pays to mention any dietary requirement when making a reservation at a restaurant or B&B, and it's essential in this meat-loving country to mention it to the host when invited to a private home.

Environment Vaughan Yarwood

THE LAND

Vaughan Yarwood is a historian and travel writer who is widely published in NZ and internationally. His most recent book is *The History Makers: Adventures in New Zealand Biography*.

New Zealand is a young country – its present shape is less than 10,000 years old. Having broken away from the supercontinent of Gondwanaland (which included Africa, Australia, Antarctica and South America) in a stately geological dance some 130 million years ago, it endured aeons of uplift and erosion, buckling and tearing, and the slow fall and rise of the sea as ice ages came and went. Straddling the boundary of two great colliding slabs of the earth's crust – the Pacific plate and the Indian/Australian plate – to this day NZ remains the plaything of nature's strongest forces.

The result is one of the most varied and spectacular series of landscapes in the world, ranging from snow-dusted mountains and drowned glacial valleys to rainforests, dunelands and an otherworldly volcanic plateau. It is a diversity of landforms you would expect to find across an entire continent rather than a small archipelago in the South Pacific.

Evidence of NZ's tumultuous past is everywhere. The South Island's mountainous spine – the 650km-long ranges of the Southern Alps – is a product of the clash of the two plates; the result of a process of rapid lifting that, if anything, is accelerating. Despite NZ's highest peak, Aoraki/Mt Cook (p260), losing 10m from its summit overnight in a 1991 landslide, the Alps are on an express elevator that, without erosion and landslides, would see them 10 times their present height within a few million years.

On the North Island, the most impressive changes have been wrought by volcanoes. Auckland is built on an isthmus peppered by scoria cones, on many of which you can still see the earthworks of *pa* (fortified villages) built by early Maori. The city's biggest and most recent volcano, 600-year-old Rangitoto Island is just a short ferry ride from the downtown wharves. Some 300km further south, the classically shaped cone of snowcapped Mt Taranaki/Egmont overlooks tranquil dairy pastures.

But the real volcanic heartland runs through the centre of the North Island, from the restless bulk of Mt Ruapehu in Tongariro National Park northeast through the Rotorua lake district out to NZ's most active volcano, White

RESPONSIBLE TRAVEL

Toitu te whenua – care for the land. Help protect the environment by following these guidelines:

- Treat NZ's forests and native wildlife with respect. Damaging or taking plants is illegal in most parts of the country.
- Remove rubbish. Litter is unsightly and can encourage vermin and disease. Rather than burying or burning, carry out what you carry in.
- In areas without toilet facilities bury toilet waste in a shallow hole away from tracks, huts, campsites and waterways.
- Keep streams and lakes pure by cleaning away from water sources. Drain waste water into the soil to filter out soaps and detergent. If you suspect contamination, boil water for three minutes, filter, or chemically treat it before use.
- Where possible use portable fuel stoves. Keep open fires small, use only dead wood and make sure the fire is out by dousing it with water and checking the ashes before leaving.
- Keep to tracks where possible. Get permission before crossing private land and move carefully around livestock.

Island, in the Bay of Plenty. Called the Taupo Volcanic Zone, this great 250km-long rift valley – part of a volcano chain known as the 'Pacific Ring of Fire' – has been the seat of massive eruptions that have left their mark on the country physically and culturally.

Most spectacular were the eruptions from the volcano that created Lake Taupo. Considered the world's most productive volcano in terms of the amount of material ejected, Taupo last erupted 1800 years ago in a display that was the most violent anywhere on the planet within the past 5000 years.

You can experience the aftermath of volcanic destruction on a smaller scale at Te Wairoa (the Buried Village; near Rotorua on the shores of Lake Tarawera. Here, partly excavated and open to the public, lie the remains of a 19th-century Maori village overwhelmed when nearby Mt Tarawera erupted without warning. The famous Pink and White Terraces (one of several claimants to the popular title 'eighth wonder of the world') were destroyed overnight by the same upheaval.

But when nature sweeps the board clean with one hand she often rebuilds with the other: Waimangu Valley, born of all that geothermal violence, is the place to go to experience the hot earth up close and personal amid geysers, silica pans, bubbling mud pools, and the world's biggest hot spring. Or you can wander around Rotorua's Whakarewarewa Thermal Village, where descendants of Maori displaced by the eruption live in the middle of steaming vents and prepare food for visitors in boiling pools.

A second by-product of movement along the tectonic plate boundary is seismic activity – earthquakes. Not for nothing has NZ been called 'the Shaky Isles'. Most quakes only rattle the glassware, but one was indirectly responsible for creating an internationally celebrated tourist attraction…

In 1931, an earthquake measuring 7.9 on the Richter scale levelled the Hawke's Bay city of Napier, causing huge damage and loss of life. Napier was rebuilt almost entirely in the then-fashionable art-deco architectural style, and walking its streets today you can relive its brash exuberance in what has become a mecca for lovers of art deco.

Travellers to the South Island can also see some evidence of volcanism – if the remains of the old volcanoes of Banks Peninsula (p236) weren't there to repel the sea, the vast Canterbury Plains, built from alpine sediment washed down the rivers from the Alps, would have eroded away long ago.

But in the south it is the Southern Alps themselves that dominate, dictating settlement patterns, throwing down engineering challenges and offering outstanding recreational opportunities. The island's mountainous backbone also helps shape the weather, as it stands in the path of the prevailing westerly winds which roll in, moisture-laden, from the Tasman Sea. As a result bush-clad lower slopes of the western Southern Alps are among the wettest places on earth, with an annual precipitation of some 15,000mm. Having lost its moisture, the wind then blows dry across the eastern plains towards the Pacific coast.

The North Island has a more even rainfall and is spared the temperature extremes of the South – which can plunge when a wind blows in from Antarctica. The important thing to remember, especially if you are tramping at high altitude, is that NZ has a maritime climate. This means weather can change with lightning speed, catching out the unprepared.

WILDLIFE

NZ may be relatively young, geologically speaking, but its plants and animals go back a long way. The tuatara, for instance, an ancient reptile unique to these islands, is a Gondwanaland survivor closely related to the dinosaurs,

The GreenDex (p434) at the end of this book lists ecofriendly places to explore, stay or dine throughout NZ. Discover more about ecotourism across the country with Leonie Johnsen's *Organic Explorer New Zealand* (www.organicexplorer. co.nz).

ENVIRONMENTAL ISSUES IN AOTEAROA NEW ZEALAND *Nandor Tanczos*

Most people think of Aotearoa New Zealand as clean and green, a place that respects the environment. We have the NZ Forest Accord to protect native forests, national parks and reserves now cover a third of the country, marine reserves continue to pop up around the coast, and our antinuclear legislation seems unassailable. A closer look, however, reveals a dirtier picture.

New Zealand has one of the highest per capita rates of greenhouse-gas emissions in the world. We are one of the most inefficient users of energy in the developed world. Public transport is negligible in most places and ecological values play little part in urban planning or building design. Add to that the ongoing battle being fought in many communities over the disposal of sewage and toxic waste into waterways, a conflict often spearheaded by *tangata whenua* (local Maori people), and the 'clean and green' label begins to look seriously compromised.

Our biggest polluting sector is pastoral farming, responsible for half of our greenhouse-gas emissions. The importation of European sheep and cattle-grazing systems has left many hillsides with marginal productivity, bare of trees and prone to erosion. Grazing threatens many waterways, with stock causing damage to stream and lake margins and run-off causing nutrient overload leading to eutrophication and algal blooms. Dairy farming, the worst culprit due to its intensity, is expanding into areas often poorly suited to this kind of land use, relying on a massive increase in the use of irrigation. Over-allocation of water has become a problem in many areas as a result. Regional councils and farming groups are fencing and planting stream banks to protect water quality, but their efforts are outstripped by the sheer growth in dairying.

The election of the centre-right National Government in 2008 has led to the unravelling of a number of important environmental protections. They have gutted the already inadequate Emissions Trading Scheme. The world-leading Resource Management Act has been significantly weakened, and the Government is proposing to open up Department of Conservation and other

---

while many of the distinctive flightless birds (ratites) have distant African and South American cousins.

Due to its long isolation, the country is a veritable warehouse of unique and varied plants, most of which are found nowhere else. And with separation of the landmass occurring before mammals appeared on the scene, birds and insects have evolved in spectacular ways to fill the gaps.

The now extinct flightless moa, the largest of which grew to 3.5m tall and weighed over 200kg, browsed open grasslands much as cattle do today (skeletons can be seen at Auckland Museum), while the smaller kiwi still ekes out a nocturnal living rummaging among forest leaf litter for insects and worms much as small mammals do elsewhere. One of the country's most ferocious-looking insects, the mouse-sized giant weta, meanwhile, has taken on a scavenging role elsewhere filled by rodents.

As one of the last places on earth to be colonised by humans, NZ was for millennia a safe laboratory for such risky evolutionary strategies, but with the arrival first of Maori and soon after of Europeans, things went downhill fast.

Many endemic creatures, including moa and the huia, an exquisite songbird, were driven to extinction, and the vast forests were cleared for their timber and to make way for agriculture. Destruction of habitat and the introduction of exotic animals and plants have taken a terrible environmental toll and New Zealanders are now fighting a rearguard battle to save what remains.

NZ is one of the most spectacular places in the world to see geysers. Rotorua's short-lived Waimangu geyser, formed after the Mt Tarawera eruption, was once the world's largest, often gushing to a dizzying height of 400m.

Birds & Animals

The first Polynesian settlers found little in the way of land mammals – just two species of bat – but forests, plains and coasts are alive with birds. Largely lacking the bright plumage found elsewhere, NZ's birds – like its endemic plants – have an understated beauty which does not shout for attention.

protected land for mining. Local communities in places like the Coromandel Peninsula are now gearing up for a rerun of the fierce environmental battles of the 1970s and '80s, which ended with the Coromandel being declared off limits to mining.

Despite these things, New Zealand has some advantages. A relatively high proportion of our energy comes from renewable hydro-generation. Farm animals, except for pigs and chickens, are almost all grass fed and free range. We are starting to get serious about waste minimisation and resource recovery. But our biggest saving grace is our small population. As a result, Aotearoa is a place well worth visiting. This is a beautiful land with enormous geographical and ecological diversity. Our forests are unique and magnificent, and the bird species that evolved in response to an almost total lack of mammalian life are spectacular, although now reduced in numbers due to introduced predators such as rats, stoats and hedgehogs.

The responsibility of New Zealanders is to make change for ecological sustainability, not just at a personal level, but at an institutional and infrastructural level. The responsibility of visitors to Aotearoa New Zealand is to respect our unique biodiversity, and to query and question: every time you ask where the recycling centre is; every time you express surprise at the levels of energy use, car use and water use; every time you request organic food at a cafe or restaurant; you affect the person you talk to.

Aotearoa New Zealand has the potential to be a world leader in ecological wisdom. We have a strong tradition to draw from – the careful relationship of reciprocity that Maori developed with the natural world over the course of many, many generations. We live at the edge of the Pacific, on the Rim of Fire, a remnant of the ancient forests of Gondwanaland. We welcome conscious travellers.

Nandor Tanczos is an activist, researcher and educator based in Ngaruawahia. He was a Member of Parliament for the Green Party until 2008.

Among the most musical is the bellbird, common in both native and exotic forests everywhere except Northland, though like many birds it is more likely to be heard than seen. Its call is a series of liquid bell notes, most often sounded at dawn or dusk.

The tui, another nectar eater and the country's most beautiful songbird, is a great mimic, with an inventive repertoire that includes clicks, grunts and chuckles. Notable for the white throat feathers which stand out against its dark plumage, the tui often feeds on flax flowers in suburban gardens but is most at home in densely tangled forest ('bush' to New Zealanders).

Fantails are commonly encountered on forest trails, swooping and jinking to catch insects stirred up by passing hikers, while pukeko, elegant swamp-hens with blue plumage and bright red beaks, are readily seen along wetland margins and even on the sides of roads nearby – be warned, they have little road sense.

B Heather and H Robertson's *Field Guide to the Birds of New Zealand* is a comprehensive guide for birdwatchers and a model of helpfulness for anyone even casually interested in the country's remarkable bird life.

If you spend any time in the South Island high country, you are likely to come up against the fearless and inquisitive kea – an uncharacteristically drab green parrot with bright red underwings. Kea are common in the car parks of the Fox Glacier (p206) and Franz Josef Glacier (p202), where they hang out for food scraps or tear rubber from car windscreens.

Then there is the takahe, a rare flightless bird thought extinct until a small colony was discovered in 1948, and the equally flightless kiwi, NZ's national emblem and the nickname for New Zealanders themselves.

The kiwi has a round body covered in coarse feathers, strong legs and a long, distinctive bill with nostrils at the tip for sniffing out food. It is not easy to find them in the wild, but they can be seen in simulated environments at excellent nocturnal houses. One of the best is the Otorohanga Kiwi House, which also has other birds, including native falcons, moreporks (owls) and weka.

To get a feel for what the bush used to be like, take a trip to Tiritiri Matangi Island. This regenerating island is an open sanctuary and one of the country's most successful exercises in community-assisted conservation.

BIRDWATCHING

The flightless kiwi is the species most sought after by birdwatchers. Sightings of the Stewart Island subspecies are common at all times of the year. Elsewhere, wild sightings of this increasingly rare nocturnal species are difficult, apart from in enclosures. Other birds that twitchers like to sight are the royal albatross, white heron, Fiordland crested penguin, yellow-eyed penguin, Australasian gannet and wrybill.

On the Coromandel Peninsula, the Firth of Thames (particularly Miranda) is a haven for migrating birds, while the Wharekawa Wildlife Refuge at Opoutere Beach is a breeding ground of the endangered NZ dotterel. There's also a very accessible Australasian gannet colony at Muriwai, west of Auckland, and one in Hawke's Bay. There are popular trips to observe pelagic birds out of Kaikoura, and royal albatross viewing on the Otago Peninsula.

Two good guides are the newly revised *Field Guide to the Birds of New Zealand*, by Barrie Heather and Hugh Robertson, and *Birds of New Zealand: Locality Guide* by Stuart Chambers.

MARINE MAMMAL–WATCHING

Kaikoura, on the northeast coast of the South Island, is NZ's nexus of marine mammal-watching. The main attraction here is whale-watching, but this is dependent on weather conditions, so don't expect to just be able to rock up and head straight out on a boat for a dream encounter. The sperm whale, the largest toothed whale, is pretty much a year-round resident, and depending on the season you may also see migrating humpback whales, pilot whales, blue whales and southern right whales. Other mammals – including fur seals and dusky dolphins – are seen year-round.

Kaikoura is also an outstanding place to swim with dolphins. Pods of up to 500 playful dusky dolphins can be seen on any given day. Dolphin swimming is common elsewhere in NZ, with the animals gathering off the North Island near Whakatane, Paihia, Tauranga, and in the Hauraki Gulf, and off Akaroa on the South Island's Banks Peninsula. Seal swimming is possible in Kaikoura and in the Abel Tasman National Park.

Swimming with sharks is also possible, though with a protective cage as a chaperone; you can do it in Tutukaka and Gisborne.

KIWI SPOTTING

The kiwi is a threatened species, and with the additional difficulty of them being nocturnal, it's only on Stewart Island (p366) that you might easily see one in the wild. They can, however, be observed in many artificially dark 'kiwi houses':

- Nga Manu Nature Reserve, Waikanae (p116)
- Pukaha Mt Bruce National Wildlife Centre, near Masterton (p121)
- Wellington Zoo (p97)
- Southern Encounter Aquarium & Kiwi House, Christchurch (p218)
- Orana Wildlife Park, Christchurch (p220)
- Willowbank Wildlife Reserve, Christchurch (p221)
- Kiwi Birdlife Park, Queenstown (p303)

Trees

No visitor to NZ (particularly Australians!) will go for long without hearing about the damage done to the bush by that bad-mannered Australian import, the brush-tailed possum. The long list of mammal pests introduced to NZ accidentally or for a variety of misguided reasons includes deer, rabbits, stoats, pigs and goats. But the most destructive by far is the possum, 70 million of which now chew through millions of tonnes of foliage a year despite the best efforts of the Department of Conservation (DOC) to control them.

Among favoured possum food are NZ's most colourful trees: the kowhai, a small-leaved tree growing to 11m, that in spring has drooping clusters of bright yellow flowers (NZ's national flower); the pohutukawa, a beautiful coastal tree of the northern North Island which bursts into vivid red flower in December, earning the nickname 'Christmas tree'; and a similar crimson-flowered tree, the rata. Rata species are found on both islands; the northern rata starts life as a climber on a host tree (that it eventually chokes).

The few remaining pockets of mature centuries-old kauri are stately emblems of former days. Their vast hammered trunks and towering, epiphyte-festooned limbs, which dwarf every other tree in the forest, are reminders of why they were sought after in colonial days for spars and building timber. The best place to see the remaining giants is Northland's Waipoua Kauri Forest, home to three-quarters of the country's surviving kauri.

Now the pressure has been taken off kauri and other timber trees, including the distinctive rimu (red pine) and the long-lived totara (favoured for Maori war canoes), by one of the country's most successful imports – *Pinus radiata*. Pine was found to thrive in NZ, growing to maturity in just 35 years, and plantation forests are now widespread through the central North Island – the southern hemisphere's biggest, Kaingaroa Forest, lies southeast of Rotorua.

You won't get far into the bush without coming across one of its most prominent features – tree ferns. NZ is a land of ferns (more than 80 species) and most easily recognised are the mamaku (black tree fern) – which grows to 20m and can be seen in damp gullies throughout the country – and the 10m-high ponga (silver tree fern) with its distinctive white underside. The silver fern is equally at home as part of corporate logos and on the clothing of many of the country's top sportspeople.

Lifestyles of New Zealand Forest Plants, by J Dawson and R Lucas, is a beautifully photographed foray into the world of NZ's forests. Far from being drab and colourless, these lush treasure houses are home to ancient species dating from the time of the dinosaurs. This guidebook will have you reaching for your boots.

NATIONAL PARKS

A third of the country – more than five million hectares – is protected in environmentally important parks and reserves that embrace almost every conceivable landscape: from mangrove-fringed inlets in the north to the snow-topped volcanoes of the Central Plateau, and from the forested fastness of the Ureweras in the east to the Southern Alps' majestic mountains, glaciers and fiords. The 14 national parks, three maritime parks and two marine reserves, along with numerous forest parks, offer huge scope for wilderness experiences, ranging from climbing, snow skiing and mountain biking to tramping, kayaking and trout fishing.

TOWERING KAURI

When Chaucer was born this was a sturdy young tree. When Shakespeare was born it was 300 years old. It predates most of the great cathedrals of Europe. Its trunk is sky-rocket straight and sky-rocket bulky, limbless for half its height. Ferns sprout from its crevices. Its crown is an asymmetric mess, like an inverted root system. I lean against it, give it a slap. It's like slapping a building. This is a tree out of Tolkien. It's a kauri.

Joe Bennett (A Land of Two Halves) referring to the McKinney kauri in Northland.

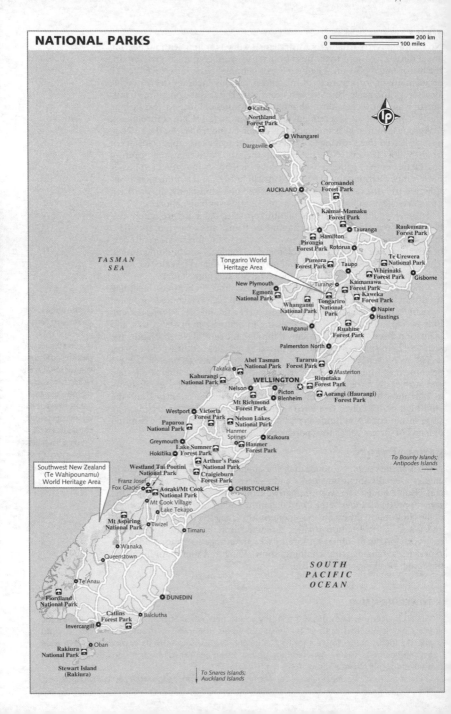

NATIONAL PARKS

0 ————————— 200 km
0 ————————— 100 miles

Kaitaia
Northland Forest Park
Whangarei
Dargaville

Coromandel Forest Park
AUCKLAND
Kaimai-Mamaku Forest Park
Tauranga
Raukumara Forest Park
Hamilton
Pirongia Forest Park
Rotorua
Te Urewera National Park
Pureora Forest Park
Taupo
Whirinaki Forest Park
Gisborne
Tongariro World Heritage Area
Turangi
Kaimanawa Forest Park
New Plymouth
Kaweka Forest Park
Egmont National Park
Whanganui National Park
Tongariro National Park
Napier
Hastings
Wanganui
Ruahine Forest Park
Palmerston North

TASMAN SEA

Abel Tasman National Park
Tararua Forest Park
Takaka
Kahurangi National Park
WELLINGTON
Masterton
Nelson
Rimutaka Forest Park
Picton
Aorangi (Haurangi) Forest Park
Blenheim
Mt Richmond Forest Park
Westport
Victoria Forest Park
Nelson Lakes National Park
Paparoa National Park
Hanmer Springs
Kaikoura
Greymouth
Lake Sumner Forest Park
Hammer Forest Park
Hokitika
Arthur's Pass National Park
Westland Tai Poutini National Park
Craigieburn Forest Park
Franz Josef
Fox Glacier
Aoraki/Mt Cook National Park
CHRISTCHURCH
Mt Cook Village
Lake Tekapo
Southwest New Zealand (Te Wahipounamu) World Heritage Area
Mt Aspiring National Park
Twizel
Timaru

Wanaka
Queenstown

SOUTH PACIFIC OCEAN

To Bounty Islands; Antipodes Islands →

Te Anau
DUNEDIN
Fiordland National Park
Catlins Forest Park
Balclutha
Invercargill
Rakiura National Park
Oban
Stewart Island (Rakiura)

To Snares Islands; Auckland Islands ↓

Three places are World Heritage areas: NZ's Subantarctic Islands, Tongariro National Park and Te Wahipounamu (p345), an amalgam of several national parks in southwest NZ that boast the world's finest surviving Gondwanaland plants and animals in their natural habitats.

Access to the country's wild places is relatively straightforward, though huts on walking tracks require passes and may need to be booked in advance. In practical terms, there is little difference for travellers between a national park and a forest park, though dogs are not allowed in national parks without a permit. Camping is possible in all parks, but may be restricted to dedicated camping grounds – check first. Permits are required for hunting (game birds), and licences are needed for inland fishing (trout, salmon); both can be bought online at www.fishandgame.org.nz.

The Department of Conservation website (www.doc.govt.nz) has useful information on the country's national parks, tracks and walkways. It also lists backcountry huts and campsites.

Active South Island

The South Island's astounding natural assets encourage even the laziest lounge lizards to drag themselves outside. Many travellers come here for the sole purpose of getting active, but the great outdoors isn't just the domain of thrill-seeking tourists. Outdoor culture is ingrained in Kiwi life: from family camping holidays to elite mountaineering, wandering into the wilderness and experiencing NZ's unpeopled majesty is the national habit.

See p379 for tips on less active sports like aerial sightseeing, fishing, sailing and golf; and p68 for the low-down on bird- and marine mammal-watching.

It will come as no surprise then that outdoor activities across the island are accessible and supremely well organised. Commercial operators can hook you up with whatever kind of experience floats your boat – from bungy jumping off a canyon to sea kayaking around a national park – but the beauty of NZ is that you can do a lot of stuff under your own steam, without tagging along on a tour. This is still a wild frontier – don't miss the chance to engage with nature one on one, a million miles from home, just you and the great void.

Adrenaline-pumping activities obviously have an element of risk – particularly white-water rafting, kayaking and anything that involves falling from a great height – but the perception of danger is part of the thrill. Despite some recent mishaps, chances of an accident remain negligible, but make sure you have travel insurance that fully covers you for any planned activities – for more info see p384.

TRAMPING

Tramping (aka bushwalking, hiking or trekking) is the perfect vehicle for a close encounter with the South Island's natural beauty. There are thousands of kilometres of tracks – some well marked, some barely a line on a map – plus an excellent network of huts enabling trampers to avoid lugging tents and (in some cases) cooking gear. Before plodding off into the forest, get up-to-date information from the appropriate authority – usually the **Department of Conservation** (DOC; www.doc.govt.nz), or regional i-SITE visitor information centres.

If you're planning your first walk, check out www.tramper.co.nz – a fantastic website with track descriptions and track ratings.

On the South Island, the most popular tracks are the Routeburn, Milford, Kepler, Queen Charlotte and Abel Tasman Coast tracks. If you've got your heart set on a summer walk along the Milford, Routeburn or any other Great Walk, check out the booking requirements and get in early. If you want to avoid the crowds, go in the shoulder season. DOC staff can help plan tramps on lesser-known tracks; see the DOC website for details.

When to Go

Tramping high season is during the school summer holidays, from two weeks before Christmas until the end of January – avoid it if you can. The best weather is from January to March, though most nonalpine tracks can be walked enjoyably at any time from about October through to April. Winter

---

VOLUNTOURISM

NZ presents a swathe of active, outdoorsy opportunities for travellers to get some dirt under their fingernails and participate in conservation programs. Programs can include anything from tree-planting and weed removal to track construction, habitat conservation and fencing. Ask about local opportunities at any regional i-SITE visitor information centre, or check out www.conservationvolunteers.org.nz and www.doc.govt.nz/getting-involved, both of which allow you to browse for opportunities by region. See also WWOOFing (p377).

(June to August) is not the time to be out in the wild, especially at altitude – some paths close in winter because of avalanche danger and lower levels of facilities and services.

What to Bring
For a primo tramp, the primary considerations are your feet and shoulders. Make sure your footwear is tough as old boots, and that your pack isn't too heavy. Adequate wet-weather gear is essential, especially on the waterlogged West Coast. If you're camping or staying in huts without stoves (eg on the Abel Tasman Coast Track), bring a camping stove. And don't forget your scroggin – a mixture of dried fruit and nuts (and sometimes chocolate) for munching en route.

Books
DOC publishes detailed books on the flora and fauna, geology and history of NZ's national parks, plus leaflets (50c to $2) detailing hundreds of walking tracks across NZ.

Lonely Planet's *Tramping in New Zealand* describes around 50 walks of various lengths and degrees of difficulty. Mark Pickering and Rodney Smith's *101 Great Tramps* has suggestions for two- to six-day tramps around the country. The companion guide, *202 Great Walks: the Best Day Walks in New Zealand*, by Mark Pickering, is handy for shorter, family-friendly excursions. *Accessible Walks*, by Anna and Andrew Jameson, is an excellent guide for elderly, disabled and family trampers, with detailed access information on 100-plus South Island walks.

New trampers should check out *Don't Forget Your Scroggin* by Sarah Bennett and Lee Slater – all about being safe and happy on the track. The *Birdseye Tramping Guides* from Craig Potton Publishing have fab topographical maps, and there are countless books covering tramps and short urban walks around NZ – scan the bookshops.

Maps
The topographical maps produced by **Land Information New Zealand** (LINZ; www.linz.govt.nz) are a safe bet. Bookshops don't often have a good selection of these, but LINZ has map-sales offices in major cities and towns, and DOC offices often sell LINZ maps for local tracks. Outdoor stores also stock them (see the boxed text, p78). LINZ's map series includes park maps (national, state and forest parks), dedicated walking-track maps, and highly detailed 'Topomaps' (you may need two or three of these for one track).

Track Classification
Tracks are classified according to various features, including level of difficulty. In this chapter we loosely refer to the level of difficulty as easy, medium, hard or difficult. The widely used track classification system is as follows:

Short Walk Well formed; allows for wheelchair access or constructed to 'shoe' standard (ie walking boots not required). Suitable for people of all ages and fitness levels.

Walking Track Easy and well-formed longer walks; constructed to 'shoe' standard. Suitable for people of most ages and fitness levels.

Easy Tramping Track or Great Walk Well formed; major water crossings have bridges and track junctions have signs. Light walking boots required.

Tramping Track Requires skill and experience; constructed to 'boot' standard. Suitable for people of average physical fitness. Water crossings may not have bridges.

Route Requires a high degree of skill, experience and navigation skills. Well-equipped trampers only.

If you don't want to be itching and scratching for weeks, bring some insect repellent on your tramp to keep the sandflies at bay (see p382).

GREAT WALKS

0 |▬▬▬▬▬▬| 200 km
0 |▬▬▬▬▬▬| 100 miles

Raglan • ○
Hamilton ○ • Tauranga
• ○ Rotorua
Taupo • ○ • ○ Gisborne
Turangi ○ Lake
New Plymouth • ○ Waikaremoana
Tongariro Track
Ohakune ○ ▣ Northern
Whanganui ○ Circuit • ○ Napier
Journey • ○ Hastings
Wanganui ○

TASMAN
SEA

Palmerston North ○ •

Takaka Abel Tasman
• ○ ▣ Coast Track
Heaphy Track ▣ • ○ Masterton
Picton
Nelson ○ • ○ WELLINGTON
Blenheim ○ •

Westport ○ •

Greymouth • ○ Hanmer • ○ Kaikoura
Springs ○
Hokitika ○ •

Franz Josef •○
Fox Glacier ○
Mt Cook Village • ○ CHRISTCHURCH
• ○ Lake Tekapo
• ○ Twizel
Routeburn • ○ Timaru
Track • ○ Wanaka
Milford ▣
Track • ○ Queenstown

Kepler ▣ ○
Track • ○ Te Anau

SOUTH
PACIFIC
OCEAN

• ○ DUNEDIN

• ○ Balclutha
Rakiura ○ • Invercargill
Track
Stewart Island ▣ ○ • Oban
(Rakiura)

Track Safety

Thousands of people tramp across the South Island without incident, but every year a few folks meet their maker in the mountains. Some trails are only for the experienced, fit and well-equipped – don't attempt these if you don't fit the bill. NZ's climatic changeability subjects high-altitude walks to snow and ice, even in summer, so always check weather and track conditions before setting off. Consult a DOC visitor centre and leave your intentions with a responsible person before starting longer walks. See also www.mountainsafety.org.nz.

The Great Walks

NZ's nine official 'Great Walks' are the country's most popular tracks and six of them are on the South Island. Natural beauty abounds, but prepare yourself for crowds, especially over summer when folks from around the globe pull on their boots.

All nine Great Walks are described in Lonely Planet's *Tramping in New Zealand,* and are detailed in pamphlets provided by DOC visitor centres. You will also find a park map handy.

To tramp these tracks you'll need to buy a Great Walk Pass, sold at DOC visitor centres near each walk, before setting out. These track-specific passes cover you for hut accommodation (from $12 to $45 per person per night, depending on the track and the season) and/or camping (free to $15 per person per night). You can camp only at designated camping grounds (note there's no camping on the Milford Track). In the off-peak season (May to September), Backcountry Hut Passes ($90, valid for 12 months) and pay-as-you-go hut tickets can be used instead of a Great

Walk Pass in many huts (see p76). Kids under 18 stay in huts and camp for free on Great Walks.

DOC has introduced a booking system for six of the Great Walks, to avoid overcrowding and protect the environment. Trampers must book their chosen hut or campsite and specify dates when they purchase a Great Walk Pass.

Abel Tasman Coast Track, Heaphy Track – bookings required year-round
Kepler Track, Milford Track, Routeburn Track – bookings required October to April
Rakiura Track – bookings not required

Bookings can be made online (www.doc.govt.nz), by email (greatwalks booking@doc.govt.nz), by phone, by fax or in person at DOC offices close to the tracks. For full details see the DOC website. There's no charge to do a day walk on any track, but you have to pay if you're staying overnight.

Other Tracks
Of course, there are a lot more walks on the South Island than just the Great ones! Try these on for size:

Arthur's Pass There are many walks in Arthur's Pass National Park; most are difficult. See p246.
Banks Peninsula Track A 35km, two-day (medium) or four-day (easy) walk over the hills and along the coast of Banks Peninsula, crossing private and public land near Akaroa. See p239.
Greenstone and Caples Tracks Two harder tracks on conservation land, just outside Fiordland National Park. They both meet up with the Routeburn Track – a great way to start or finish this popular walk. See p324.
Hump Ridge Track An excellent, three-day, 53km circuit beginning and ending at Bluecliffs Beach on Te Waewae Bay, 20km from Tuatapere. See p352.
Inland Pack Track A 27km medium tramp in Paparoa National Park, following river valleys through the karst landscape near Punakaiki on the West Coast. See p186.
Kaikoura Coast Track An easy, three-day, 40km walk over private and public land along the spectacular coastline 50km south of Kaikoura. See p146.
Matukituki Valley Walks Good medium-to-hard walks in the Matukituki Valley, in Mt Aspiring National Park near Wanaka. See p327.
North-West Circuit A hard, muddy, eight- to 12-day walk on Stewart Island. See p370.
Queen Charlotte Track A three- to five-day medium walk in the Marlborough Sounds, affording great water views. Top-notch accommodation and water transport available. See p132.

SOUTH ISLAND'S 'GREAT WALKS'

Walk	Distance	Duration	Difficulty	Description
Abel Tasman Coast Track (p166)	51km	3-5 days	Easy to medium	NZ's most popular walk (or sea kayak); beaches and bays in Abel Tasman National Park
Heaphy Track (p174)	82km	4-6 days	Medium to hard	Forests, beaches and karst landscapes in Kahurangi National Park
Kepler Track (p340)	60km	3-4 days	Easy to medium	Lakes, rivers, gorges, glacial valleys and beech forest in Fiordland National Park
Milford Track (p345)	54km	4 days	Easy	Rainforest, crystal-clear streams and 630m-high Sutherland Falls in Fiordland National Park
Rakiura Track (p370)	36km	3 days	Medium	Bird life (kiwi!), beaches and lush bush on remote Stewart Island
Routeburn Track (p324)	32km	3 days	Medium	Eye-popping alpine scenery around Mt Aspiring and Fiordland National Parks

Rees-Dart Track A 70km, four- to five-day hard tramping track in Mt Aspiring National Park, through river valleys and traversing an alpine pass. See p325.

St James Walkway This 65km, three- to five-day medium tramping track in Lake Sumner Forest Park/Lewis Pass Reserve passes through sumptuous subalpine scenery. See p245.

Wangapeka and Leslie-Karamea Tracks The Wangapeka is a four- to five-day medium tramping track along river valleys and overpasses. The Leslie-Karamea is a 90km to 100km, five- to seven-day tramp for experienced walkers only, negotiating river valleys, gorges and passes. The two tracks traverse the South Island's northwest, between Golden Bay and Karamea. See p175.

Guided Walks

Due to open in late 2010, Te Araroa (www.teararoa. org.nz) is ambitious: a 3000km walking trail from Cape Reinga in NZ's north to Bluff in the south, linking existing trails and adding new sections. Stay tuned…

Experienced, independent hikers are usually prepared to do some track research, book hut tickets, buy and cook their own food, and lug their tents across the mountains of New Zealand – but guided walks offer an alternative. If you are new to tramping or just want a more comfortable experience, quite a few companies can escort you through the wilds, usually staying in comfortable huts with meals cooked and equipment carried along for you.

Places on the South Island where you can sign up for a guided walk include Kaikoura, the Milford Track (p345), Heaphy Track and Hollyford Track (p345). Prices for a four-night guided walk start around $1500, and ascend to $2000 for deluxe guided experiences.

Backcountry Hut & Camping Fees

DOC has a huge network of backcountry huts (more than 950) in NZ's national and forest parks. There are 'Great Walk' category huts (with mattress-equipped bunks or sleeping platforms, water supply, toilets, heating, and often solar lighting, cooking facilities and a warden); 'serviced huts' (mattress-equipped bunks or sleeping platforms, water supply, heating, toilets and sometimes cooking facilities); 'standard huts' (no cooking equipment or heating); and 'basic huts' (just a shed!). Details about the services in every hut can be found on the DOC website. Backcountry hut fees per adult per night range from free to $45, with tickets bought in advance at DOC visitor centres. Children under 10 can use huts free of charge; 11- to 17-year-olds are charged half price. If you do a lot of tramping, DOC sells an annual **Backcountry Hut Pass** (adult/child $90/45), applicable to most huts except those identified in the DOC Backcountry Huts brochure – which includes many Great Walk huts in summer (for which you'll need a Great Walk Pass – see p74). Backcountry hut tickets and passes can be used to procure a bunk or campsite on some Great Walks in low season (May to September) – see p74.

Depending on the hut category, a night's stay may use one or two tickets. When you arrive at a hut, date your tickets and put them in the box provided. Accommodation is on a first-come, first-served basis.

DOC also manages 250 vehicle-accessible 'Conservation Campsites'. The most basic of these ('basic' sites) are free; 'standard' and 'serviced' grounds cost between $3 and $14 per adult per night. Serviced grounds have full facilities (flush toilets, tap water, showers and picnic tables); they may also have barbecues, a kitchen and a laundry. Standard grounds have toilets and water supply and perhaps barbecues and picnic tables.

Getting There & Away

Getting to and from trailheads can be a problem, except for popular trails serviced by public and dedicated trampers' transport. Having a vehicle only helps with getting to one end of the track (you still have to collect your car

RESPONSIBLE TRAMPING

To help preserve the ecology and beauty of the South Island, have a scan through the following tramping tips. If you went straight from the cradle into a pair of hiking boots, some of these will seem ridiculously obvious; others you mightn't have considered. Online, www.lnt.org is a great resource for low-impact hiking, and the DOC site www.camping.org.nz has plenty more responsible camping tips. When in doubt, ask DOC or i-SITE staff.

The ridiculously obvious:

- If you can, time your tramp to avoid peak season: less people = less stress on the environment and fewer snorers in the huts.
- Carry out *all* your rubbish (including unglamorous items like condoms, tampons and toilet paper). Burying rubbish disturbs soil and vegetation, encourages erosion, and animals will probably dig up what you bury anyway.
- Don't use detergents, shampoo or toothpaste in or near watercourses, even if the products are biodegradable.
- Don't depend on open fires for cooking. Instead, use lightweight kerosene, alcohol or Shellite (white gas) stoves; avoid cookers powered by disposable butane gas canisters.
- If there isn't a toilet, dig a hole and bury your by-product (at least 15cm deep, 100m from any watercourse). Cover it up with soil and a rock. In snow, dig down until you're into the dirt.
- If a track passes through a muddy patch, just plough straight on through – skirting around the outside increases the size of the bog.
- Always seek permission to camp on private land.

You mightn't have considered:

- Wash your dishes 50m from watercourses; use a scourer, sand or snow instead of detergent.
- If you *really* need to scrub your bod, use biodegradable soap and a bucket, at least 50m from any watercourse. Spread the waste water around widely to help the soil filter it.
- If open fires are allowed, use only dead, fallen wood in existing fireplaces (collecting firewood around campsites strips the forest bare in quick time). Don't surround fires with rocks, and leave any extra wood for the next happy camper.
- Keep food-storage bags out of reach of scavengers by tying them to rafters or trees.
- Feeding wildlife can lead to unbalanced populations, diseases and animals becoming dependent on handouts. Keep your dried apricots to yourself.
- If you're bunking down in local accommodation near trailheads, consider environmentally savvy places; keep an eye out for self-composting toilet systems, solar power and greywater recycling systems.

afterwards). If the track starts or ends down a dead-end road, hitching will be difficult.

Of course, tracks that are easily accessed by public transport (eg Abel Tasman) are also the most crowded. An alternative is to arrange private transport, either with a friend or by chartering a vehicle to drop you at one end then pick you up at the other. If you intend to leave a vehicle at a trailhead and return for it later, don't leave anything valuable inside – theft from cars in isolated areas is a significant problem.

EXTREME ADVENTURE

Bungy jumping was made famous by Kiwi AJ Hackett's 1986 plunge from the Eiffel Tower, after which he teamed up with champion NZ skier Henry

---

TOP GEAR

Around the South Island, here are the best places to fix a fractured tent pole or buy a warmer sleeping bag:

- Christchurch: **Snowgum** (Map p216; ☎ 03-365 4336; www.snowgum.co.nz; 637 Colombo St; ⏰ 9am-5.30pm)

- Dunedin: **Bivouac Outdoor** (Map p270; ☎ 03-477 3679; www.bivouac.co.nz; 171 George St; ⏰ 9am-5.30pm Mon-Thu, 9am-6pm Fri, 9am-4pm Sat, 10am-4pm Sun)

- Kaikoura: **R&R Sport** (Map p144; ☎ 03-319 5028; www.rrsport.co.nz; 14 West End; ⏰ 9am-7pm Mon-Sat, to 5.30pm in winter, 10am-4pm Sun)

- Nelson: **R&R Sport** (Map p152; ☎ 03-548 4999; www.rrsport.co.nz; cnr Rutherford & Bridge Sts; ⏰ 9am-5.30pm Mon-Thu, 9am-7pm Fri, 9.30am-4pm Sat, 10am-3pm Sun) Queenstown: **Outside Sports** (Map p306; ☎ 03-441 0074; www.outsidesports.co.nz; 36 Shotover St; ⏰ 8am-8pm)

- Te Anau: **Outside Sports** (Map p339; ☎ 03-249 8195; www.sportsworldteanau.co.nz; 38 Town Centre; ⏰ 9am-9pm)

- Wanaka: **Outside Sports** (Map p328; ☎ 03-443 7966; www.good-sports.co.nz; 17-23 Dunmore St; ⏰ 9am-5.30pm)

---

van Asch to turn the endeavour into a profitable enterprise. The fact that a pant-wetting, illogical activity like bungy jumping is now an everyday pursuit in NZ says much about how 'extreme sports' have evolved here. Bungy, skydiving, jetboating, paragliding and kiteboarding are all well established, but keep an eye out for weird-and-wonderful activities like zorbing (rolling down a hill inside a transparent plastic ball), quad-biking, cave rafting, river sledging (white-water body boarding) and blokarting (windsurfing on wheels). Queenstown's Shotover Canyon Swing (p305) and Ledge Sky Swing (p305) are variations on the extreme theme – all against the laws of nature, and all great fun!

Bungy Jumping

Bungy jumping (hurtling earthwards from bridges with nothing between you and eternity but a gigantic rubber band strapped to your ankles) has plenty of daredevil panache.

Queenstown is a spider's web of bungy cords, including a 43m jump off the Kawarau Bridge (which also has a bungy theatre and museum), a 47m leap from a ledge at the top of the gondola, and the big daddy, the 134m Nevis Bungy. Other South Island bungy jumps include Waiau River (near Hanmer Springs) and Mt Hutt ski field.

Skydiving

Ejecting yourself from a plane at high altitude is big business in NZ. There are plenty of professional operators, and at most drop zones the views on the way up (not to mention the way down) are sublime.

Some operators and clubs offer static-line jumps and Accelerated Free Fall courses, but for most first-timers a tandem skydive is the way to go. After bonding with a fully qualified instructor, you get to experience up to 45 seconds of high-speed free fall before the chute opens. The thrill is worth every dollar (specifically as much as $250/330/430 for a 9000/12,000/15,000ft jump). You'll pay extra for a video/DVD/photograph of your exploits.

Try tandem skydiving in Nelson, Motueka, Christchurch, Fox Glacier, Methven, Wanaka, Queenstown, Te Anau and Kaikoura.

Jetboating

The jetboat is a local invention, dreamed up by CWF Hamilton in 1957. An inboard engine sucks water into a tube in the bottom of the boat, and an impeller driven by the engine blows it out of a nozzle at the stern in a high-speed stream. The boat is steered simply by directing the jet stream. Jetboats make short work of shallow and white water because there are no propellers to damage, there's better clearance under the boat and the jet can be reversed instantly for quick braking. The jet's instant response enables these craft to execute passenger-drenching 360-degree spins almost within the length of the boat.

The 109m-high Shotover Canyon Swing in Queenstown is touted as the world's highest rope swing.

The Shotover and Kawarau Rivers near Queenstown and the Buller River near Westport are renowned jetboating waterways. The Dart River is less travelled but also good, and the Waiatoto River near Haast is a superb wilderness experience, as is the Wilkin River in Mt Aspiring National Park. Try also the Kawarau River (out of Cromwell), the Waiau River (out of Te Anau) and the Wairahurahiri River (out of Tuatapere).

Paragliding & Kiteboarding

Paragliding is perhaps the easiest way for humans to achieve assisted flight. The sport involves taking to the skies in what is basically a parachute that's been modified so it glides through the air. After a half-day of instruction you should be able to do limited solo flights, and before you know it you could be soaring through the sky, 300m high. The **New Zealand Hang Gliding & Paragliding Association** (www.nzhgpa.org.nz) rules the roost. One of the best places to learn the skills is Wanaka Paragliding (p329).

The rather literally named New Zealand Parachute Federation (www.nzpf.org) is the governing body for skydiving in NZ. Check the website for info and operator listings.

Tandem flights, where you are strapped to an experienced paraglider, are offered all over the country. Popular tandem experiences include those in Queenstown and Nelson.

Kiteboarding (aka kitesurfing), where a mini parachute drags you across the ocean on a mini surfboard, is pretty 'extreme', and can be attempted at Wellington and Nelson. You can tee up lessons at both places.

SKIING & SNOWBOARDING

Global warming is triggering a worldwide melt, but NZ remains an essential southern-hemisphere destination for snow bunnies, with downhill, cross-country and ski mountaineering all passionately pursued. Heliskiing, where choppers lift skiers to the top of long, isolated stretches of virgin snow, also has its fans. The NZ ski season is generally June to October, though it varies considerably from one ski area to another, and can run as late as November.

Unlike Europe, America or even Australia, NZ's commercial ski areas aren't generally set up as 'resorts' with chalets, lodges or hotels. Rather, accommodation and après-ski carousing are often in surrounding towns that connect with the slopes via daily shuttles.

The variety of locations and conditions makes it difficult to rate the ski fields in any particular order. Some people like to be near Queenstown's party scene; others prefer the high slopes and quality runs of Mt Hutt, uncrowded Rainbow or less-stressed club skiing areas. Club areas are publicly accessible and usually less crowded and cheaper than commercial ski fields, even though nonmembers pay a slightly higher fee. Many club areas have lodges you can stay at, subject to availability – winter holidays and weekends will be fully booked, but midweek you'll be OK.

Visitor information centres in NZ, and the New Zealand Tourism Board (NZTB) internationally, have brochures on the various ski areas and packages, and can make bookings. Lift passes can cost anywhere from $35 to $90 a day (roughly half that for children and two-thirds for students). Lesson-and-lift packages are available at most areas. Ski-equipment rental (skis, boots and poles) starts at around $40 a day; snowboard-and-boots hire starts at around $45. Prices decrease for multiday hire. Try to rent equipment close to where you'll be skiing, so you can exchange gear if there's a problem with the fit.

QUEENSTOWN & WANAKA

The Queenstown region's oldest ski field is **Coronet Peak** (☎ 0800 365 696, 03-442 4620, snow-phone 03-442 1970; www.nzski.com; daily lift pass adult/child $93/51). A multimillion dollar snow-making system and treeless slopes provide excellent skiing for all levels. The consistent gradient and the many undulations make this a snowboarder's paradise. Night skiing usually happens on Friday and Saturday, from late June to late September. Shuttles run from Queenstown, 18km away.

Visually remarkable, the **Remarkables** (☎ 03-442 4615, snow-phone 03-442 4615; www.nzski.com; daily lift pass adult/child $87/48) is also near Queenstown (28km away) – shuttle buses run during the season. It has an equal smattering of beginner, intermediate and advanced runs, with chairlifts and beginners' tows, and is a family-friendly field (kids under 10 ski free). Look for the sweeping run called Homeward Bound.

The highest and largest of the southern lakes ski areas, **Treble Cone** (☎ 03-443 7443, snow-phone 03-443 7444; www.treblecone.com; daily lift pass adult/child $89/39) is in a spectacular location 26km from Wanaka, with steep slopes suitable for intermediate to advanced skiers. Treble Cone also has numerous half-pipes and a terrain park for snowboarding.

Around 34km from Wanaka, **Cardrona** (☎ 03-443 7341, snow-phone 03-443 7007; www.cardrona.com; daily lift pass adult/child $85/42) has several high-capacity chairlifts, beginners' tows and extreme terrain for snowboarders. Buses run from

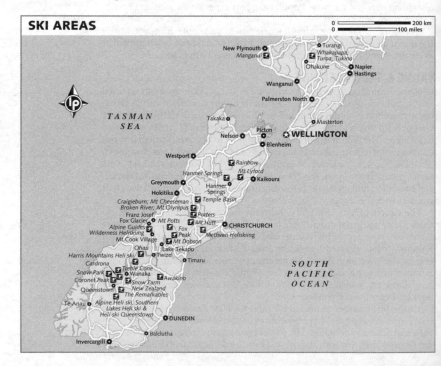

Wanaka during the ski season, and also from Queenstown. Cardrona has acquired a reputation for the services it offers skiers with disabilities, and it was the first resort on the South Island to have an on-field crèche. In summer, the mountain bikers take over.

NZ's only commercial Nordic (cross-country) ski area, **Snow Farm New Zealand** (☎ 03-443 7542; www.snowfarmnz.com; daily trail pass adult/child $35/15) is 35km from Wanaka on the Pisa Range, high above Lake Wanaka. There are 50km of groomed trails and thousands of hectares of open rolling country for classic ski touring. Huts with facilities are dotted along the top of the Pisa Range.

Snow Park (☎ 03-443 9991; www.snowparknz.com; daily lift pass adult/child $75/40) is NZ's only dedicated freestyle ski and board area, with a plethora of pipes, terrain parks, boxes, rails, hits and snow-making facilities. There's backpacker-style accommodation, a restaurant and a bar here too. It's 34km from Wanaka; 58km from Queenstown.

For info on local facilities, see Queenstown (p301) and Wanaka (p326).

SOUTH CANTERBURY

The commercial ski area **Ohau** (☎ 03-438 9885; www.ohau.co.nz; daily lift pass adult/child $68/26) lines the flanks of Mt Sutton, 42km from Twizel. Expect a high percentage of intermediate and advanced runs, excellent terrain for snowboarding and cross-country skiing, and a ski lodge to sleep in. See Lake Ohau & Ohau Forests (p260) for more accommodation info.

The 3km-wide basin at **Mt Dobson** (☎ 03-685 8039, snow-phone 0900 39 888; www.dobson.co.nz; daily lift pass adult/child $65/25), a commercial ski area 26km from Fairlie, caters for learners and has a large intermediate area, a terrain park and famously dry powder. On a clear day you can see Mt Cook and the Pacific Ocean from the Mt Dobson summit. **Fox Peak** (☎ 03-696 4808, snow-phone 03-688 0044; www.foxpeak.co.nz; daily lift pass adult/child $45/15) is a club ski area 29km from Fairlie in the Two Thumb Range. Fox Peak has four rope tows; there's good cross-country skiing from the summit. There's also dorm-style accommodation at Fox Lodge, 3km below the ski area. For info on nearby facilities, see Fairlie (p255).

Round Hill (☎ 021 680 694, snow-phone 03-680 6977; www.roundhill.co.nz; daily lift pass adult/child $65/32) is a small field with wide, gentle slopes perfect for beginners and intermediates, about 32km from Lake Tekapo village. See Lake Tekapo (p256) for details on local accommodation.

CENTRAL CANTERBURY

Mt Hutt (☎ 03-302 8811, snow-phone 03-308 5074; www.nzski.com; daily lift pass adult/child $87/48) is one of the highest ski areas in the southern hemisphere, as well as one of NZ's best. It's close to Methven and can be reached by bus from Christchurch (118km to the west). Ski shuttles run to/from both towns. The ski area's access road is a rough, unpaved ride – drivers should be extremely cautious when the weather is lousy. Mt Hutt has beginner, intermediate and advanced slopes, with a six-seater chairlift, various other lifts and heliskiing to slopes further afield. The wide-open faces are good for snowboard learners. For info on where to stay and eat in the area, see Methven (p248).

Exclusive Mt Potts is **HeliPark New Zealand** (☎ 0800 435 472, 03-303 9060; www.mtpotts.co.nz, www.helipark.co.nz; access incl 1st run $225, per subsequent run $85) – one of NZ's snow-white gems, sitting above the headwaters of the Rangitata River, 75km from Methven. It offers a helicopter-accessed skiing experience. Accommodation and meals are available at a lodge 8km from the ski area – dinner, bed and breakfast (DB&B) costs from $109. For info on the nearby town of Mt Somers, see p251.

Websites such as www .snow.co.nz, www .chillout.co.nz and www .nzski.com provide ski reports, employment opportunities, webcams and virtual tours across NZ.

The closest commercial ski area to Christchurch is **Porters** (☎ 03-318 4002, snow-phone 03-383 8888; www.skiporters.co.nz; daily lift pass adult/child $75/40), 96km away on the Arthur's Pass road. Its Big Mama is one of the steepest runs in NZ, but there are wider, gentler slopes too. There's a half-pipe for snowboarders, good cross-country runs along the ridge, and lodge accommodation (DB&B $83). For accommodation in the area, see Craigieburn Forest Park (p246).

Temple Basin (☎ 03-377 7788, snow-phone 03-383 8888; www.templebasin.co.nz; daily lift pass adult/child $60/35) is a club field 4km from the Arthur's Pass township. It's a 50-minute walk uphill from the car park to the ski-area lodges. There's floodlit skiing at night and excellent backcountry runs for snowboarders. For info on local facilities, see Arthur's Pass (p246).

Craigieburn Valley (☎ 03-318 8711 snow-phone 03-383 8888; www.craigieburn.co.nz; daily lift pass adult/child $65/35), centred on Hamilton Peak, is 40km from Arthur's Pass. It's one of NZ's most challenging club areas, with intermediate and advanced runs (no beginners). Not far away is **Broken River** (☎ 03-318 8713, snow-phone 03-383 8888; www.brokenriver.co.nz; daily lift pass adult/child $60/35), another club field, with a 15- to 20-minute walk from the car park and a real sense of isolation. See Craigieburn Forest Park (p246) and Arthur's Pass (p246) for details of local places to stay and eat.

Another cool club area in the Craigieburn Range is family-friendly **Mt Cheeseman** (☎ 03-344 3247, snow-phone 03-383 8888; www.mtcheeseman.co.nz; daily lift pass adult/child $60/30), 112km from Christchurch (the closest club to the city). Based on Mt Cockayne, it's a wide, sheltered basin with drive-to-the-snow road access. Also in Craigieburn (difficult to find, but worth the search) is **Mt Olympus** (☎ 03-318 5840, snow-phone 03-383 8888; www.mtolympus.co.nz; daily lift pass adult/child $60/30), 58km from Methven and 12km from Lake Ida. This club area has four tows that lead to intermediate and advanced runs, and there are solid cross-country trails to other areas. Access is sometimes 4WD-only, depending on conditions. Lodge accommodation is available. See Craigieburn Forest Park (p246) and Arthur's Pass (p246) for details of local places to stay and eat near Mt Cheeseman and Mt Olympus.

NORTHERN SOUTH ISLAND

There are two ski areas near Hanmer Springs. Accommodation is on-field, or you can stay in the township (p242). **Hanmer Springs** (☎ 027 434 1806, snow-phone 03-383 8888; www.skihanmer.co.nz; daily lift pass adult/child $55/25) is based on Mt St Patrick, 17km from Hanmer Springs township, with mostly intermediate and advanced runs. There are natural and groomed pipe-rides for snowboarders too. **Mt Lyford** (☎ 03-315 6178, snow-phone 03-366 1220; www.mtlyford.co.nz; daily lift pass adult/child $60/30) is 60km from both Hanmer Springs and Kaikoura, and 4km from Mt Lyford Village. It's a 'resort' in the true sense, with accommodation and plenty of food options available. There's a good mix of runs, suiting beginner, intermediate and advanced skiers and boarders, and a terrain park.

The sunny Nelson region also has a ski area, just 100km away (a similar distance from Blenheim). **Rainbow** (☎ 03-521 1861, snow-phone 0832 226 05; www.skirainbow.co.nz; daily lift pass adult/child $62/30) borders the Nelson Lakes National Park, with varied terrain, minimal crowds and good cross-country skiing. Chains are often required. St Arnaud (p158) is the closest town (32km).

OTAGO

Awakino (☎ 03-313 7229; www.skiawakino.com; daily lift pass adult/child $35/25) in North Otago is a small player on the scene, but worth a visit for intermediate skiers. Oamaru (p291) is 45km away on the coast; Omarama (p296) is 66km inland. Weekend lodge-and-ski packages are good value.

The *NZ Ski & Snowboard Guide*, published annually by Brown Bear, is a brilliant reference for powder-hounds, detailing NZ's 26 ski areas. Check it out at www.brownbear.co.nz/ski

Heliskiing

The South Island's remote heights are tailor-made for heliskiing. From July to October, operators cover a wide off-piste (off the beaten slopes) area along the Southern Alps. The cost ranges from around $750 to $1200 for three to eight runs. HeliPark New Zealand (p81) at Mt Potts is a dedicated heliski park. Heliskiing is also available at Coronet Peak, Treble Cone, Cardrona, Mt Hutt, Mt Lyford, Ohau and Hanmer Springs. Alternatively you can contact an independent operator:

Alpine Heli ski (☎ 03-441 2300; www.alpineheliski.com; Queenstown)
Backcountry Helicopters NZ (☎ 0800 583 945, 03-443 9032; www.heliskinz.com; Wanaka)
Harris Mountains Heli-ski (☎ 03-442 6722; www.heliski.co.nz; Queenstown & Wanaka)
Heli Ski Queenstown (☎ 0800 123 4354, 03-442 7733; www.flynz.co.nz; Queenstown)
Methven Heliski (☎ 03-302 8108; www.methvenheli.co.nz; Methven)
Southern Lakes Heliski (☎ 03-442 6222; www.southernlakesheliski.co.nz; Queenstown)
Wilderness Heliski (☎ 03-435 1834; www.wildernessheli.co.nz; Aoraki/Mt Cook)

MOUNTAIN BIKING

The South Island is laced with quality mountain-biking opportunities. Mountain bikes can be hired in major towns or adventure-sports centres like Queenstown, Wanaka, Nelson and Picton; all also have repair shops.

Various companies will take you up to the tops of mountains and volcanoes (eg Christchurch's Port Hills, Cardrona and the Remarkables) so you can hurtle down without the grunt-work of getting to the top first. Central Otago offers famously good mountain biking on the Alexandra goldfield trails. Also check out Twizel near Mt Cook, the Waitati Valley and Hayward Point near Dunedin, Canaan Downs near Abel Tasman National Park and Mt Hutt.

Some traditional tramping tracks are open to mountain bikes, but DOC has restricted access in many cases due to track damage and the inconvenience to walkers, especially at busy times. Never cycle on walking tracks in national parks unless it's permissible (check with DOC), or you risk heavy fines and the unfathomable ire of hikers. The Queen Charlotte Track is a good one to bike, but part of it is closed in summer.

CYCLE TOURING

On any given stretch of highway, especially during summer, you'll come across plenty of pannier-laden cyclists with one eye on the scenery and the other looking out for potholes. Not that potholes are really an issue – the roads here are generally solid. Most towns offer touring-bike hire, at either backpacker hostels or specialist bike shops. Bike service and repair shops can be found in big towns; see the regional chapters in this book.

Some excellent cycle-touring books are available, including Lonely Planet's *Cycling New Zealand,* and the *Pedallers' Paradise* booklets by Nigel Rushton (see www.paradise-press.co.nz). Anyone planning a cycling tour of the South Island should check out the self-guided tour options at www.cyclehire.co.nz.

Almost every town-to-town and over-the-mountain road attracts cyclists. If you're not after altitude, the Central Otago Rail Trail (p286) between Middlemarch and Clyde is a winner. The Little River Rail Trail (p222) in Canterbury (en route to Banks Peninsula) is also fabulous. For an off-the-beaten-highway option, try the Southern Scenic Route (p352) from Invercargill round Tuatapere to Te Anau.

The proposed $50-million **New Zealand Cycle Trail** (www.tourism.govt.nz/our-work/new-zealand-cycle-trail-project) – a national bike path from Kaitaia to Bluff – is still in the developmental stages, with some parts already open: watch this space…

Online, www.cycletour.co.nz has loads of two-wheeled info.

Classic New Zealand Mountain Bike Rides details short and long rides all over NZ (see www.kennett.co.nz). *New Zealand Mountain Biker* (www.nzmtbr.co.nz) mag comes out every two months.

SEA KAYAKING

Highly rated sea kayaking areas in NZ's south include the Marlborough Sounds (Picton) and along the coast of Abel Tasman National Park, where kayaking is almost as popular as tramping. Fiordland is also a hot spot, with a heap of tour operators in Te Anau, Milford, Doubtful Sound and Manapouri arranging spectacular trips on local lakes and fiords. Also try the Otago Peninsula, Stewart Island and Kaikoura. The **Kiwi Association of Sea Kayakers** (KASK; www.kask.org.nz) is the main NZ organisation.

For wannabe paddlers, the Sea Kayak Operators Association of New Zealand (www.skoanz.org.nz) website has a map of NZ paddling destinations and links to operators working in each area.

CANOEING

Canoeing is popular on the freshwater lakes on the South Island. Many backpacker hostels close to canoe-friendly waters have Canadian canoes and kayaks for hire or free use, and loads of commercial guided trips (for those without equipment or experience) are offered on rivers and lakes throughout the country. Many trips have an eco element such as birdwatching – a prime example is the beautiful Okarito Lagoon on the West Coast.

WHITE-WATER RAFTING & KAYAKING

There are almost as many white-water rafting possibilities as there are rivers in the country, and there's no shortage of companies to get you into the rapids. **Whitewater NZ** (www.rivers.org.nz) covers all things white-water.

Check the Whitewater NZ (www.rivers.org.nz) website for rainfall and river-flow updates around the country.

Popular South Island rafting rivers include the Shotover and Kawarau Rivers near Queenstown, while the Rangitata River (south of Christchurch) is considered one of the country's best. The northern end of the island also has great rafting options, including the Buller River near Murchison and Karamea River near Westport. Other West Coast possibilities include the Arnold and Waiho Rivers.

Rivers are graded from I to VI, with VI meaning 'unraftable'. The grading of the Shotover canyon varies from III to V+, depending on the time of year. The Kawarau River is rated IV; the Rangitata River has everything from I to V. On the rougher stretches there's usually a minimum age limit of 12 or 13 years. Safety equipment is supplied by operators. The **New Zealand Rafting Association** (NZRA; www.nz-rafting.co.nz) has an online river guide, and lists registered operators.

From September to April, the **New Zealand Kayak School** (☎ 03-352 5786; www.nzkayakschool.com) in Murchison offers intensive multiday courses in white-water kayaking from introductory to advanced levels (from $395).

HORSE RIDING

Horse riding is commonplace in NZ. Unlike in some other parts of the world where beginners get led by the nose around a paddock, here you can really get out into the countryside on a farm, forest or beach. Rides range from one-hour jaunts (from around $50) to week-long, fully catered treks.

NZ's premier kayaking magazine is *New Zealand Kayak*, published every two months – look for it in newsagencies.

On the South Island, all-day horseback adventures happen around Kaikoura, Nelson, Mt Cook, Lake Tekapo, Hanmer Springs, Queenstown, Glenorchy, Methven, Mt Hutt, Cardrona, Te Anau and Dunedin. Treks are also offered alongside Paparoa National Park on the West Coast.

For equine info online, see the **Auckland SPCA Horse Welfare Auxiliary Inc** (www.horsetalk.co.nz) website. For trek-operator listings see www.truenz.co.nz/horse trekking or www.newzealand.com.

ROCK CLIMBING

The Port Hills area above Christchurch has countless climbs, and 100km away on the road to Arthur's Pass is Castle Hill, with great friction climbs and bouldering. West of Nelson, the marble and limestone mountains of

Golden Bay and Takaka Hill provide prime climbing. Other options are Long Beach (north of Dunedin), and Mihiwaka and Lovers Leap on the Otago Peninsula.

MOUNTAINEERING

New Zealand has a proud mountaineering history – this was, after all, the home of Sir Edmund Hillary (1919–2008), who, along with Tenzing Norgay, was the first to summit Mt Everest. When he came back down, Hillary famously uttered to friend George Lowe, 'Well, George, we knocked the bastard off!'.

The Southern Alps are studded with impressive peaks and challenging climbs. The Aoraki/Mt Cook region is outstanding; others extend along the spine of the South Island from Tapuaenuku (in the Kaikoura Ranges) and the Nelson Lakes peaks in the north to the rugged southern mountains of Fiordland. Another area with climbs for all levels is Mt Aspiring National Park. To the south in the Forbes Mountains is Mt Earnslaw, flanked by the Rees and Dart Rivers.

The Christchurch-based **New Zealand Alpine Club** (NZAC; ☎ 03-377 7595; www. alpineclub.org.nz) proffers professional information, and produces the annual *NZAC Alpine Journal* and the quarterly *The Climber* magazine. Professional outfits for training, guiding and advice can be found at Wanaka, Aoraki/Mt Cook, Lake Tekapo, and Fox and Franz Josef Glaciers.

The website www.climb .co.nz has the low-down on the hottest rock-climbing spots around NZ, plus access and instruction info.

Covering 17 legendary NZ mountains, Hugh Logan's *Classic Peaks of New Zealand* is a classic mountaineering read.

SURFING IN NEW ZEALAND Josh Kronfeld

As a surfer I feel particularly guilty in letting the reader in on a local secret – NZ has a sensational mix of quality waves perfect for beginners and experienced surfers. As long as you're willing to travel off the beaten track, you can score some great, uncrowded waves. The islands of NZ are hit with swells from all points of the compass throughout the year. So, with a little weather knowledge and a little effort, numerous options present themselves. Point breaks, reefs, rocky shelves and hollow sandy beach breaks can all be found – take your pick!

Surfing has become increasingly popular in NZ and today there are surf schools up and running at most premier surf beaches. It's worth doing a bit of research before you arrive. **Surfing New Zealand** (www.surfingnz.co.nz) recommends a number of surf schools on its website. If you're on a surf holiday in NZ, consider purchasing a copy of the *New Zealand Surfing Guide*, by Mike Bhana.

Surf.co.nz (www.surf.co.nz) provides information on many great surf spots, but most NZ beaches hold good rideable breaks. Here are some ideal surfing spots in the Wellington region and on the South Island:

- **Wellington Region** Beaches such as Lyall Bay, Castlepoint and Tora
- **Marlborough & Nelson** Kaikoura Peninsula, Mangamaunu and Meatworks
- **Canterbury** Taylors Mistake and Sumner Bar
- **Otago** Dunedin is a good base for surfing on the South Island, with access to a number of superb breaks, such as St Clair Beach
- **West Coast** Punakaiki and Tauranga Bay
- **Southland** Porridge and Centre Island

NZ water temperatures and climate vary greatly from north to south. For comfort while surfing, wear a wet suit. On the South Island, use a 2-3mm steamer in summer and a 3-5mm with all the extras in winter.

Josh is a keen surfer originally hailing from the Hawke's Bay region. While representing the All Blacks (1995–2000) he successfully juggled surfing, pop music and an international rugby career.

SCUBA DIVING

New Zealand is prime scuba territory, with warm waters up north, brilliant sea life and plenty of interesting dive sites for both beginners and experts alike.

Down south, the Marlborough Sounds Maritime Park has some interesting dives, including the *Mikhail Lermontov*, the largest diveable cruise-ship wreck in the world. Fiordland is highly unusual in that the region's extremely heavy rainfall and mountain runoff leaves a layer of peaty, brown freshwater sitting on top of some of the saltwater fiords, notably Dusky Sound, Milford Sound and Doubtful Sound. The freshwater filters out light and discourages the growth of seaweed, so divers can experience amazingly clear pseudo-deep-water conditions not far below the surface. Invercargill, with its Antarctic waters, also has a diving club.

Expect to pay anywhere from $170 for a short, introductory, pool-based scuba-diving course; and from $495 for a four-day, PADI-approved, ocean dive course. One-off organised boat- and land-based dives start off at around $165.

DIVE SITES & SURF BEACHES

The **Dive New Zealand** (www.divenewzealand.com) website is a treasure-trove of underwater information, with the lowdown on dive and wreck sites, plus listings of operators, clubs and shops.

CAVING

Caving (aka spelunking) opportunities abound in NZ's honeycombed karst (limestone) regions. You'll find active local clubs and organised tours around Westport and Karamea, and Golden Bay also has some mammoth caves. For more info see the **New Zealand Speleological Society** (www.caves.org.nz) website.

Wellington Region

When you're flying into Wellington en route to the South Island, prepare yourself for some big-city sophistication and stay a few nights before kicking on further south. Art-house cinema, designer boutiques, hip bars, live music venues and late-night coffee shops – it's all here. Wellingtonians are geographically isolated and look inwards for inspiration, a habit that fosters a red-hot arts scene. Everyone seems to be in a band and looks a tad depleted, like they smoke and drink too much and spend their time molesting canvasses and scribbling poetry – except for the politicians of course. NZ's capital city manages to strike a balance between creative exuberance and an institutional mindset crucial to the day-to-day running of the country.

Wellington is also a major travel hub, full of visitors catching the ferries across Cook Strait to the South Island. Travellers file through the city, giving it a free-moving, energetic vibe. Steep hills lined with Victorian houses ascend from the harbour to spectacular view points. Wellington punches well above its weight – plan on spending a few days in the ring.

If city trappings are something you're trying to forget, there are great outdoor destinations less than an hour away. Cruise the Kapiti Coast or head over the Rimutaka Range into the Wairarapa, where the delicate flavours of pinot noir (the local grape) are apt reward for a day spent exploring the wild coast.

HIGHLIGHTS

- Getting interactive at NZ's finest museum, Wellington's **Te Papa** (p97)
- Scaling the lighthouse steps on wild and remote **Cape Palliser** (p120)
- Sampling the great coffee and quality beer that Wellingtonians demand at the city's slick **bars** (p106) and bohemian **cafes** (p105)
- Exploring **Kapiti Island** (p115) and saying hi to the takahe, one of NZ's rarest birds
- Maintaining a straight line on your bicycle as you tour the picturesque **Martinborough wineries** (p118)
- Riding the ratchety **cable car** (p96) from Lambton Quay to the leafy **Wellington Botanic Gardens** (p95)
- Ripping up the trails at **Makara Peak Mountain Bike Park** (p98)

Kapiti Island ★

★ Martinborough

★ Wellington

★ Cape Palliser

| ▓ Telephone code: 04 | ▓ www.wellingtonnz.com | ▓ www.wairarapanz.com |

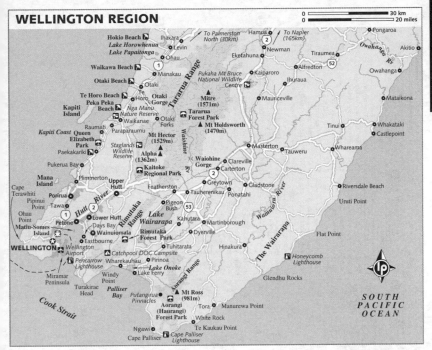

WELLINGTON REGION

Climate

When Wellington's weather turns bad, it can be *truly* foul: lacerating winds and sheets of freezing rain coming in sideways. It ain't called 'Windy Wellington' for nothing…

November to April are the warmer months and the best time to visit, with average maximums hovering around 20°C. From May to August it's colder and wetter – daily temperatures lurk around 12°C.

Getting There & Around

Wellington is a major transport hub, being the North Island port for the interisland ferries. Wellington airport is serviced by international and domestic airlines.

Easy train and bus connections make commuting into Wellington a viable option – many people travel to work (or to party) in Wellington from the hinterland. Approaching the city from the north, you'll pass through either the Kapiti Coast to the west via State Highway 1 (SH1), or the Wairarapa and heavily populated Hutt Valley to the east via State Highway 2 (SH2).

InterCity (www.intercity.co.nz) is the main North Island bus company, travelling just about everywhere. Commuter trains run from Wellington to the Kapiti Coast and the Wairarapa; long-distance **Tranz Scenic** (www.tranzscenic.co.nz) trains run from Wellington to Auckland via Palmerston North. See p109 for details on getting to/from Wellington.

WELLINGTON

pop 164,000 (city), 424,000 (region)

A small city with a relatively big reputation, Wellington is most famous for being NZ's capital. It is *infamous* for its weather, particularly the gale-force winds wont to barrel through, wrecking umbrellas and obliterating hairdos. It also lies on a major fault line. And the inner-city one-way system is like the Krypton Factor on acid.

But don't be deterred. 'Welly' is a brilliant city, as those who spend any more than a couple of days there will attest. For a starter it's lovely to look at, scattered around bushy hillsides encircling a magnificent harbour. There are super lookouts on hilltops, golden sand on the prom, and spectacular craggy shores along the South Coast. Downtown,

GREATER WELLINGTON

0   500 m
0   0.25 miles

INFORMATION
After-Hours Pharmacy	(see 12)
Air New Zealand	(see 65)
Australian High Commission	**1** C2
Automobile Association (AA)	**2** B5
Canadian Embassy	**3** B5
Fijian High Commission	**4** C3
German Embassy	**5** C2
Israeli Embassy	**6** B4
Map Shop	**7** C3
Netherlands Embassy	**8** B4
Travelex	**9** B4
UK High Commission	**10** B3
US Embassy	**11** B2
Wellington Accident & Urgent Medical Centre	**12** C8

SIGHTS & ACTIVITIES
Academy Galleries	**13** B5
Alexander Turnbull Library	(see 26)
Archives New Zealand	**14** C3
Beehive	**15** B4
Cable Car Lower Terminal	**16** B5
Cable Car Museum	(see 17)
Cable Car Upper Terminal	**17** A5
Carter Observatory	**18** A5
East by West Ferry Terminal	**19** C5
Ferg's Kayaks	**20** C5
Freyberg Pool & Fitness Centre	**21** D6
Government Buildings	**22** B4
Harbour Explorer Excursion	(see 19)
Helipro	**23** C5

Katherine Mansfield's Birthplace	**24** C2
Museum of Wellington	**25** B5
National Library Gallery	(see 26)
National Library of New Zealand	**26** B3
New Zealand Cricket Museum	**27** C8
Old St Paul's	**28** C3
Parliament House	**29** B3
Parliamentary Library	**30** B3
Wellington Botanic Gardens	**31** A5

SLEEPING ⌂
Apollo Lodge	**32** D7
Booklovers B&B	**33** D8
Capital View Motor Inn	**34** A8
Carillon Motor Inn	**35** A8
CityLife Wellington	**36** B5
Comfort & Quality Hotels	**37** B7
Copthorne Hotel	**38** D6
Downtown Backpackers	**39** C4
Majoribanks Apartments	**40** D7
Marksman Motor Inn	**41** C8
Mermaid	**42** A7
Shepherds Arms Hotel	**43** A4
Tinakori Lodge	**44** B3
Travelodge	**45** B5
Wellesley	**46** B4
Wellington Waterfront	**47** C4
Motorhome Park	
Worldwide Backpackers	**48** A6

To Omega Rental Cars (1.2km);
Ace Rental Cars (1.2km)

To SH1 (Kapiti Coast);
Moana Lodge (23km);
SH2 (Lower & Upper
Hutt; The Wairarapa);
Wellington Top 10 Holiday
Park (9km); Turners
Auctions (9km)

Aotea Quay

Westpac
Trust
Stadium

Wadestown

Thorndon Quay

Hobson St

Murphy St

Wadestown Rd

Park St

Tinakori Rd

Hill St

Town Belt

Northern
Walkway

Thorndon

Wellington
Cathedral

Molesworth St

Hawkestone St

Aitken St

Sydney St E

Sydney St W

Grant Rd

St Mary St

Glenmore St

Waterloo Quay

Thorndon Quay

Wellington Urban Mwy

Hutt Rd

Bowen St

Cenotaph

Wellington

Port of Wellington
Container Terminal

Pipitea
Quay

Featherston St

Whitmore St

Ballance St

Lambton Quay

Waring Taylor St

Bolton St

Lady Norwood
Rose Garden

To Mud Cycles (3km);
Makara Peak
Mountain Bike
Park (4km)

Wellington-Picton Ferry (Interislander Services)

Wellington-Picton Ferry (Bluebridge Services)

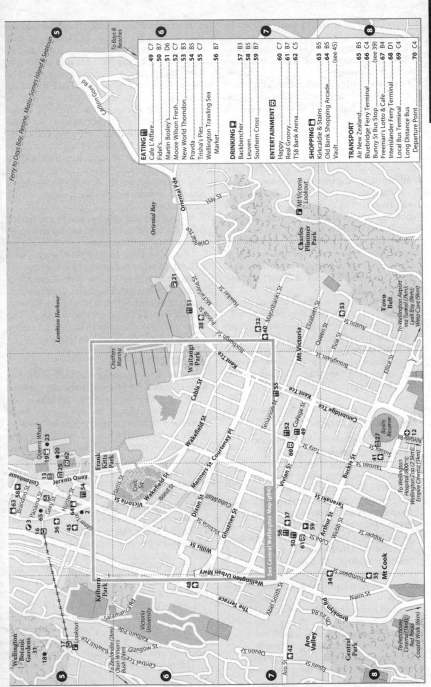

the city is compact and vibrant, buoyed by a surprising number of museums, theatres, galleries and shops. A cocktail- and caffeine-fuelled hospitality scene fizzes and pops among the throng.

Brace yourself for a roller coaster of emotions: 'You can't beat Wellington on a good day', they say, but on a bad day this city's a heartbreaker.

HISTORY

Maori legend has it that the explorer Kupe was first to discover Wellington harbour. Wellington's original Maori name was Te Whanganui-a-Tara (great harbour of Tara), named after the son of a chief named Whatonga who had settled on the Hawke's Bay coast. Whatonga sent Tara and his half-brother to explore the southern part of the North Island. When they returned over a year later, their reports were so favourable that Whatonga's followers moved there, founding the Ngati Tara tribe.

The first European settlers arrived in the New Zealand Company's ship *Aurora* on 22 January 1840, not long after Colonel William Wakefield arrived to buy land from Maori. The idea was to build two cities: one would be a commercial centre by the harbour (Port Nicholson) and the other, further north, would be the agricultural hub.

However, Maori denied they had sold the land at Port Nicholson, or Poneke, as they called it, as it was founded on hasty and illegal buying by the New Zealand Company. Land rights struggles ensued – they were to plague the country for years, and still affect it today.

By 1850 Wellington was a thriving settlement of around 5500 people; however, there was very little flat land. Originally the waterfront was along Lambton Quay, but reclamation of parts of the harbour began in 1852. In 1855 an earthquake raised part of Hutt Rd and the area from Te Aro flat to the Basin Reserve, which initiated the first major land reclamation.

In 1865 the seat of government was moved from Auckland to Wellington, due to its central location in the country.

One blustery day back in 1968 the wind blew so hard it pushed the almost-new Wellington–Christchurch ferry *Wahine* onto Barrett Reef at the harbour entrance. The disabled ship dragged its anchors, drifted into the harbour and slowly sank – 51 people perished. The Museum of Wellington (p94) has a moving exhibit commemorating this tragedy.

ORIENTATION

The city congregates in the western corner of Wellington harbour, with the city suburbs clinging to the steep valleys and hills on all sides. Lambton Quay, the city's major business thoroughfare, runs more or less parallel to the seafront (which it once was). The central business district stretches from the train station, at the northern end of Lambton Quay, southeast to Cambridge and Kent Tces.

Parliament clusters around the north end of the city, on the cusp of historic Thorndon where various embassies can be found. The waterfront along Jervois Quay, Cable St and Oriental Pde is an increasingly revitalised area and houses Te Papa museum, Waitangi Park and a man-made beach. The historic sheds of Queens Wharf have been reborn as a museum, galleries, restaurants and a coffee roaster, and joined by a couple of new buildings.

Cuba St (literate, arty types) and Courtenay Pl (young larrikins) are the main nightlife hot spots, while Willis St, Queens Wharf and Lambton Quay are peppered with eating, drinking and shopping opportunities.

The airport is 8km southeast of the city centre.

WELLINGTON REGION FACTS

Eat yourself silly: Wellington has a gut-busting number of great cafes and restaurants; bring trousers with an elasticated waistband

Drink Aro, Emporio, Fuel, Havana, Immigrant's Son, L'Affare, Mojo, Peoples, Revive and Supreme – that's pretty much every locally roasted coffee bean

Read *Big Weather: Poems of Wellington* (Mallinson Rendel, 2000), billet-doux to a hard-to-love city

Listen to *Happy Ending,* by this author's favourite Welly band, the Phoenix Foundation

Watch 'Golden Days' – the rousing short film screened on rotation at Te Papa

Swim at Oriental Bay: it's not nearly as cold as it looks

Festival Summer City (p100) – brilliant, free fun in the sun (or not…)

Tackiest tourist attraction Cuba St's bucket fountain: tacky, a bit slimy, and often malicious

Go green Check out rare NZ wildlife at Zealandia (p96), Wellington's mainland 'conservation island'

Maps

Wellington's i-SITE visitor centre has free city maps.

The **Map Shop** (Map p90; ☎ 04-385 1462; www.map-shop.co.nz; 121 Thorndon Quay; ☉ 8.30am-5.30pm Mon-Fri, 10am-1pm Sat) carries a range of NZ city and regional maps, plus topographic maps and GPS for trampers.

INFORMATION
Bookshops

Arty Bees Books (Map p94; ☎ 04-384 5339; www.artybees.co.nz; The Oaks, Manners St; ☉ 9am-9pm Mon-Thu, to 10pm Fri, 10am-10pm Sat, 11am-9pm Sun) Quality secondhand reads.

Unity Books (Map p94; ☎ 04-499 4245; www.unitybooks.co.nz; 57 Willis St; ☉ 9am-6pm Mon-Fri, 10am-5pm Sat, 11am-5pm Sun) A Wellington institution, with an excellent fiction section specialising in NZ literature.

Emergency

Wellington police station (Map p94; ☎ 04-381 2000; www.police.govt.nz; cnr Victoria & Harris Sts; ☉ 24hr)

Internet Access

Internet access rooms are plentiful; expect to pay around $3 per hour.

Cybernomad (Map p94; ☎ 04-801 5964; 43 Courtenay Pl; ☉ 9am-11pm Mon-Fri, 10am-11pm Sat & Sun)

Cyber City (Map p94; ☎ 04-384 3717; 97-99 Courtenay Pl; ☉ 9am-11pm)

iPlay (Map p94; ☎ 04-494 0088; 1st fl, 49 Manners Mall; ☉ 24hr)

Wellington i-SITE (Map p94; www.wellingtonnz.com; ☎ 04-802 4860; Civic Sq, cnr Wakefield & Victoria Sts; ☉ 8.30am-5pm Mon-Fri, 9.30am-4.30pm Sat & Sun)

Internet Resources

Feeling Great (www.feelinggreat.co.nz) Events, activities, courses and classes; run by the city council.

Positively Wellington Tourism (www.wellingtonnz.com) Official tourism website for the city.

View Wellington (www.viewwellington.co.nz) Restaurant and bar reviews, activities and special offers.

Word on the Street (www.wordonthestreet.nz) Reader-friendly, entertaining, nonadvertorial site dedicated to the best of the inner city's what, when, where and who.

Wotzon.com (www.wotzon.com) Arts and events listings in Wellington and surrounds.

Media

Capital Times (www.capitaltimes.co.nz) Free weekly newspaper with local news, gossip and gig listings.

Stuff (www.stuff.co.nz) Online news service incorporating Wellington's newspaper, the *Dominion Post*.

Medical Services

Wellington Accident & Urgent Medical Centre (Map p90; ☎ 04-384 4944; 17 Adelaide Rd, Newtown; ☉ 8am-11pm) No appointment necessary; also home to the After-Hours Pharmacy (open from 8am to 11pm).

Wellington Hospital (off Map p90; ☎ 04-385 5999; www.ccdhb.org.nz; Riddiford St, Newtown; ☉ 24hr) One kilometre south of the city centre.

Money

Major banks have branches on Courtenay Pl, Willis St and Lambton Quay. Moneychangers include the following:

City Stop (Map p94; ☎ 04-801 8669; 107 Manners St; ☉ 24hr) Convenience store; exchanges travellers cheques.

Travelex (Map p90; ☎ 04-472 8346; www.travelex.com/nz; 120 Lambton Quay; ☉ 8.30am-5.30pm Mon-Fri, 9am-4pm Sat) Foreign-exchange office. Also has a branch at the airport.

Post

Post office (Map p94; www.nzpost.co.nz; 2 Manners St) In the centre of town, with post restante.

Tourist Information

Automobile Association (AA; Map p90; ☎ 04-931 9999; www.aa.co.nz; 1st fl, 42-352 Lambton Quay; ☉ 8.30am-5pm Mon-Fri, 9am-1pm Sat)

DOC visitor centre (Department of Conservation; Map p94; ☎ 04-384 7770; www.doc.govt.nz; 18 Manners St; ☉ 9am-5pm Mon-Fri, 10am-3.30pm Sat) Bookings,

---

MAORI NZ: WELLINGTON REGION

In legend the mouth of Maui's Fish (see p51), and traditionally known as Te Whanganui-a-Tara, the Wellington area became known to Maori in the mid-19th century as 'Poneke' (a transliteration of Port Nicholas, its European name at the time).

The major *iwi* (tribes) of the region in traditional times were Te Ati Awa and Ngati Toa. Ngati Toa was the *iwi* of Te Rauparaha, who composed the now famous *Ka Mate haka* (see p54). Like most urban areas the city is now home to Maori from many *iwi*, sometimes collectively known as Ngati Poneke.

New Zealand's national museum, Te Papa (p403), presents excellent displays on Maori culture, traditional and modern, as well as a colourful *marae*. History buffs can also see the Treaty of Waitangi at the Archives New Zealand (p95).

WELLINGTON REGION

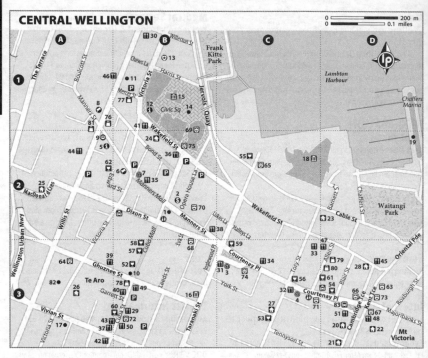

CENTRAL WELLINGTON

passes and information for national and local walks, parks, huts and camping, plus permits for Kapiti Island.

Wellington Airport Information (☎ 04-385 5104; www.wellington-airport.co.nz; Main Terminal; 24hr) Touch-screen information stations.

Wellington i-SITE (Map p94; ☎ 04-802 4860; www. wellingtonnz.com; Civic Sq, cnr Wakefield & Victoria Sts; 8.30am-5pm Mon-Fri, 9.30am-4.30pm Sat & Sun;) Staff book almost everything, and cheerfully distribute the *Official Visitor Guide to Wellington*. Internet access and cafe.

Travel Agencies

Air New Zealand (Map p90; ☎ 0800 737 000, 04-474 8950 or 04-388 9900; www.airnewzealand.co.nz; cnr Lambton Quay & Grey St; 9am-5pm Mon-Fri, 10am-1pm Sat)

STA Travel (Map p94; ☎ 04-385 0561; www.statravel. co.nz; cnr Cuba & Ghuznee Sts; 9am-5.30pm Mon-Fri, 11am-5pm Sat)

SIGHTS
Museums & Galleries

For an imaginative, interactive experience of Wellington's social and salty maritime history, swing into the **Museum of Wellington**

(Map p90; ☎ 04-472 8904; www.museumofwellington. co.nz; Queens Wharf; admission free; 10am-5pm). Highlights include a moving documentary about the tragedy of the *Wahine* (see p92), and ancient Maori legends dramatically told using tiny hologram actors and special effects. The building itself is an old Bond Store dating from 1892.

The much-loved **City Gallery** (Map p94; ☎ 04-801 3021; www.citygallery.org.nz; Civic Sq, Wakefield St; admission by donation, charges may apply for major exhibits; 10am-5pm) reopened late in 2009 after renovations and the addition of a new wing. Expect surprises: the gallery's a little cracker that secures acclaimed contemporary international artists as well as unearthing and supporting those at the forefront of New Zealand's scene. Excellent Nikau Gallery Cafe on-site.

The **New Zealand Film Archive** (Map p94; ☎ 04-384 7647, film info line 04-499 3456; www.filmarchive.org.nz; cnr Taranaki & Ghuznee Sts; admission free, movies $8; from 9am Mon-Fri, from noon Sat) was established in 1981 to protect New Zealand's moving-image history. Collections date from 1895 and represent every genre of filmmaking. The library has more than 30,000 titles you can watch for free and a big-screen program four nights a week. Combined with a cafe and gallery, it's a great place to while away the hours (or days).

Part of the New Zealand Academy of Fine Arts, **Academy Galleries** (Map p90; ☎ 04-499 8807; www.nzafa.com; 1 Queens Wharf; admission free; ☒ 10am-5pm) features works by New Zealand artists.

The muscular grey concrete of the **National Library of New Zealand** (Map p90; ☎ 04-474 3000; www.natlib.govt.nz; cnr Molesworth & Aitken Sts; admission free; ☒ 9am-5pm Mon-Fri, to 1pm Sat) is a haven to varied collections of national importance. It encompasses the **Alexander Turnbull Library**, which holds historical photographs, drawings, prints, maps and the like. Regular events are held in the **National Library Gallery** (admission free; ☒ 9am-5pm Mon-Fri, to 4.30pm Sat, 1-4.30pm Sun), which has changing exhibits. Watch for renovation-induced disruptions.

One block away, the **Archives New Zealand** (Map p90; ☎ 04-499 5595, www.archives.govt.nz; 10 Mulgrave St; admission free; ☒ 9am-5pm Mon-Fri, to 1pm Sat) is the official guardian of NZ's heritage documents. Inside are gallery displays of significant national treasures, including

the original Treaty of Waitangi (p30), NZ's founding document.

Cricket boffins will be bowled over by the historical memorabilia at the **New Zealand Cricket Museum** (Map p90; ☎ 04-385 6602; www.nzcricket.co.nz; Old Grandstand, Basin Reserve; adult/child $5/2; ☒ 10.30am-3.30pm daily Nov-Apr, Sat & Sun May-Oct). Comprehensive displays cover the history and development of NZ cricket, including the sport's arrival in the colonies and NZ's first test match in 1894. The original 1743 Addington bat is a showstopper.

Gardens & Lookouts

The expansive, hilltop **Wellington Botanic Gardens** (Map p90; ☎ 04-499 1400; www.wellington.govt. nz; admission free; ☒ dawn-dusk; P) can be conveniently visited via a cable-car ride (nice bit of planning, eh?). The hilly 25-hectare gardens boast a tract of original native forest along with varied collections including a beaut rose garden and international plant collections. Add in fountains, a cheerful playground, sculptures, duck pond, cafe, magical city views and much more, and you've got a grand day

WELLINGTON REGION IN...

Two Days

To get a feel for the lie of the land, drive up **Mt Victoria** (below), or ride the **cable car** (below) up to the **Wellington Botanic Gardens** (p95). After lunch on cool **Cuba St** (p104), immerse yourself in all things Kiwi at **Te Papa** (opposite) or the **Museum of Wellington** (p94). Drink beer by the jug at **Mighty Mighty** (p106).

The next day, fuel-up with coffee and eggs at **Cafe L'Affare** (p105) then head to **Zealandia** (below) to meet the birds and learn about New Zealand conservation, or take a snoop around the **Beehive** (opposite). For dinner try **Chow** (p104) or **Pravda** (p104), then spend your evenings **bar-hopping** (p106) along Courtenay Pl. Nocturnal entertainment could involve live music, a movie at the gloriously restored **Embassy Theatre** (p108), or a midnight snack at a late-closing cafe – or all three.

Four Days

Shake and bake the two-day itinerary, then decorate with the following: hightail it out of Wellington for some wine-tasting around **Martinborough** (p118), followed by a seal-spotting safari along the wild **Cape Palliser** (p119). The next day, take a picnic to **Paekakariki** (p114), have a swim, and then a wander around **Queen Elizabeth Park** (p114) next door.

out. The gardens are also accessible from the Centennial Entrance on Tinakori Rd (Karori bus 3).

One of Wellington's most famous attractions is the little red **cable car** (Map p90; ☎ 04-472 2199; www.wellingtoncablecar.co.nz; one-way adult/child $3/1, return $5/2; ☼ departs every 10min, 7am-10pm Mon-Fri, 8.30am-10pm Sat, 9am-10pm Sun) that clanks up the steep slope from Lambton Quay to Kelburn. At the top are a cafe, the Wellington Botanic Gardens, an observatory and the small-but-nifty **Cable Car Museum** (Map p90; ☎ 04-475 3578; www.cablecarmuseum.co.nz; admission free; ☼ 9.30am-5.30pm Nov-Apr, 10am-5pm May-Oct), which tells the cable car's story since it was built in 1902 to open up hilly Kelburn for development. Take the cable car back down the hill, or ramble down through the Botanic Gardens (a 30- to 60-minute walk, depending on your wend).

At the top of the Botanic Gardens, the **Carter Observatory** (Map p90; ☎ 04-910 3140; www.carterobservatory.org; ☼ 10am-5pm) has re-emerged after a major renovation. New features include a full-dome planetarium in which you can take a simulated trip through the universe; a multimedia display of Polynesian navigation, Maori cosmology, and European explorers; and some of New Zealand's finest telescopes and astronomical artefacts. If your lucky stars are with you, you might be able to safely see our closest star, the Sun, through the Thomas Cooke telescope's solar filter. Check the website for evening stargazing times.

For the best view of the city, harbour and surrounds, venture up to the lookout atop the 196m **Mt Victoria** (Map p90), east of the city centre. You can take bus 20 (Monday to Friday) most of the way up, or if you're feeling energetic sweat it out on the walk. If you've got your own wheels, take Oriental Pde along the waterfront and then scoot up Carlton Gore Rd.

About 3km west of the city is **Otari-Wilton's Bush** (off Map p90; ☎ 04-475 3245; www.wellington.govt.nz; 160 Wilton Rd; admission free; ☼ dawn-dusk; P), the only botanic gardens in NZ specialising in native flora. Expect to see and hear plenty of birds along the 11km of walking trails. Bus 14 from the city passes the gates.

If you have a car, take a long and winding drive around Wellington's **bays and beaches** (see www.greatharbourway.org.nz) – cruise out of town along Oriental Pde and just keep going, keeping the sea on your left. Along the largely craggy shoreline are pretty inlets, million-dollar houses and the odd cafe. You'll end up at Owhiro Bay, from where you can take Happy Valley Rd back into town. The whole loop is about 30km.

Wildlife

The groundbreaking wildlife sanctuary **Zealandia** (off Map p90; ☎ 04-920 9200; www.visitzealandia.com; Waiapu Rd; adult/child/family $15/7/37; ☼ 9am-5pm, last entry 4pm; P) is tucked in the hills about 2km west of town (buses 3, 18, 21, 22 and 23 trundle nearby). The fenced mainland 'conservation island' is home to more than 30 native bird species including kiwi, kaka, saddleback and hihi, as well as the most accessible wild population of tuatara. There are more than 30km of attractive walking tracks and a range of guided tours available. A major new exhibition centre showcases New Zealand's natural history and its world-renowned conservation story.

Wellington Zoo (off Map p90; ☎ 04-381 6755; www.wellingtonzoo.com; 200 Daniell St; adult/concession/child $15/10/7.50; ⏱ 9.30am-5pm, last entry 4.15pm; P) has a commitment to conservation and research. There's a plethora of native and non-native wildlife here, including the residents of the outdoor lion and chimpanzee parks; and the nocturnal kiwi house, which also houses tuatara. Check the website for info on 'close encounters', which allow you to meet the big cats, red pandas and giraffes (for a fee). The zoo is 4km south of the city; catch bus 10 or 23.

Notable Buildings

Three Bowen St buildings comprise NZ's seat of parliamentary power. Office workers buzz around the unmissable modernist **Beehive** (Map p90; Bowen St), which looks exactly like its name. It was designed by British architect Sir Basil Spence and built between 1969 and 1980. Controversy dogged its construction and, love it or loathe it, it's become the architectural symbol of the city.

Adjacent to the Beehive is the austere grey-and-cream **Parliament House** (Map p90; ☎ 04-471 9503; www.parliament.nz; Bowen St; tours free; ⏱ tours on the hour 10am-4pm Mon-Fri, to 3pm Sat, 11am-3pm Sun), completed in 1922. Free, one-hour tours depart from the ground-floor foyer (arrive 15 minutes prior). Next door is the 1899 neo-Gothic **Parliamentary Library** (Map p90) building.

Opposite the Beehive are the gorgeous 1876 **Government Buildings** (Map p90), some of the world's largest wooden buildings. With their chunky corner quoins and slab wooden planking, you have to look twice to realise that they aren't made of stone (knock your knuckles on a wall if you don't believe us).

The last lick of paint was splashed on **Old St Paul's** (Map p90; ☎ 04-473 6722; www.oldsaintpauls.co.nz; 34 Mulgrave St; admission by donation; ⏱ 10am-5pm) in 1866, and it still looks good-as-new from the outside. The striking interior is a stellar example of early English Gothic timberwork, with magnificent stained-glass windows and displays on Wellington's early history.

Harbour Ferries

Locals have been jumping on the cross-harbour ferry for a swim at Days Bay for decades. Book a seat on the **East by West Ferry** (Map p90; ☎ 04-499 1282; www.eastbywest.co.nz; Queens Wharf; one-way adult/child $10/5; ⏱ 6.25am-7pm Mon-Fri, 10am-5pm Sat & Sun), departing from Queens Wharf 16 times daily on weekdays, and eight times daily on weekends. It's a 30- to 40-minute chug over to **Days Bay**, where there are beaches, a park and a boatshed with canoes and rowboats for hire. A 10-minute walk from Days Bay leads to **Eastbourne**, a beachy township with cafes and other diversions.

East by West ferries also stop at **Matiu-Somes Island** (return fare adult/child $21/11), a wildlife

---

TREASURES OF TE PAPA

Te Papa (Map p94; ☎ 04-381 7000; www.tepapa.govt.nz; 55 Cable St; admission free; ⏱ 10am-6pm Mon-Wed & Fri-Sun, to 9pm Thu; P), the 'Museum of New Zealand', is an inspiring, interactive repository of historical and cultural artefacts. 'Te Papa Tongarewa' loosely translates as 'treasure box'. The building dominates the Wellington waterfront and has become a national icon – an innovative celebration of the essence of NZ.

Among Te Papa's treasures is a huge Maori collection; its own *marae;* dedicated hands-on 'discovery centres' for children; natural history and environment exhibitions; Pacific and New Zealand history galleries; and traditional and contemporary art and culture. Exhibitions occupy impressive gallery spaces with a touch of high-tech (eg motion-simulator rides and a house shaking through an earthquake). Big-name, temporary exhibitions incur an admission fee.

You could spend a day exploring Te Papa's six floors but still not see it all. To target your areas of interest head to the information desk on level two. To get your bearings, the one-hour 'Introducing Te Papa' tour ($12) is a good idea; tours leave from the info desk at 10.15am and 2pm daily in winter, more frequently in summer. Two cafes and two gift shops round out the Te Papa experience.

reserve managed by the Department of Conservation (DOC) where you might see weta, tuatara, kakariki and little blue penguins, among other critters. The island is rich in history, having once been a prisoner-of-war camp and quarantine station. Take a picnic lunch, although the eager can camp overnight (adult/child $10/5) or in a DOC house – book online at www.doc.govt.nz or at Wellington's DOC visitor centre (see p93).

On weekends you can also catch the **Harbour Explorer Excursion**, which runs between Queens Wharf and Days Bay via Somes Island, Petone and Seatoun (return fare adult/child $20/10, three daily Saturday and Sunday).

ACTIVITIES
Cycling & Mountain Biking
Wellington's good for cycling, if you don't mind hills. The excellent **Makara Peak Mountain Bike Park** (off Map p90; www.makarapeak.org.nz) in the hills of Karori is 4km west of the city centre. The main entrance is on South Karori Rd – catch bus 3 or 18. Laced through the 200-hectare park are 24km of bike tracks ranging from beginner to expert. **Mud Cycles** (off Map p90; ☎ 04-476 4961; www.mudcycles.co.nz; 338 Karori Rd, Karori; half-/full-day/weekend bike hire $30/45/70; ⏰ 9.30am-6pm Mon-Fri) has mountain bikes for hire, is close to the park, and also runs guided tours catering for all levels.

On Yer Bike (Map p94; ☎ 04-384 8480; www.onyer bikeavantiplus.co.nz; 181 Vivian St; half-day/full-day/week bike hire $30/40/150; ⏰ 8.30am-5.30pm Mon-Fri, 9am-5pm Sat)

stocks a good range of bicycles for sale and hire, and can help with info on local clubs and trails.

Walking
Wellington will be much enjoyed by walkers. It takes only an hour to amble from one end of the city centre to the other, and there is plenty of good wandering in the immediate surrounds (such as Mt Victoria, Aro Valley and Thorndon), and along one of five walkways around the city fringes (the City to Sea, the Skyline, the Southern, Northern, and Eastern – all accessible by foot or bus). The city council produces excellent 'Explore' walking maps for both inner-city heritage trails and the walkways (available from the i-SITE or at www.feelinggreat.co.nz). See Tours (p100) to connect with a walking guide.

The wild-and-woolly **Red Rocks Coastal Walk** (off Map p90; two to three hours, 8km return), 7km south of the city, follows the tumultuous volcanic coast from Owhiro Bay through Te Kopahou Reserve to Red Rocks and Sinclair Head, where there's a seal colony. Take bus 4 to Owhiro Bay Pde, then it's 1km to the quarry gate where the walk starts.

Other Activities
With all this wind and water, Wellington was made for **sailboarding** and **kiteboarding**, and there are plenty of good launching points within 30 minutes' drive of the city. **Wild Winds** (Map p94; ☎ 04-384 1010; www.wildwinds.co.nz;

KATHERINE MANSFIELD
Often compared to Chekhov and Maupassant, Katherine Mansfield is NZ's most distinguished author, known throughout the world for her short stories.

Born Kathleen Mansfield Beauchamp in 1888, at age 14 she left for Europe, where she spent most of the remainder of her short adult life. She mixed with Europe's most famous writers (DH Lawrence, TS Eliot, Virginia Woolf), and married the literary critic and author John Middleton Murry in 1918. In 1923, aged 34, she died of tuberculosis at Fontainebleau in France. It was not until 1945 that her five books of short stories (In a German Pension, Bliss, The Garden Party, The Dove's Nest and Something Childish) were combined into a single volume, Collected Stories of Katherine Mansfield.

She spent five years of her childhood at 25 Tinakori Rd in Wellington; it's mentioned in her stories Prelude and A Birthday (a fictionalised account of her own birth). The house now opens its doors as **Katherine Mansfield's Birthplace** (Map p90; ☎ 04-473 7268; www.katherinemansfield.com; 25 Tinakori Rd; adult/child $5.50/2; ⏰ 10am-4pm Tue-Sun), and is lovingly restored and maintained with a restful heritage garden. The excellent video A Portrait of Katherine Mansfield screens here and the 'Sense of Living' exhibition displays photographs of the period alongside excerpts from her writing. A doll's house has been constructed from details in the short story of the same name. Wilton bus 14 stops nearby.

Chaffers Marina, Oriental Bay; ☒ 10am-6pm Mon-Fri, to 3pm Sat, 11am-3pm Sun) runs two-hour windsurfing lessons for beginners ($110), and three-hour kiteboarding lessons from $195. Prices include equipment but not transport.

At the long-running **Ferg's Kayaks** (Map p90; ☎ 04-449 8898; www.fergskayaks.co.nz; Shed 6, Queens Wharf; ☒ 10am-8pm Mon-Fri, 9am-6pm Sat & Sun) you can punish your tendons with indoor rock climbing (adult/child $15/9), cruise the waterfront on a pair of inline skates ($15 for two hours) or paddle around the harbour in a kayak (from $15 for one hour). There's also bike hire (one hour from $20) and guided kayaking trips.

Gnarly surf rolls in from the ocean at **Lyall Bay** (off Map p90) near the airport (though it's often too choppy or too small), **Palliser Bay** (p119) and the Wainuiomata Coast, southeast of Wellington. The i-SITE can help with fishing and diving charter info.

Freyberg Pool & Fitness Centre (Map p90; ☎ 04-801 4530; www.wellingtonwaterfront.co.nz; 139 Oriental Pde; adult/child $4/2; ☒ 6am-9pm) has a heated indoor lap pool, plus a spa, sauna and gym (casual fitness classes $9.50).

WALKING TOUR

Kick-start your Wellington wander by admiring (or deploring, depending on your aesthetics) the modernist **Beehive** (1; p97), then head east along Bowen St and cross Lambton Quay to the **Government Buildings** (2; p97) – yes indeedy, they're timber, not stone.

Truck south along Lambton Quay, aka the 'Golden Mile', for all its retail revelry. Browse elegant **Kirkcaldie & Stains** (3; p109), the city's only department store. If you haven't done it yet, detour up Cable Car Lane and clank up the hillside on the **cable car** (4; p96), or continue along Lambton Quay and splash some cash at the Edwardian **Old Bank Shopping Arcade** (5; p109). Turn right onto Willis St then left at Mercer St. Civic Sq is straight ahead. Book some theatre tickets at the **Wellington i-SITE** (6; p94), duck into the **City Gallery** (7; p94) or, if you've got the kids in tow, see what's cookin' at **Capital E** (8; right).

From Civic Sq, head south for a cruise up and down **Cuba St** (9): bars, boutiques and coffee shops in the hip heart of the city. Back at Civic Sq take the City to Sea footbridge to the waterfront and stroll past the boatsheds to **Mac's Brewery Bar** (10; p106) for a quick pint of Sassy Red and a bowl of fries. Suitably

WALK FACTS

Start Beehive
Finish Courtenay Pl
Distance 3km
Duration Two hours to one day, depending on stops

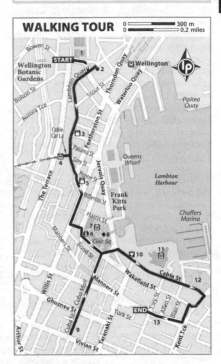

WALKING TOUR

refreshed, it's time to tackle **Te Papa** (11; p97). Once you've reached your museum maximum, pull up a patch of grass at **Waitangi Park** (12) or hurl yourself into the evening fray on **Courtenay Pl (13)**.

WELLINGTON FOR CHILDREN

With ankle biters in tow, your best bet is a visit to colourful **Capital E** (Map p94; ☎ 04-913 3720; www.capitale.org.nz; Civic Sq; events free-$12; ☒ 9am-5pm), an educational entertainment complex designed especially for kids. Expect interactive rotating exhibitions, children's theatre and TV, readings, workshops and courses. Call or check the website for the events calendar and prices.

Te Papa (p97) is fantastic for children. The Discovery Centres are loaded with interactive activities, and StoryPlace is designed for children five and under. See the dedicated Kids page on the website for more details. Along the waterfront on either side of Te Papa are **Frank Kitts Park** and **Waitangi Park**, both with playgrounds perfect for expending pent-up energy.

A ride up the **cable car** (p96) and a lap around the **Wellington Botanic Gardens** (p95) will pump plenty of fresh air into young lungs, and when darkness descends head to the **Carter Observatory** (p96) where kids can gaze at galaxies far, far away. On a more terrestrial bent, check out some living dinosaurs (aka tuatara) at the **Wellington Zoo** (p97) or **Zealandia** (p96).

For online ideas, have a look at www.feelinggreat.co.nz, operated by the city council, and follow the Young People link for a rundown on events and courses targeted at young 'uns.

TOURS

Flat Earth (☎ 0800 775 805, 04-977 5805; www.flatearth.co.nz; full-day tours $120-220) An array of themed small-group tours (city highlights, Maori treasures, food, arts and Middle-Earth filming locations).

Hammonds Scenic Tours (☎ 04-472 0869; www.wellingtonsightseeingtours.com; city tour adult/child $55/27.50, Kapiti Coast $95/47.50, Wairarapa $200/100; city tours depart 10am & 2pm, Kapiti 9am & 1.30pm, Martinborough & Wairarapa 8.30am) Runs a 2½-hour city highlights tour, four-hour tour of the Kapiti Coast, and a full-day Wairarapa experience including Cape Palliser. Dedicated Martinborough trip available ($230/115).

Helipro (Map p90; ☎ 04-472 1550; www.helipro.co.nz; Shed 1, Queens Wharf; 10/15/25/35min flights per person $95/185/225/370) Scenic helicopter flights and heli-lunch trips to the Wairarapa, Marlborough Sounds or Wellington's South Coast.

Walk Wellington (☎ 04-802 4860; www.walk.wellington.net.nz; adult/child $20/10; tours 10am daily, plus 5.30pm Mon, Wed & Fri Nov-Mar) Informative two-hour walking tours focusing on the city and waterfront, departing the i-SITE. Book online or just turn up.

Wellington Movie Tours (☎ 027 419 3077; www.movietours.co.nz; tours from adult/child $40/30) Four- to 8½-hour tours for real movie fiends – more props, clips, film sets and Lord of the Rings (LOTR) than you can point a lens at. Confirm pick-up locations when booking.

Wellington Rover (☎ 0800 426 211, 04-471 0044; www.wellingtonrover.co.nz; adult/child $40/25; departs i-SITE 9am, 11.30am & 2.30pm) The 2½-hour Explorer Tour with a hop-on/hop-off option visits places that are tricky to reach without a car (Mt Victoria, South Coast beaches, Red Rocks seal colony). Customised tours and half- and full-day LOTR trips ($90 and $150) complete with hobbit ears.

Wellington Sights (☎ 0800 775 805, 04-977 5805; www.wellingtonsights.co.nz; 2-3hr tours per adult/child $65/40) Two tours – LOTR and Snapshot.

Wild About Wellington (☎ 0274 419 010; www.wildaboutwellington.co.nz; tours from $95) Small-group walking and public-transport tours including City of Style, Sights & Bites, Wild About Chocolate or Boutique Beer Tasting. From a few hours to a full day.

Zest Food Tours (☎ 04-801 9198; www.zestfoodtours.co.nz; tours from $125) Runs 2½- to four-hour small-group city sightseeing tours; longer tours include lunch with matched wines at a top restaurant. Also Wairarapa food and wine tours (from $230).

FESTIVALS & EVENTS

Check at the Wellington i-SITE or visit www.wellingtonnz.com/event for comprehensive festival listings; most tickets can be booked through Ticketek (p108).

January/February

Summer City (☎ 04-499 4444; www.feelinggreat.co.nz) A two-month celebration commencing New Year's Eve; includes countless free outdoor events.

February

Cuba St Carnival (☎ 04-801 9390; www.cubacarnival.org.nz) NZ's largest street carnival, where the locals get uncharacteristically colourful. Biennial (odd years).

New Zealand International Sevens (☎ 04-389 0020; www.nzisevens.co.nz) The world's top seven-a-side rugby teams compete, but it's the crowd that plays up.

February/March

International Jazz Festival (☎ 04-473 0149; www.jazzfestival.co.nz) A week-long shoobedoobop featuring local and international artists. Biennial (odd years).

March

Fringe NZ (☎ 04-382 8015; www.fringe.org.nz) More than three weeks of way-out-there experimental visual arts, music, dance and theatre.

New Zealand International Arts Festival (☎ 04-473 0149; www.nzfestival.nzpost.co.nz) A month-long biennial spectacular (even years) of theatre, dance, music, visual arts and literature. International acts aplenty.

April

New Zealand Comedy Festival (www.comedyfestival.co.nz) Three weeks of hysterics. World-famous-in-New-Zealand comedians, and some truly world famous, too.

June

Matariki (www.tepapa.govt.nz) Celebrating the Maori New Year with a free festival of dance, music and other events at Te Papa.

July/August

International Film Festival (☎ 04-384 3840; www.nzff.co.nz) Two-week indie film fest screening the best of NZ and international cinema.

September

World of WearableArt (WOW; ☎ 0800 4969 746; www.worldofwearableart.com) A two-week run of the spectacular nightly extravaganza of amazing garments. Read more about WOW on p154.

November

Toast Martinborough (☎ 06-306 9183; www.toastmartinborough.co.nz) A day of hedonism around the Martinborough vineyards.

SLEEPING

Wellington accommodation is generally more expensive than in regional areas. Our price listings for the city fall into the following categories: Budget – doubles (with or without bathroom) for under $100; Midrange – doubles (with bathroom) between $101 and $200; Top End – over $201. Accommodation standards are reasonably high, and there are plenty of options right in or within easy walking distance of the city centre. One hassle is the lack of parking; if you have your own wheels, ask about car parking when you book (and be aware you'll probably have to pay for it). Sleeping reviews in this chapter feature a (P) symbol if on-site parking is available.

Wellington's budget accommodation largely takes the form of multistorey hostel megaliths. There's no 'motel alley' in Wellington, but motels are scattered around the city fringe. Being the hub of government and business, self-contained apartments are popular, and bargains can often be found at the weekends.

During the peak season (December to February), or during major festivals, book your bed well in advance.

Budget

HOSTELS

Downtown Backpackers (Map p90; ☎ 0800 225 725, 04-473 8482; www.downtownbackpackers.co.nz; 1 Bunny St; dm $23, s $62-70, d $60-92; 💻 📶) An old charmer at the railway end of town, housed in a grand art-deco building. Downtown has clean, bright rooms and plenty of character-filled communal areas (be sure to check out the carved fireplace in the bar). Budget meals in the cafe morning and night.

Base Backpackers (Map p94; ☎ 0800 227 369, 04-801 5666; www.basebackpackers.com; 21-23 Cambridge Tce; dm $25-28, d & tr with bathroom from $87; (P) 💻 📶) A slick chain hostel aimed squarely at the young 'uns. Party-perfect location (metres from Courtenay Pl), modern rooms, and the female-only floor will come as a relief to some. Bag yourself a bunkmate at the Basement Bar downstairs. The only gripe: the kitchen and lounge are tiny given the hostel's 200-plus beds. Limited parking $10 per day.

Nomads Capital (Map p94; ☎ 0508 666 237, 04-978 7800; www.nomadscapital.com; 118 Wakefield St; dm $25-31, d with bathroom from $89; 💻 📶) Smack-bang in the middle of town Nomads has good security, spick-and-span rooms, an on-site cafe-bar (free modest nightly meals) and discounts for longer stays. Kitchen and lounge spaces are short on elbow room, but heritage features (such as the amazing stairwell) stop you dwelling on the negatives.

Rosemere Backpackers (Map p94; ☎ 04-384 3041; www.backpackerswellington.co.nz; 6 MacDonald Cres; dm/s/tw/d incl breakfast $27/50/62/66; 💻) A colour-spangled former brothel a short (steep!) walk uphill from the city centre. Free internet and linen, and a couple of tent sites on the tiny lawn out front. Happy vibe.

Wellywood Backpackers (Map p94; ☎ 0508 005 858, 04-381 3899; www.wellywoodbackpackers.co.nz; 58 Tory St; dm $27, s $50, d with/without bathroom $80/70; 💻 📶) You'd have to be a zookeeper not to be impressed by this huge zebra-striped building off Courtenay Pl. Rooms are spacious, with weathered retro furniture dotted throughout the place, and unisex bathroom basins in the corridors – very social! Rock music wails over the speakers in communal areas (except the reading room).

Worldwide Backpackers (Map p90; ☎ 0508 888 555, 04-802 5590; www.worldwidenz.co.nz; 291 The Terrace; dm/d incl breakfast $27/66; 💻) In a 110-year-old house, Worldwide is the most appealing small hostel in town. Clean and homely, with winning features such as free internet, regular barbecues, and nautical reading lamps. It's youthful, down-to-earth and chilled out.

Moana Lodge (off Map p90; ☎ 04-233 2010; www.moanalodge.co.nz; 49 Moana Rd, Plimmerton; dm $29-32, d $60-90; 💻 📶) Just off SH1 and only a short train ride or drive from Wellington (25km), this exceptional backpackers right on the beach is immaculate and inviting, with friendly owners superkeen to infuse you with their local knowledge. Kayaks and golf clubs available; occasional boat trips to Mana Island. From Wellington catch the Tranz Metro Paraparaumu train to Plimmerton.

our pick **YHA Wellington City** (Map p94; ☎ 04-801 7280; www.yha.co.nz; cnr Cambridge Tce & Wakefield St; dm $30-33, d with/without bathroom $108/88; 🖳 🛜) YHA Welly wins points for the biggest and best communal areas: superior kitchens, cavernous dining areas (group dinner nights are a blast), games room, reading room and dedicated movie room with high-tech projector. Sustainable initiatives (recycling, composting and energy-efficient hot water) impress, and there's a comprehensive booking service at reception.

HOTELS & MOTELS

Cambridge Hotel (Map p94; ☎ 0800 375 021, 04-385 8829; www.cambridgehotel.co.nz; 28 Cambridge Tce; dm $23-25, s/d/tw without bathroom $61/80/85, s/d/tw/tr/f $90/99/109/130/140; 🖳 🛜) Top-quality pub accommodation at affordable prices in a heritage hotel. En suite rooms have Sky TV, phone and fridge (try for a room at the back if you're a light sleeper). The backpacker wing has a well-stocked kitchen, flash bathrooms and dorms with no natural light but sky-high ceilings. Cheap bar meals are a plus.

Shepherds Arms Hotel (Map p90; ☎ 0800 393 782, 04-472 1320; www.shepherds.co.nz; 285 Tinakori Rd; s without bathroom $65-85, d with bathroom $99-169; 🅿) With wall-to-wall heritage buildings and close to the Botanic Gardens, Thorndon makes a great home base. This well-preserved hotel serves its patrons in fitting style, with a restaurant and bar, and charming rooms upstairs. Shell out a few extra dollars for a larger room.

Carillon Motor Inn (Map p90; ☎ 04-384 8795; www.carillon.co.nz; 33 Thompson St; s/d/tw/tr $80/90/110/139; 🅿) Wow, what a relic! Carillon is a rickety old Victorian mansion that's somehow evaded the wrecking ball, developers' ambitions and renovators' brush strokes. Endearing, old-fashioned and chaotic in a *Fawlty Towers* kind of way, it's clean, central and supercheap.

Halswell Lodge (Map p94; ☎ 04-385 0196; www.halswell.co.nz; 21 Kent Tce; hotel r $90, units $135-160; 🅿 🛜) Doggone handy to all the central sights without being too noisy, Tudor-esque Halswell offers a range of options, including small, affordable hotel rooms with TV, fridge and bathroom. The upmarket lodge suites with spa are a better option if you're in the next price bracket; families pile into the two-bedroom motel units.

CAMPING

Campsites are as rare as bad coffee in Wellington. Rosemere Backpackers (see p101) can accommodate a few tents, or head to the Hutt Valley (p113). Motorhomers, however, can now enjoy the brand new and unbelievably convenient **Wellington Waterfront Motorhome Park** (Map p90; ☎ 04-384 4511; www.wwmp.co.nz; 12 Waterloo Quay; powered sites $50; 🛜); park during the day (for modest hourly rates) or stay overnight, and make use of the nice new ablution block and power supply.

Midrange
GUEST HOUSES & B&BS

Mermaid (Map p90; ☎ 04-384 4511; www.mermaid.co.nz; 1 Epuni St; s $90-150, d $100-145; 🛜) In the ubercool Aro Valley 'hood, Mermaid is a small women-only guest house in a colourfully restored villa. Each room is individually themed with artistic flair (one with private bathroom, three with shared facilities). The lounge, kitchen and deck are homely and laid-back. Great cafe, bakery and deli on your doorstep.

Tinakori Lodge (Map p90; ☎ 0800 939 347, 04-939 3478; www.tinakorilodge.co.nz; 182 Tinakori Rd; s $99-120, d $140-170 all incl breakfast; 🅿 🛜) Built in 1868 from native timbers, this lodge is in the thick of historic Thorndon, but a bit too close to the motorway for utter tranquillity. It's still a good option, with its rooms (five with bathroom; four with shared facilities) decorated in refined, motherly style. Free street-parking permits for guests.

Booklovers B&B (Map p90; ☎ 04-384 2714; www.booklovers.co.nz; 123 Pirie St; s/d from $150/180; 🅿 🖳 🛜) Booklovers is a gracious B&B run by award-winning author Jane Tolerton (her books are among the thousands shelved around the house). Four guest rooms have TV, CDs and CD/DVD player; three have en suites, one has a private bathroom. Bus 2 runs from the front gate to Courtenay Pl and the train station, and the city's 'green belt' begins right next door. Free wireless internet and limited parking.

HOTELS

Comfort & Quality Hotels (Map p90; ☎ 0800 873 553, 04-385 2156; www.hotelwellington.co.nz; 223 Cuba St; d $100-170; 🖳 🖭) Two hotels in one: the sympathetically renovated historic Trekkers building with its smaller, cheaper rooms (Comfort); and the recently built, snazzier high-rise Quality with modern styling and a swimming pool. Both share in-house bar and dining room (meals available, $14 to $28). Two solid options in the heart of Cuba.

Travelodge (Map p90; ☎ 0800 101 100, 04-499 9911; www.travelodge.co.nz; 2-6 Gilmer Tce; d $105-270; 🅿 🖳 🛜) The zillion-dollar refit is as charmless as a blancmange, but you can't argue with the location and price. An epic 132 smallish rooms, with microwaves, fridges and personal safes. In-house bar and restaurant (mains $25 to $30) will be working pretty hard to win you over with some of Welly's best on your doorstep. Parking $20 per day.

Copthorne Hotel (Map p90; ☎ 0800 782 548, 04-385 0279; www.millenniumhotels.co.nz/copthorneoriental bay; 100 Oriental Pde; d $160-290; 🅿 🖳 🛜 🖭) A tasteful refurb has this upmarket operation on ritzy Oriental Pde looking as good as gold, from the polished reception, through a seemingly endless maze of corridors, to the fancy bar and dining room. Handsome rooms are spread over two wings: the Bay wing has larger rooms with harbour views, the Roxburgh has smaller rooms, some with harbour views and some without. Parking $20 per day.

MOTELS

Apollo Lodge (Map p90; ☎ 0800 361 645, 04-385 1849; www.apollolodge.co.nz; 49 Majoribanks St; d $125-175; 🅿 🛜) Within staggering distance of Courtenay Pl, Apollo Lodge is a loose collation of 35 motel units (one and two bedrooms), ranging from old-school self-contained studios to airy suites.

Victoria Court (Map p94; ☎ 04-472 4297; www.vict oriacourt.co.nz; 201 Victoria St; r $145-200; 🅿 🛜) Our top motel choice, right in the city centre, with plenty of parking. The affable owners offer spotless, stylish studios and apartments with spas, cooking facilities, suede couches, slick blond-wood joinery and new TVs. Two disabled-access units; larger units sleep six.

Other options:

Capital View Motor Inn (Map p90; ☎ 0800 438 505, 04-385 0515; www.capitalview.co.nz; 12 Thompson St; d $120-155; 🅿 🛜) A dependable option close to Cuba St,

many rooms do indeed enjoy capital views. Undergoing gradual renovation, so ask for options.

Marksman Motor Inn (Map p90; ☎ 0800 627 574, 04-385 2499; www.marksmanmotel.co.nz; 40-44 Sussex St; units $125-275; 🅿 🛜) Clean, comfortable studios and apartments across from the Basin Reserve. Can be a tad noisy, but handy for airport runs (or the cricket).

Majoribanks Apartments (Map p90; ☎ 0800 361 645, 04-385 1849; www.apollolodge.co.nz; 38 Majoribanks St; apt for 6 per week $800; 🅿 🛜) Run by the Apollo Lodge folk.

Top End

Museum Hotel (Map p94; ☎ 0800 994 335, 04-802 8900; www.museumhotel.co.nz; 90 Cable St; r & apt Mon-Thu $190-325, Fri-Sun $150-325; 🅿 🖳 🛜 🖭) Sometimes called 'Museum Hotel de Wheels' (to make way for Te Papa, it was rolled here from its original location 120m away), the Museum is a quirky, boutique affair. Eclectic decor (chandeliers, edgy modern art), sassy staff, a decent restaurant and groovy tunes piped into the lobby make a refreshing change from homogenised business hotels. Tasty weekend/ weekly rates.

CityLife Wellington (Map p90; ☎ 0800 368 888, 04-922 2800; www.heritagehotels.co.nz; 300 Lambton Quay; d Mon-Thu from $200, Fri-Sun from $169; 🅿 🖳 🛜) Luxurious serviced apartments in the city centre, ranging from studios to three-bedroom arrangements, some with a harbour glimpse. Features include full kitchen, CD/DVD player, and in-room laundry facilities. Weekend rates are great bang for your buck. The vehicle entrance is from Gilmer Tce, off Boulcott St (parking $15 per day).

Wellesley (Map p90; ☎ 04-474 1308; www.wellesley boutiquehotel.co.nz; 2-8 Maginnity St; d $180-300) A stately central choice with buckets of old-world charm and impeccable service. Formerly a gentlemen's club, the Wellesley retains a refined vibe that makes you want to spark up a cigar. The 13 rooms are decked out with original art, antiques and the odd claw-foot bath. On-site Maginnity's restaurant and bar does everything from high tea to top shelf.

EATING

Wellington is an exciting place to eat. Considering its size, there's a bewildering array of restaurants, cafes and food-focused bars, and keen competition keeps standards high and prices reasonable. Excellent options for contemporary NZ fine dining are nicely complemented by numerous budget eateries, including oodles of noodles.

Restaurants

KK Malaysian Cafe (Map p94; ☎ 04-385 6698; 54 Ghuznee St; mains $8-14; 🕙 11.30am-2.30pm Mon-Sat, 5-9.30pm daily; Ⓥ) Decked out like a dirty protest, tiny KK is one of Wellington's most popular cheap Malaysians in a city obsessed with Southeast Asian cuisine. Satay to die for and *rendang* to put a smile on your face, accompanied by the ubiquitous roti, of course. Unlicensed.

Aunty Mena's (Map p94; ☎ 04-382 8288; 167 Cuba St; meals $9-14; 🕙 5.30-9.30pm Sun & Mon, 11.30am-9.30pm Tue & Wed, to 10pm Thu-Sat; Ⓥ) One of many Cuba St noodle houses, cheap 'n' cheerful Aunty Mena's cranks out yummy veggie/vegan Malaysian and Chinese dishes to a diverse clientele. Easy-clean, over-lit interior. Unlicensed.

Sweet Mother's Kitchen (Map p94; ☎ 04-385 444; 5 Courtenay Pl; mains $10-26; 🕙 8am-late; Ⓥ) Perpetually full, predominantly with young cool cats, Sweet Mother's serves dubious takes on the Deep South, such as burritos, nachos, the po' boys and the New Orleans muffaletta. Key lime pie is about as authentic as it gets, but we don't care. It's cheap, cute, has great cakes and gets good sun.

ourpick **Scopa** (Map p94; ☎ 04-384 6020; cnr Cuba & Ghuznee Sts; mains $14-30; 🕙 9am-late Mon-Sun) Perfect pizza, proper pasta and other authentic Italian treats. Opened in 2006, this modern *cucina* is already a Wellington institution. Slick, friendly service and consistently good food make it deservedly so. Watch the groovy 'Cubans' from a seat in the window. Lunchtime specials; sexy evenings complete with cocktails.

Great India (Map p94; ☎ 04-384 5755; 141 Manners St; mains $15-26; 🕙 noon-2pm Mon-Fri, to 3pm Sat & Sun, 5pm-late Mon-Fri; Ⓥ) This is not your average curry house. While a tad more expensive than its competitors, this place consistently earns its moniker. With any luck you'll be served by Rakesh, one of the capital's smoothest maître d's.

Miyabi Sushi (Map p94; ☎ 04-801 9688; Willis St Village, 142 Willis St; mains $15-27; 🕙 11.30am-late Mon-Fri, 5.30pm-late Sat) A steady stream of customers is testament to the satisfying food served at this low-key Japanese cafe hidden away off the main street. The smiling Mr Chuck prepares superfresh sushi, noodles, soups and set meals including teriyaki (chicken, beef or fish) with

miso soup, rice and salad – delicious and great value. The *gyoza* (pot-sticker dumplings) are hard to pass up.

Osteria del Toro (Map p94; ☎ 04-381 2299; 60 Tory St; mains $18-28; 🕙 11.30am-late Sun-Fri, 5pm-late Sat) Flamboyantly decorated in a baroque style with influences from all around the Mediterranean. The menu plucks popular classics from the region in a similar fashion. Pastas, pizzas and paella sit happily alongside souvlaki, tagine and tapas. Moreish food in Moorish surrounds; this restaurant, however, doesn't charge like a wounded bull.

Chow (Map p94; ☎ 04-382 8585; level 1, 45 Tory St; meals $18-30; 🕙 noon-midnight) Home of the legendary blue cheese and peanut wonton, Chow is a stylish pan-Asian restaurant-cum-bar: a must visit for people who love exciting food, interesting decor, and the odd cocktail. The perfect place to share food and conversation. The hip Motel bar is adjacent.

Flying Burrito Brothers (Map p94; ☎ 04-385 8811; cnr Cuba & Vivian Sts; mains $18-32; 🕙 4.30pm-late) Let it all hang out at this lively Tex-Mex cantina. Quesadillas, tortillas, tacos and tostadas laced with avocado and chilli, plus *bocaditos* (small bites, like tapas) and a kids menu, too. The extensive (and informative) tequila menu and premium margaritas will give you lift-off.

Capitol (Map p94; ☎ 04-384 2855; cnr Kent Tce & Majoribanks St; mains $20-30; 🕙 lunch & dinner Mon-Fri, brunch, lunch & dinner Sat & Sun) Simple, seasonal food using premium local ingredients, lovingly prepared with a nod to the classic Italian style. The dining room is elegant and intimate with large windows looking out onto busy Courtenay precinct. No dinner bookings are taken, but it's well worth waiting with an aperitif at the tiny bar.

Le Métropolitain (Map p94; ☎ 04-801 8007; cnr Garrett & Cuba Sts; mains $25-29; 🕙 noon-2.30pm & 5-10pm Tue-Sat) Prepare to be transported to the heart of France by your charming hosts. Expect unpretentious bistro fare in a suitably Gallic environment. Classics are well covered and include *moules,* onion soup, *steak frites,* coq au vin and escargot (yum). Cheese or scrumptious tart and a sticky wine for dessert, anyone?

Pravda (Map p90; ☎ 04-499 5570; 107 Customhouse Quay; mains $25-35; 🕙 7.30am-late Mon-Fri, 9am-late Sat) A classy downtown cafe (more chic restaurant by Wellington standards), scoring well with readers and folks that hand out culinary excellence awards. The opulent split-level space (styled in quasi-USSR mode) is a formal backdrop for enjoying well-assembled duck, chicken, fish and NZ lamb mains. Fantastic desserts and coffee.

Martin Bosley's (Map p90; ☎ 04-920 8302; 103 Oriental Pde; mains $28-47; ☿ lunch Mon-Fri, dinner Tue-Sun) Swish fish from one of the country's best chefs, in an elegant restaurant with panoramic harbour views. The degustation menu is an excellent way to sample the skills of the kitchen and is $100 very well spent. For an extra $70, you'll get wines selected to match each delicious dish. Top notch.

Logan-Brown (Map p94; ☎ 04-801 5114; 192 Cuba St; mains $39-48; ☿ noon-2pm Mon-Fri, from 5.30pm nightly) Located in a 1920s banking chamber, Logan-Brown oozes class without being pretentious or overly formal. This is seriously good food brought to you by the 2009 Wellingtonians of the Year, in their award-winning restaurant. Believe the hype, sample the paua ravioli – it's been on the menu forever and a day – and peruse the epic wine list. Bookings recommended.

Cafes

Deluxe (Map p94; ☎ 04-801 5455; 10 Kent Tce; snacks $5-8; ☿ 7am-late Mon-Fri, 8am-late Sat & Sun; Ⓥ) A stalwart of the late-night cafe scene, with off-beat, oft-changing local art adorning the walls. Teeny wee space next to the Embassy Cinema (p108) somehow serves more than 500 coffees a day and mainly vegetarian/vegan counter food and pizza slices to loyal customers.

Lido (Map p94; ☎ 04-499 6666; cnr Victoria & Wakefield Sts; brunch & lunch $5-18; dinner $16-26; ☿ 7.30am-3pm Mon, to late Tue-Fri, 9am-late Sat & Sun) Swing into Lido, at the bottom of a funky old office block, for a wide selection of consistent and reasonably priced Med-inspired food. Pancakes and pasta sit happily alongside, fish, burgers, antipasto and salad. Great coffee and sweet treats, too. Live jazz Saturday and Sunday evenings.

Felix (Map p94; ☎ 04-499 5523; cnr Wakefield & Cuba Sts; brunch $5-22, dinner $10-24; ☿ 7.30am-9pm Mon-Fri, 8.30am-8pm Sat, to 5.30pm Sun) Despite some hard edges in this modern-industrial space, Felix is still a comfortable and attractive cafe that dishes out honest food morning, noon and night. The big windows keep things bright, as do the cheery staff. Great burger and heavenly chips.

Midnight Espresso (Map p94; ☎ 04-384 7014; 178 Cuba St; meals $6-16; ☿ 7.30am-3am Mon-Fri, 8am-3am

Sat & Sun; Ⓥ) The city's original late-night cafe, with food that's hearty, tasty and inexpensive – heavy on the wholesome and vegetarian. Sit in the window with Havana coffee and cake, it's the quintessential Wellington cafe experience.

Cafe L'Affare (Map p90; ☎ 04-385 9748; 27 College St; meals $6-18; ☿ 8am-4pm) Cafe L'Affare is the centre of a small empire, from which its own beans are roasted and distributed. Its Professor Brainstorm–emporium interior is a hive of activity, with speedy baristas, crowded communal tables and a disco ball. At weekends, kids aplenty add to the cacophony, but everyone adds their cheery thanks to snappy service and wicked brekkies of eggie excellence.

Fidel's (Map p90; ☎ 04-801 6868; 234 Cuba St; meals $6-18; ☿ 7.30am-midnight Mon-Fri, 9am-midnight Sat & Sun; Ⓥ) A Cuba St institution for caffeine-craving, upbeat left-wing subversives. Eggs any-which-way, pizza and amazing salads are pumped out of the itsy kitchen, along with Welly's best milkshakes. Revolutionary memorabilia adorn the walls of the funky interior; decent outdoor areas too. A superbusy crew copes with the chaos admirably.

Nikau Gallery Cafe (Map p94; ☎ 04-801 4168; Civic Sq; lunch $11-24; ☿ 7am-4pm Mon-Fri, 8am-4pm Sat; Ⓥ) City Gallery (p94): home to fine contemporary art and its culinary equivalent served up at Nikau. Efficient service, a stylish interior and some of the best cafe fare in town make this an obvious lunch-stop while checking out the abundant artworks. Legendary kedgeree and sunny courtyard.

Quick Eats

Pandoro Panetteria (Map p94; ☎ 04-385 4478; 2 Allen St; items $3-6; ☿ 7am-5pm Mon-Fri, to 4pm Sat & Sun; Ⓥ) A fabulous Italian bakery with smooth coffee, sweet and savoury muffins, stuffed breads, scrolls, cakes and tarts.

Trisha's Pies (Map p90; ☎ 04-801 5515; 32 Cambridge Tce; pies $4-5; ☿ 8am-3.30pm Mon-Fri) Superchunky traditional pies (peppered steak, beef and mushroom) or something different (chicken, apricot and brie). Veggie and fruit options too.

Sushi of Japan (Map p94; ☎ 04-385 0290; 189 Cuba St; meals $5-9; ☿ 8.30am-6pm; Ⓥ) Superfresh, ready-to-run sushi slices that are cheap and tasty.

Crêpes a Go-Go (Map p94; 57 Manners Mall; crepes $5-9; ☿ 9am-9pm; Ⓥ) From a tiny yellow stall in the Manners Mall, a Breton batter-master whips up cheap crêpes with your choice of sweet or savoury fillings.

Burger Fuel (Map p94; ☎ 04-801 9222; 101 Courtenay Pl; burgers $5-12; 11am-10pm Sun-Thu, to 4am Fri & Sat; Ⓥ) Fast food how it should be. Tasty burgers of all description made with fresh, natural ingredients, beating the pants off Ronald and the Colonel.

Wellington Trawling Sea Market (Map p90; ☎ 04-384 8461; 220 Cuba St; meals $6-14; lunch-9pm) Locals' favourite fresh-off-the-boat fish and chips, plus oysters, scallops and whitebait in season. Burgers, too.

Phoenician Falafel (Map p94; ☎ 04-385 9997; 10 Kent Tce; meals $8-15; 11.30am-9.30pm Sun-Wed, to 11pm Thu-Sat; Ⓥ) Authentic falafel, shish and *shawarma* (kebab) served up by cheery Lebanese owners. The best kebabs in town.

Good-value (and very worldly) food courts:

BNZ Centre (Map p94; ☎ 04-499 9300; Willis St; meals $4-10; 8am-8pm Mon-Fri, 10am-4pm Sat)

Courtenay Central (Map p94; ☎ 04-382 9526; Courtenay Pl; meals $5-10; 10am-10pm)

Self-Catering

Two excellent produce markets run on Sunday mornings – next to Te Papa (Wakefield St) and on the corner of Victoria and Vivian Sts.

Commonsense Organics (Map p94; ☎ 04-384 3314; 260 Wakefield St; 9am-7pm Mon-Fri, to 6pm Sat & Sun) Organic produce (wine, fruit, veg, nuts, tea, herbs etc), and food for the intolerant.

New World Metro (Map p94; ☎ 04-417 6580; 70 Willis St; 7am-11pm Mon-Fri, 8am-11pm Sat, to 10pm Sun); Chaffers (Map p94; ☎ 04-384 8054; 279 Wakefield St; 7am-midnight); Thorndon (Map p90; ☎ 04-499 9041; Molesworth St; 7am-11pm)

Moore Wilson Fresh (Map p90; ☎ 04-384 9906; cnr College & Tory Sts; 7.30am-7pm Mon-Fri, to 6pm Sat, 9am-5pm Sun) An unsurpassed array of (predominantly NZ) produce, baking, mountains of cheese... just endless goodies. Go.

DRINKING

Wellingtonians love a late night, and it's common to see the masses heading into town at a time when normal folk would be boiling the kettle for cocoa. The city's bars and music venues ensure things keep cranking – there are a high number of reputable establishments, with plenty of live music, dance parties, quiz nights and suchlike. You'll also find a raft of great cocktails, fine wines and microbrews, as well as some impressive bar food. Indeed, many places listed below could

easily fit under Eating as well as Drinking (the legendary Matterhorn and Hummingbird, for starters).

Most of the action clusters around two hubs: Courtenay Pl – bustling, brassy, and positively let-your-hair-down; and Cuba St – edgy, groovy and sometimes too cool for school.

our pick Mighty Mighty (Map p94; ☎ 04-384 9085; 104 Cuba St; 4pm-late Wed-Sat) Possibly the hippest of the capital's drinking establishments and music venues. Inside-a-pinball-machine decor, pink velvet curtains, kitsch gewgaws and Wellington's best barmaid make this an essential port of call for those wanting to experience the best of New Zealand's bar scene. Get dancing.

Matterhorn (Map p94; ☎ 04-384 3359; 106 Cuba St; 10am-late) Perennially popular bar, with a clientele as interesting as its drinks list. Worthy winner of numerous accolades including New Zealand's best bar and restaurant. Slick and ultracool, with great attention to detail. Occasional live music provided by some of Aotearoa's freshest bands and musicians.

Malthouse (Map p94; ☎ 04-802 5484; 48 Courtenay Pl; lunch-late Mon-Sat) Beervana. An immense array of beers (both local and international) that would make even the most fervent of hopheads quiver at the knees. New Zealand *does* brew great beer, and this is the place to quaff them. Check out the *Forty Licks*–style toilets in the gents.

Vivo (Map p94; ☎ 04-384 6400; 19 Edward St; 3pm-late Mon-Fri, 5pm-late Sat) A tomelike list of approximately 700 wines from around the world, with more than 50 available by the glass. Exposed bricks and timber beams give Vivo an earthy cellarlike feel while the fairy lights look like stars set against the dark ceiling. A vinophile's delight with some decent food too.

Southern Cross (Map p90; ☎ 04-384 9085; 35 Abel Smith St; 9am-late) Welly's most stylish crowd-pleasing pub combines a laid-back restaurant, lively bar, pool table, dance floor and the best garden bar in town. Independent beer on tap and a good bowl of chips.

Mac's Brewery Bar (Map p94; ☎ 04-381 2282; cnr Taranaki & Cable Sts; 10.30am-late) Occupying a renovated warehouse on a prime waterfront site, this microbrewery does a great job of looking seriously committed to the craft. Author's favourite: Sassy Red, enjoyed in the sun while watching the skateboarders sprain

GAY & LESBIAN WELLINGTON

Wellington is open-minded and sophisticated, so G&L people fit right in almost everywhere they go. The G&L scene is small, but friendly and inclusive, as proven by one of only two gay bars in the city, **Scotty & Mal's** (Map p94; ☎ 04-802 5335; 176 Cuba St; ☾ 5pm-late). This is a stylish, welcoming bar and dance lounge where you can enjoy cocktails, small talk and quiz nights upstairs, or strut your stuff and play some pool in the sultry basement bar (DJ's Friday and Saturday).

Larger newsagents will stock the fortnightly magazine **express** (www.gayexpress.co.nz; $3), featuring the latest news, reviews and events. Useful online resources include www.gaynz.com, which has comprehensive national coverage of all things queer; and the Wellington-specific www.gayline.gen.nz, www.gaywellington.org and www.wellington.lesbian.net.nz. See www.gaystay.co.nz for G&L-hosted accommodation around town. For phone information, or just to talk, contact **Wellington Gay Welfare Group** (☎ 04-473 7878; helpline@gaywellington.org; ☾ 7.30-9.30pm).

See also Gay & Lesbian Travellers, p383.

themselves on the promenade. Excellent fish and chips.

Leuven (Map p90; ☎ 04-499 2939; 135 Featherston St; ☾ 7am-late Mon-Fri, 9am-late Sat & Sun) The menu at this beer cafe is an ode to Belgium's best: mussels come 10 different ways, the *frites* (chips) are cooked to perfection, and the big brewing guns line up at the bar (Hoegaarden, Leffe, Chimay). Popular breakfast specials (waffle, anyone?).

Hummingbird (Map p94; ☎ 04-801 6336; 22 Courtenay Pl; ☾ 9am-late) Popular with the sophisticated set, Hummingbird is usually packed – both inside in the intimate, stylish dining room and bar, and outside on street-side tables. Croony music (with regular live jazz), exciting brunch-to-supper menus, and impressive drinks including fine wines and cocktails.

Backbencher (Map p90; ☎ 04-472 3065; 34 Molesworth St; ☾ 11am-late) You might spot the odd parliamentarian on the turps at the Backbencher, a pub opposite the Beehive where rubbery puppets of NZ pollies are mounted trophy-style on the walls (David Lange is a beauty). Good weekend brunches.

Good Luck (Map p94; ☎ 04-801 9950; basement, 126 Cuba St; ☾ 5pm-late Tue-Sun) Cuba St's Chinese opium den, without the opium. This is a slickly run, sultry basement bar playing fresh hip-hop and electronica. It also brings you the thing no one else could: a middle-of-the-mall alfresco lounge – great for watching the Cuba-cade.

Molly Malone's (Map p94; ☎ 04-384 2896; cnr Courtenay Pl & Taranaki St; ☾ 11am-late) A highly polished Irish bar, complete with Guinness, live music, well-priced pub grub and a bottle store. Upstairs, the Red Head restaurant has fancier food and a balcony with rare afternoon sun.

The hip, late-night bar scene down Courtenay Place may surprise you with its density and variety. Here are just a few of the many best visited late on a Thursday, Friday or Saturday.

Betty's (Map p94; ☎ 04-803 3766; 32 Blair St) Brassy joint with apothecary theme and wraparound digital screen covering three walls.

Hawthorn Lounge (Map p94; ☎ 04-890 3724; 82 Tory St) Akin to a 1920s gentlemen's club. Play poker, drink cocktails and listen to big-band medleys.

Library (Map p94; ☎ 04-382 8593; 1/53 Courtenay Pl) Velveteen booths, books, booze and beats. Regular live music.

Vespa Lounge (Map p94; ☎ 04-385 2438; 7/21 Allen St) When everyone else is safely tucked up in bed, the Vespa crowd just keeps rolling.

ENTERTAINMENT

Wellington's entertainment scene is a bit like the Tardis: it looks small from the outside, but inside it holds big surprises. Not only does it boast its own vibrant theatres and an inordinate number of local musicians, plenty of high-quality performers visit from around New Zealand and abroad too. Hungry, appreciative crowds help things along.

Event and gig listings can be found in the *Capital Times* – the free weekly rag found all over town. Look out, also, for the *Groove Guide* (www.grooveguide.co.nz), which has a gig guide and pertinent articles.

Live Music & Clubs

Entry to most gigs and club nights can be gained via a door sale. Popular gigs, however, may well sell out, so it pays to buy advance tickets from advertised outlets – often **Real Groovy** (Map p90; ☎ 04-385 2020; www.realgroovy.conz;

cnr Cuba & Abel Smith Sts), or **Under the Radar** (www.undertheradar.co.nz). Admission prices vary depending on whom, where and when, but generally range from $5 to $70.

San Francisco Bath House (Map p94; ☎ 04-801 6797; www.sfbh.co.nz; 171 Cuba St; ☼ 5pm-late Wed-Fri, 8pm-late Sat) Wellington's best midsized live-music venue, playing host to the cream of NZ artists, as well as quality acts from abroad (Fleet Foxes, Gomez…). Somewhat debauched balcony action, five deep at the bar, but otherwise well run and usually lots of fun.

Bodega (Map p94; ☎ 04-384 8212; www.bodega.co.nz; 101 Ghuznee St; ☼ 4pm-late) A trailblazer of the city's modern live-music scene, and still considered an institution despite its move from a derelict heritage building to a concrete cavern. 'The Bodge' offers a full and varied program of gigs in a pleasant space with a respectable dance floor and filler-up food.

Garden Club (Map p94; ☎ 04-381 2341; www.thegardenclub.co.nz; 13b Dixon St; ☼ 5pm-late Wed-Sat) Three floors of dance-music-fuelled mayhem aimed primarily at a younger crowd. Level one houses the club proper with regular live acts and DJs, while the top floor is home to Welly's other gay bar. In between is a noxious den that pushes NZ's smoking laws to the limit. Well run and definitely fun.

Happy (Map p90; ☎ 04-970 1741; www.myspace.com/happybar; cnr Tory & Vivian Sts) A basement bar that picks up all the cool, stray acts (small and large) that don't seem to fit in anywhere else: spoken word, jazz fusion, acoustic singer-songwriters, electronica, short films and experimental theatre. Open performance nights only.

Sandwiches (Map p94; ☎ 04-385 7698; www.sandwiches.co.nz; 8 Kent Tce; ☼ 4pm-late Tue-Sat) Get yourself a slice of NZ's electronic artists and DJs, regular multiflavoured international acts and the capital's best sound system. Throw shapes in the edgy main room or enjoy cocktails and pizza in the sultry bar. Great club run by a dedicated team that isn't just in it for the bread.

Theatres

Wellington's accessible performing-arts scene sustains a laudable number of professional and amateur companies. Tickets for many events can be purchased from the **Ticketek box offices** (☎ 04-384 3840; www.ticketek.co.nz; ☼ 9am-5.30pm Mon-Fri, 10am-2pm Sat) at St James Theatre (Map p94) or the Michael Fowler Centre (Map p94). Discount same-day tickets for some productions are often available at the i-SITE.

BATS (Map p94; ☎ 04-802 4175; www.bats.co.nz; 1 Kent Tce; tickets $15-20; ☼ box office open 2hr before each show) Wildly alternative BATS presents cutting-edge and experimental NZ theatre – varied, cheap, and intimate.

Downstage (Map p94; ☎ 04-801 6946; www.downstage.co.nz; cnr Courtenay Pl & Cambridge Tce; tickets $25-45; ☼ box office 9am-5.30pm Mon, to show time Tue-Sat) NZ's most enduring professional theatre company with a strong presence in Wellington (established 1964). Original NZ plays, dance, comedy and musicals in a 250-seat auditorium.

Circa (Map p94; ☎ 04-801 7992; www.circa.co.nz; 1 Taranaki St; tickets adult/stand-by $35/18; ☼ box office 10am-4pm Mon-Sat) Circa's main auditorium seats 240 people, its studio 100. Cheap tickets are available for preview shows (the night before opening night), and there are stand-by tickets available an hour before the show (anything from pantomimes to international comedy).

There are four other significant venues for touring shows and one-off programs:

Michael Fowler Centre (Map p94; ☎ 04-801 4231; www.wellingtonconventioncentre.com; 111 Wakefield St) Home to the New Zealand Symphony Orchestra. The Town Hall next door hosts the occasional concert and special events.

St James Theatre (Map p94; ☎ 04-802 4060; www.stjames.co.nz; 77 Courtenay Pl) A grand old heritage auditorium hosting big productions such as the ballet and opera (www.nzballet.org.nz; www.nzopera.com).

Opera House (Map p94; 111-113 Manners St) Another heritage theatre, with heart-stopping gods, hosting sit-down concerts, touring plays and the odd musical.

TSB Bank Arena (Map p90; www.wellingtonconvention centre.com; Jervois Quay) A hangar-sized venue in which the supersized shows are held.

Cinemas

Movie times are listed in the local newspapers and at www.film.wellington.net.nz. Most cinemas have a discount day early in the week (Monday or Tuesday).

Real film buffs may want to check out the **Weta Cave** (off Map p90; ☎ 04-380 9361; www.wetanz.com; cnr Camperdown Rd & Weka St, Miramar; admission free; ☼ 11am-6pm Mon-Fri, to 4pm Sat), the minimuseum of the Academy Award–winning company that brought *LOTR, King Kong,* and *Narnia* to life.

Embassy Theatre (Map p94; ☎ 04-384 7656; www.deluxe.co.nz; 10 Kent Tce; tickets adult/child $15/9; ☼ 11am-midnight) Wellywood's cinema mothership: built in the 1920s, restored in 2003. Screens mainstream films; bar and cafe on-site.

Paramount (Map p94; ☎ 04-384 4080; www.paramount.co.nz; 25 Courtenay Pl; tickets adult/child $14.50/9;

WELCOME TO WELLYWOOD

In recent years Wellington has stamped its place firmly on the world map as the home of NZ's dynamic film industry, earning itself the nickname 'Wellywood'. Acclaimed director Peter Jackson still calls Wellington home; the success of his *Lord of the Rings* (*LOTR*) films and subsequent productions such as *King Kong* have made him a powerful Hollywood player, and have bolstered Wellington's reputation. *LOTR* fans and movie buffs can experience some local movie magic by visiting the Weta Cave (p108), or one of many film locations around the region (see p100 & p112).

noon-midnight) A lovely old complex screening largely art-house, documentary and foreign flicks.

Reading Cinemas (Map p94; ☎ 04-801 4600; www. readingcinemas.co.nz; Courtenay Central, Courtenay Pl; tickets adult/child $16/10.50; 9.30am-midnight) Mainstream new-release fodder.

Penthouse Cinema (off Map p90; ☎ 04-384 3157; www.penthousecinema.co.nz; 205 Ohiro Rd, Brooklyn; tickets adult/child $15/11; 9am-11pm) Art-deco charmer screening a smart range of films. Nice cafe too. Well worth the bus ride – take bus 7 or 8 from town.

Empire Cinema (off Map p90; ☎ 04-939 7557; www. empirecinema.co.nz; cnr Parade & Mersey St, Island Bay; tickets adult/child $16/12; 10am-midnight) A cracker indie cinema screening everything from Hollywood to Harbicht. Take bus 1 from town.

SHOPPING

Lambton Quay is known as the 'Golden Mile' for the array of flash money pits into which to pour your hard-earned dollars. To 'Buy Kiwi Made', head straight to Cuba St to score a good hit rate.

The fanciest department store in town is **Kirkcaldie & Stains** (Map p90; ☎ 04-472 5899; 165-177 Lambton Quay; 9.30am-5.30pm Mon-Thu, to 7pm Fri, 10am-5pm Sat, to 4pm Sun), NZ's answer to Bloomingdale's or Harrods, which has been running since 1863. Nearby is the **Old Bank Shopping Arcade** (Map p90; ☎ 04-922 0600; cnr Lambton Quay & Willis St; 9am-6pm Mon-Thu, to 7pm Fri, 10am-4pm Sat, 11am-3pm Sun), a dear old building home to some lovely boutique shopping (clothing, accessories and gifts).

Wellington is packed with independent designer stores and boutiques. These are a teeny tip of the iceberg:

Aquamerino (Map p94; ☎ 04-384 9290; 97 Willis St) From the sheep's back to the showroom. Hard wearing, stylish woollens of all shapes and sizes.

Hunters & Collectors (Map p94; ☎ 04-384 8948; 134 Cuba St) Off-the-rack and preloved leather (punk, skate and mod), plus shoes and accessories. Best window displays in New Zealand.

Starfish (Map p94; ☎ 04-385 3722; 128 Willis St) The fashionable Wellingtonian's favourite treat. Beautiful clothing, sustainably made.

If you're looking for something uniquely NZ, try the gift shop at Te Papa museum (p97), or these tried-and-true options:

Kura (Map p94; ☎ 04-802 4934; 19 Allen St) Contemporary indigenous art: painting, ceramics, jewellery and sculpture.

Ora Design Gallery (Map p94; ☎ 04-384 4157; 23 Allen St) The latest in Pacific and Maori art: beautiful sculpture, weaving and jewellery.

Vault (Map p90; ☎ 04-471 1404; 2 Plimmer Steps) Jewellery, clothing, bags, ceramics, cosmetics – a beautiful store with beautiful things.

Several outdoor shops gather around Mercer St, the best of which is **Bivouac Outdoor** (Map p94; ☎ 04-473 2587; 39 Mercer St; 9am-5.30pm Mon-Thu, to 7pm Fri, 10am-5pm Sat, 11am-5pm Sun).

GETTING THERE & AWAY
Air

Wellington is an international gateway to NZ. See p393 for information on international flights. **Wellington Airport** (WLG; ☎ 04-385 5100; www.wellington-airport.co.nz; 4am-1.30am) has touch-screen information kiosks in the luggage hall. There's also currency exchange, ATMs, car-rental desks, cafes, shops etc. If you're in transit or have an early flight, you can't linger overnight inside the terminal. Departure tax on international flights is adult/child $25/10.

Air New Zealand (Map p90; ☎ 0800 737 000, 04-474 8950 or 04-388 9900; www.airnewzealand.co.nz; cnr Lambton Quay & Grey St; 9am-5pm Mon-Fri, 10am-1pm Sat) offers flights between Wellington and most domestic centres, including the following:

Destination	Price	Frequency
Auckland	from $49	up to 20 daily
Christchurch	from $49	up to 14 daily
Dunedin	from $120	up to 6 daily
Queenstown	from $116	1 daily
Rotorua	from $95	up to 3 daily
Westport	from $84	2 daily

Jetstar (☎ 0800 800 995; www.jetstar.com) flies between Wellington and Auckland (from $49, three daily), and Christchurch (from $50, one daily). **Pacific Blue** (☎ 0800 670 000; www.pacificblue. co.nz) flies between Wellington and Auckland (from $65, three daily), and Christchurch (from $50, two daily).

Soundsair (☎ 0800 505 005, 03-520 3080; www.sounds air.com) flies between Wellington and Picton (from $79, up to eight daily), Nelson (from $90, up to three daily) and Blenheim (from $79, one daily).

Air2there (☎ 0800 777 000; www.air2there.com) flies between Wellington and Blenheim ($99, up to four daily), with other local destinations serviced from Paraparaumu airport, 40 minutes up the coast by car or train.

Boat

On a clear day, sailing into Wellington Harbour or through the Marlborough Sounds is magical. Cook Strait is notoriously rough, but the big ferries handle it well, and sport lounges, cafes, bars, information desks, cinemas but no pool tables. There are two options for crossing the strait between Wellington and Picton (timetables subject to change):

Bluebridge Ferries (Map p90; ☎ 0800 844 844, 04-471 6188; www.bluebridge.co.nz; adult/child $50/25) Crossing takes three hours, 20 minutes. Departs Wellington at 3am, 8am, 1pm and 9pm daily (no 3am or 9pm services Saturday). Departs Picton at 2am, 8am, 2pm & 7pm daily (no 8am service Saturday; no 2am service Sunday). Cars and campervans up to 4m long from $110; campervans under 5.5m from $150; motorbikes $50; bicycles $10.

Interislander (Map p90; ☎ 0800 802 802, 04-498 3302; www.interislander.co.nz; adult/child from $46/23) Crossing takes three hours, 10 minutes. Departs Wellington at 2.25am, 8.25am, 2.05pm and 6.25pm; departs Picton at 6.25am, 10.05am, 1.10pm, 6.05pm and 10.25pm. From November through to April there's an extra 10.25am sailing from Wellington and an extra 2.25pm sailing from Picton. Cars are priced from $101; campervans (up to 5.5m) from $126; motorbikes $46; bicycles $15.

Book ferries at hotels, by phone, online, at travel agents and with operators directly (online is the cheapest option). Bluebridge is based at Waterloo Quay, opposite the Wellington train station. The Interislander terminal is about 2km northeast of the city centre; a shuttle bus ($2) runs to the Interislander from platform 9 at Wellington train station (where long-distance buses also depart) at 7.35am, 9.35am (peak season only), 1.15pm and 5.35pm. It also meets arriving ferries, returning passengers to platform 9. There's also a taxi stand at the terminal.

Car-hire companies allow you to pick-up/drop-off vehicles at ferry terminals. If you arrive outside business hours, arrangements can be made to collect your vehicle from the terminal car park.

Bus

Wellington is a bus-travel hub, with connections north to Auckland and all major towns in between. **InterCity** (☎ 04-385 0520; www.intercity. co.nz) and **Newmans** (☎ 04-385 0521; www.newmans coach.co.nz) buses depart from platform 9 at the train station. Tickets are sold at the Intercity/Newmans ticket window in the train station. Typical fares include Auckland (from $30, 11 hours, three daily), Palmerston North (from $13, 2¼ hours, six daily), Rotorua (from $30, 7½ hours, twice daily). There are good savings when booked online.

White Star Express (☎ 0800 465 622, 04-478 4734; www.whitestarbus.co.nz) departs once daily (twice on Thursday and Friday) from Bunny St, outside the train station, running to Palmerston North ($23, 2¼ hours), Whanganui ($30, four hours) and New Plymouth ($47, 6½ hours). Connect at Palmerston North for services to Masterton, Hastings, Napier and Gisborne. Call for ticket info or visit **Freeman's Lotto & Cafe** (Map p90; 23 Lambton Quay) or the i-SITE.

Bay Xpress (☎ 0800 422 997; www.bayxpress.co.nz) has a daily service connecting Wellington with Palmerston North ($25, 2¼ hours) continuing to Hastings ($40, 4¾ hours) and Napier ($40, five hours).

Naked Bus (☎ 0900 625 33; www.nakedbus.com) runs north from Wellington to all major North Island destinations, including Palmerston North ($1 to $22, 2½ hours, two daily), Napier ($1 to $35, five hours, four times a week), Taupo (from $1 to $43, 6½ hours, one daily) and Auckland (from $1 to $34, 12 hours, one daily), with myriad stops en route. You can buy bus tickets on the ferry to Picton, connecting to the Naked Bus South Island Network. Buses depart from the Bunny St bus stop. Book online or at Wellington i-SITE; get in early for the cheapest fares.

Train

Wellington train station has four **ticket windows** (☎ 04-498 3000, ext 44324; ☺ 6.30am-8pm Mon-Thu, to 1pm Fri & Sat, to 3pm Sun), one selling tickets for Tranz Scenic trains, Interislander ferries and InterCity and Newmans coaches; the other three ticketing local/regional Tranz Metro trains (Johnsonville, Melling, Hutt Valley, Paraparaumu and Wairarapa lines).

Long-haul **Tranz Scenic** (☎ 0800 872 467; www.tranzscenic.co.nz) routes include the *Overlander* between Wellington and Auckland (from $49, 12 hours, one daily) departing Wellington at 7.25am (Friday, Saturday and Sunday only May to September); and the *Capital Connection* between Wellington and Palmerston North ($24, 2¼ hours, one daily Monday to Friday) departing Wellington at 5.17pm.

GETTING AROUND

Metlink (☎ 0800 801 700; www.metlink.org.nz) is the one-stop shop for Wellington's regional bus, train and harbour ferry networks all detailed below.

To/From the Airport

Super Shuttle (☎ 0800 748 885; www.supershuttle.co.nz; 1/2 passengers $15/21; ☺ 24hr) provides a door-to-door minibus service between the city and airport, 8km southeast of the city. It's cheaper if two or more passengers are travelling to the same destination. Shuttles meet all arriving flights.

The **Airport Flyer** (☎ 0800 801 700; www.metlink.co.nz; airport-city per adult/child $8/4.50) bus runs between the airport, Wellington and Lower Hutt (reduced service to Upper Hutt), calling at major stops. Buses run from the city to the airport between 5.50am and 8.50pm; and from the airport, between 6.30am and 9.30pm.

A taxi between the city centre and airport costs around $30.

Bus

Frequent and efficient Go Wellington, Valley Flyer, Newlands Coach Services and Mana Coach Services buses run from 7am to 11.30pm on most suburban routes. Buses depart Wellington train station, or the main bus stop on Courtenay Pl near the Cambridge Tce intersection. Colour-coded route maps and timetables are available at the i-SITE and convenience stores around town. Fares are determined by zones: there are 14 zones, and the cheapest fare is $1 for rides in the city zone, $3 for zones 1 and 2 (maximum fare $15). The Go Wellington Daytripper ticket (zones 1 to 3) costs $6, allowing unlimited bus travel for one day. The Metlink Explorer ticket ($18) gives unlimited travel off-peak and weekends on most services.

After Midnight (☎ 0800 801 700; www.metlink.org.nz) bus services depart the central entertainment strips (Courtenay Pl and Cuba St) between midnight and 4.30am Saturday and Sunday on a number of routes to the outer suburbs. Fares range from $5 to $10, depending on how far away your bed is.

Car

There are a lot of one-way streets in Wellington, the traffic is surprisingly snarly and parking can be a royal (and expensive) pain in the rump. If you've got a car or a caravan, park on the outskirts and walk or take public transport into the city centre.

Aside from the major international rental companies (see p401), Wellington has several operators that will negotiate cheap deals, especially for longer-term rental of two weeks or more, but rates generally aren't as competitive as in Auckland. Rack rates range from around $40 to $85 per day; cars are usually a few years old and in pretty good condition. Operators include the following:

Ace Rental Cars (off Map p90; ☎ 0800 535 500, 04-471 1176; www.acerentalcars.co.nz; 126 Hutt Rd; ☺ 8am-5pm)

Apex Car Rental (Map p94; ☎ 0800 300 110, 04-385 2163; www.apexrentals.co.nz; 186 Victoria St; ☺ 8am-5pm)

Omega Rental Cars (off Map p90; ☎ 0800 667 722, 04-472 8465; www.omegarentals.com; 96 Hutt Rd; ☺ 8am-5pm)

If you plan on exploring both North and South Islands, most companies suggest you leave your car at Wellington and pick up another one in Picton after crossing Cook Strait. This is a common (and more affordable) practice, and car-hire companies make it a painless exercise.

There are often cheap deals on car relocation from Wellington to Auckland (most renters travel in the opposite direction). A few companies offer heavy discounts on this route, with the catch being that you may only have 24 or 48 hours to make the journey.

Turners Auctions (off Map p90; ☎ 04-587 1400; www.turners.co.nz; 120 Hutt Park Rd, Lower Hutt; ☒ 8am-5.30pm Mon-Wed & Fri, to 8pm Thu, 9am-3pm Sat), not far from the Wellington Top 10 Holiday Park (opposite), buys and sells used cars by auction. Also check noticeboards at backpackers for cheap deals.

Taxi
Popular ranks, packed with cabs, can be found on Courtenay Place, at the corner of Dixon and Victoria Sts, on Featherston St, and outside the railway station. Some operators:
Green Cabs (☎ 0508 447 336)
Wellington City Cabs (☎ 0800 388 8000)
Wellington Combined Taxis (☎ 0800 384 444)

Train
Tranz Metro (☎ 0800 801 700; www.tranzmetro.co.nz) operates four train routes running through Wellington's suburbs to regional destinations. Trains run frequently from around 6am to 11pm, departing Wellington train station. The routes: Johnsonville, via Ngaio and Khandallah; Paraparaumu, via Porirua, Plimmerton and Paekakariki; Melling, via Petone; the Hutt Valley via Waterloo to Upper Hutt. A train service also connects with the Wairarapa, calling at Featherston, Carterton and Masterton. Timetables are available from convenience stores, the train station, Wellington i-SITE and online. Standard fares from Wellington to the ends of the five lines range from $4 to $15. A Day Rover ticket ($10) allows unlimited off-peak and weekend travel on all lines except Wairarapa.

HUTT VALLEY

pop 110,000
The Hutt Valley is home to two of Wellington's dormitory cities – imaginatively named Upper Hutt and Lower Hutt – spread out upon the terraces of the Hutt River. Dotted with a number of town centres and shopping hubs largely functional in form, the main attractions of the Hutt are its forest parks, camping options and the odd museum.

The Hutt Valley begins at the foot of the Tararua Ranges. Upper Hutt lies at the upper end (40km from Wellington city), with Lower Hutt, 15km further downstream, reaching its boundary at Petone, the historic settlement on Wellington Harbour. Visit the **Hutt City**

i-SITE (☎ 04-560 4715; www.huttvalleynz.com; 25 Laings Rd, Lower Hutt; ☒ 9am-5pm Mon-Fri, to 4pm Sat & Sun) for the local low-down.

SIGHTS & ACTIVITIES
The shell-strewn Petone foreshore is home to the art-deco **Petone Settlers Museum** (☎ 04-568 8373; www.petonesettlers.org.nz; The Esplanade; admission by donation; ☒ noon-4pm Tue-Fri, 1-5pm Sat & Sun), which recalls local migration and settlement, and presents varying exhibitions. **Jackson Street**, running parallel to the Esplanade a couple of blocks inland, is well worth a wander down for lunching and shopping. A short drive south of the Petone, **Days Bay** and **Eastbourne** make a laid-back afternoon detour via road or ferry (see p97).

Just over the hill from Lower Hutt is Wainuiomata, 14km south of which is Catchpool Valley, the main entrance to **Rimutaka Forest Park** (45 minutes' drive from Wellington). Here there's a creek-side **campsite** (adult/child $10/5) and six sole-occupancy bush huts (sleeping eight to 18) – great bases for short and long walks into the forest and gorgeous Orongorongo River valley. Book at Wellington's DOC visitor centre (see p93) or online (www.doc.govt.nz).

Lower Hutt's **NewDowse** (☎ 04-570 6500; www.newdowse.org.nz; 45 Laings Rd, Lower Hutt; admission free; ☒ 10am-4.30pm Mon-Fri, to 5pm Sat & Sun) is worth visiting for its architecture alone (the pink is positively audacious). It's also a friendly, accessible art museum showcasing NZ art, craft and design. Nice cafe.

The drive from Upper Hutt to Waikanae (on the Kapiti Coast) along the windy, scenic Akatarawa Rd passes the 10-hectare **Staglands Wildlife Reserve** (☎ 04-526 7529; www.staglands.co.nz; Akatarawa Valley; adult/child $16/8; ☒ 10am-5pm) which helps to conserve native NZ birds and animals, such as the blue duck (whio). It's 16km from SH2, 20km from SH1.

Kaitoke Regional Park, 16km north of Upper Hutt on SH2, has a pleasant **campsite** (adult/child $5/2), swimming, picnicking and walks ranging from 15 minutes to six hours long. *LOTR* fans make the pilgrimage here to size-up the fabled site of Rivendell.

SLEEPING
Harcourt Holiday Park (☎ 04-526 7400; www.harcourtholidaypark.co.nz; 45 Akatarawa Rd, Upper Hutt; unpowered/powered sites $30/32, cabins & tourist flats $45-90, motels $110; ▯) Veritably verdant park 35km northeast of Wellington (35-minute drive),

just off SH2, set in parkland by the trout-filled Hutt River. Facilities aren't as numerous as the Wellington Top 10 Holiday Park, but the location is more appealing.

Wellington Top 10 Holiday Park (off Map p90; ☎ 0800 488 872, 04-568 5913; www.wellington-top10.co.nz; 95 Hutt Park Rd, Seaview, Lower Hutt; sites $40, cabins $55-75, units $105-135, motels $120-160; 🖳) Utilitarian park 13km northeast of Wellington. Family-friendly facilities include three communal kitchens, games room, jumping pillow and a playground, but its industrial location detracts. It's a 15-minute drive from the ferry (follow the signs off SH2 for Petone and Seaview), or take Eastbourne bus 81 or 83.

KAPITI COAST

With wide, people-free beaches, the Kapiti Coast acts as a summer playground and suburban extension for Wellingtonians. The region takes its moniker from Kapiti Island, a bird and marine sanctuary 5km offshore from Paraparaumu.

In the Tararua Range, Tararua Forest Park forms a dramatic backdrop along the length of the coastline and has some accessible day walks and longer tramps.

The Kapiti Coast makes an easy day trip from Wellington, but if you're after a few restful days or are heading further north, there's some quality accommodation here. Pick up a copy of the *Kapiti Coast Arts Guide* from the local visitor information centres if you're interested in the region's abundant galleries, artists and studios.

Orientation & Information

The Kapiti Coast stretches 30km along the North Island's west coast from Paekakariki (41km north of Wellington) to Otaki. Most towns are a tale of two settlements: one along the highway (banks, petrol, hamburger joints) and another by the water (cafes, motels and houses). Paraparaumu is the biggest town here, but still runs at a beachy pace.

The most comprehensive visitor information centres are at Paraparaumu (p114) and Otaki (p116). Online, check out www.naturecoast.co.nz.

Getting There & Around

Getting here from Wellington is a breeze: just track north on SH1. By car, it's about a 45-minute drive to Paraparaumu, and an hour to Otaki, much of it by motorway.

AIR

Plans are underway to upgrade and expand Paraparaumu airport. In the meantime, **Air2there** (☎ 0800 777 000; www.air2there.com) has regular daily flights departing from the current airstrip, connecting the Kapiti Coast with Blenheim and Nelson.

BUS

InterCity (☎ 04-385 0520; www.intercitycoach.co.nz) has buses between Wellington and Palmerston North ($29 to $36, 2¼ hours, seven daily), stopping at Paekakariki ($20, 40 minutes), Paraparaumu ($22, 45 minutes) and Otaki ($29, 1¼ hours).

The daily services into/out of Wellington run by White Star Express, Naked Bus and Bay Express (see p110) also stop in major Kapiti Coast towns.

From SH1 in Paraparaumu, local buses 260, 261 and 262 run to the beach. Bus 290 heads to Otaki, and 280 and 285 to Waikanae, calling at highway settlements and the beach.

TRAIN

Tranz Metro (☎ 0800 801 700; www.tranzmetro.co.nz) commuter trains between Wellington and the coast are easier and more frequent than buses. Services run from Wellington to Paraparaumu ($10, 55 minutes, generally half-hourly off-peak between 6am and 11pm, with more services at peak times), stopping en route in Paekakariki ($9). Weekday off-peak fares (9am to 3pm) are up to $2.50 cheaper.

Tranz Scenic (☎ 0800 872 467; www.tranzscenic.co.nz) has long-distance *Overlander* trains connecting Wellington and Auckland stopping at Paraparaumu, while the weekday-only, peak-hour *Capital Connection* travelling to Wellington in the morning and back to Palmerston North in the evening, stops at Paraparaumu, Waikanae and Otaki. See p111 for details of these services.

PAEKAKARIKI
pop 1730

Paekakariki is a little seaside village stretched along a black-sand beach, serviced by a train station and passed by the highway. Almost within spitting distance of Wellington (41km to the south), it's an unhurried place to escape for a few days.

Sights & Activities

Queen Elizabeth Park (☎ 04-292 8625; qepranger@
gw.govt.nz; admission free; ☽ 8am-8pm) is a rambling 650-hectare dune-scape park behind
the beach, with plenty of opportunities for
swimming, walking, cycling and picnicking.
There are three entrances: off Wellington Rd
in Paekakariki, at MacKays Crossing on SH1,
and off the Esplanade in Raumati to the north.

About 5km north of Paekakariki, just off
SH1, the **Tramway Museum** (☎ 04-292 8361; www.
wellingtontrams.org.nz; Queen Elizabeth Park, MacKay's
Crossing; admission adult/child $5/3, with tram ride adult/
child/family $9.50/4/24; ☽ museum 10am-4.30pm daily,
trams 11am-4.30pm Sat & Sun, daily 26 Dec-late Jan) has
restored wooden trams that ran in Wellington
until 1964. A 2km track curls from the museum through Queen Elizabeth Park down
to the beach.

Stables on the Park (☎ 06-364 3336; www.stables
onthepark.co.nz; Queen Elizabeth Park, MacKay's Crossing; half-
/1-/1½hr ride $35/55/75; ☽ daily by arrangement) runs
coastal horse riding from its base behind the
Tramway Museum. The 1½-hour ride will see
you trot along the beach with views of Kapiti
Island before heading inland on park tracks.
Beginners are welcome.

Sleeping & Eating

Paekakariki Holiday Park (☎ 04-292 8292; www.
paekakarikiholidaypark.co.nz; 180 Wellington Rd; sites per
adult $13, cabins & flats $65-85) A pleasant, large,
leafy park approximately 1.5km north of the
township at the southern entrance to Queen
Elizabeth Park. Just a hop, skip and a jump
from the beach.

Paekakariki Backpackers (☎ 04-902 5967; www.
wellingtonbeachbackpackers.co.nz; 11 Wellington Rd; dm
$28, d with/without bathroom $76/66; ▣) Atop a steep
hill covered with dense gardens, two houses
combine to offer an array of rooms, many
with sea and sunset views. Ask about the
double with flash new en suite – positively
luxurious. Or maybe you'll prefer the yurt in
the front yard. Lie in bed looking out to the
sunset, and be lured to sleep by the ocean's
crashing waves.

ourpick Beach Road Deli (☎ 04-902 9029; 5 Beach
Rd; snacks $3-8, pizza $9-21; ☽ 7am-8pm Wed-Sun) Bijou
deli and pizzeria, packed with home-baked
bread and patisserie, cheese, charcuterie and
assorted imported goodies. Heaven-sent for
the highway traveller, picnic provisioner, or
those looking for a sausage to fry and a bun to
put it in. Fresh juices and ace coffee.

Finn's (☎ 04-292 8081; www.kapiticoasthotel.co.nz; 2
Beach Rd; mains $15-23; ☽ 10am-3pm Tue-Fri, 9am-3pm Sat
& Sun, 6pm-8.30pm Tue-Sun) Opened in 2007, Finn's
is the flashy, beige suit of the cutesy railway
village, but redeems itself with spacious rooms
(doubles $125 to $135), good-value meals, and
independent beer on tap. The hush glass keeps
the highway at bay.

PARAPARAUMU

pop 6840

Lower-than-low-key Paraparaumu is the
principal town on the Kapiti Coast, and a
suburban satellite of Wellington. The rough-
and-tumble beach is the coast's most developed, sustaining plenty of cafes, motels and
takeaway joints. Boat trips to Kapiti Island set
sail from here (see opposite).

The correct pronunciation is 'Pah-ra-pah-
ra-oo-moo', meaning 'scraps from an oven',
which is said to have originated when a Maori
war party attacked the settlement and found
only scraps of food remaining. It's a bit of a
mouthful to pronounce; locals usually just
corrupt it into 'Para-par-am'.

Orientation & Information

Coastlands Shoppingtown, the hub of
Paraparaumu's highway settlement, is on the
left as you head into town from Wellington.
Three kilometres west along Kapiti Rd (just
past Coastlands) is Paraparaumu Beach;
Seaview Rd is the main road here. Sleeping
and eating options are most atmospheric (and
plentiful) by the beach.

Coastlands has all the services you'll need:
banks, ATMs, post office, supermarkets and
cinema. The **Paraparaumu visitor information
centre** (☎ 04-298 8195; www.naturecoast.co.nz; Coastlands
car park, SH1; ☽ 9am-5pm Mon-Fri, 10am-3pm Sat & Sun)
is slap-bang in the middle of the Coastlands
car park. Pick up the *Nature Coast* brochure
while you're here.

Sights & Activities

Paraparaumu Beach, with its beachside park,
decent swimming and other watery activities,
is the town's raison d'être.

Paraparaumu Beach Golf Club (☎ 04-902 8200;
www.paraparaumubeachgolfclub.co.nz; 376 Kapiti Rd; 9/18
holes $55/130; ☽ 7.30am-dusk) is a challenging and
beautiful links course that is ranked among
NZ's best. It's hosted the NZ Open 12 times
and tamed Tiger in 2002. Visitors are wel-

come: call for tee times, or book online. Clubs, carts and shoes can be hired.

Another kilometre north, just off SH1 in a voluminous hangar, the **Southward Car Museum** (☎ 04-297 1221; www.southward.org.nz; Otaihanga Rd; adult/child $10/3; ☼ 9am-4.30pm) has one of Australasia's largest collections of antique and unusual cars. Check out the DeLorean and the 1950 gangster Cadillac.

Sleeping

Barnacles Seaside Inn (☎ 0800 555 856, 04-902 5856; www.seasideyha.co.nz; 3 Marine Pde; dm/s/f $28/50/90, d $62-80; ▢) Opposite Paraparaumu Beach, Barnacles is a creaky, old-style YHA hostel in a 1920s heritage building. Snug rooms are individually decorated with antique dressers and have sinks and heaters; some have electric blankets and sea views.

Wrights by the Sea (☎ 0508 902 760, 04-902 7600; www.wrightsmotel.co.nz; 387 Kapiti Rd; units $100-150; ▢ ☎) Not quite by the sea, but near enough and even closer to the golf course. A modern motel complex in the conservative style with light, airy rooms, Sky TV and off-road parking. Some with full kitchen.

Eating

Fed Up Fast Foods (☎ 04-902 6686; 40 Marine Pde; meals $5-15; ☼ 10am-9pm Mon-Thu, 9.30am-9.30pm Fri-Sun) A takeaway chippy with the usual battery of fries as well as doner kebabs and fancy burgers. Unfathomably good-value dinner deals, eggy brekkies, espresso and Kapiti ice cream. Clean-as-a-whistle dinette, plus alfresco tables with views to the blue yonder.

Mediterranean Food Warehouse (☎ 0800 334 477, 04-892 0010; Coastlands car park, SH1; meals $13-18; ☼ 9am-9pm) A handy highway pit stop, with excellent wood-fired pizza, luscious cakes, gelato, and a minimarket for picnic supplies. Food so good you'll forget you're in the middle of a car park.

Ambience Café (☎ 04-298 9898; 10 Seaview Rd; lunch $14-18, dinner $20-29; ☼ 8am-4pm Sun-Thu, to late Fri & Sat; Ⓥ) A very 'Wellington' cafe, with both light and substantial meals made with relish, such as fish cakes, the BLT, and colourful veggie options. Cake cabinet at full capacity, and great coffee (of course).

Soprano Ristorante (☎ 04-298 8892; 7 Seaview Rd; mains $21-28; ☼ 6pm-late Mon-Sat) A welcoming family-run joint with the liveliest evening atmosphere at the beach township. Pizzas, pastas and other Italian classics such as salt-imbocca. Sweet treats include the ubiquitous tiramisu and delicious homemade *limoncello* (lemon liqueur). No-nonsense, affordable food and wine in a homely environment – *bella*!

KAPITI ISLAND

Kapiti Island is the coastline's dominant feature, a 10km by 2km slice which since 1897 has been a protected reserve. It's predator-free – many bird species that are now rare or extinct on the mainland still thrive on the island. **Kapiti Island Alive** (☎ 06-362 6606; www.kapiti islandalive.co.nz; walks $20) runs one-hour guided walks and offers homestay accommodation.

The island is open to visitors, limited to around 68 people per day, and it's essential that you book and obtain a permit (adult/child $11/5) at Wellington's DOC visitor centre (p93) – in person, by phone or via email (kapiti.island@doc.govt.nz). During summer it pays to book in advance, especially on weekends. DOC also publishes the detailed *Visiting Kapiti Island* brochure.

Transport is booked separately from the permit (arrange your permit before your boat trip). Two commercial operators are licensed to take visitors to the island, both running to/from Paraparaumu Beach (which can be reached by train, see p113). Departures are between 9am and 9.30am daily, returning between 3pm and 4pm; call in the morning to confirm departure (sailings are weather dependent). All visitors receive an introductory talk; BYO lunch.

Kapiti Marine Charter (☎ 0800 433 779, 04-297 2585; www.kapitimarinecharter.co.nz; adult/child $55/30)

Kapiti Tours (☎ 0800 527 484, 04-237 7965; www.kapititours.co.nz; adult/child $55/30)

WAIKANAE
pop 6930

With a particularly nice stretch of beach, New Zealand's 2008 'Top Town' (and retirees' favourite) is a viable option as your Kapiti Coast rest stop.

About 5km north of Paraparaumu at Waikanae is the turn-off to **Nga Manu Nature Reserve** (☎ 04-293 4131; www.ngamanu.co.nz; 281 Ngarara Rd; adult/child/family $12/4/24; ☼ 10am-5pm), a 15-hectare bird sanctuary dotted with picnic areas, bush walks, aviaries and a nocturnal house with kiwi, owls and tuatara. The eels are fed at 2pm daily, and guided tours run at weekends at 1.30pm (Sunday only in winter). To get here, turn seawards from SH1 onto Te

Moana Rd and then right down Ngarara Rd and follow the signs; the sanctuary is 3.5km from the turn-off.

Old but well-maintained **Waikanae Beach Motel** (☎ 0800 486 533, 04-293 6199; www.kapitimotel. co.nz; 95 Te Moana Rd, d $110, f $140; 💻 💆) has spacious units with full kitchen facilities, about 1km from the beach. All rooms open out onto or overlook the courtyard garden and picturesque golf course beyond. The swimming pool and playground make it an ideal spot for families.

Front Room (☎ 04-905 4142; 42 Tutere St; meals $6-25; 🕑 9am-4pm Mon-Fri, 6-9pm Fri & Sat, 5-9pm Sun) has a stylish, pared-back interior and is home to food a tad more sophisticated that your average cafe. Keep an eye out for the Waikanae crab, a regional speciality. The pleasant garden out back sports a fireplace, welcome on cool evenings.

OTAKI
pop 5650

Unremarkable Otaki is primarily a gateway to the Tararua Range. It has a strong Maori history and presence: the little town has nine *marae* and a Maori college. The historic Rangiatea Church, built under the guidance of Ngati Toa chief Te Rauparaha nearly 150 years ago, tragically burnt to the ground in 1995 but has been rebuilt. This was the original burial site of Te Rauparaha.

Orientation & Information

Most services, including the train station where buses also stop, are on SH1. The main centre of Otaki, with the post office and shops, is 2km seawards on Tasman Rd. Three kilometres further on the same road brings you to Otaki's windswept beach. Note that the telephone area code in Otaki is ☎ 06, not ☎ 04 like most of the rest of the Kapiti Coast.

The **Otaki i-SITE** (☎ 06-364 7620; www.naturecoast. co.nz; Centennial Park, SH1; 🕑 9am-5pm Mon-Fri, 10am-3pm Sat & Sun) is just south of the main roundabout in an 1891 courthouse.

Activities

Two kilometres south of Otaki, scenic Otaki Gorge Rd trucks inland from SH1 and leads 19km (5km unsealed) to **Otaki Forks**, the main western entrance to **Tararua Forest Park**. Otaki Forks has picnic areas, swimming and **campsites** (unpowered sites per adult/child

$6/2), plus bush walks from 30 minutes to 3½ hours in the immediate area; longer tracks lead to huts. The i-SITE sells detailed maps and knowledgeable staff proffer information and advice about the walks. Ask at DOC in Wellington (p93) for advice on longer tracks in the park. You can tramp in the Tararua Ranges, but you must bring adequate clothing and equipment, and be well prepared for wild weather.

Sleeping & Eating

Byron's Resort (☎ 0800 800 122, 06-364 8119; www. byronsresort.co.nz; 20 Tasman Rd; unpowered/powered sites $31/35, units & motels $100-150; 💻 💆) A traditional, family-fuelled resort by the beach. The Scuttlebutt restaurant and garden bar (meals $19 to $27; open Tuesday to Sunday) is a welcome haven after a day spent at the pool, spa, sauna, tennis court and playground.

Red House Café (☎ 06-364 3022; 885 Main Rd, SH1, Te Horo; lunch $10-17, dinner $22-29; 🕑 9am-late Mon-Fri, 8.30pm-late Sat & Sun) One of the best highway pit stops round these parts is this fire-engine red cafe 5km south of Otaki. Inside it's all warm polished wood, all-day breakfasts, excellent baking and an extensive blackboard menu. Bargain two-course roast and pudding special on Sunday.

THE WAIRARAPA

The Wairarapa is the large slab of land east and northeast of Wellington, beyond the craggy Tararua and Rimutaka Ranges. Named after Lake Wairarapa (Shimmering Waters), a shallow 8000-hectare lake, the region has traditionally been a frenzied hotbed of sheep farming. More recently, wineries have sprung up – around Martinborough, most famously – which has turned the region into a decadent weekend retreat. A vigorous foodie culture has evolved alongside the wineries and restored B&B cottages.

See www.wairarapanz.com for regional info, but also check out the **Classic New Zealand Wine Trail** (www.classicwinetrail.co.nz) – a useful tool for joining the dots throughout the Wairarapa and its neighbouring wine regions of Hawke's Bay and Marlborough.

Note that the telephone area code over here is ☎ 06, not ☎ 04 like most of the rest of the Wellington region.

Getting There & Around

From Wellington, **Tranz Metro** (☎ 0800 801 700; www.tranzmetro.co.nz) commuter trains run to Masterton ($15, 1½ hours, five or six daily on weekdays, two daily on weekends), calling at seven stations including Featherston and Carterton. For other Wairarapa towns, connect with the local bus services.

Tranzit Coachlines (☎ 0800 471 227, 06-370 6600; www.tranzit.co.nz; 316 Queen St, Masterton) has a bus between Masterton and Palmerston North (one-way $21, 1¾ hours, one daily), plus local daily services (bus 200) between Martinborough and Masterton ($4) via Featherston, Greytown and Carterton.

Wairarapa Coach Lines (☎ 0800 666 355, 06-308 9352; www.waicoach.co.nz) runs between Masterton and Martinborough ($6, 1¼ hours, three daily) and meets every Featherston train for a run through to Martinborough ($4, 20 minutes, four to five daily).

MARTINBOROUGH

pop 1360

The most popular visitor spot in the Wairarapa, Martinborough is a pretty town with a leafy town square and some charming old buildings, surrounded by a patchwork of pasture and a pinstripe of grapevines. It is famed for its wineries, which draw in visitors to nose the pinot, avail themselves of its excellent eateries, and snooze it off at boutique accommodation. The best time for an overnight visit is midweek, when accommodation is cheaper (although many restaurants shut up shop on Monday and Tuesday).

Orientation & Information

Martinborough is arrowed off the SH2 from both Featherston and Greytown; it's about 20km from either town. Settler and town planner John Martin designed Martinborough's classic grid, a Union Jack street pattern centred upon a leafy square. The **Martinborough i-SITE** (☎ 06-306 5010; www.wairarapanz.com; 18 Kitchener St; ☼ 9am-5pm Mon-Fri, 10am-4pm Sat & Sun) is full of brochures and information.

Sights & Activities

With so many **wineries** scattered around town, there are no points for guessing what is the town's main attraction. This is closely followed by the excellent food that goes with it – Martinborough punches well above its weight when it comes to food cafes and restaurants.

The town's cultural hub is arguably **Circus** (see p119), a stylish art-house cinema where you can watch the cream of contemporary movies as well as eat and drink in the convivial dining room or sunny courtyard.

About 3km from town off Oxford St is **Olivo** (☎ 06-306 9074; www.olivo.co.nz; Hinakura Rd; admission free; ☼ 10am-5pm Mon-Fri), a welcoming olive grove where you can meet the owners, take a tour and tasting, and buy your oil to go.

Patuna Farm Adventures (☎ 06-306 9966; www.patunafarm.co.nz; Ruakokoputuna Rd) offers horse treks (from $40), a challenging pole-to-pole rope course (from $20), and a four-hour self-guided walk through native bush and a limestone chasm (adult/child $15/10). The chasm is open late October until Easter; other activities operate year-round.

Sleeping

A list of local B&Bs, self-contained weekend-away cottages and farmstays can be found on www.wairarapanz.com; the i-SITE can help with bookings. Expect to pay around $160 per night for two people.

our pick **Martinborough Village Camping** (☎ 06-306 8946; www.martinboroughcamping.com; cnr Princess & Dublin Sts; unpowered sites $30, cabins s/d $45/60; ☐ ☎) An appealing camping ground with grapevine views, just five minutes' walk to town. It has shady trees and the town pool over the back fence, making it a cooling oasis on sticky days. Cabins are basic but great value, freeing up your dollars for the cellar door. Bike hire available for $35 per day.

Kate's Place (☎ 06-306 9935; www.katesplace.co.nz; 7 Cologne St; dm $30, d $80; ☐) An unpretentious home stay–backpackers with a welcoming owner and a laid-back vibe, just a hop and a skip from the Square. The two dorms have solid bunks with extrawide mattresses. Mull over your day's misdemeanours on the front porch.

Claremont (☎ 0800 809 162, 06-306 9162; www.theclaremont.co.nz; 38 Regent St; d $125-160, 4-person apt $275; ☐) A classy accommodation enclave off Jellicoe St, the Claremont has two-storey, self-contained units in great nick, modern studios with spa baths, and sparkling two-bedroom apartments, all at reasonable rates (even cheaper in winter and/or midweek). Attractive gardens, barbecue areas and bike hire.

Peppers Martinborough Hotel (☎ 06-306 9350; www.martinboroughhotel.co.nz; The Square; d incl breakfast

WAIRARAPA WINE COUNTRY

Wairarapa's winemakers enjoy an impressive international reputation, but this world-renowned industry was nearly crushed in infancy. The region's first vines were planted in 1883, but the prohibition movement in 1908 soon put a cap on that corker idea. It wasn't until the 1980s that winemaking was revived, after Martinborough's *terroir* was discovered to be similar to Burgundy in France. A few vineyards soon sprang up, but the number has now ballooned to nearly 50 regionwide. Martinborough is the undisputed hub of the action, renowned for its gravels which produce particularly remarkable pinot noir and distinctive whites.

For a good introduction to Wairarapa's wines, visit Martinborough's stylish cinema, **Circus** (☎ 06-306 9442; www.circus.net.nz; 34 Jellicoe St; ⏲ screenings 3pm daily; additional screenings peak season), which screens **Vintners' Choice** (www.vintnerschoice.co.nz), a 40-minute documentary with a real-live wine tasting.

The town also plays host to New Zealand's best wine, food and music festival – **Toast Martinborough** (☎ 06-306 9183; www.toastmartinborough.co.nz; tickets $60), held annually on the third Sunday in November. Enjoyable on many levels (standing up and quite possibly lying on the grass), this is a hugely popular event and you'll have to be quick on the draw to get a ticket.

The **Wairarapa Wines Harvest Festival** (☎ 027 477 4717; www.wairarapawines.co.nz; tickets $25-35) celebrates the beginning of the harvest with an extravaganza of wine, food and family fun. It's held at a remote riverbank setting 10 minutes from Carterton on a Saturday in mid-March.

Wairarapa's wineries thrive on visitors; Martinborough's 30-odd are particularly welcoming with well-oiled cellar doors, and noteworthy food served in some gorgeous gardens and courtyards. The *Wairarapa Wine Trail Map* (available from the i-SITE and many other locations) will aid your navigations. Read all about it at www.winesfrommartinborough.com.

You can sample and purchase many wines under one gabled roof at the **Martinborough Wine Centre** (☎ 06-306 9040; www.martinboroughwinecentre.co.nz; 6 Kitchener St; tastings available; ⏲ 10am-5pm), which also sells olive oils, books, clothing and art.

Recommended Wineries

Ata Rangi (☎ 06-306 9570; www.atarangi.co.nz; Puruatanga Rd) One of the region's pioneering winemakers. Great drops across the board and cute cellar door.

$300-385; 💻 📶) Grand old hotel on the main square that's been magnificently restored, with 16 spacious, luxury rooms, each individually decorated with pizzazz. All open onto either a wide veranda or courtyard garden. Downstairs the Settlers Bar (mains $12 to $20) serves sophisticated pub nosh and local wines by the glass.

Eating & Drinking

Eating and drinking is what Martinborough's all about, with award-winning restaurants and cafes, delicatessens and food shops. Peppers Martinborough Hotel and the no-nonsense pub over the road are the best places to join the locals for a drink.

Café Medici (☎ 06-306 9965; 9 Kitchener St; breakfast & lunch $7-19, dinner $22-30; ⏲ 8.30am-4pm Wed-Mon, plus evenings summer) A perennial favourite among townsfolk and regular visitors, this airy cafe has a Florentine/Kiwiana interior and courtyard offering honest home-cooked food. Choose from the tasty counter selection including muffins, pies, quiche and famous scones. The blackboard menu is short but varied with plenty of salad options. Great coffee, too.

Trio Café at Coney Winery (☎ 06-306 8345; Dry River Rd; snacks $10, mains $24-25; ⏲ noon-3pm Sat & Sun) Wine and dine in a courtyard featuring gorgeous white roses or in the light and airy tasting room. The great-value food is sophisticated, fresh and delicious, and all made from scratch. The atmosphere is relaxed and fun, a testament to your host Tim Coney, an affable and knowledgeable character who may sing at random.

Circus (☎ 06-306 9442; www.circus.net.nz; 34 Jellicoe St; mains $18-28, tickets adult/child $14/10; ⏲ 2.30pm-late Wed-Mon) A modern microsized movie complex with two comfy studio theatres. The stylish foyer and cafe, opening out on to a rather Zen garden, offer some of the most sociable surroundings in town. Reasonably

Coney (☎ 06-306 8345; www.coneywines.co.nz; Dry River Rd) Friendly tastings and lovely restaurant (p424). Winery tours by arrangement.

Margrain (☎ 06-306 9292; www.margrainvineyard.co.nz; cnr Princess St & Huangarua Rd) Pretty winery and site of the Old Winery Cafe, a good pit stop overlooking the vines.

Vynfields (☎ 06-306 9901; www.vynfields.com; 22 Omarere Rd) Five-star, spicy pinot noir and a lush lawn on which to enjoy a platter. Organic/biodynamic wines.

Tours

If you have the time and physical ability, the best and most carbon-friendly way to explore the Wairarapa's wines is by bicycle as the flat landscape makes for puff-free cruising.

From Masterton, **March Hare** (☎ 021 668 970; www.march-hare.co.nz; tours incl all gear & a picnic $65) runs self-guided bike tours of the Opaki winegrowing area.

There are three options in Martinborough:

Christina Estate Vineyard (☎ 06-306 8920; christinaestate@xtra.co.nz; 28 Puruatanga Rd; ⏲ 8.30am-6pm) Per hour/day $15/25. Tandems for the coordinated.

Martinborough Village Camping (☎ 06-306 8946; www.martinboroughcamping.com; cnr Princess & Dublin St) Per day $35.

Martinborough Wine Centre (☎ 06-306 9040; www.martinboroughwinecentre.co.nz; 6 Kitchener St) Half-/ full day $25/35.

Numerous operators run bus tours around Martinborough and the region:

Dynamic Tours (☎ 04-478 8533; www.dynamictours.co.nz; from $225) Customised wine tours, run from Wellington.

Hammond's Scenic Tours (☎ 04-472 0869; www.wellingtonsightseeingtours.com; full-day tour adult/child $195/97.50) Full-day winery tours including gourmet lunch.

Tranzit Coachlines (☎ 0800 471 227, 06-370 6600; www.tranzit.co.nz; 316 Queen St, Masterton) Two daily tours depart from Wellington or the main Wairarapa towns. The Gourmet Wine Escape ($161) visits Martinborough vineyards and includes tastings and lunch. The Garden Gourmet Escape (adult/child $182/115) takes in two gardens, lunch at the Gladstone Country Inn, and wine tasting.

Zest Food Tours (☎ 04-801 9198; www.zestfoodtours.co.nz; tours incl lunch & wines from $230) Small-group food and wine tours (2½ to five hours) in Greytown and Martinborough.

---

priced seasonal food includes bar snacks, pizza, mains with plenty of fresh veg, and a short list of sweet delights.

French Bistro (☎ 06-306 8863; 3 Kitchener St; mains $36-40; ⏲ 6pm-late Wed-Sun) Wendy Campbell's provincial cooking in this tiny but smart family-run bistro has garnered praise both at home and abroad. Francophiles will delight at her dishes using ingredients from the region and beyond. The decor is eclectic as is the carefully selected wine list offering a variety of mainly local vintages.

CAPE PALLISER

The Wairarapa coast south of Martinborough around Palliser Bay and Cape Palliser is remote and sparsely populated. The bendy road to Cape Palliser is utterly scenic: a big ocean and black-sand beaches on one side; barren hills and sheer cliffs on the other. Look for hints of the South Island, visible on a clear day.

Standing like giant organ pipes in the Putangirua Scenic Reserve are the **Putangirua Pinnacles**, formed by rain washing silt and sand away and exposing the underlying bedrock. Accessible by a track near the car park on Cape Palliser Rd, it's an easy three-hour return walk along a streambed to the pinnacles, or take the 3½-hour loop track past hills and coastal viewpoints. For some rugged Wairarapa tramping nearby, head to **Aorangi (Haurangi) Forest Park**. For maps and access info contact DOC in Wellington (p93).

Further south is the wind-worn fishing village **Ngawi**. The first things you'll notice here are the rusty bulldozers on the beach, used to drag fishing boats ashore. Next stop is the malodorous **seal colony**, the North Island's largest breeding area. Whatever you do in your quest for a photo, don't get between the seals and the sea. If you block their escape route they're likely to have a go at you!

Get your thighs thumping on the steep, 250-step (or is it 249?) climb to **Cape Palliser Lighthouse**, from where there are yet more amazing coastal views, as far as the South Island if it's not hazy.

On the way there or back, take the short detour to the wind-blown settlement of **Lake Ferry**, overlooking **Lake Onoke**, where there's birdwatching to be enjoyed. This area is also good for exploration – discover the lake edge, the wild and woolly coastline (prime for surfing), and the cliffs behind. You'll also find the **Lake Ferry Hotel** (☎ 06-307 7831; ☉ from 11am) with its retro fitout (check out the formica), which has great views and fish and chips.

Martinborough i-SITE (p117) can help with accommodation options in the Lake Ferry and Cape Palliser area, which include camping grounds and holiday homes for rent.

GREYTOWN
pop 2000
The most popular of several small towns along SH2, Greytown has spruced itself up over recent years and is now full of Wellingtonians on the weekend. It has plenty of accommodation, some decent food, three high-street pubs, and some swanky shopping. Check out www.greytown.co.nz for more information.

Sights
Greytown was the country's first planned inland town: intact Victorian architectural specimens line the main street. The quaint **Cobblestones Village Museum** (☎ 06-304 9687; www.cobblestonesmuseum.org.nz; 169 Main St; adult/child/family $2.50/1/6; ☉ 10am-4pm) is an enclave of period buildings and various historic objects, dotted around pretty grounds inviting a lie-down on a picnic blanket. No picnic? No worries. Visit **Schoc Chocolate** (☎ 06-304 8960; www.chocolatetherapy.com; 177 Main St; ☉ 10am-5pm Mon-Fri, 10.30am-5pm Sat & Sun) in a 1920s cottage that shares the grounds. Sublime flavours, worth every single penny of 10 bucks a tablet. Truffles, rocky road and peanut brittle, too. Free tastings.

About 10km southeast of Carterton is **Stonehenge Aotearoa** (☎ 06-377 1600; www.stonehenge-aotearoa.com; tours adult $15, child $6-10; ☉ 10am-4pm Wed-Sun, tours 2pm Sat & Sun, public holidays & by appointment). Explore the southern sky – even in daylight – at this full-scale adaptation of the UK Stonehenge, orientated for its location on a grassy knoll overlooking the Wairarapa Plain. The pretour talk and

audiovisual presentation are excellent, and the henge itself a pretty surreal sight, day or night, especially when interpreted by one of its tour guides who are consummate storytellers. Self-guided tours are also available for $5.

Sleeping & Eating
Greytown Camping Ground (☎ 06-304 9837; Kuratawhiti St; unpowered/powered sites $30/36) A basic camping option (with equally basic facilities) scenically spread through Greytown Park, 500m from town.

Greytown Hotel (☎ 06-304 9138; www.greytownhotel.co.nz; 33 Main St; s/d $50/80; ☐) A serious contender for 'oldest hotel in New Zealand', the Top Pub (as it's known) is looking great for her age, having just had a major facelift. Upstairs rooms are small and basic but comfortable, with no-frills furnishings and shared bathrooms. Downstairs is a chic new dining room (classic meals $22 to $29), ol' faithful lounge-bar and popular garden-courtyard.

Oak Estate Motor Lodge (☎ 0800 843 625, 06-304 8188; www.oakestate.co.nz; cnr Main St & Hospital Rd; r $125-185) A stand of gracious roadside oaks and pretty gardens shield a smart complex of self-contained units: studios, one- and two-bedroom options.

French Baker (☎ 06-304 8873; 81 Main St; snacks $4-7, mains $13-19; ☉ 7.30am-3pm Mon, Thu & Fri, to 4pm Fri & Sat) Buttery croissants, tempting tarts and authentic breads; artisan baker Moïse Cerson is le real McCoy. Great coffee too and a compact menu of suitably Gallic offerings, such as Roquefort salad and French toast.

Cuckoo Pizza (☎ 06-304 8992; 128 Main St; mains $15-24; ☉ 11am-8.30pm Wed-Sun) Refreshingly unruly pizza joint littered with mismatched retro furniture in an old house on the main street. Try the 'moa' pizza (pepperoni, mushrooms, anchovies, olives and chilli), or pasta specials. Good coffee too.

MASTERTON & AROUND
pop 19,500
Masterton is the Wairarapa's utilitarian hub, an unselfconscious town getting on with its business. Its main claim to immortality is the 50-year-old sheep-shearing competition, the international Golden Shears (right).

Orientation & Information
State Highway 2 runs through the centre of town. From the south SH2 is named High

St, which then becomes Chapel St. Queen St runs parallel to High/Chapel St, one block east. The town's prime attractions are another block east on Dixon St where you will find the **Masterton i-SITE** (☎ 06-370 0900; www.wairarapanz. com; cnr Dixon & Bruce Sts; ✆ 9am-5pm Mon-Fri, 10am-4pm Sat & Sun).

Sights & Activities

Stretch your car-cramped legs in the 32-hectare **Queen Elizabeth Park** (Dixon St; ✆ 24hr), with its aviaries, duck lake, children's playground, minigolf and cricket oval. Opposite the park is **Aratoi Wairarapa Museum of Art & History** (☎ 06-370 0001; www.aratoi.co.nz; cnr Bruce & Dixon Sts; admission by donation; ✆ 10am-4.30pm), documenting the art and cultural heritage of the region, both Maori and Pakeha.

Occupying two historic woolsheds next to Aratoi is **Shear Discovery** (☎ 06-378 8008; www. sheardiscovery.co.nz; Dixon St; adult/child/family $5/2/10; ✆ 10am-4pm), a baaaa-loody marvellous little museum dedicated to NZ's sheep-shearing and wool-production industries.

Castlepoint, on the coast 68km east of Masterton, is an awesome, end-of-the-world place, with a reef, the lofty 162m-high Castle Rock, protected swimming and walking tracks. There's an easy (but sometimes ludicrously windy) 30-minute return walk across the reef to the lighthouse, where 70-plus shell species are fossilised in the cliffs. Another one-hour return walk runs to a huge limestone cave (take a torch), or take the 1½-hour return track from Deliverance Cove to Castle Rock. Keep well away from the lower reef when there are heavy seas. Ask the staff at Masterton i-SITE (above) about accommodation here.

Pukaha Mt Bruce National Wildlife Centre (☎ 06-375 8004; www.mtbruce.org.nz; adult/child/family $15/4/38; ✆ 9am-4.30pm) is not only an important sanctuary for native NZ wildlife (mostly birds), it's also the most readily accessible bush experience off the highway. The visitor centre has various exhibits, while outside there are aviaries, a kiwi house, virgin forest and a scenic one-hour loop track taking in some great views. Slippery eels, tuatara and other creatures also reside here. Take a walk with the ranger (10.30am and 2pm Saturday and Sunday; adult/child $25/12.50) or take the Lookout Lunch Tour (11am Sunday; adult/child $50/25 including lunch). There's a cafe on-site; it's 30km north of Masterton on SH2.

The turn-off to the main eastern entrance of the **Tararua Forest Park** is just south of Masterton on SH2; follow Norfolk Rd about 15km to the gates. Mountain streams dart through virgin forest in this reserve, known as 'Holdsworth'. At the park entrance are swimming holes, picnic areas and **campsites** (unpowered sites adult/child $6/2). Walks include short, easy family tramps, excellent one- or two-day tramps, and longer, challenging tramps for experienced bush-bods (west through to Otaki Forks). The resident caretaker (☎ 06-377 0022) has maps and hut accommodation info. Check weather and track updates before setting off, and be prepared to be baked, battered and buffeted by fickle conditions.

Festivals & Events

For wine and food related events, see p118.
Golden Shears (www.goldenshears.co.nz) Held annually in the first week of March.
Wings over Wairarapa (☎ 06-370 0900; www.wings. org.nz) An exciting three-day air show (biennial; odd years) featuring more than 70 aircraft – from the war birds through to gliders, gyros, jets and batty aerobatics.

Sleeping & Eating

Empire Lodge (☎ 06-377 1902; www.empirelodge. co.nz; 94 Queen St; backpackers dm/s/d $25/30/55, hotel s/d $80/90; ⌨) An 1870s budget hotel and backpackers, well worn and badly colour coordinated. Down its long hallways you'll discover a communal kitchen, TV room, and other surprises. Views of the Tararua Range from the rear deck. Cheap sleep in a handy location.

Copthorne Solway Park (☎ 0800 808 228, 06-370 0500; www.solway.co.nz; High St; d $130-345; ⌨ ✆) A megabuck refurb has restored this 1970s resort to glory, from its sunken bar and reputable restaurant, to its two swimming pools, tennis court and the driving range which takes up just some of its 24-hectare grounds. Lots of room options, all with classy fit-outs featuring some particularly stylish textiles.

our pick **Ten O'Clock Cookie** (☎ 06-377 4551; 180 Queen St; snacks $3-15; ✆ 7am-4.30pm Mon-Fri, 8am-2.30pm Sat) Loosen that belt and get ready to indulge. Heavenly baking, scrumptious pies, simple sandwiches and cookies of course. Take away or sit down and enjoy your treat with a decent cup of coffee or tea. Relaxed and great value, it's deserving of its many awards.

Lounge Wine Bar (☎ 06-379 6065; 78-81 Main St, Carterton; snacks & meals $5-18; ⊗ 3.30pm-late Wed-Sun; Ⓥ) A local hero saves the town of Carterton (indeed, the region) with a steady stream of live music (Friday and Saturday), local wines, independent beers and Spanish food. All this and more lapped up in a groovy 'thrift-shop' interior.

Café Cecille (☎ 06-370 1166; Queen Elizabeth Park; brunch $9-18, dinner $15-30; ⊗ 10am-3pm daily, 5-8pm Fri & Sat) In the middle of Queen Elizabeth Park is the century-old Coronation Hall, home to Café Cecille. Its wraparound veranda and simple but wholesome food make it hard to beat on a sunny day. Divine homemade chips.

Gladstone Inn (☎ 06-372 7866; 51 Gladstone Rd, Gladstone; lunch $12-28, dinner $18-30; ⊗ 11am-late) Gladstone, 18km south of Masterton, is less a town, more a state of mind. There's very little here except this proud inn, haven of thirsty locals, motorbike enthusiasts, Sunday drivers and lazy-afternoon shandy sippers who hog the tables in the glorious garden bar.

Marlborough & Nelson

For many travellers, Marlborough and Nelson will be their introduction to what South Islanders refer to as the 'Mainland'. Having left windy Wellington, and made a white-knuckled crossing of Cook Strait, folk are often surprised to find the sun shining and the temperature up to 10 degrees warmer.

Good pals, these two neighbouring regions have much in common beyond an amenable climate: both boast renowned coastal holiday spots, particularly the Marlborough Sounds and Abel Tasman National Park. There are two other national parks (Kahurangi and Nelson Lakes) and more mountain ranges than you can poke a stick at.

And so it follows that these two regions have an abundance of luscious produce: summer cherries for a starter, but most famously the grapes that work their way into the wineglasses of the world's finest restaurants. Keep your penknife and picnic set at the ready.

In high season, these regions are popular and deservedly so. Plan ahead and be prepared to jostle for your gelato with Kiwi holidaymakers.

HIGHLIGHTS

- Getting up close to **Kaikoura's wildlife** (p146), including whales, seals, dolphins and albatross
- Nosing your way through the **Marlborough Wine Region** (p140)
- Tramping the **Queen Charlotte Track** (p132) in the Marlborough Sounds
- Getting airborne above **Nelson** (p153) and **Motueka** (p161) for a spot of paragliding or skydiving
- Sea kayaking in postcard-perfect **Abel Tasman National Park** (p168)
- Getting blown away at Blenheim's **Omaka Aviation Heritage Museum** (p136), one of New Zealand's best provincial museums
- Reaching the end of the road around **Farewell Spit** (p173) where there'll be gannets and godwits for company

Telephone code: 03	www.destination marlborough.com	www.nelsonnz.com

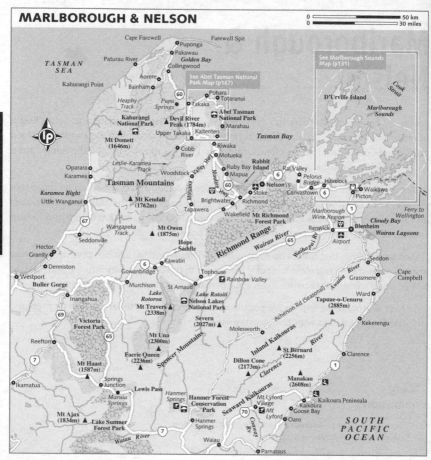

Climate

The forecast is good: Marlborough and Nelson soak up some of NZ's sunniest weather. January and February are the warmest months, with temperatures averaging 22°C; July is the coldest, averaging 12°C. It's wetter and more windswept the closer you get to Farewell Spit and the West Coast.

Getting There & Around

Soundsair (www.soundsair.com) is a local airline connecting Wellington with Blenheim, Nelson and Picton. **Air New Zealand** (www.airnewzealand.com) offers domestic flights.

Interisland Cook Strait ferries pull into Picton, often the starting point for South Island explorations. From here you can connect to almost anywhere in the South Island by bus; InterCity is the major operator, but there are also local shuttles. Tranz Scenic's *TranzCoastal* train takes the scenic route from Picton to Christchurch, via Blenheim and Kaikoura.

Renting a car is easy – there's a slew of car-hire offices in Picton.

Water transport, sea kayaking or walking are the best ways to navigate popular coastal areas, including the Marlborough Sounds and Abel Tasman National Park.

MARLBOROUGH REGION

Picton is the gateway to the South Island and the launching point for Marlborough Sounds' exploration. A cork's pop south of Picton is

---

MARLBOROUGH & NELSON FACTS

Eat Doris' bratwurst at the weekend markets in Nelson (p152) and Motueka (p161)

Drink A remarkable array of New Zealand craft beer at the Free House in Nelson (p157)

Read *Kahurangi Calling* by Gerard Hindmarsh – stories from the backcountry of northwest Nelson

Listen to Regular live music at Golden Bay's Mussel Inn (p173)

Watch The tide roll in, and then watch it roll away again…

Swim at Pelorus Bridge between Nelson and Blenheim (p145). Brrrrr!

Festival Marlborough Wine Festival (p138)

Tackiest tourist attraction The creepy Mickey Mouse and Donald Duck statues standing sentry at the Picton Foreshore playground

Go green Golden Bay (p169) – more sustainable living, untrammelled wilderness and organic food than you can lob a lentil at

---

agrarian Blenheim and the world-famous Marlborough Wine Region, and further south still Kaikoura, made famous by whales.

History

Long before Abel Tasman sheltered on the east coast of D'Urville Island in 1642 (more than 100 years before James Cook blew through in 1770), Maori traders and war parties knew the Marlborough area as Te Tau Ihu o Te Waka a Maui (the prow of Maui's canoe). Cook named Queen Charlotte Sound; his detailed reports made the area the best-known sheltered anchorage in the southern hemisphere. In 1827 French navigator Jules Dumont d'Urville discovered the narrow strait now known as French Pass. His officers named the island just to the north in his honour. In the same year a whaling station was established at Te Awaiti in Tory Channel, which brought about the first permanent European settlement in the district.

PICTON

pop 4000

Half asleep in winter, but hyperactive in summer (with up to eight fully-laden ferry arrivals per day), Picton clusters around a deep gulch at the head of Queen Charlotte Sound. It's the main traveller port for the South Island, and the best place from which to explore the Marlborough Sounds and tackle the Queen

Charlotte Track. To its credit, Picton manages to be touristy and transient but low-key and genuine at the same time.

Information

Creek Pottery (☎ 03-573 6313; 26 High St; ☻ 9am-5.30pm) Stocks souvenirs and has internet access (per hour $6).

Picton i-SITE (☎ 03-520 3113; www.destinationmarl borough.com; Foreshore; ☻ 9am-5pm Mon-Fri, to 4pm Sat & Sun) All vital tourist guff including maps and QC Track information. Internet ($6 per hr). Department of Conservation (DOC) counter staffed during summer.

Picton Library (☎ 03-520 7493; 67 High St; ☻ 8am-5pm Mon-Fri, 10am-1pm Sat) Free wi-fi internet access

Police station (☎ 03-520 3120; picton.police@police. govt.nz; 36 Broadway; ☻ 8.30am-4.30pm Mon-Fri)

Post office (Mariners Mall, 72 High St)

Sights & Activities

The *Edwin Fox* is purportedly the world's ninth-oldest wooden ship (who counts these things?). Built of teak in Bengal, the 48m, 750-tonne vessel was launched in 1853. During its chequered career it carried troops to the Crimean War, convicts to Australia and immigrants to NZ. The **Edwin Fox Maritime Museum** (☎ 03-573 6868; www.edwinfoxsociety.co.nz; Dunbar Wharf; adult/child $10/4; ☻ 9am-5pm) has maritime exhibits including the venerable old dear, preserved under cover.

Next door, the **Eco World Aquarium** (☎ 03-573 6030; www.ecoworldnz.co.nz; Dunbar Wharf; adult/child/family $19/9/49; ☻ 10am-8pm Dec-Feb, 10am-5.30pm Mar-Nov) has hundreds of fish and a veritable menagerie of native critters, including tuatara, gecko and giant weta. Fish-feeding time (11am and 2pm) is a hit with kids. Just before dusk watch the resident blue penguins returning from their fishing trips. There's also an art-house cinema here (p129).

Above the foreshore, the **Picton Museum** (☎ 03-573 8283; pictonmuseum@xtra.co.nz; London Quay; adult/child $4/1; ☻ 9am-4pm Mar-Nov, to 5pm Dec-Feb) has a collection of whale bones, shells and model ships, and displays on local history and Maori lore.

A free i-SITE map details several walks around town, including an easy 1km track along Picton Harbour's eastern side to Bob's Bay. The **Snout Walkway** (three hours return) continues along the ridge from Bob's Bay offering superb Queen Charlotte Sound views.

Diving opportunities around the Sounds include the wreck of the 577ft *Mikhail*

MARLBOROUGH & NELSON

PICTON

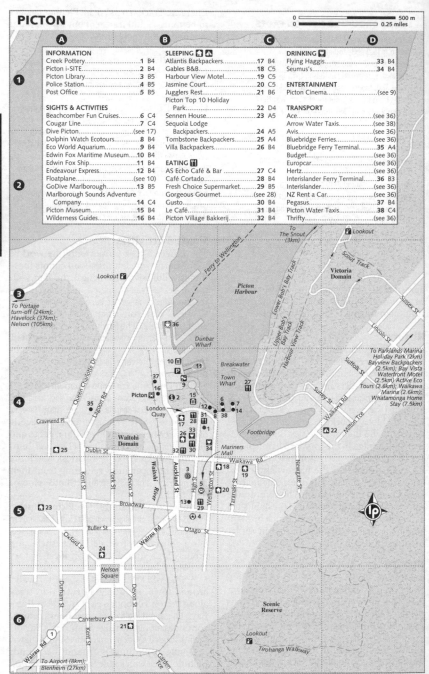

0 ——————————— 500 m
0 ——————————— 0.25 miles

INFORMATION
Creek Pottery..........................**1**	B4
Picton i-SITE..........................**2**	B4
Picton Library........................**3**	B5
Police Station........................**4**	B5
Post Office............................**5**	B5

SIGHTS & ACTIVITIES
Beachcomber Fun Cruises........**6**	C4
Cougar Line............................**7**	C4
Dive Picton.......................(see 17)	
Dolphin Watch Ecotours...........**8**	B4
Eco World Aquarium.................**9**	B4
Edwin Fox Maritime Museum...**10**	B4
Edwin Fox Ship.......................**11**	B4
Endeavour Express..................**12**	B4
Floatplane.........................(see 10)	
GoDive Marlborough...............**13**	B5
Marlborough Sounds Adventure	
Company..........................**14**	C4
Picton Museum......................**15**	B4
Wilderness Guides..................**16**	B4

SLEEPING 🏠 🏕
Atlantis Backpackers...............**17**	B4
Gables B&B...........................**18**	C5
Harbour View Motel................**19**	C5
Jasmine Court........................**20**	C5
Jugglers Rest.........................**21**	B6
Picton Top 10 Holiday	
Park..................................**22**	D4
Sennen House........................**23**	A5
Sequoia Lodge	
Backpackers.....................**24**	A5
Tombstone Backpackers...........**25**	A4
Villa Backpackers....................**26**	B4

EATING 🍴
AS Echo Café & Bar.................**27**	C4
Café Cortado.........................**28**	B4
Fresh Choice Supermarket........**29**	B5
Gorgeous Gourmet.............(see 28)	
Gusto...................................**30**	B4
Le Café.................................**31**	B4
Picton Village Bakkerij.............**32**	B4

DRINKING 🍸
Flying Haggis.........................**33**	B4
Seumus's..............................**34**	B4

ENTERTAINMENT
Picton Cinema.....................(see 9)	

TRANSPORT
Ace.................................(see 36)	
Arrow Water Taxis..............(see 38)	
Avis................................(see 36)	
Bluebridge Ferries...............(see 36)	
Bluebridge Ferry Terminal......**35**	A4
Budget............................(see 36)	
Europcar...........................(see 36)	
Hertz...............................(see 36)	
Interislander Ferry Terminal....**36**	B3
Interislander.....................(see 36)	
NZ Rent a Car...................(see 36)	
Pegasus.............................**37**	B4
Picton Water Taxis................**38**	C4
Thrifty............................(see 36)	

Lermontov, a Russian cruise ship that sank in Port Gore in 1986. Two operators offer dive courses and dive trips (both from around $185, including gear hire):

Dive Picton (☎ 0800 423 483, 03-573 7323; www. scubadive.co.nz; cnr Auckland St & London Quay)

GoDive Marlborough (☎ 0800 463 483, 03-573 9181; www.godive.co.nz; 97 High St)

Floatplane (☎ 021 704 248; www.nz-scenic-flights.co.nz; Picton Ferry Terminal) offers transfers and scenic tours (minimum two people) to Ship Cove (track transfer $125; 20-minute tour $140) and into the outer Sounds (40 minute/one hour $210/325). It also runs Cook Strait crossings from Porirua (near Wellington) to Nelson and the Abel Tasman (from $275).

Tours

There are loads of local tours, most of which focus on the Queen Charlotte Track (on foot, bike or kayak), Motuara Island bird sanctuary and other wildlife in the surrounds. See p130 for the full rundown. For winery tours around Blenheim, see p137.

Sleeping

BUDGET

Atlantis Backpackers (☎ 03-573 7390; www.atlantis hostel.co.nz; cnr Auckland St & London Quay; dm $25-28, tw/d $55/65, units $150, all incl breakfast; 🖥 🛜 🛍) Close to the ferry terminal, the basic rooms at Atlantis are cheap, but dorms are humongous (up to 28 beds). Facilities include an indoor heated pool, pool table and movie room. Basic next-door units sleep four.

Tombstone Backpackers (☎ 0800 573 7116, 03-573 7116; www.tombstonebp.co.nz; 16 Gravesend Pl; dm $25, d with/without bathroom $75/70; 🖥 🛜) Picton cemetery is across the street – a fact these hosts have turned into a marketing masterstroke. Beyond a coffin-lid door is one of the best hostels we've seen, catering to the new breed of 'flashpackers'. Hotel-worthy doubles, immaculate dorms, spa overlooking the harbour, free breakfast, sunny reading room, pool table, DVD library, free ferry pick-up and drop-off…the list goes on.

Villa Backpackers (☎ 03-573 6598; www.thevilla. co.nz; 34 Auckland St; dm $25-29, d with/without bathroom $72/63; 🖥 🛜) A blooming garden beckons you into this 1904 house with a cheery kitchen, log fires, free bikes and a spa. There are indoor and outdoor lounge areas plus in-demand en-suite rooms. Switched-on staff,

fresh flowers and free apple crumble on winter nights make this a real home away from home. The staff will also sort out your Queen Charlotte Track bookings (camping gear hire available), and more.

Sequoia Lodge Backpackers (☎ 0800 222 257, 03-573 8399; www.sequoialodge.co.nz; 3a Nelson Sq; dm $25, d with/without bathroom $78/64, all incl breakfast; 🖥 🛜) A well-managed backpackers in a colourful, high-ceilinged Victorian house. It's a little out of the centre, but a stone's throw from a pub, general store and its namesake conifers. Bonuses include quality linen, jumbo TV, videos, hammocks, barbecues, spa and nightly chocolate pudding!

Parklands Marina Holiday Park (☎ 0800 111 104, 03-573 6343; www.parktostay.co.nz; 10 Beach Rd; unpowered/powered sites $26/28, cabins $45-55, units $70-88; 🖥 🛜 🛍) Large, leafy campground with verdant bush backdrop. Three kilometres out of town, but close to pretty Waikawa Bay. Free Picton pick-up/drop-off.

Bayview Backpackers (☎ 03-573 7668; www.truenz .co.nz/bayviewbackpackers; 318 Waikawa Rd; dm $27, d with/without bathroom $78/64; 🖥) Overlooking Waikawa Bay 4km from town, Bayview feels like your house did in 1987. Or maybe your neighbour's house. Either way, it's a low-key place with friendly owners and sunny porch areas. Free kayaks and bicycles are available too.

Jugglers Rest (☎ 03-573 5570; www.jugglersrest. com; 8 Canterbury St; unpowered sites $36, dm $30, d $64-68; 🖥 🛜) Jocular hosts keep all their balls up in the air at this well-run and homely bunk-free backpackers. Peacefully located in the 'burbs, it's a 10-minute walk to the town centre or even quicker on a free bike. Cheery, private gardens are a good place to socialise with fellow travellers or soak in the outdoor bath. Closed from June to October.

Picton Top 10 Holiday Park (☎ 0800 277 444, 03-573 7212; www.pictontop10.co.nz; 70-78 Waikawa Rd; unpowered/powered sites $38/40, cabins $65-85, self-contained units $105-140; 🖥 🛜 🛍) About 500m from town, this is a well-kept park with modern, family-friendly facilities, including playground, covered barbecue area, heated swimming pool and a super recreation room.

MIDRANGE & TOP END

Gables B&B (☎ 03-573 6772; www.thegables.co.nz; 20 Waikawa Rd; s $100, d $130-160, units $155-175, all incl breakfast; 🖥) This historic B&B (once home to Picton's mayor) has three spacious, themed en-suite rooms in the main house and two more upmarket units with kitchenettes and lounges out the back. Unit prices drop if you organise your own breakfast. Lovely hosts show good humour (ask about the Muffin Club).

Bay Vista Waterfront Motel (☎ 03-573 6733; www.bayvistapicton.co.nz; 303 Waikawa Rd; d $120-165; ☎) Recently redecorated and neat as a new pin, this motel sits right at the water's edge, with lush lawn and views across Queen Charlotte Sound. All units have kitchen facilities. Located 4km from Picton (courtesy transfer available by request).

Harbour View Motel (☎ 0800 101 133, 03-573 6259; www.harbourviewpicton.co.nz; 30 Waikawa Rd; d $120-170; ☎) This tastefully decorated motel enjoys an elevated position, affording views of Picton's mast-filled harbour from its self-contained studios with timber decks.

Jasmine Court (☎ 0800 421 999, 03-573 7110; www.jasminecourt.co.nz; 78 Wellington St; d $130-210, f $185-225; ☎ ☎) Top-notch, spacious motel with plush interiors, kitchenette, free DVD player and plunger coffee. Some rooms have a spa; upstairs balconies have harbour views.

Whatamonga Home Stay (☎ 03-573 7192; www.whsl.co.nz; 425 Port Underwood Rd; d incl breakfast $155; ☎ ☎) Follow Waikawa Rd 8km around the eastern side of Picton Harbour (Waikawa Rd becomes Port Underwood Rd), and you'll bump into this classy waterside accommodation. Run by a couple of chirpy Scots, it has two detached, self-contained units with king-sized beds and balconies with magic views. Two other rooms under the main house (also

with views) share a bathroom. Free kayaks, dinghies and fishing gear are available.

Sennen House (☎ 03-573 5216; www.sennenhouse.co.nz; 9 Oxford St; d incl gourmet breakfast hamper $269-479; ☎ ☎) Tucked against a steep hillside of regenerating native bush (the odd black-faced sheep in its midst), Sennen House is an exquisitely restored, 1886 weatherboard homestead. Inside are five plush apartments and suites, each with its own entrance and kitchenette facilities, as well as sunny verandas and private lounge/dining areas.

Eating & Drinking

our pick Picton Village Bakkerij (☎ 03-573 7082; 46 Auckland St; items $2-7; ☎ 6am-3.30pm; ☑) Dutch owners bake trays of European goodies here, including interesting breads, scrumptious pies, super sandwiches, cakes and custardy, tarty treats. Look for the cut-out Amsterdam roofline stapled to the eaves.

Gorgeous Gourmet (☎ 03-573 8388; 3a High St; items $6-14.50; ☎ 7.30am-6pm Mon-Fri, 8am-4pm Sat & Sun; ☑) Hybrid sandwich shop meets microdeli, with great coffee to boot. Delectable salads, charcuterie, filled rolls, ready meals and artisan cheeses (don't go past the Over the Moon brie).

Seumus's (☎ 03-573 8994; 25 Wellington St; meals $7-24; ☎ noon-1am) An authentically snug drinking den, pouring a reliable Guinness and a good selection of whiskies. Mix it all up with hearty bar food and regular live music, and you've got the recipe for the liveliest joint in town.

Flying Haggis (☎ 03-573 6969; 27 High St; meals $8-24; ☎ noon-late) Proudly displaying a Glaswegian connection, this otherwise nondescript pub rustles up baked potatoes, toasties and fish and chips, which can be washed down with imported Scottish ales. Musos drift in from the hills occasionally and twang their guitars.

AS Echo Café & Bar (☎ 03-573 7498; Shelley Beach; meals $6-30; ☎ 10am-8.30pm daily) The deck of this old trading scow, built in 1905 but now high 'n' dry on concrete stumps, is a quirky place for a drink or home-cooked food, and a good spot to spy the comings and goings in the marina.

Gusto (☎ 03-573 7171; 33 High St; meals $12-19; ☎ 7.30am-2.30pm) This workaday joint, with friendly staff and outdoor tables, injects some class into Picton's cafe scene. Beaut breakfasts (French toast with bacon, maple syrup and berry coulis), fantastic coffee, and locally sourced mains (mussels, lamb and venison).

MAORI NZ: MARLBOROUGH & NELSON

Maori culture on the South Island is often less obvious than in the north, but that doesn't mean it's any less potent. In the Marlborough and Nelson regions, the following operators are keyed into *Maoritanga* (Maori culture):

- **Maori Tours Kaikoura** (p146) Small-group history and cultural tours around Kaikoura
- **Myths & Legends Eco-tours** (p130) Eco-oriented cultural and wildlife cruises on the Marlborough Sounds
- **Shark Nett Gallery** (p135) Contemporary Maori carving gallery

Le Café (☎ 03-573 5588; London Quay; lunch $10-20, dinner $19-28; ☷ 7.30am-10.30pm) Due credit for longevity and for food that the locals still favour; we found the space a bit tired and the service dicey when we visited. The food, however, tasted made-from-scratch: salami sandwiches, quiche, pasta and mussels, plus sweet tart for afters. Great Havana coffee and occasional live gigs.

Café Cortado (☎ 03-573 5630; cnr High St & London Quay; mains $17-29; ☷ 8am-late) A pleasant corner cafe with sneaky views of the harbour through the foreshore's pohutukawa and palms. Quite possibly your best bet for a 'sophisticated' meal in a town with limited, decent dining of an evening. The menu focuses on local fish, steak, lamb, pizzas and salads, with bar snacks available too.

Self-caterers can head to **Fresh Choice Supermarket** (☎ 03-573 6463; Mariners Mall, 100 High St; ☷ 7am-9pm).

Entertainment

Picton Cinema (☎ 03-573 6030; www.pictoncinemas.co.nz; Dunbar Wharf; adult/child $15/9; ☷ 10am-8pm) Two microtheatres within the Eco World Aquarium complex showing an excellent program of art-house movies. There is a combo-pass available for cinema and aquarium (adult/child $28/15).

Getting There & Away

Make bookings for trains, ferries and buses at Picton i-SITE and Picton Train Station.

AIR

Soundsair (☎ 0800 505 005, 03-520 3080; www.sounds air.com) flies between Picton and Wellington (adult/child $89/77, up to eight daily). There are discounts for online bookings, and a courtesy shuttle bus ($3) to/from the airstrip at Koromiko, 8km south.

BOAT

There are two operators crossing Cook Strait between Picton and Wellington, and although all ferries leave from more or less the same place, each has its own terminal. The main transport hub (and car rental offices) is at the Interislander Terminal, which also has public showers, a cafe and internet facilities. Timetables below are subject to change.

Bluebridge Ferries (☎ 0800 844 844, in Wellington 04-471 6188; www.bluebridge.co.nz; adult/child $50/25)

Crossing takes three hours 20 minutes. Departs Wellington at 3am, 8am, 1pm and 9pm daily (no 3am or 9pm services on Saturdays). Departs Picton at 2am, 8am, 2pm and 7pm daily (no 8am service on Saturdays; no 2am service on Sundays). Cars and campervans up to 4m long from $110; campervans under 5.5m from $150; motorbikes $50; bicycles $10.

Interislander (☎ 0800 802 802, in Wellington 04-498 3302; www.interislander.co.nz; adult/child from $46/23) Crossing takes three hours 10 minutes. Departs Wellington at 2.25am, 8.25am, 2.05pm and 6.25pm. Departs Picton at 6.25am, 10.05am, 1.10pm, 6.05pm and 10.25pm. From November through to April there's an extra 10.25am sailing from Wellington and an extra 2.25pm sailing from Picton. Cars are priced from $101; campervans (up to 5.5m) from $126; motorbikes $46; bicycles $15.

BUS

Buses serving Picton depart the Interislander terminal or nearby i-SITE.

InterCity (☎ 03-365 1113; www.intercitycoach.co.nz; Picton Ferry Terminal) runs services south to Christchurch ($55, 5½ hours, two daily), via Kaikoura ($35, 2½ hours, two daily) with connections to Dunedin, Queenstown and Invercargill. Services also run to/from Nelson ($34, 2¼ hours, three daily), with connections to Motueka and the West Coast; and to/from Blenheim ($15, 30 minutes, five daily). At least one bus daily on each of these routes connects with a Wellington ferry service. Keep an eye on discounted internet fares – at the time of research, Picton to Christchurch was a supercheap $25.

Smaller shuttle buses running from Picton to Christchurch (around $40, door to door) include:

Atomic Shuttles (☎ 03-349 0697; www.atomictravel. co.nz)

Naked Bus (☎ 0900 625 33; www.nakedbus.com)

Southern Link (☎ 0508 458 835, 03-358 8355; www. southernlinkcoaches.co.nz)

TRAIN

Tranz Scenic (☎ 0800 872 467, 04-495 0775; www.tranz scenic.co.nz) runs the *TranzCoastal* service daily each way between Picton and Christchurch via Blenheim and Kaikoura (and 22 tunnels and 175 bridges!), departing Christchurch at 7am, Picton at 1pm. The standard adult one-way Picton–Christchurch fare is $104, but discounted fares can be as low as $39. The service connects with the *Interislander* ferry (included in Wellington to Christchurch fares).

MARLBOROUGH & NELSON

Getting Around

Renting a car in Picton is easy-peasy – as low as $35 per day if you shop around. Most agencies allow drop-offs in Christchurch; if you're planning to drive to the North Island, most companies suggest you leave your car at Picton and pick up another one in Wellington after crossing Cook Strait. Take a punt on a cheaper local operator, or the big-namers at the Interislander terminal:

Ace (☎ 03-573 8939; www.acerentalcars.co.nz)
Apex (☎ 03-573 7009; www.apexrentals.co.nz)
Avis (☎ 03-520 3156; www.avis.co.nz)
Budget (☎ 03-573 6081; www.budget.co.nz)
Europcar (☎ 03-573 8800; www.europcar.com)
Hertz (☎ 03-520 3044; www.hertz.co.nz)
NZ Rent a car (☎ 03-573 7282; www.nzrentacar.co.nz)
Pegasus (☎ 03-577 9066; www.carrentalsblenheim. co.nz)**Thrifty** (☎ 03-573 7387; www.thrifty.co.nz)

Shuttles (and tours) around Picton and wider Marlborough are offered by **Marlborough Sounds Shuttles & Tours** (☎ 03-573 7122). Between Picton and Havelock (via Anakiwa) you can hitch a van ride on **Coleman Post** (☎ 027 255 8882; $15). It departs Picton at 8.15am and Havelock at 10.45am, with other services on request.

See right for details on water taxis servicing the Sounds.

MARLBOROUGH SOUNDS

The Marlborough Sounds are a geographic maze of inlets, headlands, peaks, beaches and watery reaches, formed when the sea flooded into deep valleys after the last ice age. Parts of the Sounds are included in the Marlborough Sounds Maritime Park – a series of small reserves punctuated by private land. To get an idea of how convoluted the sounds are, Pelorus Sound is 42km long but has 379km of shoreline. If you have your own wheels, the wiggly, verdant 35km drive along Queen Charlotte Dr from Picton to Havelock is a great Sounds snapshot (even on a rainy day).

The Queen Charlotte Track is the main lure for trampers, but the two-day Nydia Track (p145) is also worthwhile. Secluded accommodation (boutique and rudimentary) is scattered throughout the Sounds.

Tours

FROM PICTON

The bulk of Marlborough Sounds tours are based in Picton, many at the new Town Wharf.

Active Eco Tours (☎ 03-573 7199; www.sealswim ming.com; Essons Valley; full-day seal swim & sightseeing tour incl equipment adult/child $125/95; ⊙ 9am-5pm) Get underwater with speedy Sounds seals. Tours leave Picton or Waikawa; free pick-up.

Arrow Water Taxis (☎ 03-573 8229, 027 444 4689; www.arrowwatertaxis.co.nz; Town Wharf)

Beachcomber Fun Cruises (☎ 0800 624 526, 03-573 6175; www.beachcombercruises.co.nz; Town Wharf; mail run $85, cruises $69-85) Two- to four-hour cruises, some with resort lunches. Cruise/walk, cruise/bike, and QC Track options also available.

Cougar Line (☎ 0800 504 090, 03-573 7925; www.cou garlinecruises.co.nz; Town Wharf; cruises adult/child from $68/34) QC Track transport, plus various half- and full-day cruise/walk deals including the rather special (and flexible) ecocruise trip to Motuara Island bird sanctuary.

Dolphin Watch Ecotours (☎ 0800 9453 5433, 03-573 8040; www.naturetours.co.nz; Town Wharf; swimming/ viewing tour $150/100) Half-day 'swim with dolphins' and wildlife tours around Queen Charlotte Sound and Motuara Island bird sanctuary. QC Track cruise/walk options also available.

Endeavour Express (☎ 03-573 5456; www.boatrides. co.nz; Town Wharf; 1- to 4-day cruise/walk options $35-90) Backpacker-friendly company offering cruise/ walk options and QC Track transfers. Mountain bikes and camping gear for hire.

Marlborough Sounds Adventure Company
(☎ 0800 283 283, 03-573 6078; www.marlborough sounds.co.nz; Town Wharf; half- to 3-day tours $75-245) Bike-kayak-walk trips, with options to suit every inclination. The '1-day multi' guided kayak trip followed by QC Track hike ($135) or bike ($155) is a brilliant Sounds sampler. Gear rental (bikes, kayaks, camping gear) also available.

Myths & Legends Eco-tours (☎ 03-573 6901; www. eco-tours.co.nz; half-/full-day cruises $150/200) A Sounds day on the water with a local Maori family – longtime locals, storytellers and environmentalists. There are five different trips to choose from, including birdwatching and visiting Ship Cove.

Picton Water Taxis (☎ 03-573 7853, 027 227 0284; www.pictonwatertaxis.co.nz; Town Wharf; ⊙ 24hr)

Sea Kayak Adventure Tours (☎ 0800 262 5492, 03-574 2765; www.nzseakayaking.com; Anakiwa Rd, Anakiwa; half-/1-day guided tours $65/95) Guided and independent kayaking trips around Queen Charlotte and Kenepuru Sounds. Also one-day paddle and walk ($85) or paddle and bike ($120) freedom options. Kayak and mountain-bike hire from $50 per day.

Waterways Boating Safaris (☎ 03-574 1372; www. waterways.co.nz; 745 Kenepuru Rd; half-day $95, full-day $125) It's a boat tour Cap'n, but not as we know it. Buzz around majestic Kenepuru Sound in your own craft, while

MARLBOROUGH SOUNDS

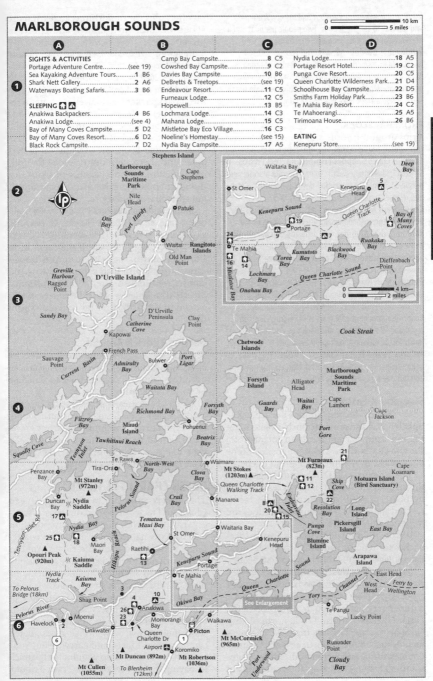

SIGHTS & ACTIVITIES	
Portage Adventure Centre............(see 19)	
Sea Kayaking Adventure Tours.......**1** B6	
Shark Nett Gallery.........................**2** A6	
Waterways Boating Safaris.............**3** B6	
SLEEPING	
Anakiwa Backpackers....................**4** B6	
Anakiwa Lodge............................(see 4)	
Bay of Many Coves Campsite.........**5** D2	
Bay of Many Coves Resort.............**6** D2	
Black Rock Campsite.....................**7** D2	

Camp Bay Campsite......................**8** C5	
Cowshed Bay Campsite..................**9** C2	
Davies Bay Campsite.....................**10** B6	
DeBretts & Treetops.....................(see 19)	
Endeavour Resort.........................**11** C5	
Furneaux Lodge...........................**12** C5	
Hopewell.....................................**13** B5	
Lochmara Lodge...........................**14** C3	
Mahana Lodge.............................**15** C3	
Mistletoe Bay Eco Village..............**16** C3	
Noeline's Homestay......................(see 15)	
Nydia Bay Campsite......................**17** A5	

Nydia Lodge................................**18** A5	
Portage Resort Hotel....................**19** C2	
Punga Cove Resort.......................**20** C5	
Queen Charlotte Wilderness Park....**21** D4	
Schoolhouse Bay Campsite............**22** D5	
Smiths Farm Holiday Park..............**23** B6	
Te Mahia Bay Resort.....................**24** C2	
Te Mahoerangi.............................**25** A5	
Tirimoana House..........................**26** B6	
EATING	
Kenepuru Store............................(see 19)	

MARLBOROUGH & NELSON

learning about the area's ecology and history. A unique and fun way to see the Sounds. Two people per boat and a maximum of five boats per guide. BYO lunch.

Wilderness Guides (☎ 0800 266 266, 03-520 3095; www.wildernessguidesnz.com; Picton Railway Station, 3 Auckland St; 1- to 4-day trip incl lunch $90-570) Guided and independent kayak/walk or kayak/bike tours on the QC Track or Nydia Track. Bike hire $50 per day.

FROM HAVELOCK
Trips around Pelorus and Kenepuru Sound generally leave from Havelock (see p135).

Captain Clay's Snapper Fishing Charters (☎ 03-574 2911; bluecottage@actrix.co.nz; Havelock Marina; per person $125, min 2 people) Half-day or longer trips. Catch and release or take it home for your tea.

Green Shell Mussel Cruise (☎ 0800 990 800, 03-577 9997; www.greenshellmusselcruise.co.nz; Havelock Marina; adult/child $120/free; ☺ departs 1.30pm) Half-day cruise on a luxury catamaran to mussel in on Kenepuru's aquaculture. Includes a feed of steamed mussels and a glass of wine. Bookings essential.

Pelorus Mail Run (☎ 03-574 1088; www.mail-boat.co.nz; Jetty 1, Havelock Marina; adult/child $120/free; ☺ departs 9.30am Tue, Thu & Fri) Popular full-day boat cruise through the far reaches of Pelorus Sound on a genuine NZ Post delivery run. Bookings essential; BYO lunch. Picton pick-up and drop-off available.

Pelorus Sound Water Taxi (☎ 03-574 2151; www.pelorusbelle.com; Jetty 1a, Havelock Marina) Taxi services and sightseeing trips made to order.

Sleeping & Eating
Some Sounds sleeping options are accessible only by boat and are deliciously isolated, but the most popular are those on (or just off) the Queen Charlotte Track (opposite). Some places close over winter; call ahead to check.

There are over 30 DOC camping grounds throughout the Sounds (many accessible only by boat), providing water and toilet facilities but not much else; cooking facilities are nonexistent.

Picton i-SITE (p125) has a list of local baches for rent, or you could try **Sounds Great Holiday Homes** (☎ 03-574 1221; www.soundsgreat.co.nz).

Queen Charlotte Wilderness Park (☎ 03-579 9025; www.truenz.co.nz/wilderness; Cape Jackson; per person 2 nights/3 days $329 or 3 nights/4 days $429) This private nature reserve allows you to venture on to the Outer Queen Charlotte Track, north of Ship Cove up to Cape Jackson. Inclusive packages includes accommodation in en-suite twins or doubles, meals and Picton transfers. Wildlife-spotting, fishing, kayaking and tramping are

on offer, plus the opportunity to learn more about the local environment and efforts to preserve it.

Hopewell (☎ 03-573 4341; www.hopewell.co.nz; Kenepuru Sound; dm from $30, d with/without bathroom from $120/98, 4-person cottage (for 2 adults) $160; ☺ closed Jun-Aug; ☐ ☎) One of NZ's best-loved backpackers, Hopewell occupies a remote corner of Kenepuru Sound, surrounded by native bush opening onto the sea. Road access is possible, but the long, bumpy drive makes a water taxi from Te Mahia far preferable. Once here, chill out or enjoy the roll-call of facilities: books, games, outdoor spa, mountain bikes, kayaks, fishing equipment, gourmet pizzas and more.

Smiths Farm Holiday Park (☎ 03-574 2806; www.smithsfarm.co.nz; 1419 Queen Charlotte Dr, Linkwater; unpowered/powered sites $32/36, cabins $60-110, motel units $130; ☐ ☎) Just east of the turn-off to Portage, Smiths is a usefully positioned caravan park with lush camping lawns and comfy, well-looked-after cabins and units. Livestock nibbles around the fences; walks extend to a nearby waterfall and glowworm dell.

Getting There & Around
The best way to get around the Sounds is by boat, and fortunately there is a plethora of operators who will oblige either to schedule or on-demand (p130).

Much of the area is accessible by car. The road is sealed to the head of Kenepuru Sound, but beyond that it's nothing but narrow gravel roads with more twists than a hurricane. To drive to Punga Cove from Picton takes two to three hours (45 minutes by boat).

QUEEN CHARLOTTE TRACK
The hugely popular, meandering Queen Charlotte Track offers gorgeous coastal scenery, isolated coves, diverse accommodation and back-to-nature campsites. The coastal forest is lush, and from the ridges you can look down on either side to Queen Charlotte and Kenepuru Sounds. The 71km track connects historic Ship Cove with Anakiwa, passing through privately owned land (40% of the track) and DOC reserves. Access depends on the cooperation of local landowners; respect their property by utilising designated campsites and toilets, and carrying out your rubbish. You can also do your bit for the track by paying the very modest $5 'Track Tribute'

fee at the Picton wharf or wherever you see a payment box.

Queen Charlotte is a well-defined track, suitable for people of average fitness. You can do the walk in sections using local water-taxi transport, or walk the whole three- to five-day journey. Sleeping options are only half a day's walk apart; boat operators will transport your pack along the track for you. Though there aren't the hordes that tramp the Abel Tasman, there's some solid summer traffic. You can do part of the trip by sea kayak (see p130).

Mountain biking is a viable alternative for fit, competent off-roaders: it's possible to ride the track in two or three days, guided or self-guided. Note that the section between Ship Cove and Kenepuru Saddle is off-limits to cyclists from December to February. During these months you can still be dropped by boat at the Saddle and ride to Anakiwa.

Ship Cove is the usual (and strongly recommended) starting point – mainly because it's easier to arrange a boat from Picton to Ship Cove than vice versa – but the track can be started from Anakiwa. There's a public phone at Anakiwa but not at Ship Cove. Between Camp Bay and Torea Saddle you'll find the going toughest. About halfway along there's an excellent viewpoint, Eatwell's Lookout, about 20 minutes off the main track.

Estimated walk times:

Track section	Distance	Duration
Ship Cove to Resolution Bay	4.5km	1½-2hr
Resolution Bay to head of Endeavour Inlet	10.5km	2-2¾hr
Endeavour Inlet to Camp Bay/Punga Cove	12km	3-4hr
Camp Bay/Punga Cove to Torea Saddle/Portage	24km	5½-7½hr
Torea Saddle/Portage to Mistletoe Bay	8km	2½-3hr
Mistletoe Bay to Anakiwa	13km	2½-3¾hr

Information
The Picton i-SITE (p125) stocks the *Queen Charlotte Track Visitor Guide* pamphlet and DOC's *Queen Charlotte Track* brochure, and is the best spot for information. Picton's Villa Backpackers is also a hotbed of info, and handles bookings. Check online details at www.qctrack.co.nz.

Tours
Most Picton-based tour companies (see p130) offer Queen Charlotte Track cruises and guided walk/bike/kayak trips.

Sleeping & Eating
Unless you're camping, it pays to book your Queen Charlotte Track accommodation *waaay* in advance, especially in summer. There are six **DOC campsites** (adult/child $6/1.50) along the track, each with toilets and a water supply but no cooking facilities. There's also a variety of resorts, lodges, backpackers and guest houses.

The following listings are arranged in order heading south from Ship Cove (where camping is not permitted). Your overnight stops will depend on how far you can/want to walk on any given day – do your research and book ahead. Not every accommodation option is covered here.

Schoolhouse Bay campsite (Resolution Bay) Beautifully situated, this is the first DOC campsite off the rank.

Furneaux Lodge (☎ 03-579 8259; www.furneauxlodge.co.nz; Endeavour Inlet; dm $30-40, chalets/studios $195/245; 🖳) One of the Sounds' stalwart resorts, Furneaux's highlights are the historic lodge building and a big flat lawn. Backpackers can choose from the old stone cottage ($10 cheaper) or in fresh, double dorms nearer the water. Fancier options are self-contained two-bedroom chalets (sleeping up to six) and swish waterfront studios. Beer, a bowl of chips or a meal ($16 to $35) are available in the bar/restaurant.

Endeavour Resort (☎ 03-579 8381; www.endeavour resort.co.nz; Endeavour Inlet; dm $30-40, cabins $75-90, motels $100-125) Proudly retro 1950s board-and-batten bach-style accommodation in one of the prettiest parts of the Sounds. It's basic, but classic, clean and tidy. Eight units spread among the gardens, most with toilet-shower and kitchen facilities. Games room and library–video room. Free kayaks and dinghies.

Camp Bay campsite (Punga Cove) On the western side of Endeavour Inlet.

Punga Cove Resort (☎ 03-579 8561; www.punga cove.co.nz; Endeavour Inlet; dm $40, lodge $140-175, chalets $175-425; 🖳 🖳) A fairly rustic resort offering self-contained studios, family and luxury A-frame chalets, most with sweeping sea views. Backpackers get a row of decent cabins and a lounge with balcony views. Ample activities (pool, spa, games, kayak and bike hire) plus a shop, restaurant (meals $26 to $37), and bar (decent beers and $22 pizza).

Mahana Lodge (☎ 03-579 8373; www.mahanahomestead.com; Endeavour Inlet; d $110-150) Ann and John's continuously improving property features a pretty waterside lawn and purpose-built lodge with four en-suite doubles (with another double in a wee bach up the back). Ecofriendly initiatives include bush regeneration and pest trapping, although of greater appeal may be the organic veggies you'll find in your optional breakfast, packed lunch, or three-course dinner ($15 to $45). Free fishing gear and kayaks are available.

Noeline's Homestay (☎ 03-579 8375; Endeavour Inlet; s/tw $30/70) Follow the pink arrows from Camp Bay to this relaxed homestay and be greeted by 70-something Noeline, 'the Universal Grandma', and her home-baked treats. It's a friendly arrangement with beds for five people, cooking facilities and great views.

Bay of Many Coves campsite (Bay of Many Coves) On a saddle above the track.

Bay of Many Coves Resort (☎ 0800 5799 771, 03-579 9771; www.bayofmanycovesresort.co.nz; 1-/2-/3-bedroom apt $500/695/950; 🖳 🖳) Honeymooning? These plush and secluded apartments are appropriately sexy. Each has a private balcony shunting you out towards the water, designer bathrooms and all mod cons. The upmarket cafe and restaurant are staffed by a crew of iron chefs. Arrive by boat or via the steep path leading down from the main track.

Black Rock campsite (Kumutoto Bay) Further along past Bay of Many Coves, above Kumutoto Bay.

Portage Resort Hotel (☎ 03-573 4309; www.portage.co.nz; Kenepuru Sound; dm $40, d $165-365; 🖳 🛜 🖳) This fancy resort is centred upon a smart lodge building with Te Weka restaurant (mains $28 to $35), lounge and view-tastic sundeck overlooking the pool patio and lush grounds. The relaxed Snapper Café (mains $15 to $30) is popular with both guests and locals. The 22-bed backpacker wing is pretty good, with small lounge and cooking facilities; tidy, moderately stylish rooms climb the price ladder from there. The on-site **Kenepuru Store** (☎ 03-573 4445; ⏰ 8am-8pm Oct-Apr, to 4.30pm May-Sep) sells newspapers, snacks, select groceries and noteworthy pies which emerge from the bakery out back (along with filled rolls and loaves to go). Underneath the Store is the **Portage Adventure Centre** (☎ 03-573 4111), an outpost of Marlborough Sounds Adventure Company

(see p130), offering trips and freedom hire of bikes and boats.

DeBretts (☎ 03-573 4522; www.stayportage.co.nz; s/d $40/80) and **Treetops** (☎ 03-573 4404; www.staytreetops.com; s/d $40/80), run by the same family, offer a combined total of six bedrooms in two homely backpackers high on the hill above Portage Resort.

Cowshed Bay campsite (Cowshed Bay) Not far from the Portage Resort Hotel.

Lochmara Lodge (☎ 03-573 4554; www.lochmaralodge.co.nz; Lochmara Bay; d $90-120, self-contained units/chalets $180-260; 🖳 🛜) A superb retreat on Lochmara Bay, reached by a side track south of the Queen Charlotte Track or by boat from Picton. Relaxation-inducing facilities include an outdoor spa, hammocks and barbeques. There are en-suite doubles, units and chalets, all set in lush surroundings, and a fully licensed cafe and restaurant serving local, wild and organic produce.

Mistletoe Bay Eco Village (☎ 03-573 4048; www.mistletoebay.co.nz; Mistletoe Bay; unpowered sites adult/child $15/5, dm $25, cabins $120, linen $7.50) On a former DOC reserve and run by a forward-thinking community trust, sweet Mistletoe Bay offers attractive camping, eight irresistible cabins sleeping up to six with communal kitchen, and a cottage with bunks for overflow. Sustainable initiatives include solar power, water conservation, recycling and waste-water treatment. There is also kayak and bike hire.

ourpick Te Mahia Bay Resort (☎ 03-573 4089; www.temahia.co.nz; Kenepuru Sound; d $148-245; 🛜) This sweetly low-key resort is north of the track, just off the main road, in a picturesque bay facing Kenepuru Sound. It has roomy, affordable self-contained units in a late-1800s house, pleasant motel units, plus new luxury self-contained apartments. There's also a store selling precooked meals, pizza, coffee and camping supplies (wine!). It also has kayaks for hire.

Davies Bay campsite (Umungata) Also a popular picnic spot, with barbecue facilities nearby.

Anakiwa Backpackers (☎ 03-574 1338; www.anakiwabackpackers.co.nz; 401 Anakiwa Rd; dm $33, d $76-96, unit (sleeps 4) $155; 🖳 🛜) This former schoolhouse (1926) greets you at the southern end of the track – a soothing spot to rest and reflect. There are two doubles (one with en suite, a four-bed dorm and beachy self-contained unit, all freshly decorated. The spirited owners will have you jumping off the jetty for joy (among other available watery activities), but also offer espresso and ice cream (hallelujah) from their little green caravan-cafe (open afternoons). Free kayak hire.

Anakiwa Lodge (☎ 03-574 2115; www.anakiwa.co.nz; 9 Lady Cobham Gr; dm $31, d $77-127; 🖳 🛜) This modern YHA backpackers, 70m from the water, has a bush and pasture backdrop. Four-bed dorms and doubles, some with en suite and DVD player. Spa, DVD library, free kayak hire and barbecue area.

Tirimoana House (☎ 03-574 2627; www.tirimoanahouse.com; 257 Anakiwa Rd; d incl breakfast $200-320; 🛜 🐾) Owned by a couple of prolific painters and about 1.5km down the road from the end of the track, this bold B&B is full to the gunwales with fabulous antique furniture. Every room has its own bathroom, sea views and balcony, plus there's a spa-with-a-view and a swimming pool. Gourmet breakfast buffet, and dinner on request.

Getting Around

Numerous boat operators service the track, allowing you to start and finish where you like. Transport costs around $90 return, $50 for a one-way drop-off (depending on where you're going), and usually includes pack transfers so you can walk with a small daypack while your heavy gear awaits you at your chosen accommodation. Bikes and kayaks can also be transported.

A full list of transport operators (many of whom offer walk/bike/kayak combos, scenic cruises and on-demand taxi services) can be found on p130.

HAVELOCK
pop 470

The highlight of tiny Havelock is its industrious harbour, which helps the town maintain the title of 'Greenshell Mussel Capital of the World'. Havelock sits at the confluence of the Pelorus and Kaiuma Rivers, 36km west of Picton, and makes a practical base from which to explore the less visited Pelorus and Kenepuru Sounds.

Located at the YHA, **Havelock Infocentre** (☎ 03-574 2104; www.havelockinfocentre.co.nz; 46 Main Rd; ⏰ 8.30am-9pm) books tours and transport, and offers regional advice. The centre doubles as a DOC agent.

Sights & Activities

Shark Nett Gallery (☎ 03-574 2877; admin@sharknett. co.nz; 129 Queen Charlotte Dr; adult/child $12/6.50; ⏰ 10am-

4pm) Overlooking the tidal Pelorus estuary, this unique gallery showcases contemporary Maori carving relating to the local Rangitane *iwi* (tribes). Tours provide an educational and evocative insight into how carving is used to record tribal *tikanga* (customs) and *whakapapa* (ancestry). There is also a cafe on-site.

Eighteen kilometres west of Havelock is **Pelorus Bridge Scenic Reserve**, a pretty forest remnant and riverside recreation area. Explore its many tracks, take a dip in the limpid (but chilly) Pelorus River, or indulge in some home-baking at the cafe. Lucky campers can stay overnight in the wonderful **DOC campsite** (☎ 03-571 6019; www.doc.govt.nz; unpowered/powered sites $20/22), managed by the cafe owners.

The **Nydia Track** (27km, 10 hours) starts at Kaiuma Bay and ends at Duncan Bay (or vice versa). Around halfway is beautiful Nydia Bay where there's a **DOC campsite** (adult/child $6/1.50) and DOC's **Nydia Lodge** (Map p131; ☎ 03-520 3002; www.doc.govt.nz; dm $15), an unhosted 50-bed lodge (four-person minimum). You'll need water and road transport to complete the journey; Blue Moon (below) runs a shuttle to Duncan Bay, or make your arrangements at the Havelock Infocentre where you can also pay your camp fees or book the lodge. **Te Mahoerangi** (Map p131; ☎ 03-579 8411; www.nydiatrack. org.nz; dm/d $30/90) offers alternative accommodation at Nydia Bay in a tranquil, ecofocused backpackers. Profits are ploughed back into local environmental protection efforts; ask about volunteering/wwoofing opportunities.

Tours

Look to the water for tours around these parts. Turn to p130 to find them (or book at the Havelock Infocentre).

Sleeping & Eating

Rutherford YHA (☎ 03-574 2104; www.yha.co.nz; 46 Main Rd; unpowered sites $24, dm/d $28/66; 🖳 🛜) A well-equipped YHA filling an 1881 schoolhouse once attended by Lord Ernest Rutherford, father of nuclear physics. Rooms are simple and comfy (doubles are nicer than dorms). It might pay to bring the earplugs.

Blue Moon (☎ 03-574 2212; www.bluemoonhavelock. co.nz; 48 Main Rd; dm $25, d $66-86; 🖳) This largely unremarkable lodge has homely rooms in the main house (one with en suite), as well as cabins and a bunkhouse in the yard (along with a spa pool). The lounge and kitchen are pleasant and relaxed, as is the sunny barbecue deck.

Havelock Motor Camp (☎ 03-574 2339; www.have
lockmotorcamp.co.nz; 24 Inglis St; unpowered/powered sites
$26/30, cabins $44; ☒) Near the marina, this well-
maintained park offers totally acceptable sites,
basic cabins and spick-and-span facilities.

Havelock Garden Motel (☎ 03-574 2387; www.
gardenmotels.com; 71 Main Rd; d $99-150) An exem-
plary family-run motel set in a large, graceful garden complete with dear old trees and
a duck-filled creek. The low and long '60s
units have been tastefully revamped to offer
homely comfort and gas cookers. You may
want to stay longer.

ourpick Wakamarinian Café (☎ 03-574 1180; 70
Main Rd; snacks $2-7; ☾ 9.30am-5pm) Heavenly home
baking in a cute cottage. Get in early to grab
one of the popular pies, or console yourself
with proper quiche and a sweet slice – the
raspberry and white-chocolate shortcake de-
fies description. Great coffee and excellent
value, too, from Beth and Laurie: Havelock's
culinary saviours.

Slip Inn (☎ 03-574 2345; Havelock Marina; meals $9-25;
☾ 8am-late) Feel appropriately maritime in this
surprisingly slick restaurant and bar in the
thick of the marina. Its signature dishes are
the mussels, as well as beer-battered blue cod,
pizza, pasta specials and home-made dessert.
Good for a cruise-by beer-stop, too.

Getting There & Away

InterCity (☎ 03-365 1113; www.intercitycoach.co.nz)
runs daily from Picton to Havelock via
Blenheim ($21, one hour, three daily), and
from Havelock to Nelson ($22, 1¼ hours,
three daily). **Atomic Shuttles** (☎ 03-349 0697;
www.atomictravel.co.nz) plies the same run. To get
between Havelock and Picton via the scenic
Queen Charlotte Drive, look up Coleman Post
(see p130).

BLENHEIM
pop 26,500

Blenheim (pronounced 'Blenum') is a dead-
flat, agricultural town 29km south of Picton
on the Wairau Plain between the Wither Hills
and the Richmond Ranges. The town offers
little to enthral or distract except for the brilliant Aviation Heritage Centre and the world-
famous wineries just over its back fence.

Information

Automobile Association (AA; ☎ 03-578 3399; www.
aa.co.nz; 23 Maxwell Rd; ☾ 8.30am-5pm Mon-Fri, from
9am Tue)

Blenheim i-SITE (☎ 03-577 8080; www.destination
marlborough.com; Railway Station, Sinclair St;
☾ 8.30am-5pm Mon-Fri, 9am-3pm Sat & Sun) Information on Marlborough and beyond. Wine trail maps and
bookings for everything under the sun.

Blenheim police station (☎ 03-578 5279; 8 Main St;
☾ 24hr)

Paperplus (☎ 03-578 3904; The Forum, Market Pl;
☾ 8.30am-5.30pm Mon-Fri, 10am-4pm Sat & Sun) Books
and magazines.

Post office (cnr Scott & Main Sts)

Travel Stop Cyber Centre (☎ 03-579 1902; Shop
17, 1 Market St; ☾ 10am-9pm Mon-Sat, to 4pm Sun)
Internet access.

Wairau Hospital (☎ 03-520 9999; www.nmdhb.govt.
nz; Hospital Rd; ☾ 24hr)

Sights & Activities

Blenheim's 'big attraction' has always been
its wineries, but the **Omaka Aviation Heritage
Centre** (Map p138; ☎ 03-579 1305; www.omaka.org.nz;
Aerodrome Rd; adult/child/family $20/8/48; ☾ 10am-4pm)
has blown the wine out of the water. Aided
by the creative geniuses that brought us *Lord
of the Rings* (Peter Jackson, Wingnut Films
and Weta Workshop), this amazing collection
of original and replica Great War aircraft is
brought to life with a series of dioramas depicting dramatic wartime scenes such as the
death of Manfred von Richthofen, the Red
Baron. Remarkable memorabilia and photographic displays deepen the experience. It's
powerful stuff, and we predict eyes on stalks
one minute, misty eyes the next. There is a
cafe and shop on-site.

On your way back into town, check out
the **Marlborough Museum** (☎ 03-578 1712; www.
marlboroughmuseum.org.nz; 26 Arthur Baker Pl off New
Renwick Rd; admission adult/child $10/5; ☾ 10am-4pm),
passionately celebrating the region's history.
Besides a replica township, vintage mechan-
icals and well-presented artefact displays,
there's the recently opened 'Wine Exhibition'
for those looking to cap-off their vineyard
experiences.

Conspicuously blue opposite Seymour
Sq, the **Millennium Art Gallery** (☎ 03-579 2001;
marlpublicart@xtra.co.nz; 13 Seymour Sq; admission by donation; ☾ 10.30am-4.30pm Mon-Fri, 1-4pm Sat & Sun) is
a contemporary gallery presenting changing
exhibitions by local and national artists.

For grand views across the Wairau Valley
and out to Cloudy Bay, take a walk or bike
ride in the 1100-hectare **Wither Hills Farm
Park** (Map p138), which could take from 30

minutes to all day, depending on the route. The two main entrances are at the top of Redwood St and the Taylor Pass Rd; pick up a map from the i-SITE or check the information panels at the gates. Ask about fire bans in high summer. Hire bikes from the Spokesman (see p142).

High Country Horse Treks (☎ 03-577 9424; www. high-horse.co.nz; 961 Taylor Pass Rd; 1/4hr rides $50/150) runs equine exploration from its base 11km southwest of town (call for directions).

Tours
WINE TOURS

Wine tours are generally conducted in a minibus, last between three and seven hours, take in four to seven wineries, and range in price

from $45 to $90 (with a few grand tours up to $200 for the day). A winery lunch is usually on the cards. Numerous operators offer various (often customised) tour options:

Bubbly Grape Wine Tours (☎ 0800 228 2253; www.bubblygrape.co.nz)

Highlight Wine Tours (☎ 03-577-9046; www. highlight-tours.co.nz)

Marlborough Wine Tours (☎ 03-578 9515; www. marlboroughwinetours.co.nz)

Na Clachan Wine Tours (☎ 03-578 8881; www. naclachan.co.nz)

Sounds Connection (☎ 0800 742 866, 03-573 8843; www.soundsconnection.co.nz)

Your other option is to get around the grapes by bike. Bike hire is available all over town, or

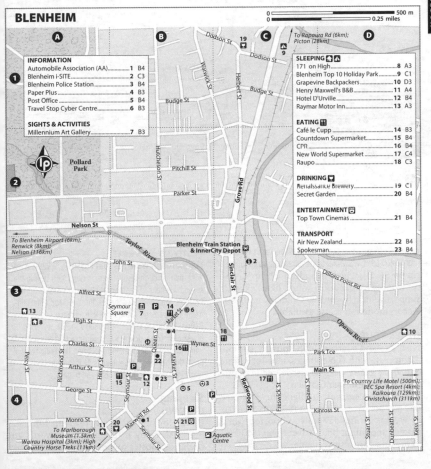

BLENHEIM

0   500 m
0   0.25 miles

To Rapaura Rd (6km);
Picton (28km)

INFORMATION
Automobile Association (AA).................1 B4
Blenheim i-SITE..................................2 C3
Blenheim Police Station.......................3 B4
Paper Plus..4 B3
Post Office...5 B4
Travel Stop Cyber Centre.....................6 B3

SIGHTS & ACTIVITIES
Millennium Art Gallery.........................7 B3

SLEEPING
171 on High.......................................8 A3
Blenheim Top 10 Holiday Park.............9 C1
Grapevine Backpackers......................10 D3
Henry Maxwell's B&B........................11 A4
Hotel D'Urville..................................12 B4
Raymar Motor Inn.............................13 A3

EATING
Café le Cupp.....................................14 B3
Countdown Supermarket....................15 B4
CPR..16 B4
New World Supermarket....................17 C4
Raupo..18 C3

DRINKING
Renaissance Brewery........................19 C1
Secret Garden..................................20 B4

ENTERTAINMENT
Top Town Cinemas...........................21 B4

TRANSPORT
Air New Zealand...............................22 B4
Spokesman.......................................23 B4

Dodson St
Dodson St
Warwick St
Herbert St
Budge St
Budge St
Hutcheson St
Pitchill St
Parker St
Groveway

Pollard Park

Nelson St

To Blenheim Airport (6km);
Renwick (8km);
Nelson (116km)

Taylor River

John St

Blenheim Train Station
& InnerCity Depot

Sinclair St

Dillons Point Rd

Opawa River

Alfred St

High St

Seymour Square

Market St

Charles St

Wynen St

Queen St

Park Tce

Main St

Richmond St

Arthur St

Henry St

George St

Percy St

Freswick St

Opawa St

To Country Life Motel (500m);
BEC Spa Resort (4km);
Kaikoura (129km);
Christchurch (311km)

Monro St

To Marlborough
Museum (1.5km);
Wairau Hospital (3km); High
Country Horse Treks (11km)

Maxwell Rd

Seymour St

Scott St

Redwood St

Kinross St

Aquatic Centre

Stuart St

Dunbeath St

Keiss St

MARLBOROUGH & NELSON

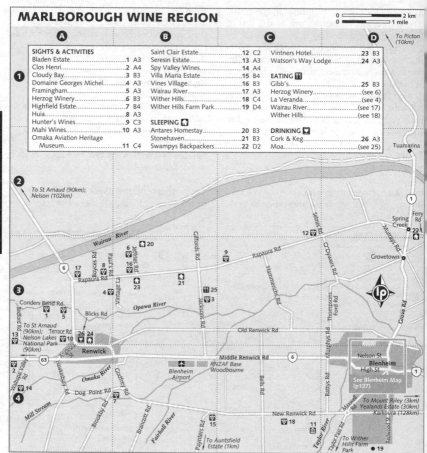

MARLBOROUGH WINE REGION

0 — 2 km
0 — 1 mile

To Picton
(10km)

SIGHTS & ACTIVITIES
Bladen Estate..........................1 A3
Clos Henri..............................2 A4
Cloudy Bay.............................3 B3
Domaine Georges Michel....4 A3
Framingham............................5 A3
Herzog Winery.......................6 B3
Highfield Estate.....................7 B4
Huia..8 A3
Hunter's Wines......................9 C3
Mahi Wines..........................10 A3
Omaka Aviation Heritage
    Museum.............................11 C4

Saint Clair Estate.................12 C2
Seresin Estate......................13 A3
Spy Valley Wines.................14 A4
Villa Maria Estate................15 B4
Vines Village........................16 B3
Wairau River.........................17 A3
Wither Hills..........................18 C4
Wither Hills Farm Park........19 D4

SLEEPING
Antares Homestay................20 B3
Stonehaven...........................21 B3
Swampys Backpackers.........22 D2

Vintners Hotel......................23 B3
Watson's Way Lodge...........24 A3

EATING
Gibb's....................................25 B3
Herzog Winery...................(see 6)
La Veranda.........................(see 4)
Wairau River....................(see 17)
Wither Hills......................(see 18)

DRINKING
Cork & Keg...........................26 A3
Moa...................................(see 25)

---

take a self-guided tour with **Wine Tours by Bike** (☎ 03-577 6954; www.winetoursbybike.co.nz; half-/full-day bike hire $40/55), which includes pick-up/drop-off, winery map, bottled water, panniers and support vehicle (if you buy too many bottles!). Accommodation is also available.

OTHER TOURS
New Zealand's largest high-country station – complete with cob cottages, a historic inn, and vistas galore – can be discovered in depth with **Molesworth Tour Company** (☎ 03-577 9897; www.molesworthtours.co.nz). It offers one- to four-day all-inclusive 4WD trips ($235 to $1500), as well as a four-day fully supported (and catered mountain bike) adventures ($1135). Wine tours are also available.

Festivals & Events
Marlborough Wine Festival (☎ 03-577 9299; www.wine-marlborough-festival.co.nz; tickets $50) During the second weekend of February at Montana's Brancott Estate. Features wine from 50 wineries, fine food and entertainment. Book accommodation well in advance.

Blues, Brews & BBQs (☎ 0800 224 224; www.bluesbrews.co.nz; tickets $28) Counteracting any potential wine-wankery, the weekend preceding the Wine Festival hosts this beer fest at Blenheim's A&P showgrounds, featuring live blues, food, booze and bogans.

Sleeping
IN TOWN
Blenheim's budget beds fill with long-stay guests working in the area's vineyards and orchards; hostel owners help find seasonal

work and offer reasonable weekly rates. There are masses of midrange motels, with rich pickings on Middle Renwick Rd west of the town centre, and a handful on SH1 towards Christchurch.

Grapevine Backpackers (☎ 03-578 6062; www.the grapevine.co.nz; 29 Park Tce; sites $17, dm $24, d $52-66, tr $78; 🖵 🛜) Inside an old maternity home just out of the centre, Grapevine is a worker-focused hostel with a brilliant sunset deck by Opawa River. There are free canoes, and bike hire is $15 per day. Avoid the three-tier bunks if vertigo is an issue.

Blenheim Top 10 Holiday Park (☎ 0800 268 666, 03-578 3667; www.blenheimtop10.co.nz; 78 Grove Rd; unpowered sites $32-36, powered sites $36-40, cabins $65-85, units & motels $90-140; 🖵 🛜 🐾) About five minutes north of town, this clean holiday park has easy-park motorhome pads and campsites spread out along Opawa River, as well as a spa, playground and the usual cabin/unit suspects. Bike hire costs $30 per day.

Henry Maxwell's B&B (☎ 0800 436 796, 03-578 8086; www.henrymaxwells.co.nz; 28 Henry St; s $80, d $120-140, all incl breakfast; 🖵 🛜) Five minutes' walk from the middle of town, this surprisingly quiet, grand old home has five homely, spacious rooms with their own bathrooms. Guests may avail themselves of their own lounge and kitchen, in-room coffee-making facilities, complimentary port, and the helpful assistance of owners Diana and Graham. There's also a full fry-up for breakfast.

Country Life Motel (☎ 03 578 7069; countrylifemotel@ clear.net.nz; Main Rd South; d $85; 🐾) It may be on SH1 on the edge of town, but as the sweeping drive, neat lawn and blooming rose garden suggest, this cheap-as-chips hotel has its merits. Shell out $20 more than you would at the backpackers and you'll get a respectable old motel unit with fridge, microwave and toaster. And there's a swimming pool.

Raymar Motor Inn (☎ 03-578 5104; raymar@slingshot. co.nz; 164 High St; d $95, extra person $20; 🛜) A recent spruce-up hasn't completely redeemed this old-timer: tacky laminex and patterned glass remain. Still, it's clean enough, central and cheap. Kitchen facilities are communal.

171 on High (☎ 0800 587 856, 03-579 5098; www.171onhighmotel.co.nz; cnr High & Percy Sts; d $125-185; 🖵 🛜) A welcoming option close to town, these tasteful splash-o-purple studios and apartments are bright and breezy in the daytime, warm and shimmery in the evening. A wide complement of facilities includes full

kitchen, Sky TV and guest laundry; staff are well-known for 'extra mile' service.

Hotel D'Urville (☎ 03-577 9945; www.durville.com; 52 Queen St; d $185-300; 🖵 🛜) Injecting some chutzpah into Blenheim's old Public Trust buildings, the 11 dazzling rooms in this boutique hotel are lavishly decorated and individually themed. Downstairs is a classy lounge bar and high-end restaurant (dinner only, mains around $38), while outside the new deck bar traps great afternoon sun.

BEC Spa Resort (☎ 03-579 4446; www.becspa.co.nz; 81 Cobb Cottage Rd; d incl breakfast $325-525; 🖵 🛜 🐾) On a knoll in the golden Wither Hills, this boutique resort basks in beautiful views and the glory of its superstylish architecture. The sophisticated owners have smattered their five en-suite, slick suites and shared living area with fabulous art, but the place manages to retain a *laissez faire* air. It's not hard to kick back in a place like this…lap-pool, spa, steamroom and on-site therapy centre. Who knew Blenheim did bliss?

WINE REGION ACCOMMODATION
The following accommodation options are beyond Blenheim and around the vines.

Swampys Backpackers (Map p138; ☎ 03-570 2180; www.swampys.co.nz; 2 Ferry Rd, Spring Creek; dm/d $25/60; 🖵) A lively hub for travellers and long-termers alike, divided between the new wing and the old grungy. There's a pub and superette nearby, plus funky lounges, two kitchens, tidy bathrooms and a chilled-out courtyard. Bike hire is also available.

Watson's Way Lodge (Map p138; ☎ 03-572 8228; www.watsonswaybackpackers.co.nz; 56 High St; dm $28, d $58-68; 🌙 closed Aug; 🖵) This traveller-focused, purpose-built hostel has three- and four-bed dorms and spick-and-span doubles (some with en suite), in a lodge set in leafy gardens dotted with fruit trees and hammocks. There are bikes for hire (special guest rate $25 per day), an outdoor claw-foot bath, and local information aplenty.

our pick **Vintners Hotel** (Map p138; ☎ 03-572 5094; www.mvh.co.nz; 190 Rapaura Rd; d $150-260; 🛜 🐾) One of the best among the vines: 16 architecturally designed suites boasting picture windows both sides making the most of vine and valley views, while inside the rooms are truly stylish boasting wet-room bathrooms and abstract art. The stylish reception building has a bar and acclaimed restaurant opening out on to a cherry-tree garden. On-to-it managers are

MARLBOROUGH WINERIES

Marlborough is NZ's vinous colossus producing around three quarters of the country's wine. At last count, there were 23,810 hectares of vines planted – that's approximately 34,000 rugby pitches! Sunny days and cool nights create the perfect microclimate for cool-climate grapes: world-famous sauvignon blanc, top-notch pinot noir, and notable gewürztraminer, riesling, pinot gris and bubbly. Spending a day or two drifting between tasting rooms and dining among the vines is a quintessential South Island experience. See p139 for sleeping options in wine country.

The majority of Marlborough's nearly 200 wineries lie within the Wairau Valley around Blenheim and Renwick with others blanketing the cooler Awatere Valley or creeping up the southern-side valleys of the Wairau. Of the 40 or so that are open to the public, those below (see Map p138) are well worth a look, providing a range of quality cellar-door experiences. For wine tours, see p137.

A Taste of the Tastings

Most tastings are free. Summer hours are given, with some wineries scaling back operations in winter. Also pick up a copy of *The Marlborough Wine Trail* map from Blenheim i-SITE, available online at www.wine-marlborough.co.nz.

■ **Auntsfield Estate** (☎ 03-578 0622; www.auntsfield.co.nz; 270 Paynters Rd; ⏰ 11am-5pm) Quality handcrafted wines from this historic and picturesque vineyard at the foot of the Wither Hills. Tours Tuesday to Saturday ($10).

■ **Bladen Estate** (☎ 03-572 9417; www.bladen.co.nz; Conders Bend Rd; ⏰ 11am-5pm) Bijou family winery that's big on charm. Award-winning cellar door.

■ **Clos Henri** (☎ 03-572 7923; www.closhenri.com; 639 SH63; ⏰ 10am-4pm Mon-Fri) French winemaking meets Marlborough terroir with *très bien* results. Beautifully restored local country church houses the cellar door.

■ **Cloudy Bay** (☎ 03-520 9147; www.cloudybay.co.nz; Jacksons Rd; ⏰ 10am-5pm) Understated exterior belies the classy interior of this blue-ribbon winery and cellar door. Globally coveted sauvignon blanc, bubbly and pinot noir.

■ **Domaine Georges Michel** (☎ 03-572 7230; www.georgesmichel.co.nz; 56 Vintage La; ⏰ 10.30am-4.30pm) A slice of France in the heart of Marlborough. Nicely balanced pinot noir, and *La Veranda* – one of our favourite places for lunch (see opposite).

■ **Framingham** (☎ 03-572 8884; www.framingham.co.nz; 19 Conders Bend Rd; ⏰ 10.30am-4.30pm) Consistent, quality wines including exceptional rieslings.

■ **Herzog Winery** (☎ 03-572 8770; www.herzog.co.nz; 81 Jeffries Rd; ⏰ 9am-5pm Mon-Fri, 11am-4pm Sat & Sun) Boutique family-owned winery and acclaimed restaurant (see opposite). Try the full-bodied montepulciano, a rare grape in these parts.

■ **Highfield Estate** (☎ 03-572 9244; www.highfield.co.nz; Brookby Rd; ⏰ 10am-5pm) Impressive views over the Wairau Valley from the tower atop this rosy Tuscan-style winery. The fizz is the biz. The restaurant is open from 11.30am to 4.30pm.

■ **Huia** (☎ 03-572 8326; www.huia.net.nz; Boyces Rd; ⏰ 10.30am-5pm) Sustainable, small-scale winegrowing and the cutest yellow tasting room in town. Delectable dry-style gewürztraminer.

■ **Hunter's Wines** (☎ 03-572 8489; www.hunters.co.nz; 603 Rapaura Rd; ⏰ 9am-5pm) Home of viti-cultural legend Jane Hunter. The garden cafe is open for lunch from 11am to 3pm, and for dinner from 6pm to 9pm, Wednesday to Saturday).

■ **Mahi Wines** (☎ 03-572 8859; www.mahiwine.co.nz; 9 Terrace Rd; ⏰ 10am-4.30pm) Knowledgeable and friendly staff who are rightly proud of Mahi's stable of fine wines, with a strong focus on single-vineyard varieties.

MARLBOROUGH & NELSON

- **Mount Riley** (☎ 03-577 9900; www.mountriley.co.nz; 10 Malthouse Rd, Riverlands; ☺ 10am-4.30pm) Family owned and operated winery producing decent, reasonably priced wines. The striking concrete sarcophagus within the vines houses the cellar door.
- **Saint Clair Estate** (☎ 03-570 5280; www.saintclair.co.nz; cnr Rapaura & Selmes Rds; ☺ 9am-5pm) Prepare to be blown away by the Pioneer Block range of sauvignon blanc; some of the finest in NZ. Cafe open from 9am to 5pm.
- **Seresin Estate** (☎ 03-572 9408; www.seresin.co.nz; 85 Bedford Rd; ☺ 10am-4.30pm) Organic and biodynamic wines and olive oils from cinematographer Michael Seresin. Shedlike cellar door (tasting $5) and groovy sculptures dotted about.
- **Spy Valley Wines** (☎ 03-572 9830; www.spyvalleywine.co.nz; Waihopai Valley Rd; ☺ 10am-4pm) Stylish, edgy architecture at this espionage-themed winery with great wines across the board. Memorable merchandise.
- **Villa Maria Estate** (☎ 03-520 8470; www.villamaria.co.nz; cnr New Renwick & Paynters Rds; ☺ 10am-5pm) One of NZ's winemaking giants with awards aplenty. Its black-label pinot noir range is oenophilic nirvana.
- **Vines Village** (☎ 03-572 8444; www.thevinesvillage.co.nz; 193 Rapaura Rd; ☺ 9am-5pm) Site of the Bouldevines cellar door (www.bouldevineswine.co.nz) and much more: Prenzel Distillery Company, olive oils, acres of quilts and a reliable cafe serving affordable homemade fare.
- **Wairau River** (☎ 03-572 9800; www.wairauriverwines.co.nz; 11 Rapaura Rd; ☺ 10am-5pm) Carbon-neutral family estate with some of Marlborough's oldest vines. Relaxing gardens and a satisfying lunch menu (see below).
- **Wither Hills** (☎ 03-578 4036; www.witherhills.co.nz; 211 New Renwick Rd; ☺ 10am-4.30pm) One of the region's flagship wineries and an architectural gem. Premium wines and an excellent lunch (see below).
- **Yealands Estate** (☎ 03-575 7618; www.yealands.com; cnr Seaview & Reserve Rd, Seddon; ☺ 10am-4.30pm) Clean, green winemaking on a grand scale, with over 1000 hectares planted. Tours of the space-age winery by arrangement.

All graped out? Cleanse your palate with Marlborough's delicious craft ales (p449).

Best Wining & Dining

With wine there must be food. This is our pick of the bunch for dining among the vines. Opening hours are for summer, when bookings are recommended.

- **La Veranda** (platters $16; ☺ 10am-5pm) Keenly priced platters of quality charcuterie, fromages and French desserts – the sort of lunch you *should* be eating at a vineyard. Eat outside or in Domaine George Michel's elegant restaurant.
- **Wairau River** (mains $17-23; ☺ noon-3pm) Mudbrick bistro with wide veranda and beautiful gardens with plenty of shade. Order a double-baked blue-cheese soufflé, or the sticky pork and peanut salad. Relaxing and thoroughly enjoyable.
- **Wither Hills** (mains $17-24, platters $28-45; ☺ 11am-4pm) Simple, well executed food in a stylish space. Pull up a beanbag on the Hockneyesque lawns and enjoy a platter or Café de Paris steak before climbing the ziggurat for impressive views across the Wairau.
- **Gibb's** (☎ 03-572 8048; 258 Jacksons Rd; mains $37-40; ☺ 6.30pm-late) It's not a winery but rather a restaurant nestled among the vineyards. Fresh and sophisticated seasonal food, with a Euro-bent and stellar wine list. Intimate evening dining in a slightly demure environment.
- **Herzog Winery** (mains $82-129, 5-course degustation menu with/without wine $191/125; ☺ 6.30-9.30pm mid-Oct–mid-May) Refined dining in Herzog's opulent dining room. Beautifully prepared food and a remarkable wine list. Less extravagant bistro lunches (☺ noon-3pm) also available.

keen to connect you with the best experiences the region has to offer.

Antares Homestay (Map p138; ☎ 03-572 9951; 106 Jeffries Rd; s/d incl breakfast $175/195, d unit $230, extra person $35; ▢ ⛆ ⛆) A four-acre property with juicy lemons, two en-suite rooms in a wing off the main house, plus a self-contained loft unit (sleeping up to five) above the garage. Bikes are available.

Stonehaven (Map p138; ☎ 03-572 9730; www.stonehavenhomestay.co.nz; 414 Rapaura Rd; d incl breakfast $185-280; ▢ ⛆ ⛆) A stellar stone-and-timber B&B nestled among the picturesque vines with three commodious guest rooms. Beds are piled high with pillows, proper continental breakfast is served in the summerhouse, dinner is offered by request with rare wines from the cellar, and bike hire is available on-site.

Eating & Drinking
Dining and drinking can be pretty hit and miss in Blenny, and some of the best food will be found yonder at the wineries and breweries (see p140 and opposite).

Café le Cupp (☎ 03-577 7311; 30 Market St; snacks $2-5, meals $6-18; ⛆ 8am-3.30pm Mon-Fri, 9am-1pm Sat) The best tearoom in town by a country mile. Ogle your way along the counter (egg sandwiches, mince savouries, luscious lamingtons, carrot cake) or get yourself a brekkie such as the full fry-up, French toast or muesli. We note the presence of the ginger gem… there is a God.

CPR (☎ 03-579 5030; 18 Wynen St; ⛆ 7am-4pm Mon-Fri, 8.30am-1pm Sat) Get a fix of Blenheim's own-roast coffee. Muffins if you're lucky, but it's really all about the beans.

Raupo (☎ 03-577 8822; 2 Symons St; lunch $12-18, dinner $22-28; ⛆ 7am-late) An airy, high-ceilinged timber-and-stone building alongside the Opawa River. During the day there's a satisfying cafe menu (brekkies, burgers, mussels, lamb shanks) and sweet treats, seguing into slightly more sophisticated fare of an evening. Sheltered outdoor seating, and soft-jazz grooves on the stereo.

Secret Garden (☎ 03-579 5025; 30 Maxwell Rd; ⛆ 9am-late; meals $16-23) A leafy oasis in a somewhat dull townscape, this sophisticated restaurant and garden bar spoils its guests with bacon butties and local coffee for breakfast before pressing on towards wild-game pies, craft beer, single malts and cigars later on. Smart service.

See also Hotel D'Urville (p138). For self-catering, hit the supermarkets:

Countdown Supermarket (☎ 03-579 2946; 51 Arthur St; ⛆ 7am-midnight)

New World Supermarket (☎ 03-520 9030; 1 Freswick St; ⛆ 7am-10pm)

Entertainment
Top Town Cinemas (☎ 03-577 8273; www.toptowncinemas.co.nz; 4 Kinross St; adult/child/concession from $11/8/10; ⛆ 10am-midnight) Major Hollywood releases in the main cinemas, with more off-the-wall stuff screening in the 'Lounge'. All tickets are $8 on Tuesdays.

Getting There & Around
AIR
Blenheim Airport is 6km west of town on Middle Renwick Rd. **Air New Zealand** (☎ 0800 747 000, 03-577 2200; www.airnewzealand.co.nz; 29 Queen St; ⛆ 9am-5pm Mon-Fri) has direct flights to/from Wellington (from $75, 12 daily), Auckland ($109, five daily) and Christchurch ($89, three daily) with onward connections.

BICYCLE
Spokesman (☎ 03-578 0433; www.bikemarlborough.co.nz; 61 Queen St; hire per half/full day incl helmet $25/40; ⛆ 8am-5.30pm Mon-Fri, 10am-1pm Sat) rents bikes; longer hire and delivery by arrangement.

BUS
InterCity (☎ 03-365 1113; www.intercitycoach.co.nz) buses run daily from the Blenheim i-SITE to Picton ($15, 30 minutes, five daily) continuing through to Nelson ($31, 1¾ hours, three daily). Buses also head down south to Christchurch ($54, five hours, two daily) via Kaikoura ($33, 1¾ hours). A couple of shuttle buses also make the stop at Blenheim on the Nelson–Picton–Christchurch run (see p129).

Ritchies Transport (☎ 03-578 5467; www.ritchies.co.nz) buses traverse the Blenheim–Picton line ($10, 25 minutes, three daily Monday to Friday during school term), departing from Blenheim Railway Station.

Naked Bus (☎ 0900 625 33; www.nakedbus.com) runs from Blenheim to many South Island destinations, including Kaikoura ($20, two hours, two daily), Nelson (from $13, 1¾ hours, one to two daily) and Motueka ($27, 3¾ hours, one daily). Buses depart the i-SITE. Book online or at the i-SITE; cheaper fares for advance bookings.

REAL BEER

It's not all about the wine…Marlborough produces some quality craft beers too. Quaff some at the following establishments dedicated to the world's oldest beverage, a fine antidote to all that sauvignon blanc:

- **Cork & Keg** (☎ 03-572 9328; Inkerman St, Renwick; ✆ noon-late) English-style country boozer with a pleasant beer patio and pub grub. Moa, West Coast and Benger Gold Cider on tap.

- **Moa** (☎ 03-572 5146; www.moabeer.co.nz; Jacksons Rd; ✆ noon-late summer, noon-late Fri-Sun winter) Winemaker's son Josh Scott brews an excellent range of bottle-fermented beers and thirst-quenching ciders at his tasting room-cum-bar in the thick of Marlborough's wineries. Nice garden overlooking the vines. Pricey platters.

- **Renaissance** (Map p137; ☎ 03-579 3400; www.renaissancebrewing.co.nz; 1 Dodson St; ✆ 11am-late Tue-Fri, 10am-late Sat & Sun) Sample quality Renaissance ales at the Dodson Street Bistro & Ale House, next door to the brewery. The malty Stonecutter Scotch Ale is fulsome and delicious. A selection of other craft beers, including Emerson's, 666 and 8-Wired, as well as some decent food too.

MARLBOROUGH & NELSON

TAXI

Call for bookings or for a post wine-touring ride back to your hotel with **Marlborough Taxis** (☎ 03-577 5511).

TRAIN

Tranz Scenic (☎ 0800 872 467, 04-495 0775; www.tranzscenic.co.nz) runs the *TranzCoastal* service, stopping daily at Blenheim en route to Picton ($27, 27 minutes, departing 11.46am) heading north, and Christchurch ($95, five hours, departing 1.33pm) via Kaikoura ($48, two hours) heading south. There are often decent discounts on the fares listed here.

KAIKOURA

pop 3850

Take SH1 132km southeast from Blenheim (or 183km north from Christchurch) and you'll wind around the panoramic coast to Kaikoura, a picture-perfect peninsula town backed by the snowcapped peaks of the Seaward Kaikoura Range. There are few places in the world with such awesome mountains so close to the sea, and such a proliferation of wildlife so close at hand: whales, dolphins, NZ fur seals, penguins, shearwaters, petrels and wandering albatross all stop by or make this area home.

Marine animals are abundant here due to ocean-current and continental-shelf conditions: the seabed gradually slopes away from the land to a depth of about 90m, then plunges to more than 800m – warm and cold water converges. When the southerly current hits the continental shelf it creates an upwelling, bringing nutrients up from the ocean floor into the feeding zone.

Until the 1980s, no one wanted to know about Kaikoura: it was a sleepy crayfishing town ('Kai' meaning food, 'koura' meaning crayfish) with grim prospects. These days it's a tourist mecca, with quality accommodation and many other enticements including eye-popping wildlife tours.

History

In Maori legend, Kaikoura Peninsula (Taumanu o Te Waka a Maui) was the seat where the demigod Maui sat when he fished the North Island up from the depths of the sea. The area was heavily settled before Europeans arrived – at least 14 Maori *pa* (fortified village) sites have been identified, and excavations show that the area was a moahunter settlement about 800 to 1000 years ago. The largest moa egg ever found (240mm long, 178mm in diameter) was unearthed in 1857 at a burial site near the present-day Fyffe House.

In 1828 Kaikoura's beachfront was the scene of a tremendous battle. A Ngati Toa war party, led by chief Te Rauparaha, bore down on Kaikoura, killing or capturing several hundred of the Ngai Tahu tribe.

James Cook sailed past the peninsula in 1770, but didn't land. His journal states that 57 Maori in four double-hulled canoes came towards the *Endeavour*, but 'would not be prevail'd upon to put along side'. Europeans established a whaling station here in 1842, and the town remained a whaling centre until 1922. Sheep farming and agriculture also flourished. After whaling ended, the sea and fertile farmland continued to sustain the community.

Information

Global Gossip (☎ 03-319 7970; 19 West End; ☻ 9am-9pm) Internet access.

Kaikoura i-SITE (☎ 03-319 5641; www.kaikoura.co.nz; West End; ☻ 9am-5pm Mon-Fri, to 4pm Sat & Sun, extended hr in summer) Helpful staff make tour, accommodation and transport bookings, and help with DOC-related matters.

Paperplus/post office (☎ 03-319 6808, 41 West End; ☻ 8.30am-5.30pm Mon-Fri, to 7pm Sat, to 4pm Sun) A decent bookshop with post office counter.

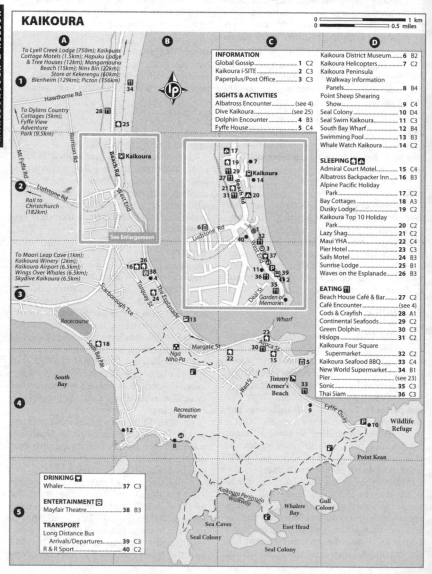

KAIKOURA

0 _____ 1 km
0 _____ 0.5 miles

INFORMATION
Global Gossip 1 C2
Kaikoura i-SITE 2 C3
Paperplus/Post Office 3 C3

SIGHTS & ACTIVITIES
Albatross Encounter .... (see 4)
Dive Kaikoura .... (see 25)
Dolphin Encounter 4 B3
Fyffe House 5 C4
Kaikoura District Museum 6 B2
Kaikoura Helicopters 7 C2
Kaikoura Peninsula
  Walkway Information
  Panels 8 B4
Point Sheep Shearing
  Show 9 C4
Seal Colony 10 D4
Seal Swim Kaikoura 11 C3
South Bay Wharf 12 B4
Swimming Pool 13 B3
Whale Watch Kaikoura 14 C2

SLEEPING 🏠 🏕
Admiral Court Motel 15 C4
Albatross Backpacker Inn 16 B3
Alpine Pacific Holiday
  Park 17 C2
Bay Cottages 18 A3
Dusky Lodge 19 C2
Kaikoura Top 10 Holiday
  Park 20 C2
Lazy Shag 21 C2
Maui YHA 22 C3
Pier Hotel 23 C3
Sails Motel 24 B3
Sunrise Lodge 25 B1
Waves on the Esplanade 26 B3

EATING 🍴
Beach House Café & Bar 27 C2
Café Encounter .... (see 4)
Cods & Crayfish 28 A1
Continental Seafoods 29 C3
Green Dolphin 30 C3
Hislops 31 C3
Kaikoura Four Square
  Supermarket 32 C2
Kaikoura Seafood BBQ 33 C4
New World Supermarket 34 B1
Pier .... (see 23)
Sonic 35 C3
Thai Siam 36 C3

DRINKING 🍷
Whaler 37 C3

ENTERTAINMENT 🎭
Mayfair Theatre 38 B3

TRANSPORT
Long Distance Bus
  Arrivals/Departures 39 C3
R & R Sport 40 C2

Sights

Kaikoura's oldest surviving building is **Fyffe House** (☎ 03-319 5835; www.fyffehouse.co.nz; 62 Avoca St; adult/child/family $7/2/15; ☺ 10am-6pm daily Nov-Apr, to 4pm Thu-Mon May-Oct). Built by Scotsman George Fyffe, cousin of Kaikoura's first European settler, Robert Fyffe, it started life as a small cottage in 1842 (with whale vertebrae for foundations) and was completed in 1860. There's plenty to see inside and out, including the original brick oven, historical displays and gardens.

Kaikoura District Museum (☎ 03-319 7440; kk.museum@xtra.co.nz; 14 Ludstone Rd; adult/child $3/50c; ☺ 12.30-4.30pm Mon-Fri, 2-4pm Sat & Sun, extended summer hr) includes the old town jail (1910), historical photos, Maori and colonial artefacts, and an exhibit on the region's whaling era (check out the sperm-whale jaw).

The 30-minute **Point Sheep Shearing Show** (☎ 03-319 5422; www.pointsheepshearing.co.nz; Fyffe Quay; adult/child $10/5; ☺ shows 1.30pm & 4pm) at the Point B&B is fun and educationally ovine. You can also feed a ram, and lambs between September and February. Classic NZ!

Near the Point Kean car park is the smelly **seal colony**. The seals laze around in the grass and on the rocks, wondering why everyone is looking at them. Give the seals a wide berth (10m), and never get between them and the sea – they will attack if they feel cornered and can move surprisingly fast.

If you haven't yet exceeded your annual wine intake around Blenheim, sip a few local drops at **Kaikoura Winery** (☎ 03-319 7966; www. kaikourawinery.co.nz; tasting $5, tour & tasting $15; ☺ 10am-5.30pm, tours 11am, 2pm, 4pm), 2km south of town off SH1. The building and views more than make up for the unremarkable wines (our pick is the bubbly).

Not far from the winery is **Maori Leap Cave** (☎ 03-319 5023; mary.and.scott@xtra.co.nz; SH1; 40min tours adult/child $12/5; ☺ tours on the hour 10.30am-3.30pm), a sea-formed limestone cave discovered in 1958. Tours depart the Caves Restaurant, 3km south of town. Book at the restaurant or i-SITE.

Activities

The **Kaikoura Peninsula Walkway** is a must-do if humanly possible. Starting from the town, this three- to four-hour loop heads out to Point Kean, along the cliffs to South Bay, then back to town over the isthmus. En route you'll see fur seals, and red-billed seagull and shearwater (aka mutton bird) colonies.

Lookouts and interesting interpretive panels abound. Collect a map at the i-SITE or follow your nose.

There's a safe swimming **beach** in front of the Esplanade, and a **pool** (adult/child $3/1.50; ☺ 10am-5pm Nov-Mar) if you have a salt aversion.

The whole coastline, with its rocky formations and abundant marine life, offers fabulous snorkelling and diving. **Dive Kaikoura** (☎ 0800 348 352, 03-319 6622; www.divekaikoura.co.nz; Yarmouth St; half-day $250) runs small-group trips and diver training.

Mangamaunu Beach, 15km north of Kaikoura, has wicked surf (a 500m point break when it's working). **Board Silly Surf Adventures** (☎ 0800 787 352, 03-319 6464; boardsilly@clear.net.nz; 3hr lesson adult/ child $80/65) can teach you to surf, or if you already can, it'll hire you a wetsuit and board ($40). R&R Sport (p149) also hires out boards and wetties.

A bit further north is the Clarence River, the bouncy Grade II rapids of which can be rafted with **Clarence River Rafting** (☎ 03-319 6993; www.clarenceriverrafting.co.nz; 5hr trip $30/50) offers. Longer trips are available.

Farmy **Fyffe View Ranch Adventure Park** (☎ 03-319 5069; www.kaikourahorsetrekking.co.nz; Chapmans Rd off Postmans Rd; ½hr/1hr treks $30/50; ☺ 10.30am-2pm) offers horse treks including a sunset trek (with/without supper $95/75). Bone-shaking mountain kart luge, farm-animal feeding and woodshed archery are also available.

Based at Kaikoura Airport, **Skydive Kaikoura** (☎ 0800 843 759; www.skydivekaikoura. co.nz; 9000/11,000/13,000ft $259/319/359), otherwise known as Sarah and Henk, will bring you down to earth in its own personal style. Handicam ($129) and photo packages ($39) are available.

If you're here in winter, you can **ski** yourself silly at nearby Mt Lyford (p82). When there's snow on the slopes, shuttle buses run from Kaikoura to the mountain; enquire at the i-SITE.

Tours

Tours are big business in Kaikoura. It's all about marine mammals: don't miss the chance to see whales (sperm, pilot, killer, humpback and southern right), dolphins (Hector's, bottlenose and dusky) and NZ fur seals up close. During summer, book whale- and dolphin-watching tours a few weeks ahead, and give yourself some leeway to allow for lousy weather.

WHALE-WATCHING

A whale-watch tour is an unforgettable experience, either by boat, plane or helicopter. Aerial options are shorter and pricier, but allow you to see the whole whale, as opposed to just a tail, flipper or spout from a boat.

Kaikoura Helicopters (☎ 03-319 6609; www.world ofwhales.co.nz; Railway Station; 15-60min flight from $100-455) Reliable whale-spotting flights (standard tour 30 minutes $195 for three or more people), plus jaunts around the peninsula, Mt Fyffe, and peaks beyond.

Whale Watch Kaikoura (☎ 0800 655 121, 03-319 6767; www.whalewatch.co.nz; Whaleway Station (ha-ha); 3hr tour adult/child $145/60) With knowledgeable guides and fascinating 'world of whales' onboard animation, Kaikoura's biggest operator heads out (with admirable frequency) in boats equipped with hydrophones (underwater microphones) to pick up whale soundings. It'll refund 80% of your fare if no whales are sighted (success rate: 98%). Sailings may be cancelled if the weather turns to custard, so if this trip is a must for you, allow a few days flexibility.

Wings over Whales (☎ 0800 226 629, 03-319 6580; www.whales.co.nz; 30min flight adult/child $165/75) Light-plane flights departing from Kaikoura Airport 7km south of town. Spotting success rate: 95%.

DOLPHIN & SEAL SPOTTING

Dolphin Encounter (☎ 0800 733 365, 03-319 6777; www.dolphin.co.nz; 96 The Esplanade; swim adult/ child $165/150, observation $80/40; ⏰ tours 8.30am & 12.30pm year-round, plus 5.30am in summer) Here's your chance to rub shoulders with pods of dusky dolphins on three-hour tours; wet suits, masks and snorkels are provided. Limited numbers, so book in advance.

Kaikoura Kayaks (☎ 0800 452 456, 03-319 7118; www.kaikourakayaks.co.nz; 19 Killarney St; seal tours adult/child $85/70; ⏰ tours 8.30am, 12.30pm & 4.30pm Nov-Apr, 9am & 1pm May-Oct) Guided sea-kayak tours to view fur seals and explore the peninsula's coastline. Kayaking lessons, freedom hire and kayak fishing also available.

Seal Swim Kaikoura (☎ 0800 732 579, 03-319 6182; www.sealswimkaikoura.co.nz; shore-based tour adult/ child $70/60, boat-based tour $90/70; ⏰ tour Oct-May) Two-hour guided snorkelling tours.

Top Spot Seal Swim (☎ 03-319 5540; shore-based tour adult $70) Two-hour guided snorkelling tours.

BIRDWATCHING

Bird-nerds fly at the opportunity for a close encounter with pelagic species: albatross, shearwaters, shags, mollymawks and petrels.

Albatross Encounter (☎ 0800 733 365, 03-319 6777; www.oceanwings.co.nz; 96 The Esplanade; adult/child $110/55;

⏰ tours 9am & 1pm year-round, plus 6am in summer) is run by the same folks as Dolphin Encounter.

FISHING TRIPS

Fish Kaikoura (☎ 0800 768 020, 03-319 6277; www. fishkaikoura.co.nz; ½hr trip $55/75) Short-and-sweet fishing (sea perch and blue cod) and crayfishing trips, launching from Kaikoura Beach. Ask about longer trips. No fish: no charge!

Kaikoura Fishing Charters (☎ 03-319 6888; www. kaikourafishing.co.nz; ¾hr trip $100/110) Dangle a line from the good ship *Takapu*, then take your filleted, bagged catch home to eat. Trips depart from South Bay Wharf.

WALKING TOURS

Kaikoura Coast Track (☎ 03-319 2715; www. kaikouratrack.co.nz; package $185) A three-day, 40km, self-guided walk through private farmland and along the photogenic Amuri Coast, 50km south of Kaikoura. The price includes three nights' farm-cottage accommodation and pack transport; BYO sleeping bag and food (some supplies and meals available). A two-day mountain-bike option costs $85.

Kaikoura Wilderness Walks (☎ 0800 945 337, 03-319 6966; www.kaikourawilderness.co.nz; 1-/2-night package $995/1395) offers more creature comforts than the Coast Track walk with the bonus of expert guides. Two-day/one-night, or three-day/two-night trips (graded easy to moderate) through forests and alpine landscapes, with secluded lodgings. Prices include Kaikoura pick-up/drop-off, meals and pack transfers.

OTHER TOURS

Kaikoura Mountain Safaris (☎ 021 869 643; www. kaikouramountainsafaris.co.nz; half-day tour adult/child $100/55, 1-day tour adult/child $175/125) Journey into the backcountry in a 4WD or Unimog — three different tours (two to three daily) taking in alpine vistas, remote farms and the Clarence River valley.

Maori Tours Kaikoura (☎ 0800 866 267, 03-319 5567; www.maoritours.co.nz; 3½hr tour adult/child $115/65; ⏰ tours 9am & 1.30pm) Unique and fascinating half-day, small-group tours laced with Maori hospitality and local lore. Visit ancient sites, hear legends and understand indigenous use of trees and plants. Advance bookings required.

Festivals & Events

Seafest (☎ 0800 4732 337, 03 319 5641; www.seafest. co.nz; tickets $30; ⏰ early Oct) If you take your seafood seriously, time your visit with Kaikoura's annual fish fiesta on the first Saturday in October (and book your ticket and bed well in advance). Seafest showcases the region's piscatorial prowess: stallholders sell seafood and wine, and there are live bands, family entertainment, and a big Friday-night bash to kick things off.

Sleeping

Book ahead in summer, and during Seafest.

BUDGET

Dusky Lodge (☎ 03-319 5959; www.duskylodge.com; 67 Beach Rd; dm $24-26, d $58-80; 🖥 🛜 🐟) What a whopper! Easily Kaikoura's biggest hostel, the Dusky is an industrious, social place with facilities to cope (including three lounge areas and three kitchens). The crowning glory is the outdoor deck with heated pool, spa and mountain views. Live it up in 'luxury doubles' with en suite and flat-screen TV. There is also a restaurant on-site.

Lazy Shag (☎ 03-319 6662; lazy-shag@hotmail.com; 37 Beach Rd; dm/s/d $25/50/65; 🖥 🛜) The name refers to a local bird species, not the behaviour of guests (but don't rule it out…). This smart lodge occupies a prime spot, with cafes left and right and a party-prone deck taking in mountain views. All rooms have bathroom; there's a separate TV lounge and pleasant back yard.

Sunrise Lodge (☎ 03-319 7444; sunrisehostel@xtra.co.nz; 74 Beach Rd; dm/tr $28/74, tw $60-65; 🖥 🛜) Run by an enthusiastic couple of corporate escapees, this comfortable, sociable lodge continues to garner great feedback from travellers. All rooms are bright and comfortable, and the three-share rooms are bunk-free. Bonuses include free bikes, Friday pub nights, and free nightly sunset tours in a minivan – the perfect introduction to Kaikoura.

Albatross Backpacker Inn (☎ 0800 222 247, 03-319 6090; www.albatross-kaikoura.co.nz; 1 Torquay St; dm/s/d $28/48/65, 6-bed unit $150; 🖥 🛜) This high-quality backpackers in two sweet heritage buildings (one a former post office) is clean, tidy, close to the beach but sheltered from the breeze. As well as a laid-back lounge and separate one for televiewers, there are decks and verandas to chill out on. Homely rooms sport colourful, youthful linen.

Maui YHA (☎ 0800 278 299, 03-319 5931; www.yha.co.nz; 270 The Esplanade; dm $32, d $76-106; 🖥 🛜) This YHA takes the award (as it often does) for location: waterfront, with unimpeded views across the bay to the pine-lined esplanade and mighty peaks beyond. Many rooms enjoy similar views, as does the big-window dining room which you'll find in the same state as

the rest of this purpose-built (1962) hostel: tidy, but slightly crummy in the corners. Half-/full-day bike hire $20/30.

Kaikoura Top 10 Holiday Park (☎ 0800 363 638, 03-319 5362; www.kaikouratop10.co.nz; 34 Beach Rd; unpowered/powered sites $35/38, cabins $55-85, units/motels $95-180; 🖥 🛜 🐟) Invisible behind a massive hedge, this busy, well-maintained campground offers family-friendly facilities (heated pool, spa, trampoline) and cabins and units of the usual Top 10 standard.

Alpine Pacific Holiday Park (☎ 0800 692 322, 03-319 6275; www.alpine-pacific.co.nz; 69 Beach Rd; unpowered/powered sites $38/40, cabins $70, units/motels $120-160; 🖥 🛜 🐟) A quiet little creekside park with mountain outlook, proudly trimmed lawns, a nice pool and barbecue pavilion. Good quality facilities include a spotless kitchen (BYO utensils), and cabins and units slightly more stylish than average. Reduced rates in winter.

MIDRANGE

Pier Hotel (☎ 03-319 5037; www.thepierhotel.co.nz; 1 Avoca St; s/d incl continental breakfast from $75/115; 🛜) A classic heritage hotel with views from sunrise to sunset, the Pier is being gradually restored to glory. The bar and restaurant are now well-known, but its upstairs lodgings – even with their worn fittings and the odd creaky door – have yet to receive their full appreciation.

Bay Cottages (☎ 03-319 5506; www.baycottages.co.nz; 29 South Bay Pde; cottages/motels $90/120) Here's a great value option on South Bay, a few kilometres south of town: five tourist cottages with kitchenette and bathroom sleeping up to four, and two slick motel rooms with stainless-steel benches, low-voltage lighting and flat-screen TVs. The friendly owner may even take you crayfishing in good weather.

Sails Motel (☎ 03-319 6145; www.sailsmotel.co.nz; 134 The Esplanade; d $95-110, apt $120-140) There are no sea (or sails) views at this motel, so the cherubic owners have to impress with quality. Their four secluded, tastefully appointed units are down a driveway in a garden setting (private outdoor areas abound). The apartment sleeps four.

Kaikoura Cottage Motels (☎ 0800 526 882, 03-319 5599; www.kaikouracottagemotels.co.nz; cnr Old Beach & Mill Rds; d $95-140; 🛜) This enclave of eight modern tourist flats is looking mighty fine, surrounded by attractive native plantings now in full flourish. Oriented for mountain views, the self-contained units sleep four between an open plan studio-style living room and one private bedroom. Soothing sand-and-sky colour scheme and quality chattels.

Admiral Court Motel (☎ 0800 555 525, 03-319 5525; www.kaikouramotel.co.nz; 16 Avoca St; d/q from $115/180; ☐ ☞) Away from the town traffic, this solid outfit offers clean, good-value self-contained units (studios and two-bedrooms) with Sky TV. Generally nondescript decor with the odd artful touch hinting at personality and pride.

Dylans Country Cottages (☎ 03-319 5473; www. dylanscottages.co.nz; 268 Postmans Rd; cottages incl breakfast $150) On the grounds of the delightful 'Lavendyl' lavender farm, northwest of town, these two self-contained cottages make for an aromatic escape from seaside fray. One has a private outdoor bath and a shower emerging from a tree; the other an indoor spa and handkerchief lawn. Homemade bread, preserves and free-range eggs for breakfast. Sweet, stylish, and romantic. Closed from May to August.

TOP END

Waves on the Esplanade (☎ 0800 319 589, 03-319 5890; www.kaikouraapartments.co.nz; 78 The Esplanade; apt $190-325; ☞) Can't do without the comforts of home? Here you go: luxury two-bedroom apartments with Sky TV, DVD player, two bathrooms, laundry facilities and full kitchen. Oh, and superb ocean views from the balcony. Rates are for up to four people.

Hapuku Lodge & Tree Houses (☎ 0800 524 5672, 03-319 6559; SH1 at Hapuku Rd; www.hapukulodge.com; d $390-850; ☐ ☞ ☑) Twelve kilometres north of Kaikoura, this fabulous place is perfect for

an indulgent escape. Warm contemporary decor and designer furniture anoint the well-appointed lodge suites, self-contained apartments and gorgeous 'tree houses' (built in a manuka grove at treetop level to snare sea views over the dunes). New additions include an in-house bar and restaurant (guest-only), and swimming pool, spa and sauna. Divine!

Eating & Drinking

Café Encounter (☎ 03-319 6064; 96 The Esplanade; snacks $4-22; ☯ 7am-5pm; ☑) Housed in the Dolphin Encounter complex (p146), this cafe is more than just somewhere to wait for your trip. Good counter food, and coffee plus cakes, crepes, bagels, toasties and daily specials, such as hot smoked salmon on focaccia. Sea and esplanade views from the sunny patio.

Beach House Café & Bar (☎ 03-319 6030; 39 Beach Rd; mains $8-20; ☯ 9am-4pm) Serving the best brunch and coffee in town, this chipper roadside cafe garners more than its fair share of the passing trade. Sit on the front terrace or back deck and reconstitute with green eggs and ham, fish and chips or seafood chowder. Good counter food, too.

Whaler (☎ 03-319 3333; 49-51 West End; ☯ 3pm-late; mains $14-38) A lively leviathan of a pub with good people-watching from the front seats, pool tables, big screens and a spartan deck upstairs. Monteith's and Murphy's on tap and a Neil Young soundtrack.

Store at Kekerengu (☎ 03-575 8600; SH1, Kekerengu; mains $16-42; ☯ 7.30am-7pm) A good place for a pit stop, being halfway between Blenheim and Kaikoura. Your best bet is the counter food or coffee and cake, rather than the overpriced à

CRAY CRAZY

Among all of Kaikoura's munificent marine life, the one species you just can't avoid is the crayfish. The cray's delicate white flesh dominates restaurant menus and takeaway blackboards. Unfortunately (some say unnecessarily), it's pricey – at a restaurant, you'll shell out (pardon the pun) around $50 for half a cray or nigh on $100 for the whole beast. At fishmongers you'll pay export price, around $85 per kg. You can also buy fresh, cooked or uncooked crays from **Cods & Crayfish** (☎ 03-319 7899; 81 Beach Rd; ☯ 8am-6pm) and iconic **Nins Bin** (☎ 03-319 6454; SH1; ☯ 8am-6pm), a surf-side caravan 23km north of town. Upwards of $35 should get you a decent specimen.

Fish-and-chip takeaways usually offer a half-cray with salad and chips for a similar price. Try **Continental Seafoods** (☎ 03-319 5509; 47 Beach Rd; ☯ 7am-9pm), or the alfresco **Kaikoura Seafood BBQ** (☎ 027 376 3619; Fyffe Quay; ☯ 10.30am-dark), a roadside stall near the seal colony – the fish or scallop sandwiches (white bread of course) are worthy, affordable alternatives if crayfish doesn't float your boat. Alternatively, take a fishing tour (p146), or buddy-up with a local who might take you crayfishing and share the spoils.

la carte menu. Enjoy it by the fire in the rustic interior, or out on the wide sun decks, with magical sea-peeks.

ourpick Pier Hotel (☎ 03-319 5037; 1 Avoca St; lunch $14-22, dinner $25-36; ✹ noon-3pm & 5pm-late) Wide views of bay and mountains beyond make this the grandest dining room in town. A cheerful crew serves up generous portions of honest food, such as fresh local fish, venison medallions and crayfish for those with fat wallets. The enticing public bar has reasonably priced beer and bar snacks, historical photos, and a garden bar. What more could you want?

Thai Siam (☎ 03-319 6992; 54 West End; mains $17-28; ✹ noon-2.30pm, 5pm-10pm) Cheerful, vaulted space on the main drag serving a typically expansive Thai menu of over 45 mains including a good selection of Asian salads. The $10 lunch special is a bargain.

Sonic (☎ 03-319 6414; West End; ✹ 3pm-late Mon-Fri, noon-late Sat & Sun; mains $20-31) A casual bar-eatery on West End's southern end, with a pool table, oceans of Mac's beer and occasional live music. Grab a sundowner on the covered deck or terrace and look out to sea through the grand Norfolk pines on the esplanade.

Hislops (☎ 03-319 6971; 33 Beach Rd; lunch $9-21, dinner $20-36; ✹ 9am-9pm, closed Tue & Wed in winter; Ⓥ) This snappy, feel-good cafe maintains its reputation for fresh, wholesome food. Start the morning with fruit salad and toasted muesli, then come back at night for organic meats plus great seafood, veg and vegan choices. The caramelised-pumpkin and blue-cheese salad is delicious.

Green Dolphin (☎ 03-319 6666; 12 Avoca St; mains $29-38; ✹ 5pm-late) Quality Kaikoura fish Asian style, and the omnipresent bovine, ovine and lobstery treats, all made with care and a fondness for good local produce. On busy nights, book ahead or nurse a cocktail or aperitif in the pleasant bar or garden. Those with foresight should plump for a table with a view by the floor-to-ceiling windows.

Self-catering options:

Kaikoura Four Square Supermarket (☎ 03-319 5332; 31-33 West End; ✹ 8am-7pm)

New World Supermarket (☎ 03-319 5723; 124 Beach Rd; ✹ 8am-8pm)

Entertainment

Mayfair Theatre (☎ 03-319 5859; 80 The Esplanade; adult/child $10/6; ✹ 6.30pm-10pm Thu-Sat, daily in summer)

Resembling a pink liquorice allsort, this seafront picture house screens almost-recent releases.

Getting There & Away
BUS

InterCity (☎ 03-365 1113; www.intercity.co.nz) buses run between Kaikoura and Nelson ($64, 3½ hours, one daily), Picton ($35, 2¼ hours, two daily) and Christchurch ($31, 2¾ hours, two daily). Buses belch into the car park next to the i-SITE (tickets and info inside).

Naked Bus (☎ 0900 625 33; www.nakedbus.com) also runs to/from Kaikoura to most South Island destinations, departing from the i-SITE. Book online or at the i-SITE; cheaper fares for advance bookings.

TRAIN

Tranz Scenic (☎ 0800 872 467, 04-495 0775; www.tranz scenic.co.nz) runs the *TranzCoastal* service, stopping at Kaikoura on its daily run between Picton ($58, two hours 20 minutes) and Christchurch ($60, three hours). The northbound train departs Kaikoura at 9.54am; the southbound at 3.28pm. Discount fares (as low as Picton/Christchurch $28/29) are often available online.

Getting Around

Hire bicycles from **R&R Sport** (☎ 03-319 5028; 14 West End; 1hr/half-/full-day hire $10/20/30; ✹ 9am-7pm Mon-Sat, to 5.30pm in winter, 10am-4pm Sun). Maui YHA (p147) also hires bikes.

There's no public transport to Kaikoura Airport, but **Kaikoura Shuttles** (☎ 03-319 6166; www.kaikourashuttles.co.nz) will shunt you there cheaply.

NELSON REGION

The Nelson region, centred upon Tasman Bay but stretching north to Golden Bay and Farewell Spit, and south to Nelson Lakes, is a popular travel destination for both international visitors and locals. It's not hard to see why. Not only does it boast three national parks (Kahurangi, Nelson Lakes and Abel Tasman), but it can also satisfy nearly every other whim, from food, wine and craft beer, to arts and festivals, ecotourism and adventure sports, to that most precious of pastimes for which the region is well known: lazing about in the sunshine.

NELSON
pop 43,500

Dishing up a winning combination of great weather, beautiful surroundings, popular arts events, and a high number of charming wooden houses, Nelson is hailed as one of New Zealand's most 'liveable' cities. While Nelsonians are generally stereotyped as colourful, arty types wont to attend yoga classes and grow their own vegetables, they are in fact a much more diverse group likely to include sun-seeking retirees, heritage fanatics, wealthy entrepreneurs, outdoor enthusiasts, and various takes on the common- or garden-variety family. There are also the itinerant – large numbers of people like you and me, just passing through, who get suckered in by this energetic town and its proximity to some very sunny fun.

Information

BOOKSHOPS

Litter Arty (Map p152; ☎ 03-546 8009; litterarty@ tasman.net; 91 Hardy St; ☼ 10am-5.30pm Mon-Fri, 9.30-2.30pm Sat) Quirky secondhand book exchange.

Page & Blackmore Booksellers (Map p152; ☎ 03-548 9992; www.pageandblackmore.co.nz; 254 Trafalgar St; ☼ 9am-5.30pm Mon-Fri, to 4pm Sat, 10am-4pm Sun) Independent bookseller.

EMERGENCY

Ambulance, fire service & police (☎ 111)

Nelson police station (Map p152; ☎ 03-546 3840; cnr St John & Harley Sts; ☼ 24hr)

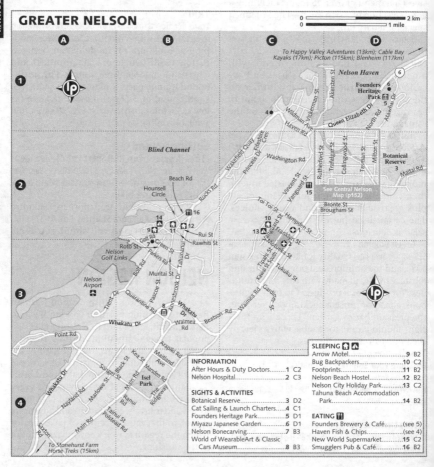

GREATER NELSON

To Happy Valley Adventures (13km); Cable Bay Kayaks (17km); Picton (115km); Blenheim (117km)

Nelson Haven

Blind Channel

See Central Nelson Map (p152)

Botanical Reserve

Nelson Golf Links

Nelson Airport

To Stonehurst Farm Horse Treks (15km)

INFORMATION	
After Hours & Duty Doctors	1 C2
Nelson Hospital	2 C3

SIGHTS & ACTIVITIES	
Botanical Reserve	3 D2
Cat Sailing & Launch Charters	4 C1
Founders Heritage Park	5 D1
Miyazu Japanese Garden	6 D1
Nelson Bonecarving	7 B3
World of WearableArt & Classic Cars Museum	8 B3

SLEEPING 🏠 🏕	
Arrow Motel	9 B2
Bug Backpackers	10 C2
Footprints	11 B2
Nelson Beach Hostel	12 B2
Nelson City Holiday Park	13 C2
Tahuna Beach Accommodation Park	14 B2

EATING 🍴	
Founders Brewery & Café	(see 5)
Haven Fish & Chips	(see 4)
New World Supermarket	15 C2
Smugglers Pub & Café	16 B2

INTERNET ACCESS
Aurora (Map p152; 161 Trafalgar St; ☺ 9am-late)
Boots Off Traveller Centre (Map p152; 53 Bridge St; ☺ 9.30am-late)

INTERNET RESOURCES
Backpack Nelson (www.backpacknelson.com) Information for the budget-bound.
Eat Drink Nelson (www.eatdrinknelson.co.nz) Culinary guide to restaurants, cafes, wines and gourmet produce.
Nelson NZ (www.nelsonnz.com) Official Nelson tourism website.
Nelson Wines (www.wineart.co.nz) Local wineries and galleries.

MEDICAL SERVICES
After Hours & Duty Doctors (Map p150; ☎ 03-546 8881; 96 Waimea Rd; ☺ 8am-10pm) After-hours attention and general practitioners.
Nelson Hospital (Map p150; ☎ 03-546 1800; www.nmdhb.govt.nz; Waimea Rd; ☺ 24hr) Emergency doctor and dentist; entry off Tipahi St.

MONEY
Banks and ATMs pepper Trafalgar St.

POST
Post office (Map p152; 209 Hardy St)

TOURIST INFORMATION
Automobile Association (AA; Map p152; ☎ 03-548 8339; www.aa.co.nz; 45 Halifax St; ☺ 8.30am 5pm Mon-Fri, from 9am Tue)
Nelson i-SITE (Map p152; ☎ 03-548 2304; www.nelsonnz.com; cnr Trafalgar & Halifax Sts; ☺ 8.30am-5pm Mon-Fri, 9am-5pm Sat & Sun) Pick up a copy of the *Nelson/Tasman Region Visitor Guide*. The DOC information desk has the low-down on national parks and walks (including Abel Tasman and Heaphy tracks).

Sights
HISTORIC BUILDINGS
The enduring symbol of Nelson is the art-deco **Christ Church Cathedral** (Map p152; ☎ 03-548 1008; www.nelsoncathedral.org; Trafalgar Sq; admission free; ☺ 8am-7pm summer, to 5pm winter), lording over the city from the top of Trafalgar St. Work began in 1925 but was delayed, and arguments raged in the 1950s over whether the design should adhere to original plans or embrace modern trends. The architectural hybrid was finally completed in 1965 and consecrated in 1972, 47 years after the foundation stone hit the dirt.

Just west of the cathedral, **South Street** (Map p152) contains a row of improbably quaint workers' cottages, built between 1863 and 1867: those in the know say it's the oldest fully intact street in NZ. Some cottages are available as accommodation (see p156).

MUSEUMS & GALLERIES
The **Nelson Provincial Museum** (Map p152; ☎ 03-548 9588; www.nelsonmuseum.co.nz; cnr Hardy & Trafalgar Sts; admission by donation; ☺ 9am-5pm Mon-Fri, 10am-4.30pm Sat & Sun) is one of Nelson's showpieces. The modern space is filled with cultural heritage and natural history exhibits with a regional bias, and there's a great rooftop garden. Charges may apply for major exhibits.

Adjacent to Queen's Gardens, the **Suter** (Map p152; ☎ 03-548 4699; www.thesuter.org.nz; 208 Bridge St; adult/child/concession $3/50c/$1; ☺ 10.30am-4.30pm) is Nelson's bastion of high art, with changing exhibitions, musical and theatrical performances, films, a craft shop and cafe.

Nelson has an inordinate number of commercial galleries, all of which are listed in the *Art & Crafts Nelson City* brochure (with walking trail map) available from the i-SITE. Our favourites:
Flamedaisy Glass Design (Map p152; ☎ 03-548 4475; www.flamedaisy.com; 324 Trafalgar Sq; ☺ 10am-5pm Mon-Fri, to 4pm Sat) Boutique glass-blowing studio.
Jens Hansen (Map p152; ☎ 03-548 0640; www.jenshansen.com; 320 Trafalgar Sq; ☺ 9am-5pm Mon-Fri, to 2pm Sat) Gold and silversmith workshop producing contemporary jewellery (including the accursed ring for the *Lord of the Rings* movies).
Refinery Artspace (Map p152; ☎ 03-548 1721; www.refineryartspace.org; 31 Halifax St; ☺ 9am-5pm Mon-Fri, 10am-2pm Sat) Frequently changing local exhibitions, retail art and workshops.
South St Gallery (Map p152; ☎ 03-548 8117; www.nelsonpottery.co.nz; 10 Nile St W; ☺ 8am-4.30pm Mon-Fri, 10am-4pm Sat & Sun) An extensive collection of kooky, classy and colourful pottery.

While you're in these parts, don't miss Höglund (p160) and the Cool Store Gallery (p160) not far from Nelson city.

PARKS & MARKETS
Founders Heritage Park (Map p150; ☎ 03-548 2649; www.founderspark.co.nz; 87 Atawhai Dr; adult/child/family $7/5/15, under 12yr free; ☺ 10am-4.30pm), near the waterfront 1km from the city centre, houses a replica historic village with a bakery, chocolatier, museums, and more importantly

Founders Brewery & Café (Map p150; ☎ 03-548 4638; www.foundersbrewery.co.nz; meals $13-16, tastings $5, tours & tastings $7; ☺ 10am-8pm, to 4.30pm in winter), NZ's first certified organic brewery. Take a tour, or sip the finished product over a cafe lunch: Tall Blonde, Red Head, Long Black, Generation Ale and Fair Maiden brews. If you're only visiting the brewery there's no admission charge to the park. Also on-site is a weekly **farmers market** (admission free; ☺ 3-6pm Fri).

Walking tracks in Nelson's **Botanical Reserve** (Map p150; Milton St; admission free; ☺ 24hr) ascend Botanical Hill, where a spire proclaims it NZ's geographical centre. NZ's first-ever rugby match was played at the foot of the hill on 14 May 1870: Nelson Rugby Club trounced the lily-livered pansies from Nelson College 2-0.

Just down the road from Founders Park is serene **Miyazu Japanese Garden** (Map p150; Atawhai Dr; admission free; ☺ 24hr), full of sculptures, lanterns and ducks on placid ponds. Sit for a while and ponder something profound.

Don't miss **Nelson Market** (Map p152; ☎ 03-546 6454; Montgomery Sq; ☺ 8am-1pm Sat), a frenzy of fresh produce, food stalls, fashion, local arts, crafts and buskers. **Monty's Sunday Market** (☺ 9am-1pm Sun) is a flea market on the same site.

Activities

Nelson offers boundless opportunities to embrace the great outdoors (something to do with the sunshine?). The clear blue skies are particularly welcome: this is a real NZ hot

spot for paragliding, kiteboarding and hang gliding. Most operators are some way out of town, but will pick-up or drop-off in Nelson.

Tandem paragliding costs around $180, while introductory courses are around $250. Operators include the following:

Adventure Paragliding & Kiteboarding (☎ 0800 212 359, 03-540 2183; www.skyout.co.nz)

Cumulus Paragliding (☎ 03-929 5515; www.cumulus-tandems.co.nz)

Nelson Paragliding (☎ 0508 359 669, 03-544 1182; www.nelsonparagliding.co.nz)

Vertical Limits (Map p152; ☎ 03-545 7511; www.verticallimits.co.nz; 34 Vanguard St; ☉ noon-9pm Mon-Fri, to 4pm Sat & Sun)

An introduction to kiteboarding will cost you around $170:

Adventure Paragliding & Kiteboarding (see above)

Kitescool (☎ 021 354 837; www.kitescool.co.nz)

Kite Surf Nelson (☎ 0800 548 363; www.kitesurfnelson.co.nz)

Hang gliding is arranged through one of two operators: **Nelson Hang Gliding Adventures** (☎ 03-548 9151; www.flynelson.co.nz; flight $165) and **Hang Gliding New Zealand** (☎ 0800 212 359, 03-540 2183; www.hanggliding.co.nz; flight $180).

Rock climbing on the limestone cliffs around Golden Bay and Takaka is popular with the wiry bods. Vertical Limits (above) runs half-/full-day rock-climbing trips ($65/130), plus an indoor climbing wall in Nelson ($16 per day including equipment). Tandem paragliding is also available.

Strap yourself onto a 'skywire' and soar through the air at **Happy Valley Adventures** (off Map p150; ☎ 03-545 0304; www.happyvalleyadventures.co.nz; 194 Cable Bay Rd), a 15-minute drive northeast along SH6. The 1.65km-long Skywire (a chairlift/flying-fox hybrid) dangles you up to 150m above the native forest; rides cost $85/55 per adult/child. Quad-bike tours start at $80/20 per driver/passenger for one-hour forest rides, and 2½-hour horse treks cost $95.

Four kilometres down the road from Happy Valley Adventures is **Cable Bay Kayaks** (off Map p150; ☎ 0508 222 532, 03-545 0332; www.cablebaykayaks.co.nz; Cable Bay Rd), offering guided sea-kayaking trips (half-/full-day from $85/135) exploring the local coastline and marine life.

Cat Sailing & Launch Charters (Map p150; ☎ 03-547 6666; www.sailingcharters.co.nz; from $70) runs reasonably priced half-day, full-day and overnight sailing trips. Options include harbour cruises, fishing trips, the 'Wednesday night races' and Abel Tasman overnighters. **Sail Nelson** (☎ 03-546 7275; www.sailnelson.co.nz) offers charters (around $100 per hour) and official Yachting NZ 'learn-to-sail' courses (two days, $500).

Back on solid ground, **Stonehurst Farm Horse Treks** (off Map p150; ☎ 0800 487 357, 03-542 4121; www.stonehurstfarm.co.nz; RD 1, Richmond; 1hr/half-day rides $65/145), 22km south of town, offers kids' pony rides, one-hour farm rides, 2½-hour sunset and 'musterers', and a half-day riverside ride.

Hit the hillside mountain-bike trails with **Biking Nelson** (☎ 021 861 725; www.bikingnelson.co.nz),

MARLBOROUGH & NELSON

THE WONDROUS WORLD OF WEARABLEART

Nelson exudes creativity: it's hardly surprising that NZ's most inspiring fashion show was born here. It began humbly in 1987 when creator Suzie Moncrieff held a local off-beat fashion show. The concept was to create a piece of art that could be worn and modelled. The idea caught on, and the World of WearableArt Awards Show became an annual event. Wood, papier mâché, paua shell, earplugs, soft-drink cans, ping-pong balls, foodstuffs and more have been used to create garments; 'Bizarre Bra' entries are showstoppers.

The awards show has been transplanted to Wellington (p101), but you can ogle entries at Nelson's **World of WearableArt & Classic Cars Museum** (WOW; Map p150; ☎ 03-547 4573; www.wowcars.co.nz; 1 Cadillac Way; adult/child $20/8; ◷ 10am-5pm). High-tech galleries include a carousel mimicking a catwalk, and glow-in-the-dark room.

More car than bra? Under the same roof are 50 mint-condition classic cars and motorbikes. Exhibits change, but may include a 1959 pink Cadillac, a yellow 1950 Bullet Nose Studebaker convertible and a BMW bubble car. You can view another 70 jalopies in *The Classic Collection* next door ($8 extra). Cafe and art gallery on-site.

---

which runs three-hour guided rides including equipment for $99, and hire half-/full day $40/60.

Artisic types will love Stephan's bonecarving courses at **Nelson Bonecarving** (Map p150; ☎ 03-546 4275; www.carvingbone.co.nz; 87 Green St, Tahunanui; day course $79). He'll supply all materials, tools, instruction, encouragement and cups of tea (plus free pick-up/drop-off in town if needed); you supply inspiration and talent and you'll emerge with your very own bone carving.

Tours

Avocado Adventures (☎ 03-548 2311; www.avocado adventures.co.nz) Personalised small-group adventures around the region.

Bay Tours (☎ 0800 229 868, 03-548 6486; www.baytoursnelson.co.nz; half-/full-day tours from $78/130) Nelson city, region, wine, food and art tours. The full-day scenic tour includes a visit to Kaiteriteri and a cruise in Abel Tasman National Park.

JJ's Quality Tours (☎ 0800 229 868, 03-548 6486; www.jjstours.co.nz; tours from $78) Scenic, wine-focused and craft tours, plus a half-day brewery trail visiting four boutique breweries.

New Zealand Nature Tours (☎ 0800 326 868, 03-539 4477; www.newzealandnaturetours.com; tours from $123) Wine, scenic and nature tours around Nelson, Marlborough, Golden Bay and the West Coast.

Simply Wild (☎ 03-548 8500; www.simplywild.co.nz) A swathe of half- to five-day active wilderness adventures: walking, mountain biking, sailing, caving, rafting and canoeing around Nelson's national parks. Prices on application.

Tasman Helicopters (☎ 03-528 8075; www.tasman helicopters.co.nz; tours from $150) A host of chopper flights and tours, including D'Urville Island, trout fishing, lunch tours and flights over Farewell Spit, and Kahurangi and Abel Tasman National Parks.

Festivals & Events

Nelson Jazz & Blues Festival (☎ 03-547 7211; www.nelsonjazzfest.co.nz) Sixty scoobedoobop events over eight days in January. Local and international acts in halls and on street corners, regionwide.

Nelson Summer Festival (☎ 03-546 0200; www.nelsonfestivals.co.nz) One-month family-focused frenzy, from mid-January to mid-February. Buskers, outdoor cinema, theatre and concerts.

Marchfest (☎ 03-548 3887; www.marchfest.com) A celebration of beer, wine, music and more beer. Just one day in April, but see www.deadgoodbeerevents.com for Nelson's quarterly beer fetes.

Nelson Arts Festival (☎ 03-546 0212; www.nelson festivals.co.nz) Over 10 days in October; events include a street carnival, exhibitions, cabaret, writers, theatre and music.

Sleeping
BUDGET

ourpick Accents on the Park (Map p152; ☎ 0800 888 335, 03-548 4335; www.accentsonthepark.com; 335 Trafalgar Sq; sites $30, dm $20-28, d with/without bathroom $92/60; ▯ 🖙) Prepare to be dazzled. This perfectly positioned hostel has a hotel feel with its professional staff, balconies, on-site cafe-bar (with Mother's home cooking and movie nights with free popcorn), soundproofed rooms, quality linen, superclean bathrooms and bikes for hire. Bravo! (Book early.)

Bug Backpackers (Map p150; ☎ 03-539 4227; www.thebug.co.nz; 226 Vanguard St; dm $23-26, d $62-70; ▯ 🖙) A fresh, excellent hostel about 15 minutes' walk to town, occupying a converted villa and brand-new building next door. The Bug emits joie de vivre, with an unashamedly bold colour scheme and swarm of cutesy VW Beetle paraphernalia. Quality beds, nice kitchens, girls' dorm, and a homely backyard. Free bikes and pick-up/drop-offs.

Paradiso Backpackers (Map p152; ☎ 0800 269 667, 03-546 6703; www.backpackernelson.co.nz; 42 Weka St; unpowered sites $36, dm/d $25/64; ☐ 🖧 🎥) Club Med for the impoverished, Paradiso is a sprawling place that lures a backpacker-body-beautiful crowd to its poolside terrace. There are two kitchens, a high-rotation hammock, volleyball court and sauna. Book in advance to cut yourself a slice of the action.

Trampers Rest (Map p152; ☎ /fax 03-545 7477; 31 Alton St; dm/s/d $26/42/62; ☐ 🖧) With just a few beds (no bunks), much-loved Trampers is hard to beat for a homely environment. The enthusiastic owner is a keen tramper and cyclist, and provides comprehensive local information and free bikes. There's a small kitchen, book exchange, piano, and Bruce Springsteen on the stereo.

Green Monkey (Map p152; ☎ 03-545 7421; www.the greenmonkey.co.nz; 129 Milton St; dm/d $26/62; ☐ 🖧) Small, homely, comfortable option (carpeted; good linen), run by a friendly English couple. There are just two dorms, and two doubles with TV. Sit and chat among the fruit trees or toast yourself by the log fire. Free bikes and evening cake.

Tasman Bay Backpackers (Map p152; ☎ 0800 ??? 572, 03-548 7950; www.tasmanbaybackpackers.co.nz; 10 Weka St; unpowered sites $36, dm $27-27, d $64-85; ☐ 🖧) Typical of Nelson's breed of quality backpackers, this well-designed hostel has airy communal spaces, hypercoloured rooms, a sunny outdoor deck and a well-used hammock. Good freebies: bikes, breakfast during winter, and chocolate pudding year-round.

Nelson YHA (Map p152; ☎ 03-545 9988; www.yha. co.nz; 59 Rutherford St; dm/s/d from $31/63/84, d with bathroom $104; ☐ 🖧) A spotless, purpose-built, central hostel with high-quality facilities including a soundproof TV room (free videos and DVDs), two well-organised kitchens, and sunny outdoor terrace. Tour and activity bookings are a given, but some extra-mile care and attention is quite likely too.

Tahuna Beach Accommodation Park (Map p150; ☎ 0800 500 501, 03-548 5159; www.tahunabeach.co.nz; 70 Beach Rd; powered & unpowered sites $34, cabins/units $50-110; ☐ 🖧) A few minutes' walk from the beach, 5km from the city, this huge park is

home to thousands in high summer and you'll find it hellish or bloody brilliant depending on your mood. Supermarket, minigolf and playgrounds in situ.

Nelson City Holiday Park (Map p150; ☎ 0800 778 898, 03-548 1445; www.nelsonholidaypark.co.nz; 230 Vanguard St; powered & unpowered sites $36, cabins/units $60-120; ☐) The closest option to town: convenient, well-maintained, clean, but cramped (although the motel units are pretty good). Limited campsites by the creek out back.

Other backpacker options:

Footprints (Map p150; ☎ 03-546 5441; www.foot prints.co.nz; 31 Beach Rd; dm/s/d/apt from $25/32/68/130; ☐ 🖧) Ask for a room with a window in this well-run, multi-option place in a breezeblock former druid hall near Tahunanui beach.

Nelson Beach Hostel (Map p150; ☎ 03-548 6817; www.nelsonbeachhostel.co.nz; 25 Muritai St; dm/d $26/60; ☐ 🖧) Chilled-out place close to Tahunanui Beach, 4km from town. Free bikes are available, plus there's a pub across the road.

Palace Backpackers (Map p152; ☎ 03-548 4691; www.thepalace.co.nz; 114 Rutherford St; dm/d incl breakfast $25/60; ☐ 🖧) A big, old grungy place with plenty of character and appealing balconies.

MIDRANGE & TOP END

Te Maunga (Map p152; ☎ 03-548 8605; temaungahouse@ xtra.co.nz; 15 Dorothy Annie Way; s $80, d $90-120; 🖧) Aptly named ('the mountain'), this is a grand old family home on a knoll with exceptional views. Two doubles and a single, with their own bathrooms, are filled with characterful furniture and made up with good linens. Your buttery breakfast can be walked off up and down *that* hill. It's only a five-minute climb (15 minutes in all, from town), but only the leggy ones will revel in it. Closed from May to September.

Lynton Lodge (Map p152; ☎ 03-548 7112; www. holidayguide.co.nz/Nelson/LyntonLodge.aspx; 25 Examiner St; apt $95-130) On the hill near the Cathedral with city views, unashamedly dated Lynton Lodge offers self-contained apartments and a guest-house vibe – try for one of the balcony units. Affable host, grassy garden and superclose to town.

Sussex House (Map p152; ☎ 03-548 9972; www.sussex .co.nz; 238 Bridge St; s $110-150, d $150-180; ☐ 🖧) In a historic riverside home, the Sussex has five appealing en-suite B&B rooms, all named after famous composers (Strauss, Beethoven, Mozart et al). Wraparound balcony, views, gardens and French-speaking hosts.

MARLBOROUGH & NELSON

Cedar Grove (Map p152; ☎ 0800 233 274, 03-545 1133; www.cedargrove.co.nz; cnr Trafalgar & Grove Sts; studios $130-180, d $170-220; ☐) A big old cedar landmarks this smart, modern block of spacious apartments just three minutes' walk to town. Its range of studios and doubles are plush and elegant, with cooking facilities and all the business trimmings (phone, fax, internet jack).

Palazzo Motor Lodge (Map p152; ☎ 0800 472 5293, 03-545 8171; www.palazzomotorlodge.co.nz; 159 Rutherford St; studios $130-225, apt $225-290; ☐ ☜) Hosts with the most offer a cheerful welcome at this popular modern Italian-style motor lodge. The stylish studios and one- and two-room apartments feature enviable kitchens (with quality glassware/crockery, decent cooking utensils and dishwasher) and luxurious textiles. The odd bit of dubious art is easily forgiven. There are spa bath units, and breakfast is available.

Arrow Motel (Map p150; ☎ 03-546 4030; www.arrow motel.co.nz; 24 Golf Rd; d $145-160, q $205-225, 6-bed r $240-300; ☐ ☜ ☜) There are one- to three-bedroom options at this tidy motel within walking distance of Tahunanui beach, owner-operated by cheery, enviro-committed folk. All units are self-contained; some have balcony views of the campground and estuary behind. There is also a small pool.

South Street Cottages (Map p152; ☎ 03-540 2769; www.cottageaccommodation.co.nz; 1, 3 & 12 South St; d $215, apt $240) Stay on NZ's oldest preserved street in one of three endearing, two-bedroom self-contained cottages built in the 1860s. Each has all the comforts of home, including kitchen, laundry, log fire and courtyard garden; breakfast provisions supplied. There is a two-night minimum stay. The owners also have a modern two-bedroom apartment on the same street.

Eating
RESTAURANTS

Stefano's (Map p152; ☎ 03-546 7530; 91 Trafalgar St; pizzas $9-25; ☜ 9am-10pm; ☑) Located upstairs in the State Cinema complex, Stefano's wouldn't win any awards for its decor. This Italian-run joint, however, does get top marks for traditional pizza – thin, crispy and delicious. Escape the movie-time madness and smell of popcorn on one of two balcony tables.

When in Rome (Map p152; ☎ 03-548 1586; 278 Hardy St; mains $10-19; ☜ noon-2pm Mon-Sat, 5pm-late daily) With its swanky Roman-chic fit-out, you might expect to pay Euro prices here. Fear not, the food at this new Italian joint is reasonably priced and darn tasty too. Ample portions of proper pasta, interesting salads and thin, crispy pizzas: *bellissimo.*

Indian Café (Map p152; ☎ 03-548 4089; 94 Collingwood St; mains $12-23; ☜ noon-2pm Mon-Fri, 5pm-late daily) This open-plan, saffron-coloured Edwardian villa houses an Indian restaurant that keeps the *bhaji* raised with impressive interpretations of Anglo-Indian standards, such as chicken tandoori, rogan josh and beef madras. Share the mixed platter to start, then mop up your mains with one of 10 different breads.

Smugglers Pub & Café (Map p150; ☎ 03-546 4084; 8 Muritai St; mains $15-34; ☜ 11am-late) This maritime-themed pub was shipshape when last we boarded, with friendly staff dishing out hearty meals to hungry landlubbers. A dependable family option serving pub grub favourites such as roast-of-the-day, burgers and fish and chips. Good patio area.

Lambretta's (Map p152; ☎ 03-545 8555; 204 Hardy St; mains $16-28; ☜ 7.30am-10pm Mon-Sat, to 5pm in winter, 8.30am-3pm Sun) Feeding what seems like half of Nelson, Lambretta's is a continually busy diner-style joint with ample seating inside and out. Family friendly, the big-eatin' offerings include breakfast, lunch and dinner (pizza, pasta, salad) and hearty counter food along the lines of humongous muffins, pies, filled croissants and sandwiches. Good coffee, too.

Hopgood's (Map p152; ☎ 03-545 7191; 284 Trafalgar St; lunch $14-20, dinner $33-36; ☜ 11am-2pm Thu & Fri, 5.30-late Mon-Sat) Tongue-and-groove-lined Hopgood's is perfect for a romantic dinner or holiday treat. The food is decadent and skilfully prepared but unfussy, allowing quality local ingredients to shine. The Asian crispy duck followed by pork belly with watercress and apple purée was a knockout. Desirable, predominantly Kiwi wine list.

CAFES

Swedish Bakery & Café (Map p152; ☎ 03-546 8685; 54 Bridge St; snacks $2-7; ☜ 8.30am-4pm Mon-Fri, 9am-1.30pm Sat) Delicious breads, croissants, pastries and cakes from the resident Scandinavian baker. Lovely fresh filled rolls such as meatball and beetroot relish, or smoked-salmon bagels. Take your goodies away or eat in the bijou cafe.

Morrison St Café (Map p152; ☎ 03-548 8110; 244 Hardy St; meals $12-19; ☜ 7.30am-4pm Mon-Fri, 8.30am-3pm Sat, 9am-3pm Sun) Part cafe, part gallery, Morrison St is a polished operator, with a menu that sticks out of the cafe crowd. Enjoy raspberry and cinnamon butter pancakes for brekkie, then sneak back for a zingy Burmese chicken salad or an afternoon pick-me-up of coffee and cake.

DeVille (Map p152; ☎ 03-545 6911; 22 New St; meals $15-25; ☷ 9am-4pm Mon-Sat) Indoor-outdoor DeVille is a cool place, with a pebble-covered courtyard dotted with couches, mirror mosaics and established greenery. Feast on bagels, veggie burgers, nachos and thumpin' breakfasts away from hustle and bustle.

QUICK EATS

Penguino Ice Cream Café (Map p152; ☎ 03-545 6450; Montgomery Sq; items $2-9; ☷ 11am-5pm) Queuing for Penguino's superb gelato and sorbet, made daily on the premises, is a Nelson ritual. The boysenberry sorbet is a medal winner.

Tozzetti Panetteria (Map p152; ☎ 03-546 8484; 41 Halifax St; items $4-7; ☷ 7am-4pm Mon-Fri, to noon Sat; Ⓥ) You'll smell fresh bread baking before you see Tozzetti, a pocket-sized bakery serving beautiful breads, sandwiches and sweet treats.

Falafel Gourmet (Map p152; ☎ 03-545 6220; 195 Hardy St; meals $9-22; ☷ 10am-6pm Mon-Thu, to 8pm Fri, to 4pm Sat) A cranking Middle-Eastern joint dishing out the best kebabs in town, full of salad.

Haven Fish & Chips (Map p150; ☎ 03-548 7969; 268 Wakefield Quay; fish & chips $7-8; ☷ 11.30-1.30pm & 4.30pm-7.30pm Tue-Sun) Pick your own fillet, then eat your meal by the waterfront. What could be better?

SELF-CATERING

Mediterranean Foods (Map p152; ☎ 03-546 7964; 23 Halifax St; ☷ 9am-5.30pm Mon-Fri, to 2pm Sat) A terrific deli with great charcuterie, cheese, dried pasta et al, as well as sit-down coffee and sandwiches.

New World Supermarket (Map p150; ☎ 03-548 9111; cnr Vanguard & Gloucester Sts; ☷ 9am-9pm)

Organic Greengrocer (Map p152; ☎ 03-548 3650; cnr Tasman & Grove Sts; ☷ 9am-6pm Mon-Fri, to 3pm Sat; Ⓥ) Stocks foods for the sensitive, plus produce, organic tipples and natural bodycare.

Drinking

ourpick Free House (Map p152; ☎ 03-548 9391; 95 Collingwood St; ☷ 4pm-late Mon-Fri, noon-late Sat, to 6pm Sun) Come rejoice at this church of ales. Tastefully converted from its original, more reverent purpose, it's now home to an excellent, oft-changing selection of NZ craft beers. You can imbibe inside or out and even bring

a takeaway curry from the Indian Café opposite. Hallelujah.

Sprig & Fern (Map p152; ☎ 03-548 1154; 280 Hardy St; ☷ 2pm-late Mon-Fri, 10am-late Sat & Sun) Equally hopheaded, the Sprig & Fern brewery in Richmond supplies an extensive range of beers to S&F pubs springing up around the region. Nearly 20 brews on tap, from lager through to doppelbock and berry cider. No pokies, no TV, just decent beer, food, occasional live music and a pleasant outdoor area.

Vic (Map p152; ☎ 03-548 7631; 281 Trafalgar St; ☷ 11am-late) A commendable example of a Mac's Brewbar, with trademark, quirky Kiwiana fit-out including a striped, knitted stag's head. Quaff a few handles of ale, maybe grab a bite to eat (mains $13 to $30) and tap a toe to regular live music (Tuesday to Saturday). Good afternoon sun and people-watching from streetside seating.

Entertainment

Phat Club (Map p152; ☎ 03-548 3311; www.phatclub.co.nz; 137 Bridge St; admission from $5; ☷ 10pm-late Wed-Sat) DJs spin techno, dub, drum 'n' bass, breaks and hip-hop, while big-name international and national bands frequently grace the stage. Ambassadors of the local dance-music scene for almost a decade.

State Cinema 6 (Map p152; ☎ 03-548 8123; www.statecinema6.co.nz; 91 Trafalgar St; adult/child $14.50/9; ☷ 10am-midnight) is the place to see mainstream, new-release flicks.

The theatre at the Suter (p151) often hosts drama, music and dance.

Getting There & Away

AIR

Air New Zealand (Map p152; ☎ 0800 737 000, 03-546 3100; www.airnewzealand.co.nz; cnr Trafalgar & Bridge Sts; ☷ 9am-5pm Mon-Fri) has direct flights to/from Wellington (from $79, up to 12 daily), Auckland (from $99, up to 10 daily) and Christchurch (from $79, up to six daily).

Soundsair (☎ 0800 505 005, 03-520 3080; www.soundsair.com) flies daily between Nelson and Wellington (from $90, up to three daily).

Air2there (☎ 0800 777 000; www.air2there.com) flies between Nelson and Paraparaumu on the Kapiti Coast ($135, one daily), and onward to Wellington ($45, Fridays).

BUS

Book Abel Tasman Coachlines, InterCity and Interislander ferries at the **Nelson SBL Travel Centre**

(Map p152; ☎ 03-548 1539; www.nelsoncoaches.co.nz; 27 Bridge St).

Abel Tasman Coachlines (☎ 03-548 0285; www.abeltasmantravel.co.nz; departs SLB Travel Centre, Bridge St) operates services to Motueka ($12, one hour, four daily), Takaka ($32, two hours, two daily), Kaiteriteri ($20, two hours, four daily) and Marahau ($20, two hours, four daily). In summer buses also run to Totaranui ($20) and the Heaphy Track ($52).

Atomic Shuttles (☎ 03-349 0697; www.atomictravel.co.nz) runs from Picton to Nelson ($24, 2¼ hours, twice daily) continuing from Nelson to West Coast centres like Greymouth ($40, 5¾ hours, one daily) and Fox Glacier ($65, 9½ hours, one daily). Services depart Nelson i-SITE.

Naked Bus (☎ 0900 625 33; www.nakedbus.com) South Island destinations ex-Nelson include Blenheim (from $14, 1¾ hours, up to two daily), Motueka ($11, one hour, one daily) and Westport ($34, 3¾ hours, one daily). Buses depart the i-SITE. Book online or at the i-SITE; cheaper fares for advance bookings.

InterCity (☎ 03-548 1538; www.intercity.co.nz; departs SLB Travel Centre, Bridge St) runs from Nelson:

Destination	Price	Duration	Frequency
Christchurch	$71	7hr	1 daily
Greymouth	$80	6hr	1 daily
Kaikoura	$64	3½hr	1 daily
Picton	$34	2hr	1-3 daily
Westport	$59	3¾hr	1 daily

See p169 for services to/from Abel Tasman National Park and p172 for services around Golden Bay including the Heaphy Track. Note that many operators run reduced timetables from May to September.

Getting Around
TO/FROM THE AIRPORT
A taxi to the airport costs about $21, or **Super Shuttle** (☎ 0800 748 885, 03-522 5100; www.supershuttle.co.nz; 1/2 passengers $15/18; ⏱ 24hr) offers door-to-door service to/from Nelson Airport, 6km southwest of town. It's cheaper if two or more passengers are travelling to the same destination.

BICYCLE
Hire a bike from **Stewarts Avanti Plus Nelson** (Map p152; ☎ 03-548 1666; www.avantiplusnelson.co.nz; 114 Hardy St; hire per day $35-95, per week from $140;

⏱ 8am-5.30pm Mon-Fri, 9am-4pm Sat). City and mountain bikes, plus touring bikes, repairs and equipment.

BUS
Nelson Suburban Bus Lines (SBL; ☎ 03-548 3290; www.nelsoncoaches.co.nz; 27 Bridge St; adult $3.80; departs SLB Travel Centre, Bridge St) operates local services from Nelson to Richmond via Tahunanui and Stoke until about 6pm weekdays, 4.30pm on weekends. It also runs the **Late Late Bus** (tickets $3; ⏱ hourly 10pm-3am Fri & Sat) from Nelson to Richmond via Tahunanui, departing the Westpac Bank on Trafalgar St.

Departing Wakatu Sq, **The Bus** (Map p152; ☎ 03-548 3290; www.nelsoncoaches.co.nz; tickets adult $2) runs roughly hourly from 7am to 5pm on four routes to outlying areas (including Tahunanui).

TAXI
Nelson City Taxis (☎ 0800 108 855, 03-548 8225)
Sun City Taxis (☎ 0800 422 666, 03-548 2666)

NELSON LAKES NATIONAL PARK
Pristine Nelson Lakes National Park surrounds two mirrorlike glacial lakes – Rotoiti and Rotoroa – fringed by beech forest with a backdrop of forested mountains. There's an unexpected hint of Fiordland about the place, minus the crowds – an unusual sense that you're well off the tourist trail.

Part of the park, east of Lake Rotoiti, is classed as a 'mainland island' where an aggressive conservation scheme aims to eradicate introduced pests (possums, stoats), and regenerate native flora and fauna. There's excellent tramping, including short walks, lake scenery and also winter skiing at Rainbow ski field (p82). The park is flush with bird life, and is famous for brown-trout fishing.

Orientation & Information
To get here take SH6 south from Nelson towards Murchison, or SH65 southwest from Blenheim; the journey will take about 1¼ hours either way. The park itself is accessible from both Lake Rotoiti and Lake Rotoroa. The main town is diminutive St Arnaud near Lake Rotoiti. Lake Rotoroa, 11km off the highway, sees far fewer visitors (mainly trampers, sandflies and fisherfolk), although there is some accommodation down this way.

The **DOC visitors centre** (☎ 03-521 1806; www.
doc.govt.nz; View Rd, St Arnaud; ⏰ 8am-5pm peak
summer) proffers park information (weather,
activities, hut tickets) plus displays on park
ecology and Maori history. See also www.st
arnaud.co.nz.

Activities

There are many spectacular walks allowing
you to appreciate this rugged landscape, but
before you tackle them, stop by the DOC visitor centre for maps, track/weather updates
and to leave intentions.

The five-hour **Mt Robert Circuit Track** starts
south of St Arnaud and circumnavigates the
mountain, with options for a side trip along
Robert Ridge. Alternatively, the **St Arnaud
Range Track** (five hours return), on the east
side of the lake, climbs steadily to the ridgeline
via Parachute Rocks. Both tracks are strenuous, but reward with jaw-dropping views of
glaciated valleys, arête peaks and Lake Rotoiti.
Only attempt these walks in fine weather. At
other times they are both pointless (no views)
and dangerous.

Short walks at Rotoiti, most starting from
the car park at Kerr Bay, include the **Bellbird
Walk** (15 minutes), **Honeydew Walk** (45 minutes), **Peninsula Nature Walk** (1½ hours), **Black
Hill Walk** (1½ hours) and **Loop Track** (1½ hours).

Walks around Lake Rotoroa include the
Nature Walk (25 minutes), **Porika Lookout Track**
(one to three hours return) at the northern
end of the lake, and **Braeburn Walk** (two hours
return) on the western side.

The 80km five- to seven-day **Travers–Sabine
Circuit** from St Arnaud is a tramp for the hardy
and experienced, with backcountry skills
essential.

Sleeping & Eating

DOC campsite (☎ 03-521 1806; unpowered/powered
sites Oct-May $20/24, Jun-Sep $14/16) Located on
the shores of Lake Rotoiti at Kerr Bay, this
inviting site has toilets, hot showers (summer only) and a kitchen. Three kilometres
from St Arnaud, West Bay campsite has the
bare necessities and is open in summer only.
Bookings are essential over the Christmas and
Easter holidays.

Travers-Sabine Lodge (☎ 03-521 1887; www.nelson
lakes.co.nz; Main Rd, St Arnaud; dm/d $26/59; 🖳 🛜)
This modern lodge is a great base for outdoor adventure, being a short walk to Lake
Rotoiti, inexpensive, clean and comfortable.

It also has particularly cheerful technicolour
linen in the dorms, doubles and a family
room. The owners are experienced adven-
turers themselves, so tips come as standard;
tramping equipment and snowshoes available for hire.

Nelson Lakes Motels (☎ 03-521 1887; www.nelson
lakes.co.nz; Main Rd, St Arnaud; d $110-129; 🖳 🛜) Next
to the Travers-Sabine Lodge and run by the
same people, these log cabins and newer
board-and-batten units offer all the creature
comforts, including kitchenettes and Sky TV.
Bigger units sleep up to six.

Alpine Lodge (☎ 03-521 1869; www.alpinelodge.co.nz;
Main Rd, St Arnaud; d $145-180; 🖳 🛜) This lodge
tries its darnedest to create an alpine mood.
There's a range of accommodation, the pick
of which are the split-level doubles with mezzanine bedroom, spa and pine timberwork
aplenty. A fairly spartan budget chalet (dorm/
double $25/65) is clean and warm, and head-
ing for renovations. The in-house restaurant
is a snug, family affair, serving crowd-pleasing
meals (mixed grill, nachos, $17 to $33) and a
children's menu.

Part of the same complex, **Alpine Lodge Café**
(☎ 03-521 1288; Main Rd, St Arnaud; meals $9-27; ⏰ 8am-
5pm Wed-Mon) is a toasty spot decked out in
retro-Kiwiana. Youthful, on-to-it crew serve
up a short, snappy menu, wholesome counter
food and Supreme Coffee. Cool tunes on the
stereo.

St Arnaud Alpine Village Store (☎ 03-521 1854; Main
Rd, St Arnaud; ⏰ 7.30am-8.30pm) The settlement's
only general store sells groceries, petrol, good
beer and possum-wool socks. Mountain-bike
hire per half-/full-day is $20/40. It also has
sandwiches, pies and milkshakes, and from
4.30pm to 8.30pm the owners crank up the
fish-and-chip shop ($4 to $9).

Tophouse Historic Hotel (☎ 03-521 1848; www.top
house.co.nz; Tophouse Rd; s/d $75/135, chalets d $135) Nine
kilometres from St Arnaud off the Blenheim
road, the hilltop Tophouse was built in 1887.
Rich in history, this rare cob highway inn has
big open fires and a preloved interior. It has
comfy beds with good linen, home cooking
(cake and coffee, venison pies, a $45 four-
course dinner – bookings are essential) and
cheerful hospitality. Reopened after 40 years,
'New Zealand's smallest bar' serves good local
beer with a little elbow room; the garden bar
has fantastic St Arnaud Range views. Out in
the back paddock are four chalets sleeping
up to five.

Getting There & Around

Nelson Lakes Shuttles (☎ 03-521 1900, 021 490 095; www.nelsonlakesshuttles.co.nz) provides on-demand transport from St Arnaud to the Mt Robert car park (all prices per person are $10), Lake Rotoroa ($25), Murchison ($30) and further afield, including Nelson ($30), Picton ($35) and the Heaphy Track ($60). Minimum numbers apply, depending on destination; check the website for up-to-the-minute movements.

Rotoiti Water Taxis (☎ 03-521 1894, 021 702 278; www.rotoitiwatertaxis.co.nz) runs to/from Kerr Bay and West Bay to Lakehead Jetty ($75, up to four people) and Coldwater Jetty ($90, up to four people). Kayaks, canoes and rowboats can also be hired from $40 per half-day; fishing trips and scenic lake cruises by arrangement.

NELSON TO MOTUEKA

From Richmond, south of Nelson, SH60 heads northwest to Motueka. This stretch of Tasman Bay teems with local holidaymakers: there's plenty of accommodation, art-and-craft activity, vineyards, fruit stalls and swimming to draw you off the highway. The area is also flap-happy with bird life, particularly Arctic migrant waders.

Sights & Activities

WINERIES

The Nelson region has a significant winemaking industry, and although it can't challenge Marlborough's marketing juggernaut, there are enough quality wineries here to keep the average vinophile busy – 23 at last count; the *Nelson Wine Guide* pamphlet (www.wineart.co.nz) lists them. Chardonnay, pinot noir and aromatic varietals are favoured. See p154 for local wine tours, or tackle the vineyards via a loop from Nelson to Motueka along coastal SH60 and back through the inland Moutere Hwy. Wineries are open for tastings and sales; several have cafes and restaurants.

A few of our fave local wineries:

Neudorf (☎ 03-543 2643; www.neudorf.co.nz; 138 Neudorf Rd, Upper Moutere; ✆ 11am-5pm) Moss-covered barnlike complex; gorgeous pinot noir and some of the country's finest chardonnay.

Seifried (☎ 03-544 5599; www.seifried.co.nz; cnr SH60 & Redwood Rd; ✆ 10am-5pm) One of the region's biggest wineries, at the turn-off to Rabbit Island, and home to a pleasant garden restaurant.

Waimea (☎ 03-544 4963; www.waimeaestates.co.nz; SH60, Richmond; ✆ 11am-5pm) Jazzy cafe and tables by the vines.

Woollaston (☎ 03-543 2817; www.woollaston.co.nz; SH60, Richmond; ✆ 11am-5pm) Multilevel winery set into the hillside with tussock roof, gallery and picturesque surrounds. Enjoy a platter on the lawn.

OTHER SIGHTS & ACTIVITIES

There are loads of craft outlets along these routes too; for details pick up the *Nelson's Creative Pathways* or *Nelson Art Guide* brochures from the Nelson i-SITE and around.

View and/or buy vitreous masterpieces at **Höglund Glass Art** (☎ 03-544 6500; www.hoglundartglass. com; 52 Landsdowne Rd, Appleby; ✆ 10am-5pm), a five-minute drive west of Richmond. The furnace operates between Christmas and Easter: come watch Ola the master and his trainees, who blow most days during this time.

Just up the road (SH60) is the turn-off to **Rabbit Island**, a recreation reserve boasting unspoilt swimming beaches and pine forests. We didn't see any rabbits when we visited, but plenty of walkers, boaters, swimmers and sunbathers. The bridge to the island closes at sunset; overnight stays are not allowed.

Further along, the picturesque Waimea Inlet and twin villages of **Mapua** and **Ruby Bay** sit at the mouth of the Waimea River, one of NZ's biggest estuaries and a haven for bird life. Clustered around Mapua's town wharf are chi-chi shops and art galleries, the best of which is the **Cool Store Gallery** (☎ 03-540 3778; www.coolstoregallery.co.nz; 7 Aranui Rd, Mapua; ✆ 11am-5pm). Packed with high-quality local art, it's brilliant for browsers, while those with dough may find it impossible to leave empty-handed. With the kids in tow, nip into **Touch the Sea** (☎ 03-540 3557; www.seatouchaquarium. co.nz; 8 Aranui Rd, Mapua; adult/child/family $8.50/5/19; ✆ 10am-5.30pm), a small aquarium where you're allowed to touch anything you can reach in the tank.

Sleeping & Eating

Consult staff at Nelson or Motueka i-SITEs for a host of out-of-the-way homestays, cottages and B&Bs in the area.

Mapua Leisure Park (☎ 03-540 2666; www.mapua leisurepark.co.nz; 33 Toru St, Mapua; unpowered/powered sites $32/34, cabins $70-85, motels $115-135; 🖳 🛜 🐾) This is 'NZ's only clothes-optional leisure park' but you don't *have* to nude-up, and the buff option is only available from February to March. It's a bit ragged around the edges, but the location and swimming are sweet, and there are tennis and volleyball courts, kayak hire, pool, sauna, spa and a waterfront cafe.

Clayridge House (☎ 03-540 2548; www.clayridge. co.nz; 77 Pinehill Rd, Ruby Bay; B&B s/d $180/250, cottages $180-200, extra person $25; 🖳) On a property high above Ruby Bay with sea views across Tasman Bay to Nelson, surrounded by orchards and vineyards, this is the perfect place to unwind. There's a choice of B&B guest rooms or modern two-bedroom, self-contained cottages (two-night minimum stay for the cottages).

Golden Bear Brewing Company (☎ 03-540 3210; 12 Aranui Rd; snacks $3-16; 🕑 noon-10pm Thu-Sat, to 8pm Sun) New brewery by the wharf with tuns of stainless steel out back. Eight quality beers on tap – brewed using only South Island ingredients – and authentic Mexican food (burritos, quesadillas and huevos rancheros) to stop you from getting a sore head. Takeaway beers and tours available.

Jester House (☎ 03-526 6742; SH60, Tasman; meals $13-20; 🕑 9am-5pm) A perennially popular highway stop, as much for its tame eels (which you can feed) as for the peaceful sculpture gardens that encourage you to linger over lunch. A short, simple menu puts a few twists into the staples (wild pork burger, lavender shortbread), and there's Mussel Inn beers and local wine. It's 8km to Mapua or Motueka.

Smokehouse (☎ 03-540 2280; www.smokehouse. co.nz; Mapua Wharf; mains $26-33; 🕑 9am-9pm) Hamish the white heron surveys proceedings at this water's-edge eatery, which serves fresh, wood-smoked fish and a bevy of seafood dishes in salty surroundings. Its shop next door has excellent fish and chips as well as smoked fish and pâté to go.

MOTUEKA
pop 6900

Motueka (pronounced Mott-oo-ecka, meaning 'Island of Wekas') has morphed from something quite ordinary into a place that the locals are proud to call home. A bustling town servicing a large urban and pretty rural area, visitors will find it a handy pit stop en route to Golden Bay and the Abel Tasman and Kahurangi National Parks. Closer to home, however, are all vital amenities, ample accommodation, cafes, roadside fruit stalls, and a clean and beautiful river offering swimming and fishing.

Information

Cyberworld (☎ 03-528 8090; www.abeltasmaninform ation.co.nz; 178 High St; 🕑 9am-9pm) Internet access and associated services, plus local info and bookings.

Motueka i-SITE (☎ 03-528 6543; www.motuekaisite. co.nz; 20 Wallace St; 🕑 8.30am-5pm Mon-Fri, 9am-4pm Sat & Sun) An excellent centre with helpful staff, able to making bookings from Kaitaia to Bluff and offer local national park expertise and necessaries.

Motueka police station (☎ 03-528 1220; 68 High St; 🕑 24hr)

Take Note/post office (☎ 03-528 6600; 207 High St; 🕑 8am-5.30pm Mon-Fri, 9am-4pm Sat, 10am-4pm Sun) Bookshop moonlighting as a post office.

Sights & Activities

To get a grip on the town, visit the i-SITE and collect the *Motueka Art Walk* pamphlet, detailing sculpture, mural and occasional peculiarities around town. This will take you past the **Motueka District Museum** (☎ 03-528 7660; savepast@ihug.co.nz; 140 High St; admission by donation; 🕑 10am-4pm Mon-Sat, closed Mon in winter). It has displays recreating the region's colonial past, plus a cafe.

On Sunday the car park behind the i-SITE fills up with trestle tables for the **Motueka Sunday Market** (☎ 03-540 2709; Wallace St; 🕑 8am-1pm Sun): produce, jewellery, buskers, arts, crafts and Doris' divine bratwurst.

Ten minutes' walk from the town centre is one of New Zealand's best small airstrips, offering pleasurable spectating (coffee cart on-site in summer). Visitors have three eye-popping/pant-wetting options for getting airborne (accessed off College St). **Skydive Abel Tasman** (☎ 0800 422 899, 03-528 4091; www.skydive. co.nz; jumps 12,000ft/13,000ft $279/299) offers tandem skydiving. Move over Taupo: we've jumped both and think Mot takes the cake (presumably so do the many sports jumpers who favour this drop zone, some of whom you may see rocketing in). DVDs and photos cost extra; free pick-up/drop-off from Motueka and Nelson.

Rather soar than plummet? **Tasman Sky Adventures** (☎ 0800 114 386, 027 229 9693; www.skyad ventures.co.nz) offers a rare opportunity to fly in a microlight. Keep your eyes open and blow your mind on its 30-minute scenic flight above Abel Tasman National Park ($155). Wow. And there's tandem hang gliding for the eager (15/30 minutes, 2500ft/5280ft $185/275).

Next stop is one for the courageous: aerobatics in an open cockpit Pitt-Special with

MARLBOROUGH & NELSON

MOTUEKA

INFORMATION	
Cyberworld	**1** C2
Motueka i-SITE	**2** C2
Mouteka Police Station	**3** C1
Take Note/Post Office	**4** C2

SIGHTS & ACTIVITIES	
Abel Tasman Wilson's Experiences	**5** C2
Bike Tasman	(see 23)
Motueka District Museum	**6** C2
Motueka Sunday Market	**7** C2
Sea Kayak Company	**8** C4
Skydive Abel Tasman	**9** A3
Tasman Sky Adventures	**10** A3
U-fly Extreme	**11** A3

SLEEPING 🏨 🏕	
Avalon Manor Motel	**12** C2
Bakers Lodge	**13** C1
Equestrian Lodge Motel	**14** C2
Hat Trick Lodge	**15** C1
Lagoon Lodge	**16** C4
Laughing Kiwi	**17** C2
Motueka Top 10 Holiday Park	**18** C1
Nautilus Lodge	**19** C1
Rowan Cottage	**20** C1
White Elephant	**21** B2

EATING 🍴	
Chokdee	(see 22)
MoTown Pizzeria & Juice Bar	**22** C1
Motueka Deli	**23** C2
New World Supermarket	**24** C2
Patisserie Royale	**25** C2
Red Beret	**26** C2

Simply Indian	**27** C1
Up the Garden Path	**28** C3

ENTERTAINMENT 🎭	
Gecko Theatre	**29** C2

Map labels: To Eden's Edge Backpacker Lodge (5km); Resurgence (15km); Kaiteriteri (13km); Marahau (18km); Takaka (57km); Parker St; Fearon St; Jocelyn Ave; Wilkie St; Saxon St; Thorp St; Poole St; York St; Clay St; Pah St; Greenwood St; Greenwood St; Grey St; Wallace St; Wilkison St; Taylor Ave; Tudor St; Motueka Golf Course; Harbour Rd; Whakarewa St; Green La; Motueka Airstrip; Queen Victoria St; College St; King Edward St; High St; Woodland Ave; Goodman Reserve; Old Wharf Rd; Thorp St; Trewavas St; Tasman Bay; Courtney St; Coastal Hwy; Motueka Quay; Motueka Beach; Wharf Rd; To Nelson (49km); Moutere Inlet; High St S; Saltwater Swimming Pool; Ward St; George Quay; Port Motueka

U-fly Extreme (☎ 0800 360 180, 03-528 8290; www.uflyex treme.co.nz; 20min $285). No experience necessary, just a strong stomach. Weaklings can take a scenic flight in the Cessna (minimum two people half-/one hour $135/265).

Energetic but more sane folk can hire bikes from **Bike Tasman** (☎ 0508 254 464, 021 958 890; www.biketasman.co.nz; 195 High St; half-/full day $40/60). Guided tours available (from $79).

Sleeping
BUDGET

Lagoon Lodge (☎ 03-528 8652; www.happyapple backpackers.co.nz; 500 High St; sites per person $14, dm/s/d $27/40/60; 🖳 🛜) Formerly the Happy Apple; new owners have made many improvements to this hostel, freshly paint-licked and swad-

dled in new soft furnishings. Rooms are divided between the house (nice doubles) and dorm wing. The action's all in the quiet yard out back where there's an expansive lawn (camping allowed), gardens, lounging areas and spa pool.

ourpick Eden's Edge Backpacker Lodge (☎ 03-528 4242; www.edensedge.co.nz; 137 Lodder Ln, Riwaka; sites $15, dm $30, d with/without bathroom $80/70, tr with/without bathroom $105/100; 🖳 🛜 🞉) Surrounded by orchards just five minutes' drive to Motueka, this new lodge comes pretty darn close to backpacker heaven. Well-designed facilities include a spotless kitchen, inviting communal areas and ample deck space. Dreamy 10m rainwater pool, and all within walking distance of beer, ice cream, coffee and fresh bread.

Motueka Top 10 Holiday Park (☎ 0800 668 835, 03-528 7189; www.motuekatop10.co.nz; 10 Fearon St; unpowered & powered sites $40, cabins $50-60, units/motels $105-150; 🖳 🛜 🕭) A busy park at the northern end of town, with all the bells and whistles including cabin and motel options. Grassy campsites are peppered with shady native trees, and the central amenities block is fresh out of the box. Prices take a tumble either side of December and January. Local wine tours by arrangement.

Other hostels:

Bakers Lodge (☎ 03-528 0102; www.bakerslodge. co.nz; 4 Poole St; dm $23, d with/without bathroom $75/65, f with/without bathroom $125/115; 🖳 🛜) A roomy YHA just off the main street. Ceilings are tall, facilities are in reasonable shape, and there are plenty of common areas, including two kitchens and barbecue terrace. Legendary evening muffins.

Hat Trick Lodge (☎ 03-528 5353; www.hattricklodge. co.nz; 25 Wallace St; dm $25, d with/without bathroom $70/62; 🖳 🛜) A purpose-built lodge with little personality. It is, however, clean and tidy with a pleasant kitchen-dining area and two 2nd-storey deck areas.

Laughing Kiwi (☎ 03-528 9229; www.laughingkiwi. co.nz; 310 High St; dm $24-26, d with/without bathroom $66/60; 🖳 🛜) A two-block combo of rambling old house and a modern, purpose-built bunkhouse. The new section is a better bet, with airy kitchen and sundeck. Free spa.

White Elephant (☎ 03-528 6208; www.white elephant.co.nz; 55 Whakarewa St; dm $24, d with/without bathroom $74/70; 🖳 🛜) Dorms in a high-ceilinged colonial villa have a creaky charm, but our pick is the en-suite cabins in the garden.

MIDRANGE & TOP END
Numerous midrange B&Bs and holiday homes are secreted in the surrounds – ask the i-SITE for suggestions.

Equestrian Lodge Motel (☎ 0800 668 782, 03-528 9369; www.equestrianlodge.co.nz; Avalon Ct, off Tudor St; d $110-135, q $160-195; 🖳 🛜 🕭) No horses, no lodge, but no matter. This is a lovely option: quiet, close to town, with expansive lawns, rose gardens and shady corners. Family-friendly amenities include several trampolines and a heated pool (and spa). Rooms are clean but do need a spruce-up (in progress, thankfully).

Nautilus Lodge (☎ 0800 628 845, 03-528 4658; www.nautiluslodge.co.nz; 67 High St; d $110-220; 🖳 🛜) Probably the best motel north of Christchurch, with 12 high-class units dressed in adobe. Rooms feature subtle wall colours, European

slatted beds, beautiful bathrooms, flat-screen TVs and plush linen. Good off-season rates; spas and kitchenettes in bigger units.

Avalon Manor Motel (☎ 0800 282 566, 03-528 8320; www.avalonmotels.co.nz; 314 High St; d $125-225; 🖳 🛜) Prominent L-shaped motel on the highway heading into town from Nelson. Massive four-star rooms have a contemporary vibe, with cooking facilities, Sky TV, free videos and DVDs. Sumptuous studios have king-size beds and huge flat-screen TVs. There's also a garden and guest barbecue.

Also recommended:

Resurgence (☎ 03-528 4664; www.resurgence.co.nz; Riwaka Valley Rd, Riwaka; lodge $545-645, chalets $445-595; 🖳 🛜 🕭) Choose a luxurious en-suite lodge room or self-contained chalet at this magical 50-acre bushland retreat 15 minutes' drive north of Motueka, and half an hour's walk from the picturesque source of the Riwaka River. Lodge rates include cocktails and a four-course dinner as well as breakfast, or you can fire up the barbecue if you're staying in one of the chalets. Chalet rates are for B&B; lodge dinner extra ($90).

Rowan Cottage (☎ 03-528 6492; www.rowancottage. net; 27 Fearon St; d incl breakfast $110-150) Chomp into an organic breakfast in one of two private rooms – choose the studio with outdoor deck and spa. Cheaper sans breakfast.

Eating & Drinking
Red Beret (☎ 03-528 0087; 145 High St; meals $9-19; 🕒 8am-5pm; 🅥) Slick and chic family-run affair that's raised the bar of Mot's cafe scene. Tasty and generous à la carte menu – egg brekkies, steak sandwiches, BLE(egg)T – plus salads galore and the best counter food in town.

MoTown Pizzeria & Juice Bar (☎ 03-528 6060; 107 High St; meals $9-21; 🕒 11am-late; 🅥) Retro-styled MoTown is a fun place to chew the fat with your friends over decent pizza and fresh juice. Eat up in the little mezzanine lounge or down in the diner with its formica tables and '60s musical motifs. Cutesy named pizzas (the Diana Ross, Smokey Robinson) boast traditional and sensible gourmet toppings.

Simply Indian (☎ 03-528 6364; 130 High St; mains $15-21; 🕒 11am-2pm & 5.30-9pm Mon-Sat, 5.30-9pm Sun; 🅥) As the name suggests: no-nonsense curry in a no-frills setting. The food, however, is consistently good and relatively cheap. Expect the usual suspects such as tikka, tandoori, madras and vindaloo, and the ubiquitous naan prepared eight different ways. Takeaways are available.

Up the Garden Path (☎ 03-528 9588; 473 High St; meals $15-30; ☺ 9am-5pm Mon-Sun; **V**) Perfect for lunch or a peppy coffee, this licensed cafe-gallery kicks back in an 1890s house amid idyllic gardens. Unleash the kids in the play-room and linger over your cheese platter, seafood chowder, laksa, pasta or lemon tart. Vegetarian, gluten- and dairy-free options, too.

Chokdee (☎ 03-528 0318; 109 High St; mains $16-26; ☺ 11am-2pm & 5.30-late; **V**) is Siamese for 'good luck', but you shouldn't need it at this reliable and homely Thai restaurant. Plenty of spicy and fragrant offerings including tom yum soup, technicolour curries and oodles of noodles and rice dishes. The $9 lunch specials are great value. Takeaways are available.

For fast food and self-catering:

Motueka Deli (☎ 03-528 0385; 195 High St; ☺ 9am-5.30pm Mon-Fri, to 1pm Sat & Sun) Fancy picnic supplies (prosciutto, imported cheese) and delicious local ice cream.

New World Supermarket (☎ 03-528 6245; 271 High St; ☺ 8am-8.30pm)

Patisserie Royale (☎ 03-528 7200; 152-154 High St; ☺ 6am-4.30pm) Delightful sweet treats, sandwiches, quiche and pies.

Entertainment

Gecko Theatre (☎ 03-528 4272; www.geckotheatre.co.nz; 23b Wallace St; adult/child $12/9; ☺ 5pm-midnight) When the weather closes in, pull up an easy chair at this wee, independent theatre for interesting art-house flicks. Cheap tickets ($9) are available on Mondays and Tuesdays.

Getting There & Away

All services depart Motueka i-SITE. See p169 for transport to/from the Abel Tasman Coast Track.

Abel Tasman Coachlines (☎ 03-528 8850; www.abeltasmantravel.co.nz) runs between Motueka and Nelson ($12, one hour, up to five daily), Marahau ($10, 30 minutes, three or four daily), Kaiteriteri ($10, 25 minutes, three or four daily) and Takaka ($23, one hour, two daily). In summer these services connect with Golden Bay Coachline services to the Heaphy, Abel Tasman and other Golden Bay destinations; from May to September all buses run less frequently.

Golden Bay Coachlines (☎ 03-525 8352; www.goldenbaycoachlines.co.nz) run from Motueka to Takaka ($23, one hour, two daily) and Collingwood

($42, 1½ hours, one daily). In summer services run from Takaka around once daily to Wainui carpark ($16) and Totaranui ($20) with Heaphy Track drops on request (from Motueka, $51).

Naked Bus (☎ 0900 625 33; www.nakedbus.com) runs from Motueka to Nelson ($11, one hour, one daily). Book online or at the i-SITE; cheaper fares for advance bookings.

MOTUEKA TO ABEL TASMAN
Kaiteriteri

Known simply as 'Kaiteri', this seaside hamlet 13km from Motueka is the most popular resort town in the area. On a sunny summer's day, its gorgeous, golden, safe-swimming beach feels more like Noumea than NZ, with more towels than sand. Despite a real-estate boom riding the Kiwi quintessence right out of town, Kaiteri remains a fun place to holiday with the kids, and a buzzy gateway to Abel Tasman National Park (various trips depart Kaiteriteri beach, though Marahau is the main base). Kaiteri now also boasts an all-comers mountain bike park – you'll bump into bike hire all over the show, or get the good oil from Abel Tasman Mountain Biking (see opposite).

SLEEPING & EATING

Kaiteri Lodge (☎ 03-527 8281; www.kaiterilodge.co.nz; Inlet Rd; dm $20-35, d $80-160, f $120-200; ☐) Modern, purpose-built lodge with small, simple rooms – mainly en-suite doubles. A nautical navy-and-white colour scheme has been splashed throughout; communal facilities (kitchen, laundry, barbecue, bike hire) are excellent.

Kaiteriteri Beach Motor Camp (☎ 03-527 8010; www.kaiteriteribeach.co.nz; Sandy Bay Rd; unpowered & powered sites $30, cabins $43-75; ☐ ☎) A gargantuan 430-site park in pole position across from the beach. It's hugely popular (make your summer bookings in winter), but it's large enough to cope, and there's an on-site general store. Showers cost a paltry 50c.

Torlesse Coastal Motels (☎ 03-527 8063; www.torlessemotels.co.nz; Kotare Pl, Little Kaiteriteri; d $120-190, q & f $195-280; ☎) Just 200m from Little Kaiteriteri Beach (around the corner from the main beach) is this congregation of roomy hillside units with kitchens and laundries. The two-bedroom units have lofty ceilings; most have water views.

Bellbird Lodge (☎ 03-527 8555; www.bellbirdlodge.com; Sandy Bay Rd; d incl breakfast $275-325; ☐ ☎) An upmarket B&B 1.5km up the hill from Kaiteri

Beach, offering bush and sea views, extensive gardens, fluffy towels, spectacular breakfasts (croissants, French toast, poached pears etc) and gracious hosts. Dinner by arrangement in winter, when local restaurant hours are irregular.

Shoreline (☎ 03-527 8507; cnr Inlet & Sandy Bay Rds; meals $14-28, dinner $17-30; ☺ 8am-9pm) A spiffy, modern cafe-bar-restaurant right on the beach. Punters chill on the sunny deck, lingering over panini, pizzas, pasta or fresh fish, but you can also just pop in for coffee and a jumbo muffin. Erratic winter hours; takeaway booth out the back.

Beached Whale (☎ 03-527 8114; Inlet Rd; dinner $20-32; ☺ 4pm-late) Adjacent to Kaiteri Lodge, Beached Whale is a casual, family-friendly affair serving palatable mains (wood-fired pizzas, steaks, fish and chips), with the lodge owner strumming a guitar most evenings. Closed May to September.

GETTING THERE & AWAY
Kaiteriteri is serviced by Abel Tasman Coachlines (see opposite).

Marahau

Further along the coast from Kaiteriteri and 18km north of Motueka, Marahau is the main gateway to the Abel Tasman National Park. From here you can book water taxis, hire kayaks, swim with seals or wander off on foot into the park. Marahau itself doesn't really feel like a town – more like a loose affiliation of houses and businesses.

Abel Tasman Mountain Biking (☎ 0800 808 018, 03-527 8176; www.abeltasmanmountainbiking.co.nz; Abel Tasman Centre, Franklin St, Marahau; half- to 2-day tours $84-339) offers two-wheeled options for experiencing the Abel Tasman area, Kaiteriteri MTB Park, and Canaan Downs/Rameka Track (p169).

If you're in an equine state of mind, **Marahau Horse Treks** (☎ 03 527-8425; clydesdaleadventures@yahoo.com; Harvey Rd) and **Pegasus Park** (☎ 0800 200 888; www.pegasuspark.co.nz; Sandy Bay Rd), both on Sandy Bay Rd, offer chance to belt along the beach on a horse, your hair streaming out behind you (children's pony rides $30 to $35, two-hour rides $80 to $85).

SLEEPING & EATING
Barn (☎ 03-527 8043; Harvey Rd; unpowered sites $15, dm $25-27, d $60-70; ☐ ☜) Architecturally chaotic, this rustic, tranquil place surrounded by

eucalypts offers no-frills microcabins, and bunks and attic doubles in the main house. The star of the communal facilities is the fab new social deck (shade sails, beanbags, outdoor baths), but there are also the necessaries including a separate kitchen for the cabins/campers, tour bookings and secure parking.

Old MacDonald's Farm (☎ 03-527 8288; www.oldmacs.co.nz; Harvey Rd; unpowered/powered sites $28/40, dm $25, cabins/units $80-140; ☐ ☜) Hang out with your farmyard friends (including llamas) at this rambling 100-acre property offering backpacker huts, cabins, campsites and self-contained units. There are swimming holes in the river, and bushwalks nearby. Ee-aye-ee-aye-oh.

Marahau Beach Camp (☎ 0800 808 018, 03-527 8176; www.abeltasmancentre.co.nz; Franklin St; unpowered & powered sites $30, dm/d/cabins $20/45/70; ☐ ☜) An established camping ground on Marahau Beach with beds from backpacker dorms to serviceable cabins. Marahau Sea Kayaks (p168), Marahau Water Taxis (p169) and Abel Tasman Mountain Biking (left) operate from the Abel Tasman Centre out the front; Hooked on Marahau (p166) and the camp shop (groceries, beer and wine) are also situated here.

Ocean View Chalets (☎ 03-527 8232; www.accommodationabeltasman.co.nz; Marahau Beach Rd; d $118-165, q $235-255; ☜) Well-priced cypress-lined chalets, 300m from the Abel Tasman Track with views across Tasman Bay to Fisherman Island. Positioned on a leafy hillside for maximum privacy, the chalets are self-contained, some with wheelchair access. Breakfast and packed lunches available.

Abel Tasman Marahau Lodge (☎ 03-527 8250; www.abeltasmanmarahaulodge.co.nz; Marahau Beach Rd; d $130-240; ☐ ☜) Enjoy halcyon days in this arc of 12 lovely studios and self-contained units with pitched ceilings, fan, TV, phone and microwave. There's also a fully equipped communal kitchen for self-caterers, plus spa and sauna. Cuckoos, tui and bellbirds squawk 'n' warble in the bushy surrounds.

Park Café (☎ 03-527 8270; Harvey Rd; snacks $4-8, meals $9-18; ☺ 8am-10pm mid-Sep–May; ⓥ) Pretty much on the start of the Abel Tasman Coast Track, this breezy, licensed cafe is perfectly placed for fuelling up or restoring the waistline. High-calorie options include egg breakfast, fat cake, toasted sandwiches, nachos and pizza. Fine views and decent drinks make this a good spot for your sundowner.

MARLBOROUGH & NELSON

Hooked on Marahau (☎ 03-527 8576; Franklin St; meals $13-33; ☺ 6pm-late Oct-May, 8am-late Dec-Apr) This place has the natives hooked – dinner reservations are prudent. The art-bedecked interior (local stuff) opens onto an outdoor terrace with meal-distracting views. Lunch lurks around sandwiches and salads, while the dinner menu hauls up fresh fish of the day, green-lipped mussels and NZ lamb.

GETTING THERE & AWAY
Marahau is serviced by Abel Tasman Coachlines (see p164).

ABEL TASMAN NATIONAL PARK
The accessible, coastal Abel Tasman National Park is NZ's most visited. The park blankets the northern end of a range of marble and limestone hills extending from Kahurangi National Park; its interior is honeycombed with caves and potholes. There are various tracks in the park, including an inland route, although the Coast Track is what everyone is here for.

Abel Tasman Coast Track
This 51km, three- to five-day track is one of the most scenic in the country, passing through native bush overlooking golden beaches lapped by gleaming azure water. Numerous bays, small and large, are like a travel brochure come to life. Visitors can walk into the park, catch water taxis to beaches and resorts along the track, or kayak along the coast.

It's hard to believe, but the Coast Track was once little known beyond the Nelson/Tasman region, but the trail has now been well and truly 'discovered'. In summer hundreds of trampers tackle the track at the same time (far more than can be accommodated in the huts – bring your tent). Track accommodation works on a booking system: huts and campsites must be prebooked year-round. There's no charge for day walks – if you're after a taster, the 2½-hour stretch from Torrent Bay to Bark Bay is as photogenic a stretch as any.

Between Bark Bay and Awaroa Head is an area classified as the **Tonga Island Marine Reserve** – home to a seal colony and visiting dolphins. Tonga Island itself is a small island offshore from Onetahuti Beach.

For a full description of the route, see Lonely Planet's *Tramping in New Zealand* or DOC's *Abel Tasman Coast Track* brochure.

INFORMATION
The track operates on a **Great Walks Pass** (sites/huts per person Oct-Apr $12/30, May-Sep $12/8) system. Children are free but booking is still required. The **Great Walks Helpdesk** (☎ 03-546 8210; great walksbooking@doc.govt.nz) offers information and can make bookings. You can also book on-line (www.doc.govt.nz) or in person at the Nelson, Motueka and Takaka i-SITES, where staff can offer suggestions to tailor the track to your needs and organise transport at each end. Fees apply to all bookings other than those made online. Try to book your trip well ahead of time, especially if you're planning on staying in huts between December and March.

WALKING THE TRACK
The Abel Tasman area has crazy tides (up to 6m difference between low and high tide), which has an impact on walking. Two sections of the main track are tidal, with no high-tide track around them: Awaroa Estuary can only be crossed 1½ hours before and two hours after low tide, and the narrow channel at Onetahuti Beach must be crossed within three hours either side of low tide. The estuaries at Torrent and Bark Bay have tracks around them for use during high tide. Tide tables are posted along the track; regional i-SITES also have them. To be immune from the tides, many visitors kayak the track; see p168. Note that you can't pick up kayaks within the park, only at either end (Kaiteriteri and Marahau in the south; Pohara in the north).

Take additional food so you can stay longer should you have the inclination. Bays around all the huts are beautiful, but definitely bring plenty of sandfly repellent and sunscreen.

Estimated walking times from south to north:

Route	Time
Marahau to Anchorage Hut	4hr
Anchorage Hut to Bark Bay Hut	3hr
Bark Bay Hut to Awaroa Hut	4hr
Awaroa Hut to Totaranui	1½hr

Many walkers finish at Totaranui, the final stop for the boat services and bus pick-up point, but it is possible to keep walking around the headland to Whariwharangi Hut (three hours) and then on to Wainui (1½ hours), where buses service the car park.

ABEL TASMAN NATIONAL PARK

0 ————— 4 km
0 ————— 2 miles

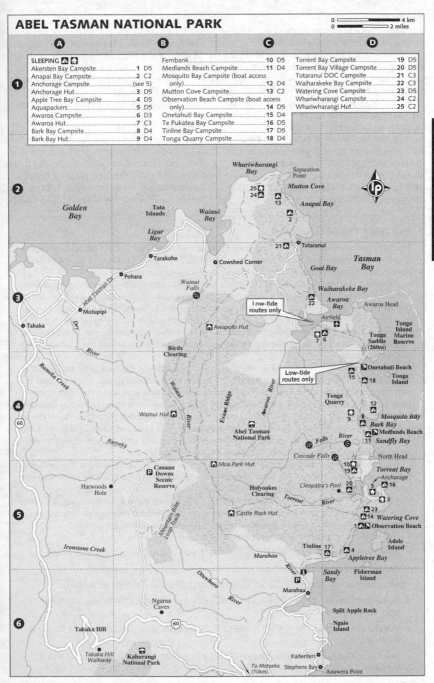

SLEEPING 🏕️ 🏠

Akersten Bay Campsite.....................1	D5
Anapai Bay Campsite........................2	C2
Anchorage Campsite....................(see 5)	
Anchorage Hut...............................3	D5
Apple Tree Bay Campsite..................4	D5
Aquapackers....................................5	D5
Awaroa Campsite.............................6	D3
Awaroa Hut.....................................7	C3
Bark Bay Campsite...........................8	D4
Bark Bay Hut...................................9	D4

Fernbank..10	D5
Medlands Beach Campsite..............11	D4
Mosquito Bay Campsite (boat access only)...................................12	D4
Mutton Cove Campsite....................13	C2
Observation Beach Campsite (boat access only)...................................14	D5
Onetahuti Bay Campsite.................15	D4
Te Pukatea Bay Campsite...............16	D5
Tinline Bay Campsite.......................17	D5
Tonga Quarry Campsite...................18	D4

Torrent Bay Campsite......................19	D5
Torrent Bay Village Campsite..........20	D5
Totaranui DOC Campsite.................21	C3
Waiharakeke Bay Campsite.............22	C3
Watering Cove Campsite.................23	D5
Whariwharangi Campsite................24	C2
Whariwharangi Hut.........................25	C2

MARLBOROUGH & NELSON

Golden
Bay

Tata
Islands

Ligar
Bay

Tarakohe

Pohara

Motupipi

Takaka

Rameka Creek

Dry River

Abel Tasman Dr

Wainui
Falls

Birds
Clearing

Wainui Hut

Abel Tasman
National Park

Rameka

Harwoods
Hole

Canaan
Downs
Scenic
Reserve

Mountain Bike Loop Track

Castle Rock Hut

Ironstone Creek

Takaka Hill

Takaka Hill
Walkway

Kahurangi
National Park

Ngarua
Caves

Whariwharangi
Bay

Separation
Point

Mutton Cove

Wainui
Bay

Cowshed Corner

Awapoto Hut

Moa Park Hut

Holyoakes
Clearing

Otuwhero River

Marahau
River

Marahau

Anapai Bay

Totaranui

Goat Bay

Waiharakeke Bay

Awaroa
Bay

Awaroa Head

Airfield

Low-tide
routes only

Tonga
Saddle
(260m)

Tonga
Island
Marine
Reserve

Low-tide
routes only

Onetahuti Beach

Tonga
Island

Tonga
Quarry

Mosquito Bay

Bark Bay

Medlands Beach

Sandfly Bay

Falls River

Cascade Falls

North Head

Cleopatra's Pool

Torrent Bay

Anchorage

Torrent River

Watering Cove

Observation Beach

Adele
Island

Tinline

Appletree Bay

Marahau

Sandy
Bay

Fisherman
Island

Split Apple Rock

Ngaio
Island

Kaiteriteri

Stephens Bay

To Motueka
(10km)

Anawera Point

Tasman
Bay

Exian Ridge

Awaroa River

Evans Ridge

Wainui River

TOURS

See opposite for information about water taxis to the park and for information on flights. Tour companies usually offer free Motueka pick-up/drop-off, with Nelson pick-up available at extra cost:

Abel Tasman Sailing Adventures (☎ 0800 467 245, 03-527 8375; www.sailingadventures.co.nz; Kaiteriteri; full day $75-190, overnight from $270) A range of well-priced catamaran trips, plus private skippered charters.

Abel Tasman Seal Swim (☎ 0800 252 925, 03-527 8383; www.sealswim.com; Aqua Taxi Base, Marahau; 5hr seal swim adult/child $169/130, seal watch $90/70) Tide-scheduled trips to the seal colony.

Abel Tasman Tours & Guided Walks (☎ 03-528 9602; www.abeltasmantours.co.nz; $195) Small-group,

day-long walking tours (minimum two people) include packed lunch and water taxis.

Abel Tasman Wilson's Experiences (Map p162; ☎ 0800 221 888, 03-528 2027; www.abeltasman.co.nz; 265 High St, Motueka; half-day cruise $70, cruise & walk $55-70, kayak & walk $89-195) Impressive array of cruises, walks, kayak and combo tours. Luxurious beachfront lodges at Awaroa and Torrent Bay for guided-tour guests.

Sleeping & Eating

At the southern edge of the park, Marahau is the main jumping-off point for the Abel Tasman National Park. From the northern end of the park, the nearest towns with accommodation are Pohara and Takaka. The whopping **Totaranui DOC Campsite** (☎ 03-528 8083;

PADDLING THE ABEL TASMAN

The Abel Tasman Coast Track has long been trampers' territory, but its main attractions – scenic beaches, isolated coves and rock formations – make it an equally seductive spot for sea kayaking. Fortunately, kayaking can easily be combined with walking and camping.

It needn't necessarily be a matter of hiring a kayak then looking after yourself from that point (although it is possible to do that) – a variety of professional outfits are able to float you out on the water, and the possibilities and permutations for guided or freedom trips are vast. You can kayak from half a day up to three days, camping ($12 per night) or staying in DOC huts ($30 per night), baches, even a floating backpackers (p169), either fully catered for or self-catering. You can kayak one day, camp overnight then walk back, or walk further into the park and catch a water taxi back.

Most sea-kayaking operators have plenty of experience, offering similar trips at similar prices. Marahau is the main base, but trips also depart Kaiteriteri. A popular choice if time is tight is a half-day guided kayak trip in the south of the park, followed by a walk along the track between Bark Bay and Torrent Bay. This will cost around $160 including water taxis. Three-day trips usually drop you at the northern end of the park, then you paddle back (or vice versa) and cost around $550 including food. One-day guided trips are around $190 and two-days around $360.

Freedom rentals (double-kayak and equipment hire) are around $100 per person for two days; most companies do not allow solo hires.

Peak season runs from November to Easter, but you can paddle year-round. December to February is the busiest time – it's worth timing your visit earlier or later. In winter you'll see more bird life, and the weather is surprisingly amenable.

Instruction is given to everyone and most tour companies have a minimum age of either eight or 14 depending on the trip. Camping gear is usually provided on overnight trips; if you're disappearing into the park for a few days, most operators provide free car parking.

These are the main players in this competitive market. Shop around.

- **Abel Tasman Kayaks** (☎ 0800 732 529, 03-527 8022; www.abeltasmankayaks.co.nz; Main Rd, Marahau)
- **Golden Bay Kayaks** (p172) Self-guided tours from the park's northern end.
- **Kahu Kayaks** (☎ 0800 300 101, 03-527 8300; www.kahukayaks.co.nz; Sandy Bay Rd, Marahau)
- **Kaiteriteri Kayaks** (☎ 0800 252 925, 03-527 8383; www.seakayak.co.nz; Kaiteriteri Beach & Marahau Beach Rd, Marahau)
- **Marahau Sea Kayaks** (☎ 0800 529 257, 03-527 8176; www.msk.net.nz; Abel Tasman Centre, Franklin St, Marahau)
- **Sea Kayak Company** (Map p162; ☎ 0508 252 925, 03-528 7251; www.seakayaknz.co.nz; 506 High St, Motueka)

www.doc.govt.nz; unpowered sites adult/child $12/6) is also in the north, 32km from Takaka on a narrow, winding road (12km of it unsealed). It's serviced by buses from October to April (right). Sites at Totaranui from December to mid-February are now allocated via ballot. Download a booking form from the DOC website, submit it to Takaka DOC (p170) between specified dates (usually the first week in July) and cross your fingers. There are no powered sites.

Along the Coast Track there are four huts: Anchorage (24 bunks), Bark Bay (34 bunks), Awaroa (26 bunks) and Whariwharangi (20 bunks), plus 19 designated campsites – BYO stove. None of these have cooking facilities – BYO stove. Some of the campsites have fireplaces but, again, you must carry cooking equipment. Hut and camp passes should be purchased before you enter the park (see p166). From Christmas Day to February, huts and campsites fill to the rafters (book with DOC).

Other sleeping options in the park, accessible on foot, by kayak or water taxi, but not by road, include the following:

Aquapackers (☎ 0800 430 744, 027 230 7002; www.aquapackers.co.nz; dm/d incl breakfast$65/180) The *MV Parore* (a former Navy patrol boat) and *Catarac* (a 13m catamaran), moored permanently in Anchorage Bay, provide unusual but buoyant backpacker options. Facilities are basic but decent; prices include bedding and dinner.

Fernbank (☎ 027 369 9555; www.abeltasmanaccommodation.co.nz; Torrent Bay; d $160, extra adult/child $15/10) Fernbank comprises two classic holiday homes at Torrent Bay; each self-contained house can sleep up to seven and is only a minute from the beach. BYO linen (or pay an extra charge) and food.

Abel Tasman Wilson's Experiences (right) has two lodges on the track but these are largely reserved for those travelling on its tours. That said, it's worth enquiring about availability as staff will fit you in if they can.

Getting There & Away
AIR
If you're time-poor but funds-rich, consider a fly-in option; the following companies fly to Awaroa, and offer scenic flights:

Abel Tasman Air (☎ 0800 304 560, 03-528 8290; www.abeltasmanair.co.nz) Flies to Awaroa from Motueka ($175) or Nelson ($265). Scenic flights available; Heaphy Track connections as well.

Tasman Helicopters (p154) Motueka to Awaroa by helicopter costs from $150, one-way.

BUS
Abel Tasman Coachlines (☎ 03-528 8850; www.abeltasmantravel.co.nz) runs from Nelson to Motueka, then on to the following:

Destination	Price	Duration	Frequency
Kaiteriteri	$10	25min	3 daily
Marahau	$10	30min	3-4 daily
Takaka	$23	1hr	2 daily

Golden Bay Coachlines (☎ 03-525 8352; www.goldenbaycoachlines.co.nz) runs from November to April from Takaka around once daily to Wainui carpark ($16) and Totaranui ($20).

Getting Around
The beauty of Abel Tasman is that it's easy to get to/from any point on the track by water taxi, either from Kaiteriteri or Marahau. Typical one-way prices from either Marahau or Kaiteriteri: Anchorage and Torrent Bay ($32), Bark Bay ($37), Tonga ($39), Awaroa ($42), Totaranui ($44). Some operators:

Abel Tasman Aqua Taxi (☎ 0800 278 282, 03-527 8083; www.aquataxi.co.nz; Kaiteriteri & Marahau)

Abel Tasman Sea Shuttle (☎ 0800 732 748, 03-527 8688; www.abeltasmanseashuttles.co.nz; Kaiteriteri)

Abel Tasman Wilson's Experiences (Map p162; ☎ 0800 221 888, 03-528 2027; www.abeltasmannz.com; 265 High St, Motueka) Offers an explorer pass (adult/child $135/67.50) for unlimited taxi travel on three days over a five-day period.

Marahau Water Taxis (☎ 0800 808 018, 03-527 8176; www.abeltasmancentre.co.nz; Abel Tasman Centre, Franklin St, Marahau)

GOLDEN BAY

MOTUEKA TO TAKAKA
From Motueka, SH60 takes a stomach-churning meander over Takaka Hill. On the way it passes dramatic lookouts over Tasman Bay and Abel Tasman National Park before swooping down towards Takaka and Collingwood. The best way to tackle this region is with your own wheels.

Takaka Hill (791m) butts-in between Tasman Bay and Golden Bay. Just below the summit (literally) are the **Ngarua Caves** (☎ 03-528 8093; janetdavid@paradise.net.nz; SH60; adult/child $15/5; ☽ 45min tours hourly 10am-4pm Sep-May, open

Sat & Sun only Jun-Aug), where you can see myriad subterranean delights including moa bones. Access is restricted to tours – you can't go solo spelunking.

Also just before the summit is the turn-off to **Canaan Downs Scenic Reserve** (Map p167), reached at the end of the 11km gravel road. This area starred as Chetwood Forest in the *Lord of the Rings* movies, but **Harwood's Hole** is the most famous feature here. It's one of the largest *tomo* (caves) in the country at 357m deep, 70m wide, with a 176m vertical drop. The cave is a 30-minute walk from the car park. Be careful as you approach the precipice – accidents have occurred. Only *very* experienced cavers should attempt to explore the cave itself. Off-road cyclists quite rightly find Canaan's magical landscape irresistible, and the new **mountain bike loop track** (14km, two hours, intermediate) offers varied terrain, a bit of technical stuff and wonderful views. From here you can link with the Rameka Track; more tracks are currently being planned. Bikes and drop-offs can be negotiated from Takaka (see right) or Marahau (see p165).

Close to the zenith also lies the **Takaka Hill Walkway**, a three-hour loop walk through marble karst rock formations, native forest and private farmland (owned by the Harwoods, of Hole fame), and **Harwood Lookout**, affording fine views down the Takaka River Valley to Takaka and Golden Bay.

TAKAKA
pop 1230

Laid-back to near-horizontal, Takaka is Golden Bay's business centre, and the last 'big' town as you head towards the South Island's northwest extremity, Farewell Spit. The local community of rootsy artists and bearded, dreadlocked types rubs shoulders with hardened farmers and crusty fisherfolk in harmonious equilibrium.

Information

DOC office (☎ 03-525 8026; www.doc.govt.co.nz; 62 Commercial St; ☯ 8.30am-4pm Mon-Fri) Information on Abel Tasman and Kahurangi National Parks, the Heaphy Track, Farewell Spit and Cobb Valley. Sells hut passes.
Golden Bay i-SITE (☎ 03-525 9136; www.golden baynz.co.nz; Willow St; ☯ 9am-6pm summer; 10am-5pm Mon-Fri, to 4pm Sat & Sun winter) A friendly little information centre with all necessary information and a booking service.

Unlimited Copies 07 (☎ 03-525 8355; 4 Commercial St; ☯ 9am-5pm) Internet access ($6 per hour) and associated usefulness.

Sights & Activities

Simply called 'Pupu', **Te Waikoropupu Springs** are the largest freshwater springs in NZ and reputedly the clearest in the world. About 14,000L of water per second surges from underground vents dotted around the Pupu Springs Scenic Reserve, including one with 'dancing sands' propelled upwards by water gushing from the ground. The water looks enticing, but swimming is a no-no. From Takaka, head 4km northwest on SH60, turn inland at Waitapu Bridge and follow Pupu Springs Rd for 3km. From the car park, a walkway (30 minutes return) leads to a slightly scruffy glassed viewing area.

Close by is **Pupu Hydro Walkway**, a two-hour circuit through beech forest, past engineering and gold-mining relics to the restored (and operational) Pupu Hydro Powerhouse, built in 1929. To get here, take the 4km gravel road (signed 'Pupu Walkway') off Pupu Springs Rd.

On the road to Pohara you'll see a signpost to **Labyrinth Rocks Park** (Scotts Rd; admission free; ☯ dawn-dusk), two wondrous hectares of limestone canyons and native bush making for a fascinating stroll. Down at Clifton you'll find the **Grove** (signposted down Clifton Rd), offering further geological and botanical delights.

An abundance of excellent mountain bike tracks await exploration by beginner and hard-core alike. **Quiet Revolution Cycle Shop** (☎ 03-525 9555; quietrev@hotmail.com; 11 Commercial St; per day $20-40; ☯ 9am-5pm Mon-Fri, to 12.30pm Sat) hires town and mountain bikes, has local track information and will straighten your wonky spokes. **Escape Adventures** (☎ 03-525 8783; www. escapeadventures.co.nz; behind the Post Shop; per day $35-75; ☯ 9am-5pm Mon-Sat) will do similar and offers bespoke guided tours and GPS-mapped track info.

Remote Adventures (☎ 0800 150 338, 03-525 6167; www.remoteadventures.co.nz) offers scenic flights around the Bay for as little as $35.

The **Golden Bay Museum** (☎ 03-525 6268; www. virtualbay.co.nz/gbmuseum; Commercial St; admission free; ☯ 10am-4pm, closed Sun in winter) is a jumble of historical memorabilia. Stand-out exhibits include a diorama depicting Abel Tasman's 1642 Golden Bay landing and some dubious human taxidermy. Sharing the same building is **Golden Bay Gallery** (☎ 03-525 9990; Commercial St;

admission free; 10am-4.30pm, closed Sun in winter), a good example of just one of Golden Bay's many galleries and artist studios. Collect a copy of the *Guide to Artists in Golden Bay* leaflet for more along those lines.

On the Anatoki River 6km south of town, **Bencarri Nature Park & Café** (03-525 8261; www.bencarri.co.nz; McCallum Rd; adult/child/family $12/6/35, meals $8-16; 10am-5pm, closed April–mid-Sep) is home to farm animals including llamas and a longhorn. The prime attraction, though, is feeding the fat, tame river eels, which can live to be 100, and have apparently been here since 1914.

Fish for salmon next door at the **Anatoki Salmon Farm** (03-525 7251; www.anatokisalmon.co.nz; McCallum Rd; admission & fishing gear free, salmon price per kg $19; 9am-5pm). The owners will clean and smoke your catch, so you can eat it on the spot. If you're not up for DIY, you can also buy fresh or smoked fish.

Tours
Unsurprisingly, tours revolve around the great outdoors.

Bush & Beyond (03-528 9054; www.bushandbeyond.co.nz; day/multiday walks from $150/1150) Offers various tramping trips including Mt Arthur or Cobb Valley day walks ($195) through to a guided five-nighter on the Heaphy Track ($1395).

Kahurangi Guided Walks (03-525 7177; www.kahurangiwalks.co.nz) Specialises in small-group tours including five-day walks along the Heaphy Track or Abel Tasman Coast Track ($1300), and day trips up the Cobb Valley ($140).

Southern Wilderness (0800 666 044, 03-546 7349; www.southernwilderness.com) Guided four- to five-day tramps on the Heaphy Track ($1495 to $1595) and day walks in Nelson Lakes National Parks ($220).

See p174 for Farewell Spit tours.

Sleeping
Kiwiana (0800 805 494, 03-525 7676; http://kiwianabackpackers.co.nz; 73 Motupipi St; sites per person $18, dm/s/d $27/42/64;) Beyond the welcoming garden is a cute cottage where rooms are named after classic Kiwiana (the jandal, Buzzy Bee...). There's a free outdoor spa and a converted garage full of treasures: wood-fired stove, pool table, CD player, books, games and bikes for guest use.

Annie's Nirvana Lodge (03-525 8766; www.nirvanalodge.co.nz; 25 Motupipi St; dm/d $28/66;) It's clean, it's tidy, and it smells good: dorms in the main house, four doubles at the bottom of the wonderful courtyard garden. We just loved this YHA hostel and its friendly owner. Fluffy the cat sealed the deal – what a charmer. Bike hire is $5 per day.

Golden Bay Motel (0800 401 212, 03-525 9428; www.goldenbaymotel.co.nz; 132 Commercial St; d $95-135, extra person $20;) It's golden, all right: check out the paint job. Clean, spacious, self-contained units with decent older-style fixtures and decent older-style hosts. The rear patios overlook a lush green lawn with playground.

Anatoki Lodge Motel (0800 262 333, 03-525 8047; www.anatokimotels.co.nz; 87 Commercial St; d $105-155;) Rhododendrons ahoy at this tidy motel, with studios and one- and two-bedroom units, all with kitchenette, lounge-dining area, and private patio. Solar-heated pool.

Shady Rest (03-525 9669; www.shadyrest.co.nz; 139 Commercial St; d incl breakfast $130-230;) A short walk along the main road from town, this two-storey dear place has four double rooms (two en suite) freshly dressed in fitting style. Expect wood panelling and heavy drapes galore, with modern bathrooms lending some sparkle. The back garden is great, with streamside seating and a bath in the grotto.

Eating & Drinking
Although Takaka proffers some reasonable hospitality, you may find better options out of town.

Dangerous Kitchen (03-525 8686; 46a Commercial St; meals $11-28; 10am-10pm Mon-Sat) Dedicated to Frank Zappa ('In the kitchen of danger, you can feel like a stranger'), DK specialises in gourmet pizzas and strong coffee, hefty slabs of cake and bumper burritos. Mellow and laid-back, with sun-trap courtyard out back, and people-watching patio on the main drag.

Brigand Café Bar (03-525 9636; 90 Commercial St; lunch $14-28, dinner $16-32; 11am-late Mon-Sat) Mainstay of the local entertainment scene; get to the Brigand for Thursday open mic and look out for other gigs. Behind steel gates and a lush garden, Brigand serves sandwiches and chips, chowder and meaty mains in a relaxed, pubby atmosphere.

The **Telegraph Hotel** (03-525 9445; cnr Commercial & Motupipi Sts; mains $15-26; 11am-late) and the **Junction Hotel** (03-525 9207; 15 Commercial St; mains $12-23; 11am-late) are old-fashioned pubs if you fancy a quiet lager or pub meal.

Your best bets for quick eats include the **Top Shop** (03-525 9387; 9 Willow St; items $2-9;

MARLBOROUGH & NELSON

🕑 6am-6pm Mon-Fri, 7.30am-6pm Sat & Sun), a dairy, tearoom and takeaway at the entrance to town. High-rating pies. Across the road is **Fresh Choice** (☎ 03-525 9383; 13 Willow St; 🕑 8am-8pm) supermarket. In the middle of town, tucked into the Library Carpark is **Paul's Coffee Caravan** – no food, but the best brew in town.

Entertainment

Village Theatre (☎ 03-525 8453; www.villagetheatre.org. nz; 34 Commercial St; adult/child $12/6; 🕑 2-10pm) Catch a flick at Takaka's cinema, screening newish releases.

Getting There & Around

Abel Tasman Coachlines (☎ 03-528 8850; www.abeltas mantravel.co.nz) runs between Takaka and Nelson ($32, 2½ hours, two daily). This company works in with **Golden Bay Coachlines** (☎ 03-525 8352; www.goldenbaycoachlines.co.nz) which connects Takaka with Collingwood ($19, 25 minutes, two daily), the Heaphy Track ($28, one hour, one daily), Totaranui ($20, one hour, one daily) and other stops en route.

Golden Bay Air (☎ 0800 588 885, 03-525 8725; www. goldenbayair.co.nz) flies daily between Wellington and Takaka ($99 to $165) and on-demand between Takaka and Karamea for Heaphy Track trampers (minimum two people, per person $169).

Remote Adventures/Star Line (☎ 0800 150 338, 03-525 6167; www.remoteadventures.co.nz) offers daily flights between Takaka and Nelson (from $90).

If you need a cab, call **Takaka Taxi Service** (☎ 0800 825 252).

POHARA

pop 350

About 10km northeast of Takaka is pint-sized Pohara, a beachside resort with a population that quadruples over summer. It's more 'yup-pified' than other parts of Golden Bay, with large modern houses cashing in on sea views, but an agreeable air persists and there's some good accommodation.

The beach is on the way to the northern end of the Abel Tasman Coastal Track; the largely unsealed road into the park passes **Tarakohe Harbour** (Pohara's working port), and **Ligar Bay** which has a lookout and a memorial to Abel Tasman, who anchored here in December 1642.

Rawhiti Cave and its vast, striking entrance is an awesome sight, located between Takaka

and Pohara. Take Packard Rd 2.5km from Motupipi, or contact **Kahurangi Guided Walks** (☎ 03-525 7177; www.kahurangiwalks.co.nz), which runs three-hour tours ($35).

Golden Bay Kayaks (☎ 03-525 9095; www.golden baykayaks.co.nz; Pohara beachfront; half-day guided tours adult/child $75/35, 3-day freedom hire $135) rents out kayaks for hour-long paddles, or can launch you on a three-day exploration of Abel Tasman National Park from Tarakohe Harbour south to Marahau or Kaiteriteri.

Sleeping & Eating

Pohara Beach Top 10 Holiday Park (☎ 0800 764 272, 03-525 9500; www.poharabeach.com; Abel Tasman Dr; unpow-ered & powered sites $36-42, cabins $58-89, motels/units $108-158; 🖳 🛜) Wow, what a big 'un! On a long grassy strip 'tween the dunes and the main road, the location is primo, but in summer it can feel more like a suburb than the seaside. There's a general store out the front.

Nook (☎ 0800 806 665, 03-525 8501; www.thenook guesthouse.co.nz; Abel Tasman Dr; unpowered sites $30, dm/ tw/d $28/56/70, cottage $120-160) Low-key, nook-sized backpackers with timber floors, and rooms opening out on to homely gardens. A self-contained straw-bale cottage sleeps six, while in the back paddock is a house truck and space for tents. Bikes available; TV banned.

Sans Souci Inn (☎ 03-525 8663; www.sanssouci inn.co.nz; 11 Richmond Rd; s/d/f $80/105/150; 🕑 closed Jul-mid-Sep) Meaning 'no worries' in French, that'll be your mantra after staying in one of Sans Souci's seven Mediterranean-flavoured, mud-brick rooms. Guests share a lovely plant-filled, mosaic communal bathroom with composting toilets, as well as an airy lounge and kitchen flowing out on to the semitropical courtyard. Dinner in the on-site restaurant ($30 to $33; bookings essential) is highly recommended; breakfast is by request.

Sandcastle (☎ 0800 433 909, 03-525 9087; www.golden bayaccommodation.co.nz; Haile Lane; d $90-110; 🛜) It sounds like a regal beach fantasy, but it's actu-ally a cluster of bird-bombarded, ecofriendly chalets with a wood-fired sauna, outdoor spa pool, and an emphasis on family frivolities. Look for the sign 600m past the Penguin Café & Bar. Great value.

Penguin Café & Bar (☎ 03-525 6126; 818 Abel Tasman Dr; lunch $12-19, dinner $18-29; 🕑 4-10pm Mon & Tue, 11am-10pm Wed-Sun) A buzzy spot with a large outdoor area, suited to sundowners and thirst-quenchers on sunny days. Open fire and pool table for the odd inclement day. Brunch treats include pizzas, burgers and bar snacks; dinner mains are meatier.

Totally Roasted Café (☎ 03-525 9396; Abel Tasman Dr; meals $10-18; ☽ 8.30am-5pm) A sure bet for primo coffee from its own-roast organic beans, this 'el rancho' style walled garden cafe is also a winner for all-day breakfast. The full fry-up is a cracker, but the home-baked cakes, muffins and pastries aren't bad either.

Getting There & Away

Golden Bay Coachlines (☎ 03-525 8352; www.golden baycoachlines.co.nz) runs from Takaka to Pohara on the way to Totaranui ($10, 15 minutes, one daily).

COLLINGWOOD & AROUND

Far-flung Collingwood (population 250) is the last town in this part of the country, and has a real end-of-the-line, frontier vibe. It's busy in summer, though for most people it's simply a launch spot for the Heaphy Track or trips to Farewell Spit.

The **Collingwood Museum** (☎ 03-524 8131; Tasman St; admission by donation; ☽ 10am-4pm) fills a tiny, unstaffed corridor with a quirky collection of saddlery, Maori artefacts, moa bones, shells and old typewriters, while the next-door **Aorere Centre** houses multimedia presentations, including the works of the wonderful pioneer photographer, Fred Tyree.

No Collingwood visit would be complete without dipping into **Rosy Glow Chocolate House** (☎ 03-524 8348; 54 Beach Rd; chocolates $3-5; ☽ 10am-5pm Sat-Thu). Chocoholics will go nuts for hand-made confection produced with love.

Sleeping

Innlet Backpackers & Cottages (☎ 03-524 8040; www.goldenbayindex.co.nz; Main Rd; unpowered sites $42, dm/d $29/68, cottage/units $70-180; ☐) A great option 10km from Collingwood on the way to Pakawau. The main house sustains elegant backpacker rooms, and there are various campsites and cabins around the property including a self-contained cottage sleeping six to eight people. The environmentally conscious owners offer kayak and bike hire.

Somerset House (☎ 03-524 8624; www.backpackers collingwood.co.nz; Lower Gibbs Rd; dm/s/d incl breakfast $29/45/70; ☐ ☞) A small, low-key hostel in a creaky, historic building on the hill with views from the deck. Graft tramping advice from the knowledgeable owners who offer tramper

transport, free bikes, and freshly baked bread for breakfast.

Beachcomber Motel (☎ 0800 270 520, 03-524 8499; www.collingwoodbeachcomber.co.nz; Tasman St; d $100-135; ☐ ☞) Clean, spacious self-contained units in excellent nick, wedged between the road and the estuary. Good-value family-sized units have nifty mezzanine floors.

Eating & Drinking

Mussel Inn (☎ 03-525 9241; SH60, Onekaka; all-day menu $4-16, dinner $21-26; ☽ 11am-late, closed Jul-Aug) Halfway between Takaka and Collingwood, this earthy tavern-cafe-brewery is a Bay institution. A totem pole with crucified mobile phones heralds the mood: this is no place for urban trappings, just excellent beer, wholesome food (mussels, seasonal scallops, fresh fish and steak), open fires and live music. Try a handle or two of 'Captain Cooker', a brown beer brewed naturally with manuka, or the delicious 'Pale Whale Ale'.

Courthouse Café (☎ 03-525 8472; cnr Gibbs & Tasman Sts; meals $8-28; ☽ 9am-5pm Thu-Mon, plus 6-9pm Fri & Sat) A sophisticated cafe in the 1901 Collingwood courthouse preparing à la carte meals from locally grown organic produce and fresh seafood. Local art; good coffee; interesting wine list. One of the Bay's best dining experiences.

our pick **Naked Possum Café** (☎ 03-524 8433; Kaituna River, 10km from Collingwood; meals $10-24; ☽ 10am-6pm Sat-Thu, to 10pm Fri) Relax at this splendid, nouveau-rustic joint after exploring the adjacent Kaituna Track and its goldmining relics and pretty river forks (two hours return). Outdoor fire, ample lawn, great beer and a possum tannery. Wild game a speciality. Book your spot at the popular Friday evening steak barbecue or Sunday roasts.

Getting There & Away

Golden Bay Coachlines (☎ 03-525 8352; www.goldenbaycoachlines.co.nz) runs from Takaka to Collingwood ($19, 25 minutes, two daily).

FAREWELL SPIT & AROUND

Bleak, exposed and unusual, **Farewell Spit** is a wetland of international importance, and a renowned bird sanctuary – the summer home of thousands of migratory waders, notably the godwit (which flies all the way from the Arctic tundra), Caspian terns and Australasian gannets. The 35km beach features colossal, crescent-shaped dunes, from where panoramic views extend across Golden

Bay and a vast low-tide salt marsh. Walkers can explore the first 4km of Spit via a network of tracks, but beyond that point access is via tour only (see below).

The Spit pit stop is **Farewell Spit Visitor Centre** (☎ 03-524 8454; Farewell Spit; ⏰ 9.30am-6.30pm), 24km north of Collingwood, which provides local information and handles Spit tour bookings. It shares its hilltop abode with **Paddlecrab Café** (meals $11-24), a memorable spot for coffee and cake or an honest lunch. How's about those views?

Tours

Two operators run tours of the Spit exploring all the sights, from fossilised shellfish and bird colonies to an old lighthouse. Tours depart daily at low tide (visit websites or ring the visitor centre for schedules) and light refreshments are usually included.

Farewell Spit Eco Tours (☎ 0800 808 257, 03-524 8257; www.farewellspit.com; Tasman St, Collingwood; tours $90-150) Operating for more than 60 years, this outfit runs a range of tours from three to 6½ hours, taking in the Spit, lighthouse, gannets and godwits. Tours depart Collingwood.

Farewell Spit Nature Experience (☎ 0800 250 500, 03-524 8992; www.farewellspittours.com; tours $90-110) Four-hour Spit tours depart Farewell Spit Visitor Centre; six-hour tours depart the Old School Café, Pakawau.

Other Activities

Remote, desolate **Wharariki Beach** is 6km from the turn-off to the visitor centre along an unsealed road, then a 20-minute walk from the car park over farmland (part of the DOC-administered Puponga Farm Park). It's a wild introduction to the West Coast, with mighty dune formations, looming rock islets just offshore and a seal colony at its eastern end (keep an eye out for seals in the stream on the walk here). As inviting as a swim here may seem, there are strong undertows – what the sea wants, the sea shall have…

Befitting a frontier, this is the place to saddle up: **Cape Farewell Horse Treks** (☎ 03-524 8031; www.horsetreksnz.com; 23 McGowan St, Puponga) is en route to Wharariki Beach. Treks in this wind-blown country range from 1½ hours ($50, to Pillar Point) to three hours ($105, to Wharariki Beach), with longer (including overnight) trips by arrangement.

KAHURANGI NATIONAL PARK

Kahurangi, meaning 'Treasured Possession', is the second largest of NZ's national parks and

undoubtedly one of the greatest. Its 452,000 hectares are a hotbed of ecological wonderment: 18 native bird species, over 50% of all NZ's plant species, including over 80% of its alpine plant species, a karst landscape and the largest known cave system in the southern hemisphere (explored by local caving groups, but only for the experienced).

Heaphy Track

One of the best-known tracks in NZ, the four-to six-day, 78km Heaphy Track doesn't have the spectacular scenery of the Routeburn or Milford Tracks, but revels in its own distinct beauty. Almost entirely within Kahurangi National Park, track highlights include the mystical Gouland Downs, and the nikau-palm-dotted coast, especially around Heaphy Hut (spend a day or two here at least). At low tide you can cross the Heaphy River mouth; the Crayfish Point section should only be tackled within one hour either side of low tide.

There are seven huts en route, each accommodating around 20 people; all have gas stoves, except Brown and Gouland Downs, which need wood. There are nine campsites along the route, with limited capacity (eight campers maximum at James Mackay Hut, as many as 40 at Heaphy Hut). Huts/campsites cost $15/8 per adult per night from May to September, $25/12 from October to April; all must be prebooked through DOC, or the i-SITE.

INFORMATION

The best spot for detailed Heaphy Track information and bookings is the DOC counter at the Nelson i-SITE (p151). You can also book at the Golden Bay i-SITE in Takaka (p170), online at www.doc.got.nz, or by post, email (greatwalksbookings@doc.govt.nz) or phone (☎ 03-546 8210). See also www.heaphytrack.com.

For a detailed track description, see Lonely Planet's *Tramping in New Zealand*.

WALKING THE TRACK

Most people tramp southwest from the Collingwood end to Karamea. From Brown Hut the track passes through beech forest to Perry Saddle. The country opens up to the swampy Gouland Downs, then closes in with sparse bush all the way to MacKay Hut. The bush becomes more dense towards Heaphy Hut, with beautiful nikau palms growing at lower levels.

The final section is along the coast through nikau forest, and partly along the beach. Unfortunately, sandflies love this beautiful stretch too! The climate here is surprisingly mild, but don't swim in the sea as the undertows and currents are vicious. The lagoon at Heaphy Hut is good for swimming, and the Heaphy River is full of fish.

Kilometre markers crop up along the track – the zero marker is at the track's southern end at Kohaihai River near Karamea. Estimated walking times:

Route	Time
Brown Hut to Perry Saddle Hut	5hr
Perry Saddle Hut to Gouland Downs Hut	2hr
Gouland Downs Hut to Saxon Hut	1½hr
Saxon Hut to James MacKay Hut	3hr
James MacKay Hut to Lewis Hut	3½hr
Lewis Hut to Heaphy Hut	2½hr
Heaphy Hut to Kohaihai River	5hr

Other Kahurangi Tracks

After tackling the Heaphy north to south, you can return to Golden Bay via the more scenic (though harder) **Wangapeka Track**. It's not as well known as the Heaphy, but many consider the Wangapeka a more enjoyable walk. Taking about five days, the track starts 25km south of Karamea at Little Wanganui, running 52km east to Rolling River near Tapawera. There's a chain of huts along the track.

The five to seven day **Leslie-Karamea Track** is a medium-to-hard tramp, connecting the Cobb Valley near Takaka with Little Wanganui, finishing on part of the Wangapeka Track.

See www.doc.govt.nz for detailed information on both tracks, and some excellent full-day and overnight walks around the **Cobb Valley**, **Mount Arthur** and **The Tablelands**.

Tours

See p171 to find operators running day-long and multiday trips in Kahurangi National Park.

Getting There & Away

Abel Tasman Coachlines (☎ 03-528 8850; www.abel tasmantravel.co.nz) will get you as far as Takaka ($23, one hour, two daily). From there you can connect with **Golden Bay Coachlines** (☎ 03-525 8352; www.goldenbaycoachlines.co.nz) which will get you to the Heaphy Track via Collingwood ($28, one hour, one daily).

Heaphy Track Help (☎ 03-525 9576; www.heaphy trackhelp.co.nz) offers car relocations ($200 to $300, depending on the direction and time), food drops, shuttles and advice.

Golden Bay Air (☎ 0800 588 885, 03-525 8725; www. goldenbayair.co.nz) flies on demand between Takaka and Karamea (minimum two people, per person $169). **Remote Adventures** (☎ 0800 150 338, 03-525 6167; www.remoteadventures.co.nz) also offers Karamea pick-ups by air (price on application).

Wadsworths Motors (☎ 03-522 4248; Main Rd, Tapawera) services the eastern ends of the Wangapeka Track, on demand. Price on application.

For transport details at the Karamea end of proceedings see p185.

MARLBOROUGH & NELSON

The West Coast

What a difference a mountain range makes. Hemmed in by the wild Tasman Sea and the peaks of the Southern Alps, the West Coast (aka Westland) is like nowhere else in New Zealand.

Opposite ends of the coast have a remote end-of-the-road feel. In the north the surf-battered coast highway leads to sleepy Karamea, the preferred getaway for alternative lifestylers drawn by its isolation and surprisingly mild climate. The southern end of spectacular State Hwy 6 continues to Haast, an entrée to the excitement and awe of the surrounding wilderness.

With less than 1% of NZ's population scattered amid almost 9% of the country's area, West Coast locals have adapted to become a rugged and individual breed. They may not be too concerned with what's happening in the country's cities, but in the West Coast's heritage pubs you'll be guaranteed a warm welcome that's tinged with a laconic sense of humour. Just don't be too surprised if 'closing time' is viewed as a recommendation, not a directive.

The coast's sublime scenery can be almost too popular, and during summer a phalanx of campervans and tourist buses tick off the 'Must See' Punakaiki Rocks and Franz Josef and Fox Glaciers. The thing is, they are truly 'Must See', and even if you're sharing your glacial gaze, it's not too hard to return to the heartland of the West Coast in laid-back coastal hamlets such as Okarito, Granity and Jackson Bay.

HIGHLIGHTS

- Crafting your own unique keepsake at **Barrytown Knifemaking** (p187)
- Kayaking through the bird-adorned channels of the **Okarito Lagoon** (p200)
- Getting wet 'n' wild on the rivers around **Murchison** (p177)
- Marvelling at nature's beautiful fury at the Pancake Rocks at **Punakaiki** (p186)
- Going underground in the limestone caverns of the **Oparara Basin** (p183)
- Hunting out authentic local greenstone in the craft shops of **Hokitika** (p197)
- Exploring the West Coast's true wilderness on a back-of-beyond river trip around **Haast** (p209)
- Feeling just a tad insignificant compared to the imposing ice flows of the **Franz Josef** (p202) and **Fox Glaciers** (p206)

Oparara Basin ★

Murchison ★

Punakaiki ★
Barrytown ★

Hokitika ★

Okarito Lagoon ★
Fox Glacier ★ ★ Franz Josef Glacier

★ Haast

- Telephone code: 03　　■ www.west-coast.co.nz　　■ www.westcoast.org.nz

THE WEST COAST

THE WEST COAST

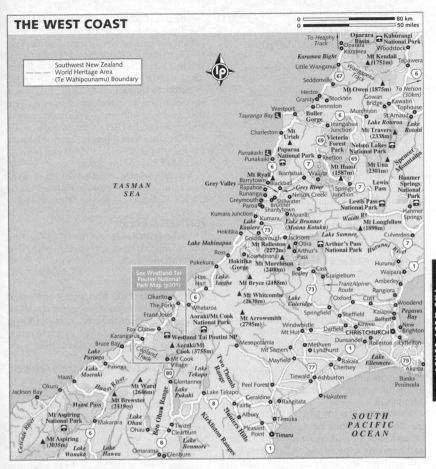

Climate
During summer the coast roads flood with campervans, but May to September can be warm and clear with fewer crowds and cheaper accommodation. At around 5m annually, the West Coast has serious rainfall (Westland = Wetland), but Westland sees as much sunshine as Christchurch. When it's pouring in the east it's just as likely to be fine here.

Getting There & Around
Air New Zealand flies between Westport and Wellington, and Hokitika and Christchurch.

Coaches and shuttles connect to centres like Christchurch, Dunedin, Queenstown and Nelson; major players are Atomic Shuttles, InterCity and Naked Bus.

The *TranzAlpine*, one of the world's great train rides, links Greymouth and Christchurch; see p193.

MURCHISON
pop 850
Up-and-coming Murchison, 125km southwest of Nelson (95km east of Westport) on the Buller Gorge Heritage Hwy/State Hwy 6 (SH6), is the northern gateway to the West Coast. It's an Upper Buller Gorge service town offering lots of summertime ways to get active on the water.

Information
The **Murchison i-SITE** (☎ 03-523 9350; www.murchisonnz.com; 47 Waller St; � 10am-6pm, reduced winter

---

THE WEST COAST FACTS

Eat A whitebait pizza at Hokitika's Fat Pipi Pizza (p197)

Drink An organic Green Fern lager at Westport's West Coast Brewing Co (p180)

Read Keri Hulme's *The Bone People*, set around peaceful Okarito (p200)

Listen to Karamea's laid-back community radio station on 107.5FM (p184); they'll even let you choose your own tracks

Watch *Bad Blood* (1982), an engrossing portrayal of the Kowhitirangi incident (p198)

Swim at You're joking, right? With water this cold, stick to the spa

Festival Go bush-food crazy at Hokitika's Wild-foods Festival (p196)

Tackiest tourist attraction Pukekura's Bush-mans Museum (p199). Just don't tell them you've got friends in Auckland, OK?

Go green Volunteer in the organic vegie garden at Rongo Backpackers in Karamea (p184)

---

hours) has info on local activities and transport. There are no banks in town; the postal agency is on Fairfax St. The **Commercial Hotel** (cnr Waller & Fairfax Sts) has internet access.

Sights & Activities

Fishing, mountain biking, rafting and kayaking all feature in the area surrounding Murchison.

Ultimate Descents (☎ 0800 748 377, 03-523 9899; www.rivers.co.nz; 51 Fairfax St; half-/full-day rafting $120/220, half-day kayaking $125) offers white-water rafting and kayaking trips on the Buller, including half-day, gentler family excursions (adult/child $105/85). Helirafting trips cost from $450 and you can combine rafting with fishing (two days, $395).

The **New Zealand Kayak School** (☎ 03-523 9611; www.nzkayakschool.com; 22 Grey St; kayaks per day $50, 4-day intro course $795; ☙ Sept-Apr) hires out (to experienced paddlers only) and sells kayaks, and runs professional courses for all levels; price includes transport and accommodation but BYO food.

White Water Action Rafting Tours (☎ 0800 100 582, 03-523 9581; www.whitewateraction.com; Waller St; half-day rafting adult/youth $120/105), behind the i-SITE, runs half-day trips with a riverside lunch. Challenging Grade III and V rapids interspersed with adrenaline-elevating optional 9m cliff jumps.

The area is threaded with **mountain-bike trails** like the west bank of the Matakitaki River (16km return) or the Maruia Saddle Trip (83km return). Check the i-SITE for maps and hire bikes from **Murchison Motels** (☎ 0800 166 500, 03-523 9026; www.murchisonmotels.co.nz; 53 Fairfax St).

Murchison Museum (☎ 03-523 9335; 60 Fairfax St; admission by donation; ☙ 10am-4pm) showcases local memorabilia, with vintage farm equipment and photos of the 1929 earthquake aftermath.

Murchison **trout fishing** is superb. Half-day guided trips cost around $350 (two people); the i-SITE has the lowdown.

Try **gold panning** (equipment hire $10) in Lyell Creek, the Buller River or the Howard Valley; the i-SITE hires out pans and shovels.

Festivals & Events

The **Buller Festival** (www.bullerfestival.co.nz) kayaking and rafting extravaganza is held over the first weekend in March.

Sleeping

Riverview Holiday Park (☎ 03-523 9591; riverview.hp@ xtra.co.nz; Riverside Tce; unpowered/powered sites $24/26, d $44) Located near the river north of town, this park has motel rooms, recently refurbished cabins and the excellent River View Café (opposite).

our pick **Lazy Cow** (☎ 03-523 9451; lazycow@xnet. co.nz; 37 Waller St; dm/d $28/66; ☐ ☞) It's easy to be a lazy cow here – so comfy it feels like home. Free muffins are an easy up-sell and there are small and homely surrounds with, according to the owners, the best shower in New Zealand. You be the judge.

Hu-Ha Bikepackers (☎ 03-548 2707; smidgley@ihug. co.nz; SH6; unpowered sites $28, dm/d without bathroom $23/60, d with bathroom $70) This laid-back, cyclist-friendly farm 45km north of Murchison has dorms and doubles (including some new en suite options), and plenty of farm animals, including the biggest and most relaxed pig you'll ever meet. The house sits above the road, 10km north of Kawatiri Junction. Cash only.

Commercial Hotel (☎ 03-523 9848; thecommercial hotel@xtra.co.nz; cnr Waller & Fairfax Sts; s/d without bathroom $40/75; ☐) Excellent value with comfortable rooms and art-deco touches. All rooms have shared facilities.

River Song (☎ 03-523 9011; www.riversong.co.nz; 30 Fairfax St; d from $95) Two minutes' walk from town, these newish self-contained cottages have big decks and gardens. Postkayaking massages are available.

Murchison Lodge (☎ 03-523 9196; www.murchison
lodge.co.nz; 15 Grey St; s $125-185, d $150-210, all incl breakfast) Surrounded by native trees, this B&B
overlooks the Buller River. Nice interior
design touches add to the comfortable feel.
The friendly hosts are around to spin yarns
of kayak adventures had just steps from the
front door.

Murchison Motels (☎ 0800 166 500, 03-523 9026;
www.murchisonmotels.co.nz; 53 Fairfax St; d $130-170)
Tucked behind Rivers Cafe, with snazzy
one- and two-bedroom units. There's also
an eight-bed cottage, and mountain bikes for
hire (half-/full day $15/30).

Triple Tui (☎ 03-548 4481; www.tripletui.co.nz; 3360
Dry Weather Rd; d $130-180 (min 3 nights); ☷ Sept-May)
What happens, when two busy Aucklanders
decide to follow their dream and leave the big
smoke? How about two luxury log cabins set
in 50 beautiful acres in the Tadmore Valley,
35 minutes north of Murchison? Both private cabins include solar water heating and
electricity from Triple Tui's own mini hydro-
electricity plant. Once you've explored nearby
walking trails, fire up the gas barbecue and
open a bottle of wine. Bookings essential.

Eating & Drinking

Commercial Hotel (☎ 03-523 9696; cnr Waller & Fairfax
Sts; lunch $10-17, dinner $19-27; ☷ 8am-9pm; 🖳) Set
yourself up for rafting with a good breakfast,
and celebrate a big day on the river with a few
beers and a robust pub meal.

River View Café (☎ 03-523 9591; Riverview Holiday
Park; pizza $14-21; ☷ 10am-8pm Oct-Apr; 🖳) This
open-air cafe is the cat's meow when the
weather is fine. Sit back and enjoy the riverside
location, have a gourmet pizza and a bottle of
Murchison Moonlight Ale as kayakers drift by.

Rivers Cafe (☎ 03-523 9009; 51 Fairfax St; mains $18-
30; ☷ 9am-9pm Oct-Mar, 10am-2pm Thu-Mon Apr-Sep) has
everything from chicken kebabs and falafel to
rib-eye steaks and roast dinners. Make a hard
decision between an organic coffee or a frothy
pint of Monteith's beer.

Getting There & Away

Buses passing through Murchison from the
West Coast to Picton include **Atomic Shuttles**
(☎ 03-349 0697; www.atomictravel.co.nz) and **InterCity**
(☎ 03-365 1113; www.intercity.co.nz), and **Naked
Bus** (www.nakedbus.com) heads both north and
south from here. Atomic stops at the i-SITE,
InterCity & Naked Bus at Beechwoods Café
on Waller St.

BULLER GORGE

The road from Murchison to the coast was
shaken up by the 1929 and 1968 earthquakes
but still snakes through Buller Gorge. The
gorge is a base for white-water rafting and
kayaking; see opposite.

About 14km west of Murchison is the **Buller
Gorge Swingbridge** (☎ 0800 285 537; www.bullergorge.
co.nz; SH6; bridge crossing adult/child $5/2; ☷ 8am-7pm
Oct-Apr, 9am-5.30pm May-Sep), NZ's longest (110m).
Across the bridge are some excellent short
walks, one to the White Creek Faultline, epi-
centre of the 1929 earthquake. Coming back,
ride the 160m **Comet Line flying fox** (seated ride
adult/child $30/15, 'Supaman' style ride $45, Tandem $30/15).
Goldrush Jet (adult/child $75/50) runs 40-minute jet-
boat trips, departing under the bridge.

Further west the road forks at Inangahua
Junction. Continue to the coast through
Lower Buller Gorge on SH6, or head south
to Greymouth via Reefton on SH69. SH6 is
longer but more interesting.

There's a **DOC camping ground** (adult/child $6/1.50)
on SH6 at Lyell, Upper Buller Gorge, 10km
northeast of Inangahua Junction.

Buller Gorge is dark and foreboding; pri-
meval ferns and cabbage trees cling to steep
cliffs; toi toi (tall native grass) flanks the road
between gorge and river. The road at Hawks
Crag negotiates an overhang just high enough
to fit a bus under, and was hacked out of the
road by hand.

Buller Adventure Tours (☎ 0800 697 286, 03-789
7286; www.adventuretours.co.nz; SH6), located 4km
from the coast, has white-water rafting on
the Grade III to IV 'Earthquake Slip' rapids
(adult/youth $120/105); 1¾-hour jetboat rides
(adult/youth $79/65); two-hour riverbank
horse treks (adult/youth $80/75); and 1¾-
hour quad-bike rides ($140).

Berlins (☎ 0800 526 405, 03-789 0295; www.xtreme
adventures.co.nz; SH6; dm $25-30, d $62) is a stylish cafe-
meets-backpackers on the site of the old Berlins
Hotel. A recent re-fit has spruced the place up a
bit too. You'll also find a restaurant (mains $14
to $17.50; open 9.30am till late) that doubles as
a damn fine pub. Berlins is a well-positioned
stop for cyclists en route to the West Coast.
Don't miss the pics on the wall of the Buller
River flowing at dangerously high levels.

WESTPORT
pop 4850

The port of Westport made its fortune in coal
mining, though the main mine is at Stockton,

THE WEST COAST

MAORI NZ: THE WEST COAST

For Maori, the river valleys and mountains of the West Coast were the traditional source of *pounamu* (greenstone), and the lustrous jade still dominates the craft shops and galleries of Greymouth and Hokitika. In Hokitika, visit the Mana Pounamu exhibit at the West Coast Historical Museum (p194) to polish your knowledge of the precious rock before admiring the classy carving done by Aden Hoglund at Jagosi Jade (p198). If you're lucky enough to be staying at Awatuna Homestead (p196) near Hokitika, owner Hemi recounts stories of the early migration of Pacific peoples to NZ.

38km north. The town itself is of little interest, but is a good base for active adventures in the Buller Gorge and Charleston ranges. Otherwise head north to relaxed Karamea (for the Heaphy Track), or continue south to the Punakaiki Rocks. Fans of Animal Planet should check out the seal colony (see p182) west of town.

Orientation

The town sprawls where the east bank of the Buller River meets the Tasman Sea. Palmerston St is the main drag, while Brougham St goes northeast to Karamea. Free town and regional maps are available at the i-SITE.

Information

The major banks are along Palmerston St.
Buller Hospital (☎ 03-788 9030; Cobden St)
Department of Conservation office (DOC; ☎ 03-788 8008; 72 Russell St; ☒ 8am-noon & 1-4.30pm Mon-Fri) Tickets for the Wangapeka Track and general tramping info.
Habitat Sports (204 Palmerston St) Internet access $6 per hour.
Police station (☎ 03-788 8310; 13 Wakefield St)
Post office (cnr Brougham & Palmerston Sts)
Take Note (☎ 03-789 8731; 106 Palmerston St) Bookshop.
Westport i-SITE (☎ 03-789 6658; www.westport. org.nz; 1 Brougham St; ☒ 9am-6pm Nov-Mar, to 4pm Apr-Oct) Provides information on local tracks, walkways, tours, accommodation, transport, and DOC hut tickets for the Heaphy Track.

Sights

The **Coaltown Museum** (☎ 03-789 8204; Queen St; www.geocities.com/coaltownnz; adult/child $12/5; ☒ 9am-

4.30pm) includes an interactive walk through a faux mine. Rusty mining artefacts sit beside a brewery, photographic displays and a huge operational steam dredge.

The **West Coast Brewing Co** (☎ 03-789 6201; www. westcoastbrewing.com; 10 Lyndhurst St; ☒ 8.30am-5.30pm Mon-Fri, 11am-5.30pm Sat) crafts seven different beers, including the organic Green Fern lager and the Good Bastards dark ale. Tastings are available and highly recommended – these folks know their beer.

Activities

From Charleston, south of Westport, **Norwest Adventures** (☎ 0800 116 686, 03-788 8168; www.caveraft ing.com) runs cave-rafting trips (Underworld Rafting, $145, four hours) into the glowworm-filled Nile River Caves. If you want the glow without the flow (no rafting), it's $90 per person. Both options start with a rainforest railway ride, available separately (adult/child $20/15, 1½ hours). The Adventure Caving trip ($295, five hours) includes a 30m abseil into Te Tahi *tomo* (hole) with rock squeezes, waterfalls, prehistoric fossils and trippy cave formations.

Westport's sparkling new **swimming pool** aka **Solid Energy Centre** (☎ 03-789 8316; Pakington St; adult/child/family $5/2.50/12.50; ☒ 6am-9pm Mon-Thu, to 8pm Fri, 8am-5pm Sat & Sun) is a state-of-the-art facility with swimming pool, squash courts, workout facilities and gymnasium – just in case it happens to rain.

Festivals & Events

The **Buller Gorge Marathon** (www.bullermarathon.org. nz) traverses a scenic riverside route on the second weekend in February. The **Cape Classic Surfing** gets radical at Tauranga Bay on late October's Labour Day weekend.

Sleeping

Bazil's Hostel (☎ 0800 303 741, 03-789 6410; www. bazils.com; 54 Russell St; dm/d/q $25/58/80; ☐ ☎) Mr Fawlty is notably absent at the sprawling Bazil's. Facilities are uniformly good, including excellent kitchens to bring out your inner celebrity chef, and there are beds to suit every budget. If you're travelling in a group of four, ask about the excellent-value mini-apartments ($80). Larger groups from backpacker buses sometimes swing by.

Westport Holiday Park (☎ 03-789 7043; www.west portholidaypark.co.nz; 31-37 Domett St; unpowered/powered sites $32/34, d $90-145; ☐) A-frame 'chalets' stud this bushy glade with decent amenities, a minigolf course for the kiddies and plenty of room to pitch your tent too.

Cosmopolitan Hotel (☎ 03-789 6305; coshotel@ ihug.co.nz; 136 Palmerston St; s$55, d$75) This classic Kiwiana pub offers affordable rooms upstairs from the lively downtown watering hole. The rooms are compact (small) but despite being directly upstairs from a bar – surprisingly quiet.

Westport Motels (☎ 03-789 7575; www.west portmotels.co.nz; 32 The Esplanade; d $85-140; 🖳 🖳) Surrounded by trees, this spot has comfortable beds, outdoor tables, a spa and a swimming pool. Several family units can accommodate bigger broods. Up and down the Esplanade you'll find other midrange motels if this one is full-up.

Chelsea Gateway Motor Lodge (☎ 0800 660 033, 03-789 6835; www.chelseagateway.co.nz; 330 Palmerston St; ste $130-230; 🖳 🛜) The exterior's never going to threaten the Architect of the Year Awards, but there's design salvation with the well-appointed interiors. There are standard suites, two- and three-bedroom family units, and flasher spa units.

Eating & Drinking

Dirty Mary's (☎ 03-789 7959; 198 Palmerston St; mains $7-18; 🕑 8am-late; 🖳) Start your day with fair-trade coffee and a breakfast burrito or bagel. If you sleep in, rest assured there are fine lunches on offer. At night things get raucous with good pizzas and wine and beer.

our pick **Yellow House Cafe** (☎ 03-789 8765; 243 Palmerston St; lunch $14-17, dinner $25-30; 🕑 8am-late, reduced winter hours; 🖳 🛜 Ⓥ) This relaxed and sunny spot has warm wooden floors, the best coffee in town, and a tasty organic tinge to the menu. Try the dips and homemade bread with a glass of wine from nearby Marlborough, or have a latte and hitch your laptop to the wi-fi network.

Denniston Dog Saloon (☎ 03-789 5030; 18 Wakefield St; mains $15-30; 🕑 11am-late; 🖳) Lots of wild West Coast wood and Kiwiana antiques give the Denniston Dog a rustic air. Then again, a couple of beers, some tasty scallops and a good steak probably have the same effect. 'The Dog' is both bar and restaurant. After you're watered and fed, take the locals on at pool. Occasional touring bands raise the roof.

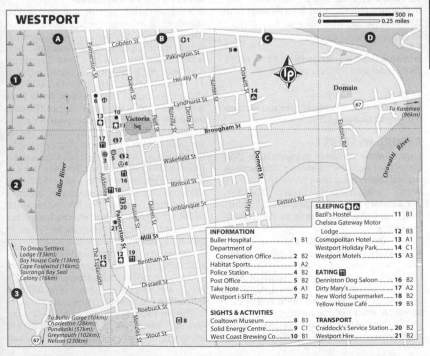

WESTPORT

0 _____ 500 m
0 _____ 0.25 miles

INFORMATION	
Buller Hospital	1 B1
Department of Conservation Office	2 B2
Habitat Sports	3 A2
Police Station	4 B2
Post Office	5 B2
Take Note	6 A1
Westport i-SITE	7 B2

SIGHTS & ACTIVITIES	
Coaltown Museum	8 B3
Solid Energy Centre	9 C1
West Coast Brewing Co	10 B1

SLEEPING 🏠 🛖	
Bazil's Hostel	11 B1
Chelsea Gateway Motor Lodge	12 B3
Cosmopolitan Hotel	13 A1
Westport Holiday Park	14 C1
Westport Motels	15 A3

EATING 🍴	
Denniston Dog Saloon	16 B2
Dirty Mary's	17 A2
New World Supermarket	18 B2
Yellow House Café	19 B3

TRANSPORT	
Craddock's Service Station	20 B2
Westport Hire	21 B2

To Omau Settlers Lodge (13km); Bay House Hotel (13km); Cape Foulwind (16km); Tauranga Bay Seal Colony (16km)

To Buller Gorge (10km); Charleston (28km); Punakaiki (57km); Greymouth (102km); Nelson (230km)

To Karamea (96km)

For self-catering, try **New World supermarket** (☎ 03-789 7669; 244 Palmerston St; ⏰ 8am-8.30pm).

Getting There & Around

AIR

Air New Zealand (☎ 0800 737 000; www.airnz.co.nz) has two flights per day to/from Wellington (from $129, 50 minutes).

BUS

InterCity (☎ 03-365 1113; www.intercity.co.nz) buses depart from **Craddock's Service Station** (☎ 03-789 7819; 197 Palmerston St) to Nelson ($45, 3½ hours, 3.55pm daily), Greymouth ($25, two hours, 11am daily) and Franz Josef Village ($56, 6½ hours, 11am daily).

Naked Bus (www.nakedbus.com) goes to Nelson ($20, 3½ hours, 3.25pm daily) and Greymouth ($20, 1½ hours, 11am daily), departing from the i-SITE.

East West Coach (☎ 0800 142 622, 03-789 6251) operates a Christchurch service ($55, five hours, 8am daily) departing from Craddock's and returning from Christchurch at 2pm.

Karamea Express (☎ 03-782 6757; info@karamea-express.co.nz) links Westport and Karamea ($30, 1½ hours, 11.30am Monday to Friday May to October, plus Saturday from November to April), departing from the i-SITE.

CAR

Hire some wheels at **Wesport Hire** (☎ 03-789 5038; 294 Palmerston St)

TAXI

Buller Taxis (☎ 03-789 6900) can take you to/from the airport (around $20).

AROUND WESTPORT

Depending on the season, anything from 20 to 200 NZ fur seals dot the rocks at the **Tauranga Bay Seal Colony**, 16km from Westport. Pups are born from late November to early December. For a month afterwards, land-bound mums tend their young before venturing out on feeding forays.

The **Cape Foulwind Walkway** (1½ hours' walk return) extends from the seal colony near its southern end, 4km along the coast to Cape Foulwind, passing a replica of Abel Tasman's astrolabe (a navigational aid) and a lighthouse. The walk's northern end is car-accessible from Lighthouse Rd.

The Maori called the cape Tauranga, meaning 'Sheltered Anchorage'. The first European

here was Abel Tasman in December 1642, naming it Clyppygen Hoek (Rocky Point). When James Cook moored the *Endeavour* here in March 1770, a furious storm made it anything but a 'sheltered anchorage'; hence the cape's modern name.

From the car park it's a five-minute walk to the seal colony lookout. The cliffs are unstable, so stick to the path.

A short stroll from the Cape Foulwind tavern you'll find **Omau Settlers Lodge** (☎ 03-789 5200; www.omausettlerslodge.co.nz; 1054 Cape Rd, Cape Foulwind; s/d incl breakfast $145/155). These contemporary and stylish units offer rest, relaxation and huge buffet breakfasts. A hot tub surrounded by bush maximises the take-it-easy quotient.

One of NZ's best restaurants, the `ourpick` **Bay House Cafe** (☎ 03-789 7133; Tauranga Bay, Cape Foulwind; lunch mains $18-22, dinner mains $22-33; ⏰ 10.30am-late Mon-Fri, from 9am Sat & Sun) is sophisticated without being stuffy. The chefs use local ingredients like piko piko (fern shoots) and horopito (NZ peppertree) in preparing seafood, West Coast venison and Canterbury lamb. The wine list is easily the best on the West Coast.

WESTPORT TO KARAMEA

North along SH67, the road is pressed against the rocky shoreline by verdant hills. The first town beyond Westport is Waimangaroa, where there's a turn-off to **Denniston**, 9km inland and 600m above sea level. Denniston was once NZ's largest coal producer, with 1500 residents in 1911. By 1981 this had shrunk to eight. The **Denniston Bridle Track** follows sections of the fantastically steep **Denniston Incline**. The incline was an engineering spectacular – empty coal trucks were hauled back up the 45-degree slope by the weight of descending loaded trucks. An information kiosk and the **'Friends of the Hill' museum** (⏰ summer weekends only) bring to life the harsh conditions experienced by the miners and their families. Four kilometres north of Waimangaroa is the **Britannia Track** (four hours return), winding towards the Britannia Battery's gold-mining detritus.

At Granity, 30km north of Westport, head 5km uphill to the semi-ghost town of **Millerton**, and a further 3km to **Stockton**, home of NZ's largest operational coal mine. The **Millerton Incline Walk** (20 minutes return) takes in parts of the old incline, a bridge and an old dam. Granity's now a sleepy haven for alternative lifestylers, and just north at Hector you can sometimes see Hector's dolphins, NZ's smallest dolphins.

Further north at Ngakawau, just south of Hector, is the **Charming Creek Walk** (six hours return), an all-weather trail following an old coal line through the Ngakawau River Gorge. Alternatively, pursue the track 10km beyond the return point to **Seddonville**, a small bush town on the Mohikinui River. The short **Chasm Creek Walkway** links Seddonville with SH67.

A good base is the **Charming Creek B&B** (☎ 03-782 8007; www.bullerbeachstay.co.nz; d $75-220; 🖳) in Ngakawau. The rooms are stylish, clean and, well, charming. There's a wood-fire hot tub that overlooks the Tasman Sea – set to be a holiday highlight for every indulger. Budget-minded travellers can bunk down in the beachside caravan for a taste of true Kiwiana style.

Further north, the Seddonville road leads to **Rough and Tumble Bush Lodge** (☎ 03-782 1337; www.roughandtumble.co.nz; s/d $300/450; 🖳). In a gentle bend of the Mohikinui River, this luxury ecolodge is surrounded by walking trails and pristine bush. The beautiful isolation is ambushed each night with gourmet food. Advance bookings are essential and rates include all meals. Worth a splurge.

At the Mohikinui River mouth, 3km off the highway, is the not-so-gentle **Gentle Annie Beach**, and the **Gentle Annie Coastal Enclave** (☎ 03-782 1826; www.gentleannie.co.nz; De Malmanche Rd, Mohikinui; unpowered sites $20, dm $25, cabins $150-180). The surf hammers the coast and the wind shakes the palms at this isolated place that's perfect for quiet contemplation. There's camping, a basic backpacker lodge, and rustic cabins sleeping up to eight. The Cabbage Tree Beach Cottage is a low-key masterpiece of rugged Kiwi architecture.

Between Mohikinui and Little Wanganui the road meanders over **Karamea Bluff**, with rata and matai forests, and expansive views of the Tasman Sea below.

KARAMEA
pop 420

The relaxed town of Karamea is literally the end of the road – the end of SH67 and near the southern ends of the Heaphy and Wangapeka Tracks. Debate rages about continuing the road through to Nelson, as any highway would need to bisect the Kahurangi National Park. Don't hold your breath waiting for a resolution. With a subtropical maritime climate, Karamea is often warmer and drier than the rest of the coast, and is actually further north than Wellington. A take-it-easy mix of locals and chilled-out imports means it's ideal for jumping off the well-trod tourist trail for a few lazy days. When you feel like getting active again, there's good caving, mountain biking and tramping.

Information
The **Karamea visitor information centre** (☎ 03-782 6652; www.karameainfo.co.nz; Market Cross; ⏲ 9am-5pm daily Jan-Apr, to 5pm Mon-Fri, to 1pm Sat May-Dec; 🖳) has the local low-down, internet access, maps and DOC hut tickets. For detailed information on negotiating the Heaphy Track, see www.heaphytrack.com.

Sights
North of Karamea in the **Oparara Basin** are spectacular limestone arches and the unique Honeycomb Hill Caves (ancient home of the moa), the surrounding karst landscape blanketed by primitive rainforest. Moss-laden trees droop over the Oparara River, illuminated by light filtering through a dense forest canopy.

Ten kilometres along the road to the start of the Heaphy Track, turn off at McCallum's Mill Rd and go 15km past the sawmill along a winding gravel (sometimes rough) road to the arches. It's an easy walk (45 minutes return) through old-growth forest to the 200m-long, 37m-high **Oparara Arch**, spanning its namesake river. Its arch-rival is the **Moria Gate Arch** (43m long, 19m high), accessed via a similar track (one hour return). At the time of writing the switched-on Oparara Valley Trust was planning a further series of walking trails. Ask at the visitor information centre about joining a customised tour, including a guided bush walk.

Other quirky calcified features are **Mirror Tarn** (an easy 20 minutes return), a tree-lined tarn full of reflections, and the **Crazy Paving & Box Canyon Caves** (10 minutes return, BYO torch), a cracked-up cave-floor formation and a roomy cave system with fossils on the ceiling. Beyond these, in a protected area of Kahurangi National Park are the superb **Honeycomb Hill Caves & Arch**, only accessible by a prebooked **guided tour** (☎ 03-782 6652; adult/child $75/35); ask at the visitor information centre. These caves contain the bones of nine different moa species and the extinct giant

Haast eagle. Gentle river **kayaking trips** (trips $75; mid-Dec–Apr) are also on offer, but only outside the breeding season of the rare kow-hiowhio (blue duck).

Activities

The Karamea River has good swimming, fishing, whitebaiting and kayaking, but ask a local or use common sense before jumping in. **Karamea Outdoor Adventures** (03-782 6181; sylvia.mike@slingshot.co.nz; Bridge St) offers kayaking and mountain-biking trips, including taking on the **K-Road** (bike hire only $35, including transport $55), a purpose-built mountain-bike trail (27km return) along logging roads.

The Little Wanganui, Oparara and Kohaihai Rivers have good swimming holes. Again, ask a local. There are good beaches too but also squadrons of sandflies; lashings of repellent (or wind) will help.

Longer walks around Karamea include the **Fenian Track** (four hours return) leading to **Cavern Creek Caves** and **Adams Flat**, where there's a replica gold-miners hut; a steep tramp for the reasonably fit to the 1084m **Mt Stormy** (eight hours return); and the first leg of the **Wangapeka Track** to Belltown Hut. Shorter walks include the **Lake Hanlon** (30 minutes return), **Big Remu** (45 minutes return), **Flagstaff** (one hour return) and **Zig Zag Track** (one hour return) walks.

If the prospect of walking the entire **Heaphy Track** tires you, just walk as far as the **Heaphy Hut** (five hours, adult/child $25/free), stay overnight, and then head back. Heaphy Track huts must be booked in advance, regardless of season, through DOC or the Karamea visitor information centre. Alternatively, walk as far as **Scotts Beach** (1½ hours return), passing nikau palm groves along the way, or continue to **Crayfish Point**. For detailed information on the Heaphy and Wangapeka Tracks, see p174 and p175.

Helicopter Charter Karamea (03-782 6111; www.adventuresnz.co.nz; 79 Waverley St) will chopper you to anywhere in the area. Options include a one-day helihike ($400 per three persons) where you are dropped off at the Heaphy Hut and walk back to Kohaihai at the southern end of the track.

Sleeping

Wangapeka Backpackers Retreat & Farmstay (03-782 6663; www.wangapeka.co.nz; Atawhai Farm, Wangapeka Valley; campsites per person $10, dm $20, s/d $40/65;) Laid-back and friendly farmstay that's a good place to recharge after completing the Wangapeka Track. Dorms are basic but there's a wood-fired bush bath. Campers are welcome and meals are available. Turn down Wangapeka Rd just north of Little Wanganui and follow the signs. It's a 20km drive south of Karamea.

Karamea Holiday Park (03-782 6758; www.karamea.com; Maori Point Rd; unpowered/powered sites $22/24, cabins $30-40, d $70) Set among native bush, 3km south of Market Cross, this is the ideal place to perfect your whitebaiting skills.

Last Resort (0800 505 042, 03-782 6617; www.lastresort.co.nz; 71 Waverley St; sites $24, dm $30, d $75-150) New owners are doing a great job in resurrecting this iconic Karamea property. Options stretch from tent sites to comfortable motel units. Dissolve into a spa or massage to lose any post-Heaphy aches and pains.

Rongo Backpackers (03-782 6667; www.rongobackpackers.com; Waverley St; unpowered sites per 2 Rongolians $50, dm/d $27/76;) Part neohippie artists' haven and part organic vegie garden, this uberrelaxed hostel even has its own community radio station (107.5 FM or www.karamearadio.com). Popular with long-term guests who often end up working within – either tending the garden or as de facto daytime DJs.

Karamea Farm Baches (03-782 6838; www.karameamotels.com; Bridge Rd; cabins $80-100) Most people would modernise these six 1960s cabins after buying them, but owners Paul and Sanae have kept the retro-Kiwiana ambience here gloriously intact, including riotous carpet last seen at your nana's place. If that sounds like your style – you'll love it.

Karamea River Motels (03-782 6955; www.karameamotels.co.nz; Bridge St; r $120-140) Accommodation at this rural motel ranges from studios to two-bedroom units. The new owners are putting their stamp on the hotel – sprucing it up and freely distributing a friendly vibe.

Karamea Beachfront Farmstay B&B (03-782 676; www.westcoastbeachaccommodation.co.nz; SH67; d incl breakfast $160-180) This friendly farmstay has three comfortable rooms and 2.5km of pristine beachfront 15km south of Karamea. Your host studied cooking in France, so expect the breakfast to be a cut above.

Eating & Drinking

Last Resort (03-782 6617; 71 Waverley St; lunch mains $8-12, dinner mains $22-30; 7am-late) The pleasant ambience of the dining area ushers in the best cuisine in town. Dine at either the all-day cafe, or the flasher evening restaurant with local tastes like Karamea reef and beef ($29.50).

Saracens Café (☎ 03-782 6600; 99 Bridge St; mains $10-15; ☷ 11am-late) The best place in town for a quick bite and a coffee, Saracens morphs into a live-music venue with occasional gigs on summer evenings.

Karamea Village Hotel (☎ 03-782 6800; Waverley St; mains $18-22; ☷ 11am-11pm) Treat yourself to life's simple pleasures. A game of pool or darts with the locals, a pint of Monteith's Original Ale, and a whitebait-fritter sandwich ($12). Sorted.

Just behind Saracens, the **Bush Lounge** (☎ 03-782 6711; ☷ mains $15-20; 6pm-late) aligns a rustic interior with a suitably rustic menu.

Getting There & Away

If you're driving from Westport to Karamea, fill up in Westport as there's no petrol until Karamea, 98km away.

Karamea Express (☎ 03-782 6757; info@karamea-express.co.nz) links Karamea and Westport (adult/child $27/17, 1½ hours, 7.50am Monday to Friday May to October, plus Saturday from November to April), departing from Last Resort.

Karamea Express also services Kohaihai at the southern end of the Heaphy Track, departing Kohaihai at 1pm and 2pm during summer; phone for prices and off-season times. It also services the Wangapeka Track on demand. There are phones at both trailheads to arrange transport out to Karamea.

You can also fly from Karamea to Takaka (around $175 per person) then walk back on the Heaphy Track; contact the visitor information centre for details.

Ask at Rongo Backpackers (opposite) about transport to trailheads (Heaphy $10 per person, Wangapeka $15 per person), and to other destinations in the area including the Oparara Basin ($35 per person).

WESTPORT TO GREYMOUTH

SH6 along the surf-pounded coastline proffers fine Tasman Sea views; so fine that Lonely Planet's *Best of Travel* dubbed the West Coast highway one of the planet's 10 best road trips. Fill up in Westport if you're low on petrol and cash – there's no fuel until Runanga, 92km away, and the next ATM is in Greymouth. The main attractions along this stretch are the geologically fascinating Pancake Rocks

at Punakaiki. To break the journey, consider the following.

our pick **Beaconstone** (☎ 027 431 0491; www.beaconstone.co.nz; Birds Ferry Rd; dm/d $25/65; ☷ Oct-Jun) is 17km south of Westport on 52 serene hectares. Solar power, an organic garden and energy-efficient appliances make a bold ecofriendly and sustainable statement. This ubercool establishment is overflowing with character and charm. Beaconstone only has room for 12 guests so booking ahead is recommended.

Jack's Gasthof (☎ 03-789 6501; jack.schubert@xtra.co.nz; SH6; sites $10, d $50; ☷ Oct-May) is 23km south of Westport on the Little Totara River. Laconic Jack swapped Berlin for this gentle spot more than 20 years ago. There are two cruisy doubles, and a pizzeria (mains $16 to $30; open 11am till late) serving pizzas made with organic vegies grown outside the door. Watch out for Jack's huge (and hugely friendly) dog.

For a taste of the region's old mining past, swing into **Mitchell's Gully Gold Mine** (☎ 03-789 6553; www.mitchellsgullygoldmine.co.nz; SH6; adult/child $10/free; ☷ 9am-4pm), 22km south of Westport, with a tumbledown water wheel, old rail tracks and hillside tunnels (BYO torch).

Charleston, 28km south of Westport, boomed during the 1860s gold rush, with 80 hotels, three breweries, and hundreds of thirsty gold-diggers staking claims along the Nile River. Though it was a hot spot in the old days, most will struggle to find reason to hang out here for too long these days. The only pub left is the **Charleston European Tavern** (☎ 03-789 8862; SH6; mains $16-26; ☷ 9am-late), now doing double-duty as a cafe during the day and a boozer at night. It's the base for underground, water-laden trips offered by Norwest Adventures (p180).

Next door, the **Charleston Motel** (☎ 03-789 7599; www.charlestonmotel.co.nz; SH6; d $110) offers comfortable units just off the highway.

Those wanting to sleep under canvas should refer to the **Charleston Motor Camp** (☎ 03-789 6773; www.charlestonmotorcamp.co.nz; SH6; sites per person $10; cabins per person $25) Nothing fancy, but the price is right.

The broken coastline from Fox River to Runanga will remind Californians of Big Sur. Woodpecker Bay, Tiromoana, Punakaiki, Barrytown, Fourteen Mile, Motukiekie, Ten Mile, Nine Mile and Seven Mile are **beaches** sculpted by relentless ocean fury.

Punakaiki & Paparoa National Park

Located midway between Westport and Greymouth is Punakaiki, a small settlement beside the rugged 38,000-hectare Paparoa National Park. For most travellers, it's a quick stop for an ice cream and a squiz at the Pancake Rocks; a shame because there's excellent tramping on offer and some tragically underused charismatic accommodation options.

INFORMATION

The **Paparoa National Park visitor information centre** (☎ 03-731 1895; punakaiki@doc.govt.nz; SH6; ✆ 9am-5pm Oct-Dec, to 6pm Jan-May, to 4.30pm Jun-Sep) has info-laden displays on the park, and details on activities, accommodation and trail conditions. Online see www.punakaiki.co.nz.

SIGHTS

Punakaiki is famous for its fantastic **Pancake Rocks** and **blowholes**. Through a layering-weathering process called stylobedding, the Dolomite Point limestone has formed into what looks like piles of thick pancakes. When the tide is right (tide times are posted at the visitor information centre), the sea surges into caverns and booms menacingly through blowholes. See it on a windy and wild day and be reminded that Mother Nature really is the boss. An easy 15-minute walk loops from the highway out to the rocks and blowholes.

Paparoa National Park is also blessed with sea cliffs, the mountains of the Paparoa Range, rivers, diverse flora and a Westland petrel colony, the world's only nesting site of this rare sea bird.

ACTIVITIES

Tramps in the national park are detailed in the DOC *Paparoa National Park* pamphlet ($1), and include the **Inland Pack Track** (two to three days), a route established by miners in 1867 to dodge difficult coastal terrain. The **Croesus Track** (one to two days), covered by another DOC leaflet (50c), is a tramp over the Paparoa Range from Blackball to Barrytown, passing historic gold-mining areas. Register at the Greymouth or Paparoa visitor information centres before setting out. Some inland walks are susceptible to river flooding; check conditions before you depart.

Shorter options include the **Truman Track** (30 minutes return) and the **Porari River Track** (2½ hours return), which follows a spectacu-lar limestone gorge. The **Fox River Tourist Cave** (three hours return) is open to amateur explorers. BYO torch and wear good walking shoes.

Punakaiki Canoes (☎ 03-731 1870; www.riverkayaking.co.nz; SH6; canoe hire 2hr/full day $35/55) rents canoes and kayaks near the Pororari River bridge. Guided tours start from $70. **Punakaiki Horse Treks** (☎ 03-731 1839; www.pancake-rocks.co.nz; SH6; 2½-hr ride $125; ✆ Oct-May), based at Hydrangea Cottages, conducts four-legged outings alongside the national park.

TOURS

Green Kiwi Tours (☎ 03 731 1843; www.greenkiwitours.co.nz; guided walking tours from $60, caving from $100) runs info-rich excursions throughout the region with an ecofriendly focus. Trips centered around native flora, fauna and local history are on offer as well as caving excursions.

SLEEPING & EATING

Punakaiki Beach Hostel (☎ 03-731 1852; www.punakaiki beachhostel.co.nz; 4 Webb St; tents per person $20, dm/s/d $28/50/70; 🖥 🛜) A sandy, beach-bumming hostel with a deep, sea-view veranda and an outdoor spa, just a short stroll from Pancake Rocks and the beach. They were mid-tidy when we came by, so you can expect a fresh feel to the place.

Te Nikau Retreat (☎ 03-731 1111; www.tenikaure treat.co.nz; Hartmount Pl; dm $23, d $60-85, cabins $90; 🖥) This unconventional accommodation option is set aesthetically amid the rainforest. Several buildings populate the property, all with their own character. From straightforward dorms in a chilled setting all the way through to cabins that take indoor-outdoor flow to a new level (the kitchen is in an attached greenhouse). There is even a stargazer hut for those who want to sleep under the night sky.

Punakaiki Beach Camp (☎ 03-731 1894; beach camp@xtra.co.nz; 5 Owen St; unpowered & powered sites $30, d $45) This park is drenched with salty scents and studded with clean, old-style cabins and shipshape amenities.

Rocks Homestay (☎ 03-731 1141; www.therocks homestay.com; 33 Hartmount Pl; s/d incl breakfast from $135/195) Three kilometres north of Punakaiki (100m north of the Truman Track), this house looks over wild scrub to the rolling sea. The breakfasts are tasty, and dinner is available by arrangement. Once you've had your fill of pancakes, the sunny conservatory promotes curling up with a good book.

Hydrangea Cottages (☎ 03-731 1839; www.pancake-rocks.co.nz; SH6; d $140-295) On a hillside overlooking Pancake Rocks, these five stand-alone and self-contained cottages are constructed classily from recycled rimu and local river stones. Punakaiki Horse Treks is based here.

Punakaiki Crafts (☎ 03-731 1813; SH6; coffee & cake $7; ☯ 9am-4.30pm, gallery to 7pm) Good coffee, cakes and slices share an interesting gallery showcasing local artists.

Wild Coast Café (☎ 03-731 1873; SH6; mains $18-26; ☯ 8am-9pm; 💻 ☷) Beside the visitor information centre is this tourist-swollen cafe, serving pancake stacks, good pies and ice creams. Those in need of a dub-dub-dub fix can jump on the internet here for $3 per hour.

Punakaiki Tavern (☎ 03-731 1188; SH6; mains $19-31; ☯ 8.30am-late) Most nights the punters are a mix of local and international, and the pub menu with steak, fish and pasta has a similar slant. When you're done, stick a pin in a map of the world to show how far you've come.

GETTING THERE & AWAY
InterCity (☎ 03-365 1113; www.intercity.co.nz) links to Westport ($19) and Greymouth ($25). **Naked Bus** (www.nakedbus.com) has a similar service along SH6 to Westport ($22) and Greymouth ($12). Both companies stop allowing enough time to check out Pancake Rocks.

The Coast Road
SH6 from Punakaiki to Greymouth is flanked by white-capped waves and rocky bays on one side, and the steep, bushy Paparoa Ranges on the other.

Steve used to design women's lingerie, but now he runs one of the South Island's most surprising attractions, **Barrytown Knifemaking** (☎ 0800 256 433; www.barrytownknifemaking.com; SH6; classes $120). Put aside a day (9.30am to 3.30pm) as Steve and wife Robyn steer you through the process of making your own knife. We're talking the whole shebang here, from hand-forging the blade to crafting a handle from native rimu timber. Between the knifemaking, there's lunch, archery, axe-throwing lessons, and a stream of entertainingly bad jokes from Steve. Bookings recommended and transport can be arranged from Greymouth or Punakaiki.

Barrytown, 16km south of Punakaiki, has the **All Nations Hotel** (☎ 03-731 1812; allnations@xtra.co.nz; SH6; unpowered sites $20, dm/d $28/70). Its coaster-covered walls are opposite the western end of the Croesus Track, handy for trampers desperate for a beer and a bed (definitely in that order). Also serves pub meals and attracts backpacker buses.

Ti Kouka House (☎ 03-731 1460; www.tikoukahouse.co.nz; SH6; d incl breakfast $295) is all rugged sea views, global antiques and lots of recycled wood, including history-laden doors and windows. Three luxury rooms stud this excellent B&B, which has a luscious backdrop of subtropical rainforest. Think Santa Fe adobe style meets West Coast rustic.

For food, try **Darcy's Buffalo Bar & Grill** (☎ 03-731 1151; SH6, Barrytown; mains $10-22; ☯ 11am-late), a spacious cafe perched above the road with lots of outdoor seating.

Breakers (☎ 03-762 7743; www.breakers.co.nz; SH6; d incl breakfast $200-330; ☷), 14km north of Greymouth, is one of the best-kept secrets on the coast. Breakers sits on a stunning spot overlooking the sea with fine surfing opportunities at hand for the intrepid. The rooms are beautifully appointed and the hosts are friendly.

GREY VALLEY
From Murchison, an alternative to the SH6 coast route is to turn off at Inangahua Junction and travel inland across winding valley roads via Reefton, and over the mountains into the Grey Valley.

Amid the regenerating forests, small towns are reminders of futile farming attempts, and of the gold rush of the 1860s.

Reefton
pop 1000
Reefton is an unconcerned little hamlet in the heart of superb tramping and trout-fishing country. As early as 1888, Reefton had its own electricity supply and street lighting, ahead of everywhere else in NZ. If you've crossed Lewis Pass from Christchurch, this is the first sizeable town you come to.

INFORMATION
The **Reefton i-SITE** (☎ 03-732 8391; www.reefton.co.nz; 67 Broadway; ☯ 8.30am-6pm Nov-Mar, to 4.30pm Apr-Oct; 💻) has very helpful staff, and a one-room recreation of the Quartzopolis Mine (50c). At the time of writing, plans were afoot to introduce mine tours in the area.

SIGHTS & ACTIVITIES
Quite a few shops on Broadway date from the 1870s, and the town feels like a Western

movie backdrop. For more information buy the *Historic Reefton* leaflet ($1).

The community-run **Blacks Point Museum** (Franklin St, Blacks Point; adult/child/family $5/3/15; ⏰ 9am-noon & 1-4pm Wed-Fri & Sun, 1-4pm Sat Oct-Apr), 2km east of Reefton on the Christchurch road, is inside a former Methodist church and crammed with prospecting paraphernalia. Up the road is the still-functional **Golden Fleece Battery** (adult/child $1/free; ⏰ 1-4pm Wed & Sun Oct-Apr), used for crushing gold-flecked quartz.

You can also have a chat with the guys at the **Bearded Miner Company** (☎ 03-732 8377; Broadway; admission by donation; ⏰ 11am-4pm). Friendly bearded types will sit you down in a 1860s-style miners hut and give you a cup of billy tea. You might wonder why they haven't formed a ZZ Top tribute band.

If you want to dig a bit deeper check out the **Globe Gold Mine Tours** (☎ 027 442 4777; www.reefton gold.co.nz; adult/child $45/28; ⏰ tours 1.30pm Tue-Sat). This new operation takes in many of the gold-flavoured attractions in town including the Bearded Miners and Blacks Point Museum. The real highlight is the chance to get up close and personal with a working gold mine – hard hat and high-vis vest provided.

Short walks around town include the **Powerhouse Walk** (40 minutes return) and **Reefton Heritage Walk** (30 minutes return). The **Murray Creek Track** (two to seven hours return), from Blacks Point, takes in abandoned coal and gold mines.

There's good tramping in the 182,000-hectare **Victoria Forest Park** (NZ's largest forest park), overgrown by five different species of beech tree. Consider the three-day **Kirwans**, **Lake Christabel** and **Robinson River Tracks** or the two-day **Big River Track** with good **mountain biking** opportunities. Ask at the i-SITE for information and maps.

SLEEPING & EATING
Reefton Motor Camp (☎ 03-732 8477; roa.reuben@xtra. co.nz; 1 Ross St; unpowered/powered sites $20/25, d $40) On the Inangahua River at the eastern end of town, this park is encircled by birdsong and stately fir trees.

Old Nurses Home (☎ 03-732 8881; reeftonretreat@ hotmail.com; 104 Shiel St; dm/s/d $25/33/54; 💻 🛜) In Reefton they're good at transforming stately old buildings into cosy hostels. With colourful duvets and pretty gardens and patios, there's nary a whiff of this place's more buttoned-down institutional past.

Reef Cottage (☎ 0800 770 440, 03-732 8440; www. reefcottage.co.nz; 51-55 Broadway; d $100-150) This 1867 cottage, popular with couples and groups of up to eight, was formerly a solicitor's office. There's plenty of heritage timber, warming the mood for the (occasional) West Coast downpour. Adjoining the cottage, the Reef Cottage Café (meals $8 to $20) serves gourmet pies, cakes, quiches, pastas and salads.

Alfresco (☎ 03-732 8513; 16 Broadway; mains $12-25; ⏰ 11am-7pm) With a family bistro atmosphere, Alfresco serves up meat and seafood grills and a half-dozen tasty pizzas. There are gas heaters or tables inside if the alfresco gets too fresco. They also have charming accommodation in the adjacent building – a double room will run you $60 to $120 and you won't be disappointed.

DRINKING
Wilson's (☎ 03-732 8800; 32 Broadway; mains $12-20; ⏰ 11am-11pm) Sleepy Reefton could be the most laid-back place you'll ever visit, but if you do need to slow down, then the two garden bars (count 'em…) at Wilson's will do the trick. Occasional bands raise the excitement level to somewhere under fever pitch.

GETTING THERE & AWAY
East West Coach (☎ 0800 142 622, 03-789 6251; east westco@xtra.co.nz) runs daily to Westport ($22, 1¼ hours) and Christchurch ($44, 3¾ hours). **Atomic Shuttles** (☎ 03 349 0697; www.atomictravel.co.nz) swings by on its service linking Nelson ($40, six hours) and Franz Josef ($32, 5¾ hours).

State Highway 7 to Greymouth
At Hukarere, 21km south of Reefton, turn east and drive 14km to **Waiuta**, once a burgeoning gold town, now a spectral collection of remnants. The Birthday Reef was unearthed here on King Edward VII's birthday in 1905. By 1906 the Blackwater Mine was booming, and the town's population swelled to 500. In 1951 the mine collapsed and Waiuta was abandoned virtually overnight.

The lonesomely ruinous atmosphere makes Waiuta worth the trip. It's a leafy drive through beech forest, the last 7km on a winding, narrow dirt road. **Waiuta Lodge** (adult/child $15/7.50, plus key deposit $10) is a 30-bunk building with full kitchen facilities. Book and collect the key at the **Reefton i-SITE** (☎ 03-732 8391; www. reefton.co.nz; 67 Broadway, Reefton).

BLACKBALL

Northeast of the Grey River, about 25km north of Greymouth, Blackball is a working town established in 1866 to service gold diggers; coal mining kicked in between 1890 and 1964. The National Federation of Labour (a trade union) was conceived here, born from influential strikes in 1908 and 1931.

On the road 1km from Blackball is the trailhead of the **Croesus Track** (DOC leaflet $1), tracking 18km across the Paparoa Range to Barrytown on the West Coast. Do it in a day if you're keen/mad, or stay overnight at DOC's **Ces Clark Hut** (adult $10), halfway along. Book the hut through the Greymouth i-SITE (p190) before you start walking.

The hub of Blackball society is the **Formerly the Blackball Hilton** (☎ 0800 4252 252 255, 03-732 4705; www.blackballhilton.co.nz; 26 Hart St; dm/d $30/110), designated a New Zealand Historic Place. The 'formerly' was added after a certain global hotel chain got antsy. There are B&B doubles and funky dorms. The beer's cold, the pub atmosphere is good value and the kitchen has just been re-fit to ensure the meals are Hilton worthy. Full of character, this establishment alone makes the trip off the main highway well worth the eclectic diversion.

The **Blackball Salami Co** (☎ 03-732 4111; www.blackballsalami.co.nz; 11 Hilton St; ⏰ 8am-4pm Mon-Fri, 9am-3pm Sat) sells low-fat venison and beef salami. If you're planning a barbecue pick up some tasty snarlers as they say in Kiwi-speak – that's sausages for the uninitiated.

LAKE BRUNNER

At Stillwater, detour to Lake Brunner, aka Moana Kotuku (Heron Sea). Locals reckon Lake Brunner and the Arnold River have the world's best **trout fishing** – not an uncommon boast in NZ. Hire a fishing guide in Moana (at the Moana Hotel) or corner a local for advice. Moana is going ahead with lots of flash new holiday homes, but peace and quiet is usually just a boat ride away

Walks include the **Velenski Walk** (20 minutes one-way) from the motor camp through native forest; the **Arnold Dam Walk** (45 minutes return), which crosses a swing bridge over the Arnold River; and the **Rakaitane Track** (45 minutes return) through mixed podocarp forest with glowworms.

Lake Brunner Motor Camp (☎ 03-738 0600; lake.brunner@paradise.net.nz; Ahau St; powered sites $26, s $20) is in dire need of a tidy or perhaps a bulldozer – but it is the best and only budget option in town.

The **Lake Brunner Resort** (☎ 03-738 0083; www.lakebrunnerresort.net.nz; Ahau St; d $145-320) is a step above most places in town with slick facilities, tidy rooms and nice views. The resort's restaurant (mains $15 to $20; open noon till 9pm) does old-school favourites like chicken Kiev. If you're looking for a fishing guide, immerse yourself in the hotel's garden bar and throw out a few lines.

The **Lake Brunner Country Motel** (☎ 03-738 0144; www.lakebrunnermotel.co.nz; 2014 Arnold Valley Rd; tent sites $24, powered sites $35, cabins $52-119) has cabins, cottages and campervan sites ringed by native bush. It's a quiet and peaceful location, made more relaxing with a spa and the regular chorus of birdsong. It's 2km west of Moana; on your right if you're coming from Greymouth.

The **Station House Cafe** (☎ 03-738 0158; 40 Koe St; lunch $12-18, dinner $20-28; ⏰ noon-10pm, from 10am in summer) is on a hillside opposite the Moana Railway Station, where the *TranzAlpine* train pulls in. Aimed at the train-folk but no matter how you got here – it's the best food in town.

GREYMOUTH
pop 10,000

Welcome to the 'Big Smoke' of Westland. Crouched at the mouth of the Grey River (early European settlers had a lot of stuff to name, OK?), the West Coast's largest town has a proud gold-mining history, and a legacy of occasional river floods, now somewhat alleviated by a flood wall.

On the main road and rail route through Arthur's Pass and across the Southern Alps from Christchurch, Greymouth sees its fair share of travellers taking advantage of outstanding budget accommodation. Once you've enjoyed the tasty Monteith's Brewery tour, outdoor adventures including rafting, kayaking, canyoning and quad-biking can fill another couple of days. Motorcyclists and motorcycling enthusiasts rock in over Labour Weekend for October's Downtown Street Racing.

Orientation

The town centre is on the Grey River's south bank, 1km from the river mouth, and around the intersection of Mackay and Tainui Sts.

THE WEST COAST

Free town and regional maps are available at the i-SITE and the **Automobile Association** (AA; ☎ 03-768 4300; www.aatravel.co.nz; 84 Tainui St).

Information

Major banks huddle around Mackay and Tainui Sts. There's internet access at the i-SITE and at the library.

DP:One Cafe (108 Mawhera Quay) Internet access.
Greymouth Hospital (☎ 03-768 0499; High St)
Greymouth i-SITE (☎ 0800 473 966, 03-768 5101; www.greydistrict.co.nz; cnr Herbert & Mackay Sts; ⊙ 8.30am-7pm Mon-Fri, 9am-6pm Sat, 10am-5pm Sun Nov-Apr, reduced hours May-Oct; ⌨) Very helpful crew and DOC information.
Paper Plus (☎ 03-768 5175; 62 Mackay St) Bookshop.
Police station (☎ 03-768 1600; 45-47 Guinness St)
Post office (Tainui St)

Sights

History House Museum (☎ 03-768 4028; www.history-house.co.nz; Gresson St; adult/child $5/2; ⊙ 10am-4pm Mon-Fri) documents Greymouth's gold-prospecting history.

The **Left Bank Art Gallery** (☎ 03-768 0038; www.leftbankart.co.nz; 1 Tainui St; ⊙ 10am-2pm winter, to 4pm summer) houses contemporary NZ jade carvings. Prints, paintings and photographs also get an airing.

Jade Country Greymouth (☎ 03-768 0700; 1 Guinness St; admission free; ⊙ 8.30am-8pm Oct-Apr, to 5pm May-Sep) has original jade jewellery costing from $30 to thousands of dollars. There's a walk-through Jade Trail display on the precious *pounamu*, and the Jade Boulder Café (mains $10 to $21; open 8.30am till 4pm) serves organic coffee, whitebait and other 'wild food' that's more difficult to catch.

Not happy with your photos? **Stewart Nimmo Gallery** (☎ 03-768 6499; www.stewartnimmo.co.nz; cnr Mackay & Tainui Sts; admission free) is the place to stock up on some pro shots of the stellar West Coast scenery.

Activities

The **Point Elizabeth Walkway** (three hours return) heads north of Greymouth into the Rapahoe Range Scenic Reserve. The **Floodwall Walk** from Cobden Bridge towards Blaketown is shorter (30 minutes return).

Wild West Adventure Co (☎ 0800 147 483, 03-768 6649; www.nzholidayheaven.com; 8 Whall St) runs rafting excursions (priced from $160 to $845), a three-hour river cruise ($145) aboard a 'Jungle Boat' and a 5½-hour 'Dragons

Cave' blackwater rafting expedition ($160). Inflatable kayak trips start at $225.

On Yer Bike (☎ 0800 669 372, 03-762 7438; www.onyerbike.co.nz; SH6, Coal Creek; 2hr ride adult/child $140/120), 5km north of Greymouth, gets down 'n' dirty on quad-bikes and rugged go-karts. Take a two-hour 'Bush 'n' Bog' ride or jump into the amphibious 8WD 'Argo' (one-hour trips $70).

The **surf** at Cobden Beach and Seven Mile Beach in Rapahoe is consistent, but too dangerous for swimming.

Tours

Kea Heritage Tours (☎ 0800 532 868; www.keatours.co.nz; day tours $70-275) Well-informed guides visit West Coast locations like Blackball, Punakaiki and the glaciers. The four-day Te Ara Pounamu tour ($1595) from Greymouth to Queenstown follows the greenstone trading route traditionally used by Maori.

Monteith's Brewing Co (☎ 03-768 4149; www.monteiths.co.nz; cnr Turumaha & Herbert Sts; admission $15; ⊙ tours 11.30am, 2pm, 4pm, 6pm) Finish this excellent 1¼-hour-long tour in the bar by working your way through Monteith's eight brews. Bookings recommended, especially for the 6pm tour ($25) which kicks on for a barbecue at one of three downtown eateries.

Sleeping
BUDGET

Neptunes International Backpackers (☎ 0800 003 768, 03-768 4425; www.neptunesbackpackers.co.nz; 43 Gresson St; dm/d $18/45; ⌨ ☎) This two-storey hostel has a prime location in the heart of town. A nautical theme permeates everything, and you won't find any bunks here. This worn-in property is getting dangerously close to worn-out, but the price is right.

Noah's Ark Backpackers (☎ 0800 662 472, 03-768 4868; www.noahsarkbackpackers.co.nz; 16 Chapel St; unpowered sites $34, dm/s/d $22/43/54; ⌨ ☎) Originally a monastery, Noah's now has eccentric animal-themed rooms and a sunset-worthy balcony. In true Ark style, the camping price is for two people. Mountain bikes and fishing rods are provided free of charge.

South Beach Motel & Motorpark (☎ 0800 101 222, 03-762 6768; www.southbeach.co.nz; 318 Main South Rd; unpowered/powered sites $25/30, d $45-135; ⌨) This low-rise motel and cabin complex propositions with a pastel-hued Miami accent, but the well-established nikau palms bring it firmly back to good old Enzed. Use of a spa and the internet are both gratis. Campervans and tents also welcome.

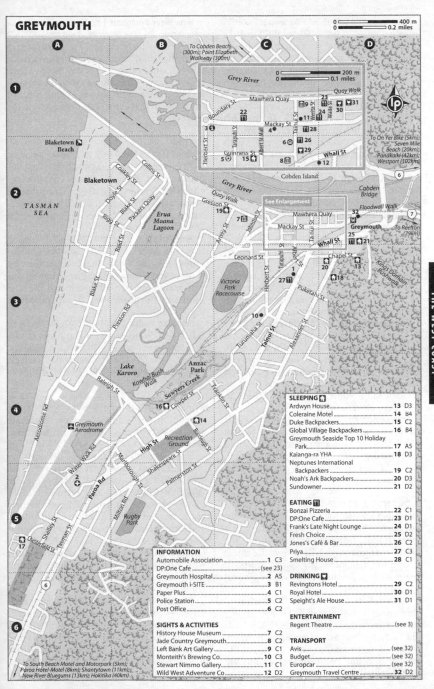

THE WEST COAST

INFORMATION
Automobile Association	1	C3
DP:One Cafe	(see 23)	
Greymouth Hospital	2	A5
Greymouth i-SITE	3	B1
Paper Plus	4	C1
Police Station	5	C2
Post Office	6	C2

SIGHTS & ACTIVITIES
History House Museum	7	C2
Jade Country Greymouth	8	C2
Left Bank Art Gallery	9	C1
Monteith's Brewing Co	10	C3
Stewart Nimmo Gallery	11	C1
Wild West Adventure Co	12	D2

SLEEPING
Ardwyn House	13	D3
Coleraine Motel	14	B4
Duke Backpackers	15	C2
Global Village Backpackers	16	B4
Greymouth Seaside Top 10 Holiday Park	17	A5
Kaianga-ra YHA	18	D3
Neptunes International Backpackers	19	C2
Noah's Ark Backpackers	20	D3
Sundowner	21	D2

EATING
Bonzai Pizzeria	22	C1
DP:One Cafe	23	D1
Frank's Late Night Lounge	24	D1
Fresh Choice	25	D2
Jones's Café & Bar	26	C2
Priya	27	C3
Smelting House	28	C1

DRINKING
Revingtons Hotel	29	C2
Royal Hotel	30	D1
Speight's Ale House	31	D1

ENTERTAINMENT
Regent Theatre	(see 3)	

TRANSPORT
Avis	(see 32)	
Budget	(see 32)	
Europcar	(see 32)	
Greymouth Travel Centre	32	D2

Kaianga-ra YHA (☎ 03-768 4951; www.yha.co.nz; 15 Alexander St; dm $27, s/d $60/68; 🖳 🛜) Built in 1938 as a Marist Brothers' residence, this hostel is big, clean, functional and well behaved – everything you'd expect from YHA. Shatter the monastic ambience by playing guitar on the veranda.

Duke Backpackers (☎ 03-768 9470; www.duke.co.nz; 27 Guinness St; dm $27, s $45, d $64-75; 🖳 🛜) This purple palace has spared no expense when it comes to paint. Duke's is a lively place with an in-house bar, ample social areas and some cool free extras like soup, half-hour internet when you book in and a free second beer at the bar. It's loud, raucous, and popular with groups – love it or hate it.

ourpick Global Village Backpackers (☎ 03-768 7272; www.globalvillagebackpackers.co.nz; 42-54 Cowper St; sites/dm/s/d/tr/q $30/25/60/60/90/108; 🖳 🛜) A collage of African and Asian art is infused with a passionate travellers' vibe here. Free kayaks – the Lake Karoro wetlands reserve is just metres away – and mountain bikes are on tap, and relaxation comes easy with a spa, sauna and riverside barbecue.

Greymouth Seaside Top 10 Holiday Park (☎ 0800 867 104, 03-768 6618; www.top10greymouth.co.nz; 2 Chesterfield St; unpowered/powered sites $36/40, d $55-115; 🖳) This well-appointed beachside park is 2.5km south of town. Cabins sleep six and the good-value self-contained units sleep up to eight. Kid-friendly distractions include an adventure playground.

Ardwyn House (☎ 03-768 6107; ardwynhouse@hot mail.com; 48 Chapel St; s/d without bathroom incl breakfast $55/90) This old-fashioned B&B nestles amid steep gardens on a quiet dead-end street. Mary, the well-travelled host, cooks a splendid breakfast.

MIDRANGE & TOP END

Sundowner (☎ 0800 080 859, 03-768 4666; www.sun downer.co.nz; 14 Smith St; d $105-115; 🖳 🛜) Just a short walk from the train station, the Sundowner impresses with a versatile range of options, from cheaper family units to newer studios. Brightly coloured duvets will brighten your day.

Coleraine Motel (☎ 0800 270 027, 03-768 077; www. colerainemotel.co.nz; 61 High St; d $139-200; 🖳 🛜) Rattan furniture, spa baths and king-size beds add up to the best accommodation in town. We're talking about the luxury units, but the cheaper one- and two-bedroom studios are not far behind.

New River Bluegums (☎ 03-762 6678; www.blue gumsnz.com; 985 Main South Rd; d incl breakfast $165; 🖳 🛜) Stay either in the cosy upstairs room in the rustic family home, or settle into a private self-contained cabin. Either way there's a farm to be explored, sheep to be shorn (in season), and huge cooked breakfasts to look forward to. Work off that extra rasher of bacon on the tennis court.

Eating

DP:One Cafe (☎ 03-768 4005; 108 Mawhera Quay; meals $6-15; 🕒 8am-5pm, closed Sunday; 🖳 🛜) This bohemian room plugs the grungy cred of a big-city cafe into the artsy vibe of a ramshackle garage sale. The menu features healthy pies, focaccias, salads and cakes, plus good coffee and wicked smoothies.

Jones's Café & Bar (☎ 03-768 6468; 37 Tainui St; lunch $8-15, dinner $19-30; 🕒 11.30am-2pm, 5.50-9pm) Jones's bills itself as a blues bar, but the vibe is more yawn than Stevie Ray Vaughan. It's extremely popular with locals and the trad meat and fish dishes are as dependable as the 12-bar blues.

Smelting House (☎ 03-768 0012; 102 Mackay St; mains $10-16; 🕒 8am-5pm) This is the sort of cafe that entices you to settle in for a lengthy stay. Heaps of mags – check, great coffee – check, tasty bagels, sandwiches and breakfast choices galore – check. Check it out.

Priya (☎ 03-768 7377; 84 Tainui St; mains $13-16; 🕒 noon-12.30pm & 5-10pm; Ⓥ) An explosion of subcontinental Indian spices on temperate West Coast tastebuds, this seasoned performer is heavily patronised. There's chilled Kingfisher beer and a healthy range of vego delights.

ourpick Frank's Late Night Lounge (☎ 03-768 9075; 115 Mackay St; mains $13-20; 🕒 5pm-late Thu-Sat; Ⓥ) Effortlessly cool and retro late-night lounge-bar-cafe. A mirror ball hovers blithely above rescued 1950s furniture while Sinatra and Dean Martin bubble away as the soundtrack. An eclectic list of teas and NZ's best boutique beers partner a small global menu with surprises like Tibetan *momos* (dumplings) and Moroccan fish. Occasional live gigs complete the picture.

Bonzai Pizzeria (☎ 03-768 4170; 31 Mackay St; mains $15-25; 🕒 8am-late Mon-Sat, from 3pm Sun) The name's (kind of) Japanese; the decor is pure 1970s NZ, and the Italian-tinged pizzas, pasta and soup all come reader-recommended. Be sure to save room for one of the awesome home-made cakes.

Self-caterers should check out **Fresh Choice** (☎ 03-768 7545; 174b Mawhera Quay; ☯ 7am-9pm) supermarket.

Drinking

Speight's Ale House (☎ 03-768 0667; 130 Mawhera Quay; mains $20-30; ☯ 11am-late) In a 1909 waterfront building, Dunedin's finest beer has crossed the Southern Alps to take on Monteith's. With Greymouth's best wine list and tasty farm-style meals on offer, it's easy to see why locals have adopted Speight's as their *other* favourite beer.

Royal Hotel (☎ 03-768 4022; 128 Mawhera Quay; ☯ 11am-late) The Royal is an old-fashioned pub with affable Brit owners who welcome all comers with gusto. Grab a beer, get chatting, or watch the football (soccer) on Sky TV.

Revingtons Hotel (☎ 03-768 7055; 46 Tainui St; ☯ 8.30am-late) Alternate between a Monteith's in Revy's Sports Bar, or a Guinness or Kilkenny next door in Danny Doolan's. Steaks and venison pie tick the box marked 'Pub Grub' (mains $12 to $25).

Entertainment

Regent Theatre (☎ 03-768 0920; www.regentgrey mouth.co.nz; cnr Herbert & Mackay Sts; adult/child $12/6) has movies and occasional live performances.

Getting There & Around

The **Greymouth Travel Centre** (☎ 03-768 7080; www. westcoasttravel.co.nz; railway station, 164 Mackay St; ☯ 9am-5pm Mon-Fri, 10am-3pm Sat & Sun; ☐ ☏) books all forms of transport, including buses, trains and interisland ferries, and has luggage-storage facilities. This is also the bus depot and offers wi-fi access.

BUS

InterCity (☎ 03-365 1113; www.intercity.co.nz) has daily 1.30pm buses north to Westport ($25, two hours) and Nelson ($60, six hours), and south to Franz Josef ($42, 3½ hours) and Fox Glaciers ($45, 4¼ hours). Prices vary depending on season and availability.

Naked Bus (www.nakedbus.com) runs north to Nelson and south to Queenstown stopping at Hokitika, Franz Josef and Fox Glaciers, Haast and Wanaka.

Atomic Shuttles (☎ 03-349 0697; www.atomictravel. co.nz) runs daily to Queenstown ($70, 10½ hours, departs at 7.30am), with daily services to Fox Glacier ($35, 4¼ hours, departing 3.15pm), Picton ($60, 7½ hours, departing 1.15pm), and Hokitika ($15, one hour, departing 2pm).

CAR

Greymouth Travel Centre has the following branches of the major hire companies:
Avis (☎ 03-768 0902; www.avis.com)
Budget (☎ 03-768 4343; www.budget.co.nz)
Europcar (☎ 03-768 9980; www.europcar.co.nz)

A local company is **Alpine West** (☎ 0800 257 736, 03-736 4002; www.alpinerentals.co.nz; 11 Shelley St).

TAXI

Try **Greymouth Taxis** (☎ 03-768 7078). To the airport is around $20.

THE WEST COAST

THE TRANZALPINE

The **TranzAlpine** (☎ 0800 872 467, 03-768 7080; www.tranzscenic.co.nz; adult/child $118/70, rates vary seasonally) is one of the world's great train journeys. Traversing the Southern Alps between Christchurch and Greymouth, and from the Pacific Ocean to the Tasman Sea, the *TranzAlpine* tracks through a sequence of unbelievable landscapes. Leaving Christchurch at 8.15am, it speeds across the flat, alluvial Canterbury Plains to the Alps' foothills. Here it enters a labyrinth of gorges and hills called the Staircase, a climb made possible by three large viaducts and a plethora of tunnels.

The train emerges into the broad Waimakariri and Bealey Valleys and (on a good day) the vistas are stupendous. The beech-forested river valley gives way to the snowcapped peaks of Arthur's Pass National Park. At Arthur's Pass itself (a small alpine village), the train enters the longest tunnel, the 8.5km 'Otira', burrowing under the mountains to the West Coast.

The western side is just as stunning, with the Otira, Taramakau and Grey River valleys, patches of podocarp forest, and the trout-filled Lake Brunner (Moana Kotuku), fringed with cabbage trees. The train rolls into Greymouth at 12.45pm, heading back to Christchurch an hour later, arriving at 6.05pm.

This awesome journey is diminished only when the weather's bad, but if it's raining on one coast, it's probably fine on the other.

THE COAST TO COAST

Kiwis really are a mad bunch – take, for instance, the **Coast to Coast** (www.coasttocoast.co.nz), which has grown to become the most coveted one-day multisport race in the country. This annual race starts in Kumara on the West Coast and ends in Christchurch. Intrepid racers start in the wee hours of the morning with a gentle 3km run, followed by a 55km cycle that will wake you up quicker than a 6am espresso. Next it's a 33km mountain run over Goat Pass – you know any pass named after a goat isn't going to be flat. From there all there is to do is ride your bike another 15km, paddle your kayak 67km and get back on the bike for the final 70km.

After all this the strong, the brave and the uberfit will arrive in Christchurch to much fanfare. The course is 243km long and the top competitors will dust it off in just under 11 hours – with mortals taking almost twice that. The race is held annually in mid-February and is good fun to go and watch – if you're not up for racing.

AROUND GREYMOUTH

From Greymouth to Hokitika SH6 crawls along the wild West Coast beside surging waves and tortured driftwood.

Providing context for West Coast history, **Shantytown** (☎ 03-762 6634; www.shantytown.co.nz; Rutherglen Rd, Paroa; adult/child $25/10; ☺ 8.30am-5pm), 8km south of Greymouth and 3km inland from SH6, recreates an 1860s gold-mining town, complete with post office, pub and Rosie's House of Ill Repute. There's gold panning ($5 extra for adults), trains to ride, and a sawmill.

Popular with locals and highway explorers, the **Paroa Hotel-Motel** (☎ 0800 762 6860, 03-762 6860; www.paroa.co.nz; 508 Main South Rd; d $125-140; ☞) is located opposite the Shantytown turn-off and has spacious, garden-fronted units. Its restaurant, **Ham's** (mains $16-23; ☺ 7am-8pm), plates meaty schnitzels amid a blokey display of rugby jerseys.

Heading east across Arthur's Pass on SH73, 39km from Greymouth, the tiny settlement of **Jacksons** is nestled beside the Taramakau River. Campervan travellers and tenters can stay at **Jacksons Retreat** (☎ 03-738 0474; www.jacksonscampervanretreat.co.nz; unpowered/powered sites $20/39), with superb facilities set in 15 acres. The owners run scenic jetboat trips on the Taramakau River (adult/child from $110/55) and just up the road the historic **Jackson's Tavern** (☎ 03-738 0457; ☺ 11am-11pm) is perfect for a pie and a pint.

HOKITIKA

pop 3100

Visit Hokitika's wide and quiet streets in the off season, and you might be excused for thinking you've stumbled into a true Wild West town. Across summer though, there's no room for rogue tumbleweeds in the expansive thoroughfares, and 'Hoki' gets as busy with visitors as when the town was a thriving port during the 1860s gold rush. Only now, green (stone), and not gold, is the colour of choice.

Orientation

The town forms a grid at the mouth of the Hokitika River around Weld and Tancred Sts. Free town maps are available at the **Westland i-SITE** (☎ 03-755 6166; hkkvin@xtra.co.nz; 7 Tancred St).

Information

Look for banks on Weld and Revell Sts.
Bookworms 102 Books (26b Weld St.; ☺ 9am-5pm) Buys/sells/exchanges books.
DOC office (☎ 03-756 9100; 10 Sewell St; ☺ 8am-4.45pm Mon-Fri)
Hokitika Travel Centre (☎ 03-755 5251; 64 Tancred St; ☺ 8.30am-5pm Mon-Fri) Books scenic flights and transport. Based inside the National Kiwi Centre.
Photo Corner (☎ 03-755 7768; 15 Weld St) Internet access including wi-fi.
Police station (☎ 03-756 8310; 50 Sewell St)
Post office (Revell St)
Take Note (☎ 03-755 8167; cnr Weld & Revell Sts) Maps, mags and West Coast books.
Westland i-SITE (☎ 03-755 6166; www.hokitika.org; 7 Tancred St; ☺ 10am-6pm Mon-Fri, to 4pm Sat & Sun)
Westland Medical Centre (☎ 03-755 8180; 54a Sewell St; ☺ 8.30am-10pm)

Sights

Hoki's premier attractions are its arts-and-crafts shops; see p197.

The **West Coast Historical Museum** (☎ 03-755 6898; enquiries@hokitikamuseum.co.nz; Tancred St.; adult/child $5/1; ☺ 8am-6pm) has old photos, Maori artefacts, river and pub-life displays, and the southern hemisphere's biggest Meccano set (a gold dredge replica). The Mana Pounamu exhibition is the ideal primer before you hit the shops looking for greenstone treasures.

Pick up the free *Hokitika Heritage Walk* leaflet from the i-SITE and wander the **Gibson Quay Heritage Waterfront**, imagining when the wharves were choked with old-time sailing ships.

The rather tired **National Kiwi Centre** (☎ 03-755 5251; natkiwi@xtra.co.nz; 60 Tancred St; adult/child/ family $14/8/36; ⏰ 9am-5pm Mon-Fri) has seen better days, but at least you'll see a kiwi – peer into the dimly lit enclosure and see what's rummaging about. There are also turtles, tuatara, and 150-year-old eels that get fed every day at 10am, noon and 3pm.

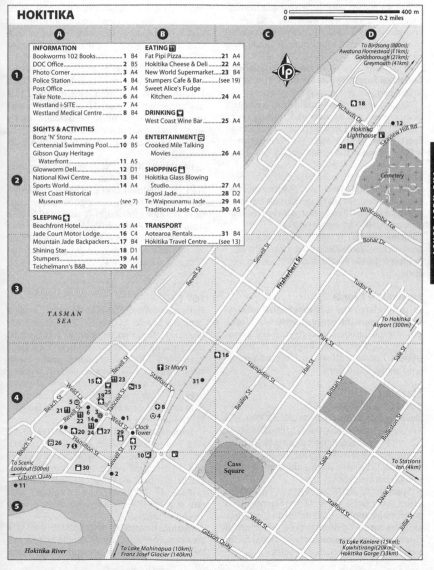

HOKITIKA

0 _____ 400 m
0 _____ 0.2 miles

INFORMATION
Bookworms 102 Books................1 B4
DOC Office.................................2 B5
Photo Corner.............................3 A4
Police Station.............................4 B4
Post Office.................................5 A4
Take Note..................................6 A4
Westland i-SITE.........................7 A4
Westland Medical Centre............8 B4

SIGHTS & ACTIVITIES
Bonz 'N' Stonz...........................9 A4
Centennial Swimming Pool........10 B5
Gibson Quay Heritage
  Waterfront.............................11 A5
Glowworm Dell.........................12 D1
National Kiwi Centre.................13 B4
Sports World.............................14 A4
West Coast Historical
  Museum...........................(see 7)

SLEEPING
Beachfront Hotel......................15 A4
Jade Court Motor Lodge............16 C4
Mountain Jade Backpackers.......17 B4
Shining Star.............................18 D1
Stumpers.................................19 A4
Teichelmann's B&B...................20 A4

EATING
Fat Pipi Pizza...........................21 A4
Hokitika Cheese & Deli..............22 A4
New World Supermarket............23 B4
Stumpers Cafe & Bar...........(see 19)
Sweet Alice's Fudge
  Kitchen.................................24 A4

DRINKING
West Coast Wine Bar................25 A4

ENTERTAINMENT
Crooked Mile Talking
  Movies..................................26 A4

SHOPPING
Hokitika Glass Blowing
  Studio...................................27 A4
Jagosi Jade..............................28 D2
Te Waipounamu Jade...............29 B4
Traditional Jade Co..................30 A5

TRANSPORT
Aotearoa Rentals.....................31 B4
Hokitika Travel Centre.........(see 13)

To Birdsong (800m);
Awatuna Homestead (11km);
Goldsborough (21km);
Greymouth (41km)

Richards Dr

Hokitika Lighthouse

Seaview Hill Rd

Cemetery

Whitcombe Tce

Bonar Dr

Tudor St

To Hokitika Airport (300m)

Sale St

Brittan St

Rolleston St

To Stations Inn (4km)

Davie St

Jollie St

Stafford St

Weld St

Fitzherbert St

Seaville St

Park St

Hampden St

Hall St

Bealey St

Sale St

Cass Square

TASMAN SEA

Revell St

St Mary's

Stafford St

Weld La

Beach St

Weld St

Clock Tower

Hamilton St

Sewell St

To Scenic Lookout (500m)
Gibson Quay

Hokitika River

To Lake Mahinapua (10km);
Franz Josef Glacier (140km)

Gibson Quay

To Lake Kaniere (15km);
Kowhitirangi (20km);
Hokitika Gorge (33km)

Just north of town, a short stroll from SH6 leads to a **glowworm dell**. Evening darkness maximises the show.

Activities

Dabble in jade carving with Steve Gwaliasi at **Bonz 'N' Stonz** (☎ 0800 214 949, 03-755 6504; www.bonz-n-stonz.co.nz; 16 Hamilton St; full-day workshop $80-150; ☽ 8.30am-5pm Mon-Sat). Design, carve and polish your own jade, bone or paua masterpiece. Prices vary with materials and design complexity, and bookings are recommended in summer – allow four hours to create your wearable art.

If it rains, get really wet in the heated **Centennial Swimming Pool** (☎ 03-755 8119; 53 Weld St; adult/child $4/2; ☽ 9am-5pm Sep-May).

A good range of mountain-bike trails lurk nearby amid old forestry and mining trails. Hire bikes and get trail maps and advice from **Sports World** (☎ 03-755 8662; 33 Tancred St; bike hire per hr $25; ☽ 8am-5pm Mon-Fri, 9am-1pm Sat).

Tours

Scenic Waterways (☎ 03-755 7239; www.paddleboat cruises.com; adult/child $30/15; ☽ tours 2pm Dec-Apr, on demand May-Nov) Runs 1½-hour paddleboat tours on Mahinapua Creek, 10km south of Hokitika.

Wilderness Wings (☎ 0800 755 8118; www.wilder nesswings.co.nz; Hokitika Airport; flights from $320) Has four-hour flights over Hokitika, Aoraki (Mt Cook) and the glaciers.

Festivals & Events

In early March the **Wildfoods Festival** attracts 20,000 curious and brave gourmands. Check out www.wildfoods.co.nz to find out about tasty goodies like huhu bugs and mountain oysters. Less adventurous palates can sample wild venison and pork.

Sleeping

BUDGET & MIDRANGE

Mountain Jade Backpackers (☎ 0800 838 301, 03-755 8007; mtjade@minidata.co.nz; 41 Weld St; dm $21, d $41-44; ☐ ☎) What this concrete housing block lacks in atmosphere it makes up for in value. Cheap sleeps are to be found in this ultracentral mass-market backpackers.

Stumpers (☎ 0800 788 673, 03-755 6154; www.stumpers .co.nz; 2 Weld St; dm $25, d 50-80; ☐ ☎) Stumpers has comfortable rooms above its bustling cafe-bar. Doubles have TVs, dorms have a maximum of three beds, and most rooms have shared facilities. En suite doubles are $10 extra.

Shining Star (☎ 03-755 8921; www.shiningstar.co.nz; 11 Richards Dr; unpowered/powered sites $25/32, d $85-160; ☐ ☎) Sprawling and versatile beachside spot with everything from camping to classy new seafront units. Kids will love the menagerie, including ducks and alpacas straight from Dr Doolittle's appointment book. Mum and Dad might prefer the spa and sauna.

Birdsong (☎ 03-755 9179; www.birdsong.co.nz; SH6; dm/s $28/55, d $70-88; ☐ ☎) Just north of town, this hostel has sea views and an atmosphere that is hard to rival. Don't let the out-of-the-way location deter you; the art-filled house will seduce you into extending your stay.

Jade Court Motor Lodge (☎ 0800 755 885, 03-755 8855; www.jadecourt.co.nz; 85 Fitzherbert St; d $95-140) Priding itself on superior hospitality, this midrange déjà vu special is a slight standout among a sea of same-same hotels. Nearby along Fitzherbert St are several other motels, so you won't have to look far if Jade Court is full.

Beachfront Hotel (☎ 03-755 8344; www.beach fronthotel.co.nz; 111 Revell St; d $125-300; ☎) This split-personality hotel raises the bar in Hoki. The original rooms are a good budget option; though offer nothing remarkable (the noise from the adjacent pub can be an issue at times). The rooms in the Ocean View Wing are another story. Modern decor, flat-screen TVs and seaside views add up to a top-notch choice.

TOP END

Stations Inn (☎ 0508 782 846, 03-755 5499; www.stations .co.nz; Blue Spur Rd; d $170-250) King-sized beds feature in these cottages amid rolling hills and rocking alpacas. Brand-new units have flat-screen TVs and spa baths, and a short stroll away is a heritage restaurant with an award-winning relationship with venison, beef and lamb (mains $26 to $35; open from 6pm daily). Follow Hampden St and Hau Hau Rd to Blue Spur Rd.

Teichelmann's B&B (☎ 0800 743 742, 03-755 8232; www.teichelmanns.co.nz; 20 Hamilton St; d $195-240) Once home to surgeon, mountaineer and professional beard-cultivator Ebenezer Teichelmann, now a luxurious B&B with amicable hosts. All rooms have en suites, and if you're a bit shy consider the more private Teichy's Cottage.

Awatuna Homestead (☎ 0800 006 888, 03-755 6834; www.awatunahomestead.co.nz; 9 Stafford Rd, Awatuna; d incl breakfast $280-360) Set down a quiet road 11km north of Hokitika, the family-run Awatuna Homestead has three lovely guest rooms and a self-contained apartment. Dinner is available by prior arrangement, and in the evening owners Hemi and Pauline recount cultural stories of the discovery of NZ by the early Pacific explorers.

Eating & Drinking

Sweet Alice's Fudge Kitchen (☎ 03-755 5359; 27 Tancred St; per slice $6; ☽ 10am-4pm Mon-Fri, to 2pm Sat & Sun) Treat yourself with a slice of Alice's handmade, all-natural fudge. Your biggest decision of the day could be which flavour to choose. Go for the uberclassic mint-chocolate or spice it up with 'boozy fruit and nut'.

Hokitika Cheese & Deli (☎ 03-755 5432; 84 Revell St; mains $7-16; ☽ 8am-4pm) This airy and open cafe and cheesery is a fine place to start the day. Brunch and light meals are the main forte with fresh coffee and aged cheese at the ready. The chicken and mushroom pies alone are worth a visit.

Stumpers Cafe & Bar (☎ 03-755 6154; 2 Weld St; mains $12-28; ☽ 7am-late) Eating at Hokitika's pubs is pretty uninspiring, but Stumpers is the best of them with a cafe-style atmosphere and a (slightly) more imaginative kitchen dishing up colourful food from blue cod to green-lipped mussels.

our pick **Fat Pipi Pizza** (☎ 03-755 6263; 83a Revell St; pizza $19-24; ☽ 5pm-late Thu-Sun; **V**) Vegetarians, carnivores and everyone in between will be salivating for the pizza made with love right before your eyes. If you're in town during whitebait season (September to mid-November) try the Fat Pipi whitebait pizza. Plan to take away – there's no seating to be found here.

West Coast Wine Bar (☎ 03-755 5417; 108 Revell St; ☽ 11am-4pm Mon-Sat, till late Fri) No, you're not seeing things. Upping the posh factor to unseen West Coast heights – they also have cheese platters and marinated olives to nibble on. Don't be scared; they also have beer, if all that sounds too decadent.

If you are self-catering, check out **New World** (☎ 03-755 8390; 116 Revell St; ☽ 8am-7pm Mon-Sat, 9am-6pm Sun) supermarket.

Entertainment

Crooked Mile Talking Movies (☎ 03-755 5309; www. crookedmile.co.nz; 36 Revell St; tickets adult/child $11/6) Vintage building, plus old couches, plus organic chocolate and house bar, plus art-house films, equals – perfect night out.

Shopping

Most of Hokitika's crafty shops are on Tancred St, where things of stone and wood (and glass, gold, bone and shell) are worked into shape. Staff love to talk *pounamu*, and in some studios you can watch carvers in action. Be aware that some shops sell jade imported from Europe and Asia, as local greenstone can often be difficult and expensive to discover in the NZ wilderness.

Traditional Jade Co (☎ 03-755 5233; 2 Tancred St) This family-run studio distils the jade hype into something meaningful. Watch talented artists carving classic Maori greenstone designs.

Te Waipounamu Jade (☎ 03-755 8304; 19 Sewell St) Te Waipounamu is scrupulously authentic, selling only NZ *pounamu* handcrafted into both traditional and contemporary designs – all with an aesthetic flavour.

THE WEST COAST

WHITEBAIT FEVER

Author of *The Bone People* Keri Hulme once opined, 'I'm not particularly serious about anything except whitebaiting'. Okarito's most famous resident recluse may have been commenting on behalf of the entire West Coast, because from September to mid-November, the region's rivers and marine estuaries are crowded with fisherfolk of all ages keen to net a few precious kilos of immature-stage inanga (river smelt). Catches in recent years have been lower than normal, and in 2007 prices for the wee beasties reached $150 per kilogram. With some whitebaiters securing up to 15kg on a good day, it can be a lucrative business. Little wonder it's a practice enjoyed by a wide range of keen Coasters, all with their own distinct financial goals. Teenagers save up for a shiny mobile phone while Mum might be eyeing a new digital TV receiver. The experienced old-timers are usually just happy to make enough for beer money and pay for their riverside crib (cottage) or caravan for a few more weeks.

Try a whitebait fritter wrapped in fresh white bread, or head to Hokitika's Fat Pipi Pizza (above) for its tasty whitebait pizza.

Jagosi Jade (☎ 03-755 6243; 246 Sewell St; ☺ 8.30am-4pm Mon-Fri) Carver Aden Hoglund produces traditional and modern Maori designs from jade sourced from around the South Island.

Hokitika Glass Blowing Studio (☎ 03-755 7775; 28 Tancred St; ☺ 9am-4pm Mon-Fri) Specialising in glass art and covering a continuum from garish to glorious. Wear a T-shirt if you've come to watch the glass-blowers; it can get a tad toasty.

Getting There & Around

AIR

Hokitika Airport is on Airport Dr (off Tudor St), 1.5km east of the centre of town. **Air New Zealand** (☎ 0800 737 000, 09-357 3000; www.airnz.co.nz) has four flights daily (from $65 one-way) to/from Christchurch.

BUS

InterCity (☎ 03-365 1113; www.intercity.co.nz) buses depart from outside the **National Kiwi Centre** (03-755 5251; 60 Tancred St) daily for Greymouth ($14, 45 minutes, departing 12.30pm), Nelson ($65, seven hours, departing 12.30pm) and Fox Glacier ($39, 3½ hours, departing 2.55pm).

Atomic Shuttles (☎ 03-349 0697; www.atomictravel.co.nz) departs i-SITE to Fox Glacier ($35, 3½ hours, departing 8am and 3.15pm), Greymouth ($15, one hour, departing 11.30am and 4.50pm) and Queenstown ($70, 10 hours, departing 8am).

Naked Bus (www.nakedbus.com) heads north to Greymouth, and south to Queenstown stopping at Franz Josef and Fox Glaciers, Haast and Wanaka.

CAR

Car-hire branches at Hokitika Airport:
Avis (☎ 03-768 0902; www.avis.com)
Budget (☎ 03-768 4343; www.budget.co.nz)
Hertz (☎ 03-768 0196; www.hertz.co.nz)

A local company good for day rentals is **Aotearoa Rentals** (☎ 03-755 5222; hokitikacc@xtra.co.nz; Hokitika Car Court, 65 Fitzherbert St).

TAXI

Try **Hokitika Taxis** (☎ 03-755 5075).

AROUND HOKITIKA

A 33km farmland drive or cycle gets you to **Hokitika Gorge**, a ravishing ravine with turquoise waters. Glacial flour (suspended rock particles) imbues the milky hues. Cross the swing bridge for a couple of short forest walks. To get here, head up Stafford St past the dairy factory and follow the signs.

Kowhitirangi, en route to the gorge, was the scene of a massive 12-day manhunt involving the NZ army in 1941. Unhinged farmer Stanley Graham shot dead four Hokitika policemen, disappeared into the bush then returned to murder three others, eventually being killed himself. A grim roadside monument lines up the farmstead site through a stone gun shaft. The 1982 film *Bad Blood* re-enacts the awful incident.

A gravel forest road (lousy for big vehicles) circumnavigates **Lake Kaniere**, passing **Dorothy Falls**, **Kahikatea Forest** and **Canoe Cove**. The Westland i-SITE and DOC in Hokitika have info on other local walks, including the **Lake Kaniere Walkway** (four hours one-way), along the lake's western shore, and the **Mahinapua Walkway** (2½ hours one-way), through the reserve on Lake Mahinapua's northeast side to a wildlife-engorged swamp.

There are **DOC camping grounds** (adult/child $6/1.50) at **Goldsborough**, 17km from Hoki on the 1876 'gold trail'; **Hans Bay**, 19km from Hokitika on Lake Kaniere's eastern shore; and 10km south of Hokitika at **Lake Mahinapua**.

HOKITIKA TO WESTLAND TAI POUTINI NATIONAL PARK

From Hokitika it's 140km south to Franz Josef Glacier. Most travellers fast forward without stopping, but there are some interesting historical highlights, and tramping, kayaking, and birdwatching opportunities along the way. **InterCity** (☎ 03-365 1113; www.intercity.co.nz) and **Atomic Shuttles** (☎ 03-349 0697; www.atomictravel.co.nz) are transport options offering stops along SH6.

Ross

Ross is a town of glories lost, 30km south of Hokitika. It's where the unearthing of NZ's largest gold nugget, the 2.772kg 'Honourable Roddy', caused a kerfuffle in 1907. The **Ross visitor information centre** (☎ 03-755 4077; www.ross.org.nz; 4 Aylmer St; ☺ 9am-5pm Dec-Feb, to 3pm Mar-Nov) features a scale model of the town in its shiny years ($2).

Opposite is the **Miner's Cottage Museum** (admission free; ☺ 9am-5pm), in an 1885 cottage containing two old pianolas and a replica Roddy. The recreated **Ross Gaol** next door will make you glad you're not staying there for the night.

The **Water Race Walk** (one hour return) starts near the museum, passing old gold-diggings, caves, tunnels and a cemetery. Try **gold panning** at the visitor information centre ($10), or hire a pan ($10) and head to Jones Creek to look for Roddy's great, great grandnuggets.

The **Empire Hotel** (☎ 03-755 4005; basilcybil@xtra.co.nz; 19 Aylmer St; unpowered/powered sites $15/20, s $40, d $60-75) has a row of basic cabins and backpacker dorms, with authentic old-timer pub rooms upstairs. Tent and campervan travellers are also welcome to kip down in the adjacent yard. The bar is one of the West Coast's hidden gems – imported directly from a bygone era, it reeks of authenticity and unsaid cool. Classic Kiwiana, and well up in the running for the South Island's best watering hole.

The rustic **Roddy Nugget Cafe & Bar** (☎ 03-755 4245; 5 Moorhouse St; meals $6-15; ⏰ 7am-11pm) is a country cafe serving homemade meals, including some stellar blueberry pancakes. Occasionally the bar, and on fine days the outdoor beer garden, threatens to recreate the energy of the town's glory days.

Ross to Okarito

South of Ross the bush closes in and mist and rain often cling to the verdant surroundings.

About 16km south of Ross, the **Old Church** (☎ 03-755 4000; SH6; unpowered sites $12.50, dm/d $20/50) stands remotely on the Kakapotahi River. Bikes, kayaks and fishing are on offer but BYO food as there's no nearby shop.

PUKEKURA

Just north of Lake Ianthe, carved out of the dense bush, is this tiny place, population two.

The tour buses descend on the **Bushmans Centre** (☎ 03-755 4144; www.pukekura.co.nz; SH6; admission free; ⏰ 9am-6pm), an overly rustic cafe-shop with a pathological distrust of possums, animal rights activists and Aucklanders. Inside is a souvenir shop and the **Bushmans Museum** (adult $4), laying on blokey bush humour with a 20-minute video on local industry, anti-possum displays and some giant eels. The cafe offers snacks like possum jerky, possum pie and possum pâté. Outside in a paddock are chamois and thar that look happier than the caged possums inside.

Across the road is the Puke Pub and the **Wild Foods Restaurant** (☎ 03-755 4008; mains $10-15; ⏰ noon-late), specialising in 'road kill' dishes like 'wheel-tread possum' and 'headlight delight'. (Motto: 'You kill 'em, we'll grill 'em').

Pukekura Lodge (☎ 03-755 4008; SH6; unpowered & powered sites $15, dm $15, d $40) has four rustic rooms right next door. There's a **DOC camping ground** (adult/child $6/1.50) beside Lake Ianthe, 6km south of Pukekura.

HARI HARI

About 22km south of Lake Ianthe, Hari Hari made headlines in 1931 when swashbuckling Australian aviator Guy Menzies completed the first solo trans-Tasman flight from Sydney. Menzies crash-landed the *Southern Cross Junior* into the La Fontaine swamp. Menzies' flight took 11¾ hours, 2½ hours faster than fellow Australian Charles Kingsford Smith in 1928. At the southern end of town is a replica of his trusty biplane. Internet access is available at the Pioneer Cottage Craft Store at the north end of town.

The **Hari Hari Coastal Walk** (aka Doughboy Walk or Coastal Pack Track; 2¾ hours return) is a well-trodden low-tide loop passing the Poerua and Wanganui Rivers. The walk starts 20km from SH6, the last 8km unsealed; follow Wanganui Flats Rd then La Fontaine Dr. There's tidal info at the trailhead, or ask at the Ross visitor information centre.

Flaxbush Motels (☎ 03-753 3116; flaxbush123@xtra.co.nz; SH6; d $50-150; 🖳) This decidedly bohemian establishment has gone through something of a reinvention the past few years. Amenities have been spruced up and new facilities added. Cabins and units cover a wide range of budgets. The owners are certainly animal lovers, with peacocks wandering the grounds and a pet possum that has its own room – in the house.

The **Hari Hari Motor Inn** (☎ 03-753 3026; hhmi@paradise.net; SH6; unpowered/powered sites $19/22, dm/d $18.50/100) has serviceable doubles but doesn't have a shared kitchen for campers. The bistro (mains $11 to $29; open noon till late) is Hari Hari's only evening eatery, with tasty pizzas, steak and roasts and cold pints of beer.

WHATAROA & THE KOTUKU SANCTUARY

Near Whataroa, 35km south of Hari Hari, is NZ's only nesting site for the kotuku (white heron), roosting here between November and February. The herons then fly off individually to reconsider the single life over winter.

White Heron Sanctuary Tours (☎ 0800 523 456, 03-753 4120; www.whiteherontours.co.nz; SH6, Whataroa; adult/child $110/45; ⏰ 4 tours daily late Oct-Mar) has the only DOC concession to see the herons, with

2½-hour 'jetboat ecotours' (the jetboat doesn't bug the birds). Year-round a scenic rainforest tour without the herons is available for the same price.

Next door is the **Sanctuary Tours Motel** (☎ 0800 523 456, 03-753 4120; www.whiteherontours.co.nz; SH6, Whataroa; cabins $55-65, d $95-125), with basic cabins with shared facilities ($8 extra for bedlinen), and enthusiastically painted motel units.

Okarito

Another 15km south of Whataroa is the Forks and the turn-off to peaceful Okarito, 13km further on the coast. Keri Hulme's Booker Prize–winning bestseller, *The Bone People*, is set in this unpeopled region. The reclusive author is one of a few score permanent residents in this peaceful coastal hamlet. Okarito has no shops, so stock up on food and supplies at New World in Hokitika.

From the southern end of the Strand, there are a couple of coastal walks to **Three Mile Lagoon** (three hours return; low tide only) and to **Okarito Trig** (1½ hours return). Expect Southern Alps and Okarito Lagoon views.

Okarito Nature Tours (☎ 0800 524 666, 03-753 4014; www.okarito.co.nz; kayak rental per half-/full day $50/60) hires out kayaks for paddles into peaceful **Okarito Lagoon**, a fish-laden buffet for waterbirds. The lagoon is NZ's largest unmodified wetland, an intricate ecosystem of shallow water and tidal flats surrounded by rainforest. Guided tours are available (from $75), and overnight rentals ($80) allow the experienced to check out deserted North Beach or Lake Windemere.

Also explore the lagoon with **Okarito Boat Tours** (☎ 03-753 4223; www.okaritoboattours.co.nz), morning and evening sightseeing tours starting at $45. Bookings are recommended for the nature tour, which departs in the mornings for better wildlife-viewing potential (two hours, $75).

Okarito Kiwi Tours (☎ 03-753 4330; www.okarito kiwitours.co.nz; $60) run nightly expeditions (two to three hours). Numbers are limited to eight kiwi fans per night, so booking is recommended during summer. The company will also pick you up from Franz Josef, and it boasts a 90% success rate in spying the iconic birds.

Okarito Campground (off Russell St; adult/child $7.50/free) is a breezy patch of community-managed greenery complete with barbecues, toilets, hot showers ($1) and a public telephone. Drop your cash in the honesty box and you're sweet as.

An old 1892 school building is now the community-run **Okarito YHA Hostel** (☎ 03-379 9970; www.yha.co.nz; The Strand; dm $21). This charming heritage building is in fact the smallest youth hostel in NZ. You can't book individual beds; you can only hire out the whole hostel. There's room for 12 and it's only $60 a night so get a gang together and go for it.

The **Okarito Beach House & Royal Hostel** (☎ 03-753 4080; www.okaritobeachhouse.com; The Strand; dm $25, d $60-90) has a variety of accommodation options – all filled with charm. The weathered, self-contained 'Hutel' ($90) is worth every cent. The Summit Lodge has commanding views and the best dining-room table you've ever seen. This property is popular with groups, so be sure to book your bed well in advance.

WESTLAND TAI POUTINI NATIONAL PARK

Literally the biggest highlights of the Westland Tai Poutini National Park are the Franz Josef and Fox Glaciers. Nowhere else at this latitude do glaciers come so close to the ocean.

The glaciers' staggering development is largely due to the West Coast's endless rain. Snow falling in the glaciers' broad accumulation zones fuses into clear ice at 20m depth then surges down valleys. The glaciers are particularly steep, so the ice travels a long way before it finally melts.

The rate of descent is mind-blowing: wreckage of a plane that crashed into Franz Josef in 1943, 3.5km from the terminal face, made it down to the bottom 6½ years later – a speed of 1.5m per day. Big Franz usually advances about 1m per day, but sometimes ramps it up to 5m per day, over 10 times faster than the Swiss Alps' glaciers.

Some say Franz Josef is the superior ice experience, and while it's visually more impressive, the walk to Fox is shorter, more interesting and gets you closer to the ice (80m versus 200m).

Beyond the glaciers, the park's lower reaches harbour deserted Tasman Sea beaches, rising up through colour-splashed podocarp forests to NZ's highest peaks. Virtually unique in the world, diverse ecosystems huddle next to each other in interdependent ecological sequence. Seals frolic in the surf as deer sneak through the forests. The resident endangered

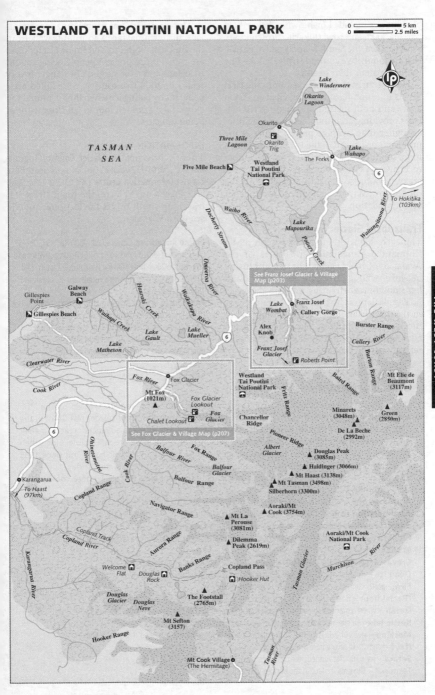

WESTLAND TAI POUTINI NATIONAL PARK

bird species include kowhiowhio, kakariki (a parrot), kaka and rowi (Okarito brown kiwi), as well as kea, the South Island's native parrot. Kea are inquisitive and endearing, but feeding them threatens their health.

Heavy tourist traffic often swamps the twin towns of Franz Josef and Fox Glacier, 23km apart and both picture-postcard tourist villages providing accommodation and facilities at higher-than-average prices. Franz is the more action-packed of the two, but Fox has a more subdued alpine charm. From December to February, visitor numbers can get a little crazy in both, so consider travelling in the off season (May to September) for cheaper accommodation.

Franz Josef Glacier

The early Maori knew Franz Joseph as Ka Roimata o Hine Hukatere (Tears of the Avalanche Girl). Legend tells of a girl losing her lover who fell from the local peaks, and her flood of tears freezing into the glacier.

The glacier was first explored by Europeans in 1865, Austrian Julius Haast naming it after the Austrian emperor. The glacier started advancing again in 1985 after a period of retreat (see the boxed text, below).

The glacier is 5km from Franz Joseph village, the terminal face a 40-minute walk from the car park. Both Fox and Franz glacier faces are roped off to prevent people being caught in icefalls and river surges. The danger is very real – in 2009 two tourists were killed after being hit by falling ice when they ventured too close. Take a guided tour to get close without being too close.

INFORMATION

There's internet at **Glacier Country Tours & Kayaks** (☎ 03-752 0230; 20 Cron St) and **Scott Base Tourist Information Centre** (☎ 03-752 0288; SH6), and there's an ATM on the main street – if travelling south this is the last one you will see until Wanaka.

Alpine Adventure Centre (☎ 0800 800 793, 03-752 0793; www.scenic-flights.co.nz; SH6) Books activities and screens the 20-minute *Flowing West* movie (adult/child $12/6) on a giant screen. Nice visuals, shame about the 1980s soundtrack.

Franz Josef visitor information centre (☎ 03-752 0796; www.glaciercountry.co.nz, www.doc.govt.nz; SH6; ☙ 8.30am-6pm Dec-Feb, to 5pm Mar-Nov) Also the regional DOC office; has an excellent display, weather information and tramping-condition updates.

GLACIERS FOR DUMMIES

During the last ice age (15,000 to 20,000 years ago) the Franz Josef and Fox Glaciers reached the sea; in the ensuing thaw they may have crawled back further than their current positions. In the 14th century a mini ice age descended and for centuries the glaciers advanced, reaching their greatest extent around 1750. The terminal moraines from this time are still visible. Since then the West Coast's twin glaciers have both ebbed and advanced on a cyclic basis, and since 1985 it's estimated the Franz Josef glacier has actually advanced by up to 70 cm per day.

If you get rained in during your time in glacier country, here are a few glacier-geek conversation starters for the pub.

Ablation zone – where the glacier melts.

Accumulation zone – where the snow collects.

Bergschrund – a large *crevasse* in the ice near the glacier's starting point.

Blue ice – as the accumulation zone (*névé*) snow is compressed by subsequent snowfalls, it becomes *firn* and then *blue ice.*

Crevasse – a crack in the glacial ice formed as it crosses obstacles while descending.

Dead ice – isolated chunks of ice left behind when a glacier retreats.

Firn – partly compressed snow en route to becoming *blue ice.*

Glacial flour – finely ground rock particles in the milky rivers flowing off glaciers.

Icefall – when a glacier descends so steeply that the upper ice breaks into a jumble of ice blocks.

Kettle lake – a lake formed by the melt of an area of isolated *dead ice.*

Moraine – walls of debris formed at the glacier's sides (lateral moraine) or end (terminal moraine).

Névé – snowfield area where *firn* is formed.

Seracs – ice pinnacles formed, like *crevasses,* by the glacier rolling over obstacles.

Terminal – the final ice face at the bottom of the glacier.

Medical centre (☎ 03-752 0700; SH6; ⏱ 8.30am-5pm Mon-Fri, doctor 9am-noon Mon-Thu, summer only)
Postal agency (cnr Condon St & SH6) At the Mobil station.

ACTIVITIES
Independent Walks
Several glacier viewpoints are accessed from the glacier car park, including **Sentinel Rock** (20 minutes return) and the **Ka Roimata o Hine Hukatere Walk** (1½ hours return), leading you to the terminal face.

Other longer walks include the **Douglas Walk** (one hour return), off the Glacier Access Rd, which passes moraine from the 1750 advance and Peter's Pool, a small 'kettle lake'. The **Terrace Track** (30 minutes return) is an easy amble over bushy terraces behind the village with Waiho River views. The rough **Callery-Waiho Walk** (four hours return) heads off from the village to the Douglas Swing Bridge, optionally extending to Roberts Point. The **Alex Knob Track** (eight hours return) runs from the Glacier Access Rd to the 1303m peak of Alex Knob. Look forward to three glacier lookouts and views to the coast (cloud cover permitting).

Check out the glacier in the morning or evening, before the cloud cover sets in or after it lifts. Expect fewer tour buses as well.

Guided Walks & Helihikes
Small group walks with experienced guides (boots, jackets and equipment supplied) are

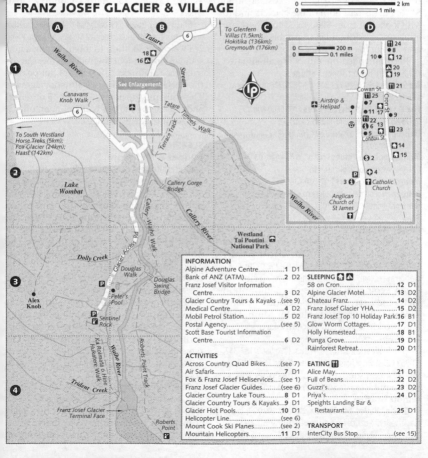

FRANZ JOSEF GLACIER & VILLAGE

offered by **Franz Josef Glacier Guides** (☎ 0800 484 337, 03-752 0763; www.franzjosefglacier.com). Half-/full-day walks are $105/160 per adult (slightly cheaper for children). Full-day trips have around six hours on the ice, half-day trips up to two hours. Full-day ice-climbing trips ($250 including training) and three-hour heli-hikes with two hours on the ice ($390) are also available. Helihikes take you further up the glacier to explore blue-ice caves, seracs and pristine ice formations.

Aerial Sightseeing
Forget sandflies and mozzies. The buzzing you're hearing is more likely to be helicopters and planes cruising past the glaciers and Aoraki (Mt Cook). Most flights also include a snow landing. A 20-minute flight to the head of Franz Josef or Fox Glacier costs around $180. Flights past both of the glaciers and to Mt Cook cost from $280 to $340. These are adult prices; kids under 15 pay between 60% and 70% of the adult price. Shop around.

Recommended operators are all situated on SH6 in Franz Josef Village:

Air Safaris (☎ 0800 723 274, 03-752 0716; www.air safaris.co.nz)

Fox & Franz Josef Heliservices (☎ 0800 800 793, 03-752 0793; www.scenic-flights.co.nz)

Helicopter Line (☎ 0800 807 767, 03-752 0767; www. helicopter.co.nz)

Mount Cook Ski Planes (☎ 0800 368 000, 03-752 0714; www.mtcookskiplanes.com)

Mountain Helicopters (☎ 0800 369 432, 03-752 0046; www.mountainhelicopters.co.nz) Also runs shorter 10-minute flights ($105).

Other Activities
Take a guided kayak trip on Lake Mapourika (7km north of Franz) with **Glacier Country Tours & Kayaks** (☎ 0800 423 262, 03-752 0230; www. glacierkayaks.com; 20 Cron St; 3hr tours $90). Trips include ecological commentary, mountain views and a serene channel detour. The family deal ($220) is good value for Mum, Dad and two kids. You can also hire kayaks ($60 for 2½ hours).

South Westland Horse Treks (☎ 0800 187 357, 03-752 0223; www.horsetreknz.com; Waiho Flats Rd; treks $60-240), 5km south of town, runs one- to six-hour equine excursions across farmland and remote beaches.

Glacier Valley Eco-Tours (☎ 0800 999 739; www. glaciervalley.co.nz) offers three-hour walks ($65) that are leisurely and packed with local

knowledge. Similar walks are offered down at Fox Glacier.

Faster-paced (and certainly noisier) are the four-wheeled outings from **Across Country Quad Bikes** (☎ 0800 234 288, 03-752 0123; www.across countryquadbikes.co.nz Air Safaris Bldg, SH6). Rockin' and rollin' rainforest quad-bike trips (two hours, adult/child $150/75) are joined by off-road adventures on 8WD Argo amphibious vehicles (one hour, $60). Heliquad adventures (2½ hours, $395) traverse the mountains and coastline by air before taking on a remote West Coast beach.

Join **Glacier Country Lake Tours** (☎ 0800 525 386, 03-752 0244; www.laketours.co.nz; 64 Cron St) on placid Lake Mapourika. Fishing and ecotour excursions (1½ hours, $98) are both available.

Hire bikes from Chateau Franz, Glow Worm Cottages or Across Country Quad Bikes.

Glacier Hot Pools (☎ 0800 044 044; www.glacierhot pools.co.nz; Cron St; adult/child $22.50/16; ⏱ noon-10pm) is a welcome addition to town, setting a new standard for outdoor thermal bathing. Carved from the rainforest, this series of hot pools is the perfect après-hike or rainy-day activity. There are private pools ($40 per 45 minutes) and massages ($80 per half-hour) on offer if you want to really indulge.

SLEEPING
Budget & Midrange
Rainforest Retreat (☎ 0800 873 346, 03-752 0220; www. rainforestretreat.co.nz; 46 Cron St; unpowered/powered sites $22/30, dm $21-27, d $99-209; 🖳 🛜) Campsites and dorms share first-rate facilities (including sauna and spa), and there are also en suite cottages and elevated self-contained 'tree houses' ($259 to $329) that sleep up to seven. The Monsoon Bar – motto: 'It rains, we pour' – is a social option on rainy days.

Chateau Franz (☎ 0800 728 372, 03-752 0738; www. chateaufranz.co.nz; 8 Cron St; dm $23-26, d $53-95; 🖳 🛜) When the weather outside is frightful, this is a decent option to hide away for the night. Nice extras like a spa pool, free soup, popcorn and DVDs aplenty are a nice touch. The ramshackle feel of the place, with mismatched everything, will either appeal or annoy – take your pick.

Glow Worm Cottages (☎ 0800 151 027, 03-752 0172; www.glowwormcottages.co.nz; 27 Cron St; dm from $24, d $55-110; 🖳 🛜) After a day of adventure, relax at this quiet haven trimmed by native ferns. Be back by 6pm and there's free vegie soup on offer. If the rain settles in, chill out in the spa or with a good DVD.

Franz Josef Glacier YHA (☎ 03-752 0754; www.yha. co.nz; 2-4 Cron St; dm $28-30, s $55, d $75-96; 🖳 🛜) A high-standard, colourful place with over 100 beds (linen provided) in 36 heated rooms. There are three family rooms, a Kiwi sauna (keep your bathers on please) and the rainforest at the back door. The needs of travellers with disabilities are well catered for.

Franz Josef Top 10 Holiday Park (☎ 0800 467 897, 03-752 0735; www.mountainview.co.nz; SH6; unpowered/ powered sites $42, d $55-300; 🖳 🛜) This recently tidied up campground has a sleeping option for every budget. Plenty of tent sites pepper the property, while slightly posher units will suit the alfresco-sleeping disinclined.

Alpine Glacier Motel (☎ 0800 757 111, 03-752 0226; www.alpineglaciermotel.com; 14 Cron St; d $150) Standard motel offerings for the dorm-weary traveller in a U-shaped configuration. Two units have spas, and king-sized units have cooking facilities.

Top End

58 on Cron (☎ 0800 662 766, 03-752 0627; www.58oncron. co.nz; 58 Cron St; d $170-225; 🛜) No prizes for the name, but with trendy, dark-chocolate decor and flash furniture, this new bush-side spot is one of FJ's classier motels.

Punga Grove (☎ 0800 437 269, 03-752 0001; www.punga grove.co.nz; 40 Cron St; d $190-250) Priding itself on top-notch service, Punga is a quality motel on the rainforest verge. Split-level self-contained family units mix it up with spacious studios. Splurge on a luxury rainforest studio with leather couches.

Glenfern Villas (☎ 0800 453 633, 03-752 0054; www. glenfern.co.nz; SH6; d $205-260) A handy 3km out of the tourist hubbub, these self-contained designer villas sit amid nikau palms and have private decks and gardens. Pour yourself a glass of wine and toast your holiday and the nearby alpine peaks.

Holly Homestead (☎ 03-752 0299; www.holly homestead.co.nz; SH6; d $260-420) Guests are welcomed with fresh home baking at this luxury wisteria-draped 1920s B&B. Five gorgeous rooms all have en suites, and a new guest suite features a private deck just made for early evening wine-tasting. Kids under 12 will have to sleep in the car.

EATING & DRINKING

Full of Beans (☎ 03-752 0139; SH6; mains $5-17; 🕒 7.30am-late) This cruisy cafe offers superlative

coffee – the best in town – and tasty home-made cakes from go to whoa. Good-value lunch offerings include burgers, Thai curry and chicken pies that are a particular favourite among locals.

Speights Landing Bar & Restaurant (☎ 03-752 0229; SH6; mains $10-30; 🕒 7.30am-late) From early to late, under the market umbrellas at this cosy pub-cafe is the place to be. Burgers, soups, pasta and wraps give you plenty of opportunity to overhear other travellers going gaga over the glaciers.

Guzzi's (☎ 03-752 0085; 18 Cron St; pizza $12-24; 🕒 noon-late; 🆅) Choose your own toppings – including plenty of vegie options – at this bright yellow and purple pizza and takeaway shack with a matching cute-as-a-button delivery van. Plan to take away; Guzzi's is sans seats.

Alice May (☎ 03-752 0740; cnr Cowan & Cron Sts; mains $12-30; 🕒 4pm-late) At this rustic Nordic-style lodge transplanted from somewhere near the Arctic Circle there's no smorgasbord on offer, but plenty of meaty meals like pork ribs and venison stew. Park yourself on a rustic barstool for happy hour (4pm to 7pm).

Priya's (☎ 03-752 0060; 70 Cron St; mains $14-20; 🕒 lunch 11.30am-2.30pm, dinner 5pm-late) If you're in dire need of a curry fix this is your best option in town. The atmosphere leaves much to be desired – harsh overhead fluorescent lights and a minibar with all the ambience of a takeaway-shop waiting area. The food on the other hand is full of flavour. Mouth- (and eye-) watering curries are the house speciality and they don't disappoint.

GETTING THERE & AROUND

InterCity (☎ 03-365 1113; www.intercity.co.nz) has daily buses south to Fox Glacier ($11, 40 minutes, departing 8am and 5.05pm) and Queenstown ($62, eight hours, departing 8am); and north to Nelson ($84, 10 hours, departing 9.15am). Book at the YHA or Scott Base Tourist Information Centre; buses depart from the YHA.

Atomic Shuttles (☎ 03-349 0697; www.atomictravel. co.nz) has daily services south to Queenstown ($50, 7¼ hours, departing 10.15am) via Fox Glacier ($15, 30 minutes), and north to Greymouth ($30, 2½ hours, departing 2.40pm), leaving from the Alpine Adventure Centre.

Glacier Valley Eco Tours (☎ 03-752 0699; www.glacier valley.co.nz) runs shuttles to the glacier car park (return trip $12.50).

Naked Bus (www.nakedbus.com) runs north to Hokitika and Greymouth, and south to Queenstown stopping at Fox Glacier, Haast and Wanaka.

Fox Glacier

Sir William Fox was NZ's prime minister, and anything but a shy and retiring type, when he named the river of ice in 1872. Even if you've already been to Franz Josef Glacier, it's still worth checking out Fox. Take a walk around beautiful Lake Matheson, and dive into Fox's array of glacier-related attractions: glacier walks, flights and travellers wearing thermals.

INFORMATION

There are no banks or ATMs in town; the BP petrol station is the last fuel stop until Haast, 120km south. Get online at the Internet Outpost, beside the Helicopter Line office.

DOC South Westland Area Office (☎ 03-751 0807; SH6; ☺ 9am-noon & 1-4.30pm Mon-Fri) No longer a general visitor information centre, but has the usual DOC information and weather/track updates.

Fox Glacier Guiding (☎ 0800 111 600, 03-751 0825; www.foxguides.co.nz; SH6) Books most activities and transport; includes postal services and a money exchange.

Fox Glacier Health Centre (☎ 03-751 0836, after hours 027 464 1193; SH6) The nurse here can patch you up on weekday mornings from 9am to noon and most afternoons, and there's a doctor from 2pm to 5pm on Thursdays.

ACTIVITIES
Independent Walks

It's 1.5km from Fox Village to the glacier turn-off, a further 2km to the car park. The terminal face is 30 to 40 minutes' walk from there, finishing 80m from the ice.

Short walks around the glacier include the **Moraine Walk** (over a major 18th-century advance) and **Minnehaha Walk**. The **River Walk** extends to the **Chalet Lookout Track** (1½ hours return) leading to a glacier lookout.

About 6km down Cook Flat Rd is the turn-off to **Lake Matheson**. It's an hour's walk around the lake, and at the far end (on a clear day) are improbably photogenic views of Mt Tasman and Mt Cook reflected in the water. Visit during the early morning or when the sun is low in the late afternoon.

Follow Cook Flat Rd for its full 21km (unsealed for the final 12km) to the remote black sand and rimu forest of **Gillespies Beach**, from where there's a dune track to **Galway Beach** (3½ hours return). The **Mt Fox Walk** (1021m above sea level; eight hours return), off the highway 3km south of town, makes for a challenging hike, only recommended for well-equipped trampers.

Glacier Walks & Helihikes

Guided walks (equipment provided) are organised by **Fox Glacier Guiding** (☎ 0800 111 600, 03-751 0825; www.foxguides.co.nz; SH6). Half-day walks cost $95/75 per adult/child; full-day walks are $145 (over-13s only). If you're fit, consider the full-day stroll, which takes you further up the glacier; BYO lunch.

Helihikes cost $395 per person, while a day-long introductory ice-climbing course costs $235 per adult. From October to April, there are also easy-going two-hour interpretive walks to the glacier (adult/child $49/35). Longer guided helitrek adventures are also available.

Skydiving & Aerial Sightseeing

With Fox Glacier's backdrop of Southern Alps, rainforest and ocean, it's hard to imagine a better place to jump out of a plane. **Skydive Glacier Country** (☎ 0800 751 0080, 03-751 0080; www. skydiving.co.nz; Fox Glacier Airfield, SH6, Fox Glacier Village) is a professional outfit that challenges Isaac Newton with thrilling leaps from 12,000ft ($295) or 9000ft ($245). Digitise your terror with a DVD/photograph package ($180/35). Smile as you scream.

Aerial sightseeing costs at Fox parallel those at Franz Josef. The recommended operators are all on SH6 in Fox Glacier Village:
Fox & Franz Josef Heliservices (☎ 0800 800 793, 03-751 0866; www.scenic-flights.co.nz)
Helicopter Line (☎ 0800 807 767, 03-751 0767; www. helicopter.co.nz)
Mount Cook Ski Planes (☎ 0800 368 000, 03-752 0714; www.mtcookskiplanes.com; SH6, Franz Josef Village)
Mountain Helicopters (☎ 03-751 0045; www. mountainhelicopters.co.nz)
Southern Lakes Helicopters (☎ 0800 800 732, 03-751 0803; www.heli-flights.co.nz)

SLEEPING

Ivory Towers (☎ 03-751 0838; www.ivorytowerslodge. co.nz; Sullivan Rd; sites $18, dm/s $28/55, d $70-85, f $95 🖵 ⛭) This top-notch hostel is tidy, laid-back and colourful, draped in greenery and endowed with good facilities. The friendly staff is accommodating and the tidy facilities will entice you to extend your stay.

Fox Glacier Holiday Park (☎ 0800 154 366, 03-751 0821; www.foxglacierholidaypark.co.nz; Kerrs Rd; unpowered/ powered sites $34/38, cabins $62, d $95-194; 🖳 🛜) This park has a range of different sleeping options to suit all budgets. Recent renovations have improved what was already a good choice. New showers, a playground for the kiddies and barbecue facilities are a welcome addition.

ourpick **Lake Matheson Motels** (☎ 0800 452 2437, 03-751 0830; www.lakematheson.co.nz; Cook Flat Rd; d $135-190) This unassuming property has been finished off with a real sense of care. From the outside it looks pretty ordinary, but inside the rooms come into their own. The owners have continued to pour profits back into the facilities. You'll find ultratidy rooms with up-market amenities that contradict the midrange price.

Heartland Hotel Fox Glacier (☎ 03-751 0839; cnr SH6 & Cook Flat Rd; d $140-180; 🖳 🛜) This freshly re-booted hotel was in fact the first building in Fox Glacier. Decaying exteriors have been spruced up to complement the tidy interior. Some of the older rooms are still on the to-do

list – be sure to have a look before you shell out.

Rainforest Motel (☎ 0800 724 636, 03-751 0140; www.rainforestmotel.co.nz; Cook Flat Rd; d $145-150) Rustic log cabins on the outside with coolly neutral decor on the inside; now with the added attraction of Sky TV for those rainy West Coast days.

Fox Glacier Lodge (☎ 03-751 0888; www.foxglacier lodge.co.nz; Sullivan Rd; d $180-230) Beautiful timber adorns the exterior and interior of this attractive property. It has that mountain chalet vibe that'll look great in your slide show. Top-notch facilities and a home-away-from-home feel seal the deal.

Reflection Lodge (☎ 03-751 0707; www.reflection lodge.co.nz; Cook Flat Rd; d $190-210; 🖳) Funky '60s ski-lodge style with flash new bathrooms. Blur your eyes a little – well, maybe a bit more – and you could almost be in an old James Bond movie. The West Coast's friendliest little dog brings you back to supercomfy reality.

Westhaven (☎ 03-751 0084; www.thewesthaven. co.nz; SH6; d $195-215; 🖳) These architecturally precise suites are a classy combo of corrugated steel and local stone amid burnt red and ivory

THE WEST COAST

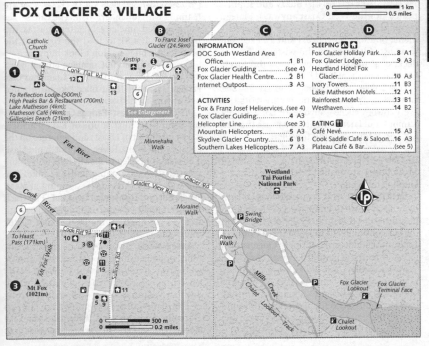

FOX GLACIER & VILLAGE

INFORMATION	
DOC South Westland Area Office.............................1 B1	
Fox Glacier Guiding..............(see 4)	
Fox Glacier Health Centre........2 B1	
Internet Outpost........................3 A3	

ACTIVITIES	
Fox & Franz Josef Heliservices..(see 4)	
Fox Glacier Guiding................4 A3	
Helicopter Line...................(see 3)	
Mountain Helicopters............5 A3	
Skydive Glacier Country...........6 B1	
Southern Lakes Helicopters......7 A3	

SLEEPING	
Fox Glacier Holiday Park..........8 A1	
Fox Glacier Lodge................9 A3	
Heartland Hotel Fox Glacier......10 A3	
Ivory Towers....................11 B3	
Lake Matheson Motels..........12 A1	
Rainforest Motel..................13 B1	
Westhaven.......................14 B2	

EATING	
Café Nevé.........................15 A3	
Cook Saddle Cafe & Saloon...16 A3	
Plateau Café & Bar...............(see 5)	

walls. The deluxe king rooms have spas and there are comfy chairs for relaxing outside.

EATING & DRINKING
our pick **Matheson Café** (☎ 03-751 0878; Lake Matheson Rd; mains $10-17; ☽ 7.30am-late) Near the shores of Lake Matheson, this cafe does everything right: slick interior design, inspiring mountain views, strong coffee and upmarket Kiwi fare. Get your sketchpad out and while away the afternoon.

High Peaks Bar & Restaurant (☎ 03-751 0131; Cooks Flat Rd; bar meals $14-24, restaurant mains $27-34; ☽ 6pm-late) Angled towards Mt Cook, High Peaks combines eating and drinking. Forget the calories, this is enjoyment food: steaks, pastas, fish and chips, roasts, chunky soups and stews. Have another Monteith's and wait for the clouds to part.

Café Nevé (☎ 03-751 0110; SH6; mains $15-30; ☽ 8am-late) Smart choices on the menu include pizza and award-winning ways with beef and lamb, and there's home-baked cookies and cakes available throughout the day. If you're going for a wander grab one of the takeaway focaccia sandwiches.

Plateau Café & Bar (☎ 03-751 0058; cnr Sullivan Rd & SH6; mains $18-30; ☽ 10am-late) Buzzy and sophisticated (for the West Coast anyway), Plateau combines snappy service with an eclectic menu, boutique Kiwi beers and an excellent wine list. Chill out on the wisteria-covered deck, or if the sky is grey, enjoy the lovely warm atmosphere inside.

Cook Saddle Cafe & Saloon (☎ 03-751 0700; SH6; meals $18-30; ☽ 8am-late) The menu trots out every cowboy cliché - anyone for Lone Ranger Lamb? - but later at night it's a more than an OK corral for locals and travellers.

GETTING THERE & AROUND
Most buses stop outside the Fox Glacier Guiding building.

InterCity (☎ 03-365 1113; www.intercity.co.nz) runs daily buses north to Franz Josef ($11, 40 minutes, departing 8.30am and 3.25pm), the morning bus continuing to Nelson ($85, 11 hours). Daily southbound services run to Queenstown ($58, 7½ hours, departing 8.45am).

Atomic Shuttles (☎ 03-349 0697; www.atomictravel.co.nz) runs daily to Franz Josef ($15, 30 minutes, departing 9am and 1.55pm), continuing to Greymouth ($35, 3¼ hours). Southbound buses run daily to Queenstown ($45, 6½ hours, departing 11am).

Fox Glacier Shuttle (☎ 0800 369 287) will drive you to Lake Matheson or Fox Glacier and allow you enough time for a stroll ($12 return, minimum two people).

Naked Bus (www.nakedbus.com) runs north to Franz Josef Glacier, Hokitika and Greymouth, and south to Queenstown, stopping at Haast and Wanaka.

SOUTH TO HAAST
About 26km south of Fox Glacier, along SH6, the **Copland Valley** is the western end of the **Copland Track**. Treat yourself to one of the best pay-offs of any walk in Aotearoa. Six to seven hours tramping will get you to the **Welcome Flat DOC Hut** (per night $15), where thermal springs bubble just metres from the hut door. Backcountry Hut Passes don't apply here, but you can buy tickets at any West Coast DOC office or visitor information centre.

Popular with Haast–Fox cyclists and Copland Track trampers, the **Pine Grove Motel** (☎ 03-751 0898; SH6; unpowered & powered sites $20, d $50-90) is 8km south of the trailhead. Units are affordable and in reasonable shape.

Like some sort of gigantic edible aquarium, the fish ponds at the **Salmon Farm Café & Shop** (☎ 03-751 0837; SH6; meals $10-32; ☽ 8am-4pm) are teaming with lunch, err, fish. The cafe serves salmon-filled omelettes, platters, pastas and fresh pâté. It's $1 to feed the fish, but the plump little buggers don't look hungry.

There's a basic **DOC camping ground** (adult/child $6/1.50) 70km south of Fox Glacier at **Lake Paringa**, a tranquil trout-filled lake surrounded by swaying forest boughs.

The historic **Haast–Paringa Cattle Track** hoofs off from SH6 (just south of Lake Paringa, 43km northeast of Haast) and emerges on the coast by the Waita River, just north of Haast. The track's first leg to **Blowfly Hut** (four hours return) is an easy-going half-day hike. The full walk takes three days, stopping at **Maori Saddle Hut** and **Coppermine Creek Hut**. The track can get muddy – check conditions and pay hut fees ($5 per night) at the DOC Haast visitor information centre (opposite).

Lake Moeraki, 31km north of Haast, is another rippling fishing lake. An easy 40-minute walk from here brings you to **Monro Beach**, a west-facing gravel beach copping the full Tasman Sea force. There's a breeding colony of Fiordland crested penguins here (July to December) and fur seals. **Wilderness Lodge Lake Moeraki** (☎ 03-750 0881; www.wildernesslodge.co.nz;

SH6; d incl breakfast & dinner $780-980) is a spectacular oasis of ecofriendly accommodation in a vibrant wilderness setting. The rooms are plush, the included meals are bordering on decadent and the activities on offer are top notch. Pricy, yes, but the quality of services is worth every cent.

About 5km south of Lake Moeraki is the much-photographed **Knights Point** (named after a surveyor's dog) where the Haast road was eventually opened in 1965. Deep waters just offshore and uninterrupted Antarctic swells make this a favoured eatery for seals, birds and sometimes whales.

Ship Creek, 15km north of Haast, has a lookout platform and two interesting interpretive walks: the **Dune Lake Walk** (30 minutes return) and the **Kahikatea Swamp Forest Walk** (20 minutes return).

HAAST REGION

The Haast region is a major nature refuge, with enormous stands of rainforest thriving alongside extensive wetlands. The area's kahikatea and flame red rimu forests, swamps, sand dunes, seal and penguin colonies, bird life and sweeping beaches ensured its inclusion in the Southwest New Zealand (Te Wahipounamu) World Heritage Area. Birding buffs might see fantails, bellbirds, kereru (NZ pigeons), falcons, kaka, kiwi and morepork.

Haast
pop 300

Some 120km south of Fox Glacier, Haast crouches around the mouth of the wide Haast River in three distinct pockets: Haast Junction, Haast Village and Haast Beach. After the jaw-dropping scenery of the glaciers or Haast Pass, the area is a functional service hub, but local operators are waiting on your call to transport you deeper into some of NZ's most spectacular wilderness areas.

Haast is also big on whitebaiting; see the boxed text, p197.

INFORMATION

The **DOC Haast Visitor Information Centre** (☎ 03-750 0809; www.doc.govt.nz; cnr SH6 & Jackson Bay Rd; ◷ 9am-6pm Nov-Mar, to 4.30pm Apr-Oct) has wall-to-wall regional information and every half-hour it screens the all-too-brief Haast landscape film *Edge of Wilderness* (adult/child $3/free).

TOURS

Take a hair-tousling 2½-hour 'sea to mountain' ecojetboat trip on the wild Waiatoto River with **Waiatoto River Safaris** (☎ 03-750 0780; www.riversafaris.co.nz; Jackson Bay Rd; adult/child $199/129; ◷ trips 10am, 1pm & 4pm), departing from the Waiatoto River Bridge 30km south of Haast.
Haast River Safari (☎ 0800 865 382, 03-750 0101; www.haastriver.co.nz; adult/child $132/55; ◷ cruises 9am & 2pm), based in the Red Barn between Haast Village and the visitor information centre, runs more leisurely 90-minute covered-jetboat cruises on the Haast River.

Round About Haast (☎ 03-750 0890; www.roundabouthaast.co.nz; tours $65-135) runs local boat and minibus tours. Out on Jackson Bay you'll see seals, dolphins and (seasonally) penguins, while the bus takes you to beaches, estuaries and forests, with walks and local folklore thrown in.

SLEEPING

Wilderness Accommodation (☎ 03-750 0029; www.wildernessaccommodation.co.nz; Marks Rd; dm/s $24/40, d $65-90; 💻) Your best budget option in town is everything a hostel should be. It's cheap, the facilities are clean, the dorm rooms are spacious and the staff friendly. The large leafy glassed-in courtyard is a fine place to catch up on your journal when the 'Wet Coast' weather doesn't play ball.

Haast Beach Holiday Park (☎ 0800 843 226, 03-750 0860; haastpark@xtra.co.nz; Jackson Bay Rd; unpowered & powered sites $28, dm $25, d $45-110) Close to the beach about 15km south of Haast, this caravan park has old but functional facilities. The Hapuka Estuary Walk (p210) is across the road.

Haast Lodge (☎ 0800 500 703, 03-750 0703; www.haastlodge.com; Marks Rd; sites $30, dm/d $25/60; 💻) There's a bit much beige and shiny lino going on, but the functional rooms here are spotlessly clean and the whole shebang is very well managed.

Aspiring Court Motel (☎ 0800 500 703, 03-750 0777; www.aspiringcourtmotel.com; Marks Rd; d $79-140; 💻) Just as clean and well-run as the associated Haast Lodge – these comfortable motel units are just next door.

Heartland World Heritage Hotel (☎ 0800 696 963, 03-750 0828; www.world-heritage-hotel.com; SH6; d $184-260; 💻) This sprawling hotel is staking its claim as the most comfy place to stay in town. The Frontier Café is open for lunch (mains $12 to $22) and dinner (mains $18 to $32), and the bar has big live-sport-friendly TVs and pool tables. Live bands occasionally rouse the friendly and laid-back locals.

ourpick **Collyer House** (☎ 03-750 0022; www.collyerhouse.co.nz; Jackson Bay Rd; s/d incl cooked breakfast $250) This gem of a place has thick bathrobes, quality linen, beach views and an owner as passionate about photography as she is about ensuring her guests have a fantastic stay. This all adds up to make Collyer House an indulgent and aesthetic choice. Follow the signs off SH6 for 12km down Jackson Bay Rd.

EATING & DRINKING

Fantail Café (☎ 03-750 0055; Marks Rd; breakfast & lunch $10-15, dinner $15-27; ☾ 8am-9pm) With cafe fodder like toasted sandwiches, and fish and chips the speciality – what you see is what you get. Nothing fancy, but the grub is good and the views, especially from the table out front, are awesome.

Hard Antler (☎ 03-750 0034; Marks Rd; dinner $18-27; ☾ dining 11am-9pm) Raucous as hell on a Friday night, and all the better for it. An expanding array of deer antlers, pool tables and darts, and robust pub grub (lamb, steak and pork) make this an unpretentious spot.

GETTING THERE & AWAY

InterCity (☎ 03-365 1113; www.intercity.co.nz) and **Atomic Shuttles** (☎ 03-322 8883; www.atomictravel.co.nz) buses stop at the visitor information centre on their Fox to Wanaka runs. **TrackNET**(☎ 0800 483 262, 03-249 7777; www.tracknet.net) also swings through linking Queenstown and Greymouth.

Naked Bus (www.nakedbus.com) runs north to the glaciers, Hokitika and Greymouth, and south to Queenstown, stopping at Wanaka.

Haast to Jackson Bay & Cascade River

From Haast Junction a side road heads to Jackson Bay, with numerous wilderness walks along the way.

Near Okuru is the **Hapuka Estuary Walk** (20 minutes return), an information-packed boardwalk loop winding its way through a sleepy whitebait sanctuary.

The road continues west from Arawhata Bridge to the isolated fishing hamlet of **Jackson**

Bay. Southern Alps views from here are unforgettable, and there are colonies of Fiordland crested penguins near the road. Migrants arrived here in 1875 under a doomed assisted-immigration scheme, their farming fantasies mercilessly shattered by never-ending rain and the lack of a wharf, not built until 1938. Today fishing boats bob on the bay, gathering lobster, tuna, tarakihi and gurnard.

Dining at the **Craypot** (☎ 03-750 0035; meals $7-20; ☾ noon-5pm Sep-Easter, to 8pm in summer), is more than a classic Kiwi dining experience – it's verging upon essential. So fresh it was swimming yesterday fish and chips, whitebait sandwiches and mixed grills are served up in an absolute waterfront location. The rustic old caravan with views of snowy peaks is pretty hard to beat.

Walks at Jackson Bay include the **Smoothwater Bay Track** (three hours return) and the **Wharekai Te Kau Walk** (40 minutes return) to Ocean Beach, a tiny bay that hosts pounding waves and some interesting rock formations.

HAAST PASS

Turning inland from Haast towards Wanaka (145km, 2½ hours), SH6 snakes alongside the Haast River, climbing up to Haast Pass and Mt Aspiring National Park. As you move inland the vegetation thins away until you reach the 563m pass – snow country covered in tussock and scrub. There are some stunning waterfalls en route (especially if it's been raining), tumbling down just minutes from the highway: **Fantail** and **Thunder Creek** falls are worth a look. There's also the **Bridle Track** (1½ hours one-way) between the pass and Davis Flat. See the DOC booklet *Haast Pass/Tioripatea Highway: Walking Opportunities* ($1).

The Haast Pass road (Tioripatea, meaning 'Clear Path' in Maori) opened in 1965; before then Maori walked this route bringing West Coast greenstone to the Makarora River in Otago. The pass (and river and township) take their European name from geologist Julius Haast, who passed through in 1863.

There are food and fuel stops at Makarora and Lake Hawea. If you're driving north, check your fuel gauge: Haast petrol station is the last one before Fox Glacier, 120km north.

Christchurch & Canterbury

The good people of Canterbury are probably only half-joking when they say it would be good if the South Island was a separate country, but when you consider the region surrounding them you can understand their parochial pride and confidence.

Christchurch is undoubtedly one of New Zealand's most liveable cities, combining an easy-going provincial charm with the emerging energy and verve of a metropolis. Modern bars and restaurants complement Gothic architecture, and locals know how lucky they are to blend all the attractions of a city with the relaxed ambience of a small town.

To the east, the volcanically uplifted hills of Banks Peninsula conceal a wealth of hidden bays and isolated beaches, forming a backdrop for kayaking and wildlife cruises with an eventual sunset return to the Francophile attractions of Akaroa. To the north are the up-and-coming vineyards of the Waipara Valley and the take-it-easy spa town of Hanmer Springs. Westwards the preferred weekend backyard of active Cantabrians builds quickly from the well-ordered farms of the Canterbury Plains to the rough-and-tumble wilderness of the Southern Alps.

Summertime attractions include tramping along the braided rivers and alpine valleys around Arthur's Pass or mountain biking around the turquoise lakes of the Mackenzie Country. During winter, the attention switches to the mountains, with skiing at Mt Hutt. Throughout the seasons, the country's tallest peak stands sentinel over Canterbury, and indeed all the South Island – whether you fly over it or walk around it, you'll never forget your first view of Aoraki/Mt Cook.

CHRISTCHURCH & CANTERBURY

HIGHLIGHTS

- Exploring the history of **Christchurch** (p213) by tram, river punt or two legs
- Marvelling at the views of the Mackenzie Country from atop **Mt John** (p257)
- Discovering funky restaurants and friendly locals in raffish **Lyttelton** (p235)
- Taking a soothing soak at Lake Tekapo's **Alpine Springs & Spa** (p257)
- Negotiating the outer reaches of **Banks Peninsula** (p236) by bike, kayak and boat
- Tramping in the shadow of NZ's highest peak in **Aoraki/Mt Cook National Park** (p260)
- Being surprised by the size of the Canterbury Plains on a balloon flight from **Methven** (p248)

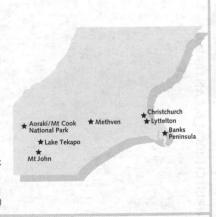

★ Christchurch
★ Lyttelton
★ Banks Peninsula
★ Methven
★ Aoraki/Mt Cook National Park
★ Lake Tekapo
★ Mt John

■ Telephone code: 03   ■ www.christchurchnz.com   ■ www.mtcooknz.com

CHRISTCHURCH & CANTERBURY

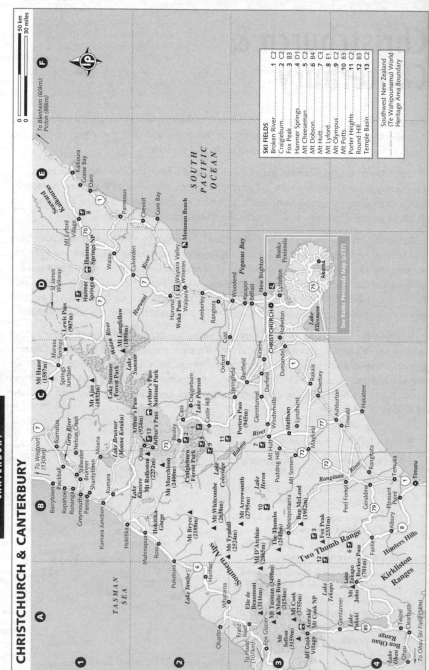

SKI FIELDS	
Broken River...............................	1 C2
Craigieburn..................................	2 C2
Fox Peak......................................	3 B3
Hanmer Springs..........................	4 D1
Mt Cheeseman............................	5 C2
Mt Dobson..................................	6 B4
Mt Hutt.......................................	7 C3
Mt Lyford...................................	8 E1
Mt Olympus.................................	9 C2
Mt Potts......................................	10 B3
Porter Heights............................	11 C2
Round Hill....................................	12 B3
Temple Basin................................	13 C2

---- Southwest New Zealand
(Te Wahipounamu) World
Heritage Area Boundary

Climate

Canterbury is one of NZ's driest regions. Moisture-laden westerlies from the Tasman Sea hit the Southern Alps and dump their rainfall on the West Coast before reaching the eastern South Island. The result? Canterbury has an annual rainfall of only 750mm, compared with a soaking 5000mm on the West Coast.

Getting There & Around

Christchurch has an international airport serviced by several domestic airlines flying to key destinations around NZ.

Bus and shuttle operators scurry along the east coast, connecting Canterbury's coastal (and near-coastal) settlements with northern destinations such as Picton and Nelson, and southern towns like Dunedin. Operators connect Christchurch to Arthur's Pass, the West Coast and Mt Cook.

Rail options for east-coast and coast-to-coast travel are provided by Tranz Scenic; its *TranzAlpine* service connects Christchurch and Greymouth, and its *TranzCoastal* trains chug north to Picton, with connections to the North Island. For information on getting to and from Christchurch, see p233.

CHRISTCHURCH

pop 344,100

Traditionally the most English of the NZ cities, Christchurch is now embracing the increasingly multicultural nature of urban NZ society. Change is coming through more diverse immigration, and a cosmopolitan tinge is being added to the city's earlier conservatism. There's still plenty to remind visitors of Christchurch's English past though, with a grand Anglican cathedral rising from a stately square, punts gliding down the sleepy Avon River, and trams rattling contentedly along Worcester St. But scratch the surface a little, and a more dynamic Christchurch is reflected in the restored laneways and squares around Lichfield St, High St's hip cafe scene, and locals' immense pride in their beautifully maintained Arts Centre.

HISTORY

Though it still has the Gothic architecture and wooden villas bequeathed by its founders, Christchurch has strayed from the original urban vision. The settlement of Christchurch in 1850 was an ordered Church of England enterprise, and the fertile farming land was deliberately placed in the hands of the gentry. Christchurch was meant to be a model of class-structured England in the South Pacific, not just another scruffy colonial outpost. Churches were built rather than pubs, and wool made the elite of Christchurch wealthy. In 1862, Christchurch was incorporated as a very English city, but its character slowly changed as other migrants arrived; new industries followed, and the city forged its own aesthetic and cultural notions. Like Auckland and Wellington, the city's economic and sporting rivals in the north, Christchurch is becoming a more multicultural society, and increasing immigration is alerting parochial Cantabrians to the wider world around them.

ORIENTATION

Cathedral Sq is the centre of town and is punctuated by the spire of ChristChurch Cathedral. The western inner city is dominated by the Botanic Gardens.

Christchurch is compact and easy to walk around, but slightly complicated by the river twisting through the centre and constantly crossing your path.

Colombo St runs north–south through Cathedral Sq and is the main shopping strip. Southeast the up-and-coming area around Lichfield St and High St has interesting boutiques, galleries, cafes and restaurants. Oxford Tce also features good eating and drinking near the Avon River.

Maps

Christchurch's i-SITE distributes free tourist maps, and maps and road atlases.

Map World (Map p216; ☎ 03-374 5399; www.map world.co.nz; cnr Manchester & Gloucester Sts) has NZ city and regional maps, guidebooks, and trampers' topographic maps.

INFORMATION
Bookshops

Arts Centre Bookshop (Map p216; ☎ 03-365 5277; www.booksnz.com; Arts Centre, 2 Worcester St) Excellent NZ-oriented titles.

Scorpio Books (Map p216; ☎ 03-379 2882; 79 Hereford St) Travel, history and Maori culture.

Smith's Bookshop (Map p216; ☎ 03-379 7976; 133 Manchester St) Secondhand book nirvana.

Whitcoulls (Map p216; ☎ 03-379 4580; 111 Cashel St)

CHRISTCHURCH & CANTERBURY FACTS

Eat Amid the up-and-coming restaurant scene in Lyttelton (p235)

Drink A beer from one of Canterbury's microbreweries, such as Brew Moon (p242), Three Boys or the Wigram Brewing Company

Read The World's Your Lobster by Lyttelton local and well-known newspaper-columnist Joe Bennett

Listen to The occasional negative comment when you tell Christchurch folk you actually quite like Auckland

Watch The mighty Canterbury Crusaders Super 14 Rugby team at Christchurch's Holy Grail pub (p231)

Swim at Akaroa, with the dolphins (p239), or soak at Hanmer Springs Thermal Reserve (p242)

Festival Free street performances at Christchurch's World Buskers Festival (p225)

Tackiest tourist attraction Christchurch's floral clock (p222)

Go green At the ecofriendly Onuku Farm Hostel (p241)

Emergency

Ambulance, fire service & police (☎ 111)
Police station (Map p216; ☎ 03-363 7400; cnr Hereford St & Cambridge Tce) There is also a police kiosk in Cathedral Sq.

Internet Access

The going rate in Christchurch is around $3 an hour. Most accommodation also offers internet services, including wi-fi.

dub dub dub (Map p216; 140 Gloucester St; 🛜)
E Blah Blah (Map p216; 77 Cathedral Sq; 🛜) Also offers mobile-phone rentals, wi-fi, and luggage storage.
high://NET (Map p216; 230 High St; 🛜)

Internet Resources

Christchurch & Canterbury (www.christchurchnz.com) Official tourism website for the city and region.
Christchurch.org.nz (www.christchurch.org.nz) Operated by the Christchurch City Council.
Local Eye (www.localeye.info) Online regional portal.

Laundry

Central City Laundrette (Map p216; ☎ 03-379 6622; 247 Armagh St; wash & dry per load $10; ⏱ 7.30am-5.30pm Mon-Fri & 9am-4pm Sat)

Media

Cityscape (www.cityscape-christchurch.co.nz) Entertainment and events magazine available in inner-city cafes and retailers.

Indulge (www.brownbear.co.nz) Eating, drinking and shopping.
Press (www.stuff.co.nz) Christchurch's newspaper, published Monday to Saturday.

Medical Services

24 Hour Surgery (Bealey Ave Medical Centre; Map p216; ☎ 03-365 7777; cnr Bealey Ave & Colombo St; ⏱ 24hr) North of town; no appointment necessary.
After-hours pharmacy (Map p216; ☎ 03-366 4439; 931 Colombo St; ⏱ 6-11pm Mon-Fri, 9am-11pm Sat & Sun, plus public holidays) Beside the 24 Hour Surgery.
Christchurch Hospital (Map p216; ☎ 03-364 0640, emergency dept 03-364 0270; 2 Riccarton Ave)

Money

The intersection of Hereford and Colombo Sts is home to major banks.

Travelex i-SITE (Map p216; Cathedral Sq); United Travel (Map p216; cnr Colombo & Armagh Sts)

Post

Post office (Map p216; 736 Colombo St)

Tourist Information

Adventure Centre (Map p216; ☎ 0800 847 486, 03-366 0302; www.adventures.net.nz; 69 Cathedral Sq; ⏱ 9am-8pm Mon-Fri, 10am-6pm Sat & Sun) One-stop adventure booking centre with branch at 94 Worcester St (Map p216; ⏱ 9am-6pm).
Airport information desks (☎ 03-353 7774) Open to meet all incoming flights for booking transport and accommodation.
Automobile Association (AA; Map p216; ☎ 03-964 3650; Unit 19/293 Durham St N; 8.30am-5pm Mon-Fri)
Christchurch i-SITE (Map p216; ☎ 03-379 9629; www.christchurchnz.com; Cathedral Sq; ⏱ 8.30am-5pm, later in summer) Transport, activities and accommodation.
Department of Conservation (DOC; Map p216; ☎ 03-371 3700; www.doc.govt.nz; Level 4, Torrens House, 195 Hereford St; ⏱ 8.30am-5pm Mon-Fri) Has information on South Island national parks and walkways.

SIGHTS
Cathedral Square

Cathedral Sq is where locals and tourists meet, giving the city's flat centrepiece a lively bustle. Featured here is the 18m-high *Metal Chalice* **sculpture**, created by Neil Dawson to acknowledge the new millennium.

ChristChurch Cathedral (Map p216; ☎ 03-366 0046; www.christchurchcathedral.co.nz; Cathedral Sq; admission free; ⏱ 8.30am-7pm Oct-Mar, 9am-5pm Apr-Sep) was consecrated in 1881 and has an impressive rose window, wooden-ribbed ceiling and tile work

GREATER CHRISTCHURCH

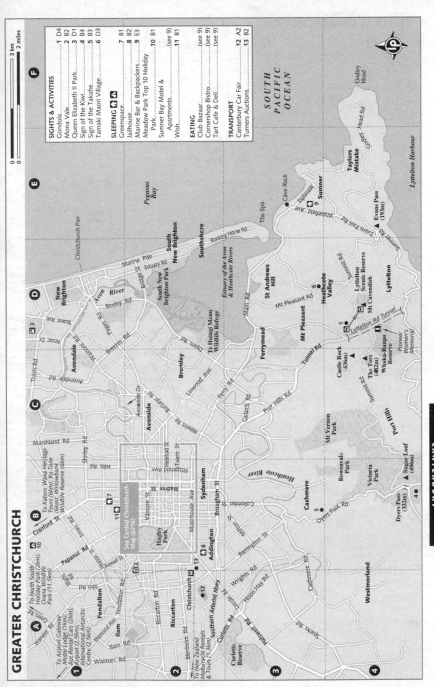

0 — 3 km
0 — 2 miles

SIGHTS & ACTIVITIES	
Gondola................................1	D4
Mona Vale.............................2	B2
Queen Elizabeth II Park............3	D1
Sign of the Kiwi.....................4	B4
Sign of the Takahe..................5	B3
Tamaki Maori Village................6	D3

SLEEPING	
Greenspace...........................7	B1
Jailhouse..............................8	B2
Marine Bar & Backpackers..........9	E3
Meadow Park Top 10 Holiday	
Park.................................10	B1
Sumner Bay Motel &	
Apartments.......................(see 9)	
Wish..................................11	B1

EATING	
Club Bazaar..........................(see 9)	
Cornershop Bistro...................(see 9)	
Tart Cafe & Deli.....................(see 9)	

TRANSPORT	
Canterbury Car Fair.................12	A2
Turners Auctions.....................13	B2

CHRISTCHURCH &
CANTERBURY

CENTRAL CHRISTCHURCH

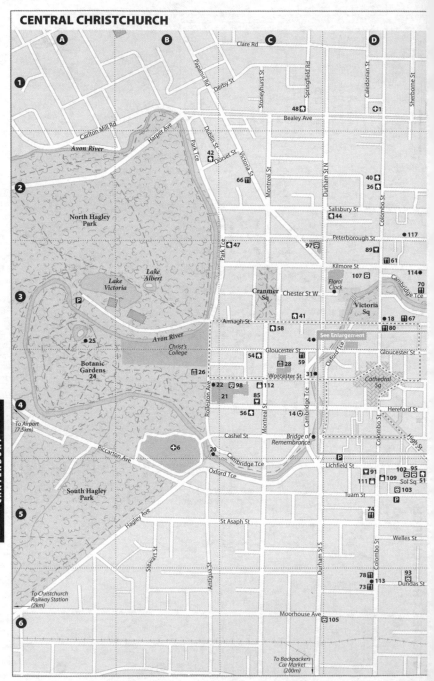

emblazoned with the distinctive Fylfot Cross. Climb halfway up the Gothic church's 63m-high **spire** (adult/child/family $5/2/10, tokens at the visitor centre). Guided 45-minute tours (🕐 tours 11am & 2pm Mon-Fri, 11am Sat & 11.30am Sun) are by donation. Self-guided audio tours cost $10.

Southern Encounter Aquarium & Kiwi House (Map p216; ☎ 03-359 0581; www.southernencounter.co.nz; Cathedral Sq; adult/child/family $17/7/41; 🕐 9am-5pm), is beside the i-SITE and has eels, seahorses, turtles and other marine life with specific feeding times. Don't expect too much from the **kiwi enclosure** (🕐 10.30am-4.30pm), as the endangered birds are hypersensitive to sound and light.

Banks of the Avon

The **Botanic Gardens** (Map p216; ☎ 03-941 8999; www. ccc.govt.nz/parks/botanicgardens; Rolleston Ave; admission free; 🕐 grounds 7am-1hr before sunset, conservatories 10.15am-4pm; 🅿) comprise 30 riverside hectares planted with 10,000-plus specimens of indigenous and introduced plants. There are

CHRISTCHURCH & CANTERBURY

conservatories and thematic gardens to explore, lawns to sprawl on, and a cafe at the **Botanic Gardens visitors centre** (Map p216; ☎ 03-941 8999; Rolleston Ave; ☻ 9am-4pm Mon-Fri, 10.15am-4pm Sat & Sun). Get the kids active in the playground adjacent to the cafe. **Guided walks** (adult/child $5/free; ☻ walks 1.30pm Sep-Apr) depart daily from the Canterbury Museum (right), or you can ride around the gardens in the electric **'Caterpillar'** train. Hop-on, hop-off **tickets** (www.gardentour. co.nz; adult/concession $15/6; ☻ 10am-4pm) are valid for two days and include a commentary.

Mona Vale (Map p215; ☎ 03-348 9660; www.mona vale.co.nz; 63 Fendalton Rd; admission free; ☻ 9.30am-5pm Oct-Apr, to 4pm May-Sep; P) is a charming Elizabethan-style homestead on 5.5 hectares of landscaped gardens, ponds and fountains. Dine in the cafe inside the riverside homestead, wander the gorgeous grounds, or take a half-hour Avon River **punt** (per person $20; ☻ Oct-Apr). Tasty picnic hampers (per couple $27 to $65) need to be ordered by noon the day prior. Mona Vale is just northwest of Hagley Park by bus 9.

Arts Centre

The former Canterbury College site (later Canterbury University), with its enclave of Gothic Revival buildings, is now the excellent **Arts Centre** (Map p216; www.artscentre.org.nz; 2 Worcester St; admission free; P), where arts and craft outlets share the premises with cinemas, a live theatre, restaurants and cafes. Visit the workshop and gallery of **Te Toi Mana** (☎ 03-366 4943; toimanamaori@xtra.co.nz) for traditional and contemporary Maori carving and design. **Visually Maori** (☎ 03-379 7855; visually.maori@xtra.co.nz) also showcases interesting Maori art.

There's a good **market** (☻ 10am-4pm Sat & Sun) selling craft and gourmet food items, often with live entertainment and plenty of cheap food stalls.

The **Arts Centre visitors centre** (Map p216; ☎ 03-363 2836; 2 Worcester St; ☻ 9.30am-5pm) is inside the clock tower on Worcester St. The helpful staff can provide information on free **guided tours** (☻ 10.30am-3.30pm) of the complex, including the **Rutherford's Den** (www.rutherfordsden.org.nz; ☻ 10am-5pm) exhibit celebrating the life and work of Ernest Rutherford, the NZ physicist who first split the atom in 1917.

Tramway

Trams were introduced to Christchurch streets in 1905 but were discontinued as a means of transport 50 years later. Restored **trams** (☎ 03-366 7830; www.tram.co.nz; adult/child $15/5; ☻ 9am-9pm Nov-Mar, to 6pm Apr-Oct) now operate a 2.5km inner-city loop that takes in local attractions and shopping areas. Tickets are valid for 48 hours and can be bought from the driver. Expect the odd live jazz band to join you in summer and look forward to travelling through the glass atrium at Cathedral Junction. One tram is fitted out as a **restaurant** (☎ 03-366 7511; dinner packages $73-125; ☻ 7.30pm-late Sep-May, from 7pm Jun-Aug).

At the time of writing, plans were progressing to extend the existing line to incorporate High St and Cashel St in time for the 2011 Rugby World Cup.

You can get combo tickets (adult/child/family $35/12/80) for the tram and gondola (p221) — purchase from the tram or gondola staff. If you're planning on punting on the Avon (left) similar combo tickets including the tram (adult/child $30/15) are also available. A triple pass for tram, gondola and punting (adult/child/family $50/20/120) incorporates three of Christchurch's iconic attractions.

Canterbury Museum

The absorbing **Canterbury Museum** (Map p216; ☎ 03-366 5000; www.canterburymuseum.com; Rolleston Ave; donation $2; ☻ 9am-5pm Apr-Sep, to 5.30pm Oct-Mar) has a wonderful collection of items of significance to NZ. Highlights include the Maori gallery, with some stunning *pounamu* (greenstone) pieces on display; the coracle in the Antarctic Hall used by a group shipwrecked on Disappointment Island in 1907; and a wide array of stuffed bird life from the Pacific and beyond. Don't miss the statuesque Emperor penguin. Guided tours (donations appreciated) run from 3.30pm to 4.30pm on Tuesday and Thursday. Kids will enjoy the interactive displays at Discovery (admission $2).

Christchurch Art Gallery

Set in an eye-catching metal-and-glass construction built in 2003, the city's **art gallery** (Map p216; ☎ 03-941 7300; www.christchurchartgallery.org.nz; cnr Worcester & Montreal Sts; admission free; ☻ 10am-5pm Thu-Tue, to 9pm Wed) has an engrossing permanent collection divided into historical, 20th-century and contemporary galleries, plus temporary exhibitions featuring NZ artists. **Guided tours** (free; ☻ tours 11am Mon-Sun, plus 2pm Sat & Sun & 7.15pm Wed) provide an excellent overview, or you can hire an audio guide ($5) for a self-guided tour. Ask at i-SITE (p214) for the *Cultural Precinct* brochure detailing other nearby galleries.

International Antarctic Centre

The **International Antarctic Centre** (off Map p215; ☎ 0508 736 4846, 03-353 7798; www.iceberg.co.nz; 38 Orchard Rd; adult/child/family $55/36/145, audio guide $6; ☼ 9am-7pm Oct-Mar, to 5.30pm Apr-Sep; P) is part of a huge complex built for the administration of the NZ, US and Italian Antarctic programs. See penguins and learn about the icy continent via historical, geological and zoological exhibits, including videos of life on Scott Base. There's also an aquarium of creatures gathered under the ice in McMurdo Sound, and an 'Antarctic Storm' chamber where you get a firsthand taste of minus 18°C wind chill (check at reception for 'storm' forecasts). Admission includes unlimited rides on the **Hägglund**, an all-terrain vehicle that negotiates an outdoor adventure course. An optional extra is the **Penguin Backstage Pass** (adult/child $20/15) taking visitors behind the scenes of the Penguin Encounter. Transport options include the City Flyer airport bus (p234) – it's just a short walk from the main terminal – or the Penguin Express shuttle departing Cathedral Sq on the hour from 9am (adult/child return $6/3).

Science Alive!

Inside the city's old train station, **Science Alive!** (Map p216; ☎ 03-365 5199; www.sciencealive.co.nz; 392 Moorhouse Ave; adult/child/family $14/10/45; ☼ 10am-5pm; P) is crammed with ever-changing interactive exhibits, from optical illusions to things that children can push, pull and climb. Kids will love the climbing wall and NZ's highest vertical slide. If the sprogs get bored with reality, movie make-believe (p232) is right next door.

Wildlife Reserves

Orana Wildlife Park (off Map p215; ☎ 03-359 7109; www.oranawildlifepark.co.nz; McLeans Island Rd; adult/child/family $24/8/56; ☼ 10am-5pm; P) has an excellent walk-through native bird aviary, a nocturnal kiwi house and a reptile exhibit featuring the wrinkly tuatara. Most of the grounds are devoted to Africana, including lions, rhinos, giraffes, zebras, lemurs, oryx and cheetahs, and Asia is well represented with an array of Sumatran tigers. Guided walks start from the native bird feed at 10.45am and around the African lion enclosure at 2.30pm. Check the website – under 'Exciting Encounters' – for other regular walks and daily feeding times. The Orana Wildlife Park shuttle departs Cathedral Sq at 10am and 1pm daily.

MAORI NZ: CHRISTCHURCH & CANTERBURY

Only 5% of NZ's Maori live on the South Island: the south was settled a few hundred years later than the north, with significant numbers coming south only after land became scarcer on the North Island. Before that, Maori mostly travelled to the south in search of moa, fish and, of course, West Coast *pounamu* (greenstone).

The major *iwi* (tribe) of the South Island is Ngai Tahu (www.ngaitahu.iwi.nz), ironically now one of the country's wealthiest, because it is so much richer in land (per person) than the North Island tribes. In Christchurch, as in other cities, there are urban Maori of many other *iwi* as well.

Ko Tane (☎ 03-359 6226; www.kotane.co.nz; 60 Hussey Rd; dancing-tour-dinner package adult/child $110/54; ☼ packages 5.30pm & 6.30pm Oct-May, 6.30pm Jun-Sep) at Willowbank Wildlife Reserve (opposite) features traditional dancing, a wildlife tour and buffet dinner. Forego the wildlife tour and/or dinner for a cheaper night out – the performance only is $48/24 per adult/child. Another option is to incorporate a paddle in a traditional *waka* (Maori canoe) with Katoro Waka Heritage Tours (opposite), also based at Willowbank.

The Chronicles of Uitara performance at the **Tamaki Maori Village** (Map p215; ☎ 03-366 7333; www.christchurchinfo.co.nz; adult/child under 5yr/child 5-15yr $126/free/73) brings to life early interaction between Maori and European settlers. The evening is set in a recreated Maori village, and concludes with a traditional *hangi* (Maori feast).

More contemporary is the bone carving done by the 'Bone Dude', John Fraser, who trains visitors to do their own carving at his studio (p222), and the work at the Te Toi Mana gallery (p219) at the Arts Centre.

As well as at Christchurch's Canterbury Museum (p219), you'll unearth Maori artefacts at museums in Akaroa (p238) and Okains Bay (Maori & Colonial Museum; p238).

Two Days

After breakfast at one of **High Street's cafes** (p229), jump on the **tramway** (p219) and do a full loop to get your bearings. Disembark at the **Arts Centre** (p219) to explore the historic area's galleries, and recharge with lunch at **Dux de Lux** (p230). Walk off your meal in the pretty **Botanic Gardens** (p218), and head to the **Antigua Boatsheds** (below) for a late-afternoon **Avon punt** (below). End the day eating and bar-hopping around the interesting nooks and crannies of **Poplar Street** and **SOL Square** (p230).

On day two, check out the **Canterbury Museum** (p219) and the **Christchurch Art Gallery** (p219), before heading out of town to ride the **gondola** (below) and do some mountaintop walking. In the evening, jump on a bus to the excellent restaurants at **Lyttelton** (p235) or **Sumner** (p228).

Four Days

Follow the two-day itinerary, then head to **Akaroa** (p236) to explore its wildlife-rich harbour, and the peninsula's beautiful outer bays. On day four it's time for **shopping** (p232) in funky High St, before chilling at the **International Antarctic Centre** (opposite) or paddling a Maori canoe and enjoying a traditional Maori feast at **Willowbank Wildlife Reserve** (below).

Willowbank Wildlife Reserve (off Map p215; ☎ 03-359 6226; www.willowbank.co.nz; 60 Hussey Rd; adult/child under 5yr/child 5-15yr/family $25/free/10/65; ⏱ 9.30am-dusk; Ⓟ), about 6km north of the city, is another good animal reserve focusing on native NZ animals and hands-on enclosures with alpacas, wallabies and deer. Tours are held several times a day, and Willowbank's escorted after-dark tours are a good opportunity to see NZ's national bird, the kiwi. Evening Maori performances also take place here (see opposite). Another area of Willowbank is **Katoro Waka Heritage Tours** (off Map p215; ☎ 0800 528 676; www.katoro.co.nz; adult/child from $70/35), blending Maori folklore with a paddle in a traditional *waka* (war canoe) and a visit to a *pa* (Maori village).

Gondola

The **gondola** (Map p215; ☎ 03-384 0700; www.gondola.co.nz; 10 Bridle Path Rd; return adult/child/family $24/10/59; ⏱ 10am-9pm; Ⓟ) whisks you from the Heathcote Valley terminal to the cafe-restaurant complex on Mt Cavendish (500m) in 10 minutes. Expect great views over Lyttelton Harbour and towards the Southern Alps. Paths lead to the Crater Rim Walkway, or you can gondola up and cycle down (see right). Lyttelton bus 28 travels here. Secure a combo deal (adult/child/family $35/12/80) if you're planning on also riding the tram (see p219).

ACTIVITIES

Christchurch's most popular activities are gentler than the adrenaline-fuelled pursuits of Queenstown and Wanaka. Christchurch is better suited to punting down the Avon River, cycling through the easy terrain of Hagley Park, or negotiating the walking trails at Lyttelton Harbour. The city's best swimming is at Sumner and New Brighton beaches, and there is good skiing at nearby Mt Hutt (p81).

Boating

Dating from 1882, the photogenic green-and-white **Antigua Boatsheds** (Map p216; ☎ 03-366 5885; www.boatsheds.co.nz; 2 Cambridge Tce; kayaks per hr from $10, rowboats/paddleboats per 30min/hr $20/30; ⏱ 9am-5pm) rents out various self-propelled vessels for independent Avon River exploration. There's also an excellent **cafe** (mains $10-20; ⏱ 7am-5pm), which is a great spot for brunch or lunch. The boatsheds are the starting point for **Punting on the Avon** (☎ 03-366 0337; www.punting.co.nz; 30min trip adult/child $20/10; ⏱ 9am-6pm Oct-Apr, 10am-4pm May-Sep), where someone else does all the work during a half-hour return trip in a flat-bottomed boat. There is another departure point for punting from the landing stage at the Worcester St bridge. A combination ticket (adult/child $30/15) is available that includes the Tramway (p219).

Cycling

City Cycle Hire (☎ 0800 424 534, 03-377 5952; www.cyclehire-tours.co.nz; half/full day $25/35) will deliver bikes to where you're staying. Mountain bikes (half/full day $30/45) will get you nicely off road. It also offers day trips (adult/child $95/50) on the Little River Rail Trail (p222) and you can pedal downhill from the gondola

---

THE SLOW ROAD TO LITTLE RIVER

The Little River Rail Trail will eventually traverse 45km from the Christchurch suburb of Hornby to the Banks Peninsula hamlet of Little River. At the time of writing, all sections excluding a 14km stretch were open. See www.littleriverrailtrail.co.nz for the latest information. Join the trail 20km from Little River at Motukarara for the best of the ride. Ask at the Christchurch i-SITE (p214) about bike rental and public transport options. Rail trail day trips including transport can be booked with City Cycle Hire (p221) and Natural High (below). Natural High can also rent out bikes and offer advice for multiday self-guided cycling trips incorporating the Little River Rail Trail.

---

terminal (p221) on a mountain bike ($50). Price includes the gondola ride up the mountain. Bookings are essential.

Natural High (☎ 0800 444 144; 03-982 2966; www.naturalhigh.co.nz) rents touring and mountain bikes (per day/week from $40/154), and can advise on guided and self-guided bicycle touring through Canterbury and the South Island.

See p224 for details of two-wheeled guided city tours.

Walking

The i-SITE has information on Christchurch walks. Within the city are the **Riverside Walk** and various historical strolls, while further afield is the excellent clifftop walk to **Taylors Mistake** (2½ hours).

For great views of the city, take the walkway from the **Sign of the Takahe** (Map p215) on Dyers Pass Rd. The various 'Sign of the…' places in this area were originally roadhouses built during the Depression as rest stops. Now they vary from the impressive tearooms at the Sign of the Takahe to a simple shelter at the Sign of the Bellbird, and are referred to primarily as landmarks. This walk leads up to the **Sign of the Kiwi** (Map p215) through Victoria Park and then along Summit Rd to Scotts Reserve, with several lookout points along the way.

You can walk to Lyttelton on the **Bridle Path** (1½ hours), which starts at Heathcote Valley (take bus 28). The **Godley Head Walkway** (two hours return) begins at Taylors Mistake, crossing and recrossing Summit Rd, and offers beautiful views on a clear day.

The **Crater Rim Walkway** (nine hours) around Lyttelton Harbour goes some 20km from Evans Pass to the Ahuriri Scenic Reserve. From the gondola terminal on Mt Cavendish, walk to **Cavendish Bluff Lookout** (30 minutes return) or the **Pioneer Women's Memorial** (one hour return).

Other Activities

Queen Elizabeth II Park (Map p215; ☎ 03-941 6849; www.qeiipark.org.nz; Travis Rd, New Brighton; pool adult/child $5/3; ⏰ 6am-9pm Mon-Fri, 7am-8pm Sat & Sun) has indoor pools (including a wave pool), waterslides, a gym and squash courts. Take bus 43. Closer to town is the **Centennial Leisure Centre** (Map p216; ☎ 03-941 7080; www.centennial.org. nz; 181 Armagh St; adult/child $5/3; ⏰ 6am-9pm Mon-Fri, 7am-7pm Sat & Sun), with a heated indoor pool.

The closest **beaches** to the city are Waimairi, North Beach, New Brighton and South Brighton; buses 5, 49 and 60 head here. Sumner (see p228), to the city's southeast, is also popular with good restaurants (take bus 3), while further east at Taylors Mistake are some good **surfing** breaks.

Several **skiing** areas lie within a two-hour drive of Christchurch (see p81). Other active options accessible from Christchurch include cruising on Lyttelton Harbour (p235), rafting on the Rangitata River (p255), tandem skydiving, tandem paragliding, hot-air ballooning, jetboating the Waimakariri River and horse trekking. Inquire at i-SITE (p214).

Creative types should book a session with the **Bone Dude** (Map p216; ☎ 03-379 7530; www.the bonedude.co.nz; 229B Fitzgerald Ave; from $60; ⏰ 9am-noon & 1-4pm Mon-Fri, Sat 10am-1pm). Allow three hours to craft your own bone carving in a creative and supportive environment. Owner John Fraser of Ngati Rangitihi ancestry provides a range of traditional Maori templates, or you can work on your own design. Sessions are limited to 12 carvers, so booking is highly recommended. It's a 15-minute walk from the city, or catch bus 70.

WALKING TOUR

Start your day in **High Street** (1; p232) with a leisurely breakfast at C1 Espresso (p230) before checking out nearby boutiques and galleries. Detour down Poplar St to explore the interesting shops of the **Lichfield Lanes** (2; p230) precinct, and make a note of which bars to return to after dark. Return to High St and continue to the intersection

WALKING TOUR

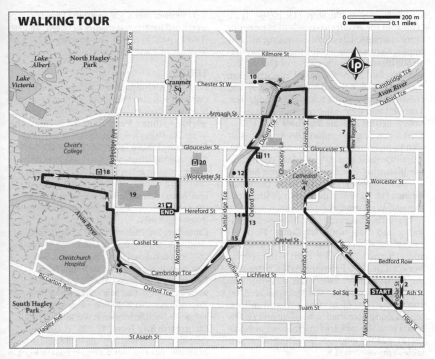

WALK FACTS

Start High St
Finish Dux de Lux
Distance About 5km
Duration Three hours to one day, depending on stops

of Manchester St and Lichfield St. Turn left into Lichfield St and then left again into His Lordship's Lane to explore the quirky design stores around **SOL Sq** (**3**; p230). Return to High St and follow the pedestrian mall to Colombo St. At the time of writing the tramway was being extended along High St, so maybe watch out for passing trams. Follow Colombo St to **Cathedral Sq** (**4**; p214). If you've got time, climb the spire of ChristChurch Cathedral (p214). From Cathedral Sq walk along Worcester St with the cathedral on your left. Turn left into the expansive glass atrium of **Cathedral Junction** (**5**). Take care because it's also a regular thoroughfare for the **Christchurch Tramway** (**6**; p219). Cross Gloucester St and walk up pretty **New Regent**

Street (**7**), full of pastel-coloured Spanish Mission architecture.

Follow the tramline left down Armagh St, and then turn right up Colombo St. To your left is the greenery of **Victoria Square** (**8**). In Victoria Sq admire the statues of Queen Victoria and the English explorer Captain James Cook. You are in NZ's most English city, after all.

Head left down the path opposite Oxford Tce and cross the bridge over the gentle **Avon River** (**9**; p218) to smell the time at the **Floral Clock** (**10**). Return to the statue of James Cook and turn right to follow the banks of the river. At Armagh St turn right and cross the Armagh St Bridge. Turn left before the Belgian Beer Café (look for the Stella Artois sign) and, keeping the river on your left, follow the meandering path. Turn left at the Gloucester St bridge and turn right into Oxford Tce for a coffee or lunch stop at **Caffe Roma** (**11**; p230).

Carry on along Oxford Tce to the Worcester St Bridge where you can arrange to go **punting on the Avon** (**12**; p221). Back on dry land, follow Oxford Tce to reach the bars and restaurants known locally as 'the Strip' (13; p230). It's a great spot for an alfresco lunch in summer or more energetic late-night carousing all year round. Keep an eye out for the Water Wheel on Mill Island (14) on the corner of Oxford Tce and Hereford St. At the end of 'the Strip' turn right at the Bridge of Remembrance (15) and cross Durham St S to reach Cambridge Tce. Turn left and follow the riverside path to the candy-striped Antigua Boatsheds (16; p221). Rent a rowboat to explore the Avon at your own pace. Punting can also be arranged here.

Follow Rolleston Ave and lose yourself in the blooming beauty of the Botanic Gardens (17; p218) before continuing to the Canterbury Museum (18; p219) on the corner of Rolleston Ave and Worcester St.

Leave the museum at the Hereford St entrance and cross to the Arts Centre (19; p219) to explore diverse galleries and workshops and – if you've timed it right – the regular weekend market. From the Arts Centre visit the Christchurch Art Gallery (20; p219) on the corner of Worcester St and Montreal St. After you've had your fill of visual arts and culture, return along Montreal St to while away a few hours with the excellent microbrews at Dux de Lux (21; p230). Good luck in scoring an outside table. You've earned it.

CHRISTCHURCH FOR CHILDREN

There's no shortage of kid-friendly sights and activities in Christchurch. If family fun is a priority, consider planning your travels around NZ's biggest children's festival, KidsFest (www.kidsfest.org.nz). It's held every July and is chock-full of shows, workshops and parties. The annual World Buskers Festival (opposite) in late January is also bound to be a hit.

For picnics and open-air frolicking, visit the Botanic Gardens (p218); there's a playground beside the cafe, and the kids will love riding on the Caterpillar train. Extend your nature-based experience with a wildlife reserve (p220), or take a ride on the gondola (p221), before burning off excess energy in a rowboat or paddleboat from the Antigua Boatsheds (p221). At the engrossing International Antarctic Centre (p220), kids will love the storm chamber, the Hägglund Ride, and (of course) the penguins. Educational and attention-getting factors are also high at the Discovery centre at Canterbury Museum (p219), and Science Alive! (p220); at the latter you can try your hand at minigolf on a glow-in-the-dark course.

If the weather's good and the kids are restless, head for the waterslides of Queen Elizabeth II Park (p222), or hit the beaches (p222) at Sumner or New Brighton.

TOURS

Numerous companies conduct tours of the city and will also transport you out to nearby towns (Lyttelton, Akaroa) and sites further afield (Arthur's Pass, Hanmer Springs, the Waipara Valley). Ask at the i-SITE (p214).

Canterbury Leisure Tours (☎ 0800 484 485, 03-384 0999; www.leisuretours.co.nz; tours from $100) Offers touring options in and around Christchurch, with everything from three-hour city tours to full-day Akaroa, Mt Cook, Arthur's Pass and Kaikoura outings (day tours are fine if you're short on time, but these places really deserve more in-depth visits).

Canterbury Sightseeing (☎ 027 321 0116; www. christchurchsightseeing.co.nz; tours from $260) Offer themed sightseeing tours around the region with a focus on food and wine, especially the vineyards of the Waipara Valley.

Canterbury Wine Tours (☎ 0800 081 155; www. waiparavalley.co.nz; tours from $75) Experience three Waipara vineyards on the half-day trip, or make a day of it and sample four different wineries with lunch ($119).

Christchurch Bike Tours (☎ 0800 733 257; www. chchbiketours.co.nz; tours from $35) Pedal around on fun, informative, two-hour tours in a city just made for biking. Tours depart from i-SITE, and bookings are recommended. Foodies should ask about the special 'Farmers Market' ($45) and 'Gourmet Christchurch' ($110) tours.

Christchurch Personal Guiding Service (Map p216; ☎ 03-379 9629; tours $15; ☽ tours 10am & 1pm Oct-Apr, 1pm May-Sep) Nonprofit organisation offering informative, two-hour city walks. Get tickets from the i-SITE or the red-and-black kiosk in Cathedral Sq.

Christchurch Sightseeing Tours (☎ 0508 669 660, 03-366 9660; www.christchurchtours.co.nz; tours $40-46) Offers comprehensive half-day city tours year-round, a 3½-hour circuit of private gardens in spring and summer, and twice-weekly tours of heritage homes.

Hassle Free Tours (☎ 0800 427 753, 03-385-5755; www.hasslefree.co.nz; tours from $215) Options include a 4WD alpine safari, jetboating on the Waimakariri River, and visiting the location of Edoras from the Lord of the Rings trilogy. The scenery is stunning, but don't expect to see anything from the original set.

Ghost Walk (☎ 03-963 0870; tour $20; ☽ tours 9pm Wed-Fri Oct-Mar, 8pm Wed-Fri Apr-Sep) Dr Aloysius Mort (actually an actor from the Court Theatre) leads spooky night-time strolls through the Gothic cloisters of the Arts Centre. Book at the i-SITE or the Court Theatre (p231).

Unlimited NZ (☎ 03-960 9119; www.unlimitednz. co.nz; adult/child $315/210) Day trips incorporating the

TranzAlpine train (p193) and tramping around Arthur's Pass.

FESTIVALS & EVENTS
Check at the i-SITE or www.bethere.co.nz for a comprehensive listing. Some notable regular events:

January
World Buskers Festival (☎ 03-377 2365; www.world buskersfestival.com) National and international talent entertain passers-by on the city's streets for 10 days in late January. Don't forget to put money in the hat.

January-March
Garden City SummerTimes (☎ 03-941 8999; www. summertimes.co.nz) Say g'day to summer at a huge array of outdoor events. Sweet as.

February-March
Festival of Flowers (☎ 03-365 5403; www. festivalofflowers.co.nz) Christchurch's gardens bloom with the ChristChurch Cathedral Carpet of Flowers and the Wearable Flowers Parade. From mid-February to mid-March.

March
Ellerslie Flower Show (☎ 03-379 4581; www. ellerslieflowershow.co.nz) Hagley Park comes alive in mid-March with NZ's biggest flower show.

July
Christchurch Arts Festival (☎ 03-365 2223; www. artsfestival.co.nz) Biennial midwinter arts event (held in odd-numbered years).

November
NZ Cup and Show Week (☎ 03-379 9629; www. nzcupandshow.co.nz) Includes the NZ Cup horse race, fashion shows, fireworks and the centrepiece A&P Show (Agricultural & Pastoral Show; www.theshow.co.nz) where the country comes to town. Also includes Southern Amp (www.southernamp.co.nz), the South Island's biggest outdoor music festival.

SLEEPING
Christchurch has many hostels, most of them within a 10-minute shuffle of Cathedral Sq. Several budget stalwarts are found around Latimer Sq, with a few smaller options to the east. There are also several well-established hostels near the Botanic Gardens.

Motels are clustered around Bealey Ave and Papanui Rd, north of the centre, and Riccarton Rd, west of town beyond Hagley

Park. A number of top-end hotels are around Cathedral Sq.

Consider also staying in either Lyttelton (p235) or Sumner (p228). Both are pleasant waterfront 'burbs easily reached by public transport and with lots of good eating.

Budget
CAMPING
North South Holiday Park (off Map p215; ☎ 0800 567 765, 03-359 5993; www.northsouth.co.nz; cnr John's & Sawyers Arms Rds, SH1; unpowered/powered sites $30/32, cabins & units $52-117; P 🖳 🛜 🔊) This place is just five minutes from the airport, and a good first night after picking up your campervan. Facilities include a pool, sauna and playground and newer motel units. Airport transfers are available.

Meadow Park Top 10 Holiday Park (Map p215; ☎ 0800 396 323, 03-352 9176; www.christchurchtop10. co.nz; 39 Meadow St; sites $37-46, cabins & chalets $64-126, motel units $136-176; P 🖳 🛜 🔊) Wall-to-wall campervans here, while other accommodation ranges from cabins to motel units. Also well equipped for leisure activities, with an indoor pool, and games rooms and playground for the kids.

Closer to the city, Stonehurst (below) offers powered campervan sites.

HOSTELS
Stonehurst (Map p216; ☎ 0508 786 633, 03-379 4620; www.stonehurst.co.nz; 241 Gloucester St; campervan sites $35, dm $21, s from $50, d $55-65; P 🖳 🛜 🔊) Versatility plus, with three buildings covering half a city block. There's everything from campervan sites to dorms and three-bedroom tourist flats (see p227). Decide in advance what you're after (eg don't get a poolside bunk room if you want some quiet times) and book ahead at peak times. The city centre is a short walk away.

Foley Towers (Map p216; ☎ 03-366 9720; foley .towers@backpack.co.nz; 208 Kilmore St; dm $23-26, d with/ without bathroom $64/58; P 🖳 🛜) Sheltered by well-established trees, Foley Towers provides well-maintained rooms encircling quiet inner courtyards and a friendly welcome in dorms warmed by underfloor heating.

Old Countryhouse (Map p216; ☎ 03-381 5504; www. oldcountryhousenz.com; 437 Gloucester St; dm $24-31, d $56-78; P 🖳 🛜) Well loved for its easygoing ambience, the Countryhouse features two separate villas with handmade wooden furniture, a reading lounge, and a lovely garden filled with native ferns. It's slightly further out than other hostels, but still only 1km east of Latimer Sq; bus 21 stops opposite.

Vagabond Backpackers (Map p216; ☎ 03-379 9677; vagabondbackpackers@hotmail.com; 232 Worcester St; dm/s/d $25/39/58; P 💻 🛜) Small, friendly place reminiscent of a big share-house. There's an appealing garden, rustic but comfy facilities, and frisbees and barbecues reinforce that you're definitely in NZ.

Coachman Backpackers (Map p216; ☎ 0800 692 622, 03-377 0908; www.coachmanbackpackers.co.nz; 144 Gloucester St; dm/d from $25/66; 💻 🛜) Centrally located in a heritage building with stained glass, timber panelling and a grand staircase. Most of the light-filled rooms come with a private bathroom.

Frauenreisehaus (Map p216; ☎ 03-366 2585; www.womanshostel.co.nz; 272 Barbadoes St; dm/s/tw $26/43/66; P 💻) Sorry guys, this welcoming hostel is for women only. It offers free bikes and laundry, a huge selection of books and DVDs, two well-equipped kitchens and a garden full of fresh herbs. Reconfirm before you arrive.

ourpick Jailhouse (Map p215; ☎ 0800 524 546, 03-982 7777; www.jail.co.nz; 338 Lincoln Rd; dm/s/d $26/49/70; P 💻 🛜) Housed in an old prison that was built in 1874 and only decommissioned in 1999, the Jailhouse is one of NZ's most unique hostels. Twins and doubles are a bit on the small side (remember, it was a prison), but it's still an exceptionally well-run and friendly spot. The city is a pleasant 25-minute walk through Hagley Park, but the upside is that the Jailhouse is quieter than some central hostels.

Dorset House (Map p216; ☎ 03-366 8268; www.dorsethouse.co.nz; 1 Dorset St; dm/s/d $27/55/74; P 💻 🛜) This 145-year-old wooden villa has a large regal lounge with log fire, pool table, DVDs, and beds instead of bunks. It's a short stroll to Hagley Park. From November to April it also rents out a couple of nearby self-contained flats (double/quad $89/142) sleeping up to four.

Chester Street Backpackers (Map p216; ☎ 03-377 1897; www.chesterst.co.nz; 148 Chester St E; dm/tw/d $27/58/60; P 💻 🛜) This relaxed wooden villa is painted in bright colours and has a huge library in the sunny front room and the world-renowned 'Car-be-cue' in the boot of an old Ford Anglia. Chester St's friendly cat is a regular guest at barbecues. It's popular so try and book ahead. Across the road is the cosy self-contained Entwhistle Cottage (opposite).

Base Christchurch (Map p216; ☎ 0800 227 369, 03-982 2225; www.stayatbase.com; 56 Cathedral Sq; dm $27.50-31; 💻 🛜) Slick and busy hostel pitching itself to young travellers out for social good times. It's right on Cathedral Sq with loads of modern facilities, including plusher women-only 'Sanctuary' dorms.

Central City YHA (Map p216; ☎ 03-379 9535; www.yha.co.nz; yha.christchurch@yha.co.nz; 273 Manchester St; dm $30, d with/without bathroom $95/80; 💻 🛜) Comfortable bunks and beds; huge, spotless lounges and kitchens; a pool table; and helpful staff characterise this well-equipped, efficiently run hostel.

Also recommended:

Around the World Backpackers (Map p216; ☎ 03-365 4363; www.aroundtheworld.co.nz; 314 Barbadoes St; dm/d $22/50; P 💻) Owned by a friendly family, Around the World gets rave recommendations for its 'Kiwiana' decor and sunny back garden.

Charlie B's (Map p216; ☎ 03-379 8429; www.charliebs.co.nz; 268 Madras St; dm $24.50-$27.50, s $55, d $60-65; 💻 🛜) This spacious, centrally located option has a grassy lawn made for relaxation.

Thomas's Hotel (Map p216; ☎ 03-379 9536; www.gaanz.com; 36 Hereford St; dm $25-28, d $65-130; P 💻 🛜) Well-run budget spot near the Arts Centre with a huge array of different rooms; a good option for groups.

New Excelsior Backpackers (Map p216; ☎ 0800 666 237, 03-366 7570; www.newexcelsior.co.nz; cnr Manchester & High Sts; dm $27-30; d with/without bathroom $75/63; 💻 🛜) Well placed for the restaurants, nightlife and shopping around nearby High and Lichfield Sts.

Midrange
GUEST HOUSES AND B&BS

Greenspace (Map p215; ☎ 03-377 8832; www.greenspace.co.nz; 5/48 Trafalgar St, St Albans; d with/without breakfast $140/110; P 💻) This ecofriendly and sunny bed and breakfast – the hosts actually live up the road – oozes privacy with its secluded garden location beside a stream and a stand of native bush. The decor includes retro Kiwiana touches, and there's a well-chosen selection of Kiwi music to ease you in and out of every day. It's an easy 20-minute walk to town, or catch bus 14 or 16.

ourpick Wish (Map p215; ☎ 03-356 2455; www.wishnz.com; 38 Edgeware Rd, St Albans; s/d incl breakfast $110/140; P 💻 🛜) The rooms and beds at the stylish and modern Wish are supercomfy, but it could be the locally sourced, sustainable and organic breakfasts that you recommend to other travellers. Contemporary NZ art dots the walls, and the huge native-timber kitchen table is just made for catching up for an end-of-day glass of wine. Central Christchurch is a 15-minute walk away, or bus 14 or 16 stops virtually outside.

Entwhistle Cottage (Map p216; ☎ 03-377 2001; www.chesterst.co.nz; 147 Chester St E; d $125; P) This colonial-style self-contained cottage is aligned to Chester Street Backpackers (opposite). Built in 1870, it's now charmingly modern with a sunny courtyard that could hinder your opportunity to look around Christchurch. There are two bedrooms, with additional guests costing $15. A two-night minimum applies. A port-a-cot, highchair and loads of toys makes it a good option for families.

Orari B&B (Map p216; ☎ 03-365 6569; www.orari.net.nz; 42 Gloucester St; d incl breakfast $190-230; P 🛜) Orari is a late-19th-century home that has been stylishly updated with light-filled, pastel-toned rooms, inviting guest areas, and a lovely front garden. Art connoisseurs take note: it's right across the road from Christchurch Art Gallery. Wine connoisseurs can look forward to complimentary wine. Newly built self-contained three-bedroom apartments are equally comfortable (from $300 per night).

On Armagh St are several character-filled homes offering guest-house accommodation: **Windsor Hotel** (Map p216; ☎ 0800 366 1503, 03-366 1503; www.windsorhotel.co.nz; 52 Armagh St; s/d/tr/q incl breakfast $98/140/180/200; P 🖳 🛜) Trimmed with stately red bricks, this heritage abode has 40 simple, sunny and very comfortable rooms. All facilities are shared (fluffy bathrobes provided). Say hi to the friendly dog usually monopolising the front porch. **Croydon House** (Map p216; ☎ 03-366 5111; www.croydon.co.nz; 63 Armagh St; s $110-140, d $140-180, all incl breakfast; P) Flower-filled window boxes decorate this B&B in a charming 1920s building. Rooms have shared facilities or private bathroom. The shared garden is a lovely spot after a busy day, and there is a special toy-filled room for families.

HOTELS & APARTMENTS

Hotel SO (Map p216; ☎ 0508 165 165, 03-968 5050; www.hotelso.co.nz; 165 Cashel St; s $69, d $89-135; P 🖳 🛜) The sleek Hotel SO has (very) compact rooms that are an ode to whip-smart, ergonomic design. Look forward to flat-screen TVs, flash bathrooms, and iPod docks in hip surroundings. The hotel is close to Christchurch's nightlife precinct, so expect some after-dark noise at the weekend. Note that not all rooms have windows.

Living Space (Map p216; ☎ 0508 454 846, 03-964 5212; www.livingspace.net; 96 Lichfield St; d $80-120; 🖳 🛜) Pitched somewhere between handy central digs for nightlife-loving visitors and compact studios for longer-term visitors, Living Space has minikitchens, high-speed internet and Sky TV. There's also an industrial-strength shared kitchen and DVD theatres. Rates are cheaper at weekends and longer-stay discounts are available.

Hotel off the Square (Map p216; ☎ 0800 633 843, 03-374 9980; www.offthesquare.com; 115 Worcester St; d $140-180, apt $280; 🖳 🛜) This boutique hotel provides a stylish antidote to clinical business hotels. No two rooms are alike, and the place radiates warmth, with vibrant colours and lots of original art and plants. Loft-style apartments provide a self-contained option.

MOTELS

Stonehurst (Map p216; ☎ 0508 786 633, 03-379 4620; www.stonehurst.co.nz; 241 Gloucester St; motel d $110-210, q $260, apt per week $805-1400; P 🖳 🛜 🕱) The place to go for great deals on a variety of motel rooms (from studios to two-bedroom units) and fully self-contained tourist flats sleeping up to six (good for groups and not much more expensive than a hostel). Stonehurst is central, modern and superbly equipped, and there's also backpacker accommodation (see p225).

Airport Gateway Motor Lodge (off Map p215; ☎ 0800 242 8392, 03-358 7093; www.airportgateway.co.nz; 45 Roydvale Ave; d/q from $125/165; P 🖳 🛜) Handy for those early flights, this lodge has a variety of rooms with good facilities; airport pick-ups at no extra charge.

Colombo in the City (Map p216; ☎ 0800 265 662, 03-366 8775; www.motelcolombo.co.nz; 863 Colombo St; d $140-155, apt $165-240; P 🖳 🛜) has attractive units that are luxuriously equipped (Sky TV, CD players, double glazing, spa baths). Next door, **CentrePoint on Colombo** (Map p216; ☎ 0800 859 000, 03-377 0859; www.centrepointoncolombo.co.nz; 859 Colombo St; d $145-165, apt $175-290; P 🖳 🛜) is a lookalike with all the same supercomfortable facilities, and the bonus of friendly Kiwi-Japanese management. Cathedral Sq is just 500m away and both motels are near good ethnic restaurants.

Also recommended is the **Focus Motel** (Map p216; ☎ 03-943 0800; www.focusmotel.com; 344 Durham St N; d $140-350; P 🖳 🛜), a sleek, centrally located new opening with big-screen TVs and supermodern decor.

SEASIDE AT SUMNER

Just 12km southeast of Christchurch by bus 3, the beachy suburb of Sumner is a relaxing place to stay. Commute to central Christchurch for sightseeing and return to Sumner for good restaurants and a cinema at night.

Marine Bar & Backpackers (Map p215; ☎ 03-326 6609; www.themarine.co.nz; 26 Nayland St; dm/s/d $25/35/55, s/d with bathroom $45/65, all incl breakfast; P 🖵 🛜) A welcoming, social place with top-notch facilities. Some doubles open onto a large upstairs balcony. Downstairs is a bar with pool tables and a sunny outdoor area.

Sumner Bay Motel and Apartments (Map p215; ☎ 0800 496 949, 03-326 5969; www.sumnermotel. co.nz; 26 Marriner St; d $155-205; P 🛜) Studios and one- and two-bedroom units all have balcony or courtyard, quality furnishings and Sky TV and DVD players. Bikes and surfboards can be rented.

Cornershop Bistro (Map p215; ☎ 03-326 6720; 32 Nayland St; brunch $10-17, dinner mains $22-27; 🕙 9.30am-late Wed-Fri, from 8.30am Sat & Sun) Superior French-style bistro that never forgets it's in a relaxed beachside suburb. Spend longer than you planned to lingering over brunch.

Tart Café & Deli (Map p215; ☎ 03-326 7111; 26 Marriner St; brunch $10-15; 🕙 7.30am-5pm Mon-Fri, 8.30am-6pm Sat & Sun) Bright and airy Cape Cod–style decor combines with superior cafe fare including bagels, eggs lots of ways, and just maybe the South Island's biggest and best sausage rolls.

Club Bazaar (Map p215; ☎ 03-326 6155; 15 Wakefield St; pizza $11-30; 🕙 3pm-late, from noon Sun, closed Tue) Surf-themed pizza 'n' pasta bar with tables made from retro longboards. And yes, it does have Hawaiian pizza.

Top End

Hambledon (Map p216; ☎ 03-379 0723; www.hambledon. co.nz; 103 Bealey Ave; ste $250-295, apt $380; P 🖵 🛜) This sumptuous antique-furnished heritage mansion has elegantly old-fashioned en-suite rooms (some with four-poster beds) that will take your mind off modern-day worries. Complimentary beer and wine may also help achieve that aim. The larger Camellia Apartment is wonderfully self-contained with a private garden, a sunny kitchen, and lots of interesting books.

George (Map p216; ☎ 0800 100 220, 03-379 4560; www.thegeorge.com; 50 Park Tce; r from $350-620; P 🖵 🛜) The George has 53 handsomely decorated rooms and suites on the fringe of Christchurch's sweeping Hagley Park. Discreet staff attend to every whim, there are two excellent restaurants, and ritzy features including plasma TVs, luxury toiletries and glossy magazines.

EATING

The variety of Christchurch's dining options has increased in recent years. There's a good array of ethnic eateries along Colombo St north of Cathedral Sq from Kilmore to Salisbury Sts, and High St and the nearby Lichfield Lanes feature good cafes. Along the 'Strip' on the eastern side of Oxford Tce between Hereford and Cashel Sts, restaurants with outdoor tables are a good place to tuck into various shared tapas platters, steak and seafood.

Restaurants

Tatsumi Kitchen & Pub (Map p216; ☎ 03-366 1038; Chancery Lane, 100 Gloucester St; small plates $8-13, mains $14-18; 🕙 11.30am-2.30pm & 6pm-late Thu-Tue) Grab a table, or prop yourself at the bar with a handle of draught Asahi beer and choose from an almost-too-big selection of Japanese snacks and small plates. The sushi and sashimi is supremely fresh, and there's a tad more innovation – soft shell crabs or fish carpaccio anyone? – than your usual Japanese eatery. Lunch specials ($15) are particularly good value.

Mum's (Map p216; ☎ 03-365 2211; cnr Colombo & Gloucester Sts; mains $10-20; 🕙 11am-11pm) No-nonsense food just like Mum used to make. That's if you grew up in Seoul or Tokyo anyway. More than a few Japanese and Korean language students regularly co-opt Mum's as their tasty home-away-from-home, and the sushi, sashimi and bowls of *ramen* noodles remain authentic.

our pick Bodhi Tree (Map p216; ☎ 03-377 6808; 808 Colombo St; dishes $11-19; 🕙 6-10pm Tue-Sun; V) Christchurch's only Burmese restaurant is also one of the city's best eateries. Don't come expecting bold flavours from neighbouring Thailand, but look forward to subtle food crafted from exceptionally fresh ingredients.

Standout dishes include the *le pet thoke* (pickled tea leaf salad) and the *ciandi thoke* (grilled eggplant). Meat and seafood also feature. Dishes are entrée-sized so drum up a group and sample lots of different flavours. Bookings are essential.

Memphis Belle (Map p216; ☎ 03-389 4590; 391 Worcester St, Linwood; pizza $15-24; ✌ 5-9.30pm Tue-Thu & Sun, to 11pm Fri & Sat) The shortish trek from central Christchurch is definitely worth it for the city's best pizza. Look forward to retro furniture and thin-crust savoury marvels that put to shame the international chains. Cash only and bookings are recommended.

Bicycle Thief (Map p216; ☎ 03-379 2264; 21 Latimer Sq; mains $15-30; ✌ 8am-late Mon-Fri, from 5pm Sat) Tom Waits on the stereo, a corner spot overlooking leafy Latimer Sq, and an excellent wine and beer list. What more could you want? How about great thin-crust pizzas and lovingly prepared rustic Italian cuisine? Cafe, bar or restaurant? You choose.

Nobanno (Map p216; ☎ 03-943 1616; cnr Armagh & Colombo Sts; mains $17-24; ✌ 11.30am-2.30pm & 5pm-late) NZ's only Bangladeshi restaurant dishes up subcontinental flavours that are slightly more subtle and subdued than the sometimes overt spiciness of Indian cuisine. The seafood – including prawn and fish curries – is especially good.

Indochine (Map p216; ☎ 03-365 7323; 209 Cambridge Tce; mains $20-32; ✌ 5pm-late Mon-Sat) Indochine's menu travels seamlessly from China to Thailand, and it's usual for the mains to also feature a brave pan-Asian fusion focus. The successful experimentation continues on the cocktail list, which includes the mighty Indochine Mojito, blending vanilla-infused rum and palm sugar.

Chinwag (Map p216; ☎ 03-365 7363; 161 High St; mains $20-34; ✌ 5pm-late) Designer Thai food comes to Christchurch with subtle spins on the traditional Thai cookbook. Start the night with a heady Wild Thang cocktail and graduate to zingy, zesty dishes including green curry with prawns and baby corn. Bookings recommended. There is another branch dubbed Chinwag II (☎ 03-366 4544) at 131 Victoria St, with the same opening hours.

Liquidity (Map p216; ☎ 03-365 6088; 128 Oxford Tce; mains $26-35; ✌ 10am-late) Liquidity's eclectic and stylish decor mixing chandeliers and warm timber tones combines with a diverse and proudly local menu. Free-range chicken with Israeli couscous and prime Canterbury lamb

are a cut above other players on 'the Strip'. Later at night good cocktails and plenty of European beer on tap fuels Liquidity's eventual metamorphosis into a bar. Eclectic beats kick off most nights from 10pm. The morning after it's a good riverside option for brunch ($13 to $20).

Cafes

Christchurch does cafes very, very well, and is undoubtedly a challenger to funky Wellington as the country's caffeine capital.

Avon Café & Bakery (Map p216; ☎ 03-366 0836; cnr Gloucester St & Cambridge Tce; snacks $6-10; ✌ 8am-4pm) Life is really quite simple. Sometimes all you need is a takeaway coffee beside the banks of the Avon River.

our pick Lunes (Map p216; ☎ 03-379 7221; 126 Lichfield St; coffee & cake $6-10; ✌ 8am-5pm) Just maybe the perfect Christchurch cafe: Lunes mixes cool jazz, a professorial approach to making coffee, and perfect midafternoon treats like baked New York cheesecake. Only open for six weeks when we dropped by, and already easily our favourite caffeine haunt in town.

Lotus Heart (Map p216; ☎ 03-379 0324; 595 Colombo St; mains $6-14; ✌ 8am-4pm Mon-Fri; Ⓥ) This organic, vegetarian eatery does curries, freshly squeezed juices and filled pita pockets. There's another more central branch above the i-SITE in Cathedral Sq with longer opening hours, which operates as a more spacious restaurant with tasty veg pizzas and casseroles (mains $8 to $16).

dose (Map p216; ☎ 03-374 9907; 90 Hereford St; mains $7-16; ✌ 7am-4pm Mon-Fri, 8am-3pm Sat) Cunningly mismatched furniture, bold local art, and high art-deco ceilings add up to a top place for wickedly strong coffee, superlative bagels, and quite probably Christchurch's best eggs Benedict.

NG Café (Map p216; ☎ 03-366 8683; 212 Madras St; snacks $8-12; ✌ 9am-4pm Mon-Fri, from 10am Sat) A former warehouse now incorporates an open-plan gallery and clothing boutique. Old meets new with a combination of iconic Kiwi snacks such as Anzac biscuits and relaxing world music beats. Soups and sandwiches tick the box marked 'comfort food'.

Under the Red Verandah (off Map p216; ☎ 03-381 1109; Cnr Tancred & Worcester Sts; breakfast $8-18, lunch $14-24; ✌ 7.30am-5pm Tue-Fri, 8.30am-4pm Sat & Sun) This lovely old villa is always packed with regulars, especially on bustling weekend mornings. Weekdays are slightly less busy, but still a good time for lots of organic and gluten-free baking, and mains including grilled haloumi on ciabatta and wonderfully robust oaty pancakes. The on-site deli and gallery space are further reasons to make the flat 30-minute walk from town.

Caffe Roma (Map p216; ☎ 03-379 3879; 176 Oxford Tce; mains $9-19; ⏱ 7am-4pm) Often voted Christchurch's best spot for breakfast, a relaxed attitude at Caffe Roma means goodies such as salmon with hash browns are available until 3.30pm every day.

C1 Espresso (Map p216; ☎ 03-379 1917; 150 High St; mains $10-15; ⏱ 7am-10pm Mon-Fri, 8.30am-10pm Sat, to 5.30pm Sun) C1 is a versatile spot with a global selection of teas and coffees, lots of local beers, and everything from robust breakfasts to bagels, wraps and burritos. Check out the selection of framed postcards and plan your next escape.

Joe's Garage (Map p216; ☎ 03-366 8317; 194 Hereford St; mains $10-15; ⏱ 7am-4pm) The pride of Queenstown comes to Christchurch and brings along good-value breakfasts and lunches.

Quick Eats

Food and coffee stands are set up daily in Cathedral Sq, or there are many ethnic flavours at the eclectic food stalls at the Arts Centre weekend market (p233).

Copenhagen Bakery & Café (Map p216; ☎ 03-379 3935; PricewaterhouseCoopers Centre, 119 Armagh St; pies $4; ⏱ 7am-5pm Mon-Fri) A regular winner in the Supreme Pie Awards – try the chicken satay – but also highly regarded by locals for tasty sandwiches and cakes.

Little Saigon (Map p216; ☎ 03-365 5889; 547 Colombo St; snacks $8-10; ⏱ 11.30am-3pm & 5-9pm) Cheap and cheerful with all your Vietnamese favourites, including excellent fresh spring rolls.

High to Hereford Food Court (Map p216; 250 High St & 150 Hereford St; mains $10-15; ⏱ 11am-5pm) Spotless food court that travels from Greece and India, to Cambodia, China and Italy.

Burgers & Beer Inc (Map p216; ☎ 03-366 3339; 178 High St; burgers $12.50; ⏱ 11am-late) Quirkily named gourmet burgers – try the Moroccan-spiced Woolly Sahara Sand Hopper – and lots of Kiwi brews.

Self-Catering

New World Supermarket (Map p216; South City Centre, Colombo St; ⏱ 7.30am-9pm).

Pak N Save Supermarket (Map p216; 297 Moorhouse Ave; ⏱ 8am-10pm)

DRINKING

Christchurch sees numerous restaurants and cafes packing away their dinner menus later in the evening and distributing cocktail, wine and beer lists. Riverside Oxford Tce ('the Strip') is popular with a younger crowd, but the most interesting spots for late-night shenanigans are in the Lichfield Lanes area around SOL ('South of Lichfield') Sq and Poplar St.

our pick Cartel (Map p216; ☎ 021 576 857; His Lordships Lane, SOL Sq; ⏱ 4pm-late) Cartel may look like the end result of a garage sale at your quirky uncle's house, but inside the retro interior is a wine list and cocktails to die for. In cooler months, pull up a bean bag in front of the toasty outdoor fire and look forward to music you thought only you knew about. There's only room for 30 punters, but that doesn't stop Cartel from hosting occasional DJs and live bands.

Dux de Lux (Map p216; ☎ 03-366 6919; cnr Hereford & Montreal Sts; ⏱ 10.30am-late) Quality microbrewed beers underpin this Christchurch icon. There's good food too, especially seafood and vegetarian, and live music features at least four nights a week. On weekend afternoons the garden bar is the place to be after exploring the Arts Centre market.

Indochine (Map p216; ☎ 03-365 7323; 209 Cambridge Tce; ⏱ 5pm-late Mon-Sat) If you can't score a dinner reservation at this popular eatery, swing by for one of its Asian-inspired cocktails.

Twisted Hop (Map p216; ☎ 03-962 3688; 6 Poplar St; ⏱ noon-late) If you think a bar specialising in English-style cask-conditioned beer is old-fashioned, think again. The architectural élan of the Twisted Hop is reinforcing Poplar St as Christchurch's coolest drinking hub. Mix in an excellent wine list, a tasty tapas menu and boutique beers from around NZ, and you've got a spot that could soon become your surrogate local bar.

Cleaners Only (Map p216; SOL Sq; ⏱ 5pm-late Wed-Sun) Good luck finding this place – it's tucked away in the corner of SOL Sq – but once inside you'll be in Christchurch's quirkiest bar. Apparently it used to be the lunchroom for cleaners at nearby warehouses, and a gloriously retro ambience is still intact, complete with comfy old sofas from your first student flat.

Thirsty Weta (Map p216; ☎ 03-372 9232; 56 Lichfield St; ⏱ 5pm-late Wed-Thu, 4pm-late Fri & Sat) Not so long ago, the NZ beer scene was as dull as dishwater. Now you can try more than 70 Kiwi microbrews at this slim space incongruously located in Christchurch's retail hub. If you're a bit peckish, have a gourmet pie, or order in from the Indian restaurant upstairs.

Le Plonk (Map p216; ☎ 03-377 7724; 211 Manchester St; ☺ 3pm-late Mon-Fri, 4pm-late Sat & Sun) This wine bar offers superior NZ vintages, lush leather lounges and live jazz on Thursdays from 8pm. A high class of bar snacks kicks off around $8.

Holy Grail (Map p216; ☎ 03-365 9816; 88 Worcester St; ☺ 11am-late) In a converted art-deco theatre, the raucous Holy Grail is about as subtle as an All Blacks fan's reaction to a bad refereeing decision. Watch live sport on a huge 10m screen from the indoor grandstand – if you're watching the Canterbury Crusaders rugby team, wearing red and black is recommended, but not mandatory.

Lyme (Map p216; ☎ 03-365 2393; 817 Colombo St; ☺ 4.30pm-late Wed-Sat) Good for a drink before or after diving into the restaurant strip along Colombo St, Lyme was named NZ's best new bar a few years back. The award-winning bartenders still make damn fine cocktails, and on Friday nights it's a good place to meet young professionals celebrating the end of the working week.

Bard on Avon (Map p216; ☎ 03-377 1493; cnr Gloucester St & Oxford Tce; ☺ 11am-late) The Bard has an authentic English ambience and plenty of traveller-friendly events such as the pub quiz (Sunday at 7pm) and live music from Thursday to Saturday. The pub is a few blocks from 'the Strip', and the better for it.

Tap Room (Map p216; ☎ 03-365 0547; 124 Oxford Tce; ☺ 11am-late) An always-busy option on 'the Strip' with Monteith's beers on tap and bands covering tunes you can sing along to.

Foam Bar (Map p216; ☎ 03-365 2926; 30 Bedford Row; ☺ 5pm-late Wed-Sat) Sophisticated back-alley bar, worth seeking out for its chilled-out crowd, art-bedecked walls and DJ-spun tunes. Expect occasional live bands and jam sessions.

ENTERTAINMENT

Christchurch's vigorous bar-club scene is centred on Lichfield St (usually from 10pm Wednesday to Saturday), while many Oxford Tce bars/restaurants transform with DJs and impromptu dance floors. Nightclub admission ranges from free to $15, though bigname DJ events can cost upwards of $40. Live music in pubs, bars and cafes is mostly free. See www.jagg.co.nz for listings. The weekly

Groove Guide lists local gigs, too; pick it up at **Real Groovy Records** (Map p216; ☎ 03-366-7140; 179 Tuam St; ☺ 9am-6pm Mon-Sat, 10am-5pm Sun) just off Sol Sq. Most gigs are also advertised at Real Groovy, and it is often the booking agent for local and international acts.

Christchurch is the hub of the South Island's performing-arts scene, with several excellent theatres. The major ticketing company is **Ticketek** (Map p216; ☎ 03-377 8899; http://premier.ticketek.co.nz), with outlets inside the Town Hall and the Isaac Theatre Royal.

Performing Arts
Town Hall (Map p216; ☎ 03-366 8899; 86 Kilmore St) The riverside town hall and its two main spaces (the 2500-seat Auditorium and the 1000-seat James Hay Theatre) are the main venues for local performing arts such as orchestras, choirs and bands. The venue's acoustics are excellent.

Isaac Theatre Royal (Map p216; ☎ 03-366 6326; www.isaactheatreroyal.co.nz; 145 Gloucester St) Another versatile stalwart of the local scene, with offers including the Royal New Zealand Ballet, the Canterbury Opera and occasional touring plays.

Court Theatre (Map p216; ☎ 0800 333 100, 03-963 0870; www.courttheatre.org.nz; 20 Worcester St) In the Arts Centre, this theatre performs everything from Beckett and Chekhov to popular NZ playwrights such as Roger Hall. The resident Court Jesters troupe stages its long-running improvised comedy show, *Scared Scriptless*, Friday and Saturday nights at 10pm ($15). Also popular is the theatre's regular Ghost Walk (see p224).

Cinemas
Movies are listed in the local newspapers. Adult tickets cost around $16, children $10, and most cinemas are cheaper on Tuesdays. From late July to mid-August, the NZ International Film Festival (www.nzff.telecom.co.nz) comes to town.

Arts Centre Cinemas (Map p216; ☎ 03-366 0167; www.artfilms.co.nz; Arts Centre, Worcester St) Comprises two venues (the Academy and Cloisters) at the Arts Centre.

Metro Gold Cinema (Map p216; ☎ 03-377 5705; 105 Worcester St) Another Arts Centre Cinemas branch, this one near ChristChurch Cathedral.

Other options:
Hoyts Moorhouse (Map p216; ☎ 0508 446 987; www.hoyts.co.nz; 392 Moorhouse Ave) For all the latest Hollywood blockbusters.

Regent on Worcester (Map p216; ☎ 0508 446 987; www.hoyts.co.nz; 94 Worcester St) Shows art-house and mainstream titles.

Rialto (Map p216; ☎ 03-379 9404; www.rialto.co.nz; cnr Moorhouse Ave & Durham St) Art-house central with plenty of foreign flicks and the occasional mini film festival.

Live Music

Dux de Lux (Map p216; ☎ 03-366 6919; www.thedux.co.nz; cnr Hereford & Montreal Sts; ☑ 10.30am-late) Invites ska, reggae, rock, pop and dub artists to cater to crowds at least four nights a week. On a sunny day the outdoor tables are a mass of raised glasses of the Dux's excellent micro-brewed beers.

Southern Blues Bar (Map p216; ☎ 03-365 1654; 198 Madras St; ☑ 7.30am-late) NZ's oldest blues venue is still going strong; gigs kick off nightly around 10.30pm. Expect a friendly crowd of musos, office workers and the confidently unfashionable.

Yellow Cross (Map p216; SOL Sq; ☑ noon-late) An eclectic live-music haven amid the largely manufactured beats of SOL Sq is a good thing. Wood-fired pizzas and Euro brews are the icing on the cake.

Bedford (Map p216; ☎ 03-374 9988; www.thebedford.co.nz; 46 Bedford Row; ☑ vary by event) The brick building dates back to 1903, but now the sprawling Bedford hosts a thoroughly modern mix of up-and-coming international bands and the best of Kiwi acts with a rocky tinge.

Goodbye Blue Monday (Map p216; 03-961 3353; www.goodbyebluemonday.co.nz; Poplar Lane; ☑ 5pm-late Mon-Sat) Tucked away in Poplar Lane, Goodbye Blue Monday's mismatched retro couches are a cool spot for a drink early in the evening, and then the ambience usually morphs to include live bands and DJ beats, often with an indie accent. It's the preferred venue of about-to-be-famous Kiwi bands. It's also the only place, *anywhere*, you'll find Bodgie Beer's organic Pilsner.

Al's Bar (Map p216; www.alsbar.co.nz; 33 Dundas St; ☑ 8pm-late Wed-Sat) Live music is definitely the hero at Al's Bar, with the cosy brick-lined space and excellent sound system drawing a diverse mix of local and international acts.

Nightclubs

Double Happy (Map p216; ☎ 03-374 6463; 182 Cashel St; ☑ 8pm-late Wed-Sun) The city's best bar-club hybrid with great cocktails, Euro beers on tap and an ever-changing diet of dub, house and soul. Perfect for chilled late-night/early-morning denizens.

Base (Map p216; ☎ 03-377 7149; www.thebase.co.nz; 92 Struthers Lane; ☑ from 9pm Thu-Sat) Down a slightly seedy side alley a few doors along from SOL Sq. Specialises in electro, house and trance. Admission is cheaper until midnight.

Ministry/Propaganda (Map p216; ☎ 03-379 2910; www.ministry.co.nz; 90 Lichfield St) Two venues in one big space combining an intimate lounge bar and an always-pumping club. House and drum and bass is the usual recipe, but the occasional metal night with live bands ambushes things.

Sport

AMI Stadium (Map p216; tickets ☎ 03-377 8899, http://premier.ticketek.co.nz; www.amistadium.co.nz; 30 Stevens St) This stadium hosts cricket internationals, but it's best known as Canterbury's rugby heartland. Watch the Crusaders in Super 14 action from February to May. The stadium got a whizzbang makeover for the 2011 Rugby World Cup.

Casino

Christchurch Casino (Map p216; ☎ 03-365 9999; www.christchurchcasino.co.nz; 30 Victoria St; ☑ 24hr)

SHOPPING

Colombo St, High St and the pedestrianised Cashel St are all crammed with credit-card-hungry places. Head to the funky southern end of High St (between Lichfield and St Asaph Sts) for the creative output of young NZ fashion designers, and in nearby Poplar St and His Lordship's Lane, design shops share the laneways with bars and restaurants. For a wider range of arts and crafts, visit the Arts Centre and the shops in the art galleries.

Arts Centre (Map p216; ☎ 03-363 2836; www.artscentre.org.nz; 2 Worcester St) Dozens of craft shops and art galleries selling pottery, jewellery, woollen goods and handmade toys. Visually Maori and Te Toi Mana are your best options for Maori art and design (see p219).

Arts Centre market (Map p216; ☑ 10am-4pm Sat & Sun) Every weekend the Arts Centre is host to a craft and produce market.

REAL Aotearoa (Map p216; ☎ 03-377 5418; www.realaotearoa.co.nz; 101 Cashel St) Eclectic Kiwi design from pottery to glassware.

Untouched World (Map p216; ☎ 03-962 6551; www.untouchedworld.com; 301 Montreal St) At the Arts Centre, Untouched World has quality NZ-made clothing. Clothes may be made of 'mountainsilk' (machine-washable fine merino wool) or 'merinomink' (a blend of merino wool and possum fur).

Ballantynes (Map p216; ☎ 03-379 7400; cnr Colombo & Cashel Sts) Venerable Christchurch department store selling men's and women's fashions, cosmetics, travel goods and speciality NZ gifts.

For camping gear, hiking boots and outdoor equipment, head to **Snowgum** (Map p216; ☎ 03-365 4336; 637 Colombo St) or **Mountain Designs** (Map p216; ☎ 03-377 8522; 654 Colombo St) near the intersection of Colombo and Lichfield Sts.

GETTING THERE & AWAY
Air
Christchurch airport (off Map p215; ☎ 03-358 5029; www.christchurchairport.co.nz) is the South Island's main international gateway. For details of international flights, see p393. The airport has excellent facilities, including currency exchange, ATMs, baggage storage (8am to 6.30pm), plus travel centres (☎ 03-353 7774) in both the domestic terminal (7.30am to 8pm) and the international terminal (open for all international flight arrivals). Departure tax on international flights is $25, with children under 12 exempt. Prices listed below are for one-way flights.

Air New Zealand (Map p216; ☎ 0800 737 000, 03-363 0600; www.airnz.co.nz; 549 Colombo St; 9am-5pm Mon-Fri, 9.30am-1pm Sat) also offers numerous direct domestic flights with connections to other centres. There are direct flights to and from Auckland ($59 to $239, 20 flights per day), Blenheim ($79 to $179, three daily), Dunedin ($59 to $169, eight daily), Hamilton ($109 to $259, three daily), Hokitika ($65 to $135, five daily), Invercargill ($79 to $189, eight daily), Napier ($99 to $229, two daily), Nelson ($89 to $219, eight daily), New Plymouth ($139 to $229, one daily), Palmerston North ($99 to $189, four daily), Queenstown ($59 to $199, five daily), Rotorua ($129 to $259, three daily), Tauranga ($99 to $239, one daily), Wanaka ($169 to $199, one daily) and Wellington ($49 to $1792, 15 daily). Check www.grabaseat.co.nz for last-minute deals.

Jetstar (☎ 0800 800 995; www.jetstar.com) offers direct flights to and from Auckland ($49 to $219, six daily), Queenstown ($59 to $189, one daily) and Wellington ($99 to $169, one daily).

Pacific Blue (☎ 0800 670 000; www.flypacificblue. com) flies to and from Auckland ($90 to $230, two daily) and Wellington ($60 to $180, two daily).

Bus
InterCity (Map p216; ☎ 03-365 1113; www.intercity.co.nz; 123 Worcester St; 7am-5.15pm Mon-Sat, to 5.30pm Sun) buses depart from Worcester St, between the cathedral and Manchester St. Northbound buses go twice daily to Kaikoura (from $14, 2¾ hours), Blenheim (from $24, five hours) and Picton (from $25, 5½ hours), with connections to Nelson (from $71, eight hours). One daily bus also goes southwest to Queenstown direct (from $49, eight hours). There are also services to Wanaka (from $79, seven hours) that involve a change in Tarras. Heading south, two buses run daily along the coast via the towns along SH1 to Dunedin (from $37, six hours), with connections via Gore to Invercargill (from $53, 9¾ hours) and Te Anau (from $59, 10½ hours).

Naked Bus (www.nakedbus.com) heads north to Picton and Nelson, south to Dunedin and southwest to Queenstown. Buses leave from opposite the Holy Grail pub at 88 Worcester St.

Shuttles run to Akaroa, Arthur's Pass, Dunedin, Greymouth, Hanmer Springs, Picton, Queenstown, Twizel, Wanaka, Westport and points in between; see the i-SITE (p214).

Train
Christchurch railway station (Map p215; ☎ 0800 872 467, 03-341 2588; Troup Dr, Addington; ticket office 6.30am-3.30pm Mon-Fri, to 3pm Sat & Sun) is serviced by a free shuttle that picks up from various accommodation; ring the i-SITE (p214) to request pick-up.

The *TranzCoastal* runs daily each way between Christchurch and Picton via Kaikoura and Blenheim, departing from Christchurch at 7am and arriving at Picton at 12.13pm; the standard adult one-way fare to Picton is $83, but fares can be discounted to $59.

The *TranzAlpine* has a daily route between Christchurch and Greymouth via Arthur's Pass (see p193); the standard adult one-way fare is $137, but fares can be discounted to $89. Ask about any current specials.

Contact **Tranz Scenic** (☎ 0800 872 467; www.tranzscenic.co.nz).

GETTING AROUND
To/From the Airport
The airport is 12km from the city centre.

Super Shuttle (☎ 0800 748 885; www.supershuttle.co.nz) operates 24 hours and charges $17 for one person between the city and the airport, plus $4 for each additional person. A cheaper alternative is the **Seven Dollar Bus** (8am-5pm; one-way $7), which runs every 20 minutes between the airport and Cathedral Sq.

The airport is serviced by the **City Flyer bus** (☎ 0800 733 287; www.redbus.co.nz; adult/child $7.50/4.50), which runs from Cathedral Sq between 5.30am and 11.30pm Monday to Friday and 7.30am to 11.30pm Saturday and Sunday (from the airport 35 minutes later). Pick up the red City Flyer timetable at the i-SITE (p214).

A taxi between the city centre and airport costs around $40 to $45.

Car & Motorcycle
HIRE

Major car- and campervan-rental companies all have offices in Christchurch, as do numerous smaller local companies. Operators with national networks often want cars to be returned from Christchurch to Auckland because most renters travel in the opposite direction, so special rates may apply on this northbound route. For reliable national rental companies, see p401.

Some smaller-scale companies:

Ace Rental Cars (off Map p215; ☎ 0800 202 029, 03-360 3270; www.acerentalcars.co.nz; 20 Abros Pl)

First Choice (Map p216; ☎ 0800 736 822, 03-365 9261; www.firstchoice.co.nz; 132 Kilmore St)

New Zealand Motorcycle Rentals & Tours (off Map p215; ☎ 03-348 1106; www.nzbike.com; 22 Lowther St) Also does guided motorbike tours.

Omega Rental Cars (Map p216; ☎ 0800 112 121, 03-377 4558; www.omegarentalcars.com; 20 Lichfield St)

Pegasus Rental Cars (Map p216; ☎ 0800 354 506, 03-365 1100; www.rentalcars.co.nz; 127 Peterborough St)

PURCHASE

Many vehicles are offered for sale on noticeboards at hostels, cafes and internet places. Check out **Backpackers Car Market** (Map p216; ☎ 03-377 3177; www.backpackerscarmarket.co.nz; 33 Battersea St; 9.30am-5pm), or the weekly **Canterbury Car Fair** (Map p215; ☎ 03-338 5525; Wrights Rd entrance; 9am-noon Sun) held at Addington Raceway. **Turners Auctions** (Map p215; ☎ 03-343 9850; www.turners.co.nz; 1 Detroit Place) buys and sells used cars by auction; vehicles priced under $7000 are auctioned at 6pm on Tuesday and Thursday.

Online see www.trademe.co.nz and www.autotrader.co.nz.

Public Transport

The Christchurch **bus network** (Metro; ☎ 03-366 8855; www.metroinfo.org.nz; 6.30am-10.30pm Mon-Sat, 9am-9pm Sun) is inexpensive and efficient. Most buses run from The Crossing (Map p216), with its pedestrian entrance on Colombo St opposite Ballantynes. The exchange has an information desk here; alternatively, get timetables from the i-SITE (p214). A cash fare to anywhere in the city costs $2.80, including one free transfer within two hours. Metrocards allow two-hour/full-day travel for $2.10/4.20, but the cards must be loaded up with a minimum of $10.

For information on the following two services, contact **Red Bus** (☎ 0800 733 287; www.redbus.co.nz). The big yellow **Central City Shuttle** (fare free; 7.30am-10.30pm Mon-Fri, 8am-10.30pm Sat, 10am-8pm Sun) is an inner-city service (as far north as Peterborough St, south to Moorhouse Ave) with about 20 pick-up points. The **After Midnight Express** (fare $6; midnight-4am Sat & Sun) operates hourly on five suburban routes, most of them departing Oxford Tce.

Taxi

Christchurch's main taxi companies:
Blue Star (☎ 0800 379 979)
First Direct (☎ 0800 505 555)
Gold Band (☎ 0800 379 5795)

AROUND CHRISTCHURCH

LYTTELTON
pop 3100

Southeast of Christchurch are the prominent Port Hills, which slope down to the city's port at Lyttelton Harbour. Christchurch's first European settlers landed here in 1850 to embark on their historic trek over the hills. With attractive heritage architecture and eclectic cafe-bars, it's now a popular weekend getaway and dining destination for in-the-know foodies. Lyttelton is still a working port, and the raffish charm of the old waterfront pubs contrasts with the gentrifying scene just up the hill along London St.

Regular ferries and boat cruises provide access to sheltered islands and across the water to sleepy Diamond Harbour. If you've got your own transport, the harbour road wends a scenic 15-minute route to pretty

Governors Bay with a couple of good spots for lunch.

The **Lyttelton visitor information centre** (☎ 03-328 9093; www.lytteltonharbour.co.nz; 20 Oxford St; ☺ 9am-5pm Sep-May, to 4pm Jun-Aug) has accommodation and transport information.

Sights

Lyttelton is linked to Christchurch via a **road tunnel**, but there's a more scenic (and 10km longer) route along the narrow **Summit Rd**, which has breathtaking city, hill and harbour views, and vistas of the Southern Alps; see the *Lyttelton Port Hills Drive* pamphlet ($1).

Lyttelton Museum (☎ 03-328 8972; Gladstone Quay; admission by donation; ☺ 2-4pm Tue, Thu, Sat & Sun) has interesting maritime exhibits such as wreck-recovered artefacts and ship models, plus Lyttelton memorabilia including a 19th-century pipe organ and an Antarctic gallery (both Scott and Shackleton used the port as a base).

The neogothic **Timeball Station** (☎ 03-328 7311; 2 Reserve Tce; adult/child/family $7/2/15; ☺ 10am-5.30pm), built in 1876, was where (for 58 years) a huge time ball was hoisted on a mast and then dropped at exactly 1pm, Greenwich Mean Time, allowing ships in the harbour to set their clocks and thereby accurately calculate longitude. The time ball is still dropped at 1pm on days when the station is open. Access requires a short, steep climb.

Tours

Black Cat (☎ 0800 436 574, 03-328 9078; www.blackcat.co.nz; 17 Norwich Quay; cruises adult/child $60/25; ☺ tour 1.30pm) operates two-hour Christchurch Wildlife Cruises on Lyttelton Harbour, where you may see rare Hector's dolphins, blue penguins and various seabirds. A free shuttle bus for participants leaves Cathedral Sq in Christchurch at 12.50pm. Black Cat also shuttles across to nearby **Quail Island** (adult/child $20/10; ☺ trips 10.20am & 12.20pm Dec-Mar, 12.20pm Apr & Sep-Nov, no sailings May-Aug), and to pretty Diamond Harbour (adult/child $10/5; 23 times daily).

Enquire at the visitor information centre about other ways to get active on the harbour, including kayaking and sailing.

Sleeping & Eating

A few B&Bs dot the surrounding hills; the visitor information centre can help with bookings.

Dockside Accommodation (☎ 03-325 5707; www.dockside.co.nz; 22 Sumner Rd; apt $80-120; 🖳 🛜) Three

homely self-contained apartments each sleep up to four. They're a short, easy walk from town, or you can stay put and enjoy the harbour views from your private deck. It's the kind of place that feels just like home.

Lyttelton Lounge (☎ 03-328 7114; 17 Oxford St; baked goods $4-6; ☺ 8am-4.30pm Mon-Sat, 9am-4.30pm Sun) Dub reggae, freshly baked muffins and supercharged coffee feature at this atmospheric wood-lined haven. Linger for a while before looking for treasures at the vintage and secondhand shops just down the hill.

Lyttelton Roasting Company (☎ 03-328 8096; 29 London St; mains $6-17; ☺ 7.30am-4.30pm Tue-Fri, from 8am Sat & Sun) The best coffee in town – and maybe in all of Canterbury – is roasted daily at this bohemian spot with incredibly high ceilings and an eclectic breakfast and lunch menu. Try the Armenian yoghurt cake as you linger for the regular Saturday afternoon live music.

our pick **Monster Yakitori** (☎ 03-328 9166; 29 London St; per 2 skewers $7-11; ☺ 5pm-late Wed-Sun) Classic cocktails and boutique Kiwi beers and wines provide the liquid sustenance for an extended bout of grazing and drinking at this quirky anime-themed yakitori bar. All the skewered goodies are grilled as you wait; our favourite is the ebi bacon – prawns wrapped in bacon with plum wasabi. DJs kick in most Saturday nights from 10pm.

Volcano Cafe (☎ 03-328 7077; 42 London St; mains $27-33; ☺ 5pm-late) The vaguely Mexican but exceedingly friendly Volcano is a festive, retro-style cafe serving seafood risotto, enchiladas and good curries and pastas. The attached Lava Bar has a cheaper bar menu.

West round the harbour, the **Governor's Bay Hotel** (☎ 03-329 9433; www.governorsbayhotel.co.nz; Main Rd, Governors Bay; mains $15-30; ☺ 11am-10pm) serves tasty burgers, fish and chips, and more innovative meals of chargrilled tuna or curry prawn laksa. Enjoy a beer on the cool veranda dotted with memoirs of the hotel's 140 years of history. Upstairs there is accommodation in simple but sunny rooms with shared bathrooms (doubles $100).

Across the road, **She Chocolat** (☎ 03-328 9285; www.shechocolat.com; 79 Main Rd, Governors Bay; mains $15-26; ☺ 10am-4pm Wed-Fri, to 5pm Sat & Sun) serves excellent brunches and lunches with an organic and new-age tinge. After kumara (sweet potato) oatcakes, make room for locally made Belgian chocolate and take in the harbour views.

Lyttelton's growing rep as a foodie destination is enhanced by the Saturday **farmers market** (www.lyttelton.net.nz; ☺ 10am-1pm Sat) held in the local school on Oxford St. Also check out **Ground** (☎ 03-328 7275; www.ground.co.nz; 44a London St; ☺ 9.30am-7.30pm Mon-Thu, to 8pm Fri & Sat, 10am-5pm Sun), ground zero for the best of Kiwi food, wine and beer. For a quick bite there's megasandwiches ($6.50) and an excellent brunch menu ($7 to $18). If you're staying the night in Lyttelton, it also does gourmet takeaway meals.

Drinking & Entertainment

Wunderbar (☎ 03-328 8818; www.wunderbar.co.nz; 19 London St; ☺ 5pm-late Mon-Fri, 1pm-late Sat & Sun) Wunderbar is a top spot to see NZ's more interesting acts, from raucous rock to late-night/early-morning dub. The funky decor alone is worth a trip to Lyttelton. Look for the sign on London St that says 'Sorry, nice people only' and head down the steps. Be nice.

Lava Bar (☎ 03-328 7077; 42 London St; ☺ 5pm-late) Flowing on from Volcano Cafe (naturally) and open for sociable boozing (and snacking) nightly. Has an outdoor terrace crammed with quirky artistic touches, which may seem only slightly quirky after a few drinks.

Harbour Light (☎ 03-328 8615; www.harbourlight. co.nz; 24 London St; admission $15-25) This wonderful old theatre (built in 1916) straddles old and new Lyttelton with regular live gigs showcasing jazz, Celtic and world music. Check the website for what's on; there's normally gigs around three nights a week. On show nights, drinks and food are served.

Getting There & Away

Buses 28 and 35 run from Christchurch to Lyttelton (25 minutes). From Lyttelton by car, you can continue around Lyttelton Harbour on to Akaroa. This winding route is longer and more scenic than the route via SH75 between Christchurch and Akaroa.

AKAROA & BANKS PENINSULA

Banks Peninsula and its hills were formed by two giant volcanic eruptions. Small harbours such as Le Bons, Pigeon and Little Akaloa Bays radiate out from the peninsula's centre, giving it a cogwheel shape. The historic town of Akaroa is a highlight, as is the absurdly beautiful drive along Summit Rd around the edge of the original crater.

Akaroa means 'Long Harbour' in Maori and is the site of the country's first French settlement; descendants of the original French settlers still reside here. Located 83km from Christchurch, it's a charming town that strives to recreate the feel of a French provincial village, down to the names of its streets (rues Lavaud, Balguerie, Jolie) and houses (Langlois-Eteveneaux), plus a few choice eateries. The Gallic pretence can sometimes be a tad forced, but it's still an undeniably picturesque spot, especially if you use it as a base for exploring the incredible landscapes and bays of the surrounding area.

If you're not in a hurry, it's worth spending a few leisurely days in the excellent budget accommodation that dots the outer bays of Banks Peninsula. Most accommodation will arrange pick-up in Akaroa after you arrive from Christchurch.

History

James Cook sighted the peninsula in 1770. Thinking it was an island he named it after the naturalist Sir Joseph Banks. The Ngai Tahu tribe, who occupied the peninsula at the time, were attacked at the fortified Onawe *pa* (Maori village) by the Ngati Toa chief Te Rauparaha in 1831 and their population was dramatically reduced.

In 1838, whaling captain Jean Langlois negotiated the purchase of Banks Peninsula from local Maori and returned to France to form a trading company. With French-government backing, 63 settlers headed for the peninsula in 1840. But only days before they arrived, panicked British officials sent their own warship to raise the flag at Akaroa, claiming British sovereignty under the Treaty of Waitangi. Had the settlers arrived two years earlier, the entire South Island could have become a French colony, and NZ's future may have been quite different.

The French did settle at Akaroa, but in 1849 their land claim was sold to the New Zealand Company, and in 1850 a large group of British settlers arrived. The heavily forested land was cleared and soon farming became the peninsula's main industry.

Information

Akaroa visitor information centre (Map p238; ☎ 03-304 8600; www.akaroa.com; 80 Rue Lavaud; ☺ 9am-5pm) Information on tours, activities and accommodation, including good farmstays.

Bank of New Zealand (Map p238; Rue Lavaud) With an ATM; opposite the visitor information centre.

Bon-E-Mail (Map p238; ☎ 03-304 7447; 41 Rue Lavaud; ☻ 9am-8pm; ☎) Internet access including wi-fi. There is also wi-fi at the cafe at Tree Crop Farm (see right).

Sights

The **Akaroa Museum** (Map p238; ☎ 03-304 1013; cnr Rues Lavaud & Balguerie; adult/child/family $4/1/8; ☻ 10.30am-4.30pm Oct-Apr, to 4pm May-Sep) is spread over several historic buildings, including the old courthouse, the tiny Custom House by Daly's Wharf, and one of NZ's oldest houses, Langlois-Eteveneaux. It has modest displays on the peninsula's once-significant Maori population, a courtroom diorama, a 20-minute audiovisual on peninsular history, and Akaroa community archives.

The quirky **Tree Crop Farm** (off Map p238; ☎ 03-304 7158; www.treecropfarm.com; admission $10; ☻ 10am-5pm in good weather only; ☎) is 1.8km off the main road through Akaroa (take Rue Grehan). This private wilderness garden is perfect for wandering on established tracks, relaxing on sheepskin-covered couches on the ramshackle veranda, or flicking through magazines and playing board games. A drink and snack is included in the admission price (try the berry juice). Rustic and romantic accommodation ($200 to $250) and a spa are also available here.

At Barrys Bay, on the western side of Akaroa Harbour (12km from Akaroa), is the enticing **Barrys Bay Cheese** (Map p237; ☎ 03-304 5809;

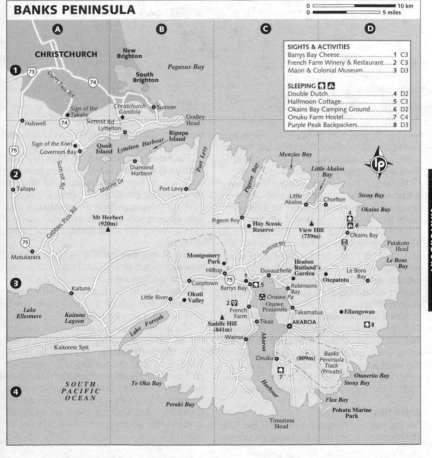

BANKS PENINSULA

0 _____ 10 km
0 _____ 5 miles

SIGHTS & ACTIVITIES
Barrys Bay Cheese..........................1 C3
French Farm Winery & Restaurant.....2 C3
Maori & Colonial Museum................3 D3

SLEEPING
Double Dutch................................4 D2
Halfmoon Cottage..........................5 C3
Okains Bay Camping Ground............6 D2
Onuku Farm Hostel........................7 C4
Purple Peak Backpackers.................8 D3

CHRISTCHURCH & CANTERBURY

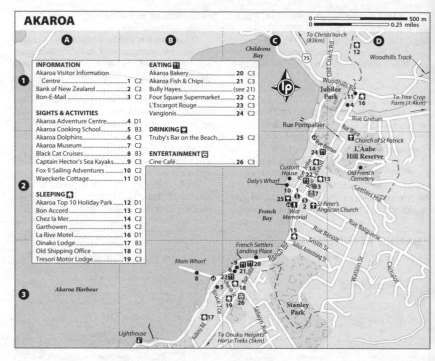

AKAROA

INFORMATION	
Akaroa Visitor Information	
Centre	1 C2
Bank of New Zealand	2 C2
Bon-E-Mail	3 C2

SIGHTS & ACTIVITIES	
Akaroa Adventure Centre	4 D1
Akaroa Cooking School	5 B3
Akaroa Dolphins	6 C3
Akaroa Museum	7 C2
Black Cat Cruises	8 B3
Captain Hector's Sea Kayaks	9 C3
Fox II Sailing Adventures	10 C2
Waeckerle Cottage	11 D1

SLEEPING	
Akaroa Top 10 Holiday Park	12 D1
Bon Accord	13 C2
Chez la Mer	14 C2
Garthowen	15 C2
La Rive Motel	16 D1
Oinako Lodge	17 B3
Old Shipping Office	18 C3
Tresori Motor Lodge	19 C3

EATING	
Akaroa Bakery	20 C3
Akaroa Fish & Chips	21 C3
Bully Hayes	(see 21)
Four Square Supermarket	22 C2
L'Escargot Rouge	23 C3
Vangionis	24 C2

DRINKING	
Truby's Bar on the Beach	25 C2

ENTERTAINMENT	
Cine Café	26 C3

www.barrysbaycheese.co.nz; 9am-5pm), where you can taste and purchase fine cheddar, havarti and gouda. Crackers and chutney are available for a spontaneous seaside snack.

Just west is the turn-off to **French Farm Winery & Restaurant** (Map p237; 03-304 5784; www.frenchfarm.co.nz; French Farm Valley Rd; platters $25-44, pizza $24-26; 10am-4pm), set in beautiful grounds with a south of France ambience. Sample French Farm's chardonnay and pinot noir ($1 per taste and all crafted from local grapes) or unwind with an antipasto platter or Akaroa salmon cakes. In summer (late October to Easter) wood-fired pizzas are served alfresco from midday.

Maori & Colonial Museum (Map p237; 03-304 8611; Okains Bay; adult/child $6/2; 10am-5pm) at Okains Bay, northeast of Akaroa, began as a private collection of indigenous and pioneer artefacts but went public 28 years ago. It features a reproduction Maori meeting house, a sacred 15th-century god stick and a war canoe.

Activities

See the visitor information centre if you like the sound of jetboating, kayaking or sailing on Akaroa Harbour, touring a working sheep farm or visiting a seal colony.

The **Banks Peninsula Track** (03-304 7612; www.bankstrack.co.nz; per person $240) is a 35km four-day walk across private farmland and around the dramatic coastline of Banks Peninsula; cost includes transport from Akaroa and hut accommodation. A two-day option ($160) covers the same ground at twice the speed.

The **Akaroa Walk** (0800 377 378, 03-962 3280; www.tuataratours.co.nz; per person $1486) is a leisurely upmarket 42km stroll across three days from Christchurch to Akaroa with good accommodation and lots of gourmet food. You'll only need to carry a daypack.

The *Akaroa – an Historic Walk* booklet ($9.50) details a walking tour starting at the 1876 **Waeckerle Cottage** (Map p238; Rue Lavaud) and finishing at the old Taylor's Emporium premises near the main wharf. The route takes in the old wooden buildings and churches that give Akaroa its character. Audio guides for self-guided walking tours are available at the visitor information centre ($10 per 90 minutes).

The **Akaroa Adventure Centre** (Map p238; ☎ 03-304 8709; Rue Lavaud; sea kayaks per hr/day $15/55, bikes per hr $15) rents out sea kayaks, bikes, golf clubs, fishing rods and windsurfing gear. For $39 (including bike hire) they'll transport you to the top of the volcanic crater around Banks Peninsula from where you can ride downhill all the way to Akaroa. Ask here about staying at Purple Peak Backpackers (p241).

Captain Hector's Sea Kayaks (Map p238; ☎ 03-304 7866; Beach Rd; www.akaroaseakayaks.co.nz; kayak hire per half-/full day $35/60) is another rental company that offers kayaks, canoes and rowboats for self-exploration.

The **Akaroa Cooking School** (Map p238; ☎ 021 166 3737; www.akaroacooking.co.nz; 81 Beach Rd; per person $175) runs popular 'Gourmet in a Day' sessions (10am to 3pm) on Fridays and Saturdays, and occasional specialised seafood and barbecue classes. All sessions end with tucking into your self-prepared feast.

Pohatu Plunge (☎ 03-304 8552; www.pohatu. co.nz) runs evening penguin-viewing tours (per adult/child $66/55). Spying the white-flippered penguin is best between August and January. Sea kayaking (adult/child $75/60) and 4WD nature tours (adult/child $90/50) are also available with the option of staying overnight in a secluded cottage ($60) in the Pohutu Nature Reserve. Book through the visitor information centre.

Surround yourself with the best of the spectacular scenery of Banks Peninsula at **Onuku Heights Horse Treks** (off Map p238; ☎ 03-304 7112; www.onuku-heights.co.nz; 166 Haylocks Rd; from $110; ⊙ Nov-May). Onuku Heights is 15 minutes from Akaroa. Follow the signs to Onuku Marae, continue uphill and turn left into Haylocks Rd.

On 2 Wheels (☎ 0800 662 943; www.on2wheels.co.nz; bike trip $80) runs cycling trips featuring 14km of glorious (mostly downhill...) riding, starting at the rim of an ancient volcano, and ending with a beachfront picnic and cold beer. Book at the Akaroa visitor information centre.

Tours

Eastern Bays Scenic Mail Run (☎ 03-304 8600; tour $50; ⊙ 9am Mon-Sat) This is a 120km, 4½-hour delivery service to remote parts of the peninsula, and visitors can travel along with the posties to visit isolated communities and bays (beachfront picnic included). The minibus departs the visitor information centre; bookings are essential as there are only eight seats available. See the visitor information centre for other tour options around Banks Peninsula.

To go spy Hector's dolphins and blue penguins, take a harbour cruise.

Akaroa Dolphins (Map p238; ☎ 0800 990 102, 03-304 7866; www.akaroadolphins.co.nz; 65 Beach Rd; adult/child $68/35; ⊙ departures 10.15am, 12.45pm & 3.15pm) Two-hour wildlife cruises, plus evening cruises and birdwatching trips by arrangement. Say hi to Murphy, wildlife-spotting dog extraordinaire for us.

Black Cat Cruises (Map p238; ☎ 03-304 7641; www. blackcat.co.nz; Main Wharf; adult/child $65/25; ⊙ departures 11am, 1.30pm & 3.40pm, more limited in winter) Two-hour cruises viewing wildlife, caves and cliffs.

Fox II Sailing Adventures (Map p238; ☎ 0800 369 7245; www.akaroafoxsail.co.nz; Daly's Wharf; ⊙ departures 10.30am & 1.30pm Dec–mid-May) History, scenery and wildlife on NZ's oldest gaff-rigged ketch.

Festivals & Events

French Fest Akaroa (www.frenchfest.co.nz) is a Gallic-inspired get-together held annually in late September/early October with an emphasis on food, wine, music and art. Don't miss (or stand on) *Le Race D'Escargots*, where sleek, highly trained snails negotiate a compact

---

SWIMMING WITH DOLPHINS

The waters around Akaroa are home to the world's smallest and rarest dolphin, the Hector's dolphin, found only in NZ waters. If viewing the dolphins on a harbour cruise (above) isn't enough, **Black Cat Cruises** (Map p238; ☎ 03-304 7641; www.blackcat.co.nz; Main Wharf; ⊙ 5 tours daily 6am-3.30pm Oct-April, 1 tour daily 11.30am May-Sep) can get you swimming alongside the dolphins (assuming it's not the calving season). Trips operate year-round and carry only 10 swimmers per trip, so book ahead. Wet suits and snorkelling gear are provided, plus hot showers back on dry land. Count on a 2½-hour outing including time in and on the water, and a $50 refund if you don't get to swim with the dolphins. Cruises have around a 98% success rate in seeing dolphins, and an 81% success rate in actually swimming with them, so it's pretty good odds. Costs are around $130/110 per adult/child for a cruise and swim, and $70/35 per adult/child for a cruise only.

course. There's also a French Waiter's Race later in the day.

Sleeping

Most Banks Peninsula accommodation is around Akaroa, but the outer bays are also blessed with excellent budget lodgings. Akaroa has some splurge-worthy, romantic B&B accommodation.

Akaroa

Akaroa Top 10 Holiday Park (Map p238; ☎ 0800 727 525, 03-304 7471; www.akaroa-holidaypark.co.nz; 96 Morgans Rd; sites $32-36, cabins & units $65-115; 🖳 🛜) On a terraced hillside above town and connected by a pathway to Woodhills Rd, this pleasant park has good harbour views and versatile options for every budget.

Chez la Mer (Map p238; ☎ 03-304 7024; www.chezlamer.co.nz; 50 Rue Lavaud; dm $25, d with/without bathroom $70/60; 🖳 🛜) Friendly backpackers with well-kept rooms and a shaded garden, complete with fish ponds, hammocks, barbecue and outdoor seating. Free bikes and fishing rods are available, and it's a TV-free zone.

Bon Accord (Map p238; ☎ 03-304 7782; www.bon-accord.co.nz; 57 Rue Lavaud; dm $27, d $60-70; 🖳 🛜) This colourful and quirky backpackers fills a compact 155-year-old house. Relax on the deck or in the two cosy lounges, or dive into the herb-filled garden to release your inner French chef. There's free bikes to get you exploring.

La Rive Motel (Map p238; ☎ 0800 247 651, 03-304 7651; www.larivemotel.co.nz; 1 Rue Lavaud; d $115-165; 🖳 🛜) Old-style motel with big rooms and good facilities; well priced considering each unit (studios, two- and three-bedroom options) is fully self-contained. New owners have recently given La Rive a makeover.

Tresori Motor Lodge (Map p238; ☎ 0800 273 747, 03-304 7500; www.tresori.co.nz; cnr Rue Jolie & Church St; d $170-200; 🖳 🛜) For designer-conscious lodgings treat yourself to the Tresori, with rich, colourful decor that's anything but bland.

Old Shipping Office (Map p238; ☎ 0800 695 2000; www.akaroavillageinn.co.nz; Church St; d $200) Self-contained apartment in a restored heritage building with an interesting past. Two bedrooms, a spacious shared lounge and a spa make the Old Shipping Office a good option for families or for two couples. No prizes for guessing the building's former incarnation.

Oinako Lodge (Map p238; ☎ 03-304 8787; www.oinako.co.nz; 99 Beach Rd; d incl breakfast $245-285; 🖳 🛜) This glorious timber mansion was built in 1865 for the then British magistrate. Almost 15 decades later, it's now a wonderfully upmarket bed and breakfast with six themed rooms, expansive bay windows with sea and garden views, and gourmet breakfasts you'll definitely want to linger over.

Garthowen (Map p238; ☎ 03-304 7419; www.garthowen.co.nz; 7 Beach Rd; s/d $265-295; 🖳 🛜) With two vintage Citroën cars, two friendly Jack Russell terriers and four supercomfortable en-suite rooms, (almost) everything comes in twos at this upscale B&B rebuilt in heritage style using recycled cedar. Breakfast on the deck comes with a side order of the best view in town.

Around Banks Peninsula

Okains Bay Camping Ground (Map p237; ☎ 03-304 8789; 1162 Okains Bay Rd; adult/child $8/5) Pine-tree-peppered ground right by the beach, with kitchen facilities and coin-operated hot showers. Pay your fees at the house at the camping ground's entrance. There's a small general store a few hundred metres down the road.

our pick Onuku Farm Hostel (Map p237; ☎ 03-304 7066; www.onukufarm.com; Onuku Rd; tent or van sites per person $15, dm/d from $28/66; 🖖 closed Jun-Aug; 🖳) An ecominded backpackers (with basic huts, tent sites and a comfy house) on a sheep farm near Onuku, 6km south of Akaroa. From November to March the owners organise swimming-with-dolphins tours ($100) and kayaking trips ($45) for guests, and will pick up from Akaroa. The same family has owned the farm since the 1860s, so you should trust them when they say there's some great walks on the 340-hectare spread.

Purple Peak Backpackers (Map p237; ☎ 03-420 0199; camping by donation, dm/d/tr $25/60/90; 🖳) This rustic surf lodge and backpackers has glorious sea views and a rugged out-of-the-way location. Accommodation is simple but clean, and during summer there's the occasional tasty seafood barbecue ($12 per person). Surfboards and gear are available for hire. Free shuttles are provided from Akaroa. See Darin at the Akaroa Adventure Centre (p239).

Halfmoon Cottage (Map p237; ☎ 03-304 5050; www.halfmoon.co.nz; Barrys Bay; dm/s/d $28/48/66; 🖖 often closed Jun-Sep) This marvellous cottage at Barrys Bay (12km from Akaroa) is a blissful place to spend a few days, lazing on the big verandas or in the hammocks dotting the lush gardens. The rooms – mostly doubles – are warmly decorated and there are free bikes and kayaks for guest use.

Double Dutch (Map p237; ☎ 03-304 7229; www.double-dutch.co.nz; 32 Chorlton Rd, Okains Bay; dm/s $28/53, d with/without bathroom $72/66; 🖳) Posh enough to be a B&B, but budget-friendly, this relaxed spot is perched in farmland on a secluded river estuary. There's a general store (and the beach) just a short walk away, but you're best to bring your own ingredients for the flash kitchen.

Eating & Drinking

L'Escargot Rouge (Map p238; ☎ 03-304 8774; 67 Beach Rd; meals $6-14; ⊙ from 8am) Tasty pies ($6), picnic fixings and French-accented breakfasts are the main attractions at the 'Red Snail'. Gourmet 'meals-to-go' ($8 to $14) are perfect for al-fresco harbourside dining.

Vangionis (Map p238; ☎ 03-308 7144; Rue Brittan; tapas $8-15, pizza $18-28; ⊙ 11am-late) Thin-crust pizzas, tapas, pasta and Canterbury beers and wines all feature at this Tuscan-style trattoria. Secure an outside table and while away the afternoon or evening. Takeaway pizzas are also available.

Bully Hayes (Map p238; ☎ 03-304 7533; 57 Beach Rd; lunch $13-20, dinner mains $22-30; ⊙ 8am-late) Named after a well-travelled American buccaneer, the menu at this sunny spot kicks off with Akaroa salmon before touching down in New York for gourmet burgers, Italy for pasta, and a lei-surely final stop in Spain for tapas. Monteith's beers and a good local wine list make it a worthwhile place to linger.

Truby's Bar on the Beach (Map p238; ☎ 03-308 7144; Rue Jolie; ⊙ 10am-late) An absolute water-front location teams with rustic outdoor seating to produce Akaroa's best place for a sundowner drink. Toasted ciabatta rolls ($9.50) and good coffee are other distractions earlier in the day.

Get yourself an all-day breakfast at **Akaroa Bakery** (Map p238; ☎ 03-304 7663; 51 Beach Rd; snacks & meals $5-15; ⊙ 7am-4pm), or takeaways from **Akaroa Fish & Chips** (Map p238; ☎ 03-304 7464; 59 Beach Rd; meals $6-10; ⊙ 10am-7pm Sun-Thu, 10.30am-8pm Fri & Sat).

The **Four Square supermarket** (Map p238; Rue Lavaud; ⊙ 9am-6pm Mon-Sat) has a good deli.

Entertainment

Cine Café (Map p238; ☎ 03-304 7678; www.cinecafe.co.nz; cnr Rue Jolie & Selwyn Ave; adult/child $15/13; ⊙ 2-10pm) Part cafe with excellent pastries and

soups, and part cinema showing art-house flicks.

Getting There & Away

The **Akaroa Shuttle** (☎ 0800 500 929; return $45) departs from outside the Christchurch i-SITE in Cathedral Sq at 8.30am and 2pm, returning from Akaroa at 10.30am, 3.35pm and 4.30pm. There's an extra departure from Christchurch at 4.30pm on a Friday. Bookings are recommended.

French Connection (☎ 0800 800 575; www.akaroabus.co.nz; return from $20) has a year-round daily departure from the Christchurch i-SITE at 8.45am, returning from Akaroa at 2.30pm and 4.30pm. During summer additional services may operate – ask at the Christchurch i-SITE.

Both companies run scenic tours from Christchurch exploring Banks Peninsula ($110).

NORTH CANTERBURY

From Christchurch, SH1 heads north for 57km through Woodend and Amberley to Waipara. From here SH1 continues north-east to Kaikoura, while SH7 branches due north to Hurunui through flat farming country and reaches Culverden. About 27km from Culverden is the turn-off from SH7 to Hanmer Springs, a thermal resort. The *Alpine Pacific Triangle Touring Guide* outlines things to see and do in this region. See also www.visithurunui.co.nz.

If you're a passionate wine buff or foodie, look for the North Canterbury Food & Wine Trail touring map at the i-SITE in Christchurch (p214). Online see www.foodandwinetrail.co.nz.

The **Brew Moon Garden Café & Brewery** (☎ 03-314 0830; 150 Ashworths Rd, Amberley; mains $15-26; ⊙ 10.30am-late Mon-Fri, 10am-late Sat & Sun) on SH75 in Amberley crafts four different beers; sample them all for $8.80. Our favourite is the gloriously hoppy Hophead IPA. Gourmet pizzas ($20 to $25) and meals including Akaroa salmon and steak sandwiches are also available.

A few kilometres up SH1, the scenic **Waipara Valley** is home to around 20 wineries. See www.waiparawines.co.nz. Sample a pinot noir or riesling and stop for lunch at one of the spectacular vineyard restaurants. **Waipara Springs** (☎ 03-314 6777; www.waiparasprings.co.nz; SH1, north of Waipara), **Pegasus Bay** (☎ 03-314 6869; www. pegasusbay.com; Stockgrove Rd, south of Waipara) and the **Mud House** (☎ 03-314 6900; www.themudhouse.co.nz; SH1, south of Waipara) are open daily for wine tasting and sales, and all have restaurant-cafes for a leisurely lunch.

The annual **Waipara Wine and Food Festival** (www.waiparawineandfood.co.nz) is held in early March.

Wine tours are available from several Christchurch-based companies (p224).

The **Pegasus Bay restaurant** (☎ 03-314 6869; www.pegasusbay.com; Stockgrove Rd, south of Waipara; mains $29-36, ☺ noon-4pm) has an old-world ambience set amid a lovely European-style garden. The menu takes advantage of superb local produce and recommends appropriate wines matches. Pegasus Bay is a regular contender for NZ's Best Winery Restaurant award.

Near the intersection with SH7 is **Waipara Sleepers** (☎ 03-314 6003; www.waiparasleepers.co.nz; 12 Glenmark Dr; unpowered/powered sites $20/25, dm $22, s $35-42, d from $48; 💻 🛜), where you can camp, bunk down in converted train carriages, and cook your own meals in the 'station house'. The local pub and general store are located close by.

HANMER SPRINGS
pop 750

Hanmer Springs, the main thermal resort on the South Island, is 10km off SH7. It's a pleasantly low-key spot to indulge in pampering in the hot pools and a flash new spa complex. There are a couple of good restaurants, and family-friendly activities include forest walks, minigolf, horse treks and jetboating.

Information

Bank of New Zealand (☺ 10am-2pm Mon-Fri) At the i-SITE. Another ATM at the Four Square supermarket.
Hanmer Springs Foodway (43 Amuri Ave; ☺ 10am-10pm) Internet access.
Hanmer Springs i-SITE (☎ 0800 733 426, 03-315 7128; www.visithanmersprings.co.nz, www.visithurunui. co.nz; 42 Amuri Ave; ☺ 10am-5pm) Books transport, accommodation and activities.
Powerhouse Café (p244) Wi-fi with a purchase.

Sights
THERMAL RESERVE

Visitors have been soaking in the waters of **Hanmer Springs Thermal Pools** (☎ 0800 442 663, 03-315 7511; www.hanmersprings.co.nz; entry on Jacks Pass Rd;

adult/child $18/7; ☺ 10am-9pm) for over 100 years. Local legend has it that the thermal springs are the fires of Tamatea that fell from the sky after an eruption of Mt Ngauruhoe on the North Island; Maoris call the springs Waitapu (Sacred Waters).

The hot spring water mixes with freshwater to produce pools of varying temperatures. In addition to mineral pools, there are landscaped rock pools, a freshwater 25m lap pool, private sauna/steam suites ($24 per half-hour), a restaurant, and a family activity area including a waterslide ($6). The adjacent **Hanmer Springs Spa** (☎ 0800 873 527, 03-315 0029; www.hanmerspa.co.nz; ☺ 10am-7pm) has massage and beauty treatments from $65.

MOLESWORTH STATION

Northeast of Hanmer Springs, Molesworth Station, at 180,500 hectares, is NZ's largest farm with the country's largest cattle herd (up to 10,000). Inquire at the i-SITE about independent visits to Molesworth, which is under DOC control. Visits are usually only possible when the Acheron Rd through the station is open from late December to early April, weather permitting. The drive from Hanmer Springs north to Blenheim on this narrow, unsealed backcountry road takes around six hours; note that the gates are only open from 7am to 7pm, and overnight camping (adult/child $6/1.50) is permitted in certain areas (no open fires allowed). Pick up the Department of Conservation *Molesworth Station* brochure from the Hanmer Springs i-SITE or download it from www.doc.govt.nz.

Trailways Safaris (☎ 03-315 7401; www.molesworth. co.nz; tours $195-665; ☺ Oct-May) offers 4WD tours of the station and the remote private land stretching north to St Arnaud. Day tours include a picnic lunch and there is a five-hour 'no frills' option.

Activities

Hanmer Springs Adventure Centre (☎ 03-315 7233; www.hanmeradventure.co.nz; 20 Conical Hill Rd; ☺ 9am-5pm) books activities, and rents mountain bikes (per hour/day from $19/45), fishing rods (per day $25) and ski and snowboard gear. Mountain biking maps ($2) are available at the i-SITE.

There are two skiing areas nearby. **Hanmer Springs Ski Field** is the closest, 17km (unsealed) from town, and **Mt Lyford Ski Field** is 60km away. They're cheaper than larger resorts (see

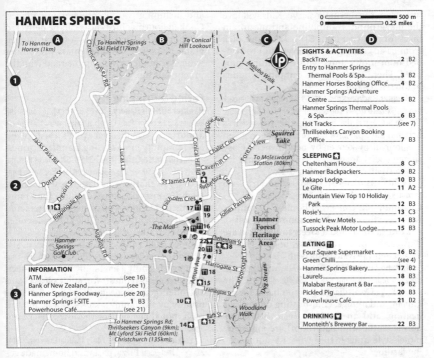

HANMER SPRINGS

SIGHTS & ACTIVITIES
BackTrax	**2** B2
Entry to Hanmer Springs Thermal Pools & Spa	**3** B2
Hanmer Horses Booking Office	**4** B2
Hanmer Springs Adventure Centre	**5** B2
Hanmer Springs Thermal Pools & Spa	**6** B3
Hot Tracks	(see 7)
Thrillseekers Canyon Booking Office	**7** B3

SLEEPING
Cheltenham House	**8** C3
Hanmer Backpackers	**9** B2
Kakapo Lodge	**10** B3
Le Gite	**11** A2
Mountain View Top 10 Holiday Park	**12** B3
Rosie's	**13** C3
Scenic View Motels	**14** B3
Tussock Peak Motor Lodge	**15** B3

EATING
Four Square Supermarket	**16** B2
Green Chilli	(see 4)
Hanmer Springs Bakery	**17** B2
Laurels	**18** B3
Malabar Restaurant & Bar	**19** B2
Pickled Pig	**20** B3
Powerhouse Café	**21** D2

DRINKING
Monteith's Brewery Bar	**22** B3

INFORMATION
ATM	(see 16)
Bank of New Zealand	(see 1)
Hanmer Springs Foodway	(see 20)
Hanmer Springs i-SITE	**1** B3
Powerhouse Café	(see 21)

p81). The Hanmer Springs Adventure Centre operates transport.

The *Hanmer Forest Recreation* pamphlet ($2) outlines short walks near town, mostly through picturesque forest. The easy **Woodland Walk** starts from Jollies Pass Rd, 1km from town, and goes through Douglas fir, poplar and redwood stands. It joins the **Majuba Walk** (1½ hours), which leads to Conical Hill Lookout and then back towards town. The i-SITE has details of longer tramps, including those in Lake Sumner Forest Park to the west.

Thrillseekers Canyon (☎ 03-315 7046; www.thrillseekerscanyon.co.nz; SH7) is the adrenaline centre of Hanmer Springs. Bungy off a 35m-high bridge ($145), jetboat the Waiau Gorge (adult/child $110/59) or go white-water rafting (Grade II to III) down the Waiau River (adult/child $145/75). Other activities include quad-biking (adult/child $99/90). Book at the Thrillseekers Canyon centre, next to the bridge where the Hanmer Springs turn-off meets SH7. Another **booking office** (☎ 03-315 7346; 37 Amuri Ave; ⏰ 10am-6pm) is in town.

Hanmer Horses (☎ 0800 873 546; www.hanmerhorses. co.nz; The Mall; 1hr rides adult/child $50/45, 2½hr treks $95)

leave from a forested setting 10 minutes from town on Rogerson Rd. Younger children can be led on a pony for 30 minutes ($20).

BackTrax (☎ 0800 422 258, 03-315 7073; www.backtrax.co.nz; cnr Jacks Pass & Conical Hill Rds; trips from $90) organises guided quad-bike trips up into the hills, and along (and across) the Hanmer River. The region is also popular for mountain biking – the Hanmer Springs Adventure Centre (see opposite) offers trail maps, advice and bike rental, and also does organised rides up over Jacks and Jollies Passes.

Hot Tracks (☎ 021 718 551; www.hottracks.co.nz; 37 Amuri Ave; adult/child from $45/35) takes all-terrain Hagglund vehicles into the forests and hills surrounding Hanmer. If you're feeling a bit gung-ho, then a self-drive option ($180) is also available.

Other activities include kayaking, scenic flights, fishing trips and claybird shooting.

Sleeping

Mountain View Top 10 Holiday Park (☎ 0800 904 545, 03-315 7113; www.mountainviewtop10.co.nz; Bath St; unpowered/powered sites $30/35, cabins & motels $65-140; 🖥 🛜) Family-friendly park a few minutes'

CHRISTCHURCH & CANTERBURY

walk from the thermal reserve. Kids will love the playground, trampoline and mountain bikes for rent (per hour $10). Take your pick from basic cabins (BYO everything) to two-bedroom motel units with everything supplied. There are two more camping grounds in town if it's full.

Hanmer Backpackers (☎ 03-315 7196; hanmerbackpackers@xtra.co.nz; 41 Conical Hill Rd; dm/s/d $27/55/58; 🖳 🛜) Centrally located, the township's original backpackers has recently been given a colourful makeover by new owners. Cosy shared social areas, free fruit, coffee and ice cream (!) all add further big ticks.

Le Gite (☎ 03-315 5111; www.legite.co.nz; 3 Devon St; dm $27, d with/without bathroom $70/60; 🖳 🛜) Charming old converted home a 10-minute walk from the centre. Large rooms (no bunks), relaxing gardens and a lovely lounge area are drawcards; for extra privacy, book a garden 'chalet' with private bathroom.

Kakapo Lodge (☎ 03-315 7472; ww.kakapolodge.co.nz; 14 Amuri Ave; dm $28, d $66-90; 🖳 🛜) The spartan YHA-affiliated Kakapo has a roomy kitchen and lounge, chill-busting underfloor heating, and an outdoor deck. Bunk-free dorms (some with bathroom) are joined by motel-style units ($100) with TV and cooking facilities.

Rosie's (☎ 03-315 7095; roxyrosie@clearnet.nz; 9 Cheltenham St; s $55-90, d $80-130, all incl breakfast) Rosie was originally from Australia, but she's now offering great Kiwi hospitality at this welcoming reader-recommended spot. Rooms offer either en-suite or shared facilities. Look forward to newly decorated bathrooms and a friendly cat.

Scenic View Motels (☎ 03-315 7419; www.hanmerscenicviews.co.nz; 10 Amuri Ave; d $130-200; 🖳 🛜) An attractive timber-and-stone complex with modern, colourful studios and two- and three-bedroom apartments. Mountain views come as standard.

Tussock Peak Motor Lodge (☎ 0800 8877 625, 03-315 5191; www.tussockpeak.co.nz; cnr Amuri Ave & Leamington St; d $145-200; 🛜) Tussock Peak has colourful decor that's an eclectic cut above other motels on Hanmer's main drag. The hardest part is choosing what kind of room: studio, one- or two-bedroom units, spas, courtyards or balconies.

Cheltenham House (☎ 03-315 7545; www.cheltenham.co.nz; 13 Cheltenham St; s $190-220, d $220-260; 🖳 🛜) Centrally located B&B with six snooze-inducing suites, all with bathroom, and including two in cosy garden cottages. Cooked gourmet breakfasts can be delivered to your room, and there's a billiard table, grand piano and complimentary pre-dinner wine. Avoid the crowds up the road with the private hot tub.

Eating & Drinking

Hanmer Springs Bakery (☎ 03-315 7714; 16 Conical Hill Rd; pies $5; 🕑 6am-4pm) Grab a takeaway coffee or a gourmet pie at this place that's a taste of old NZ in rapidly modernising Hanmer Springs.

Powerhouse Café (☎ 03-315 5252; 6 Jacks Pass Rd; meals $8.50-16.50; 🕑 8am-3pm, open late Thu-Sat in summer; 🛜) Recharge your batteries with a huge High Country breakfast, or linger for a more sophisticated lunch of whitebait fritters and Canterbury lamb. An organic fair-trade coffee is a good trade for wi-fi access.

Green Chilli (☎ 03-315 5188; The Mall; mains $14-20; 🕑 11.30am-2pm Tue-Fri & 4.30pm-9.30pm Tue-Sun) Run by a friendly Thai family, the cosy Green Chilli respects requests for 'spicy please', and also offers good-value lunch specials. Service – usually by the family's kids – can be hit and miss, but that's part of the low-key charm. Takeaways available.

Pickled Pig (☎ 03-315 7441; 47 Amuri Ave; pizza $14-22; 🕑 11am-9pm) Pizza, pasta and homemade gelato feature at this spot with an Italian accent. There's also a small deli for picnic fixings.

Malabar Restaurant & Bar (☎ 03-315 7745; 5 Conical Hill Rd; mains $28-32; 🕑 lunch 11am-3pm & dinner 5.30pm-late) This elegant eatery presents Asian cuisine from Beijing to Bangalore. Try the Malabar thali showcasing four different curries, or the mustard and star anise flavoured duck. A limited takeaway menu is available ($10 to $15).

Laurels (☎ 03-315 7788; 31 Amuri Ave; mains $30-35; 🕑 6pm-late) The most common answer to 'So, what's the most romantic place in town?', the Laurels works hard to showcase Waipara Valley wines and local produce including lamb and salmon. On cooler nights, beside the open fire is the place to be, while during summer, the action is alfresco in the delightful bricked courtyard.

Monteith's Brewery Bar (☎ 03-315 5133; 47 Amuri Ave; 🕑 11.30am-late Mon-Fri, from 9am Sat & Sun) The best (and most central) pub in town features lots of different craft beers and tasty tucker from bar snacks ($10 to $15) to full meals ($20 to $30). Platters ($44 to $52) are good value if you've just met some new friends in the hot pools across the road.

Four Square supermarket (Conical Hill Rd; 8.30am-7pm Mon-Sat, 9am-5.30pm Sun).

Getting There & Away

Hanmer Connection (☎ 0800 242 663; www.atsnz.com) runs from Hanmer Springs to Christchurch ($33, two daily).

East West Coach (☎ 0800 142 622, 03-789 6251) has a service that runs between Christchurch and Westport via the Lewis Pass and also diverts to Hanmer Springs.

LEWIS PASS HWY

At the northern end of the Southern Alps, the beautiful Lewis Pass Hwy (SH7) wiggles west from the Hanmer Springs turn-off to Lewis Pass, Maruia Springs and Springs Junction. The 907m-high **Lewis Pass** is not as steep or the forest as dense as Arthur's and Haast Passes, with mainly red and silver beech, and kowhai trees growing along river terraces.

The area has some interesting tramps; see the DOC pamphlet *Lake Sumner/Lewis Pass Recreation* ($1). Most tracks pass through beech forest with a backdrop of snowcapped mountains, lakes, and alpine tarns and rivers. The most popular tramps are around **Lake Sumner** in the Lake Sumner Forest Park and the **St James Walkway** (66km; three to five days) in the Lewis Pass National Reserve. Subalpine conditions apply; sign the intentions book at the start of the St James Walkway and at Windy Point for the Lake Sumner area before heading off.

Maruia Springs (☎ 03-523 8840; www.maruiasprings. co.nz; SH7; d $179-199, f $259;) is a small thermal resort on the banks of the Maruia River, 69km from the Hanmer turn-off. It has units (accommodation includes admission to the pools), a cafe-bar and a Japanese restaurant. In the **thermal pools** (adult/child/family $18/8/45; 8am-8.30pm) water is pumped into a gender-segregated traditional Japanese bathhouse and outdoor rock pools. It's a magical setting during a winter snowfall, but mind the sandflies in summer. Massages (per 30/50 minutes $45/65) and private spa houses (per person for 45 minutes $25) are available. Check the website for spa and accommodation special deals.

SH7 continues to **Springs Junction**, where the Shenandoah Hwy (SH65) branches north to meet SH6 near Murchison, while SH7 continues west to Reefton and down to Greymouth. Springs Junction has a petrol station and cafe.

CENTRAL CANTERBURY

Two hours west from Christchurch on SH73 is Arthur's Pass National Park. The trans-island crossing from Christchurch to Greymouth over Arthur's Pass is covered by buses and the *TranzAlpine* train (see p193).

Nowhere else in NZ does the coast rise to the mountains so quickly. From Christchurch the road traverses the Canterbury Plains and then escalates rapidly into the Porter Heights and Craigieburn skiing areas before following the Waimakariri and Bealey Rivers and Lakes Pearson and Grasmere to Arthur's Pass. Southwest of Christchurch (reached by SH73 and SH77) is the Mt Hutt ski resort and Methven.

CRAIGIEBURN FOREST PARK

Accessed from SH73, this forest park is 110km northwest of Christchurch and 42km south of Arthur's Pass. The park has many walking tracks, with longer tramps possible in the valleys west of the Craigieburn Range; see the DOC pamphlet *Craigieburn Forest Park: Day Walks* ($1). The surrounding country is also suitable for skiing and rock climbing. Dominating the vegetation is beech, tussock, totara and turpentine scrub, and even a few patches of South Island edelweiss (*Leucogenes grandiceps*).

Craigieburn has a rise of 503m so is one of NZ's best skiing areas. Its wild-country slopes suit the advanced skier.

Between the entrance to the forest park and the Broken River bridge to the south is **Cave Stream Scenic Reserve**, with a 594m-long cave with a small waterfall at one end. Take all the necessary precautions (two light sources per person etc) if doing the one-hour walk through the pitch-black cave. For details, get the DOC brochure *Cave Stream Scenic Reserve* (50c). The reserve is in the **Castle Hill area** with prominent limestone outcrops loved by rock climbers and boulderers. Scenes from the *Lord of the Rings* trilogy and *Chronicles of Narnia: The Lion, the Witch and the Wardrobe* were filmed in the area.

Sleeping & Eating

Smylie's Accommodation (☎ 03-318 4740; www.smylies. co.nz; Main Rd, Springfield; dm/s/d $26/43/58;) Welcoming YHA-associated hostel in the town of Springfield, around 30km southeast of

Craigieburn. Run by a Dutch-Japanese family, there is a popular Japanese bath, a *kotatsu* (foot warmer) and some futon-equipped rooms. A handful of self-contained motel units ($85 to $120) and a three-bedroom cottage ($180) are also available. In winter, packages including ski-equipment rental and ski-field transport are available. Nearby year-round activities include jetboating, rock climbing, mountain biking and horse trekking.

Flock Hill Lodge (☎ 03-318 8196; www.flockhill.co.nz; SH73; dm/d $30/135; ▣ ☏) High-country sheep station 44km east of Arthur's Pass, adjacent to Lake Pearson and the Craigieburn Forest Park. Backpackers can stay in rustic shearers' quarters, while large groups can opt for two-bedroom motel units or large cottages with kitchenette. After fishing, exploring, horse riding or mountain biking, recharge in the cosy bar-restaurant.

Bealey Hotel (☎ 03-318 9277; www.bealeyhotel. co.nz; s/d without bathroom $60/80, units $140-170; ▣) Just 12km east of Arthur's Pass, tiny Bealey is famous for a hoax by the local pub owner in 1993. He reckoned he'd seen a real live moa, hence the bogus Big Bird statue standing on a rocky outcrop. There are self-contained motel units and the budget Moa Lodge with eight double rooms. Enjoy expansive alpine views from the Mad Moa restaurant.

Wilderness Lodge (☎ 03-318 9246; www.wilderness lodge.co.nz; SH73; s $490-640, d $780-980, all incl breakfast & dinner; ▣) Luxurious lodge on a mountain-beech-speckled sheep station (2400 hectares worth), 16km east of Arthur's Pass. Alpine views and the world's longest driveway produce an absolute middle-of-nowhere atmosphere, and standalone studios with private spa baths feel even more remote. Soft adventure including walking, birdwatching and canoeing is on tap.

Original Sheffield Pie Shop (☎ 03-318 3876; Main Rd, Sheffield; pies $4-5; ☽ 11am-6pm) This roadside bakery in the quiet Canterbury Plains hamlet of Sheffield turns out some of NZ's best pies.

ARTHUR'S PASS
pop 62

Arthur's Pass village is 4km from the pass of the same name and is NZ's highest-altitude settlement. The 924m pass was used by Maoris to reach Westland, but its European discovery was made by Arthur Dobson in 1864, when the Westland gold rush created the need for a crossing over the Southern Alps from Christchurch. A coach road was completed within a year, but later on the coal and timber trade demanded a railway, duly completed in 1923.

The town is a handy base for tramps, climbs, views and wintertime skiing in Arthur's Pass National Park.

Information

DOC Arthur's Pass visitor information centre (☎ 03-318 9211; www.apinfo.co.nz; arthurspassvc@doc.govt.nz; SH73; ☽ 8am-5pm) has information on all park tramps, including route guides for longer hut-lined tramps. It doesn't make onward bookings or reservations, but can help with local accommodation and transport information. The centre screens a 17-minute video (adult/child $1/free) on the history of Arthur's Pass and has excellent displays – check out the 1888 Cobb & Co coach.

Purchase detailed topographical maps ($9) and hire mandatory locator beacons ($35) from DOC. DOC also advises on the park's often savagely changeable weather. Check conditions here and fill out an intentions card before venturing out. Sign in again after returning to avoid a search party being organised.

The Arthur's Pass Store has internet access. There is no ATM in Arthur's Pass.

Online see www.arthurspass.com. For specific information on weather conditions in the mountains see www.softrock.co.nz.

Sights & Activities

Near DOC is the small interfaith **chapel**, with wonderful views.

Day tramps offer 360-degree views of snow-capped peaks, many of them over 2000m; the highest is Mt Murchison (2400m). There are huts on the tramping tracks and several areas suitable for camping. Tramping is best in the drier months (January to April). The leaflet *Walks in Arthur's Pass National Park* ($2) details walks to scenic places including **Devils Punchbowl Waterfall** (one hour return), **Temple Basin** (three hours return) and **Avalanche Peak** (six to eight hours return). The pleasant **Dobson Nature Walk** (30 minutes return) is best from November to February when the alpine flowers are blooming. Recommended for fit trampers is the **Bealey Spur Track** (four to six hours return) with expansive views of the Waimakariri River valley and surrounding mountains. Longer tramps with superb alpine backdrops include

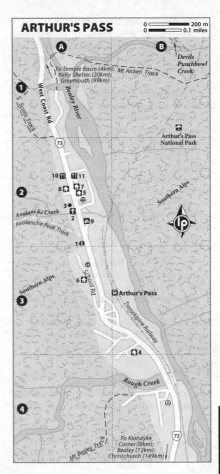

the **Goat Pass Track** (two days), and the longer and more difficult **Harman Pass** and **Harpers Pass Tracks**. These tracks require previous tramping experience as flooding can make the rivers dangerous and the weather is extremely changeable; ask DOC first.

Home in the Hills (☎ 027 451 1550; www.homeinthe hills.co.nz) offers short alpine encounters (three to five hours, $100), guided nature walks and birdwatching (two to three hours, $80), and longer personalised mountain and bush experiences.

There's also skiing at Temple Basin; see p82.

Sleeping & Eating
Camp within Arthur's Pass township at the basic **public shelter** (adult/child $6/3), opposite DOC, where there's stream water, a sink, tables and toilets. Camping is free at **Klondyke Corner**, 8km south of Arthur's Pass, and **Kelly Shelter**, 20km to the northwest; both have toilets and the water must be boiled before drinking.

Mountain House YHA Backpackers & Cottages (☎ 03-318 9258; www.trampers.co.nz; SH73; dm $27, s/d/tr/q $73/76/93/116, cottage sleeping up to 10 from $220; 🖳 🛜) has excellent dorms and private rooms on one side of the highway, and older, but still comfortable rooms across the road in what was one of NZ's earliest youth hostels. The owner is a wealth of information on local activities, and also provides transport to trailheads (p248). Self-contained cottages with cosy open fires are also available. Bookings recommended from November to April. You can sometimes camp ($20 per person) near the cottages, but you'll need to phone ahead to check availability first.

In the southern part of town, **Arthur's Pass Alpine Motel** (☎ 03-318 9233; www.apam.co.nz; SH73; d $115-135; 🖳 🛜) has simple but comfortable motel units, some recently refurbished, and with new beds. If you're snowed in there's a good DVD library and Freeview satellite TV.

Centrally located, the **Arthur's Pass Village Motel** (☎ 021 131 0616; www.apmotel.co.nz; SH73; d $145) has two luxury units with cosy leather furniture and warm, natural colours. Booking ahead from November to April is highly recommended.

The **Wobbly Kea** (☎ 03-318 9101; SH73; meals $15-24; ⏱ 9am-10.30pm Sun-Thu, to late Fri & Sat) is a friendly cafe-bar serving steaks, pasta and pizza. Takeaway pizza ($26) is also available. Breakfast at the Wobbly Kea ($13 to $19) is also a local tradition.

CHRISTCHURCH & CANTERBURY

The **Arthur's Pass Store** (☎ 03-318 9235; SH73; ☼ 7am-7pm; ▯) sells sandwiches, pies and good breakfasts. Limited groceries and petrol are very expensive; fill up in Christchurch or Greymouth.

Getting There & Around

Arthur's Pass sees buses travelling between Christchurch ($25 to $36) and Greymouth ($26); both **Atomic Shuttles** (☎ 03-349 0697; www.atomictravel.co.nz) and **West Coast Shuttle** (☎ 027 492 7488, 03-768 0028; www.westcoastshuttle.co.nz) stop here. Bus tickets are sold at the Arthur's Pass Store. In Christchurch, both companies depart from Cathderal Sq.

The *TranzAlpine* train operated by **Tranz Scenic** (☎ 0800 872 467; www.tranzscenic.co.nz) runs between Christchurch and Greymouth via Arthur's Pass. See the boxed text, p193.

The road over the pass was once winding and very steep, but the spectacular Otira viaduct has removed many of the treacherous hairpin bends.

Mountain House Shuttle (☎ 027 419 2354, 03-318 9258), based at Mountain House YHA Backpackers (p248), provides transport to various trailheads. See the Trampers Shuttle tab on www.trampers.co.nz for costs.

METHVEN

pop 1140

Methven is busiest in winter, when it fills up with snow-sports fans heading to nearby Mt Hutt. In summer, Methven town is a laid-back option with quieter (and usually cheaper) accommodation than elsewhere in the country, and a 'what shall I do today?' range of warm-weather activities including ballooning, tramping, fishing and skydiving.

Information

Bank of New Zealand (Main St) With ATM.
Medical centre (☎ 03-302 8105; Main St)
Methven i-SITE (☎ 03-302 8955; www.methveninfo. co.nz, www.amazingspace.co.nz; 160 Main St; ☼ 8am-6pm daily May-Oct, 9am-5pm Mon-Fri, 11am-4pm Sat & Sun Nov-Apr; ▯) Books accommodation, skiing packages, transport and activities. Internet available.
PC House (McMillan St; ☼ 11am-5pm Mon-Tue, to 6pm Wed-Sat) For internet access. There is also paid wi-fi at Cafe 131 (p250).

Activities

Nearby **Mount Hutt** (see p81) offers five months of skiing (June to October, weather permitting), often the longest ski season of any resort in NZ.

For mountain bikes, and ski rental and advice, see **Big Al's Snow Sports** (☎ 03-302 8003; www.bigals.co.nz; cnr Main St & Forest Dr; mountain bikes per hr/day $12/39).

Methven Heliskiing (☎ 03-302 8108; www.methven heliski.co.nz, www.heliskiing.co.nz; Main St; five-run day trips $525; ☼ May-Oct) offers trips including guide service, safety equipment and lunch. **Black Diamond Safaris** (☎ 03-302 1884; www.blackdiamond safaris.co.nz) can take you to uncrowded club ski fields by 4WD. Prices start at $150 for 4WD transport only, while $270 gets you transport, a lift pass, guiding and lunch.

Nearby Pudding Hill is a skydiving centre. **Skydiving NZ** (☎ 03-302 9143; www.skydivingnz.com; Pudding Hill Airfield) offers tandem jumps from 3600m ($369), and the **NZ Skydiving School** (☎ 03-302 9143; www.nzskydivingschool.com) has introductory courses starting at $395.

Aoraki Balloon Safaris (☎ 0800 256 837, 03-302 8172; www.nzballooning.co.nz; flights $385) offers flights that include snowcapped peaks and a champagne breakfast.

The **Mount Hutt Forest** is predominantly mountain beech; it's 14km west of Methven. Adjoining it are the **Awa Awa Rata Reserve** and the **Pudding Hill Scenic Reserve**. There are two access roads: Pudding Hill Rd leads to foot access for Pudding Hill Stream, and McLennan's Bush Rd leads to both reserves. There are many walking trails, including the water-crossing **Pudding Hill Stream Route** (two hours).

There's a good, easy walk through farmland and the impressive **Rakaia Gorge** (three to four hours return), beginning at the car park just south of the bridge on SH77. There are good picnic spots around the bridge. **Rakaia Gorge Alpine Jet** (☎ 03-318 6574; www.rivertours.co.nz; tour $68) and **Rakaia Gorge Scenic Jet** (☎ 03-318 6515; tour $65) both do 40-minute jetboat trips through the gorge.

Terrace Downs (☎ 03-318 6943; www.terracedowns. co.nz; SH72; green fees $140, club hire $45), 30km from Methven near Windwhistle, is a 'high-country resort' with a world-class 18-hole golf course. Take your pick from three restaurants of increasing sophistication, or escape the rigours of life on the road in Terrace Downs' recently opened spa (open 10am to 6pm Wednesday to Sunday).

Ask at the i-SITE about horse riding, mountain biking, fishing, scenic helicopter flights and farm tours.

METHVEN

Sleeping

Some accommodation is closed in summer, but the following are open year-round with lower prices often available outside the ski season. During the ski season, it pays to book well ahead, especially for budget accommodation.

our pick Alpernhorn Chalet (☎ 03-302 8779; www. alpenhorn.co.nz; 44 Allen St; dm $25, d $60-85; 🖳) This small, inviting home has a conservatory housing an indoor garden and a spa pool. A log fire, free internet and complimentary espresso coffee seal the deal. The bright bedrooms have been recently redecorated, and an in-house reflexologist and massage therapist is on hand if you've come a cropper on the slopes.

Snow Denn Lodge (☎ 03-302 8999; www.methven accommodation.co.nz; cnr McMillan & Bank Sts; dm/d $25/70, d with bathroom $80; 🖳 🛜) This YHA-associated lodge has appealing dining/living areas, a large kitchen, and indoor and outdoor spa pools. Prices include breakfast and equipment hire (bikes, golf clubs, fishing gear etc).

Glenthorne Station (☎ 0800 926 868, 03-318 5818; www.glenthorne.co.nz; lodge per person $25-35, holiday house per person $50, chalet per person $160) Beautifully isolated 25,800-hectare sheep station, 60km

northwest of Methven on the northern shore of Lake Coleridge. The high-country accommodation ranges from a 15-bed budget lodge (equipped with kitchen, but meals are available from the homestead), to self-contained holiday houses or DB&B (dinner, bed and breakfast) lake-view chalets. There are activities aplenty including 4WD tours, fishing, horse riding and walking.

Methven Camping Ground (☎ 03-302 8005; methven nz@hotmail.com; Barkers Rd; unpowered/powered sites $26/28, cabins $40-55) Small park in a scenic location close to the centre of town. Facilities (including a TV room) are serviceable. Tiny budget cabins are OK, but it's worth spending slightly more at a backpackers.

Big Tree Lodge (☎ 03-302 9575; www.bigtreelodge. co.nz; 25 South Belt; dm $27-29, s/tr 45/90, d $65-110; 🖳 🛜) Transformed from a one-time vicarage, this friendly and relaxed lodge has lovely wood-trimmed bathrooms, and a comfy, heritage ambience. Long-term discounts are available.

Redwood Lodge (☎ 03-302 8964; www.snowboardnz. com; 3 Wayne Pl; s $55, d $65-90, tr & q $120; 🖳 🛜) Turkish rugs and a bright decor give this family-friendly spot with single, double, triple and quad rooms plenty of charm. En-suite rooms with TV provide privacy and there's a huge shared TV lounge and kitchen.

Beluga Lodge (☎ 03-302 8290; www.beluga.co.nz; 40 Allen St; d incl breakfast $210-250; ☐) Highly relaxing B&B with king-sized beds, fluffy bathrobes, luscious bathrooms and private decks. Extreme privacy-seekers should consider the garden suite, with its own patio and barbecue. A four-bedroom cottage is also available ($350; minimum three-night stay from June to October).

Also recommended:

Skiwi House (☎ 03-302 8872; www.skiwihouse.co.nz; 30 Chapman St; dm $25, d $58; P ☐) Smaller backpackers with a family atmosphere and plenty of DVDs if the mountain is closed. Covered storage area for bicycles, and drying and tuning facilities for powderhounds.

Mount Taylor Lodge (☎ 03-302 9699; www.mount taylorlodge.co.nz; 32 Lampard St; s/d incl breakfast $90/180; ☐) Stylish 11-room lodge with wooden floors.

Breckenridge Lodge (☎ 03-302 8902; www.brecken ridgelodge.com; 49-51 South Belt; s/d/tr/q/f incl breakfast $95/115/140/165/185; ☐ ☎) Versatile lodge with a wide array of rooms, warm wooden decor, and a lounge bar. A spa pool, sauna and games room provide plenty of distraction before and after hitting the slopes.

Eating & Drinking

Cafe 131 (☎ 03-302 9131; Main St; meals $6-17; 7.30am-late; ☐ ☎) A warm space with polished timber and leadlight windows. Serves up all-day breakfasts, good-value platters, and soup, pasta, and sandwiches. Beer and wine takes over later in the day. There's also paid wi-fi.

Café Primo e Secundo (☎ 03-302 9309; 38 McMillan St; meals $10-18; 8am-5pm) A treasure trove of retro Kiwiana; the coolest part is that everything is for sale. Sandwiched in and around the souvenir teaspoons and Buzzy Bee bookends are tasty cakes, panini, and legendary bacon and egg sandwiches. You'll also unearth Methven's best coffee.

Blue Pub (☎ 03-302 8046; Main St; mains $10-30; noon-late) Drink at the bar crafted from a huge slab of native timber, or tuck into surprisingly sophisticated meals like parmesan-crusted blue cod in the quieter restaurant. Challenge the locals to a game of pool or watch rugby on the big screen (most Friday and Saturday nights from March to June).

Arabica (☎ 03-302 8455; 36 McMillan St; mains $15-20; 9am-4pm Tue-Thu & Sat, to late Fri) Coolly

cosmopolitan cafe with an all-day menu featuring brekkie items like corned beef hash with salmon cakes. Beer and wine goes well with the dinner menu available on Friday nights.

Last Post (☎ 03-302 8259; Main St; mains $25-35; 6pm-late Tue-Sat, from 5pm daily in winter) Popular après-ski rendezvous point where the day's downhill escapades are recounted over good cocktails and innovative mains like grilled yellow-fin tuna or crusted Canterbury lamb backstrap. The excellent wine list features the best of the South Island.

Also recommended:

Deli(cious) (☎ 03-302 9239; Bank St; tapas 3 for $25; 11am-3pm Mon & 9am-6pm Tue-Sat) Spanish meatballs and chorizo offer an alternative to another hostel kitchen creation.

Supervalue supermarket (cnr The Mall & MacMillan St; 7am-9pm).

Entertainment

Cinema Paradiso (☎ 03-302 1957; www.cinemaparadiso. co.nz; Main St; adult/child $14/11)

Getting There & Around

Methven Travel (☎ 03-302 8106; www.methventravel. co.nz; 93 Main St; adult/child one-way $36/18; Mon, Wed, Fri, Sat in summer, up to three times daily in winter) picks up from Christchurch. Cathedral Sq and Christchurch airport departures are available. Other companies offer this service during winter. Ask at the Christchurch i-SITE for details (p214).

Shuttles operate from Methven to Mt Hutt ski field in winter for around $35; enquiries and pick-ups are from Methven i-SITE.

MT SOMERS

Mt Somers is a small settlement just off SH72, the main road between Geraldine and Mt Hutt. The **Mt Somers Subalpine Walkway** (17km, 10 hours) traverses the northern face of Mt Somers, linking the popular picnic spots of Sharplin Falls and Woolshed Creek. Trail highlights include volcanic formations, Maori rock drawings, deep river canyons and botanical diversity. There are two huts on the tramp: **Pinnacles Hut** and **Woolshed Creek Hut** ($10 each). This route is subject to sudden changes in weather and precautions should be taken. Hut tickets and information are available at the **Mt Somers General Store** (☎ 03-303 9831; Pattons Rd). There are other shorter walks in the area.

The **Mt Somers Holiday Park** (☎ 03-303 9719; www.mountsomers.co.nz; Hoods Rd; sites $26, cabins $54-69) is small and well-maintained.

At the highway turn-off to Mt Somers is **Stronechrubie** (☎ 03-303 9814; www.stronechrubie.co.nz; SH72; d $110-160), with studios and luxury chalets scattered across bird-filled gardens. The intimate **restaurant** (mains $29-31; ✆ 6.30pm-late Wed-Sat, noon-2pm Sun) features excellent Canterbury lamb and local venison and duck. Consider a DB&B package (per two people $230 to $280).

SOUTH CANTERBURY

SH1 heading south from Christchurch along the coast passes through the port city of Timaru on its way to Dunedin and carries a lot of traffic. The inland route along SH8 is also busy, but showcases the stunning landscapes of the Mackenzie Country. Studded with the intense blue lakes of Tekapo and Ohau, SH80 veers off at Twizel in the Mackenzie Country to hug Lake Pukaki all the way to the magnificent heights of Aoraki/Mt Cook National Park.

TIMARU
pop 26,750

The port city of Timaru is a handy stopping-off point halfway between Christchurch and Dunedin. Many travellers prefer to kick on 85km further south to the smaller, more charming Oamaru, but a few good restaurants and good-value motels means Timaru is worthy of a spot of travellers' R&R. The town's name comes from the Maori name Te Maru, meaning the 'Place of Shelter'. No permanent settlement existed here until 1839 when the Weller brothers from Sydney set up a whaling station. The *Caroline*, a sailing ship that picked up whale oil, gave the picturesque bay its name.

Orientation

SH1 is known by many names as it passes through Timaru: the Hilton Hwy north of town, Evans St as it enters town and then Theodosia St and Craigie Ave as it bypasses the central business district around Stafford St. Continuing south, the highway becomes King St and then SH1 again after emerging from town. Confused?

Information

The **Timaru i-SITE** (☎ 0800 484 6278, 03-688 6163; www.southisland.org.nz; 2 George St; ✆ 8.30am-5pm Mon-Fri, 10am-3pm Sat & Sun) is across from the train station (trains in this area only carry freight, not passengers). The i-SITE has street maps, information on local walks, and also handles transport bookings. Internet is available at the i-SITE and across the road at the Off the Rail Café (p253).

Sights

South Canterbury Museum (☎ 03-687 7212; www.timaru.govt.nz; Perth St; admission by donation; ✆ 10am-4.30pm Tue-Fri, 1.30-4.30pm Sat & Sun) has historical and natural artefacts of the region. Hanging from the ceiling is a replica of the aeroplane designed and flown by local pioneer aviator and inventor Richard Pearse. Many believe his mildly successful attempts at manned flight came before the Wright brothers first flew in 1903.

At the time of writing, a **Maori Rock Art Centre** (including tours around the region to see rock art in situ) was planned near the i-SITE. Ask for an update.

Aigantighe Art Gallery (☎ 03-688 4424; www.timaru.govt.nz; 49 Wai-iti Rd; admission free; ✆ 10am-4pm Tue-Fri, noon-4pm Sat & Sun) is one of the South Island's largest public galleries, a 900-piece collection of NZ and European art from the previous four centuries set up in a 1908 mansion, and adorned externally by a sculpture garden (always open). The gallery's Gaelic name means 'at home' and is pronounced 'egg-and-tie'.

DB Mainland Brewery (☎ 03-688 2059; Sheffield St; tours $10; ✆ tours 1pm Mon-Sat) is located 6km north of town. Enclosed footwear must be worn and bookings are required.

The **Botanic Gardens** (cnr King & Queen Sts; admission free; ✆ 8am-dusk), established in 1864, have ponds, a conservatory and a notable collection of roses and native tree ferns. The gardens are south of town; enter from Queen St. Passionate rose buffs should also visit the **Trevor Griffiths Rose Garden** (Caroline Bay; admission free; ✆ open daylight hours) with more than 1000 romantic blooms set around arbours and water features. The finest display is from December to February.

Every November Timaru celebrates the **Timaru Festival of Roses** (www.festivalofroses.co.nz) with two weeks of garden tours, exhibitions and floral workshops.

Activities

One of the few safe, sheltered beaches on the east coast is Caroline Bay. There's a fun,

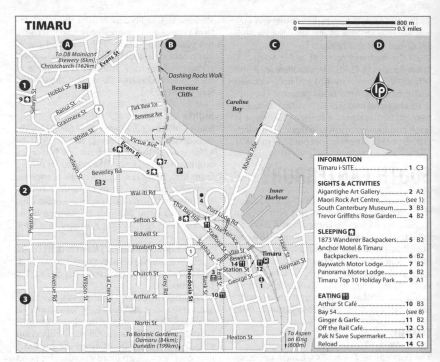

INFORMATION	
Timaru i-SITE	1 C3

SIGHTS & ACTIVITIES	
Aigantighe Art Gallery	2 A2
Maori Rock Art Centre	(see 1)
South Canterbury Museum	3 B3
Trevor Griffiths Rose Garden	4 B2

SLEEPING	
1873 Wanderer Backpackers	5 B2
Anchor Motel & Timaru	
Backpackers	6 B2
Baywatch Motor Lodge	7 B2
Panorama Motor Lodge	8 B2
Timaru Top 10 Holiday Park	9 A1

EATING	
Arthur St Café	10 B3
Bay 54	(see 8)
Ginger & Garlic	11 B2
Off the Rail Café	12 C3
Pak N Save Supermarket	13 A1
Reload	14 C3

crowded **Christmas Carnival** (www.carolinebay.org. nz) with concerts and events here beginning 26 December and running for about 10 days. The beachside **park** has a walk-through aviary, a wading pool, minigolf ($3), kids playground and a pleasant walkway.

A good one-hour **walk** heads north from town along Caroline Bay, past the Benvenue Cliffs and on to the Dashing Rocks and rock pools at the end of the bay. Ask at the i-SITE about other walks in the area.

Sleeping

1873 Wanderer Backpackers (☎ 0800 187 392, 03-688 8795; 1873wandererbackpackers@xtra.co.nz; 24 Evans St; sites/dm/s/d $16/23/29/58; 🖳) Sprawling spot with friendly owners offering transfers to/from the bus station. Rent a mountain bike, fire up the barbecue and relax in the pretty garden.

Timaru Top 10 Holiday Park (☎ 0800 242 121, 03-684 7690; www.timaruholidaypark.co.nz; 154a Selwyn St; unpowered/powered sites $32/35, cabins & motels d $65-115; 🖳 🛜) Parkland site with excellent amenities and a golf course next door that's included in your park tariff.

Panorama Motor Lodge (☎ 03-688 0097; www. panorama.net.nz; 52 The Bay Hill; d from $120; 🖳 🛜) Modern, well-appointed units with spa, sauna and gym. More greenery to soften the concrete would be nice, but Caroline Bay Park and Bay Hill's cafes are a short walk away. Family units are particularly spacious.

Aspen on King (☎ 0800 822 344, 03-688 3034; www. aspenonking.co.nz; 51 King St; d $145-155; 🖳 🛜) A three-bedroom apartment features a retro bathroom complete with a bright red bath that's straight from the Playboy mansion. Other newer units are equally spacious and crisply modern with free broadband internet. It's in a quieter location away from busy Evans St.

Busy Evans St is wall-to-wall motels, but it's worth asking for a room at the back if you're a light sleeper. The best option is **Baywatch Motor Lodge** (☎ 0800 929 828, 03-688 1886; www.baywatch timaru.co.nz; 7 Evans St; d $120-140; 🖳 🛜). Its units offer Hoff-tastic bay views, and double-glazed windows mask the worst of the road noise from SH1.

Also recommended is the **Anchor Motel and Timaru Backpackers** (☎ 03-684 5067; 42 Evans St;

backpackers dm/d $25/60, motels $49-95; (🖥 🛜)), a clean and simple property a short walk from the beach at Caroline Bay.

Eating & Drinking

Reload (☎ 03-688 6616; cnr Stafford & Beswick Sts; wraps, salads & juices $5-9; ☒ 8.30am-5.30pm Mon-Fri, to 3.30pm Sat) Self-styled 'health fuel stop' with wraps, salads and smoothies. The not-so-virtuous can recharge on coffee as they read the global array of magazines.

Off the Rail Café (☎ 03-688 3594; Station St; meals $8-17; ☒ 7.30am-5pm Mon-Fri, to 9.30pm Sat; 🖥) This funky licensed cafe is at the train station. Fire up the jukebox crammed with '70s tunes, and sample Kiwi baked goodies and more contemporary globally influenced dishes. It's open late for drinks and occasional live music on Saturday night.

Arthur St Café (☎ 03-688 9449; 8 Arthur St; snacks & meals $10-15; ☒ 7.30am-5.30pm Mon-Thu, to 8pm Fri, 8.30am-3pm Sat) Excellent coffee and cruisy Kiwi dub is always a good way to ease into the day. Timaru's funkiest eatery offers sandwiches, bagels and world-famous (in Timaru) breakfasts.

Bay 54 (☎ 03-688 4367; 56 The Bay Hill; lunch mains $10-18, dinner mains $19-32; ☒ 11am-late) Kiwi craft beers from Monteith's, classy Kiwi pub tucker, and the choice of Caroline Bay views or big-screen sport. Sorted.

Ginger & Garlic (☎ 03-688 3981; 335 Stafford St; mains $25-34; ☒ noon-2pm Mon-Fri & 5-10pm Mon-Sat) Timaru's take on sophisticated food with a subtle Asian spin is showcased at this long-running local favourite. Standouts include calamari and prawn spring rolls, and honey-spice pork on sticky miso rice. The menu also includes dishes with a European and Middle Eastern influence.

Pak N Save supermarket (cnr Ranui & Evans Sts; ☒ 8am-9pm Mon-Fri, to 7pm Sat & Sun).

Getting There & Away

InterCity (☎ 03-365 1113; www.intercity.co.nz) stops outside the train station, with buses to Christchurch ($34, 2½ hours, two daily), Oamaru ($28, one hour, two daily) and Dunedin ($37, three hours, two daily). From Dunedin connect to Queenstown, Te Anau and Invercargill.

Atomic Shuttles (☎ 03-349 0697; www.atomictravel.co.nz) stop in Timaru en route to Christchurch ($25) and Dunedin ($25). Departs Timaru from the i-SITE.

There are no direct buses from Timaru to Lake Tekapo and Mt Cook – you'll need to first get to Geraldine or Fairlie to catch buses to the Mackenzie Country.

INLAND & MACKENZIE COUNTRY

Heading to Queenstown and the southern lakes from Christchurch means a turn off SH1 onto SH79, a scenic route towards the high country and the Aoraki/Mt Cook National Park's eastern foothills. The road passes through Geraldine and Fairlie before joining SH8, which heads over Burkes Pass to the blue intensity of Lake Tekapo.

The expansive high ground from which the scenic peaks of Aoraki/Mt Cook National Park escalate is known as Mackenzie Country after the legendary James 'Jock' MacKenzie, who ran his stolen flocks in this then-uninhabited region in the 1840s. When he was finally caught, other settlers realised the potential of the land and followed in his footsteps. The first people to traverse the Mackenzie were the Maori, trekking from Banks Peninsula to Otago hundreds of years ago.

Online see www.mtcooknz.com and for information on winter activities see www.mackenziewinter.co.nz.

Geraldine
pop 2210

Geraldine has a country-village atmosphere with pretty private gardens and an active craft scene.

The **Geraldine i-SITE** (☎ 03-693 1006; www.gogeraldine.co.nz; geraldineinfo@southisland.org.nz; cnr Talbot & Cox Sts; ☒ 8.30am-5pm Mon-Fri, 10am-4pm Sat & Sun) has brochures detailing the gardens and galleries in town, and can book rural B&Bs and farmstays.

Four Peaks Plaza (cnr Talbot & Cox Sts; ☒ 9am-5pm) has a bakery, cafes and the Talbot Forest cheese shop. Also here is **Barker's** (☎ 03-693 9727), a fruit-products emporium selling (and sampling) kiwifruit wines, juices, sauces, smoothies and jams. Every Saturday during summer the town kicks into organic action with a **farmers market** (☒ 9.30am-12.30pm).

The **Vintage Car & Machinery Museum** (☎ 03-693 8005; 178 Talbot St; adult/child $7/free; ☒ 10am-4pm mid-Sep–early Jun) has more than 30 vintage and veteran cars from as far back as 1907. There's also a rare 1929 Spartan biplane.

4x4 New Zealand (☎ 03-693 7254; www.4x4newzealand.co.nz; tour $105-220) operates a range of 4WD tours in the surrounding high country, taking in sheep stations, braided rivers and *Lord of the Rings* film sites. Prices vary according to itinerary and length of tours.

The mind-bending **Medieval Mosaic** (☎ 03-693 9820; www.1066.co.nz; 10 Wilson St; admission free; ☯ 9am-5pm Mon-Fri, 10am-4pm Sat & Sun) is ideal for fans of medieval history, word games and clever-clogs mathematics. If you're feeling chilly, the world's biggest woollen jersey is also on display.

SLEEPING & EATING

Geraldine Holiday Park (☎ 03-693 8147; www.geraldineholidaypark.co.nz; 39 Hislop St; unpowered/powered sites $24/26, cabins & units $45-105; ☐) This holiday park is set amid well-established trees across the road from a grassy oval. Besides budget cabins and self-contained units, there's a TV room and playground.

Rawhiti Backpackers (☎ 03-693 8252; www.rawhitibackpackers.co.nz; 27 Hewlings St; dm/s/d/tr $30/40/68/90; ☐ ☏) Under friendly new ownership, but the standards have been kept up at this old maternity hospital that's now a sunny and spacious hostel with solar electricity and colourfully furnished rooms all with different themes such as 'French' or 'Pacific'. Mountain bikes are available and guests rave about the comfy beds. It's above town off Peel St; grab a map before setting off. If you ask them when you book, they'll usually pick you up from the bus stop.

Scenic Route Motor Lodge (☎ 0800 723 643; www.motelscenicroute.co.nz; 28 Waihi Terrace; d $110-130; ☐ ☏) This spacious motel is built in early-settler style, but the modern studios include double-glazing, Sky TV and the attention of Molly, a friendly feline who definitely thinks she runs the place. You'll find Molly and her human employees Rob and Elaine at the northern end of town.

Cafe Verde (☎ 03-693 9616; 45 Talbot St; mains $8-15; ☯ 9am-4pm) Down the lane beside the old post office is this delightful garden cafe. Grown-ups will appreciate the tasty lunch options such as salmon in filo pastry, while the kids go crazy – with a small, well-behaved 'c' please – in the sweet postage-stamp-sized playground.

Taste (☎ 03-693 8877; 7 Talbot St; mains $20-30; ☯ 5pm-late Tue-Sat) The ritziest place in town sees local farmers enjoying robust Angus steaks, and more delicate palates are catered to with scallops in filo pastry.

Geraldine's best pub meals are available for alfresco dining in the garden bar at the **Village Inn** (☎ 03-693 1004; 41 Talbot St; mains $10-17; ☯ 10am-late).

The eateries at Four Peaks Plaza (p254) are ideal for a quick bite. Newly opened on our last visit were outlets for sushi, bagels and freshly squeezed fruit juices. For a quality sugar rush, visit **Coco** (☎ 03-693 9982; 10 Talbot St; ☯ 10am-5pm Mon-Fri, to 3pm Sat, to 4pm Sun) for handmade choccies, plus designer teas, coffee, hot chocolate and cake.

ENTERTAINMENT

Geraldine Cinema (☎ 03-693 8118; Talbot St; adult/child $10/7) is a quirky local cinema with old sofas.

Peel Forest

Peel Forest, 22km north of Geraldine (signposted off SH72), is among NZ's most important indigenous podocarp (conifer) forests. A road from nearby Mt Peel station leads to **Mesopotamia**, the run of English writer Samuel Butler (author of the satire *Erewhon*) in the 1860s.

Get the *Peel Forest Park: Track Information* brochure ($1) from **Peel Forest Store** (☎ 03-696 3567; ☯ 9am-6pm Mon-Thu, to 7pm Fri & Sat, 10am-5.30pm Sun; ☐), which also stocks petrol, groceries and takeaway food, and has internet access and an on-site cafe-restaurant. The store also manages the pleasant DOC **camping ground** (☎ 03-696 3567, unpowered/powered sites $18/22, cabins $36) beside the Rangitata River, about 3km beyond the store and equipped with basic two- to four-berth cabins, showers, a kitchen, laundry and card phone. Check in at the store and ask about renting a mountain bike ($12/35 per hour/day).

More upmarket is **Peel Forest Lodge** (☎ 03-696 3703; www.peelforestlodge.co.nz; d $350), a self-contained log-cabin-style lodge deep in the forest. Bring your own food along for leisurely barbecues; meals are also available (breakfast/dinner per person $25/50) if you can't/won't cook. The owners don't live on-site so you'll need to book ahead.

Horse trekking (☎ 0800 022 536; 03-696 3703; www.peelforesthorsetrekking.co.nz; 1hr/2hr/half-day/full day $55/110/220/380) in the lush forest is also on offer even if you're not staying at the lodge. Longer multiday treks ($982 to $1673) and accommodation and horse-trekking packages ($550) are available in conjunction with Peel Forest Lodge (see above).

The magnificent podocarp forest consists of totara, kahikatea and matai. One fine example of totara on the **Big Tree Walk** (30 minutes return) has a circumference of 9m and is over 1000 years old. Local bird life includes the rifleman, kereru (NZ pigeon), bellbird, fantail and grey warbler. There are also trails to waterfalls: **Emily Falls** (1½ hours return), **Rata Falls** (two hours return) and **Acland Falls** (one hour return).

Rangitata Rafts (☎ 0800 251 251, 03-696 3534; www.rafts.co.nz; ◷ Oct-Apr) goes white-water rafting on the Rangitata River, which contains exhilarating Grade V rapids. The company's base is at Mt Peel, 13km past the camping ground, and includes budget **lodge accommodation** (unpowered sites/dm/d $20/20/48). Rafting trips can be joined from either the Rangitata lodge ($185) or from Christchurch ($195 including return transport), and include hot showers and a barbecue. Count on three hours on the river. A less frantic option for families is a Family Fun trip (adult/child $165/120) on the Grade II Lower Rangitata River. Inflatable kayaks are used, and you'll have around two hours on the river followed by a meal at the lodge.

If you can't get enough of NZ's rivers, consider a longer three-day rafting expedition with **Hidden Valleys** (☎ 03-696 3560; www.hiddenvalleys.co.nz; from $1350; ◷ Oct-Mar). One-day to one-week adventure tours around Peel Forest and the Rangitata River are also available.

Fairlie
pop 725

Fairlie is often described as 'the gateway to the Mackenzie'. To the west the landscape changes as the road ascends Burkes Pass to the open spaces of Mackenzie Country.

The **Fairlie visitor information centre** (☎ 03-685 8496; www.fairlie.co.nz; Allandale St; ◷ 10am-4pm) can provide information on nearby **mountainbiking** tracks. There's skiing 29km northwest at **Fox Peak** in the Two Thumb Range. **Mt Dobson**, 26km northwest of Fairlie, is in a 3km-wide basin (see p81). The **Ski Shack** (☎ 03-685 8088; Allandale St) has information and gear rental. Internet is available at **eat** (right).

SLEEPING & EATING

Both Main St pubs offer budget accommodation, or you can try one of the local motels from around $90.

Fairlie Gateway Top 10 Holiday Park (☎ 0800 324 754, 03-685 8375; www.fairlietop10.com; 10 Allandale Rd; unpowered & powered sites $30, cabins & units $50-150; 🖳 🛜) Tranquil, creek-side park that's perfect for families, with a large playground for the kids. Fishing gear is for hire.

Pinewood Motels (☎ 0800 858 599, 03-685 8599; www.pinewoodmotels.co.nz; 25-27 Mt Cook Rd; d from $90; 🛜) Comfortable self-contained units, including one that's wheelchair-accessible.

eat (☎ 03-685 6275; 76 Main St; mains $10-18; ◷ 8am-5pm Tue-Sun; 🖳) Family-friendly with a kid's play area, eat also drags in grown-ups with its excellent food – try a hot chicken sandwich ($17.50) – beer, wine, and speedy internet access.

Old Library Café (☎ 03-685 8999; 6 Allandale Rd; dinner mains $20-30; ◷ 11am-late; 🖳) Has elegant touches including an old pressed-metal ceiling, and serves fresh, local food such as roasted Mackenzie lamb or smoked Alpine salmon. There's also a more casual all-day menu featuring pasta, salads and soups.

Lake Tekapo
pop 315

At the southern end of its namesake lake, this town has unobstructed views across turquoise water, and a backdrop of rolling hills and mountains worthy of a Peter Jackson movie. The town has boomed in recent times, with new B&Bs, holiday homes and resort accommodation taking advantage of the epic vistas.

Lake Tekapo is a popular stop on tours of the Southern Alps, with Mt Cook– and Queenstown-bound buses popping in for a quick ice cream or coffee. Rather than rushing on, it's actually worth staying at least a couple of nights to experience the region's glorious night sky from atop nearby Mt John.

For an explanation of why this and other lakes in the region are such a vibrant shade of blue, see the boxed text, p258.

INFORMATION

Lake Tekapo i-SITE (☎ 03-680 6579; www.laketekapountouched.co.nz; Godley Hotel, SH8; ◷ 9am-5pm) handles bookings for activities and transport. Also see www.tekapotourism.co.nz.

There's internet access – including wi-fi – at the Tekapo Helicopters office (p257).

SIGHTS & ACTIVITIES

The diminutive, picturesque **Church of the Good Shepherd** (◷ 9am-5pm) beside the lake was built of stone and oak in 1935 and is a favourite for weddings given its postcard-perfect setting.

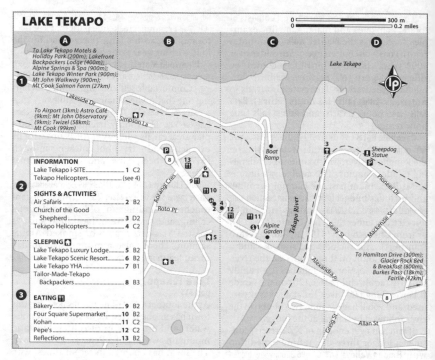

LAKE TEKAPO

0 ——————— 300 m
0 ——————— 0.2 miles

To Lake Tekapo Motels &
Holiday Park (200m); Lakefront
Backpackers Lodge (400m);
Alpine Springs & Spa (900m);
Lake Tekapo Winter Park (900m);
Mt John Walkway (900m);
Mt Cook Salmon Farm (27km)

To Airport (3km); Astro Café
(9km); Mt John Observatory
(9km); Twizel (58km);
Mt Cook (99km)

Lakeside Dr
Simpson La
Aorangi Cres
Roto Pl
Lakeside Dr

Lake Tekapo

Boat
Ramp

Sheepdog
Statue

Pioneer Dr

Tekapo River

Sealy St

Mackenzie St

Alpine
Garden

Alexandra Pl

Gregg St

Allan St

To Hamilton Drive (300m);
Glacier Rock Bed
& Breakfast (800m);
Burkes Pass (18km);
Fairlie (42km)

INFORMATION
Lake Tekapo i-SITE.............................. 1   C2
Tekapo Helicopters......................... (see 4)

SIGHTS & ACTIVITIES
Air Safaris... 2   B2
Church of the Good
   Shepherd... 3   D2
Tekapo Helicopters........................... 4   C2

SLEEPING 🛏
Lake Tekapo Luxury Lodge.............. 5   B2
Lake Tekapo Scenic Resort.............. 6   B2
Lake Tekapo YHA................................ 7   B1
Tailor-Made-Tekapo
   Backpackers................................... 8   B3

EATING 🍴
Bakery.. 9   B2
Four Square Supermarket............. 10   B2
Kohan.. 11   C2
Pepe's.. 12   C2
Reflections...................................... 13   B2

Nearby is a **statue** of a collie dog, a tribute to the sheepdogs that helped develop the Mackenzie Country. This area is at its scenic best before or after the last bus group leaves, otherwise the place is swarming with quick-stop sightseers, so come early morning or late afternoon. It's also an increasingly popular location for wedding photographic shoots for visiting Asian honeymooners. Try not to walk into their pictures.

Popular walks include the track to the summit of **Mt John** (three hours return) from just beyond the camping ground. From there, continue on to Alexandrina and McGregor Lakes, making it an all-day walk. Other walks are detailed in the brochure *Lake Tekapo Walkway* ($1).

Cruise Tekapo (☎ 027 479 7675; www.cruisetekapo. co.nz; 25/40min cruise $30/45, fishing per hr $80) can get you out and about on Lake Tekapo.

Mountain bikes can be hired (per hour/half-day $10/25) from Lakefront Backpackers Lodge and the Lake Tekapo YHA.

Mackenzie Alpine Horse Trekking (☎ 0800 628 269; www.maht.co.nz; 1/2hr ride $50/80, half-/full day $125/250) organises four-footed high-country explora-tions. Overnight camping trips ($300) are also available.

Thanks to clear skies and its distance from any main towns, Lake Tekapo has top-notch stargazing, and the area is known as one of the finest spots on the planet to explore the heavens. Join a two-hour night-time star-gazing tour operated by **Earth & Sky** (☎ 03-680 6960; www.earthandsky.co.nz; adult/child $80/45) Forty-minute daytime tours (adult/child $30/15) of the University of Canterbury observatory operate on demand from 10am to 4pm from the Astro Café on Mt John; call for start times as these can vary seasonally. On the night tour visitors can use their own cameras to delve into astrophotography with local photographer Fraser Gunn (www.laketekapo.cc).

In winter, Lake Tekapo is a base for **downhill skiing** at Mt Dobson or Round Hill and **cross-country skiing** on the Two Thumb Range.

At the western edge of the lake, the **Lake Tekapo Winter Park** (☎ 0800 353 8283, 03-680 6550; www.winterpark.co.nz; Lakeside Dr; skating adult/child $14/11, snow-tubing adult/child $15/11; 🕙 10am-10pm) features a year-round skating rink and a winter mini-snow slope for gentle snow-tubing action.

Next door, the **Alpine Springs & Spa** (www.alpine springs.co.nz; hot pools adult/child $16/9; ⏰ 10am-10pm) is open all year round with hot pools scattered amid quickly growing native trees. Private pools and saunas ($24 per hour) are also available, and spa packages start at $80. 'Skate and Soak' combo deals are available, and there's a good **cafe** (snacks $5-10; ⏰ 10am-7pm) for coffee and cake, or a snack and something stronger.

TOURS

Air Safaris (☎ 03-680 6880; www.airsafaris.co.nz; SH8) Does 50-minute 'Grand Traverse' flights over Mt Cook and its glaciers (adult/child $295/195), taking you up the Tasman Glacier, over the upper part of the Fox and Franz Josef Glaciers, and by Mts Cook, Tasman and Elie de Beaumont. A similar flight goes from Glentanner Park (see p264), but with higher prices (adult/child $340/240).

Tekapo Helicopters (☎ 0800 359 835, 03-680 6229; www.tekapohelicopters.co.nz; SH8) Has five options, from a 25-minute flight ($195) to a 70-minute trip taking in Mt Cook and Fox and Franz Josef Glaciers ($500). All flights include icefield landings and views of Mt Cook.

SLEEPING

Lake Tekapo Scenic Resort (☎ 0800 118 666, 03-680 6808; www.laketekapo.com; SH8; dm/s $22/50, d $160-190; 🖳 🛜) Not so much a self-contained resort as a central complex of basic dorms, singles and doubles, and more modern studio and family units. Lacking in character, but undeniably central, and the local pub is just next door.

Tailor-Made-Tekapo Backpackers (☎ 03-680 6700; www.tailor-made-backpackers.co.nz; 9-11 Aorangi Cres; dm $25-29, d with/without bathroom $74/62; 🖳) This hostel favours beds rather than bunks and is spread over a pair of well-tended houses on a peaceful street away from the main road. The interior is spick and span and there's a barbecue-equipped garden complete with well-established trees, birdsong and a children's playground.

Lakefront Backpackers Lodge (☎ 03-680 6227; www.laketekapo-accommodation.co.nz; Lakeside Dr; dm/d $27/80; 🖳 🛜) An impressive lakeside place owned by the nearby holiday park (about 1km from the township). Relax by the open fire in the comfy lounge area or take in the sensational views from the front deck. Rooms are modern and bathrooms are top-notch. Backpacker buses stop by so it can be a tad social.

Lake Tekapo Motels & Holiday Park (☎ 0800 853 853, 03-680 6825; www.laketekapo-accommodation.co.nz; Lakeside Dr; unpowered/powered sites $30/36, cabins & units $70-150; 🖳 🛜) Has a pretty and peaceful lakeside locale, plus everything from basic cabins to motel units with full kitchen and Sky TV. Newer chalets come with shared picnic tables, barbecues and spectacular lake vistas.

Lake Tekapo YHA (☎ 03-680 6857; www.yha.co.nz; yha.laketekapo@yha.co.nz; 3 Simpson Lane; dm/d $30/78; 🖳 🛜) Friendly, well-equipped little place with a living room adorned with open fireplaces, a piano and outstanding views across the lake to the mountains beyond.

Glacier Rock Bed and Breakfast (☎ 03-680 6669; www.glacierrock.co.nz; 35 Lochinver Ave; d incl breakfast $195-250; 🖳 🛜) This architecturally designed home doubles as an art gallery. An artist's – or maybe an architect's – eye is evident in the spacious and airy rooms. Breakfast is served in sunny rooms with huge picture windows.

Lake Tekapo Luxury Lodge (☎ 0800 525 383, 03-680 6566; www.laketekapolodge.co.nz; 24 Aorangi Cres; d incl breakfast $250-430; 🖳 🛜) Luxurious hilltop B&B set in an English-manor style home. Three of the four well-appointed rooms have great views from a back deck, and there's also a handy path leading to the village past the owner's quirky corrugated-iron artwork.

Hamilton Drive and the surrounding streets in the eastern part of town have several good B&Bs.

EATING

The dining scene at Lake Tekapo remains rather lacklustre, with most places doing OK business from the passing trade and a cavalcade of bus tours. For lunch, compile a lakeside picnic from the supermarket and the bakery.

our pick **Astro Café** (Mt John Observatory; coffee & cake $4-8; ⏰ 9am-6pm) This tiny, glass-walled pavilion atop Mt John has insanely spectacular 360-degree views across the entire Mackenzie Basin. Quite possibly one of the best locations on the planet for a cafe, and the coffee and cake is pretty good, too. On our latest visit they'd branched out into fresh ham-off-the-bone sandwiches. After dark the cafe becomes the location for astrophotography (opposite) with local photographer Fraser Gunn.

Pepe's (☎ 03-680 6677; SH8; meals $15-30; ⏰ 6pm-late) With large booths and walls decorated with skiing paraphernalia, the rustic Pepe's is a cosy little place with good pizza and pasta. Some of the names are a bit naff (Vinnie's Venison or Spag Bol Bada Bing, anyone?), but the dishes are tasty, and later at night it becomes a good spot for a few quiet ones.

Kohan (☎ 03-680 6688; SH8; lunch $10-14, dinner $22-35; ⏲ 11am-2pm Mon-Sun & 6-9pm Mon-Sat) The decor's a bit ho-hum, but you should be gazing at the lake and mountains outside anyway. The Japanese food is actually among the South Island's best, and with a salmon farm just up the road, you just know the sashimi is ultra-fresh. Lunch specials are good value.

Reflections (☎ 03-680 6808; SH8; lunch mains $10-17, dinner mains $25-32; ⏲ 8am-late) Grab an outdoor table with views to the lake – try and look past the minigolf course – then select from a decent menu that includes roasted venison or baked Mt Cook salmon. Lunchtime offerings are more casual (burgers and salads) and next door is the town's pub for more nocturnal action.

Pick up supplies at the **Four Square supermarket** (SH8; ⏲ 7am-9pm) and the nearby **bakery** (☎ 03-680 655; SH8; ⏲ 7am-4pm).

GETTING THERE & AWAY
Southbound services to Queenstown and Wanaka, and northbound services to Christchurch, are offered by **Atomic Shuttles** (☎ 03-349 0697; www.atomictravel.co.nz), **InterCity** (☎ 03-365 1113; www.intercity.co.nz) and **Southern Link Coaches** (☎ 0508 458 835; www.southernlinkcoaches.co.nz). One-way fares are around $30.

Cook Connection (☎ 0800 266 526; www.cookconnect.co.nz) operates to Mt Cook (one-way $30, one daily) and for an additional $20 you can carry on from Mt Cook to Twizel. Travel can be over more than one day.

Mt Cook Salmon Farm
Some 15km west of Lake Tekapo along SH8 is the signposted turn-off to the **Mt Cook Salmon Farm** (☎ 03-435 0585; www.mtcooksalmon.com; Canal Rd; adult/child $2/free; ⏲ daylight hr). The farm operates in a hydroelectric canal system and is 12km from the turn-off. A scenic drive along the canal has popular fishing spots and enjoys great views of Mt Cook. Stop at the farm to feed the fish, or pick up something smoked or fresh for dinner.

Lake Pukaki
On the southern shore of Lake Pukaki, 45km southwest of Lake Tekapo and 2km northeast of the turn-off to Mt Cook, is the **Lake Pukaki visitor information centre** (☎ 03-435 3280; info@mtcooknz.com; SH8; ⏲ 9am-6pm Oct-Apr, 10am-

> **BLUE CRUSH**
>
> The blazing turquoise colour of Lake Pukaki, a characteristic it shares with other regional bodies of water such as Lake Tekapo, is due to 'rock flour' (sediment) in the water. This so-called flour was created when the lake's basin was gouged out by a stony-bottomed glacier moving across the land's surface, with the rock-on-rock action grinding out fine particles that ended up being suspended in the glacial melt water. This sediment gives the water a milky quality and refracts the sunlight beaming down, hence the brilliant colour.

4pm May-Sep), with reams of information on Mackenzie Country. But the highlight here is the sterling **lookout** that on a clear day gives a picture-perfect view of Mt Cook and its surrounding peaks, with the ultrablue lake in the foreground.

Twizel
pop 1015
It wasn't long ago that New Zealanders maligned the town of Twizel, just south of Lake Pukaki. The town was built in 1968 to service construction of the nearby hydroelectric power station, and was due to be abandoned in 1984 when the construction project was completed. Now the town's tenacious residents are having the last laugh as house prices are increasing and new lakeside subdivisions are being built to take advantage of the area's relaxed lakes-and-mountains lifestyle. Mt Cook is just 63km down the road, and Twizel's range of affordable accommodation and a few pleasant eateries make it a good alternative to staying in more expensive Mt Cook Village.

Right in town is the **Twizel i-SITE** (☎ 03-435 3124; www.twizel.com; Twizel Events Centre; ⏲ 9am-6pm daily Oct-Apr, 10am-4pm Tue-Sat May-Sep; 🖳), which has internet access. In late January, the town hosts the lively Mackenzie Summer Salmon and Wine Festival.

There's an ATM in the main shopping area. Note there's no ATM at Mt Cook. Self-drive travellers should also fill up with petrol in Twizel before heading to Mt Cook.

ACTIVITIES
Nearby Lake Ruataniwha is popular for rowing, boating and windsurfing. Fishing in local

rivers, canals and lakes is also big business and there are a number of guides in the region; ask at the i-SITE.

Discovery Tours (☎ 0800 213 868, 03-435 0114; www.discoverytours.co.nz) is based in Twizel and operates guided, small-group tours around the Mackenzie Country and Aoraki/Mt Cook, including hiking and helibiking, plus a popular two-hour tour (adult/child $75/40) to the site of the Pelennor battlefield in the *Lord of the Rings* movies. You can even get to charge around like a mad thing wearing *LOTR* replica gear. A shorter one-hour *LOTR* tour (adult/child $30/5) is also available.

The wading kaki (black stilt bird) is found only in NZ and is one of the country's rarest birds. A breeding program is now attempting to increase the population and the new Ahuriri Conservation Park is part of this effort. Just south of Twizel, the **Kaki Visitor Hide** (☎ 03-435 3124; adult/child $15/7; ♥ 9.30am & 4.30pm Oct-Apr) gives you a close-up look at these elusive fellows. Bookings are essential for the one-hour tour of the hide; for more info, visit the Twizel i-SITE (you'll need your own transport to get to the hide).

Helicopter Line (☎ 0800 650 652, 03-435 0370; www.helicopter.co.nz; Wairepo Rd) flies over the Mt Cook region from a helipad beside Mackenzie Country Inn. Sightseeing flights last from 25 minutes ($220) to 60 minutes ($525) and include a snow landing.

SLEEPING

High Country Lodge & Backpackers (☎ 03-435 0671; www.highcountrylodge.co.nz; Mackenzie Dr; dm $25, d with/without bathroom $85/75, units $115-150; 🖳 🛜) This excellent value place used to be a hostel for construction workers, and new owners have smartened up the decor with colourful curtains and bed linen. A few standalone motel units also see your Kiwi pesos going a long way. They're also YHA-affiliated for additional discounts.

Parklands Alpine Tourists Park (☎ 03-435 0507; www.parklandstwizel.co.nz; 122 Mackenzie Dr; unpowered/powered sites $28/30, dm $25, cabins & cottages d $85-100; 🖳 🛜) Offering green, flower-filled grounds and accommodation in a colourfully refurbished maternity hospital. The modern self-contained cottages are particularly good value.

Mountain Chalet Motels (☎ 0800 629 999, 03-435 0785; www.mountainchalets.co.nz; Wairepo Rd; dm/d from $25/105) Recommended place with well-equipped, self-contained A-frame chalets.

The cheapest units are studios, but there are a number of two-bedroom set-ups for larger groups or families. There's also a small, laid-back lodge that's perfect for backpackers.

our pick **Omahau Downs** (☎ 03-435 0199; www.omahau.co.nz; SH8; cottages d $115, B&B d $135; ♥ closed Jun-Aug) There's nothing more relaxing than kicking back at this rural homestead 2km north of Twizel. Omahau Downs is run by a laid-back Kiwi–South African couple, and caters to all tastes with two cosy self-contained cottages sleeping up to four, and a B&B lodge with sparkling modern rooms and a view-enhanced deck looking out on the Ben Ohau Range. An essential experience is a moonlit wood-fired outdoor bath ($20). Don't make the mistake of booking for only one night.

Matuka Lodge (☎ 03-435 0144; www.matukalodge.co.nz; Old Station Rd; d incl breakfast $465-535; 🖳 🛜) Surrounded by farmland and mountain scenery, this luxury B&B blends modern design with antiques and Oriental rugs sourced on the owners' travels. A library full of well-thumbed Lonely Planet guides is testament to their wanderlust, so look forward to interesting chats over pre-dinner drinks. Also look forward to a breakfast of locally sourced free-range eggs and salmon smoked just up the road at the Twizel Aoraki Smokehouse.

Also recommended:

Colonial Motel (☎ 0800 355 722, 03-435 0100; www.colonialmoteltwizel.co.nz; 38 Mackenzie Dr; d $110-120; 🖳 🛜)

Aspen Court Motel (☎ 0800 277 364, 03-435 0274; www.aspencourt.co.nz; 10 Mackenzie Dr; d $130-150; 🖳 🛜)

EATING & DRINKING

Poppies Cafe (☎ 03-435 3308; 1 Benmore Pl; breakfast/lunch $9-18, dinner mains $24-32; ♥ 9am-late in summer, restricted hr in winter) The versatile Poppies is a classy addition to the Twizel dining scene. Lunch showcases lighter meals like Thai beef salad, and dinner is a slightly more formal experience with steak *frites* and venison escalope. Excellent pizzas ($17 to $24) occupy a tasty middle ground. Where possible, organic and locally sourced produce is used. You'll find Poppies on the outskirts of town near the Mackenzie Country Inn.

Shawty's Café (☎ 03-435 3155; 4 Market Pl; breakfast & lunch $9-19, dinner mains $20-28; ♥ 8.30am-late) Cool beats and craft microbrews create a mood that's surprisingly sophisticated for Twizel. Big breakfasts and gourmet pizzas ($12 to

$25) are a good way to start and end an active day amid the surrounding alpine vistas.

Jasmine Thai Café (☎ 03-435 3232; 1 Market Pl; lunch $10, dinner mains $10-16; ⊕ 11am-2pm & 5-10pm Tue-Sun) Thailand comes to Twizel and the zesty and zingy flavours of your favourite South East Asian beach have travelled well to get this far inland. It's BYO (bring your own), so grab a few cold beers from the Four Square supermarket to ease the authentic heat.

Hunter's Cafe & Bar (☎ 03-435 0303; 2 Market Pl; meals $18-30; ⊕ 11am-2.30pm & 5-8.30pm Mon-Thu & Sat, 11am-8.30pm Fri, 11am-2.30pm Sun) An airy space with generous mains of local produce (salmon from nearby Lake Benmore or rib-eye steak), as well as cheaper bar snacks. Later at night it morphs into a pub.

Right next door to Shawty's, its newly opened **Grappa Lounge** (⊕ 5pm-late Wed-Fri, 1pm-late Sat & Sun) is a little slice of cosmopolitan cocktail heaven that might have you staying up later than you planned. In summer there's occasional live music and DJs.

GETTING THERE & AWAY
Onward services to Mt Cook, Queenstown and Wanaka, and northbound services to Christchurch, are offered by **Atomic Shuttles** (☎ 03-349 0697; www.atomictravel.co.nz), **InterCity/Newmans** (☎ 03-365 1113; www.intercitycoach.co.nz) and **Southern Link Coaches** (☎ 0508 458 835; www.southernlinkcoaches.co.nz).

Cook Connection (☎ 0800 266 526; www.cookconnect.co.nz) operates to Mt Cook (one-way $22, one daily) and for an additional $28 you can carry on from Mt Cook to Tekapo. Travel can be over more than one day.

Naked Bus (www.nakedbus.com) travel from here to Christchurch and Queenstown/Wanaka.

Lake Ohau & Ohau Forests
Six forests in the Lake Ohau area (Dobson, Hopkins, Huxley, Temple, Ohau and Ahuriri) are administered by DOC. The numerous walks in this vast recreation grove are detailed in the DOC pamphlet *Ohau Conservation Area* ($1); huts and camping areas are also scattered throughout for adventurous trampers.

Lake Ohau Lodge (☎ 03-438 9885; www.ohau.co.nz; Lake Ohau Rd; s $94-165, d $100-190) is idyllically sited on the western shore of the rower-friendly Lake Ohau, 42km west of Twizel. Prices listed are for accommodation only (everything from backpacker-style to upmarket rooms with

deck and mountain views); DB&B packages are good value.

The lodge is the wintertime service centre for the **Ohau Ski Field** (see p81). In the summer it's a quieter retreat.

AORAKI/MT COOK NATIONAL PARK
The spectacular 700-sq-km Aoraki/Mt Cook National Park, along with Fiordland, Aspiring and Westland National Parks incorporates the Southwest New Zealand (Te Wahipounamu) World Heritage Area, which extends from Westland's Cook River down to the Fiordland. Fenced in by the Southern Alps and the Two Thumb, Liebig and Ben Ohau Ranges, more than one-third of the park has a blanket of permanent snow and glacial ice.

Of the 27 NZ mountains over 3050m, 22 are in this park. The highest is the mighty Mt Cook, and at 3755m it's the tallest peak in Australasia. Known to Maori as Aoraki (Cloud Piercer), after an ancestral deity in Maori mythology, the mountain was named after James Cook by Captain Stokes of the survey ship HMS *Acheron*.

The Mt Cook region has always been the focus of climbing in NZ. On 2 March 1882, William Spotswood Green and two Swiss alpinists failed to reach the summit of Cook after an epic 62-hour ascent. But two years later a trio of local climbers – Tom Fyfe, George Graham and Jack Clarke – were spurred into action by the news that two well-known European alpinists were coming to attempt Cook, and set off to climb it before the visitors. On Christmas Day 1884 they ascended the Hooker Glacier and north ridge, a brilliant climb in those days, and stood on the summit.

In 1913, Australian climber Freda du Faur became the first woman to reach the summit. In 1948, Edmund Hillary's party, along with Tenzing Norgay, climbed the south ridge; Hillary went on to become the first to reach the summit of Mt Everest. Since then, most of the daunting face routes have been climbed. Among the region's many great peaks are Sefton, Tasman, Silberhorn, Malte Brun, La Perouse, Hicks, De la Beche, Douglas and the Minarets. Many can be ascended from Westland National Park, and there are climbers' huts on both sides of the divide.

Mt Cook is a wonderful sight – assuming there's no cloud in the way. Most visitors arrive on tour buses, stop at the Hermitage hotel for photos, and then zoom off back down

SH80. Hang around to soak up this awesome peak and the surrounding landscape and try the excellent short walks. On the trails, look for the thar, a goatlike creature and excellent climber; the chamois, smaller and of lighter build than the thar; and red deer. Summertime brings the large mountain buttercup (the Mt Cook lily), and mountain daisies, gentians and edelweiss.

Information

The **DOC Aoraki/Mt Cook visitor information centre** (☎ 03-435 1186; mtcookvc@doc.govt.nz; 1 Larch Grove; ☷ 8.30am-5pm Oct-Apr, to 4.30pm May-Sep) advises on weather conditions, guided tours and tramping routes, and hires out beacons for trampers ($35). The centre has recently been expanded and includes excellent displays on the flora, fauna and history of the Mt Cook region. Online see www.mtcooknz.com. Most activities can be booked here or at the Activities Desk at the Sir Edmund Hillary Alpine Centre.

The **Alpine Guides shop** (☎ 03-435 1834; www. alpineguides.co.nz; Retail Centre, The Hermitage; ☷ 8am-5pm) sells travel clothing and accessories,

and mountaineering gear, and rents ice axes, crampons, daypacks and sleeping bags.

Internet access – including paid wi-fi – is available at the Old Mountaineer's Café (p265).

Stock up on groceries and petrol at Twizel or Lake Tekapo, and note that Mt Cook has no banking facilities.

Sights
TASMAN GLACIER

Higher up, the **Tasman Glacier** is a predictably spectacular sweep of ice, but further down it's downright ugly. Normally as a glacier retreats it melts back up the mountain, but the Tasman is unusual because its last few kilometres are almost horizontal. In recent decades it has melted from the top down, exposing a jumble of stones, rocks and boulders and forming a lake. In other words, in its 'ablation zone' (where it melts), the Tasman is covered in a solid mass of debris, which slows down its melting rate and makes it unsightly.

Despite this considerable melt, the ice by the site of the old Ball Hut is still estimated to be over 600m thick. In its last major advance

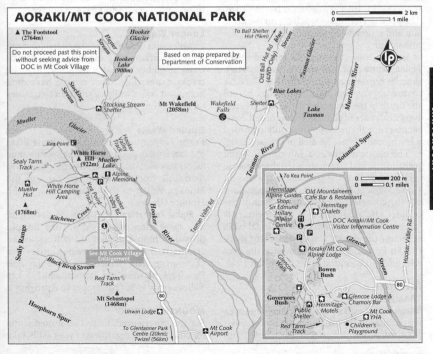

(17,000 years ago), the glacier crept south far enough to carve out Lake Pukaki. A later advance did not reach out to the valley sides, so the Old Ball Hut Rd runs between the outer valley walls and the lateral moraines of this later advance.

Like the Fox and Franz Josef Glaciers on the other side of the divide, the Mt Cook glaciers move fast. The **Alpine Memorial**, near the old Hermitage site on the Hooker Valley Track and commemorating one of the mountain's first climbing disasters, illustrates the glaciers' speed. Three climbers were killed by an avalanche in 1914. Only one of the bodies was recovered at the time, but 12 years later a second one melted out of the bottom of the Hochstetter Icefall, 2000m below where the party was buried.

HERMITAGE
With fantastic views of Mt Cook, this is arguably the most famous hotel in NZ. Originally constructed in 1884, when the trip from Christchurch took several days, the first hotel was destroyed in a flash flood in 1913; you can see the foundations in Hooker Valley, 2km from the current Hermitage. Rebuilt, it survived until 1957, when it burnt down. The present Hermitage was built on the same site and a new wing was added for the new millennium.

In late 2007, the new **Sir Edmund Hillary Alpine Centre** (☎ 0800 686 800; www.hermitage. co.nz; The Hermitage; adult/child/family from $26/13/52; ⊗ 8am-late) opened just three weeks before the death of the man regarded as the greatest New Zealander of all time. His recorded commentary for the museum was only recorded a few months before he died in January 2008.

The centre includes a full-dome digital planetarium and screen showing three feature movies as well as the specially made Mount Cook Magic 3D movie, but most poignant are the countless personal memories of the country's beloved 'Sir Ed'. A documentary is screened in the musuem on a continual basis reflecting the charity and development work that Sir Edmund Hillary achieved in the decades after his conquest of Mt Everest in 1953.

Activities
TRAMPING
Various easy walks from the Hermitage area are outlined in the brochure *Walks in Aoraki/ Mt Cook National Park* ($1), available from the visitor information centre. Always be prepared for sudden weather changes.

The trail to **Kea Point** (two hours return from the village) is lined with native plant life and ends at a platform with excellent views of Mt Cook, the Hooker Valley and the ice faces of Mt Sefton and the Footstool. You'll usually share your walk with a few inquisitive kea. The walk to **Sealy Tarns** (three to four hours return) branches off the Kea Point Track and continues up the ridge to **Mueller Hut** (dm $35); a comfortable 30-bunk hut with gas and cooking facilities.

The walk up the **Hooker Valley** (three hours return) crosses a couple of swing bridges to Stocking Stream and the terminus of the Hooker Glacier. After the second swing bridge, Mt Cook totally dominates the valley.

The Tasman Valley walks are popular for their views of the Tasman Glacier. Walks start at the end of the unsealed Tasman Valley Rd, 8km from the village. The **Tasman Glacier View track** (50 minutes return) leads to a viewpoint on the moraine wall, passing the **Blue Lakes** (more green than blue these days) on the way.

If you intend staying at any of the park's huts, register your intentions at the visitor information centre and pay the hut fee.

Longer Walks
Longer walks are only recommended for those with mountaineering experience, as conditions at higher altitudes are severe and the tracks dangerous. Many people have died here, and most walkers shouldn't consider tackling these trails.

Guided Walks
From November to March, **Ultimate Hikes** (☎ 0800 686 800, 03-435 1899; www.ultimatehikes.co.nz; full-day walk adult/child $105/65) offers a day-long 8km walk from the Hermitage through the Hooker Valley to the terminal lake of the Hooker Glacier.

Alpine Recreation (☎ 0800 006 096, 03-680 6736; www.alpinerecreation.com), based in Lake Tekapo, organises high-altitude guided treks in the area, as well as mountaineering courses and ski touring. The challenging three-day Ball Pass Trek between the Tasman and Hooker Valleys costs $650 (November to April only).

MOUNTAINEERING
For the experienced, there's unlimited scope for climbing, but regardless of your skills, take

TITANIC SCENE ON LAKE TASMAN

When you're only a few kilometres from NZ's highest mountain, the last thing you expect to see is a maze of huge icebergs straight from the planet's polar regions. It's a surreal feeling cruising in an inflatable boat (p264) amid 500-year-old islands of ice on Lake Tasman in the Aoraki/Mt Cook National Park. The ice may be centuries old, but the lake's only been around a few decades. Lake Tasman was first formed around 30 years ago, when huge swathes of ice sheared off the Tasman Glacier's terminal face.

The ice-strewn lake is a dynamic environment and there's always the danger of one of the icebergs breaking up. An icing-sugar-like dusting of snow may have fallen overnight, and even that could be enough to rebalance an iceberg and send it spinning and rotating in the frigid water. With a decent wind the location of the floating islands can change by the hour.

Come back in a few years, and the ongoing impact of climate change will have further increased the size of one of NZ's newest and coldest lakes.

every precaution as 200 people have died in climbing accidents in the park. The bleak In Memoriam book in the visitor information centre begins with the first death on Mt Cook in 1907, and since then more than 70 climbers have died on the peak.

Highly changeable weather is typical around here; Mt Cook is only 44km from the coast and weather conditions rolling in from the Tasman Sea can mean sudden storms. Unless you're experienced in such conditions, don't climb anywhere without a guide.

Check with the park rangers before attempting any climb and always heed their advice. Fill out a climbers-intentions card before starting out, so rangers can check on you if you're overdue coming out, and sign out again when you return.

Alpine Guides (☎ 03-435 1834; www.alpineguides. co.nz; Retail Centre, The Hermitage; ☷ Nov-Apr) runs guided climbs and courses, from six-day introductory Mountain Experience courses ($1995) through to six-day ascents of Mt Cook ($4950). It also rents and sells mountaineering and hiking gear from a **shop** (☷ 8am-5pm) adjacent to the Sir Edmund Hillary Centre.

Alpine Recreation (☎ 0800 006 096, 03-680 6736; www.alpinerecreation.com; ☷ Nov-Apr) also has a summertime program of climbing courses (a four-day introduction to climbing costs $1350) and guided ascents of Mt Cook or Mt Tasman ($4000).

SKI TOURING & HELISKIING

Alpine Guides (☎ 03-435 1834; www.alpineguides.co.nz; Retail Centre, The Hermitage; ☷ Jul-Sep) does tailored ski-touring, ski-mountaineering and winter alpine courses. Its specialities are glacier ski-

ing (www.skithetasman.co.nz) and heliskiing (www.wildernessheli.co.nz) on the highest peaks in NZ. Ski the Tasman and Wilderness Heliski are also available ex-Queenstown.

Southern Alps Guiding (☎ 027 342 277, 03-435 1890; www.mtcook.com) has a range of heliskiing and boarding options including Tasman Glacier ($775). Ask at the Old Mountaineers Café (p265).

Alpine Recreation (☎ 0800 006 096, 03-680 6736; www.alpinerecreation.com) has a winter (July to September) program involving two days touring in the high country around Lake Tekapo, wearing skis or snowshoes ($650), and other ways to explore the mountains on two feet.

AERIAL SIGHTSEEING

Mount Cook Ski Planes (☎ 0800 800 702, 03-430 8034; www.mtcookskiplanes.com), based at Mt Cook Airport, offers 40-minute (adult/child $375/275) and 55-minute (adult/child $495/375) flights, both with snow landings. Flightseeing without a landing is a cheaper option; try the 25-minute Mini Tasman trip (adult/child $255/210).

From Glentanner Park, the **Helicopter Line** (☎ 0800 650 651, 03-435 1801; www.helicopter.co.nz) does 20-minute Alpine Vista flights ($210), an exhilarating 30-minute flight over the Ben Ohau Range ($295), and a 45-minute Mountains High flight over the Tasman Glacier and by Mt Cook ($390). All feature snow landings.

Other operators include Air Safaris (see p257) and the Twizel branch of the Helicopter Line (see p259).

OTHER ACTIVITIES

The visitor information centre, the Hermitage, the YHA and Glentanner Park provide information and make bookings for activities and tours. Note that most of them are weather-dependent and seasonal.

Glacier Explorers (☎ 0800 686 800, 03-435 1809; www.glacierexplorers.com; adult/child $130/65) heads out on the terminal lake of the Tasman Glacier. It starts with a 20-minute walk to the shore of Lake Tasman, where you board a custom-built MAC boat and get up close and personal with 300-year-old icebergs. See the boxed text, p263. Book at the Activities Desk inside the Sir Edmund Hillary Alpine Centre (p262).

Glacier Sea-kayaking (☎ 03-435 1890; www.mt cook.com; trips $110; ⌚ mid-Apr–Oct) has three-hour kayak trips negotiating icebergs across glacial bays in the Hooker Valley.

Glentanner Horse Trekking (☎ 03-435 1855; www. glentanner.co.nz; 1/2/3hr ride $60/80/150; ⌚ Nov-Apr) leads guided treks on a high-country sheep station. All levels of experience are welcome.

Tasman Valley 4WD & Argo Tours (☎ 0800 686 800, 03-435 1809; www.mountcooktours.co.nz; adult/child $130/65) offers a three-hour return trip by 4WD and argo (8WD all-terrain vehicle) alongside the morraine walls of the Tasman Glacier. Expect plenty of alpine flora and an interesting commentary along the way. Pre-book online (recommended) or book at the Hermitage hotel activities desk (p262).

Discovery Tours (☎ 0800 213 868; www.discovery tours.co.nz; tour $395; ⌚ Oct-May) operates helibiking tours on a high-country station. Afterwards, slow down with a farm tour and meet the local sheep. It also offers guided tours blending sightseeing by van with walking, including a guided wilderness hike to the Ball Ridge (from $130, November to May).

Sleeping

Campers and walkers can use the **public shelter** (⌚ 8am-7pm Oct-Apr, to 5pm May-Sep) in the village, which has running water, toilets and coin-operated showers. Accommodation is expensive in Mt Cook Village; consider staying at Twizel (p259) and visiting Mt Cook as a day trip.

White Horse Hill Camping Area (☎ 03-435 1186; Hooker Valley; adult/child $6/3) A basic DOC-run, self-registration camping ground at the starting point for the Hooker Valley Track, 2km from Aoraki/Mt Cook village. There's running water (boil before drinking) and a new amenities block, but no electricity or cooking facilities.

Unwin Lodge (☎ 03-435 1100; www.alpineclub.org.nz; SH80; dm $25; ▯) About 3.5km before the village, this lodge belongs to the New Zealand Alpine Club (NZAC). Members get preference, but beds are usually available for climbing groupies. There are basic bunks, and a big common room with a fireplace, kitchen and excellent views up the Tasman Glacier.

Glentanner Park Centre (☎ 0800 453 682, 03-435 1855; www.glentanner.co.nz; unpowered/powered sites $32/36, dm $25, cabins $80-125) On the northern shore of Lake Pukaki, this is the nearest facility-laden camping ground to the national park and has great views of Mt Cook, 25km to the north. It's well set up with various cabins, a dormitory (open October to April), a restaurant, and books tours and activities.

Mt Cook YHA (☎ 03-435 1820; www.yha.co.nz; mt cook@yha.org.nz; cnr Bowen & Kitchener Dr; dm/d $30/100; ▯ 🛜) This excellent hostel has a free sauna, drying room, warming log fires and DVDs. Rooms are clean and spacious, and family rooms and facilities for travellers with disabilities are also available. Try and book a few days in advance. If you're mountain-bound you can store luggage here.

our pick Aoraki/Mt Cook Alpine Lodge (☎ 03-435 1860; www.aorakialpinelodge.co.nz; Bowen Dr; d $159-179, tr/q $164/164, f $200-225; ▯ 🛜) With colourful Turkish rugs and underfloor heating, the place ensures a warm welcome. Just a few years old, this cosy lodge with twin, double and family rooms is the best place to stay in the village. Shared facilities include a huge lounge and kitchen area, and the alfresco barbecue with superb mountain views will have you arguing over who's going to grill the steak. Two new, more spacious rooms on the ground floor have simply superb views of Mt Cook.

Hermitage (☎ 0800 686 800, 03-435 1809; www. hermitage.co.co.nz; Terrace Rd; r $160-585; ▯ 🛜) A sprawling complex that has long monopolised accommodation in the village and continues to leverage that position with its room rates. Rooms in well-equipped A-frame chalets (double $235) sleep up to four and include a kitchen. Also available are motel units (double from $160) and refurbished rooms (doubles $175 to $585) in various wings of the hotel proper. The higher end rooms are very smart indeed, and include cinematic views of Mt Cook through huge picture windows. Winter (May to September) sees a reduction in accommodation prices.

Eating & Drinking

Glentanner Restaurant (☎ 03-435 1855; SH80, Glentanner; meals $10-20; 🕑 9am-4pm) The decor might resemble a school cafeteria, but there's plenty of robust Kiwi tucker on offer. Steak sandwiches and fish and chips will get you through the longest of exploring days.

our pick **Old Mountaineers Café, Bar & Restaurant** (☎ 03-435 1890; Bowen Dr; mains $20-35; 🕑 11am-late; 🖳 🛜) Cosy in winter, with mountain views from outside tables in summer, this place delivers top-notch burgers, pizza, pasta and salad and is a good-value alternative to the eateries at the Hermitage. Linger to study the old black-and-white pics and mountaineering memorabilia. You might still be there for happy hour – actually two hours – when it kicks off at 5pm. Paid wi-fi access is also available.

The Hermitage (p262) has a variety of eating and drinking options. Grab a table outside on the extensive deck of the **cafe** (🕑 9am-5.30pm), or wait for dinner and dine at the **Panorama Restaurant** (dinner mains $25-40; 🕑 6pm-late), an excellent à la carte restaurant with local treats including grilled Mt Cook salmon, Canterbury lamb rack and pan-seared venison. The adjacent Alpine Restaurant offers breakfast ($17 to $38), lunch ($44) and dinner ($63) buffets.

Raise a glass to the outrageous mountain scenery at Sir Ed's Bar at the Sir Edmund Hillary Alpine Centre or the Snowline Lounge. Choose between special beer-appreciation and wine-tasting self-guided tours, and also drink in the outrageous scenery up the valley to Aoraki/Mt Cook's iconic profile (weather and cloud cover permitting, of course). The Hermitage Hotel High Tea is also available in the afternoon ($25 to $55).

A smaller, less formal **Chamois Bar** (🕑 5pm-late daily Oct-Mar, Thu-Sat only Apr-Sep) is upstairs in Glencoe Lodge, 500m from the YHA, where it entertains with a pool table, big-screen TV, and the occasional live gig. It's a good place to catch up over a burger or nachos with the international crew of mountain guides and travellers who call the village home during summer.

Getting There & Away

The village's small airport only serves aerial sightseeing companies. Some of these may be willing to combine transport to, say, the West Coast (ie Franz Josef) with a scenic flight, but flights are heavily dependent on weather.

National bus line **InterCity** (☎ 03-365 1113; www.intercitycoach.co.nz) links Mt Cook to Christchurch ($165, five hours), Queenstown ($145, four hours) and Wanaka (with a change in Tarras, 4¼ hours, $195). Buses stop at the YHA and the Hermitage, both of which handle bookings.

InterCity subsidiary **Great Sights** (☎ 0800 744 487; www.greatsights.co.nz) runs a sightseeing day trip from Christchurch ($199) and from Christchurch to Queenstown ($235) via Mt Cook.

The **Cook Connection** (☎ 0800 266 526, 021 583 211; www.cookconnect.co.nz) has shuttle services to Glentanner (one-way $15), Twizel (one-way $22) and Lake Tekapo (one-way $28). Bus services in these towns link on to major centres such as Christchurch, Queenstown, Wanaka and Dunedin. If you're travelling via Mt Cook from Lake Tekapo to Twizel or vice versa, the all-up cost is $50 and you do the travel over more than one day.

If you're driving here, it's best to fill up at Lake Tekapo or Twizel. There is petrol at Mt Cook, but it's expensive and usually involves summoning an attendant from the Hermitage (for a fee).

Dunedin & Otago

Coastal Otago has attractions both urban and rural, offering travellers a chance to escape the crowds of Queenstown, party down in the South Island's *coolest* city, and get up close and personal with the island's most accessible wildlife.

The heart of Otago is Dunedin, long credited as New Zealand's indie-music heartland and definitive student party town. With a plateful of fabulous restaurants and cafes, it's also a great place to lay off the two-minute noodles and indulge your stomach. From its stately train station (one of many grand old Victorian buildings in town), you can catch the famous Taieri Gorge Railway inland, or continue further on NZ's greatest bike trail, the Otago Central Rail Trail.

Those seeking quiet backcountry NZ will love the tiny towns of inland Otago: historic Clyde, sweet little St Bathans, Disney-cute Naseby – wonderful dots of humanity that don't see a lot of tourist traffic. If you're seeking wildlife, head to the Otago Peninsula, where penguins, albatross, sea lions and seals are easily sighted. Or visit seaside Oamaru, with its active historic district and resident penguin colonies.

Unhurried, and rife with picturesque scenery, Otago is generous to explorers who are after something a little less intense.

HIGHLIGHTS

- Air guitaring to live music or wriggling to DJ sounds in the bars and clubs of **Dunedin** (p276)
- Discovering laid-back charm along the quiet northern shore of **Otago Harbour** (p283)
- Peering at penguins, admiring albatross and staring at sea lions and fur seals on **Otago Peninsula** (p279)
- Cycling through lonely vistas of brown and gold along the **Otago Central Rail Trail** (p286)
- Reliving the days of the gold rush in the cobbled streets of the **Oamaru Historic Precinct** (p291)
- Winding through gorges, alongside canyons and across tall viaducts on the snaking **Taieri Gorge Railway** (p279)
- Exploring NZ's southern heritage in quaint backcountry villages such as **Clyde** (p285)
- Sampling excellent local beers and all-round gastronomic excellence in the cafes and restaurants of **Dunedin** (p274)

- Telephone code: 03
- www.dunedinnz.com
- www.otago.co.nz

DUNEDIN & OTAGO

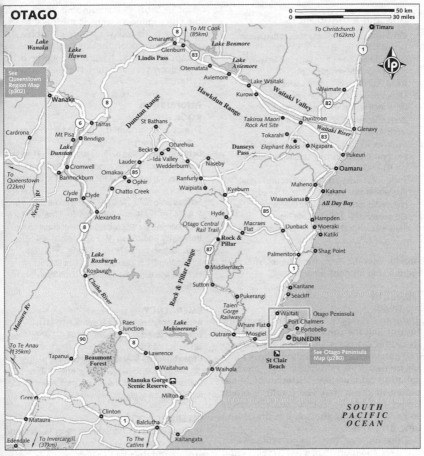

OTAGO

Climate

With the Southern Alps blocking the prevailing wet winds from the Tasman Sea, the east coast of Otago has a relatively dry climate, similar to that of Canterbury to the north. Summer days are generally warm to hot and rainfall is very low. In winter it's a different story: temperatures can drop to well below freezing, as hinted at by the name of NZ's most famous motorcycle rally, the Brass Monkey (as in 'freeze the nuts off a…').

Getting There & Around

Air New Zealand (www.airnewzealand.co.nz) flies from Dunedin to Christchurch, Wellington and Auckland. **Pacific Blue** (www.flypacificblue.co.nz) links Dunedin to Auckland and Brisbane, Australia.

Major bus and shuttle operators include InterCity, Atomic Shuttles, Bottom Bus, Catch-A-Bus, Naked Bus and Wanaka Connexions.

For more information on getting to and from Dunedin, see p278.

DUNEDIN & THE OTAGO PENINSULA

Nestled at the end of Otago Harbour, Dunedin is a surprisingly artsy town, with lots of bars and eateries. If you can unglue yourself from the city's live music and cafe scene, the rugged Otago Peninsula and northern harbour

---

DUNEDIN & OTAGO FACTS

Eat Alfresco from the diverse stalls at the Dunedin Farmers Market (p276)

Drink The fine brews from Dunedin's Emerson's and Green Man breweries (p276)

Read *Owls Do Cry* by Oamaru's Janet Frame

Listen to *... But I Can Write Songs Okay*, a compilation of 40 years of the Dunedin sound

Watch *Scarfies* (1999), about murderous Dunedin university students

Swim at St Kilda Beach or St Clair Beach (p272)

Festival Victorian Heritage Celebrations (Oamaru; late November; p294)

Tackiest tourist attraction Cromwell's giant fruit salad of apples and stone fruit at the edge of town on the main highway from Queenstown

Go green Tiptoe down to Otago Peninsula beaches in search of yellow-eyed penguins (p281)

---

provide easy day trips (or longer), rich with wildlife and outdoor activities.

DUNEDIN
pop 110,800

Dunedin's compact town centre blends the historic and the contemporary, reflected in its alluring museums, and tempting bars, cafes and restaurants. Weatherboard houses ranging from stately to ramshackle pepper its hilly suburbs, and bluestone Victorian buildings punctuate the centre. The country's oldest university provides loads of student energy to sustain thriving theatre, live-music and after-dark scenes.

Dunedin is an easy city to while away a few days, and more than a few travellers find themselves staying here longer than they expected as they recover from the noise, adrenaline and crowds of Queenstown. The excellent wildlife-viewing opportunities of the Otago Peninsula are also close at hand.

History

The Otakou area's early history was particularly bloody, involving a three-way feud between peninsular tribes that escalated in the early 19th century. This brutal warfare was closely followed by devastating diseases and interracial conflict ushered in via coastal sealing and whaling. The first permanent European settlers, two shiploads of pious, hard-working Scots, arrived at Port Chalmers in 1848, including the nephew of the patron saint of Scots poetry, Robbie Burns. That the city's founders were Scottish is a source of fierce pride today: a statue of Robbie still frowns down upon the city centre, there are a handful of civic haggis 'n' bagpipe occasions every year, and the city even has its own tartan.

Information
BOOKSHOPS

Dunedin is particularly blessed with secondhand bookshops.

Octagon Books (Map p270; 32 Moray Pl; 🕙 11am-4pm Mon-Fri, to 2pm Sat) This wonderful-smelling labyrinth of old tomes was voted one of the world's top 10 bookshops. Cash only.

Scribes (Map p270; ☎ 03-477 6874; cnr Great King & St David Sts; 🕙 10am-5.30pm Mon-Fri, 11am-4pm Sat & Sun) Dunedin's greatest selection of secondhand books.

University Book Shop (Map p270; ☎ 03-477 6976; www.unibooks.co.nz; 378 Great King St; 🕙 8.30am-5.30pm Mon-Fri, 9.30am-3pm Sat, 11am-3pm Sun) An excellent selection of fiction, poetry, Maori/Pacific and NZ titles.

EMERGENCY

Ambulance, fire service & police (☎ 111)

Dunedin Hospital (Map p270; ☎ 03-474 0999; 201 Great King St)

Urgent Doctors & Accident Centre (Map p270; ☎ 03-479 2900; 95 Hanover St; 🕙 8am-11.30pm) Deals with emergencies and has a pharmacy open outside normal business hours.

INTERNET ACCESS

Internet access is available at most hostels and accommodation. Wi-fi can be found at the airport and the Otago Museum.

Common Room (Map p270; 18 George St; 🕙 8.30am-9pm Mon-Wed, to 5pm Thu-Fri, 9am-1pm Sat) Coffee plus internet.

Net Planet (Map p270; 78 St Andrew St; 🕙 10am-late Mon-Sat, noon-late Sun; 🛜) Also has LAN and wi-fi.

PC Internet (Map p270; 237 Moray Pl; 🕙 10am-8pm; 🛜)

POST
Post office (Map p270; 233 Moray Pl)

TOURIST INFORMATION

Automobile Association (Map p270; AA; ☎ 0800 500 222, 03-477 5945; 450 Moray Pl; 🕙 8.30am-5pm Mon-Fri) For members' driving queries.

Department of Conservation (Map p270; DOC; ☎ 03-477 0677; www.doc.govt.nz, dunedinvc@doc.govt.nz;

1st fl, 77 Lower Stuart St; ☺ 8.30am-5pm Mon-Fri)
Information and maps on regional walking tracks and Great
Walks bookings.
Dunedin i-SITE (Map p270; ☎ 03-474 3300; www.
dunedinnz.com; 48 The Octagon; ☺ 8.30am-5pm
Mon-Fri, 8.45am-5pm Sat & Sun) Advice and bookings for
accommodation, activities, transport and walking tours.

Sights
Some of the most popular things to do in
Dunedin involve leaving town. See the Otago
Peninsula (p279), the Otago Central Rail Trail
(p286) and Taieri Gorge Railway (p279).

OTAGO MUSEUM
The modern and interactive **Otago Museum**
(Map p270; ☎ 03-474 7474; www.otagomuseum.govt.nz;
419 Great King St; admission by donation, guided tour $10;
☺ 10am-5pm) explores Otago's cultural and
physical past and present, from geology and
dinosaurs to the modern day. The beautifully designed Tangata Whenua gallery houses
an impressive *waka taua* (war canoe), wonderfully worn old carvings and some lovely
pounamu (greenstone) works. This is one of
the richest repositories of Maori knowledge
on the South Island. If you've already been
out on the peninsula admiring penguins and
albatrosses, the museum's collection of ancient and contemporary wildlife will fascinate.
Join themed guided tours ($10, see website for
times and themes). Children can explore at
the hands-on Discovery World (adult/child/
family $9.50/4.50/24), and there's a smart,
newly expanded cafe with surprisingly good
food. Check the website for always-excellent
temporary exhibitions and special gallery
talks.

DUNEDIN PUBLIC ART GALLERY
Explore NZ's art scene at Dunedin's expansive
and airy **Public Art Gallery** (Map p270; ☎ 03-474 4000;
www.dunedin.art.museum; 30 The Octagon; permanent exhibition free; ☺ 10am-5pm). Climb the iron staircase
for great city views. Works on permanent
show are mainly contemporary, including a
big NZ collection featuring local kids Ralph
Hotere and Frances Hodgkins, Cantabrian
Colin McCahon, and some old CF Goldie
oils. Rotating exhibits include some European
works and Kiwi masters.

OTHER MUSEUMS & GALLERIES
The eclectic collection at the **Otago Settlers
Museum** (Map p270; ☎ 03-477 5052; www.otago.settlers.

museum; 31 Queens Gardens; admission free; ☺ 10am-5pm)
gives insights into past residents, whether
Maori or Scots, whalers or farmers. Petrol
heads and trainspotters will love the old Buick
straight eight and 1872-built steam engine;
style hounds will love the original art-deco
bus depot foyer. See p272 for walking tours
covering the city's history.

At the **New Zealand Sports Hall of Fame** (Map
p270; ☎ 03-477 7775; www.nzhalloffame.co.nz; Dunedin
Railway Station, Anzac Ave; adult/child $5/2; ☺ 10am-4pm)
you can try and match bike-champ Karen
Holliday's average speed of 45.629km/h, or
check out the high-stepping style of iconic All
Black fullback George Nepia. You'll also find
out NZ continually punches above its weight
in the sporting world.

The **Temple Gallery** (Map p270; ☎ 03-477 7235; 29
Moray Pl; admission free; ☺ 10am-6pm Mon-Fri, to 2pm Sat)
was Dunedin's first synagogue (1863), and
then for 30 years a Masonic temple. The building retains marks of both, and is a fabulous
artspace. The Chills recorded their last album
here, and Dunedin bands still launch new
offerings here. Artists represented are predominantly Otago locals and include Ralph
Hotere, Donna Demente and Anita DeSoto).

OTHER SIGHTS
Follow your chocolate cravings to the massive **Cadbury World** (Map p270; ☎ 0800 223 287, 03-467
7967; www.cadburyworld.co.nz; 280 Cumberland St; full tour
adult/child/family $18/12/48, reduced tour adult/child $12/7;
☺ full tour 9am-3.30pm Mon-Fri, reduced tour 9am-3.30pm
Sat & Sun) and don a paper hairnet for the full
75-minute tour of the factory that includes
a spiel on history and production, a look at
their version of a liquid-chocolate waterfall,
and a taste of the end product. The shorter
45-minute weekend tour omits the factory
tour and concentrates on the really yummy
part.

After lots of chocolate, kick on to the
90-minute, interactive tour of **Speight's Brewery**
(Map p270; ☎ 03-477 7697; www.speights.co.nz; 200 Rattray
St; adult/child/family $20/8/42; ☺ tours 10am, noon, 2pm,
6pm, 7pm Mon-Thu, 10am, noon, 2pm, 4pm, 6pm Fri-Sun),
which has been churning out beer since the
late 1800s. Following the tour you can sample
each of Speight's six different beers.

The world's steepest residential street (or
so says the *Guinness Book of World Records*),
Baldwin St (off Map p270) has a clamber-
ing gradient of 1 in 1.286 (19°). From the
city centre, head 2km north up Great King

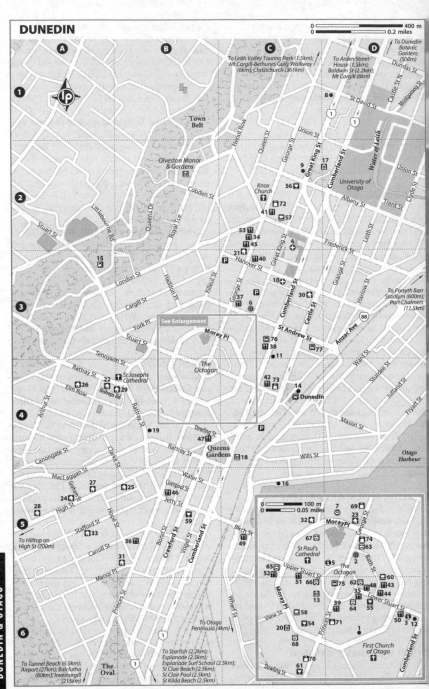

DUNEDIN

0 _____ 400 m
0 _____ 0.2 miles

St to where the road branches sharp left to Timaru. Get in the right-hand lane and continue straight ahead. This becomes North Rd, and Baldwin St is on the right after 1km. If you've any doubts about your brakes, park at the bottom. Alternatively, grab a Normanby bus at the Octagon ($1.90) and ask the driver to let you know when you're there. The annual 'Gutbuster' race in February sees up to 1000 athletes run to the top of Baldwin St and back. Every July, 10,000 oversized Jaffas (chocolate candies) are rolled down the hill for charity. In November 2009, three particularly dim Dunedin students were charged with disorderly behaviour after taking rides down Baldwin St in a chillie bin (insulated picnic cooler) being towed behind a car. Their only defence was that 'the pubs had shut' and they had nothing to do.

The **Dunedin Botanic Gardens** (off Map p270; cnr Great King St & Opoho Rd; admission free; dawn-dusk) date from the 1860s and spread across 22 peaceful, grassy and shady hectares. There's also a playground and a cafe.

Dunedin's striking Edwardian **railway station** (Map p270) celebrated its hundredth birthday recently, and claims to be NZ's most-photographed building. There are plenty of reasons to visit even without the mosaic-tile floors and the glorious stained-glass windows. The station houses the NZ Sports Hall of Fame (p269), hosts the Dunedin Farmers Market (p276), and is the departing point for the Taieri Gorge Railway (see p279).

The **Orokonui Ecosanctuary** (Map p280; 03-482 1755; www.orokonui.org.nz; 9.30am-4.30pm) occupies a 300-hectare nature reserve on Otago Harbour's north shore. Its mission is to provide a predator-free refuge to repopulate species previously exiled to smaller offshore islands. It's a good chance to see the tuatara, NZ's iconic living dinosaur unchanged for 200 million years. At the time of writing, the ecosanctuary could only be visited on a 90-minute guided walk (tour $38; 10.30am & 1.30pm), but unguided visits were also planned. Check the Dunedin i-SITE (p268) for an update.

INFORMATION
- Automobile Association (AA)........ **1** D6
- Common Room............................. **2** D5
- Department of Conservation (DOC)................................. **3** D6
- Dunedin Hospital **4** C2
- Dunedin i-SITE **5** D5
- Net Planet **6** C3
- Octagon Books.....................(see 58)
- PC Internet...........................(see 23)
- Post Office................................ **7** D5
- Scribes...................................... **8** D1
- University Book Shop.................. **9** C2
- Urgent Doctors & Accident Centre **10** C3

SIGHTS & ACTIVITIES
- Cadbury World..........................**11** C3
- Cycle Surgery............................**12** D6
- Dunedin Public Art Gallery **13** C6
- Dunedin Railway Station **14** C4
- Moana Pool...............................**15** A3
- Monarch Wildlife Cruises & Tours....................................**16** C5
- New Zealand Sports Hall of Fame.................................(see 14)
- Otago Museum..........................**17** D2
- Otago Settlers Museum **18** C4
- Speight's Brewery......................**19** B4
- Taieri Gorge Railway.............(see 14)
- Temple Gallery..........................**20** C6

SLEEPING
- 315 Euro...................................**21** C3
- Brothers Boutique Hotel............**22** A4
- Central Backpackers...................**23** D5
- Chalet Backpackers...................**24** A5
- Dunedin Palms Motel................**25** B5
- Elm Lodge.................................**26** A4
- Fletcher Lodge...........................**27** A5
- Grandview Bed & Breakfast.......**28** A5
- Hogwartz..................................**29** B4
- Living Space...............................**30** C3
- Manor House Backpackers..........**31** B5
- On Top Backpackers...................**32** C5
- Stafford Gables YHA...................**33** A5

EATING
- Anarkali....................................**34** C2
- Bacchus Wine Bar & Restaurant.............................**35** D6
- Bell Pepper Blues **36** B5
- Circadian Rhythm Café **37** C3
- Countdown Supermarket............**38** C3
- Dost...**39** D6
- Dunedin Farmers Market ....(see 14)
- Good Oil...................................**40** C3
- Governors.................................**41** C2
- Guilty by Confection **42** C4
- Izakaya Yuki..............................**43** D6
- Minami......................................**44** D6
- Modaks......................................**45** C2
- Mojo...**46** B5
- Nova Cafe............................(see 13)
- Palms Restaurant.......................**47** B4
- Perc..**48** D6
- Plato...**49** C5
- Potpourri...................................**50** D6
- Reef Seafood.......................(see 45)
- Saigon Van...........................(see 37)
- Scotia.......................................**51** C5
- Tangente...................................**52** C5
- Velvet Burger.............................**53** C2
- Velvet Burger........................(see 48)

DRINKING
- 12 Below...................................**54** C6
- Albar...**55** D6
- Captain Cook.............................**56** C2
- Carousel...............................(see 35)
- Fix..**57** C2
- Mazagran Espresso Bar..............**58** C6
- Mou Very..............................(see 34)
- Pequeno...............................(see 54)
- Sammy's....................................**59** D5
- Speight's Ale House................(see 19)
- Strictly Coffee...........................**60** D6
- Tonic..**61** C6

ENTERTAINMENT
- 10 Bar......................................**62** D6
- Bath Street................................**63** D5
- di lusso.....................................**64** D6
- Fortune Theatre.........................**65** C5
- Hoyts Cinema............................**66** C6
- Metro Cinema............................**67** C5
- Pop.....................................(see 64)
- Rialto Cinemas...........................**68** C6

SHOPPING
- Bivouac.....................................**69** D5
- Disk Den....................................**70** C6
- Fern..**71** D6
- McKinlays..................................**72** C2
- Stuart St Potters Cooperative..........................**73** C4
- Wild South.................................**74** D5

TRANSPORT
- City Bus Stop.............................**75** D6
- District Bus Stop........................**76** C3
- InterCity Depot..........................**77** C3

DUNEDIN & OTAGO

Activities

There's more walking and kayaking out on Otago Peninsula (p282).

SWIMMING, SURFING & DIVING

St Clair and St Kilda are both popular swimming beaches (though you need to watch for rips at St Clair). St Clair also has the heated, outdoor, saltwater **St Clair Pool** (off Map p270; ☎ 03-455 6352; Esplanade, St Clair Beach; adult/child $5.50/2.50; ☼ 6am-7pm Mon-Fri, 7am-7pm Sat & Sun, closed Apr-Oct).

St Clair and St Kilda have consistently good left-hand breaks, and you'll also find good surfing at Blackhead further south, and at Aramoana on Otago Harbour's north shore. **Esplanade Surf School** (off Map p270; ☎ 03-455 7728; www.espsurfschool.co.nz; lessons from $45) is based at St Clair Beach and provides equipment and lessons.

For St Clair, catch bus 8, 9, 28 or 29 ($1.90) from stand 1 at the Octagon. For St Kilda, catch bus 27 ($1.90) also from stand 1 at the Octagon

Back in town, **Moana Pool** (Map p270; ☎ 03-471 9780; 60 Littlebourne Rd; adult/child $5.50/2.50; ☼ 6am-10pm Mon-Fri, 7am-7pm Sat & Sun) has diving boards, waterslides, wave machines and a spa.

WALKING, TRAMPING & CLIMBING

The **Tunnel Beach Walkway** (Map p270; 45 minutes return; closed August to October) crosses farmland before descending the sea cliffs to Tunnel Beach. Sea stacks, arches and unusual rock shapes have been carved out by the wild Pacific, and a few fossils stud the sandstone cliffs. It impressed civic father John Cargill so much, he had a hand-hewn stone tunnel built to give his family access to secluded beachside picnics. The walk is southwest of central Dunedin. Catch a Corstorphine bus from the Octagon to Stenhope Cres and walk 1.4km along Blackhead Rd to Tunnel Beach Rd, then 400m to the start of the walkway. Strong currents make swimming here dangerous.

Catch a Normanby bus to the start of Norwood St, which leads to Cluny St and the **Mt Cargill-Bethunes Gully Walkway** (Map p270; 3½ hours return). The highlight is the view from Mt Cargill (also accessible by car). From Mt Cargill, a trail continues to the 10-million-year-old lava-formed **Organ Pipes** and, after another half-hour, to Mt Cargill Rd on the other side of the mountain.

The **Otago Tramping and Mountaineering Club** (www.otmc.co.nz) organises weekend day and overnight tramps, often to the Silver Peaks Reserve north of Dunedin. Nonmembers are welcome, but must contact trip leaders beforehand (see website for details).

Traditional rock climbing (nonbolted) is popular at **Long Beach** (off Map p280) and the cliffs at **Mihiwaka** (Map p280), both accessed via Blueskin Rd north of Port Chalmers, and **Lovers Leap** (Map p280; bolted and natural) on the peninsula. Dave Brash, Dunedin's climbing guru, has written *Dunedin Rock* detailing local climbs. Get it from the Dunedin i-SITE or at Bivouac (p278).

OTHER ACTIVITIES

Cycle Surgery (Map p270; ☎ 03-477 7473; www.cyclesurgery.co.nz; 67 Lower Stuart St; per day $35) rents out bikes and has mountain-biking info.

Hare Hill (Map p280; ☎ 0800 437 837, 03-472 8496, www.horseriding-dunedin.co.nz; 207 Aramoana Rd, Deborah Bay) runs horse treks ($75 to $210) including thrilling beach rides and farm treks.

Tours

See the Dunedin i-SITE (p268) for more specialised city tours.

First City Tours (adult/child $20/10; ☼ buses depart The Octagon 9am, 10.15am, 1pm, 2.15pm & 3.30pm) Hop-on/hop-off double-decker bus tour that loops around the city. Stops include the Otago Museum, Speight's, Botanic Gardens and Baldwin St.

Walk Dunedin (☎ 03-477 5052; 1/2hr walk $12/20; ☼ 1hr walk 7pm year-round & 9.30am Oct-Apr, 2hr walk 11am year-round) History-themed strolls around the city, organised by the Otago Settlers Museum. Meet at the i-SITE.

For viewing nearby wildlife, see p282.

Sleeping

Most accommodation is within easy walking distance of the city centre, though some spots offer a challenging uphill stroll back from town. Most motels are at the northern end of George St.

BUDGET

Dunedin Holiday Park (Map p280; ☎ 0800 945 455, 03-455 4690; www.dunedinholidaypark.co.nz; 41 Victoria Rd, campsites per adult/child $16/8, powered sites $34, cabins $44-79, units $89-110; ☐ ☏) Over the sand dunes from St Kilda Beach, this huge complex has a kids playground, barbecue area, a zillion campsites and a variety of well-equipped cabins, flats and motel units.

Arden Street House (off Map p270; ☎ 03-473 8860; www.ardenstreethouse.co.nz; 36 Arden St; dm/s/d $20/40/80, s/d incl breakfast from $55/85; 💻) North of the city up Northeast Valley, this pair of homes atop a (steep) hill share an organic garden and a very welcoming host. With a recurring leopard theme, crazy artworks and a porthole in the bathroom, the B&B is a pretty amazing space. Readers have raved about the fabulous shared dinners ($10 to $25) with neighbours, artists, wwoofers and guests. Head up North Rd toward Baldwin St, then turn right up Glendining St.

Chalet Backpackers (Map p270; ☎ 0800 242 538, 03-479 2075; www.chaletbackpackers.co.nz; 296 High St; dm/s/d $24/39/56; 💻 📶) Up a fairly steep hill, with a correspondingly fabulous view, this rambling old building quickly makes guests feel at home. The kitchen is big and sunny and festooned with flowers, and the dining room has one huge long table to help you meet your neighbours. There's also a compact garden, pool table, piano and rumours of a ghost.

Stafford Gables YHA (Map p270; ☎ 0800 600 100, 03-474 1919; www.yha.co.nz; yha.dunedin@yha.org.nz; 71 Stafford St; dm/s/d from $25/55/72; 💻 📶) Sprawling and mazelike, this century-old former hospital has a comfortable air. Rooms are fairly big and each one is unique, many with their own small balconies (ask for Room 38). The shared kitchen is truly spacious, and a dungeonlike cellar keeps the sports hounds from imposing their TV habits on everyone else. Upstairs is a sunny rooftop garden.

Elm Lodge (Map p270; ☎ 03-474 1872; www.elmlodge.co.nz; 74 Elm Row; dm/s/d $26/40/60; 💻 📶) Two sweet old houses with harbour and peninsula views, Elm Lodge is a popular choice for travellers looking to relax a while. Rooms are quaint but comfortable, and the back garden is just made for barbecues and a few cold beers. Elm Lodge is a fairly steep walk into (or particularly *out from*) town.

Central Backpackers (Map p270; ☎ 0800 423 6872; www.centralbackpackers.co.nz; 243 Moray Pl; dm/tw/d $27/58/64; 💻 📶) Located in the heart of town, this recently renovated hostel has inviting common TV lounge and kitchen areas, and a welcoming host in Gizmo the cat. Dorm rooms sleep two to 10 on bunks, and private rooms are spacious.

Leith Valley Touring Park (off Map p270; ☎ 0800 555 331, 03-467 9936; www.leithvalleytouringpark.co.nz; 103 Malvern St; powered sites $32, cabins $50, units d $79-99; 💻) A short drive from central Dunedin, this camping ground is surrounded by native bush studded with walks, glowworm caves, and a wee creek. Self-contained modern motel units are spacious, and tourist flats are smaller but have a more earthy feel (linen required). Catch the Garden Village bus from the Octagon.

our pick Hogwartz (Map p270; ☎ 03-474 1487; www.hogwartz.co.nz; 277 Rattray St; dm $27-28, s/d/tr $40/64/90; 💻 📶) The Catholic bishop's residence since the 1870s, this beautiful old building has now been converted into a wonderfully complicated warren of comfortable rooms. The five-bed dorm, the bishop's old formal dining room, would almost certainly be the grandest dorm room you have ever stayed in. There's a short, steep walk up a winding path through lush bush from Rattray St.

Also recommended:

Manor House Backpackers (Map p270; ☎ 0800 477 0484, 03-477 0484; www.manorhousebackpackers.co.nz; 28 Manor Pl; dm $22-24, d $60; 💻) Two stately old villas surrounded by gardens and trees.

On Top Backpackers (Map p270; ☎ 0800 668 672, 03-477 6121; www.ontopbackpackers.co.nz; cnr Filleul St & Moray Pl; dm $25-$26, s $50, d with/without bathroom $78/60; 💻 📶) Modern, well-located hostel atop a pool hall and bar, with large sundeck and shared barbecue area.

MIDRANGE

Living Space (Map p270; ☎ 03-951 5000; www.livingspace.net; 192 Castle St; d $89-149; 💻 📶) Living Space combines kitchenettes in funky colours, whip-smart ergonomic design and a central location. There's an on-site laundry and huge shared kitchen, conversation-friendly lounges and a private DVD cinema. Some rooms are pretty compact, but they're all you need, and represent good value. Substantial discounts kick in for longer-stay guests, and it's popular with overseas students.

Hilltop on High St (Map p270; ☎ 03-477 1053; www.hilltoponhighst.co.nz; 433 High St; d $120-170; 💻 📶) A wonderful four-bedroom villa atop a steep hill, this place is really great value for money. The fabulous shared lounge has leather armchairs and a nice little library, the kitchen sings out to cater a large meal, and the individually decorated rooms all have a touch of luxury about them. The views are stupendous.

Grandview Bed & Breakfast (Map p270; ☎ 0800 749 472, 03-474 9472; www.grandview.co.nz; 360 High St; d incl breakfast $125-195; 💻 📶) Bold colours, exposed brick walls and snazzy art-deco bathrooms are the highlights at this family-owned B&B on the slopes above town. There's more harbour views from the barbecue and deck, and lots of sunny shared spaces. The larger rooms have private spa baths.

TOP END

315 Euro (Map p270; ☎ 0800 387 638, 03-477 9929; www.eurodunedin.co.nz; 315 George St; d $150-250; 🛜) This sleek new opening is in the absolute heart of George St's daytime retail strip and after-dark eating and drinking hub. Choose from modern studio apartments or larger one-bedroom apartments with full kitchens. Decor is modern and luxurious, and soundproofing and double-glazed windows keeps George St's irresistible buzz at bay.

Dunedin Palms Motel (Map p270; ☎ 0800 782 938, 03-477 8293; www.dunedinpalmsmotel.co.nz; 185-195 High St; d $170-210; 🖳 🛜) A short stroll from the Speight's Ale House, the art-deco-style Palms has smartly decorated studios and one- and two-bedroom units arrayed around a central courtyard. You're handily just out of the CBD, but don't have to endure a long walk uphill. More expensive units feature spa baths.

Brothers Boutique Hotel (Map p270; ☎ 0800 477 004, 03-477 0043; www.brothershotel.co.nz; 295 Rattray St; d incl breakfast $170-320; 🖳 🛜) Rooms in this distinctive old 1920s Christian Brothers residence have been refurbished beyond any monk's dreams, while still retaining many unique features. The chapel room ($285) includes the original arched stained-glass windows of its past life. There are great views from the rooftop units.

Fletcher Lodge (Map p270; ☎ 03-477 5552; www.fletcherlodge.co.nz; 276 High St; d $325-450, ste $595-650, all incl breakfast; 🖳 🛜) Originally home to one of NZ's wealthy industrialist families, this gorgeous redbrick manor is just minutes from the city, but the secluded gardens feel wonderfully remote. Rooms are elegantly trimmed with antique furniture and the ornate plaster ceilings reinforce why the building is listed with the Historic Places Trust.

Eating

Whether you're looking for cheap 'n' cheerful with plastic menus, organic/vegan/herbal omelettes, or fine white linen tablecloths, Dunedin's got it.

RESTAURANTS

Izakaya Yuki (Map p270; ☎ 03-477 9539; 29 Bath St; dishes $5-12; 🕙 noon-2pm Mon-Sat & 5pm-late Mon-Sun; Ⓥ) Cute and cosy, with a huge array of small dishes on which to graze, Yuki is a lovely spot for supper or a relaxed, drawn-out Japanese meal. Make a night of it with sake or draught Asahi beer, and multiple plates of *yakitori* (grilled skewers), *gyoza* (dumplings), or sushi and sashimi. The wall-to-wall sumo wrestling videos will ensure you don't eat *too* much.

Minami (Map p270; ☎ 03-477 9596; 126-132 Lower Stuart St; meals $8-20; 🕙 noon-2pm & 5pm-late Mon-Sun) Popular for its simplicity and its prices, Minami is almost always packed with local fans of Japanese food. One half specialises in noodle dishes, while the other side is (slightly) more formal.

Saigon Van (Map p270; ☎ 03-474 1445; 66 St Andrew St; mains $10-15; 🕙 11.30am-2pm Tue-Sun & 5-10pm Mon-Sun; Ⓥ) The elegant decor looks high-end Asian, but the Vietnamese food is definitely budget-friendly. Try the combination spring rolls ($9 for six) and a bottle of Vietnamese beer to recreate lazy nights in Saigon. The bean-sprout-laden *pho* (noodle soup) and salads are also good.

Anarkali (Map p270; ☎ 03-477 1120; 365 George St; meals $11-18; 🕙 11.30am-2pm Mon-Fri & 5-10pm Mon-Sun; Ⓥ) Even the most difficult-to-please fans of Indian food rave about Anarkali. Get the sampler dinner to try a bit of everything.

Reef Seafood (Map p270; ☎ 03-471 7185; 333 George St; mains $23-35; 🕙 11.30am-2pm & 5.30pm-late Mon-Sat, from 6pm Sun) Generous plates of oysters, scallops, surf and turf, and crayfish (lobster) lure burly Otago farmers into town for their monthly slap-up meal. Lunch specials are just $10.

Palms Restaurant (Map p270; ☎ 03-477 6534; 18 Queens Garden; dinner $28-35; 🕙 noon-2pm & 6pm-late Mon-Sat; Ⓥ) Hidden away at the bottom of Dowling St, Palms has long been a landmark Dunedin eatery. Food is innovative and usually locally sourced, and daily lunch specials ($10) are excellent value. How does garlic risotto with grilled halloumi cheese or steamed clams and chorizo sound?

Scotia (Map p270; ☎ 03-477 7704; 199 Upper Stuart St; mains $30-32; 🕙 3pm-late) Now relocated from the Dunedin Railway Station to a cosy heritage town house, Scotia toasts all things Scottish with a wall-full of single malt whisky and hearty fare such as smoked salmon and chargrilled venison. The two Scottish Robbies – Burns and Coltrane – look down approvingly on a menu that also includes haggis, and duck and whisky pâté.

our pick **Plato** (Map p270; ☎ 03-477 4235; 2 Birch St; dinner mains $30-35, brunch mains $15-23; ☺ 6pm-late Mon-Sat & 11am-late Sun) A regular winner in *Cuisine* magazine's Best of NZ's gongs, Plato has a retro-themed location near the harbour and a strong beer and wine list. Try standouts like Goan fish curry or slow-braised pork belly with crispy crackling. Plato's spin on seafood is always excellent, and Sunday brunch is worth the shortish trek from the CBD. Bookings are recommended.

Bell Pepper Blues (Map p270; ☎ 03-474 0973; 474 Princes St; mains $30-39; ☺ 6pm-late Tue-Sat) One of Dunedin's finer dining options, this restaurant boasts one of the region's best-known chefs and is famous for its venison, freshly baked bread and desserts. There's a $10-per-bottle corkage fee for BYO.

Bacchus Wine Bar & Restaurant (Map p270; ☎ 03-474 824; upstairs, 12 The Octagon; mains $33-38; ☺ noon-3pm Mon-Fri & 6pm-late Mon-Sat) Bacchus is particularly nice for a meal for two or to celebrate a special occasion. There's a wine list that the god of wine himself would approve of, and more than a few dishes combine local produce with subtle Asian influences. Try the pork belly slow cooked in Asian spices.

CAFES
See p276 for where to get the best coffee in town.

Potpourri (Map p270; ☎ 03-477 9983; 97 Lower Stuart St; snacks $7-10, meals $10-14; ☺ 9.30am-3pm Mon-Fri; Ⓥ) Funky, homey and very kid-friendly, this small cafe has been fattening up Dunedin's vegetarians and vegans for almost 40 years. Tuck into big, inexpensive portions of quiche, pizza, flatbread melts and spicy samosas. There are lots of organic, free-range and gluten-free options, and takeaways are available.

Tangente (Map p270; ☎ 03-477 0232; 111 Moray Pl; meals $7.50-17; ☺ 8am-3pm Tue-Sat, 9am-3pm Sun; Ⓥ) A cheerful, welcoming space with mismatched tables, toys for the kids, a funky soundtrack, and the glorious aroma of freshly baked bread. Tangente's food is generally organic, free-range and locally sourced.

Mojo (Map p270; ☎ 03-742 1061; 329 Princes St; mains $8-18; ☺ 7am-5.30pm Mon-Fri, 8.30am-5.30pm Sat & Sun) Quite possibly Dunedin's sunniest spot for a lazy brunch, the spacious and high-ceilinged Mojo teams yummy counter food, bagels and bircher muesli, with superlative coffee all the way from Wellington. From 11am a more substantial menu – think pizza and steak sandwiches – kicks in, with wine and beer also available.

Governors (Map p270; ☎ 03-477 6871; 438 George St; mains $9-16; ☺ 7am-9pm Mon-Fri, 8am-9pm Sat & Sun) Popular with students, Governors does a nice line in early morning pancakes and other light meals. If you're feeling a little off the pace after the previous night, a strong coffee and an eggy omelette will be just what the doctor ordered.

Modaks (Map p270; ☎ 03-477 6563; 337-339 George St; meals from $9; ☺ 8am-7pm; Ⓥ) This funky little cafe and bar, with brick walls, mismatched formica tables, and couches for slouching, is popular with students and those who appreciate chilled-out reggae while they nurse a pot of tea. Sundaes, smoothies and beer make it a great escape from the heat, and grilled homemade focaccia bread with yummy, interesting toppings warm the insides in winter.

Circadian Rhythm Café (Map p270; ☎ 03-474 9994; 72 St Andrew St; curry buffet $9.50; ☺ 8.30am-9pm Mon-Sat; Ⓥ) Specialising in organic Indian curries, this all-vegan cafe is also known for its cookies and cakes. The superfriendly staff will also try to tweak things to oblige gluten-free requests. Circadian Rhythm is a music venue, with a variety of interesting acts on Friday nights from 5.30pm. Dunedin's Emerson's and Green Man beers are both available, so you don't have to be *too* healthy.

Perc (Map p270; ☎ 03-477 5462; 142 Lower Stuart St; mains $10-18; ☺ 7am-5pm Mon-Fri, 9am-5pm Sat, 10am-5pm Sun) Always busy, and for good reason, the Perc is a grand place to kick-start your day. The decor's kinda retro and kinda art deco, and there's hearty cafe fare ranging from salmon bagels and panini to warming porridge.

Good Oil (Map p270; ☎ 03-479 9900; 314 George St; mains $10-18; ☺ 8am-5pm) This sleek little cafe is Dunedin's top spot for coffee and cake. Try the lemon and sour cream cake ($4). If you're still waking up, maybe resurrect the day with innovative brunches such as kumara (sweet potato) hash with hot smoked salmon ($15).

Nova Cafe (Map p270; ☎ 03-479 0808; 29 The Octagon; mains $15; ☺ 7am-11pm Mon-Fri, from 8.30am Sat & Sun; Ⓥ) Not surprisingly, this extension of the Public Art Gallery has a stylish look about it. Cakes and snacks are famously creative, and Nova is also licensed for beer and wine. Escape into Dunedin's best choice of interesting food, travel and arts magazines.

Starfish (off Map p270; ☎ 03-455 5940; 7/240 Forbury Rd, St Clair; mains $18-30; ☺ 8.30am-late Tue-Sat, to 4.30pm

DUNEDIN & OTAGO

JUST GIVE ME THE COFFEE & NO ONE WILL GET HURT

Dunedin has some excellent coffee bars to refuel and recharge.

Fix (Map p270; ☎ 03-479 2660; 15 Frederick St; ☺ 7.30am-5pm Mon-Fri, 8.30am-3.30pm Sat, 9.30am-late Sun) Wage slaves queue at the pavement window every morning, while students and others with time on their hands relax in the courtyard. Fix don't serve food, but you can bring along your own food or takeaways.

Mazagran Espresso Bar (Map p270; ☎ 03-477 9959; 36 Moray Pl; ☺ 8am-6pm Mon-Fri, 10am-2pm Sat) The godfather of Dunedin's coffee scene, this compact wood-and-brick coffee house is the source of the magic bean for many of the city's restaurants and cafes.

Strictly Coffee (Map p270; ☎ 03-479 0017; 23 Bath St; ☺ 8am-4pm Mon-Fri) The second of Dunedin's seriously serious coffee bars, Strictly Coffee is a stylish retro coffee bar hidden down grungy Bath St. Different rooms provide varying views and artworks to enjoy while you sip and sup.

Sun-Mon) In a cosy, brick-clad space, Starfish is the best of the growing cafe and restaurant scene at St Clair Beach. Pop out on a weekday to score an outside table to enjoy your pizza and wine. Catch bus 8, 9, 28 or 29 ($1.90) from stand 1 at The Octagon.

QUICK EATS & SELF-CATERING

Inexpensive Asian restaurants are clustered along George St, just before St Andrew St. Most also do takeaways.

Dost (Map p270; ☎ 03-477 2477; 19 Princes St; mains $8-12; ☺ 10am-10pm Mon-Wed, 11am-late Thu-Sat, 11am-9.30pm Sun; Ⓥ) Life's pretty simple really. Sometimes all you want is a good-value kebab or falafel. Especially if you've just left Dunedin's premier nightlife hub.

Velvet Burger (Map p270; ☎ 03-477 7089; 150 Lower Stuart St; mains $10-18; ☺ 11.30am-late; Ⓥ) Interesting burgers with interesting names make for interesting times. Best consumed after a few beers, but Velvet Burger is also licensed if the night is young. There's another VB at 375 George St (same hours).

Guilty by Confection (Map p270; ☎ 03-474 0835; 44-46 Lower Stuart St; ☺ 9am-2pm Mon, 10am-5pm Tue-Fri, 9.30am-1.30pm Sat) Handmade chocolates, fudges and sweets.

The thriving **Dunedin Farmers Market** (Map p270; www.otagofarmersmarket.org.nz; ☺ 8am-12.30pm Sat) convenes at the Dunedin Railway Station. It's all local, all eatable (or drinkable), and mostly organic, with everything from Speight's-beer-flavoured ice cream, gourmet sausages, and Russian pancakes filled with blue cod. There's usually live music on offer, and a passionate foodie vibe. Grab felafels or espresso to sustain you while you browse, and stock up on interesting fresh meats and seafood, vegies and cheeses for your journey.

Also pick up some locally brewed Green Man organic beer.

Countdown supermarket (Map p270; 309 Cumberland St; ☺ 6am-midnight) Self-catering central.

For coffee supplies head to either Mazagran or Strictly Coffee for freshly roasted beans; see above.

Drinking

Supported by perpetually thirsty students and the city's arty vibe, Dunedin boasts great bars and pubs. Find time to try the local beers – Green Man (organic) and Emerson's (simply magnificent).

The Octagon is the heart of the city's bar scene, with no less than eight different bars at street level (plus two downstairs out of sight).

Check www.dunedinmusic.co.nz for news and listings of club nights and bands playing around town.

Albar (Map p270; ☎ 03-479 2468; 135 Lower Stuart St; ☺ 11am-late) This former butchers is now a bohemian little bar attracting just maybe the widest age range in Dunedin. Most punters are drawn by the 50 single malt whiskies, a changing array of interesting tap beers, and a concise menu of cheap-as-chips bar snacks ($4 to $8). Background music stays firmly in the background, making Albar a top spot for conversation.

Mou Very (Map p270; ☎ 03-477 2180; www.mouvery.co.nz; 357 George St; ☺ 11am-late) The tiny Mou Very may well be the world's smallest bar. It's only 1.8m wide, but is still big enough to host regular funk and soul DJ sessions most Fridays from 5pm. There's just six bar stools, so Mou Very's boho regulars usually spill out into an adjacent laneway. By day, it's a handy refuelling spot for your morning or afternoon espresso.

DUNEDIN & OTAGO

** our pick Pequeno** (Map p270; ☎ 03-477 7830; www. pequeno.co.nz; alleyway behind 12 Moray Pl; ☒ 5pm-late Mon-Fri, from 7pm Sat) Down the alleyway opposite the Rialto cinema, Pequeno attracts a slightly older, more sophisticated crowd. There are cosy leather couches, a warming fireplace, and an excellent wine selection and interesting tapas menu. Music is generally laid-back and never too loud to intrude on discussions of the latest architectural fashions.

Tonic (Map p270; ☎ 03-471 9194; www.tonicbar.co.nz; 138 Princes St; ☒ 4pm-late Tue-Fri, 6pm-late Sat) Craft beer bar with the best of Kiwi brews, and lots more interesting imports than your average pub. Limited release beers, loads of single malt whiskies and stellar cocktails appeal to an older crowd than Dunedin's student pubs. Antipasto plates and cheese boards mean you've got good reasons to stay for another drink.

12 Below (Map p270; ☎ 03-474 5055; alleyway behind 12 Moray Pl; occasional cover charge $5-10; ☒ 8pm-late Tue-Sat) In the same alleyway as Pequeno, 12 Below is a hip and intimate underground bar. There's mismatched comfy seats and couches, and nooks aplenty for chatting to mates. There's also floor space for those here to listen to live-music acts (a lot of funk and reggae) or to wriggle along with the DJ's choice of hip-hop and drum 'n' bass.

Carousel (Map p270; ☎ 03-477 4141; www.carouselbar. co.nz; upstairs 141 Lower Stuart St, ☒ 4pm-late Tue-Sat) Dark and sophisticated, with great cocktails, loungey music and a late-30s crowd looking pretty pleased with themselves to be seen somewhere so deadly cool.

Captain Cook (Map p270; ☎ 03-474 1935; 354 Great King St; ☒ 11am-late) This grand-daddy of Dunedin student pubs, with a fun garden bar that's packed with the nation's youth over winter, shrinks to a sad pokies venue over the summer months.

Speight's Ale House (Map p270; ☎ 03-477 9480; 200 Rattray St; ☒ 11am-late) Busy even through the off months, the Ale House is a favourite of strapping young lads in their cleanest dirty shirts. A good spot to watch the rugby on TV, and to try the full range of Speight's beers.

Entertainment
NIGHTCLUBS
10 Bar (Map p270; ☎ 03-477 6310; www.10bar.co.nz; 10 The Octagon; ☒ 10pm-late Thu-Sun) Deep downstairs is a complex space filled with loud music, pulsing lights and dancing bogan princesses. A cover charge kicks in at midnight.

Bath Street (Map p270; ☎ 03-477 6750; www.myspace. com/bathst; 1 Bath St; ☒ 9pm-late Tue-Sat) When all the other bars are closed, Bath Street's famously good sound system summons Dunedin's unsleeping dance crowd for drum 'n' bass, house and hip-hop.

di lusso (Map p270; ☎ 03-477 3776; 12 The Octagon; ☒ 6.30pm-late Sun-Thu, 5pm-late Fri & Sat) Grooving to a sexier-than-average house DJ, and darkly cool with crimson walls and a backlit drinks display, di lusso serves seriously good cocktails and offers a submarine perspective through to the toilets.

Pop (Map p270; ☎ 03-474 0842; downstairs, 14 The Octagon; ☒ 8pm-late Tue-Thu, 6pm-late Fri & Sat) Downstairs from di lusso, and possibly even cooler, Pop serves Dunedin's best martinis, and prides itself on seriously good DJs playing funk and house.

CINEMAS
Rates are often cheaper on Tuesdays.

Hoyts Cinema (Map p270; ☎ 03-477 3250, info line 03-477 7019; www.hoyts.co.nz; 33 The Octagon; adult/ child $15/8) Blockbuster heaven.

Metro Cinema (Map p270; ☎ 03-471 9635; www. metrocinema.co.nz; Moray Pl; adult/student $13/10) Below the Town Hall; art house and nostalgic. Backpackers – with student ID – get in for $10.

Rialto Cinemas (Map p270; ☎ 03-474 2200; www. rialto.co.nz; 11 Moray Pl; adult/child $15/9) A mix of blockbusters and art-house flicks with an extensive program of specialised festivals.

THEATRE
Fortune Theatre (Map p270; ☎ 03-477 8323; www.for tunetheatre.co.nz; 231 Upper Stuart St; adult/child $35/15) The world's southernmost professional theatre company has been running dramas, comedies, pantomimes, classics and contemporary NZ productions for almost 40 years. Shows are performed – watched over by the obligatory theatre ghost – in a Gothic-styled old Wesleyan church.

LIVE MUSIC
Sammy's (Map p270; ☎ 03-477 2185; www.sammys.co.nz; 65 Crawford St; ☒ vary by event) Dunedin's premier live-music venue draws an eclectic mix of genres from noisy-as-hell punk to chilled reggae and gritty dubstep. It's also increasingly the venue of choice for visiting Kiwi bands and up-and-coming international acts.

DUNEDIN & OTAGO

lonelyplanet.com

Chick's Hotel (Map p280; ☎ 03-472 5074; 2 Mount St, Port Chalmers; ♥ vary by event) Across in Port Chalmers, Chicks is the archetypal rock-and-roll pub, and the venue's 19th-century stone walls now play host to everything from touring alt-country bands from the States to local metal bands. If any of Dunedin's esteemed Flying Nun alumni are performing, chances are it will be here or at Sammy's. Catch bus 13 or 14 from stand 4 outside the Countdown supermarket on Cumberland St.

SPORT

Forsyth Barr Stadium (off Map p270; www.otagostadium. co.nz; Awatea St, North Dunedin) Constructed for the 2011 Rugby World Cup, Dunedin's newest sports venue is 2km from the centre of town. It's the only major stadium in NZ with a fully covered roof and will host the Highlanders Super 14 rugby team from 2012 and the Otago NPC rugby team from 2011. See www.orfu. co.nz and www.highlanders-rugby.co.nz for match schedules.

Shopping

George St is Dunedin's main shopping strip, packed with convenient but largely generic chain stores. Note the following harder-to-find and more interesting spots. Moray Pl – near the Rialto Cinemas – is a funky area.

Disk Den (Map p270; ☎ 03-477 2280; 118 Princes St) Although it mostly carries new and recent-release CDs (and their associated posters, DVDs and other tat), the Den also has a collection of old vinyl, and even some cassette tapes, handy if your rental car happens to date from the Stone Age.

Fern (Map p270; ☎ 03-477 7292; 67 Princes St; ♥ 11.30am-5.30pm Mon, 10am-5.30pm Tue-Fri, 11am-4pm Sat) Specialises in unique clothing, design and jewellery, many from up-coming Dunedin artists and designers.

Stuart St Potters Cooperative (Map p270; ☎ 03-471 8484; 14 Lower Stuart St; ♥ 10am-5pm Mon-Fri, 9am-3pm Sat) Locally designed and made pottery and ceramic art from 12 Dunedin and Otago region craftspeople.

For outdoor equipment and clothing try:
Bivouac (Map p270; ☎ 03-477 3679; 171 George St) Climbing, camping, and tramping gear, and maps and specialist guidebooks.
McKinlays (Map p270; ☎ 03-477 1389; 454 George St; ♥ 9am-5.30pm Mon-Sat) Crafting handmade boots and shoes for 130 years. Customised shoemaking and overseas delivery are both available.

Wild South (Map p270; ☎ 03-477 7856; 78 George St) Fashionable but useful outdoorsy clothes.

Getting There & Away
AIR
There are international flights into Dunedin on **Air New Zealand** (☎ 0800 737 000; www.airnewzealand.co.nz) from Sydney and Melbourne, and flights with **Pacific Blue** (☎ 0800 670 000; www.flypacificblue.co.nz) to and from Brisbane.

Air New Zealand has domestic flights to and from Auckland (from $109), Christchurch (from $59) and Wellington (from $99). Pacific Blue links Dunedin with Christchurch (from $60) and Auckland (from $100).

BUS
Most buses leave from the Dunedin Railway Station (excluding InterCity, which depart from St Andrew St). Check when you make your booking.

InterCity (Map p270; ☎ 03-471 7143; www.intercity. co.nz; 205 St Andrew St; ♥ ticket office 7.30am-5pm Mon-Fri, 11am-3pm Sat, 11am-5.15pm Sun, tickets by phone 7am-9pm daily) has direct services to Oamaru ($28, one hour 40 minutes), Christchurch ($50, six hours), Queenstown ($45, 4½ hours), Te Anau ($45, 4½ hours) and Invercargill ($43, four hours).

Southern Link (☎ 0508 458 835; www.southernlink coaches.co.nz) connects Dunedin to Christchurch ($40) and Oamaru ($28). **Coastline Tours** (☎ 03-434 7744; www.coastline-tours.co.nz) runs between Dunedin and Oamaru ($30), and will detour to Moeraki, Karitane, Seacliff or the airport if needed. **Naked Bus** (☎ 0900 625 33; www.naked bus.com) connects Dunedin with Christchurch ($18), Queenstown ($29) and Invercargill ($29).

A couple of services connect Dunedin to the Catlins and Southland. The **Bottom Bus** (☎ 03-477 9083; www.bottombus.co.nz) does a circuit from Dunedin through the Catlins to Invercargill, Te Anau, Queenstown and back to Dunedin. **Catlins Coaster** (☎ 03-477 9083; www.catlinscoaster.co.nz) connects Dunedin with Invercargill, returning via the scenic Catlins; see p361.

Other shuttles:
Atomic Shuttles (☎ 03-349 0697; www.atomic travel.co.nz) To and from Christchurch ($35), Oamaru ($20), Invercargill ($35), Queenstown ($40) and Wanaka ($40).
Catch-A-Bus (☎ 03-449-2024; www.catchabus.co.nz) Door-to-door daily between Dunedin and Wanaka ($50),

stopping at Otago Central Rail Trail towns along the way. Bikes cost an additional $10.

Knightrider (☎ 03-342 8055; www.knightrider.co.nz) Night-time service to Christchurch ($56), Oamaru ($36) and Invercargill ($46).

Wanaka Connexions (☎ 03-443 9122; www.time2.co.nz) Shuttles between Dunedin and Wanaka ($45) and Queenstown ($45).

TRAIN
Two interesting train journeys start at Dunedin's **railway station** (Anzac Ave): the Taieri Gorge Railway journey (see the boxed text, below), and the Seasider (www.seasider.co.nz), which journeys along the coast to Palmerston and back (departs 9.30am and returns 1.30pm, one-way/return $48/72). Book via the Taieri Gorge Railway.

Getting Around
TO/FROM THE AIRPORT
Dunedin Airport (off Map p270; ☎ 03-486 2879; www.dnairport.co.nz) is 27km southwest of the city. The cheapest way to reach it is by a door-to-door shuttle (per person from $15). Try **Kiwi Shuttles** (☎ 03-487 9790; www.kiwishuttles.co.nz), **Super Shuttle** (☎ 0800 748 885; www.supershuttle.co.nz) or **Southern Taxis** (☎ 03-476 6300; www.southerntaxis.co.nz).

A standard taxi ride between the city and the airport costs around $80. There is no public bus service to the airport.

BUS
City buses (☎ 0800 474 082; www.orc.govt.nz) leave from stops in the Octagon, while buses to districts around Dunedin depart a block away from stands along Cumberland St near the Countdown supermarket. Buses run regularly during the week, but services are greatly reduced (or nonexistent) on weekends and holidays. View the Dunedin bus timetable at the Dunedin i-SITE, or see www.orc.govt.nz.

For hop-on, hop-off First City Tours, see p272

CAR
The big nationwide car-rental companies all have offices in Dunedin, and you'll find a few inexpensive local outfits here too, such as **Getaway** (☎ 0800 489 761, 03-489 7614; www.getawaycarhire.co.nz) and **Driven Rentals** (☎ 03-456 3600; www.drivengroup.co.nz).

Parking is tight in the central city, and a recent council blitz has installed parking meters across pretty much all of the CBD. The cheapest are on the steepest streets (naturally). Try London St or Cargill St northwest of the centre of town.

TAXI
Dunedin Taxis (☎ 03-477 7777) and **Otago Taxis** (☎ 03-477 3333).

OTAGO PENINSULA
Otago Peninsula has the South Island's most accessible diversity of wildlife. Albatross, penguins, fur seals and sea lions provide a natural background to rugged countryside, wild walks and beaches, and interesting historical sites. Despite the host of tours exploring the peninsula, the area maintains its quiet rural air. Get the *Otago Peninsula* brochure and map from the Dunedin i-SITE and see www.otago-peninsula.co.nz.

Sights
ROYAL ALBATROSS CENTRE
Taiaroa Head, at the peninsula's eastern tip, has the world's only mainland royal albatross colony. The best time to visit is from December to February, when one parent is constantly guarding the young while the other delivers food throughout the day. Sightings are most common in the afternoon when the

---

TAIERI GORGE RAILWAY

With narrow tunnels, deep gorges, winding tracks, rugged canyons and more than a dozen stone and wrought-iron viaduct crossings (up to 50m high), the scenic **Taieri Gorge Railway** (☎ 03-477 4449; www.taieri.co.nz; Dunedin Railway Station, Anzac Ave) consistently rates highly with visitors.

The four-hour return trip aboard 1920s heritage coaches travels to Pukerangi (one-way/return $51/76), 58km away. Some trips carry on to Middlemarch (one-way/return $58/87) or you can opt for a train-coach trip to Queenstown (one-way $115). From Middlemarch, you can also bring your bike along and hit the rail trail; see the boxed text, p286. In summer (October to April), trains depart 2.30pm daily for Pukerangi, plus trips to Middlemarch or Pukerangi some mornings. In winter (May to September) trains depart for Pukerangi at 12.30pm daily.

winds pick up; calm days don't see much bird action.

The only public access is through the **Royal Albatross Centre** (☎ 03-478 0499; www.albatross.org. nz; Taiaroa Head; ☽ 9am-dusk summer, 10am-4pm winter). One-hour tours (adult/child $45/22.50) include viewing from a glassed-in hut overlooking the nesting sites. There's no viewing from mid-September to late November, and from late November to December the birds are nestbound so it's difficult to see that magnificent wingspan. On Tuesdays, the first tour runs at 10.30am.

To make sure you're going to see the birds in the air, ask the staff whether the birds are flying before you pay. You can also sometimes see albatross flying from the car park, particu-

larly from the fine cliff-top lookout out to sea. Time it for the late afternoon when winds are strongest. Pilot Beach, on the harbour side of the car park, often sees blue-eyed penguins, sea lions and fur seals.

Also on the albatross-centre site are the remains of **Fort Taiaroa** and its 1886 Armstrong Disappearing Gun, built along with other gun emplacements on the peninsula when NZ was certain a Russian invasion was imminent. The gun is loaded and aimed underground, then pops up like the world's slowest jack-in-the-box to be fired. Apparently it's still in perfect working order. The Fort Taiaroa tour (adult/child $20/10) or the Unique Taiaroa Experience (adult/child $50/25) include the guns and the birds. There's also an exhibit

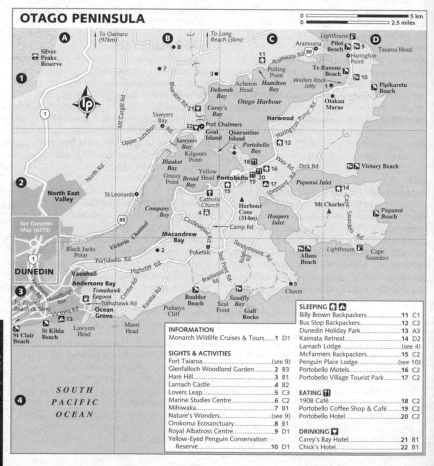

OTAGO PENINSULA

| 0 | 5 km |
| 0 | 2.5 miles |

INFORMATION
Monarch Wildlife Cruises & Tours......**1** D1

SIGHTS & ACTIVITIES
Fort Taiaroa.....................................(see **9**)
Glenfalloch Woodland Garden.........**2** B3
Hare Hill...**3** B1
Larnach Castle..................................**4** B2
Lovers Leap.......................................**5** C3
Marine Studies Centre......................**6** C2
Mihiwaka..**7** B1
Nature's Wonders.........................(see **9**)
Orokonui Ecosanctuary....................**8** B1
Royal Albatross Centre......................**9** D1
Yellow-Eyed Penguin Conservation
  Reserve.......................................**10** D1

SLEEPING
Billy Brown Backpackers..................**11** C1
Bus Stop Backpackers.......................**12** C2
Dunedin Holiday Park.......................**13** A3
Kaimata Retreat................................**14** D2
Larnach Lodge...............................(see **4**)
McFarmers Backpackers....................**15** C2
Penguin Place Lodge.....................(see **10**)
Portobello Motels.............................**16** C2
Portobello Village Tourist Park........**17** C2

EATING
1908 Café...**18** C2
Portobello Coffee Shop & Café.........**19** C2
Portobello Hotel...............................**20** C2

DRINKING
Carey's Bay Hotel.............................**21** B1
Chick's Hotel....................................**22** B1

on peninsular wildlife, and a cafe (mains $10 to $23).

Prices detailed are for December to March; rates are lower in other months.

YELLOW-EYED PENGUINS

One of the world's rarest penguins, the hoiho (yellow-eyed penguin) is found along the Otago coast, and several peninsula beaches are good places to watch them come ashore (any time after 4pm).

There are two private operators leading tours to yellow-eye colonies on private land (see following), and other tours (see p282) also visit habitats on private farmland not accessible to the public. The birds also nest at a couple of public beaches, including **Sandfly Bay**, which has a DOC hide. If you go alone, stay on the trails, view penguins *only* from the hide and don't approach these shy creatures; even loud voices can disturb them. The penguins have been badly distressed by tourists using flash photography or traipsing through the nesting grounds. Don't loiter on the beach, as this deters them from coming ashore.

The **Yellow-Eyed Penguin Conservation Reserve** (☎ 03-478 0286; www.penguinplace.co.nz; McGrouther's Farm, Harington Point Rd; tours adult/child $40/12) has replanted the penguins' breeding grounds, built nesting sites, cared for sick and injured birds and trapped predators. Ninety-minute tours include a talk on penguin conservation and close-up viewing from a system of hides. You can see the birds all year round, but summer is best. Between October and March, tours run regularly from 10.15am to 90 minutes before sunset; between April and September they're just from 3.15pm to 4.45pm. The tours are popular, so book ahead. For accommodation at the Penguin Place Lodge, see p282.

Situated just 1km past the albatross colony, and based on a large sheep farm that covers most of the peninsula's tip, **Nature's Wonders** (☎ 0800 246 446, 03-478 1150; www.natureswondersnaturally.com; Taiaroa Head; tours adult/child $50/45; ✆ tours from 10.15am) runs one-hour tours that take you up close to Stewart Island shags, NZ fur seals, and finally along a private little beach to a yellow-eyed penguin colony, where you can get within metres of the birds without disturbing them. The tour is conducted in 'go-anywhere' Argos vehicles and is an exciting combo of improbable scenery and wildlife adventure. It's worth it for the beautiful vistas alone.

BLUE PENGUINS

Blue penguins can be viewed at Pilot Beach, just below the albatross centre car park. The penguins come ashore just before dusk. Walk down the gravel road to the viewing area near the beach, and remain there until the birds have returned to their burrows. There may be as many as 80 or more in summer, but sometimes none in winter.

SEA LIONS

Sea lions are most easily seen on a tour (see p282), but are regularly present at **Sandfly Bay**, **Allans** and **Victory Beaches**. They are predominantly bachelor males vacationing from Campbell Island or the Auckland Islands. Give them plenty of space, as they can really motor over the first 20 metres.

LARNACH CASTLE

Standing proudly on the peninsula's highest point, **Larnach Castle** (☎ 03-476 1616; www.larnachcastle.co.nz; Camp Rd; castle & grounds adult/child $25/10, grounds only $10/3; ✆ 9am-7pm, to 5pm in winter) was an extravagance of the Dunedin merchant, banker and politician William Larnach. Built in 1871 to impress his French-nobility-descended wife (she apparently didn't like it much), the ostentatious, Gothic mansion is filled with exquisite antique furnishings. Larnach committed suicide in Parliament House in 1898, financially ruined, and with his latest wife and favourite son romantically linked.

The **gardens** offer fantastic views of the peninsula and harbour, and the surrounding native rainforest showcases impressive birdsong. There's a cafe in the grand ballroom, and unique accommodation (see p282). Catch the Portobello bus to Company Bay, and then it's a 4km walk uphill.

OTHER SIGHTS

Glenfalloch Woodland Garden (☎ 03-476 1006; www.glenfalloch.co.nz; 430 Portobello Rd; admission by donation; ✆ gardens 9.30am-dusk, cafe-wine bar 11am-3.30pm Mon-Fri, 11am-4.30pm Sat & Sun Sep-Apr) covers 12 hectares with flowers, walking tracks and swaying, mature trees including a 1000-year-old matai. Expect spectacular harbour views. The Portobello bus stops out the front.

The **Marine Studies Centre** (☎ 03-479 5826; www.marine.ac.nz; Hatchery Rd; adult/child/family $12/6/24; ✆ noon-4.30pm) has octopuses, seahorses, crayfish, sharks and a huge pink model squid.

Help with fish-feeding (Wednesday and Saturday 2pm to 3pm), or join a guided tour at 10.30am (adult/child/family $21/11/48 for entry plus tour). The centre showcases the work of the adjacent university-run marine laboratory.

Activities

The peninsula's coastal and farmland walkways offer stunning views and the chance to see wildlife on your own. Pick up a free copy of the detailed *Otago Peninsula Tracks* from the Dunedin i-SITE. A popular walking destination is the beautiful **Sandfly Bay**, reached from Seal Point Rd (moderate; 40 minutes) or Ridge Rd (difficult; 40 minutes). From the end of Sandymount Rd, you can follow a trail to the impressive **chasm** (20 minutes). Most trails are closed during September and October for lambing.

Wild Earth Adventures (☎ 03-489 1951; www.wild earth.co.nz; trips from $95) offers trips in double sea kayaks, with wildlife often sighted en route. Trips run between four hours and a full day, with some starting from Dunedin and some on the peninsula.

Peninsula Bike & Kayak (☎ 03-478 0724; www. bike-kayak.com) rents bikes ($25/35 per hour/day) and kayaks ($50 for two hours). Guided kayak tours, depart from Portobello and run for two or three hours ($120/170 for one/two people).

Tours

Back to Nature Tours (☎ 03-479 2009; www.backto naturetours.co.nz; adult/child $89/45)

Citibus (☎ 03-477 5577; www.transportplace.co.nz; adult/child from $90/30) Tours combining albatross and penguin viewing.

Elm Wildlife Tours (☎ 0800 356 563, 03-454 4121; www.elmwildlifetours.co.nz; standard tour $89). Small-group tours of up to six hours. Pick-up and drop-off from Dunedin is included.

Monarch Wildlife Cruises & Tours (Map p280; ☎ 03-477 4276; www.wildlife.co.nz) One-hour boat trips from Wellers Rock (adult/child $45/20), and half- ($85/30) and full-day ($210/105) tours from Dunedin. Include breeding grounds for sea lions, penguins, albatross and seals often inaccessible by land.

Otago Explorer (☎ 0800 322 240, 03-474 3300; www. otagoexplorer.com) Runs 2½-hour tours of Larnach Castle (adult/child $55/27.50) and summertime wildlife tours. Transport from Dunedin included.

Twilight Wildlife Tour (☎ 03-454 4121; www. twilighttours.co.nz; adult $91, student/child $79)

Sleeping

Portobello Village Tourist Park (☎ 03-478 0359; porto bellopark@xtra.co.nz; 27 Hereweka St, Portobello; powered sites per adult $13/15, units d $45-85, tourist flats $90-120) With lots of trees and grass, this is a pleasant place to stake your tent. There's a kids' play area, a modern kitchen and wheelchair-accessible facilities. Backpacker rooms are BYO everything, and self-contained units are smartly decorated.

Penguin Place Lodge (☎ 03-478 0286; McGrouther's Farm, Harington Point Rd; adult/child $25/10) Atop the hill and surrounded by farmland, this lodge has a good shared kitchen, a bright lounge, and basic double and twin rooms. There are views across the farm and harbour, you're close to seals and albatross, and you're next-door neighbours with the penguins. Linen costs $5 extra.

our pick **McFarmers Backpackers** (☎ 03-478 0389; mcfarmers@xtra.co.nz; 774 Portobello Rd; lodge dm/s $27/40, d $55-65, cottage d $90) On a working farm with harbour views, this rustic timber lodge and self-contained cottage are steeped in character and feel instantly like home. Lounge on the window seat or sundeck, barbecue out the back, or get warm in front of the woodburning stove. You'll almost forget you came to visit the nearby albatross and penguins. The cottage is great for families, and there are organic vegies and eggs available. The Portobello bus goes past the gate.

Bus Stop Backpackers (☎ 03-478 0330; www.bus -stop.co.nz; 252 Harington Point Rd; dm $35, cottage d $120-140; 🖳) Enjoy harbour views and salty smells from this sweet little house; watch sea lions catching their dinner without even leaving the comfy lounge. Borrow the dinghy and catch your own dinner to be cooked, smoked or barbecued. There's a triple and double in the house, or beds in a 1970s Bedford bus. A new self-contained cottage is also on offer. In season there are also organic vegies.

Portobello Motels (☎ 03-478 0155; www.portobello motels.com; 10 Harington Point Rd, Portobello; d $135-145; 🛜) Sunny, modern, self-contained units just off the main road in Portobello. Studio units have small decks overlooking the bay. One- and two-bedroom units are also available (add $25/15 per extra adult/child), but are viewless.

Larnach Lodge (☎ 03-476 1616; www.larnach castle.co.nz; Camp Rd; stable d $155, lodge d $260-280, all incl breakfast; 🖳 🛜) Larnach Castle's back-garden lodge has 12 individually decorated rooms. The Queen Victoria Room has a giant four-poster bed, and in the Goldrush Room guests sleep in an old horse-drawn carriage. Less frivolous are the atmospheric rooms in the 125-year-old Coach House with sloping Tudor ceilings. Dinner available by arrangement.

Kaimata Retreat (☎ 03-456 3443; www.kaimatanz. com; 297 Cape Saunders Rd; s/d $380/450) This luxury ecolodge has three rooms overlooking a gloriously isolated inlet on the eastern edge of Otago Peninsula. Watch sea lions and bird life from the spacious decks, or get even closer with an eco-expedition with local farmer, Dave. Be sure to include a private three-course dinner ($99 per person) from chef Dani, and don't make the mistake of staying just one night.

Eating

1908 Café (☎ 03-478 0801; 7 Harington Point Rd, Portobello; mains $20-34; 🕑 11.30am-10pm) Salmon, venison and steak are joined by fresh fish and blackboard specials, and there's a box of toys for the kids. It's a beautiful old building, cheerfully embellished with local art.

Other dining options near the 1908 Café include the Portobello Hotel, and the Portobello Coffee Shop & Café for excellent burgers ($13.50) and expensive internet. It's a good breakfast ($8 to $14) stop if you're getting an early start from Dunedin. There's takeaways at the Portobello Store, and cafes attached to Larnach Castle, Nature's Wonders, Glenfalloch Woodland Garden and the Royal Albatross Centre.

There are plenty of 'hey-let's-stop-here' places for picnics, so stock up before you leave Dunedin.

Getting There & Around

Up to 10 buses travel each weekday between Dunedin's Cumberland St and Portobello Village ($4), with one or two a day continuing on to Harington Point. Weekend services are more limited. Once on the peninsula, it's tough to get around without your own transport. Most tours will pick you up from your accommodation.

There's a petrol station in Portobello, but opening hours are unpredictable. Fill up in Dunedin before driving out.

OTAGO HARBOUR'S NORTH SHORE

The north shore of Otago Harbour provides a worthy detour from the main tourist track,

with one excellent accommodation option. The Orokonui Ecosanctuary (p271) is also worthwhile for nature buffs.

Little **Port Chalmers** (population 3000) is only 15km out of the city (15 minutes' drive, or bus 13 or 14 from stand 4 outside the Countdown supermarket on Cumberland St), but it feels a world away. Somewhere between working class and bohemian, Port Chalmers has a history as a port town but has increasingly attracted Dunedin's arty types. Dunedin's best rock-and-roll pub, **Chick's Hotel** (p277) is an essential after-dark destination, and daytime attractions include a growing range of raffish cafes, design stores and galleries.

The 150-year-old bluestone **Carey's Bay Hotel** (☎ 03-472 8022; 17 MacAndrew Rd, Carey's Bay; mains $15-25; 🕑 bar 11.30am-late Mon-Sun, restaurant 11am-3pm Mon-Thu, 11am-9pm Fri-Sun), 1km past the docks, has a bar with views of fishing boats and the harbour. There is a great collection of art from local painter Ralph Hotere, plus other Otago artworks. Meals tend to be focussed on seafood; the salmon fish cakes ($18.50) are good.

On a sheep-and-deer farm 5km down the road from Port Chalmers, **Billy Brown Backpackers** (☎ 03-472 8323; www.billybrowns.co.nz; 423 Aramoana Rd, Hamilton Bay; dm/d $27/66) has magnificent views across the harbour to the peninsula. There's a lovely rustic shared lounge with cosy woodburner, and plenty of retro vinyl to spin.

CENTRAL OTAGO

Rolling hills, grassy paddocks and a succession of tiny, charming little gold-rush towns make this region worth exploring, though most travellers barely pause for breath as they pass through. However it rewards a bit of effort: Naseby and Clyde compete for the title of NZ's cutest towns, and rugged and laconic 'Southern Man' types can be seen propping up the bar in backcountry hotels. There are also fantastic opportunities for those on two wheels, whether speeding down old gold-mining trails or taking it easy on the rail trail (see p286). Online see www.centralotagonz. com.

CROMWELL
pop 2610

Cromwell has a charming little historic precinct near the lake, and courtesy of local farms and orchards, more than a few good eateries. If you're travelling east to Dunedin or west to Queenstown, it's a good spot to stop for lunch. The nearby Bannockburn region has fine vineyards crafting excellent pinot noir, and also some lovely vineyard restaurants (the boxed text, below).

At the time of writing, the **Cromwell i-SITE** (☎ 03-445 0212; www.centralotagonz.com; 🖵 9am-6pm; 🖵) was in Cromwell's central shopping mall, but it *may* have moved to a new location on the main road from Queenstown in the life of this book.

Grab a copy of *Walk Cromwell,* which covers some cool local mountain-bike and walking trails, including the nearby gold-rush ghost-town of Bendigo. Bikes can be hired from **Cycle Surgery** (☎ 03-445 4100; www.cyclesurgery. co.nz) for $35 per day.

There is internet access at the i-SITE, and laptop users can use the LAN network ($2) at the **public library** (🖵 10am-5pm Mon-Fri, 10am-1pm Sat), also in the Cromwell mall.

Back in 1992, when the Clyde Dam was completed, it flooded the original Cromwell village including the town centre, 280 homes, six farms and 17 orchards. Many historic buildings were disassembled before the flooding and have since been restored as **Old Cromwell Town**. This pedestrianised zone sits beside the lake that swallowed the old town, and as well as featuring interesting historical buildings, there is good eating and interesting galleries. See the cool artworks at **Hullabaloo Art Space** (www.odelle.com) and interesting metalworks at **Stoop Gallery** (www.stoop. co.nz) and don't miss the Grain & Seed Café (opposite). Grab a copy of *Old Cromwell Town Historic Precinct* for a self-guided tour. During summer a **farmers market** kicks off at 8am every Sunday.

Zip around the Kawarau River on a 40-minute jetboat ride with **Goldfields Jet** (☎ 0800 111 038, 03-445 1038; www.goldfieldsjet.co.nz; adult/child $90/49).

The sinuous and hilly roads of Central Otago are perfect for negotiating on two wheels. See **Central Otago Motorcycle Hire** (☎ 03-445 4487; www.comotorcyclehire.co.nz; 271 Bannockburn Rd; motorcycle hire per day from $275) for bike hire – including Harley Davidsons. Much smaller Italian scooters ($90 per day) are perfect for zipping around the area's lakes, orchards and vineyards, and only require a car drivers' licence. The company can also advise on improbably scenic routes around Queenstown, Glenorchy and Wanaka.

Sleeping

Most of Cromwell's motels are huddled near the town's central shopping mall.

Cairnmuir Camping Ground (☎ 03-445 1956; Cairnmuir Rd, Bannockburn; sites adult/child $14/7, cabins adult/child $20/10) Peaceful grassy camping ground beside the lake 10 minutes' drive from Cromwell.

Cromwell Top 10 Holiday Park (☎ 0800 107 275, 03-445 0164; www.cromwellholidaypark.co.nz; 1 Alpha St; unpowered & powered sites $36, cabins d $60-70, units $90-170; 🖵) The size of a small European nation and packed with cabins, self-contained units and rooms of various descriptions, all set in tree-lined grounds.

Quartz Reef Creek (☎ 03-445 0404; www.quartz reefcreek.co.nz; Rapid 349, SH8, Northburn, Cromwell; d incl breakfast $130) This modern B&B enjoys lake views and a quiet location about 3km north of town. Accommodation is in three private studios, and breakfast often includes freshly baked bread and homemade preserves. Ask about the sunny upstairs studio.

SEARCHING FOR THE PERFECT PINOT NOIR

The Bannockburn Valley near Cromwell is home to NZ's finest pinot noir wines, and accounts for over half of Central Otago's total wine production. Vineyards to visit include **Mt Difficulty Wines** (☎ 03-445 3445; www.mtdifficulty.co.nz; Felton Rd, Bannockburn; platters $12-40, mains $25-28; 🖵 cellar door 10.30am-4.30pm, restaurant noon-3pm) and **Carrick Wines** (☎ 03-445 3480; www.carrick.co.nz; Cairnmuir Rd, Bannockburn; platters $12-25, mains $18-25; 🖵 cellar door 11am-4pm, restaurant noon-3pm). Both vineyards also have highly regarded restaurants open for lunch; the alfresco eateries get pretty busy, so it's worthwhile phoning ahead to book. Before you head off to Bannockburn, visit the Cromwell i-SITE and check out the handy display showcasing the area's vineyards.

Vineyard tours can be arranged through **Travel Collective** (☎ 0800 326 228, 03-445 4927; www. travelcollectivegroup.com; 8 Pinot Noir Dr; Cromwell; per person incl lunch $145).

For online information, see www.otagowine.com.

Hills of Gold (☎ 03-445 4487; www.comotorcycle hire.co.nz/accommodation; 271 Bannockburn Rd; d $140) Located 2.7km from Cromwell, and en route to the excellent Bannockburn vineyards, Hills of Gold consists of one modern and comfortable studio flat in a rural location near Lake Dunstan. A big-screen TV, audio system and private garden offer additional touches of luxury. Mountain bikes can be rented, and it's also the home base for Central Otago Motorcycle Hire (p283).

Eating & Drinking

Juice Café (☎ 03-445 2211; SH8; meals from $10; ✆ 8am-5pm) Sitting beside the state highway at the entry to town, this sunny little cafe dishes up delicious salads and world-famous-in-Cromwell fresh fruit smoothies ($6).

Grain & Seed Café (☎ 03-445 1007; Old Cromwell Town; lunch from $10; ✆ 8am-4pm) Set in a beautiful stone building that was once Jolly's Grain Store, this cute cafe serves up big, delicious, inexpensive meals. Grab an outside table beside the lake.

Thai Crom (☎ 03-445 1546; 50 The Mall; dinner mains $15-22; ✆ noon-9pm Mon-Sat, 5-9pm Sun) This Thai eatery is very authentic, with the owner's mother-in-law drifting in and out. Spice levels are carefully adhered to, there's cold Singha beer to cool the palate, and the $10 lunch specials are a tasty way to manage your daily budget.

Brewhouse Bar & Bistro (☎ 03-445 0725; 71 The Mall; mains $15-30; ✆ 11am-late) Cromwell's best spot for a quiet beer also offers robust pub meals big enough to sate the appetite of a 19th-century goldminer. Late 20th-century pop videos and big screen 21st-century sport provide other distractions. A wider than normal range of Speight's finest complements wines from just up the road.

Getting There & Away

Atomic Shuttles (☎ 03-349 0697; www.atomictravel. co.nz), **InterCity** (☎ 03-474 9600; www.intercity.co.nz), **Naked Bus** (☎ 0900 625 33; www.nakedbus.com) and **Wanaka Connexions** (☎ 03-443 9122; www.time2.co.nz) all run from Cromwell to Queenstown and Alexandra for $15 to $20, and to Dunedin for $35 to $40. Some services connect to Christchurch and Invercargill. **Catch-a-Bus** (☎ 03-449 2024; www.catchabus.co.nz) runs a convenient service linking Dunedin and Wanaka, stopping at Middlemarch, Ranfurly, Alexandra and Cromwell. Other stops near the Otago Central Rail Trail (including Naseby) can also be requested.

CLYDE
pop 850

On the banks of the emerald-green Clutha River, the little village of Clyde (www.clyde. co.nz) looks more like a cute 19th-century gold-rush film set than a real town. Despite a recent influx of retirees, Clyde retains a friendly, small-town feel, and even when holidaymakers arrive in numbers over summer, it's a great place to chill out. It's also one end of the Otago Central Rail Trail (p286).

Sights & Activities

Pick up a copy of *Walk Around Historic Clyde* available from the Alexandra i-SITE. **Clyde Historical Museum** (☎ 03-449 2711; Blyth St; adult/child $3/1; ✆ 2-4pm Tue-Sun, closed May-Oct) has random Maori and Victorian exhibits and information about the Clyde Dam.

The **Alexandra-Clyde 150th Anniversary Walk** (three hours one-way) is a riverside trail that's fairly flat with ample resting spots and shade. **Trail Journeys** (☎ 0800 724 587; www.trailjourneys.co.nz; Clyde Railhead; ✆ tours Sep-Apr) rents bikes (from $35 per day) and kayaks (from $40) and offers cycling tours.

Held on Easter Sunday, the **Clyde Wine & Food Festival** (www.promotedunstan.org.nz) showcases the region's bountiful produce and esteemed wines. For the rest of the year, visit **Central Gourmet Galleria** (☎ 03-449 3331; www.centralone.co.nz; 27 Sunderland St; ✆ 9.30am-5pm Mon-Fri, 10am-4pm Sat & Sun) for a stellar collection of award-winning local wines, many of which you won't find anywhere else.

To explore the area's boutique vineyards in a restored retro school bus, contact the **Grape Escape** (☎ 03-449 2696; tours per person $60-80).

Sleeping & Eating

In February and March, Clyde gets very busy and advance booking of accommodation is recommended.

Hartley Arms Backpackers (☎ 03-449 2700; hartley arms@xtra.co.nz; 25 Sunderland St; per person $40) In the old stables behind a beautiful 1869 building that was once the Hartley Arms Hotel, these three cosy rooms look out to a peaceful, private, stone-walled garden and share a small kitchen/lounge. Tables and chairs in the shade of the cherry tree are a fine place to stretch limbs weary from 150km of rail trail.

Dunstan House (☎ 03-449 2295; www.dunstanhouse. co.nz; 29 Sunderland St; d $100-200; 🖳) This restored Victorian-aged, balconeyed inn has lovely guests' bar and lounge areas. Rooms with en suite, individually decorated in period style, are a little pricier, but most have claw-foot tubs. Less expensive (but still flash) rooms are next door in 'Miners Lane'. Dunstan House is only open from September to May.

Bank Café (☎ 03-449 2955; 31 Sunderland St; snacks $8-10; 🕙 9am-4.30pm) Owned by a group of passionate local foodies, everything is made fresh every day at the Bank Café. That includes superlative cakes and slices, and made-to-order ciabatta sandwiches ($8) that are perfect for lunch on the rail trail.

Post Office Café & Bar (☎ 03-449 2488; 2 Blyth St; mains $12-28; 🕙 10am-9pm) Clyde's stately old 1899 post office houses a popular restaurant famous for its garden tables and gourmet versions of substantial favourites such as barbecue steak sandwiches or hotpot. The neighbouring old postmaster's house has lovely rooms (doubles from $95) with antique furnishings such as travelling trunks and bureaus.

Getting There & Away
Although no company has a dedicated stop here, buses travelling between Cromwell and Alexandra pick up and drop off in Clyde on request (it may incur a small surcharge). See p285 for details.

ALEXANDRA
pop 4620
Unless you've come here especially for the Easter Bunny Hunt or September's NZ Merino Shearing Championships, the reason to visit Alexandra is for the nearby mountain biking. Some travellers, entranced by well-shorn sheep and rabbit-free slopes, stay for seasonal fruit-picking work.

The **Alexandra i-SITE** (☎ 03-448 9515; www.central otagonz.com, www.alexandra.co.nz; 22 Centennial Ave;

TWO WHEELS GOOD: OTAGO CENTRAL RAIL TRAIL

Stretching from Dunedin to Clyde, the Central Otago rail branch linked small, inland goldfield towns with the big city from the early 20th century through to the 1990s. After the 150km stretch from Middlemarch to Clyde was permanently closed, the rails were ripped up and the trail resurfaced. The result is a year-round trail that takes bikers, walkers and horseback riders along a historic route containing old rail bridges, viaducts and tunnels. With excellent trailside facilities (toilets, shelters and information), no steep hills, gob-smacking scenery and profound remoteness, the trail attracts well over 10,000 visitors annually. Up to 95% of rail trail riders are Kiwis, so it's an excellent option for overseas visitors to combine meeting New Zealanders with experiencing a beautiful part of the country. March to April is the busiest time, when the trail is packed with urban refugees from Auckland, Wellington, Christchurch and, increasingly, Australia.

The trail can be followed in either direction. One option is to travel from Dunedin on the scenic Taieri Gorge Railway (p279), cycle from Pukerangi to Middlemarch (19km by road) and begin the trail the following day. The entire trail takes approximately four to five days to complete by bike (or a week on foot), but you can obviously choose to do as short or long a stretch as suits your plans. There are also easy detours to towns such as Naseby and St Bathans. See the map on p267 for the route. Many settlements along the route offer accommodation and dining. An evolving highlight of the rail trail is an increasing range of lodgings in restored cottages and rural farmhouses. Check out the two rail trail websites detailed below.

Zeroing the bike computer at Middlemarch, the towns through which you pass, in order of increasing distance away from Dunedin, are: Hyde (27km), Waipiata (49km), Ranfurly (59km, with a possible detour to Naseby), Wedderburn (63km), Oturehua (75km), Ida Valley (90km), Lauder (107km, with a possible detour to St Bathans), Omakau (117km), Chatto Creek (106km), Alexandra (143km), and finally Clyde (151km).

Mountain bikes can be rented in Dunedin, Middlemarch, Alexandra and Clyde. Any of the area's major i-SITEs or other information centres (including Dunedin, Cromwell and Alexandra) can provide detailed information on the trail. See www.otagocentralrailtrail.co.nz and www.otagorailtrail.co.nz to get track information, accommodation options and tour companies. The *Otago Rail Trail Guide Book* – available at information centres in the region, and online at www.otagorailtrail.co.nz – is both an excellent pre-trip planning resource and a great colour souvenir of the experience.

9am-6pm; 🖳) has internet access, and a necessary free map of this very spread-out town.

For the essential traveller's combination of internet *and* a laudromat, see **www.wash** (3 Limerick St; wash & dry per load $10; 🕙 8am-8pm; 🖳 🛜).

Sights & Activities

The modern **Alexandra Museum** (🕿 03-448 6230; 22 Centennial Ave; admission by donation; 🕙 9am-6pm) attached to the i-SITE has exhibits on geology, exploration and gold mining. The i-SITE can advise on local tour operators visiting historic gold-mining sites.

Mountain bikers will love the old gold trails weaving through the hills, and of course the **Otago Central Rail Trail** (see the boxed text, opposite). Collect relevant maps from the i-SITE, along with a series of mountain-biking pamphlets for cyclists of all levels. **Altitude Adventures** (🕿 03-448 8917; www.altitudeadventures. co.nz; 88 Centennial Ave) and **Trail Journeys** (🕿 0800 724 587; www.trailjourneys.co.nz; Clyde Railhead) both rent bikes, offer backcountry cycling tours and provide transport to trailheads.

To experience the scenery and history of the region by boat, join a 2½-hour **Clutha River Cruise** (🕿 03-449 3155; www.cluthrivercruises.co.nz; cruise $65). Book at the Alexandra i-SITE.

Sleeping

Generic motels line Centennial Ave on the way into town.

Marj's Place (☎ 03-448 7090; www.marjsplace.co.nz; 5 Theyers St; dm $25; 🖳) Two houses have myriad higgledy-piggledy rooms and a nice communal vibe, helped by the peaceful rose garden out back. Modern homestay rooms attached to the main house cost $45 per person. Cash only.

Alexandra Holiday Park (🕿 03-448 8297; www. alexandraholidaypark.com; 44 Manuherikia Rd; sites $30, cabins d $40-60; 🖳 🛜) Sitting beside the road to Ranfurly, with plenty of shade and backing onto the swimmer-friendly Manuherikia River. It's close to where the rail trail enters town. Self-contained units (sleeping up to six) start at $95 for two.

Quail Rock (🕿 03-448 7098; www.quailrock.co.nz; 5 Fairway Dr; d incl breakfast $120-150; 🖳 🛜) Perched high above town, this very comfortable B&B offers equal servings of privacy and mountain views. Homemade preserves give breakfast a unique touch, and dinners are also available. And yes, quail are often seen scratching around the rocks in the garden.

Speargrass Inn (p290) is another interesting option, 13km south towards Roxburgh.

Eating

Monteith's Brewery Bar (🕿 03-448 9189; 26 Centennial Ave; lunch $15-20, dinner $25-30; 🕙 11am-late) Opposite the i-SITE, this craft beer emporium in a stone cottage has a sunny deck, and a wide-ranging menu from cheap-and-cheerful bar snacks to more robust dinners including blue cod, lamb and pork.

Shaky Bridge Café (🕿 03-448 5111; Graveyard Gully Rd; mains $15-30; 🕙 10am-4pm Tue, Wed & Sun, 10am-late Thu-Sat) Over a 110-year-old footbridge near the rail trail, Shaky Bridge is a winery-cafe in a heritage mudbrick building with views of the Manuherikia River. Tuck into locally sourced delicacies such as venison, duck or salmon. Coffee and cake with a side order of vineyard views are perfect anytime.

Red Brick Café (🕿 03-448 9174; Centrepoint car park off Limerick St; mains $15-30; 🕙 10.30am-4pm Mon, 10.30am-late Tue-Sat, 10.30am-2pm Sun; Ⓥ) This funky cafe–wine bar is positioned beside an Alexandra shoppers' car park, the last place you'd expect to find a cafe so stylish or scallops so perfectly seared. Most ingredients (and wines) are locally sourced.

Also recommended:

Courthouse Café (🕿 03 448 7818; 8 Centennial Ave; 🕙 8am-5pm) Providing plenty of evidence of Alex's best coffee.

Foursquare (91 Tarbert St) Self-catering central.

Getting There & Away

See the Cromwell section (p283) for buses that pass along this route. From Alex you can head northwest past Cromwell towards Queenstown, south past Roxburgh and Lawrence towards the east coast or northeast along the Pig Root (see below).

ALEXANDRA TO PALMERSTON

Northeast of Alexandra, an irrigated strip of land tags alongside the highway, with the Dunstan and North Rough Ranges rising impressively on either side. This is the Manuherikia Valley, which tumbles into the Maniototo Plain as State Hwy 85 (SH85). From here to Palmerston and the sea, the scenic, winding road is charmingly known as the Pig Root.

Chatto Creek Tavern (🕿 03-447 3710; www.chatto creektavern.co.nz; SH85; meals $8-28) is a cute stone hotel from the 1880s right beside the rail trail and the highway. Pop in for a whitebait fritter (in season) or steak sandwich, or rest your weary calf muscles in a dorm bed ($20) or double room ($60).

Made up of half a handful of historic buildings, and home to just 50 souls, tiny **Ophir** lies across the Manuherikia River and lays claim to the country's largest range of temperatures (from 35°C above to 22°C below). Take the gravel exit south off SH85 to rattle across the cute, 1870s wooden-planked Dan O'Connell Bridge, a bumpy but scenic crossing. **Black's Hotel** (☎ 03-447 3826; steven.chapman@clear.net.nz; s/d incl breakfast $80/110) has cycle-friendly accommodation.

Back on SH85, Omakau and Lauder are good stops if you're a hungry rail-trailer with a sore bum and a need for a bed. Good-value rooms, excellent food and local company are all on tap at the **Omakau Commercial Hotel** (☎ 03-447 3715; omakaucommercial@xtra.co.nz; 1 Harvey St; s/d $45/80). Accommodation in nearby Lauder includes **Pedal Inn** (☎ 03-447 3460; benandcatherine@farmside.co.nz; SH85, Lauder; d $120), which has two brand-new self-contained units on a working farm, and the cosy **Muddy Creek Cutting** (☎ 03-447 3682; muddycreekcutting@clear.net.nz; per person $60), a charmingly restored 1930s mudbrick farmhouse. Dinners with a local, organic spin are also available ($40 per person).

Take the turn-off north, into the foothills of the imposing Dunstan Range and on to diminutive **St Bathans**, 17km from SH85. This once-thriving gold-mining town of 2000 people is now home to only half-a-dozen permanent residents. **Blue Lake** is an accidental attraction: a large hollow filled with amazingly blue mineral water that's run off abandoned gold workings. Walk around the alien-looking lake's edge to a lookout (one hour return).

The **Vulcan Hotel** (☎ 03-447 3629; www.stbathansnz.co.nz; Main Rd; dm/d $50/100) dates from 1863, has rooms to let, and does pub meals (mains $20 to $25). Considering it has a population of only six people (plus one labrador and a ghost or two), you'll find the bar here pretty busy on a Friday night as thirsty shearers from around the valley descend en masse. The Vulcan also rents some empty houses nearby. Guide (the black lab) will escort you down to a handful of cute cottages (doubles from $100 to $220 per night) including the old gaol. He's also very keen on his battered old rugby ball. Try not to lose it like we almost did.

If you can manage it, get along to the annual Wooden Cup rugby match in September where St Bathans (and helpers) take on the lads from Becks down the road – a near-legendary celebration of small-town rugby. You won't find a room empty for miles around, but might get a campsite at the rugby domain.

Back on SH85, the road swings around to run southeast and passes the historic **Wedderburn Tavern** (☎ 03-444 9548; www.wedderburntavern.co.nz; SH85; dm/d $40/90). Seven kilometres later is the turn-off for Naseby, or it's straight through to Ranfurly.

Naseby
pop 100

Cute as a button, surrounded by forest, and dotted with 19th-century stone buildings, Naseby is the kind of small town where life moves slowly. That the town is pleasantly obsessed with the fairly insignificant world of NZ curling indicates there's not much else going on. It's that lazy small-town vibe, along with good mountain biking and walking trails through the surrounding forest, that makes Naseby an interesting place to stay for a couple of days.

Naseby Information & Crafts (☎ 03-444 9961; Derwent St), in the old post office, has information on local walks and bike trails. For more mountain-biking information and to hire a bike, head to **Kila's Bike Shop** (☎ 03-444 9088; kilasbikeshop@xtra.co.nz; Derwent St; per day $35) near the Black Forest Café. **Naseby Forest Headquarters** (☎ 03-444 9995; Derwent St) is also good for maps of walks through the Black Forest.

All year round, you can shimmy after curling stones at the indoor ice rink at the **Naseby Alpine Park** (☎ 03-444 9878; www.curling.co.nz; Channel Rd; curling per hr $15; ◷ 10am-5pm). Curling tuition is also available.

From June to August there's ice skating at an adjacent outdoor rink, and a **seasonal ice luge** (☎ 03-444 9270; www.lugenz.co.nz; ◷ Jul-Aug) runs for a thrilling 360m down a nearby hillside. The luge is open to the public, but booking ahead is essential.

Set in 17 acres of woods, **Larchview Holiday Park** (☎ 03-444 9904; www.larchviewholidaypark.co.nz; Swimming Dam Rd; sites per person $13, cabins $45, self-contained cottages $75; ▯ 🛜) has an alpine feel, a small on-site playground and swimming at a dam nearby. There are also basic timber cabins and cottages.

Mountain View Accommodation (☎ 03-444 9972; www.mountainviewaccommodation.co.nz; 13a Channel Rd; d $95-120) has comfortable lemony flats attached to the owners' house with plush bedding, and the more expensive options have cooking facilities. On the hill across the road, the cottage is a steal at $130 for two ($20 per extra adult). A new self-contained three-bedroom house ($150 for two, plus $25 per extra adult) is a good option for families.

A mudbrick hotel dating from 1863, **Ancient Briton** (☎ 03-444 9990; www.ancientbriton.co.nz; 16 Leven St; s $60, d from $105) has a rambling range of basic-to-comfortable accommodation. Have some traditional pub grub (mains from $17 to $27), or prop yourself up at the bar to admire the trophies of the pub's 'Blue Hats' curling team and get to know the locals.

Fresh baking and good coffee features at the **Black Forest Café** (☎ 03-444 9820; 5 Derwent St; meals from $10; ☑ 9am-5pm), gorgeous inside with its stone walls, bright colours and warm polished wood. The wide-ranging menu features bagels, panini and creamy smoothies using local Central Otago fruit.

The Ancient Briton pub has a courtesy van and will pick up from Ranfurly or the rail trail. If prebooked, **Catch-a-bus** (☎ 03-449 2024; www.catchabus.co.nz) stops in Naseby on its Dunedin–Cromwell route. If you're driving, take the exit off SH85, just north of Ranfurly. From Naseby, you can wind your way northeast through spectacular scenery to **Danseys Pass** and through to Duntroon and the Waitaki Valley (p296).

Ranfurly
pop 840

Ranfurly is trying hard to cash in on its art-deco buildings – much of the town was rebuilt in the architecture of the day after a series of fires in the 1930s – and a few attractive buildings and antique shops line its sleepy main drag. The town holds an annual **Art Deco Festival** (www.ranfurlyartdeco.co.nz) on the last weekend of February.

The **Maniototo visitor information centre** (☎ 03-444 1005; www.maniototo.co.nz; Charlemont St; ☑ 10am-4pm daily Oct-Apr, Mon-Fri May-Sep; ☐) is in the old train station. Grab a copy of *Rural Art Deco – Ranfurly Walk* for a self-guided tour.

The **Old Post Office Backpackers** (☎ 03-444 9588; www.oldpobackpackers.co.nz; 11 Pery St; dm/s/d $25/40/60) is popular with rail-trailers. The art-deco **Ranfurly Lion Hotel** (☎ 03-444 9140; www.ranfurly hotel.co.nz; 10 Charlemont St; s $50, d from $70; ☐) has 16 comfortable rooms, a couple of bars, and does substantial pub meals (dinner from $20 to $27). All you'll need after a long day on two wheels and one bike seat.

Cheery and warm, with an open fire, local art and the Maniototo sports wall of fame, **E-Central Café** (☎ 03-444 8300; 14 Charlemont St; mains $7-15; ☑ breakfast & lunch) is definitely the best lunch option in town. Home-baked panini and giant toasties will find favour. For Ranfurly's best coffee, look for the train-shaped espresso caravan at the northern end of town.

To explore the rugged terrain made famous by local landscape artist Grahame Sydney, contact **Maniototo 4WD Safaris** (☎ 03-444 9703; www.maniototo4wdsafaris.co.nz; per person half-/full day $80/140).

A daily **Catch-a-Bus** (☎ 03-449 2024; www.catchabus.co.nz) shuttle passes through Ranfurly on its way between Wanaka and Dunedin. Rent bikes from **Ranfurly Bike Hire** (☎ 03-444 9245; 20 Charlemont St; per day $35).

Waipiata

About 10km southeast of Ranfurly and right on the rail trail, tiny Waipiata has the **Waipiata Country Hotel** (☎ 03-444 9470; www.waipiatahotel.co.nz; dinner mains $19-22; ☐), good for a cool beer and a comfy bed ($60 per person). There's a sunny CYO ('Cook Your Own') barbecue area, and the restaurant menu includes goodies such as Pig Root Spare Ribs and Bike Faster Pasta.

[our pick] **Peter's Farm Lodge** (☎ 0800 427 548, 027 686 1692; www.petersfarm.co.nz, peter@otagorailtrail.co.nz; Tregonning Rd; per person $35-45) Set on farmland 4km from Waipiata, this lodge has simple, comfortable rooms in a rustic 19th-century farmhouse. Shared dining tables encourage an end-of-the-day social vibe. Kayaks, fishing rods and gold pans are all available for no extra charge, so it's worth staying a couple of nights. Peter also runs the nearby Tregonnings Cottage ($45 per person), built in 1880, but now with a modern well-equipped kitchen. He'll also pick you up for nix from the Waipiata stop on the rail trail.

Ranfurly to Dunedin

After Ranfurly, SH85 runs 62km to Palmerston, then 55km south to Dunedin or 59km north to Oamaru. Another option is to hop on the southbound SH87 directly to Dunedin, 129km via **Hyde** and Middlemarch.

In Hyde, the **Otago Central Hotel** (☎ 03-444 4800; www.hydehotel.co.nz; dm $50, d $140-200, all incl breakfast) provides boutique accommodation. Linger with the friendly local terrier in the sunny terrace cafe for a second espresso before setting out on two wheels again.

With the Rock and Pillar Range as an impressive backdrop, the small town of **Middlemarch** (pop 200; www.middlemarch. co.nz) is one end of the Taieri Gorge Railway (see p279), and also a start or end-point of the Otago Central Rail Trail (see p286). Rent bikes and gear from **Cycle Surgery** (☎ 03-464 3630; www.cyclesurgery.co.nz; Snow Ave, Middlemarch; per day $35). The company has another branch at the other end of the rail trail in Clyde.

At the famous **Middlemarch Singles Ball** held across Easter in odd-numbered years, southern men from the region gather to woo city gals.

Blind Billy's Holiday Camp (☎ 03-464 3355; www. middlemarch-motels.co.nz; Mold St, Middlemarch; campsites per person $22, dm $22, cabins d $60) has a range of cheap accommodation (including self-contained units for $100 to $110 for two people, $40 for extras), meals and excellent advice for bikers.

On a family-owned farm also just a few hundred metres from the rail trail, **Trail's End** (☎ 03-464 3474; www.trailsend.co.nz; 91 Mason Rd, Middlemarch; d incl breakfast $130) combines secluded luxury cabins with views of the Rock and Pillar Mountain Range, and has the muscle-easing diversion of a spa pool.

Opposite the railway station, **Quench Café & Bar** (☎ 03-464 3070; 29 Snow Ave, Middlemarch; mains $10-30; ⏲ 8am-late) is versatility plus, with breakfast goodies such as the Cajun Corn Fritter Stack ($10 – recommended if you're beginning the rail trail), and ice-cold Speight's on tap (*definitely* recommended if you've just finished the trail: you'll have earned it).

ALEXANDRA TO DUNEDIN

Heading south from Alexandra, SH8 winds along rugged, rock-strewn hills above Lake Roxburgh, then follows the Clutha River as it passes lush farms and orchards and cool, shady forestry plantations. En route are a number of small towns, many from gold-rush days.

Only 13km south of Alexandra, **Speargrass Inn** (☎ 03-449 2192; www.speargrassinn.co.nz; SH8; d $140) has three units in attractive gardens behind a charming 1860s building with elegant guest areas. An on-site **restaurant** (mains $15-30; ⏲ 10am-5pm Mon, Wed & Thu, 10am-late Fri-Sun) offers cosmopolitan tastes including seared salmon, and mushroom and blue cheese tart.

From here, the road passes through Roxburgh, Lawrence and the **Manuka Gorge Scenic Reserve**, a scenic route through wooded hills and gullies. SH8 joins SH1 in Milton.

Roxburgh

The orchards surrounding Roxburgh provide excellent roadside stalls and equally plentiful seasonal fruit-picking work. **Roxburgh i-SITE** (☎ 03-446 8920; 120 Scotland St; ⏲ 9.30am-4pm) has information on mountain biking and water sports.

Villa Rose Backpackers (☎ 03-446 8761; www.villa rose.co.nz; 79 Scotland St; dm $30, units $95) is an old-fashioned villa with spacious dorm rooms and a huge modern kitchen. Newly built heritage-style self-contained units are super-comfortable. The manager can help sort out seasonal fruit-picking work, and provide discounted weekly rates.

For more luxury, **Lake Roxburgh Lodge** (☎ 03-446 8220; www.lakeroxburghlodge.co.nz; Lake Roxburgh Village; studios $120-150, 2-bdrm d $180) has comfortable stylish units. Staff will help you arrange tours, day trips, bike rides and kayaking, or you can just chill in the lakeside restaurant.

Stop at Roxburgh's iconic **Jimmy's Pies** (☎ 03-444-8596; 143 Scotland St; pies $3-5; ⏲ 7.30am-5pm). Renowned across the South Island since 1960, Jimmy's pastry delights are at their best just out of the oven. Try the apricot and apple flavour – you're in orchard country after all. Heading south, you'll find Jimmy's on your right just as you're leaving town.

Lawrence
pop 480

Lawrence is in a valley surrounded by farmland and forestry plantations. The **visitor information centre** (☎ 03-485 9222; www.lawrence.co.nz; 17 Ross Pl; ⏲ 9.30am-4.30pm, closed for lunch) advises on gold-rush sites, walking and mountain-bike trails, and jetboating.

Dating from 1875, **Marama Lodge** (☎ 03-485 9638; www.maramalodge.co.nz; SH8; lodge d incl breakfast $90-120, units $80-90) has a big guest lounge and impressive country-style rooms. Self-contained units are less grand, but very comfortable. Breakfast and dinner options are available.

The two one-bedroom flats and three studio units at **Jafas Motels** (☎ 03-485 9005; www.

jafaslawrence.co.nz; d $120; 🖥 🛜) are comfortable and modern. Rent a mountain bike ($40 per day) to explore the surrounding countryside.

Lemon Tree Café (☎ 03-485 9965; 28 Ross Pl; brunch $7.50-17; 🕙 9am-5pm Oct-May, 10am-4pm Thu-Tue Jun-Sep) is the finest eatery between Dunedin and Gore. This relaxed oasis in rural Otago serves vaguely Mediterranean fare with lots of organic ingredients. If it's a sunny day, sit outside in the garden.

CLUTHA DISTRICT
The mighty Clutha River is NZ's highest-volume river, and is dammed in several places to feed hydroelectric power stations. **Balclutha** is South Otago's largest town but is of little interest to travellers other than as a place to stock up on supplies before setting off into the Catlins (p666). The **Balclutha i-SITE** (☎ 03-418 0388; balclutha@i-SITE.org; 4 Clyde St) has local info and internet access. For more local information, see www.cluthacountry.co.nz.

NORTH OTAGO & WAITAKI

The broad, braided Waitaki River rushes across the northern boundary of Otago, setting the boundary with Canterbury to the north. South of the river on the coast lies Oamaru, a town of penguins and glorious heritage architecture. The Waitaki Valley itself is an alternative route inland, featuring freaky rock formations, Maori rock paintings and ancient fossils. The area is also one of NZ's newest winemaking regions (see p297).

OAMARU
pop 12,000
Nothing moves very fast in Oamaru: tourists saunter, locals languish and penguins waddle. Even oft-celebrated heritage modes of transport – penny farthings and steam trains – reflect an unhurried pace. For travellers, the town focuses mostly on penguins and the historic district, but eccentric gems such as the South Island's yummiest cheese factory, cool galleries and a peculiar live-music venue provide other distractions.

A history of refrigerated-meat shipping made Oamaru prosperous enough in the 19th century to build the imposing limestone buildings that grace the town today. In its 1880s heyday, Oamaru was about the same size as Los Angeles was at the same time. Oamaru also has an affinity with the arts that may well be rooted in its claim to Janet Frame (see the boxed text, p293), but extends to a lively arty and crafty community today.

Information
ATMs line Thames St, Oamaru's main street.
Oamaru i-SITE (☎ 03-434 1656; www.visitoamaru. co.nz; 1 Thames St; 🕙 9am-6pm; 🖥) Mountains of information including details on local walking trips and wildlife. There's internet, bike hire, and an interesting 10-minute DVD on the history of the town. Daily penguin viewing times are also posted outside.
Post office (cnr Coquet & Severn Sts)
Small Bytes Computing (191 Thames St; 🕙 9am-4.30pm; 🖥 🛜) Internet access, including paid wi-fi, is incorporated into the transport booking centre at Lagonda Tearooms.

Sights
HARBOUR-TYNE HISTORIC PRECINCT
Oamaru has some of NZ's best-preserved historic commercial buildings, particularly around the harbour and Tyne St, an area designated the Historic Precinct. They were built from the 19th century, largely using the local limestone (known as Oamaru stone or whitestone) in fashionable classic forms, from Gothic revival to neoclassical Italianate and Venetian palazzo. Pick up the free *Historic Oamaru* pamphlet, and see www.historic oamaru.co.nz. On Thames St, Oamaru's expansive main drag – laid out to accommodate the minimum turning circle of a bullock cart – don't miss the **National Bank** at No 11 and the **Oamaru Opera House** at No 92.

The fascinating area of narrow streets in the historic precinct is now home to bookshops, antique stores, galleries, vintage clothing shops and craft bookbinders. The **Woolstore** (1 Tyne St) has a cafe and souvenirs, and the **Auto Museum** (☎ 03-434 1556; adult/child $6/ free; 🕙 10am-4.30pm) is perfect for *Top Gear* fans (the racing cars from the 1930s through '80s are particularly cool). Upstairs, there's a **craft market** (🕙 10am-4pm Sun). Around the corner at the **Photo Shoppe** (☎ 03-434 3372; 🕙 10.30am-1pm, 2-4pm), you can get an old-style photo of yeeself in period dress-ups for $30. Oamaru's best-known artist, Donna Demente is one of the artists running the nearby **Grainstore Gallery** (☎ 027-261 3764; 🕙 noon-4pm Mon-Fri, 10am-4pm Sat & Sun).

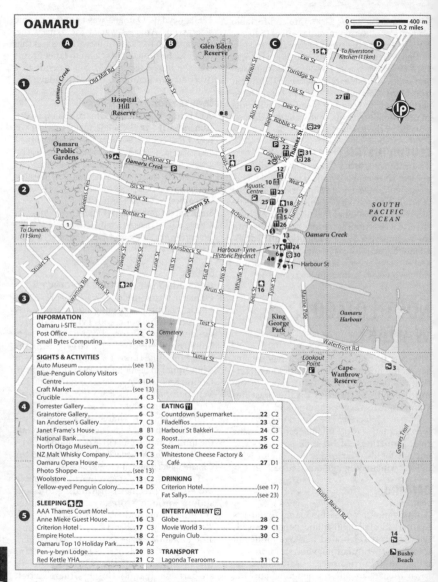

OAMARU

INFORMATION
Oamaru i-SITE	**1** C2
Post Office	**2** C2
Small Bytes Computing	(see **31**)

SIGHTS & ACTIVITIES
Auto Museum	(see **13**)
Blue-Penguin Colony Visitors Centre	**3** D4
Craft Market	(see **13**)
Crucible	**4** C3
Forrester Gallery	**5** C2
Grainstore Gallery	**6** C3
Ian Andersen's Gallery	**7** C3
Janet Frame's House	**8** B1
National Bank	**9** C2
North Otago Museum	**10** C2
NZ Malt Whisky Company	**11** C3
Oamaru Opera House	**12** C2
Photo Shoppe	(see **13**)
Woolstore	**13** C2
Yellow-eyed Penguin Colony	**14** D5

SLEEPING
AAA Thames Court Motel	**15** C1
Anne Mieke Guest House	**16** C3
Criterion Hotel	**17** C3
Empire Hotel	**18** C2
Oamaru Top 10 Holiday Park	**19** A2
Pen-y-bryn Lodge	**20** B3
Red Kettle YHA	**21** C2

EATING
Countdown Supermarket	**22** C2
Filadelfios	**23** C2
Harbour St Bakkeri	**24** C3
Roost	**25** C2
Steam	**26** C2
Whitestone Cheese Factory & Café	**27** D1

DRINKING
Criterion Hotel	(see **17**)
Fat Sallys	(see **23**)

ENTERTAINMENT
Globe	**28** C2
Movie World 3	**29** C1
Penguin Club	**30** C3

TRANSPORT
Lagonda Tearooms	**31** C2

Also check out the Oamaru limestone being carved at **Ian Andersen's gallery** (www.ianandersensculptor.co.nz; 15 Tyne St) and buy some smaller works to take home. Across the road at **Crucible Gallery** (16 Tyne St) are nice bronzes and custom-made jewellery. Art buffs should seek out the *Oamaru Arts & Crafts* brochure at the Oamaru i-SITE.

At the end of Harbour St, the **NZ Malt Whisky Company** (☎ 03-434 8842; www.nzmaltwhisky.co.nz; 14 Harbour St; ❧ 10am-5pm) uses the upper story of a handsome 130-year-old warehouse to mature barrel-loads of single-malt and blended whisky. Sample whisky and port for $2 per snifter, or there's a guided tour ($15 including four snifters) at 11am and 3pm.

The cafe-bar serves snacks and meals from $6, and you can buy bottles of the good stuff at the shop. It's definitely worth climbing the labyrinthine wooden stairs to the art gallery (free admission) on the upper floors.

On Sundays ride the old **steam train** (www. oamaru-steam.org.nz; adult/child/family one-way $5/2/12, return $8/3/18; 11am-4pm) from the historic district to the waterfront area. The two steam trains date from 1877 and 1924, although in winter they're occasionally replaced by a diesel.

PENGUINS

In an old limestone quarry near the waterfront, Oamaru's **blue-penguin colony** sees little blue penguins surfing in and wading ashore at the **visitors centre** (03-433 1195; www.penguins. co.nz; Waterfront Rd; adult/child $22/10; 9am-sunset). The penguins arrive just before dark (around 5.30pm in midwinter and 9.30pm midsummer) and it takes them about an hour to all come ashore. You'll see the most penguins (up to 150) in November and December; in the cold months from March to August there may be only 30 to 50 birds. Optimum viewing times for each night are posted at the Oamaru i-SITE. Use of camera flashes is prohibited. It can be cool, so dress warmly.

To understand the centre's conservation work, take the 30-minute daytime behind-the-scenes tour (self-guided adult/child $10/4 or guided $17.50/7.50). Forward bookings can be made on www.penguins.co.nz, and packages combining night viewing and the behind-the-scenes tour are also available.

If you head towards the penguin visitors centre around dark, and wait quietly in the car park, you'll see a few penguins waddling across the car park about the time the penguin centre empties out and people head back to their cars and buses. If you want to contribute towards the health of the penguins, pop into the centre and drop some coins in the donation box – their conservation efforts have helped increase the bird population dramatically.

Do not under any circumstances wander around the rocks beside the sea here at night looking for penguins. It's damaging to their environment as well as stuffing up studies on the effect of humans on the little birds.

There are large hides and good trails to the **yellow-eyed penguin colony** at Bushy Beach, where the penguins come ashore in late afternoon to feed their young. Two hours before dark is the best time to see them. Despite their Maori name, *hoiho* (noisy shouter), they're extremely shy; if they see or hear you they'll head back into the water. **Graves Trail**, a 2.5km low-tide walk, starts from the end of Waterfront Rd and follows the rugged coastline around to

---

OAMARU IN FRAME

One of NZ's best-known novelists, Janet Frame, is intimately linked with Oamaru. The town, disguised in her novels as 'Waimaru', was Frame's home throughout most of her early years. Her writing is often described as 'dense', with early books also somewhat grim, a reflection of her own troubled life. But they are also unique in the construction of their stories and the nature in which the story is told. Later books remain intense, with wordplays, mythological clues and illusions, but are less gloomy.

It was in 1951 that Frame, a (misdiagnosed) sufferer of schizophrenia at Seacliff Lunatic Asylum (p299), found sudden recognition as a writer, happily causing her doctors to rethink her planned lobotomy. Released, with frontal lobe intact, she moved on to gain international recognition in 1957 with her first novel *Owls Do Cry*, in which 'Waimaru' features strongly. Her subsequent literary accomplishments include *Faces in the Water* (1961), *The Edge of the Alphabet* (1962), *Scented Gardens for the Blind* (1963), *A State of Siege* (1967) and *Intensive Care* (1970). Keep an eye out in NZ bookstores and you'll find new or secondhand copies. Or get Jane Campion's film version of *An Angel at my Table*, based on the second volume of Frame's autobiographical trilogy, to watch on DVD.

Many of the settings for these novels can be found in Oamaru. Pick up a free copy of *Janet Frame's Oamaru* from the Oamaru i-SITE and follow the 1½-hour self-guided tour.

Frame received numerous NZ and international awards, and was twice short-listed for the Nobel Prize for literature, most recently in 2003. She died the following year.

Janet Frame's childhood house is also open for viewing (2-4pm Nov-Apr) at 56 Eden St.

DUNEDIN & OTAGO

the yellow-eyed colony at Bushy Beach. Watch out for fur seals, and do not use a flash when photographing the penguins.

FORRESTER GALLERY
Housed in a beautiful, columned 1880s bank building, **Forrester Gallery** (☎ 03-434 1653; www.forrestergallery.com; 9 Thames St; admission free; ☷ 10.30am-4.30pm) has an excellent collection of regional art, and hosts diverse temporary exhibits, including contemporary media. This fantastic gallery is a good place to see works by Colin McCahon (p49), renowned for his darkly melancholic style.

OTHER SIGHTS
The **Oamaru public gardens** (main entry on Severn St) were first opened in 1876 and are a lovely place to chill out on a hot day, with endless lawns, waterways, bridges and a children's playground.

In the grand 19th-century library, the **North Otago Museum** (☎ 03-434 1652; www.northotagomuseum.co.nz; 60 Thames St; admission free; ☷ 10.30am-4.30pm Mon-Fri, 1-4.30pm Sat & Sun) has exhibits on Maori and Pakeha history, writer Janet Frame, architecture and geology.

Activities
Contact Rob at **Vertical Ventures** (☎ 03-434 5010, 021 894 427; www.verticalventures.co.nz) to rent mountain bikes ($45 per day), or join guided mountain-biking trips along forest tracks and coastal roads. To get vertical, join an abseiling or climbing group. Locations include the Elephant Rocks (p296).

Festivals & Events
Oamaru Wine & Food Festival (www.oamaruwineandfoodfest.co.nz) Third Sunday in February; showcase of North Otago's food and wine scene.

Victorian Heritage Celebrations (www.historicoamaru.co.nz) Oamaru livens up for five days in late November with locals wearing Victorian garb, penny-farthing races, and singing, dancing and theatre.

Tours
Living History Players (☎ 0800 548 344; www.livinghistorynz.com; adult/child/family $25/15/75) Professional actors bring to life the 'Secrets of the Old Town' in 50-minute walking tours leaving nightly at 7pm from the i-SITE.

MP3 Self-Guided Tour ($15) MP3 players available at the i-SITE.

Penguins Crossing (☎ 03-477 9083; www.travelheadfirst.com; adult/child/family $46/23/115) Door-to-door

2½-hour tour taking in the blue and yellow-eyed colonies. Price includes admission to the blue penguin colony. Pick up times vary from 4pm to 7pm throughout the year.

Ralph's Rambles (☷ on demand) Short ($20) and long ($30) tours of Oamaru highlights, and tours of Janet Frame literary sites. Tours range from 45 minutes to three hours ($50). Enquire at the i-SITE.

Victorian Oamaru Passport Tours Guided tours ($10) leave from the i-SITE daily at 10am from November to April.

Sleeping
Empire Hotel (☎ 03-434 3446; www.empirebackpackersoamaru.co.nz; 13 Thames St; dm/s/d $25/35/56; ☐ ☎) This 150-year-old hotel has been fitted out with cosy but modern backpackers' rooms. The two kitchens are spacious, the communal TV room is warmed by a nice wood burner, and bathrooms are clean and modern. Sitting right on the main street, it's the best-located accommodation in Oamaru.

Red Kettle YHA (☎ 03-434 5008; www.yha.co.nz; cnr Reed & Cross Sts; dm/d $28/60; ☷ closed May-Aug; ☐ ☎) This red-roofed cottage has colourfully painted inner walls, a well-equipped kitchen, and a cosy lounge. A good old-school vinyl collection will keep you and fellow guests entertained. It's on a quiet side street, a short walk from the town centre.

Oamaru Top 10 Holiday Park (☎ 0800 280 202, 03-434 7666; www.top10.co.nz; Chelmer St; unpowered/powered sites $34/38, cabins d $60, self-contained d $80-150; ☐ ☎) Grassy and well maintained, with trees out the back and the public gardens next door. Cabins are basic, but units with kitchen and varying levels of self-contained comfort are much nicer.

Anne Mieke Guest House (☎ 03-434 8051; www.theoamarubnb.com; 47 Tees St; s/d incl breakfast $60/85) The decor is a tad chintzy, and the ambience hushed like your Nana's house, but visitors are guaranteed harbour views at this good-value B&B. Look forward to spotless shared bathrooms and a spacious guest lounge.

Criterion Hotel (☎ 03-434 6247; www.criterion.net.nz; 3 Tyne St; s/tw/d without bathroom $80/100/130, d with bathroom $160, all incl breakfast) Period rooms at this 1877 hotel are smallish, but the guest lounge is large, and both are lovingly restored. Also includes home baking and preserves in a homey dining room. Downstairs there's the distraction of one of the South Island's best pubs.

AAA Thames Court Motel (☎ 0800 223 644, 03-434 6963; www.aaathamescourt.co.nz; 252 Thames St; d $105-

130; 🖥 📶) Good option for families with its comfortable, newly renovated units and a play area for kids. Extra people $15 each. There's also a cheaper self-contained caravan ($70).

Pen-y-bryn Lodge (☎ 03-434 7939; www.penybryn.co.nz; 41 Towey St; s/d incl breakfast $556/888; 🖥) Just past its 120th birthday, this old manor has lavish period rooms and guest areas. Rates include a full breakfast, predinner drinks in the drawing room, and a five-course, gourmet dinner in the fabulous dining room. Retire afterwards to the billiard room and show off on the full-sized billiards table.

Oamaru's motel mile kicks off at the northern end of town as SH1 morphs into Thames St.

Eating

Steam (☎ 03-434 3344; 7 Thames St; 🕙 8.30am-4.30pm Mon-Fri, 10am-4.30pm Sat & Sun). Steam specialises in coffees and fruit juices, and is a good spot to stock up on freshly ground coffee for your own travels.

Whitestone Cheese Factory & Café (☎ 03-434 8098; www.whitestonecheese.co.nz; 3 Torridge St; snacks & mains $5-10; 🕙 9am-5.30pm) The home of tasty, award-winning organic cheeses. Try the creamy Mature Windsor Blue or the ultrarich Mt Domet Double Cream. Buy cheese to take away, or dine here on various cheesy treats after you've tried the range of samples for a gold coin donation. The cheese rolls are an Otago delicacy, and there are also local fruit juices and Central Otago wines.

Roost (☎ 03-434 1165; 30 Thames St; meals $5-15; 🕙 8.30am-4.30pm Mon-Sat, 9am-4pm Sun) Good for the day's first coffee, and the toasted sandwiches ($7 to $12) make it a worthwhile lunch option, too. Grab a seat out the back to soak up the afternoon sun.

our pick **Riverstone Kitchen** (☎ 03-431 3505; 1431 SH1; mains $15-30; 🕙 9am-5pm Mon & Wed, 9am-late Thu-Sun, closed Tue Nov-Feb, closed Tue & Wed Mar-Oct; Ⓥ) This spacious haven 12km north of Oamaru on SH1 blends leather couches and polished concrete for a sophisticated ambience. The menu showcases simply prepared produce and local flavours, with standout options including lamb with smoked eggplant and free-range scrambled eggs with pesto on ciabatta. Beers include the best of the South Island and the North Island, and you can also pick up organic jams and preserves in the cool on-site deli.

Filadelfios (☎ 03-434 8884; 70 Thames St; pizzas $21.50-31.50; 🕙 11.30am-late; Ⓥ) A brick restaurant-bar that specialises in rather special pizzas and pastas. Read other travellers' notes on the wall while you wait for your meal to arrive. Dips and antipasto are also popular, particularly late at night when it becomes a lively bar.

In the historic precinct, the **Harbour St Bakkeri** (☎ 434 0444; Harbour St; 🕙 8am-4pm Tue-Sun) has beaut gourmet pies and the South Island's best sourdough bread – just perfect with a slab of local Whitestone cheese.

The central **Countdown Supermarket** (cnr Thames & Coquet Sts; 🕙 7am-9pm) is well stocked for self-caterers.

Drinking

Fat Sallys (☎ 03-434 8368; 84 Thames St; closed Mon) Popular with locals, especially early on when they're often tucking into a substantial pub meal. Come along on a Wednesday night for the rollicking pub quiz.

our pick **Criterion Hotel** (3 Tyne St) This restored property is the ultimate corner pub in Oamaru's heritage district. The canny owner maintains an ever-changing selection of draught brews and there's also excellent pub food. Don't blame us if you progress to the single malt heaven also on offer. Oamaru's historic district once boasted 13 boozers, and the Criterion is the only one still operating.

Entertainment

Penguin Club (☎ 03-434 1402; www.thepenguinclub.co.nz; Emulsion Lane off Harbour St; admission $10-15) Tucked down a seedy industrial alley off a 19th-century street, the Penguin's bizarre location matches its acts: everything from Flying Nun stalwarts the Clean to punky/grungy/rocky/country locals. Big national acts and up-and-coming international acts sometimes drop by, too. Fridays are open-stage jam night with free admission. If there's something on at Penguin – *anything* – go and see it. It's nominally Members Only, so ask at the Oamaru i-SITE about scoring a guest pass.

Movie World 3 (☎ 03-434 1077, info line 03-434 1070; www.movieworld3.co.nz; 239 Thames St; adult/child $13/8) Cheaper on Tuesdays.

Globe (12 Coquet St; 🕙 Fri & Sat) is the town's nightclub. The cafe Filadelfios (left) is another good late-night nightspot with occasional live music.

Getting There & Around

Bookings can be made through i-SITE and at the booking office at the **Lagonda Tearooms** (191

Thames St; 9am-4.30pm). Buses and shuttles also depart from this location.

The following buses and shuttle buses go to Dunedin (1¾ hours) and Christchurch (3½ hours).

Atomic Shuttles (03-349 0697; www.atomictravel. co.nz) Dunedin/Christchurch $20/30.

Coastline Tours (03-434 7744; www.coastline-tours. co.nz) Runs between Dunedin and Oamaru ($30), and will detour to Moeraki, Karitane, Seacliff or Dunedin airport if needed.

InterCity (03-474 9600; www.intercity.co.nz) Dunedin/Christchurch $28/40.

Knightrider (0800 317 057; www.knightrider.co.nz) Dunedin/Christchurch $31/41.

Naked Bus (0900 625 33; www.nakedbus.com) Dunedin/Christchurch $11/$16

Southern Link (0508 458 835; www.southernlink. co.nz) Dunedin/Christchurch $11/16.

WAITAKI VALLEY

The flat-bottomed pastoral Waitaki Valley is a little-travelled route but includes some unique sights and scenery between the turn-off at SH1 and Omarama. Predominantly farmland, the valley is also an outdoorsy paradise, and a place to shoot ducks, catch trout and salmon, and waterski on the strikingly blue hydrolakes. This is a possible route to Wanaka and Queenstown if you're heading south, or to Twizel and Mt Cook if you're heading north.

After following SH83 almost to Duntroon, detour left at the signposted turn-off to Danseys Pass. Just on your left, under an impressive limestone overhang on a hill with great views to the mountains, you'll find the Maraewhenua **Maori rock paintings**. The charcoal-and-ochre paintings date back several centuries, tracing everything from pre-European hunting to sailing ships, as well as more contemporary tributes to 1980s Kiwi funk band Supergroove.

Follow the road southish another 4km then turn left towards Ngapara. Two kilometres further on in a peaceful sheep paddock are **Elephant Rocks**. Sculpted by wind, rain and rivers, these huge limestone boulders lie about like giant slumbering animals. The bizarre landscape was utilised as Aslan's Camp in the NZ-filmed *Narnia* blockbuster (2005). If you're feeling adventurous, continue over Danseys Pass to Naseby (p288) from 2km back at the intersection.

Back on SH83 at Duntroon is the **Vanished World Centre** (03-431 2024; www.vanishedworld.

co.nz; 7 Campbell St; adult/family $5/10; 10am-4pm Oct-Jun, 11am-3pm Sat & Sun Jul-Sep), with small but interesting displays of 25-million-year-old fossils, including NZ's shark-toothed dolphins and giant penguins. There's also a selection of books on geology, history and talking lions. If you're really into fossils and geology, pick up a copy of the Vanished World Fossil Trail map outlining 20 different locations around North Otago. Just west of Duntroon is the **Takiroa Maori Rock Art Site**, with more drawings dating back many centuries; the fluidity of the shapes is still clear enough to be admired.

Tiny **Kurow** is at the junction of the Waitaki and Hakataramea Rivers. For good coffee and home baking, stop at the **Te Kohurau Restaurant & Café** (03-436 0603). Pop into the **Kurow Heritage & Information Centre** (03-436 0950; museum@kurow.co.nz; SH83) , which has an interesting local museum. Instead of continuing west from Kurow on SH83, take the 21km scenic detour over the Aviemore dam, around the northern lake shore past walking tracks and scenic campsites ($10), then over the huge Benmore dam earthworks. Rejoin SH83 just west of Otematata.

Omarama
pop 360

At the head of the Waitaki Valley, surrounded by mountain ranges, the Omarama area is at the centre of fabulous landscapes. The bizarre moonscape of the **Clay Cliffs** (admission $5) is the result of two million years of erosion on layers of silt and gravel that were exposed along the active Osler fault line. The cliffs are on private land; the turn-off is 3.5km north of Omarama, then it's another 10km on an unsealed road.

Wrinkly Rams (03-438 9751; www.thewrinklyrams. co.nz; SH8; adult/child/family $20/10/50; 2 or 3 shows daily 10.30am-4.30pm) does 30-minute stage shows of merino sheep being shorn using both modern and traditional methods, along with a sheepdog show. A barbecue lunch is included. Attached is one of the town's better restaurants.

Busy times in town include the Omarama **rodeo** (28 December) and the Omarama **sheepdog trials** (March).

The area's westerlies and warm summer thermals allow for world-class gliding over the hills and spectacular Southern Alps, and a **national gliding meet** is held here in December or January. Two companies will get you aloft from around $285.

Glideomarama.com (☎ 03-438 9555; www.glide omarama.com)
Southern Soaring (☎ 0800 762 746; www.soaring. co.nz)

If your legs are weary after mountain biking or hiking, or you just want to cosy up with your significant other, pop into the **Omarama Hot Tubs** (☎ 03-438 9703; www.hottubsomarama.co.nz; 25 Omamara Ave; ☒ 10am-10pm). The concept, combining private hot tubs (per person $30 to $40), and private 'wellness pods' ($125 for two people) including intimate, personal saunas, is Japanese, but with the surrounding mountain ranges and a pristine night sky, you could only be on the South Island of New Zealand. The chemical-free mountain water is changed daily, and used water is recycled for irrigation.

Omarama Hot Tubs also doubles as the local information office, and can assist with accommodation and transport information.

SLEEPING & EATING

Buscot Station (☎ 03-438 9646; SH8; dm/s/d $21/43/52; ☒) A slightly chintzy, but very comfortable farmhouse on a huge farm with big, open views. Large doubles in the main house and a large modern dormitory out back are all comfortable. Tony shares his kitchen and lounge, as well as his theories on farming and politics. You'll find the turn-off to Buscot's 10km north of Omarama.

Omarama Top 10 Holiday Park (☎ 03-438 9875; www.omaramatop10.co.nz; SH8; unpowered/powered sites $30/35, cabins d $45-80; ☒ ☜) Streamside and duckponded, this is a peaceful green space to

camp in. Cabins are compact; larger en suite and self-contained units cost $105 for two.

Heritage Gateway Hotel (☎ 03-438 9850; www. heritagegateway.co.nz; SH8; d $135-165; ☒ ☜) A large complex of comfortable, modern rooms (all with en suite) and a restaurant-bar on the road towards Queenstown.

Wrinkly Rams (☎ 03-438 9751; SH8; breakfast $10-15, dinner $20-30; ☒ 7am-9pm) Restaurants attached to tourist attractions can be dodgy, but the dinners here (pan-fried cod, tender lamb shanks) are quite delicious. Big glass windows and outside tables give a nice view of the mountains while you eat. Wines from the nearby Waitaki Valley (see the boxed text, below) also feature.

Omarama Hotel (☎ 03-438 9713; cnr SH8 & SH83; meals $15-25) Good pub food and displays of local sheepdog competition winners.

GETTING THERE & AWAY

From Omarama head north up SH8 past beautiful Lake Ohau to Twizel and Mt Cook, or southwest through striking Lindis Pass towards Cromwell and Queenstown. Stop before Lindis Pass to add your own roadside cairn.

Omarama is on the main route from Christchurch, and both **Atomic Shuttles** (☎ 03-349 0697; www.atomictravel.co.nz) and **InterCity** (☎ 03-474 9600; www.intercity.co.nz) swing by.

OAMARU TO DUNEDIN

It's 114km along SH1 from Oamaru to Dunedin and all too easy to blast up at the open-road speed limit without stopping on

---

WAITAKI WINE ON THE WAY UP

The wines of nearby Central Otago already have a robust global reputation, but a few winemaking pioneers in North Otago's Waitaki Valley are also making international wine experts drink up and take notice.

Just 6km east of Kurow on SH83, the **Kurow Winery** (☎ 03-436 0443; www.kurowwinery.co.nz; Duntroon; ☒ cellar door 11am-5pm) only kicked off in 2007, but it already has an excellent reputation for fresh, well-balanced riesling and smoky and spicy pinot noir. When we visited, they were putting the finishing touches to their new tasting room. Drop by for an antipasto platter.

Pinot gris and pinot noir are the stars at **Sublime Wine** (☎ 03-436 0089; www.sublimewine.co.nz; 511 Grants Rd, RD7K, Oamaru), a compact, family-owned vineyard around 2km further east on SH83 past the Kurow Winery. The well-travelled owners also operate the funky **Sublime Bed & Breakfast** (thelodge@sublimewine.co.nz; d incl breakfast $150; ☜). The rambling old homestead is surrounded by vineyards and mountain valleys, and a twin and double room are decorated with an eclectic combo of old advertising signs, retro furniture and distressed wooden floors. Special Taste of Waitaki three-course dinners ($50 per person including wine) showcasing local produce are available. Ask Steve about his time as a bass player for some of NZ's biggest bands.

the way. There are some really delightful places to stay along here though, and they alone justify spending more time. The narrow, ocean-hugging road travelling south from Oamaru provides a break from SH1, and has some gorgeous coastal views; take Wharfe St out of town (following the signs for Kakanui).

About 5km south of Oamaru, **Old Bones Backpackers** (☎ 03-434 8115; www.oldbones.co.nz; Beach Rd; dm/s/d $30/43/60; 💻 🗢) is beautifully designed, with rooms off a sunny, central space that encourages a safe, communal feeling. Close enough to the sea to hear the surf at night, this is a place to just relax in front of the huge windows looking over farmland to the sea, or get stuck into your favourite book. One of NZ's best hostels.

Also near the beach, at All Day Bay 16km from Oamaru, is **Coastal Backpackers** (☎ 03-439 5411; www.coastalbackpackers.co.nz; Waianakarua Rd, All Day Bay; dm/d $26/54, self-contained d $85). With a big garden and good swimming at the beach, you may find yourself extending your stay here. Choose from rooms in the main lodge, a compact cabin for two, or the self-contained unit in the main house. When we visited, the friendly Welsh–Kiwi owners were juggling tending their cherry orchard, looking after their baby llamas, and planning the reopening of their rambling garden pub. Not a bad life, really.

Rejoining SH1 again at Waianakarua, backtrack a couple of hundred metres north to the **Olive Grove Lodge and Holiday Park** (☎ 03-439 5830; www.olivebranch.co.nz; SH1, Waianakarua; sites per adult/child $12/6, powered sites $24, dm/d $25/60; 💻). Surrounded by farm, encircled by the Waianakarua River, and with birdsong and shady trees, this is an extremely popular camping ground for Kiwis around summer. The backpacker rooms are brightly painted, with interesting artworks, and the sunny communal lounge is a treat. Kids will love the adventure playground and highland cattle; parents will love the spa, eco lifestyle, organic vegies and peaceful vibe. En suite rooms (doubles $70, $15 extra for a third person) are good options for families.

Further south on SH1, 30km south of Oamaru, stop to check out the **Moeraki Boulders** (*Te Kaihinaki*), a collection of large spherical boulders on a stunning stretch of beach, scattered about like a giant kid's discarded marbles. Try to time your visit with low tide. There's a perfectly fine restaurant here, but it would be criminal to not dine at Fleur's (right).

Moeraki township is a charming little fishing village that you really should visit before it's overrun by retired folk from Christchurch. It's a nice 1½-hour walk along the beach between the village and the boulders, or head in the other direction towards the Kaiks wildlife trail and a cute old wooden lighthouse – a great spot to see yellow-eyed penguins and fur seals up close. For such a small town, Moeraki has nurtured the creation of more than its fair share of national treasures, from Francis Hodgkins' paintings to Keri Hulme's *The Bone People*…and Fleur Sullivan's cooking.

our pick **Fleur's Place** (☎ 03-439 4480; www.fleursplace.com; Old Jetty, Moeraki; mains $20-35; 🕐 10.30am-late Wed-Sat) has a rumble-tumble look about it, but this stylish timber hut serves up some of the South Island's best food. The speciality is seafood, fresh off the boats that are moored only metres away, and it's equally popular among locals for an evening drink and occasional live music. Head for the upstairs deck and smell the ocean while you tuck into fresh chowder, tender mutton bird, or whatever fish the boats caught last night. From 8am Friday to Tuesday, the adjacent **Fleur's Place Food 2 Go** caravan offers a very affordable taste of the Fleur's experience with seafood chowder ($10), smoked mussels ($8) and *kadoka* (raw fish salad; $8). It's also a handy spot for an alfresco espresso with an outlook of Moeraki's perfect little fishing harbour. Bookings for the restaurant are strongly recommended, but they'll probably squeeze you in if you arrive between the busy lunch and dinner times.

Moeraki Motel (☎ 03-439 4862; www.moerakibeachmotel.co.nz; cnr Beach & Haven Sts; d $95) has self-contained units with balconies, while the **Moeraki Village Holiday Park** (☎ 03-439 4759; www.moerakivillageholidaypark.co.nz; 114 Haven St; campsites $26, powered sites $26, d $45-125; 💻 🗢) occupies a small field above the road into town and has cabins and motel units.

A growing number of Moeraki locals are also opening their houses as B&B accommodation.

Detouring off SH1 to the coast again towards Karitane, you wind down the scenic coastal road to **Seacliff**.

our pick **Asylum Backpackers** (☎ 03-465 8123; Russell Rd, Seacliff; dm/s/d $25/40/62; 🕐 Nov-May; 💻), on the grounds of the former Seacliff Lunatic Asylum, is a lovely chilled-out place. The communal lounge, complete with giant palm, has an excellent selection of music, or there's kayaking and fishing ($35), surfing ($15), cycling (free) or horse riding ($55) to be done. The horses occasionally look in the hostel's windows. Many people come here for a day and stay for weeks, those with mechanical skills sometimes pitching in to help with the 50-odd wonderful old classic cars (1920s to '60s), or with restoring the old bluestone building. Cash only.

The rest of the old asylum grounds are now the **Truby King Reserve**, with parklands, overgrown gardens and native forest – perfect a picnic or a stroll. Even though it's a beautiful park, it's a site with a scary, horrible history. Far too many people were essentially imprisoned here, and far too many of them were brutalised by the experience, or by the staff – these were the days when lobotomies and desexing operations were still de rigueur. Almost 30 women, locked in their dorms, were killed in a fire here in 1942. Among Seacliff's most famous residents was one of NZ's greatest novelists, Oamaru's Janet Frame (see p293). If you wander through the gardens you'll find a plaque recording some of her thoughts.

Queenstown & Wanaka

If Queenstown didn't exist, someone would have to invent it. With a cinematic background of mountains and lakes you actually have seen in the movies, and a 'what can we think of next?' array of adventure activities, it's little wonder that the South Island's premier tourist town tops many travellers' Kiwi itineraries. This Disneyland of derring-do will prompt you to scrabble for a hundred synonyms for 'exciting' and 'thrilling' when writing in your travel journal, but lurking in and around the tangle of bungy cords are experiences that will last longer than a shriek-inducing 10 or 20 seconds.

Venture out on the Greenstone and Routeburn Tracks for extended outdoor thrills amid arguably New Zealand's most stunning scenery, or sample world-beating wines in world-beating surroundings in the Gibbston Valley. If you listen really closely, you might even hear the screams of glee across the road at bungy's birthplace, the Kawarau River.

Slow down (slightly) in Wanaka, Queenstown's junior sibling, now offering its own menu of outdoor adventure and a growing restaurant and bar scene. Explore Mt Aspiring National Park to reinforce that you're only a short drive from true NZ wilderness.

Slow down even more in sleepy Glenorchy, a scenic reminder of what Queenstown and Wanaka were before the adventure groupies moved in. Reduce your speed further in Arrow-town to consider the town's gold-mining past over dinner in a quiet bistro. The following day there'll be plenty of opportunities to jump back into the region's cavalcade of fun.

HIGHLIGHTS

- Sampling superb wines amid the dramatic scenery at **Gibbston Valley** (p316)
- Relaxing and dining in **Arrowtown** (p319) after the last of the day-trippers have left
- Doing things you've only dreamed about in **Queenstown** (p305), the adrenaline-rush capital of NZ
- Walking the peaceful **Routeburn Track** (p324)
- Exploring by horseback, kayak and jetboat the upper reaches of Lake Wakatipu from sleepy and stunning **Glenorchy** (p322)
- Watching a flick at **Cinema Paradiso** (p333) in Wanaka, with pizza during intermission
- **Bar-hopping** (p316) and **dining** (p314) in cosmopolitan Queenstown

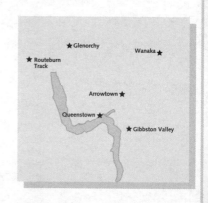

- Telephone code: 03
- www.queenstown-nz.co.nz
- www.queenstown-vacation.com

QUEENSTOWN & WANAKA

QUEENSTOWN & WANAKA
0   50 km
0   30 miles

QUEENSTOWN REGION

Surrounded by the soaring indigo heights of the Remarkables, crowned by Coronet Peak, and framed by the meandering coves of Lake Wakatipu, it's little wonder that Queenstown is a show-off. The town wears its 'Global Adventure Capital' badge proudly, and most visitors take the time to do crazy things they've never done before. But a new Queenstown is also emerging, with a cosmopolitan restaurant and arts scene and excellent vineyards. Go ahead and jump off a bridge or out of a plane, but also make time to slow down and experience Queenstown without the adrenaline. And once you've eased up, look forward to more of the same in historic Arrowtown or beautiful Glenorchy.

QUEENSTOWN
pop 11,000

No one has ever visited Queenstown and said, 'I'm bored'. Looking like a small town, but displaying the energy of a small city, Queenstown offers a mountain of activities. If your 'Things to Do' list contains bungy jumping, caving, rafting, sledging, jetboating, skiing, skydiving and hang gliding, trained operators are waiting on your call right now.

Maximise bragging rights with your souvenir T-shirt in the town's atmospheric restaurants, laid-back cafes and bustling bars. Be sure to also find a lakeside bench at sunrise or dusk and immerse yourself in one of NZ's most beautiful views. It's a pretty good option for an alfresco afternoon picnic as well.

Confident Queenstown is well used to visitors with international accents, so expect great tourist facilities, but also great big crowds, especially in summer and winter. Autumn (March to May) and spring

Climate

Summer (December to February) has long days with temperatures up to 30°C, but January also sees the region's highest rainfall. This elevated region gets crisp winters (June to August) with daytime temperatures around 5°C to 10°C, dipping to freezing or below at night, and lots of mountaintop snow. Autumn (March to May) is pleasant with relatively warm temperatures (15°C to 20°C), while spring (September to November) is slightly cooler.

Getting There & Around

Air New Zealand links Auckland, Wellington and Christchurch to Queenstown, with connections to Wanaka. Jetstar flies to Auckland, Christchurch and Rotorua from Queenstown. Bus and shuttle companies criss-cross Otago from Dunedin to Queenstown and Wanaka. Several divert south to Te Anau and Invercargill, and others migrate north to Christchurch or travel through the Haast Pass and up the West Coast. The major operators include InterCity, Atomic Shuttles, Naked Bus, Tracknet and Wanaka Connexions.

MAORI NEW ZEALAND

Kiwi Haka (p318) perform nightly atop the Queenstown gondola, and Te Maori (p303) perform cultural shows during the day at the Kiwi Birdlife Park. Two Queenstown galleries worth checking out for contemporary Maori art and design are Kapa (p318) and toi o tahuna (p318). For active travellers, Kawarau Jet operates highly rated jetboat cultural tours with Maori guides (p306).

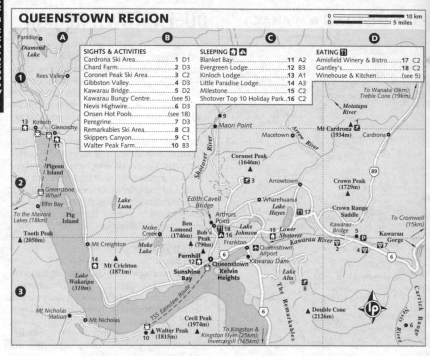

QUEENSTOWN REGION

SIGHTS & ACTIVITIES		SLEEPING		EATING	
Cardrona Ski Area	1 D1	Blanket Bay	11 A2	Amisfield Winery & Bistro	17 C2
Chard Farm	2 D3	Evergreen Lodge	12 B3	Gantley's	18 C2
Coronet Peak Ski Area	3 C2	Kinloch Lodge	13 A1	Winehouse & Kitchen	(see 5)
Gibbston Valley	4 D3	Little Paradise Lodge	14 A3		
Kawarau Bridge	5 D2	Milestone	15 C2		
Kawarau Bungy Centre	(see 5)	Shotover Top 10 Holiday Park	16 C2		
Nevis Highwire	6 D3				
Onsen Hot Pools	(see 18)				
Peregrine	7 D3				
Remarkables Ski Area	8 C3				
Skippers Canyon	9 C1				
Walter Peak Farm	10 B3				

(October to November) are slightly quieter, but Queenstown's a year-round destination. The town's restaurants and bars are regularly packed with a mainly young crowd that really know how to enjoy themselves on holiday. If you're a more private soul, drop in to see what all the fuss is about, but then get out and about by exploring the sublime wilderness further up the lake at Glenorchy.

History
The region was deserted when the first Pakeha (white person) arrived in the mid-1850s, although there is evidence of previous Maori settlement. Sheep farmers came first, but after two shearers discovered gold on the banks of the Shotover River in 1862, a deluge of prospectors followed. Within a year Queenstown was a mining town with streets, permanent buildings and a population of several thousand. It was declared 'fit for a queen' by the NZ government, hence Queenstown was born. Lake Wakatipu was the principal means of transport, and at the height of the boom there were four paddle steamers and 30 other craft plying the waters.

By 1900 the gold had petered out and the population was a mere 190. It wasn't until the 1950s that Queenstown became a popular holiday destination. In recent years Queenstown has wrestled with rising water levels in Lake Wakatipu and, in 1999, a third of the town was severely flooded. To thwart a repeat occurrence, there was an initial proposal to permanently lower lake levels. Instead, the town has decided to raise floor levels and put other flood-mitigation measures in place.

Orientation
Queenstown's town centre is compact and pedestrian-friendly, with most tourist facilities situated along Shotover St, Beach St and the Mall. The airport is 8km east of town; see p319.

Information
EMERGENCY
Ambulance, fire service & police (☎ 111)
Queenstown Medical Centre (Map p306; ☎ 03-441 0500; www.qmc.co.nz; 9 Isle St; ☽ 8.30am-8pm) Emergency care and a pharmacy.

INTERNET ACCESS

Most hostels also offer internet access.

Budget Communications (Map p306; O'Connell's Shopping Centre) Has laptop access and stacks of computers.

Global Gossip (Map p306; 27 Shotover St)

Internet Laundry (Map p306; 1 Shotover St) Surf as you wash.

MONEY

ATMs and banks are scattered throughout town.

POST

Post office (Map p306; 13 Camp St)

TOURIST INFORMATION

Department of Conservation visitor information centre (DOC; Map p306; ☎ 03-442 7935; queenstownvc@ doc.govt.nz; 38 Shotover St; ☷ 8.30am-5pm May-Nov, to 6pm Dec-Apr) Backcountry Hut Passes and weather and track updates; on the mezzanine floor above Outdoor Sports.

Info & Track Centre (Map p306; ☎ 03-442 9708; www.infotrack.co.nz; 37 Shotover St) Info on transport to trailheads.

Queenstown i-SITE (Map p306; ☎ 0800 668 888, 03-442 4100; www.queenstown-vacation.com; Clocktower Centre, cnr Shotover & Camp Sts; ☷ 7am-7pm Dec-Apr, to 6pm May-Nov) Also check www.queenstown-nz.co.nz.

TRAVEL AGENCIES

Kiwi Discovery (Map p306; ☎ 0800 505 504, 03-442 7340; www.kiwidiscovery.com; 37 Camp St) Tramping packages, ski transport and equipment hire.

Real Journeys (Map p306; ☎ 0800 656 501, 03-249-7416; www.realjourneys.co.nz; Steamer Wharf, Beach St) Huge range of lake trips and tours.

Station (Map p306; ☎ 03-442 5252; www.thestation.co.nz; cnr Camp & Shotover Sts) Houses AJ Hackett Bungy and Shotover Jet.

Sights

Hop on the **Skyline Gondola** (Map p304; ☎ 03-441 0101; www.skyline.co.nz; Brecon St; adult/child/family return $23/12/59; ☷ 9.30am-6.30pm) for fantastic views of Queenstown, the lake and the mountains. At the top are a cafe, a restaurant with regular Maori cultural shows, and souvenir shops. Walking trails include the **loop track** (30 minutes return) or you can try the Luge (p309). The energetic can forgo the gondola and hike to the top – take the upper, left-hand gravel track from the trailhead on Lomond Cres for an hour's uphill hike.

The **Kiwi Birdlife Park** (Map p306; ☎ 03-442 8059; www.kiwibird.co.nz; Brecon St; adult/child $35/15; ☷ 9am-5pm Oct-Mar, to 6pm Apr-Sep, shows 11am & 3pm) is your best bet to spy a kiwi. There are also 10,000 native plants and scores of birds, including the rare black stilt, kea, morepork and parakeets. Stroll around the sanctuary, watch the conservation show and tiptoe quietly into the darkened kiwi houses. The conservation shows also incorporate a cultural show by the Te Maori performers. Kids under 15 get in free with a paying adult.

Williams Cottage (Map p306; cnr Marine Pde & Earl St; ☷ 10am-5pm Mon-Sat) is Queenstown's oldest home. An annexe of Arrowtown's Lake District Museum and Gallery (p320), it was built in 1864 and remains close to its original condition, including 1930s wallpaper. The cottage and its 1920s garden are now home to the very cool Vesta shop (p318) and cafe (p315).

Around the corner is the **Church of St Peter** (Map p306; www.stpeters.co.nz; cnr Church & Camp Sts; ☷ services 10am Wed, 10.30am Sun), another oasis of calm. The gift of a faithful parishioner, this pretty wood-beamed building has a beautiful organ and colourful stained glass. Take a look at the cedar-wood lectern, which was carved by Ah Tong, a Chinese immigrant, in the 1870s.

Underwater Observatory (Map p306; ☎ 03-442 6142; Queenstown Bay Jetty; admission free; ☷ 9am-5pm) has

QUEENSTOWN & WANAKA

QUEENSTOWN

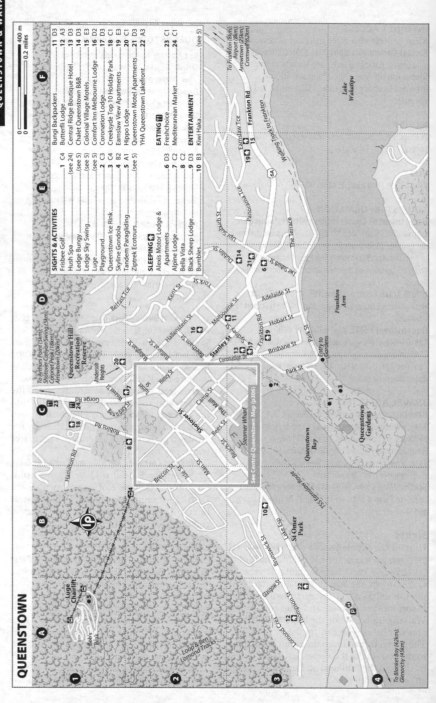

See Central Queenstown Map (p306)

six giant windows showcasing life under the lake. Brown trout abound, and based on their generous size, look to be impossibly well fed. Keep a keen eye out for freshwater eels and the favourite of the kiddies – the scaup (diving ducks), which dive down and swim right past the windows.

Activities

Purchase ombination tickets for a variety of Queenstown's more heart-stopping activities from **Queenstown Combos** (☎ 0800 423 836, 03-442 7318; www.combos.co.nz).

Some activity operators have an office where you can book directly, but for most head to the Queenstown i-SITE (p303).

BUNGY JUMPING

Queenstown is famous for bungy jumping, and **AJ Hackett Bungy** (Map p306; ☎ 03-442 7100; www.bungy.co.nz; Station, cnr Camp & Shotover Sts) is the activity's best-known representative. Prices for the following include transport out of town and gondola rides where relevant.

The historic 1880 **Kawarau Bridge** (Map p302; per person $175), 23km from Queenstown, became the world's first commercial bungy site in 1988 and allows you to leap 43m. Next door, the **Kawarau Bungy Centre** (Map p302; ☎ 03-442 1177; SH6; ☟ 8am-5.45pm) has a **Secrets of Bungy Tour** (adult/child/family incl transport $45/35/125), which tells the story of bungy and lets the faint-hearted get a feel for the experience – minus the leap.

Atop Queenstown's gondola, the 47m-high **Ledge Bungy** (Map p304; per person $175) is the only place you can bungy after dark.

The gold-standard jump is the truly awe-inspiring/terrifying/crazy (choose one) 134m-high **Nevis Highwire** (Map p302; per person $250), where you jump from a pod suspended over the Nevis River. AJ Hackett's 3Thrillogy (per person $450) combines the Kawarau, Ledge and Nevis jumps.

BUNGY VARIATIONS

Shotover Canyon Swing (off Map p304; ☎ 0800 279 464, 03-442 6990; www.canyonswing.co.nz; per person $199, additional swings $39) is not your average backyard swing. If you can't force yourself to jump, they can release you in a variety of creative ways – backwards, in a chair, upside down; if you can dream it, you can swing it. From there it's a 60m free fall and a wild swing across the canyon at 150km/h. Not for the faint-hearted – it's one of the best buzzes in town.

The new swinger on the block is the **Nevis Arc** (Map p304; ☎ 03-442 4007; www.nevisarc.co.nz), at AJ Hackett's Nevis Highwire Bungy site. Billed as the world's highest swing (120m) here you can fly with a friend in tandem ($300) or go it alone ($170).

Same, same but different is the **Ledge Sky Swing** (Map p304; $120), at AJ Hackett's Ledge

---

QUEENSTOWN IN...

Two Days

Start your day with a breakfast burrito at **Halo** (p316) before heading to Shotover St to book your adrenaline-charged activities for the next day. Spend the rest of the day visiting **Williams Cottage** (p303), **Skyline Gondola** (p303) and **Kiwi Birdlife Park** (p303), before boarding the exciting **Shotover Jet** (p306) or taking a lake cruise on the **TSS Earnslaw** (p311). Wind up with a walk through **Queenstown Gardens** (p309) to capture dramatic views of the Remarkables at dusk. Have a sunset drink at **Pub on Wharf** (p317) or **Monty's** (p317), before dinner at the **Cow** (p315) or **Wai Waterfront Restaurant & Wine Bar** (p315). The evening's still young so head to **Minibar** (p317) or **Bardeaux** (p317). Devote the next day to bungy jumping, skydiving, whitewater rafting or perusing the art galleries in Church Lane. Enjoy dinner at **Winnies** (p317), and stay on for the live music or DJs.

Four Days

Follow the two-day itinerary, then head to **Arrowtown** (p319) to wander the enigmatic **Chinese settlement** (p320), browse the local shops and eat a gourmet lunch. The following day drive along the shores of Lake Wakatipu to tiny **Glenorchy** (p322). Have lunch at **Glenorchy Café** (p323) and then strap on your hiking boots and head into **Mt Aspiring National Park** (p327) to do some wonderful short tramps in the vicinity of the **Routeburn Track** (p324). If you'd rather exercise your arms, go kayaking across the lake at **Kinloch** (p323).

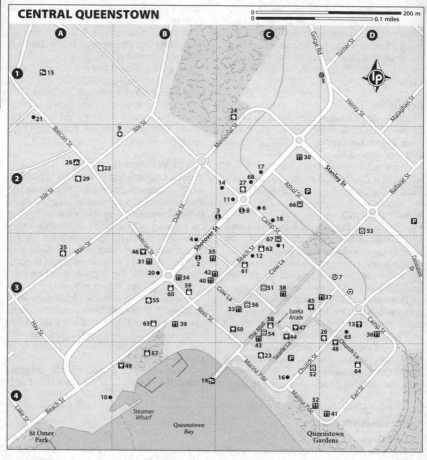

CENTRAL QUEENSTOWN

Bungy site. A shorter swing, but stunning views of Queenstown as you scream your lungs out.

JETBOATING

The Shotover and Kawarau are Queenstown's most popular rivers to hurtle along; the lengthier and more scenic Dart River is less travelled (see p322). Trips depart from Queenstown or go via minibus to the river and awaiting jetboat.

Shotover Jet (☎ 0800 746 868; www.shotoverjet.co.nz; adult/child $109/69) does half-hour trips through the rocky Shotover Canyons, with lots of thrilling 360-degree spins. **Kawarau Jet** (Map p306; ☎ 0800 529 272, 03-442 6142; www.kjet.co.nz; Queenstown Bay Jetty; adult/child $95/55) does one-hour trips on

the Kawarau and Lower Shotover Rivers, and a special wine-tasting five-hour trip (adult/child $229/142) that includes lunch at the Gibbston Winery and some wine sampling along the way.

Skippers Canyon Jet (☎ 03-442 9434; www.skip perscanyon.co.nz; adult/child $109/69) incorporates a 30-minute blast in the narrow gorges of Skippers Canyon in its three-hour trips, which cover the region's gold-mining history.

WHITE-WATER RAFTING

The choppy Shotover and calmer Kawarau Rivers are both great for rafting. Trips take four to five hours with two to three hours on the river. There's generally a minimum age of 13 years.

Companies include **Queenstown Rafting** (☎ 0800 723 8464, 03-442 9792; www.rafting.co.nz), **Extreme Green Rafting** (☎ 03-442 8517; www.nzraft.com) and **Challenge Rafting** (☎ 0800 423 836, 03-442 7318; www.raft.co.nz); prices start at around $175.

Family Adventures (☎ 03-442 8836; www.familyadventures.co.nz; adult/child $155/110) offers gentler (Grade I to II) trips on the Shotover suitable for children three years and older that include swimming, snacks and all sorts of family-flavoured frivolity.

RIVER SURFING & WHITE-WATER SLEDGING
Hang onto a body board and 'surf' down the Kawarau River with **Serious Fun** (☎ 0800 737 468, 03-442 5262; www.riversurfing.co.nz) or **Mad Dog River Boarding** (☎ 03-442 7797; www.riverboarding.co.nz). Trips take about four hours (1½ hours in the water), cost around $150 and run from September to June.

Frogz Have More Fun (☎ 0800 437 649, 03-441 2318; www.frogz.co.nz) lets you steer purpose-built, buoyant sledges down the challenging full-day descent of the Kawarau River ($370) and the more mellow half-day roller-coaster of the Roaring Meg ($149).

CANYONING
Canyoning.co.nz (☎ 03-441 3003; www.canyoning.co.nz; per person $155) runs half-day trips in the nearby 12-Mile Delta Canyons incorporating water slides, rock jumps and abseiling – even a zipline. Canyoning in the remote Routeburn Valley ($195) is possible with Canyoning .co.nz and with **Routeburn Canyoning** (☎ 0800 222 696, 03-441 4386; www.gycanyoning.co.nz; per person $195).

OVERHEARD #1

'My favourite questions from passengers on the jetboat are "Does the boat run on rails?" and "How long did it take to make the canyon out of all that fake rock?"' – Brett Black, Shotover Jet Driver.

ESPRESSO, LATTE OR DECAF?

Got your head around what's on offer in Queenstown yet? The number of ways to explore the great outdoors can be a little overwhelming, so here's a handy ready-reckoner based on your desired thrill level.

- **Espresso** – Launch yourself into the extreme thrills of the Shotover Canyon Swing (p305) or the Nevis Highwire (p305). Expect to be babbling like an adrenaline-pumped travelling fool for a few hours afterwards.

- **Latte** – Combine tangible thrills with a more leisurely look at the stupendous scenery around you with a mountain-top departure on a mountain bike or hang glider (below).

- **Decaf** – Ride a jetboat (p306) through the twisting and turning ravines of the Shotover River (it feels life-threatening, but it's actually very safe), or take a leisurely paddle in a kayak (p323) on the beautiful upper reaches of Lake Wakatipu at Kinloch.

FLYING, GLIDING & SKYDIVING

Tandem Paragliding (Map p304; ☎ 0800 759 688, 03-441 8581; www.paraglide.net.nz; per person $199, if you are on the gondola by 9am $169) takes off from the top of the gondola, while **Flight Park Tandems** (☎ 0800 467 325; www.tandemparagliding.com; from 1140m/1620m $179/205) offers spectacular views from Coronet Peak.

Those wanting to stay tethered can opt for the more relaxed paraflight. Glide 200m above the lake thanks to **Queenstown Paraflights** (Map p306; ☎ 0800 225 520; www.paraflights.co.nz; Queenstown Bay Jetty; solo per adult/child $129/109, tandem $95/75), who pull you airborne by boat. Soar with **Skytrek Hang Gliding** (☎ 0800 759 873; www.skytrek. co.nz; per person $210) from Coronet Peak or the Remarkables.

Extreme Air (☎ 0800 727 245; www.extremeair.co.nz; day/month $295/2200) can train you at its paragliding and hang-gliding school.

The good folk at skydiving outfit **NZONE** (☎ 0800 376 796, 03-442 5867; www.nzone.biz; from $249) will toss you out of a perfectly good airplane – attached to somebody who knows how to open the parachute.

SKIING

The Remarkables (p80) and Coronet Peak ski fields (p80) are the region's key snow-sport centres (see Map p302). Tune into 99.2FM from 6.45am to 9am to hear snow reports.

For serious skiers, check out **Heli Ski Queenstown** (☎ 03-442 7733; www.flynz.co.nz; from $895), **Harris Mountains Heli-Ski** (☎ 03-442 6722; www.heliski. co.nz; from $775) or **Southern Lakes Heliski** (☎ 03-442 6222; www.southernlakesheliski.co.nz; from $675).

Ski equipment hire companies:
Gravity Action (Map p306; ☎ 03-442 5277; 19 Shotover St)

Green Toad (Map p306; ☎ 03-442 5311; 48 Camp St)
Outside Sports (Map p306; ☎ 03-441 0074; Shotover St)
Snowrental (Map p306; ☎ 03-442 4187; 39 Camp St)

MOUNTAIN BIKING

There's excellent mountain biking around Queenstown. **Fat Tyre Adventures** (☎ 0800 328 897; www.fat-tyre.co.nz; from $195) takes small tours off the main trails. Tours cater to different abilities with day tours, multiday tours, helibiking and singletrack riding. Bike hire and trail snacks are included.

If you're not keen on strenuous uphill pedalling, chat to the folks at **Vertigo** (Map p306; ☎ 0800 837 8446, 03-442 8378; www.vertigobikes.co.nz; 4 Brecon St). They run guided downhill rides into Skippers Canyon and from the top of the gondola. Both options are $149, and they have helibiking trips on offer too.

Places to hire bikes:
Outside Sports (Map p306; ☎ 03-441 0074; 36 Shotover St; per half-/full day from $30/50) Has mountain bikes – hard tail and full suspension – road bikes, tandems and kids' bikes.
Queenstown Bike Hire (Map p306; ☎ 03-442 6039; cnr Marine Pde & Church St; per hr from $14)
Vertigo (Map p306; ☎ 0800 837 8446, 03-442 8378; www.vertigobikes.co.nz; 4 Brecon St) Has a laundry list of bikes (per half-/full day from $30/50), including full-on DH bikes.

TRAMPING & CLIMBING

Pick up a free copy of *Queenstown Walks and Trails* from the DOC visitor information centre (DOC; Map p306; ☎ 03-442 7935; queenstownvc@doc.govt.nz; 38 Shotover St) for local tramping tracks ranging from easy one-hour strolls to tough eight-hour slogs.

The peaceful **Queenstown Gardens** (Map p304) has a number of walking trails to follow. You can also haul yourself up to **Bob's Peak**, where the gondola lands. It's not a particularly scenic walk but the views at the top are excellent. Another short climb is up 900m **Queenstown Hill** (Map p304; two to three hours return); access is from Belfast Tce.

For a spectacular view, climb 1746m **Ben Lomond** (Map p302; six to eight hours return), accessed from Lomond Cres (Map p304). It's a difficult tramp requiring high-level fitness and shouldn't be underestimated; consult DOC on this and the region's other tramps.

Guided Nature Walks (☎ 03-442 7126; www.nzwalks.com; adult/child from $103/60) offers excellent walks in the area, including a Walk and Wine option and helihikes. **Encounter Guided Day Walks** (☎ 03-442 8200; www.ultimate hikes.co.nz; ☽ Oct-Apr) offers day walks on the Routeburn Track (adult/child $145/85), the Milford Track (adult/child $165/95) and near Mt Cook (adult/child $105/65), as well as multiday trips.

For climbers, **Climbing Queenstown** (☎ 03-450 2119; www.climbingqueenstown.com) offers a variety of vertigo-inducing experiences. It has rock climbing (from $169), abseiling (adult/child $99/59), Via Ferrata (climbing fixed metal rungs, rails, pegs and cables – all attached to the cliff face; adult/child $159/89) and mountaineering (from $250). All activities are guided by highly professional and qualified guides.

For outdoor gear:

Outside Sports (Map p306; ☎ 03-441-0074; 36 Shotover St) Has the largest selection of retail outdoor gear in town and hires almost everything you might need for the great outdoors.

Small Planet Sports Co (Map p306; ☎ 03-442 6393; 17 Shotover St) New and used outdoor equipment.

HORSE TREKS

Ride through a stunning landscape on a 324-hectare working farm with **Moonlight Stables** (☎ 03-442 1229; www.moonlightcountry.co.nz; adult/child $99/65). **Shotover Stables** (☎ 03-442 7486; www.shotoverstables.net; adult/child $65/40) offers gentle rides with bush trekking and a river crossing.

FISHING

The rivers and lakes around Queenstown are home to brown and rainbow trout. All companies practise catch-and-release. Half-day guided trips start at $120.

Some fishing companies:

Stu's Guiding Service (☎ 03-248 8890; www.born tofish.co.nz) Located in Athol 77km south of Queenstown. Offers guided fly-fishing, lessons and multiday trips. Prices drop for two or more patrons.

Fly Fishing (☎ 03-442 5363; www.wakatipu.co.nz) Helifishing, lake trolling, lure fishing and fly-fishing.

Stu Dever Fishing Charters (☎ 03-442 6371; www. fishing-queenstown.co.nz) Salmon and trout fishing from the 34ft launch *Chinook*. Owner Stu can arrange for your catch to be cooked at a local restaurant.

OTHER ACTIVITIES

Ziptrek Ecotours (Map p304; ☎ 0800 947 8735; www. ziptrek.com; adult/child $119/69), the new kid on the adventure tourism block, is also the talk of the town. Incorporating a series of zip-lines (flying foxes), this harness-clad thrill-ride takes you from treetop to treetop high above Queenstown. Ingenious design and ecofriendly values are a bonus on the adrenaline-fuelled two-hour tour.

Hop on a three-wheeled cart to ride the **Luge** (Map p304; ☎ 03-441 0101; www.skyline.co.nz; Brecon St; 2/3/5 rides incl gondola ride $35/40/45) at the top of the gondola. Nail the 'scenic' run once, and then you're allowed on the advanced track with its banked corners and tunnel.

Frisbee Golf (Map p304; www.discgolf.co.nz) has a marked course in Queenstown Gardens. Tees are indicated by numbered arrows on the ground and targets are either trees or

---

THE ADVENTURE PRESCRIPTION

- Do you like driving in a really fast sports car? Try jetboating.
- Do you like letting go and losing control? Try bungy jumping.
- Do you crave control and want to be in charge? Try mountain biking or rock climbing.
- Do you like roller-coaster rides and aren't bothered by having messed-up hair? Try rafting or river boarding.
- Do you own jeans and aren't afraid of chafing? Try horseback riding.
- Have you always wanted to be strapped to some stranger and fall out of an airplane? Try tandem skydiving.
- Do you speak Elvish and like short people? Try a *Lord of the Rings* tour.

chain baskets. BYO frisbee. Nearby is the **Queenstown Ice Rink** (Map p304; ☎ 03-441 8000; www.queenstownicerink.co.nz; adult/child incl skate hire $15/12; ☺ 9am-5.30pm Mon-Thu, 9am-9pm Fri, 10.30am-5pm Sat & Sun); come for a skate or a game of ice hockey.

The **Central Otago Wine Experience** (Map p306; ☎ 03-409 2226; www.winetastes.com; 14 Beach St; tasting cards $20; ☺ 10am-10pm) has more than 80 wines to try. A $20 tasting card provides samples of around eight to 10 different wines.

You can also golf, minigolf, quad bike, sail, dive and more. See the Queenstown i-SITE or any booking agencies. For a paddle on the lake, rent a kayak at **Queenstown Bike Hire** (Map p306; cnr Marine Pde & Church St).

Slow down by easing into **Hush Spa** (Map p304; ☎ 03-4009 0901; www.hushspa.co.nz; cnr Gorge & Robins Rds; 30/60min massage from $65/120; ☺ 9am-9pm Tue-Fri, to 7pm Sat) for a massage, aroma stone therapy or a deep bath soak. Call the **Mobile Massage Co** (☎ 027 442 6161; www.queenstownmassage.co.nz; ☺ 9am-9pm) for an in-room massage (one hour $110).

Onsen Hot Pools (Map p302; ☎ 03-442 5707; www.onsen.co.nz; 160 Arthurs Point Rd; adult/child $46/10; ☺ 11am-10pm) has private Japanese-style hot tubs with mountain views. Book ahead and one will be warmed up for you.

Walking Tour

From Beach St, start your walk round the har-bourfront, watching for the **TSS Earnslaw** (**1**; opposite) chugging into Queenstown Bay. Stop at **Patagonia** (**2**; p315) for coffee, ice cream or hot chocolate, before heading out on the jetty to the **Underwater Observatory** (**3**; p303) to see what lies beneath. Continue along the beach to **Queenstown Gardens** (**4**) to soak up the quiet or try **Frisbee Golf** (**5**; p309). Complete the garden's loop trail and return up Marine Pde to **Williams Cottage** (**6**; p303) for a little history, retail therapy and lunch. Take a right on Church St to see the pretty **Church of St Peter** (**7**; p303), and then zigzag through the lanes to the Mall to explore some local **boutiques** (**8**; p318). Next, visit the **Central Otago Wine Experience** (**9**; above), as much to appreciate the local pinot as to steel your nerves for your visit to the **Station** (**10**; p303) to book your bungy jump for the next day. Head to Brecon St and visit the **Kiwi Birdlife Park** (**11**; p303) to spy the elusive, long-beaked balls of feathers and then hop on the **Skyline Gondola** (**12**; p303) for a peaceful (and steep) ride up Bob's Peak. Admire the quite Remarkable view before negotiating the graceful but exciting corners on the **Luge** (**13**; p309). Brave souls can glide

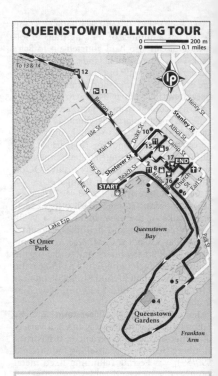

QUEENSTOWN WALKING TOUR

0 ——— 200 m
0 ——— 0.1 miles

WALK FACTS

Start Beach St
Finish Minibar
Distance 3.5km
Duration Three to four hours

---

back down with **Tandem Paragliding** (**14**; p308). From the gondola's base, it's a stroll downhill back into town for dinner at **Fishbone Bar & Grill** (**15**), followed by drinks in Eureka Arcade at **Bardeaux** (**16**; p317) or **Minibar** (**17**; p317). You're on your own now.

Queenstown for Children

While Queenstown is brimming with activities, many of them have age restrictions that may exclude the youngest in your group. Nevertheless, you shouldn't have any trouble keeping the youngsters busy.

For a high that will make sugar rushes seem passé, take wilder kids on the Shotover Jet (p306). For older kids, consider a tamer variation on the classic bungy jump with the Ledge Sky Swing (p305) or go tandem with them on

Queenstown Paraflights (p308). At Kawarau Bungy Centre (p305) kids can watch people plunging off the bridge, experience a virtual jump and explore the bungy museum. For tiny tots who don't want to miss out on the fun, **Zoom** (Map p306; ☎ 0800 124 224; Brecon St Hill; child $10; ⏰ 11am-5pm Wed-Sun) is a bungy trampoline that safely bounces them 8m into the air.

The Skyline Gondola (p303) offers a slow-moving activity from dizzying heights. At the top of the hill lies a wonderfully curvy Luge (p309) suitable for ages three and up.

Kids who are aspiring Dr Doolittles will love the Kiwi Birdlife Park (p303). Its conservation shows are especially geared to the younger crowd. Queenstown Gardens (p309) is a great place to let your children stretch their legs, and has a good beachside playground near the entrance on Marine Pde. Also in the park, Queenstown Ice Rink (opposite) is great for a rainy day.

Several places in town hire out child-sized mountain bikes (p308). Queenstown Bike Hire (opposite) hires out pogo sticks ($5 per day), foot scooters ($5 per day) and baby buggies ($15 per day), plus toboggans ($10 per day) in winter. Rookies (p318) hires out snowsuits for children aged one to 14 years, while most ski-hire shops (p308) have gear for tykes.

Consider also lake cruises on the *TSS Earnslaw* (right) and 4WD tours of narrow, snaking Skippers Canyon (right). Family rafting trips are run by Family Adventures (p307).

For more ideas and information (including a good list of babysitters) pick up a free copy of *Kidz Go!* from the i-SITE. The mini-magazine has an excellent guide to how old children should be for the wide range of activities around Queenstown, and if they're fussy eaters, there's a summary of kids' menus available around town.

Tours

AERIAL SIGHTSEEING

For a bird's-eye view, join a flightseeing tour.
Air Fiordland (☎ 0800 103 404, 03-442 3404; www. airfiordland.com; from $325) Flights around Milford Sound, Queenstown and surrounding area. Includes wine tasting.
Jag Air (☎ 03-442 3177; www.jagair.co.nz; per person $220) To see the sights upside down, take a 15-minute aerobatic flight.
Milford Sound Scenic Flights (☎ 03-442 3065; www. milfordflights.co.nz; adult/child from $325/195) Takes you south to Milford, does a fly-by and brings you back.

Over the Top Helicopters (☎ 03-442 2233; www. flynz.co.nz; from $225) Heaps of flight options taking in the best of the best views in Queenstown and beyond.
Sunrise Balloons (☎ 0800 468 247, 03-442 0781; www.ballooningnz.com; adult/child $375/245) Cruise the lake and mountain breezes in a hot-air balloon.

4WD TOURS

Nomad Safaris (☎ 03-442 6699; www.nomadsafaris. co.nz; adult/child $149/75) Runs four-hour tours with a *Lord of the Rings* flavour. Visit filming locations used for the iconic trilogy. If you're 'Bored of the Rings', Nomad has trips on offer that simply take in stunning scenery and hard-to-get-to backcountry vistas. It'll even let you drive ($260), or you can ride a quad-bike ($220).
Off Road Adventures (☎ 03-442 7858; www.offroad. co.nz; adult/child $140/70) Does similar tours, with a *Lord of the Rings* tour taking in filming locations. Also offers dirt-bike ($229) and quad-bike ($190) tours.
Skippers Canyon Heritage Tours (☎ 03-442 5949; www.queenstown-heritage.co.nz; adult/child $150/75) Skippers Canyon is reached by a narrow, winding road built by gold panners in the 1800s. This scenic but hair-raising 4WD route runs from Arthurs Point towards Coronet Peak and then above the Shotover River, passing gold-rush sights. Join a four-hour tour brimming with gold-mining stories and including a picnic. Specialist wine tours are also available.

LAKE CRUISES

The stately, steam-powered *TSS Earnslaw* (Map p306) will celebrate its centenary of continuous service in 2012. The elegant lady of the lake continues to churn across Lake Wakatipu at 13 knots. Once the lake's major means of transport, it originally carried more than 800 passengers. Climb aboard for the standard 1½-hour Lake Wakatipu tour (adult/child $48/20) or take a 3½-hour excursion to the high-country **Walter Peak Farm** (Map p302; adult/child $68/20) for sheep-shearing demonstrations and sheep-dog performances. Other tours include barbecue lunches, dinner or horse trekking. Book through **Real Journeys** (Map p306; ☎ 0800 656 503; www.realjourneys.co.nz; Steamer Wharf, Beach St).

MILFORD SOUND

Day trips via Te Anau to Milford Sound (p347) take 12 to 13 hours and cost around

---

OVERHEARD #2

'The water doesn't taste too salty for the ocean.' – Remark from an unnamed tourist after swimming in Lake Wakatipu.

QUEENSTOWN ON A BUDGET

A visit to Queenstown doesn't have to break the budget. Play **Frisbee golf** (p309) in the Queenstown Gardens, or hire a bike or **kayak** (p310) at the lakefront. Catch the bus to Arrowtown to the quirky boutique cinema **Dorothy Browns** (p321), or spy on the diving ducks at the **Underwater Observatory** (p303). Head to the **Mediterranean Market** (p316) for supplies for a lakeside picnic, or peruse the stalls at Queenstown's Saturday morning **arts & crafts market** (p318).

$225/115 per adult/child, including a two-hour cruise on the sound. Bus-cruise-flight options are also available, as is pick-up from the Routeburn Track finish line. Operators:
Great Sights (☎ 0800 744 487; www.greatsights.co.nz)
Kiwi Discovery (Map p306; ☎ 03-442 7340; www.kiwi discovery.com)
Real Journeys (Map p306; ☎ 0800 656 503, 03-442 7500; www.realjourneys.co.nz; Steamer Wharf, Beach St)

The **BBQ Bus** (☎ 03-442 1045; www.milford.net.nz; adult/child $174/98) takes smaller groups (up to 22 people) and you can look forward to sausages and marinated beef kebabs with herbivore options available too.

To save on travel time and cost, consider visiting Milford from Te Anau (p338).

WINERY TOURS

A guided tour of the region's vineyards means being able to enjoy a drink without having to get behind the wheel.
Appellation Central Wine Tours (☎ 03-442 0246; www.appellationcentral.co.nz; from $155) Runs tasty tours, including an all-day excursion ($195) that also dips into local cheeses. See the boxed text, p316.
Queenstown Wine Trail (☎ 03-442 3799; www.queenstownwinetrail.co.nz; adult from $118) Offers informative, unhurried tours; choose from a five-hour tour with tastings at four wineries or a shorter tour ($136) with lunch included.

OTHER TOURS

Hop on a **Double-Decker Bus Tour** (Map p306; ☎ 03-441 4421; $48; ☺ tours depart Queenstown 9.30am & 1.30pm) to historic Arrowtown (p319), taking in Gibbston Valley Wines (see the boxed text, p316) and Lake Hayes. You'll have 50 minutes to look around Arrowtown. Tours depart from in front of O'Connell's Shopping Centre.

Festivals & Events

Gibbston Harvest Festival (www.gibbstonharvest festival.com; Gibbston) Wine buffs should time their visit to coincide with this annual festival – food, wine and good times all on offer.
Queenstown Winter Festival (www.winterfestival. co.nz) This festival in late June/early July provides wacky ski and snowboard activities, live music, a Mardi Gras party, fireworks and plenty of frigid frivolity.

Sleeping

Queenstown has endless places to stay, but many visitors seeking accommodation. Midrange travellers won't find much choice; consider a top-end place or go for one of the excellent budget options and spend up on activities. Places book out and prices rocket during the peak summer (December to February) and ski (June to September) seasons; book well in advance at these times. Rooms with guaranteed lake views often have a surcharge.

The **Queenstown Accommodation Centre** (Map p306; ☎ 03-442 7518; www.qac.co.nz; cnr Camp & Shotover Sts) has a range of holiday homes and apartments on its books (and its website), with prices ranging from around $200 to $500 per week. There is often a minimum-stay period.

BUDGET

Bumbles (Map p304; ☎ 03-442 6298, 0800 286 2537; www.bumblesbackpackers.co.nz; cnr Lake Esplanade & Brunswick St; sites/dm/d $15/28/60; 🖳 🛜) This popular hostel has recently upped its game with some tidy renovations. Being just down the lake from the heart of town makes for a prime location and one of the best views going. The compact common facilities make for a community living feel, and the modern amenities travellers have come to expect make this hotel a wise choice.

Butterfli Lodge (Map p304; ☎ 03-442 6367; www.butterfli.co.nz; 62 Thompson St; dm/d $24/58; 🖳) This smaller hostel sits in a quiet hillside suburb. Commandeer the barbecue on the deck and take in beaut views as you turn your steaks and sausages. Rooms don't have a huge amount of character, but are modern and well maintained.

Nomads (Map p306; ☎ 03-441 3922; www.nomads hostels.com; 5 Church St; dm $25-34, tw/d $110/130; 🖳 🛜) Blessed with stunning exterior architecture and a prime location, this brand-new hostel is on a fast-track to being the one to beat. Inside, the facilities are top-notch, with en suites aplenty, massive kitchens and other bonuses such as an on-site internet cafe and travel agency. The only downside is the size of the establishment – it's massive.

YHA Queenstown Lakefront (Map p304; ☎ 03-442 8413; www.yha.co.nz; 88-90 Lake Esplanade; dm/d from $26/74; 🖳 🛜) This friendly alpine lodge has staff well versed in Queenstown's myriad activities. Rooms are basic but clean; some rooms and the dining area have lake and mountain views. It's somewhat rambling but facilities are good, with a well-equipped kitchen and loads of board games, DVDs and books. Queenstown's nightlife is a 10- to 15-minute lakeside stroll away.

Black Sheep Lodge (Map p304; ☎ 03-442 7289; www.blacksheepbackpackers.co.nz; 13 Frankton Rd; dm/d $27/70; 🖳 🛜) This place keeps younger social types happy with a spa, a pool table and a truckload of DVDs. Rooms are basic, but it's a friendly affair and provides plenty of R&R before your next Queenstown outdoor adventure. Kick off a big night in the on-site bar.

Shotover Top 10 Holiday Park (Map p302; ☎ 03-442 9306; www.shotoverholidaypark.co.nz; 70 Arthurs Pt Rd; sites $35, d $60-140; 🖳 🛜) High above the Shotover River, this family-friendly park is 10 minutes' drive from the hustle and bustle of Queenstown. Fall out of your campervan straight onto the famous Shotover Jet (p306).

Creeksyde Top 10 Holiday Park (Map p304; ☎ 0800 786 222, 03-442 9447; www.camp.co.nz; 54 Robins Rd; sites $45, d $60-165; 🖳 🛜) In a garden setting, this pretty spot has accommodation ranging from basic tent sites to self-contained motel units. An ecofriendly green tinge is added with a disciplined approach to recycling and a commitment to increase planting of native trees.

Also recommended:

Bungi Backpackers (Map p304; ☎ 03-442 8725; www.bungibackpackers.co.nz; 15 Sydney St; dm $23-26, d $53; 🖳 🛜) Relaxed hostel with hammocks and a grassy volleyball court. A spa pool and complimentary veggie soup add a touch of home-away-from-home comfort.

Southern Laughter (Map p306; ☎ 03-442 8828; www.southernlaughter.co.nz; 4 Isle St; dm $25-28, tw $56, d $58-68; 🖳 🛜) Funky hostel with various kitchens scattered throughout the sprawling complex. Check out the retro B&W pics of old Queenstown before strolling into town to see new Queenstown.

Alpine Lodge (Map p304; ☎ 03-442 7220; www.alpinelodgebackpackers.co.nz; 13 Gorge Rd; dm $26, d $62; 🖳 🛜) Friendly, smaller hostel with international staff who've experienced every adventure activity on offer around town.

Hippo Lodge (Map p304; ☎ 03-442 5785; www.hippolodge.co.nz; 4 Anderson Heights; dm $28, s/d from

$40/65; 🖳 🛜) Well-maintained, relaxed hostel with good views and a correspondingly high number of stairs. Pitch a tent for $18 per person.

Last Resort (Map p306; ☎ 03-442 4320; www.tlrqtn.com; 6 Memorial St; dm $30; 🖳 🛜) Super-central, smaller hostel with a tiny brick-and-timber bridge crossing a bubbling brook in the backyard; just a minute from where most transport will drop you off.

MIDRANGE

Queenstown Lakeview Holiday Park (Map p306; ☎ 0800 482 735, 03-442 7252; www.holidaypark.net.nz; Brecon St; sites $36, d $120-160; 🖳 🛜) A short stroll from the gondola, this park has a big open field to camp in and great facilities. A few larger trees would soften the slightly spartan ambience for campers, but there are also flasher motel units and lodges.

Colonial Village Motels (Map p304; ☎ 03-442 7629; www.colonialvillage.co.nz; 136 Frankton Rd; s/d $115/120) Older-style motel units with gorgeous lake views have been spruced up with classy bed linen and minikitchens. Expect a bit of daytime road noise, but after dark it is considerably quieter.

Lomond Lodge (Map p306; ☎ 03-442 8235; www.lomondlodge.com; 33 Man St; d $130-160; 🖳 🛜) The decor is a bit old-fashioned, but the owners have plenty of ideas to make the most of your stay in Queenstown. Share your own ideas with fellow travellers in the communal kitchen and at the garden barbecue. Larger family apartments ($250 for up to four people) are also available.

Milestone (Map p302; ☎ 03-441 4460; www.themilestone.co.nz; Ladies Mile, RD1; s/d $140/185) This welcoming B&B is 10 minutes' drive from Queenstown, but with ponds, waterfalls and 300 roses set on 4 acres, it feels wonderfully remote. The charming house is filled with antiques, and for $75 per person the friendly Turnbull family will prepare you dinner, complete with local wines. A self-contained cottage is also available at the same good-value rate.

Queenstown Motel Apartments (Map p304; ☎ 0800 661 668, 03-442 6095; www.qma.co.nz; 62 Frankton Rd; d $145) This well-run spot combines newer units with spa bathrooms, trendy decor and private minigardens, and older 1970s-style units that represent good value for larger groups of budget travellers.

Also recommended:

Little Paradise Lodge (Map p302; ☎ 03-442 6196; www.littleparadise.co.nz; Glenorchy-Queenstown Rd; s $45, d $120-140; 🔋) Wonderfully eclectic, this slice of arty paradise is the singular vision of the Swiss owner.

Each rustic room features wooden floors, quirky artwork and handmade furniture. Outside, the fun continues with a natural swimming pool and well-crafted walkways along a nearby hillside. Breakfast and boat hire both go for $15. The lodge is on the Queenstown-Glenorchy bus route; see p324 for bus info.

Comfort Inn Melbourne Lodge (Map p304; ☎ 03-442 8431; www.mmlodge.co.nz; 35 Melbourne St; s/d from $75/115) Choose from cheaper rooms with shared bathrooms in Melbourne House or splash out a little more for an en-suite room at Melbourne Lodge next door.

Bella Vista (Map p304; ☎ 03-442 4468; www.bellavista motels.co.nz; 36 Robins Rd; d $150; ☎) Identical to the rest of Bella Vista's Kiwi empire – like all its siblings, clean and good value.

TOP END

Coronation Lodge (Map p304; ☎ 0800 420 777, 03-442 0860; www.coronationlodge.co.nz; 10 Coronation Dr; d $170; ▯ ☎) Right beside the Queenstown Gardens, this recently opened lodge has plush bed linen, cosy wooden floors, Turkish rugs and Sky TV. In a town that's somewhat lacking in good midrange accommodation, Coronation Lodge is highly recommended. Two larger rooms have kitchenettes.

Alexis Motor Lodge & Apartments (Map p304; ☎ 03-409 0052; www.alexisqueenstown.co.nz; 69 Frankton Rd; d $170; ▯ ☎) With energetic family owners, this modern hillside motel with self-contained units is an easy 10-minute walk to town along the lakefront. Molly the dog is always a dependable walking partner, and Louis the cat sometimes comes along too. Ask for an end unit with snap-happy views.

our pick Chalet Queenstown B&B (Map p304; ☎ 0800 222 457, 03-442 7117; www.chalet.co.nz; 1 Dublin St; d $195; ☎) This recently renovated B&B has become the new standard for boutique accommodation in Queenstown. Perfectly appointed rooms sparkle with modern amenities like flat-screen TVs, art that stops you in your tracks and bed linen that will leave you laid up. Be sure to book well ahead so you can secure one of the rooms with a lake view – easily one of the best vistas in town.

Central Ridge Boutique Hotel (Map p304; ☎ 03-442 8832; www.centralridge.co.nz; 4 Sydney St; d incl breakfast $245-455) Visitors rave about the breakfasts, but there's plenty more to be effusive about, such as pre-dinner canapés with Central Otago wines, underfloor heating and spacious, modern bathrooms. With only 14 rooms here, you're guaranteed a winning way with personal service.

Earnslaw View Apartments (Map p304; ☎ 0800 226 652, 03-442 7629; www.earnslawviewapartments.co.nz; 21 Earnslaw Tce; d from $285; ▯ ☎) Thoroughly modern self-contained accommodation for the thoroughly modern self-contained family ($435 for up to six people). The stunning lake and mountain views have been around for much longer.

Dairy (Map p306; ☎ 0800 333 393, 03-442 5164; www.thedairy.co.nz; 10 Isle St; s/d incl breakfast $450/480; ▯ ☎) Once a corner store, the Dairy's now a luxury guest house with 13 rooms packed with classy touches like designer bed linen, silk cushions and luxurious mohair rugs. Rates also include freshly baked afternoon tea. From June to September three-night packages are great value for skiers (double $825 to $945).

Evergreen Lodge (Map p302; ☎ 03-442 6636; www.evergreenlodge.co.nz; 28 Evergreen Pl, Sunshine Bay; d $795; ▯ ☎) Handcrafted wooden furniture from a local Queenstown artisan combines with 21st-century accoutrements like DVD players and wireless internet in the four pristine rooms at this modern lodge. Add in a supremely private location with unfettered views of the Remarkables, complimentary beer and wine, and a sauna and gym, and you've got a very relaxing escape from Queenstown's international hoi polloi.

Eichardt's Private Hotel (Map p306; ☎ 03-441 0450; www.eichardtshotel.co.nz; cnr Marine Pde & Searle Lane; d $1425-1645) Originally opened in the 1860s, this reopened and restored boutique hotel enjoys an absolute lakefront location. Each of the five giant suites has a fireplace, lake views and a blend of antique and modern decor. King-sized beds, heated floors and lake-sized bath tubs provide the ideal welcome after a tough day cruising the vineyards of Central Otago.

Eating

Queenstown's town centre is peppered with busy eateries. Many target the tourist dollar, but dig a little deeper and you'll discover local favourites covering a surprising range of international cuisines. At the more popular places, it's wise to make a reservation for weekend dining.

RESTAURANTS

@Thai (Map p306; ☎ 03-442 3683; 3rd fl, 8 Church St; mains $15-25; ☷ noon-10pm) The title of best Thai in town is a hard-fought battle here in QT – and the winner is @Thai. Find the semi-hidden set of stairs and head on up for a great meal.

The pad Thai is worth writing home about and the *hor-mok* seafood red curry will blow your mind.

Winnies (Map p306; ☎ 03-442 8635; 1st fl, 7 The Mall; pizza $15-25; ☺ noon-late; ☎) Winnies' cool and sassy international team serve up a global array of pizzas with a Thai, Mexican or Moroccan accent. Occasional live music and DJs keep the energy levels up long after you've finished your last slice. Part-bar and part-restaurant, Winnies always seems busy – guess why.

our pick **Cow** (Map p306; ☎ 03-442 8588; Cow Lane; mains $18-30; ☺ noon-midnight) Tucked into a hidden corner of Cow Lane, this is a classic QT eatery. Housed in a former cow shed (hence the name of the restaurant and the street), the Cow hasn't changed its menu since 1976 – and is damn proud of it. Amazing pizzas, simple pasta and stellar garlic bread will leave you satisfied. The atmosphere is cramped with low-slung ceilings, a roaring fire, thick wooden tables and rustic candlelight.

Solero Vino (Map p306; ☎ 03-442 6082; 25 Beach St; mains $19-35; ☺ 11am-late) This tiny French restaurant is hard to find but impossible to forget. Exquisite food is presented in a simple and elegant style. Traditional fare such as escargot and salmon are cooked to perfection. If you're lucky, the soup of the day will be the gazpacho and you'll be in gastronomic nirvana.

Bella Cucina (Map p306; ☎ 03-442 6762; 6 Brecon St; mains $22-29; ☺ 6pm-late) A top-shelf Italian eatery has been long overdue in Queenstown – as of 2008 that role has been taken by this beautiful kitchen. Fresh pasta and risotto are highlights while the pizza is good for sharing. Beautiful, simple food done just right.

Gantley's (Map p302; ☎ 03-442 8999; Arthurs Point Rd; mains $30-40; ☺ 6.30pm-late) An atmospheric dining experience in a historic 1863 stone-and-timber house at Arthurs Point. The contemporary NZ cuisine and highly regarded (and award-collecting) wine list are worth the journey. Reservations are essential; a courtesy bus is run to and from town for à la carte diners.

Botswana Butchery (Map p306; ☎ 03-442 6994; Marine Pde; mains $30-50; ☺ noon-late) This stylish and new face on the local culinary scene is a breath of fresh air. Opulent and aesthetic interior design makes way for a wine list that rivals anywhere in town. The meals are a divine combination of seasonal vegetables augmenting prime cuts of beef, lamb, poultry

and seafood. There is an emphasis upon taste in all avenues – whether that is the design of the interior, the creative plating or the elegant flavours that permeate the memorable meals.

Wai Waterfront Restaurant & Wine Bar (Map p306; ☎ 03-442 5969; Steamer Wharf, Beach St; mains $35-50; ☺ 11am-10pm) Small and intimate, Wai (meaning 'water' in Maori) is white-linen classy with lake and mountain views. It's known for lamb and seafood, and the Oyster Bar does the world's favourite bivalve in 17 different ways. The seven-course degustation menu ($115 without wine and $175 with wine) is a splurge-worthy opportunity for a great culinary adventure. Think about it seriously. It's actually less than you'll spend on another round of outdoor adventure activities, and will last a lot longer.

CAFES & QUICK EATS

Joe's Garage (Map p306; ☎ 03-442 5282; Searle Lane; mains $6-20; ☺ 7am-3pm) Joe's is the perennial favourite among locals looking for their morning coffee rescue. The hipster environment flies dangerously close to *too cool for school* but pulls back on the throttle before it's too late. Great coffee and fantastic brunchy food is all found at this locals' hang-out.

our pick **Patagonia** (Map p306; ☎ 03-442 9066; 50 Beach St; coffee & chocolate $5-7; ☺ 10am-10pm; ☎) Delicious hot chocolate, homemade choccies, and Queenstown's best ice cream. What more do you want? How about a lakefront location and free wi-fi? Patagonia's open until 10pm, so it's your best bet for a late-night coffee.

Vesta (Map p306; ☎ 03-442 5687; cnr Marine Pde & Earl St; mains $6-10; ☺ 10am-5pm Mon-Sat) Sometimes it's a good thing when you can't work out exactly what something is. In the case of Vesta, just examine the evidence: a gloriously overgrown 1920s-style garden, a gallery and gift shop specialising in NZ design, and a compact wee cafe serving coffee and cake just made for mid-afternoon recharging. To confuse things, Vesta is housed in Williams Cottage (p303), Queenstown's oldest home, and now an interesting museum.

Kappa Sushi Cafe (Map p306; ☎ 03-441 1423; Level 1, 36a The Mall; sushi $6-10, mains $13-29; ☺ noon-2.30pm Mon-Fri, 6pm-late Mon-Sat) Queenstown's best Japanese eatery is also its most casual. Scarily fresh tuna and salmon feature in good-value bento boxes for lunch. Later at night linger longer with excellent tempura and Japanese beer and sake. In summer watch the passing parade in the Mall from the upstairs deck.

Vudu Cafe (Map p306; ☎ 03-442 5357; 23 Beach St; breakfast $6-15, lunch & dinner $8-25; ☺ 8am-late; 🖳) This local favourite has been sorting out caffeine fixes for ages. Food-wise it boxes above its weight with great eggs, soup and a veggie lasagne that'll put you off meat forever. The funky surrounds, with local art on the walls, complete the scene.

Habebes (Map p306; ☎ 03-442 9861; btwn Beach & Shotover Sts; meals $7-12; ☺ 10am-5pm; Ⓥ) Superhealthy and decadently delicious. Salads and wraps are the go here – a recent relocation means they've expanded to have two tables – so dash and dine at the beach.

Fergburger (Map p306; ☎ 03-441 1232; 42 Shotover St; burgers $9-15; ☺ 9am-5am) Less of a burger joint and more of a rite of passage for every Queenstown visitor, Ferg serves up the best burgers in town till way past your bedtime. All tastes are catered for including vegetarians, fish lovers and, of course, carnivores. The burgers are huge and the atmosphere festive – this could very well be the best burger stop in all of Aotearoa.

Halo (Map p306; ☎ 03-441 1411; Camp St; mains $12-16; ☺ 7am-10pm) A stylish and sunny place that effortlessly blurs the line between breakfast, lunch and dinner. The breakfast burrito will set you up for a day's adventuring. Come back at night for a Caribbean jerk chicken burger and a glass of local wine. It's beside St James Church.

SELF-CATERING

Mediterranean Market (Map p304; ☎ 03-442 4161; cnr Gorge & Robins Rds; ☺ 8am-6.30pm Mon-Sat, 10am-6pm Sun) This is the place to fill up a basket for a lakeside picnic. There are fresh pastas, sauces, Asian cuisine, good local produce and a fantastic deli and bakery. Have coffee and cake at the attached cafe while you make up your mind.

Around the corner, the well-stocked **Freshchoice** (Map p304; 64 Gorge Rd; ☺ 7am-midnight) is Queenstown's big supermarket. In town, the **Alpine Supermarket** (Map p306; cnr Stanley & Shotover Sts; ☺ 8am-9pm Mon-Fri, 9am-9pm Sat & Sun) has most staples, and next door there's a handy bottle store.

Drinking

Drinking is almost a competitive sport in Queenstown, and there's a good range of options for after-dark carousing. Gone are

---

RIVER WATER OR PINOT NOIR? YOU CHOOSE

More gung-ho visitors to Queenstown might be happiest dangling off a giant rubber band, but as they're submerged in the icy Kawarau River, they'll be missing out on some of Central Otago's most interesting vineyards just up the road. A glass of the area's outstanding pinot noir, or a mouthful of river water? Mmm…tough choice.

On a spectacular river terrace near the Kawarau Bridge, AJ Hackett's original bungy partner Henry van Asch has set up the **Winehouse & Kitchen** (Map p302; ☎ 03-442 7310; www.winehouse. co.nz; mains $15-30; ☺ 10am-5pm). A beautifully restored wooden villa includes a garden cafe and the opportunity to try van Asch's Freefall and Rock Ferry wines, as well as his own van Asch label.

Almost opposite, a winding and scenic road leads to beautiful **Chard Farm** (Map p302; ☎ 03-442 6110; www.chardfarm.co.nz; ☺ 11am-5pm), and a further 700m along is **Gibbston Valley** (Map p302; ☎ 03-442 6910; www.gvwines.co.nz), the area's largest wine producer. Try its pinot noir and take a tour of the impressive wine cave. There are also a 'cheesery' and a restaurant.

A further 4km along SH6, **Peregrine** (Map p302; ☎ 03-442 4000; www.peregrinewines.co.nz; ☺ 10am-5pm) produces excellent sauvignon blanc, pinot noir and pinot gris, and hosts occasional outdoor concerts during summer, sometimes featuring international names.

Further west near the shores of Lake Hayes, the **Amisfield Winery & Bistro** (Map p302; ☎ 03-442 0556; www.amisfield.co.nz; small plates $16.50; ☺ 11.30am-8pm Tue-Sun) is a regular winner of *Cuisine* magazine's Best NZ Winery Restaurant gong. The highly regarded eatery serves tapas-sized plates perfect for sharing with a few friends on the sunny deck, and Amisfield's pinot noir has been awarded internationally.

Ask at the Queenstown i-SITE for maps and information about touring the Gibbston Valley. Alternatively, visit www.gibbstonvalley.co.nz for more info about this compact wine-growing area with its own unique microclimate. You could also join a wine tour (p312) to keep safe.

the days of the all-night party; bars now shut promptly at 4am.

Bardeaux (Map p306; ☎ 03-442 8284; Eureka Arcade, 11 The Mall; ☺ 6pm-4am) Down a narrow alleyway, this small, low-key wine bar is all class. Under a low ceiling await plush leather armchairs and a fireplace made from Central Otago's iconic schist rock. No beanies, rugby jerseys or work boots allowed.

Monty's (Map p306; ☎ 03-441 1081; Church St; ☺ 11am-late) On warm summer days the patio at Monty's is prime real estate. Same goes for the fire inside when the snow flies. With Monteith's beer on tap, this is a great place for a quiet drink with a predominantly local crowd. Most nights the band cranks up and gets the crowd tapping their feet as they down a few.

Pub on Wharf (Map p306; ☎ 03-441 2155; Steamer Wharf; ☺ 10.30am-late) The newest pub in town is also one if its most stylish. Ubercool interior design is shoved to the fore with handsome woodwork, lighting fit for a hipster hideaway and animal heads on the wall to remind you you're still in NZ. Mac's beer on tap, scrummy nibbles and a decent wine list make this a great place to settle in for the evening.

Surreal (Map p306; ☎ 03-441 8492; 7 Rees St; ☺ 11am-late) With funky music, low lighting and red-velvet booths, this is a private spot for a quiet drink – until later in the evening when things kick off and the dance floor comes to life. Happy hour from 10pm.

Winnies (Map p306; ☎ 03-442 8635; 1st fl, 7 The Mall; ☺ noon-late; ☏) A deservedly popular place with a laid back ambience, retractable roof, pool table and patio. Daily happy hour from 9pm brings the crowds and the atmosphere keeps 'em around.

Minibar (Map p306; ☎ 03-441 3212; Eureka Arcade, 11 The Mall; ☺ 4pm-4am) Beer, beer and more beer. More than 100 local and international beers are poured in this compact space. A cool name for a cool bar, oozing with style.

Buffalo Club (Map p306; ☎ 03-442 4144; 8 Brecon St; ☺ 3pm-late) Lit by candles and an enormous campfire in the middle of the room, this is a popular after-work hang-out. Pool tables and sports on the big-screen TV make it a low-key spot to kick off the night. Happy hour from 5pm.

Barmuda (Map p306; ☎ 03-442 7300; Searle Lane; ☺ 3pm-3am) A huge open fire makes Barmuda's atmospheric courtyard the place to be in

cooler weather. In summer live jazz on Friday and Saturday nights is sometimes on the cards.

Barup (Map p306; ☎ 03-442 7067; cnr Searle Lane & Eureka Arcade; ☺ 5pm-4am) Take the stairs up (no surprises there…) to this intimate cocktail bar, which is removed from the ground-level hustle and bustle downstairs around Eureka Lane.

Entertainment

Pick up the *Source* (www.thesourceonline .com), a free weekly flyer with a gig guide and events listings. Also check the posters at **Play It Again** (Map p306; ☎ 03-442 8940; O'Connell's Shopping Centre, Beach St) for local events. Live music and clubbing are a nightly affair and most Queenstown venues stay open until the wee hours. Most DJ and live-music gigs are free, though you will encounter inexpensive cover charges in some nightclubs.

LIVE MUSIC

Dux de Lux (Map p306; ☎ 03-442 9688; 14 Church St) Lots of live bands and DJs with everything from reggae to drum 'n' bass.

Buffalo Club (Map p306; ☎ 03-442 4144; 8 Brecon St) DJs spin nightly with a top-forty flavour and a raucous atmosphere.

Monty's (Map p306; ☎ 03-441 1081; Church St) On Wednesday to Saturday nights a live cover band will be strumming out the hits and the singalongs.

Pig & Whistle (Map p306; ☎ 03-442 9055; 41 Ballarat St) Covers bands playing songs you can unashamedly sing along to.

NIGHTCLUBS

Surreal (Map p306; ☎ 03-441 8492; 7 Rees St) DJs with house, retro, open-mic and the odd break beat thrown in.

Subculture (Map p306; ☎ 03-442 7685; downstairs 12-14 Church St) Skilful locals and out-of-towners toy with turntables to make drum 'n' bass, hip-hop, dub and reggae noises that get the crowds moving.

Debajo (Map p306; ☎ 03-442 6099; Cow Lane) The perennial end-of-night boogie spot – house and big-beat gets the dance floor heaving till closing time.

Tardis Bar (Map p306; ☎ 03-441 8397; Skyline Arcade, 20 Cow Lane) A good dance bar with regular DJs playing hip-hop, dancehall and dub. Like Dr Who's phone booth, it's surprisingly roomy inside.

Revolver Bar (Map p306; ☎ 03-441 8911; 54 Shotover St) Occasionally hosts gigs from well-known NZ bands and solo artists.

HAKA

Kiwi Haka (Map p304; ☎ 03-441 0101; www.skyline.co.nz; Brecon St; adult/child incl gondola $53/27; ⊙ from 5.30pm) To witness traditional Maori dancing and singing, come watch this group at the top of the gondola. There are multiple 30-minute shows nightly, but bookings are essential.

CINEMA

Reading Cinemas (Map p306; ☎ 03-442 9990; www.readingcinemas.co.nz; 11 The Mall; adult/child $15.50/10.50) Mainly Hollywood blockbusters, but occasional art-house and Kiwi flicks too.

Shopping

Queenstown is a good place to shop for souvenirs and gifts. Start exploring and you're likely to discover some unusual goods. Lots of shops specialise in outdoor and adventure gear; prices are competitive and there's a good range. Begin your shopping along the Mall, Shotover St and Beach St. Also try the area around Church Lane joining Church St and Earl St for an expanding array of galleries, or follow your nose to **Central Otago Wine Experience** (Map p306; ☎ 03-409 2226; www.winetastes.com; 14 Beach St; ⊙ 10am-10pm) to understand what makes the local wines special.

CLOTHING

Detour (Map p306; ☎ 03-442 7918; O'Connell's Mall) The place to go for fashion-forward urban hipsters and style bunnies looking for the latest cool threads.

CSTM (Map p306; ☎ 03-441 2344; www.cstmprint.com; The Mall) Don't settle for a T-shirt you don't like – head into CSTM and custom make the shirt of your dreams. No worries if you're lacking on the creative front, they have a fine selection of pre-made options too.

rookies (Map p306; ☎ 03-442 8153; 49 Beach St) If you forgot the kids' snowsuits, rent or buy clothes from rookies to keep them cosy. Designer kids clobber for warmer seasons is also available.

OUTDOOR GEAR

Outside Sports (Map p306; ☎ 03-441 0074; 32 Shotover St) Long-standing outdoor outfitters with plenty of gear to get you ready for camping, hiking, skiing or climbing.

Kathmandu (Map p306; ☎ 03-409 0880; 88 Beach St) A well-known and good-value chain with regular sales making things even cheaper. Join its 'Summit Club' for extra discounts.

DESIGN, MUSIC & ART

Vesta (Map p306; ☎ 03-442 5687; cnr Marine Pde & Earl St) In the historic surroundings of Williams Cottage, this shop has contemporary housewares, jewellery, gift cards, baby clothes, perfumes and accessories. Most of it is designed and made in NZ.

Kapa (Map p306; ☎ 03-442 4401; 29 Rees St) Has an array of quirky and eclectic NZ design infused with a healthy dose of contemporary Maori culture.

Koha (Map p306; ☎ 03-442 8887; 18 Beach St) Meaning 'gift' in Maori, Koha sells authentic and unique gifts. Everything for sale here is from NZ including jewellery, beauty products and designer clothing.

toi o tahuna (Map p306; ☎ 03-409 0787; Church Lane) Exclusively NZ art, with around half the work from contemporary Maori artists. Ask gallery owner Mark Moran for the free 'Galleries & Artist Studios in the Wakatipu' guide – proof that Queenstown's definitely about more than leaping off bridges wearing a giant rubber band.

Play It Again (Map p306; ☎ 03-442 8940; O'Connell's Shopping Centre, Beach St) Has CDs and DVDs including a good Kiwi music section.

Arts & crafts market (Map p306; www.marketplace.net.nz; ⊙ 9am-4.30pm Nov-Apr, 10am-3.30pm May-Oct) On Saturdays visit this creative market at Earnslaw Park on the lakefront beside Steamer Wharf.

Getting There & Away

AIR

Air New Zealand (Map p306; ☎ 0800 737 000, 03-441 1900; www.airnz.co.nz; 8 Church St) has direct daily flights between Queenstown and Auckland (from $139), Wellington (from $149) and Christchurch (from $89) with connections

---

OVERHEARD #3

'On the road to Kingston there are several signs warning of Road Slumps. It's good fun to tell the passengers that these are some seldom-seen native animal. The truth is, it's nothing more than a pothole.' – unnamed Queenstown tour guide

to Wanaka. **Jetstar** (☎ 0800 800 995; www.jetstar. com) has direct daily flights to Auckland (from $139) and Christchurch (from $100).

BUS
Book seats for **InterCity** (☎ 03-442 4100; www.inter city.co.nz) trips in the i-SITE. It offers daily bus services from Queenstown to Christchurch ($50), Te Anau ($30), Milford Sound ($80), Dunedin ($40) and Invercargill ($45), plus a daily West Coast service to the glaciers ($60) via Wanaka ($17) and Haast Township ($36). Buses leave from the Athol St bus terminal (Map p306). Note that some buses may be branded Newmans.

Naked Bus (www.nakedbus.com) travels to West Coast, Te Anau, Christchurch, Dunedin and Invercargill.

The **Bottom Bus** (www.bottombus.co.nz) does a loop service around the south of the South Island (see p361). Book at the **Info & Track Centre** (Map p306; ☎ 03-442 9708; 37 Shotover St).

Shuttles charge around $20 to $25 to Wanaka, $40 to Dunedin, $30 to Te Anau and $50 to Christchurch. Book at i-SITE.
Atomic Shuttles (☎ 03-349 0697; www.atomictravel. co.nz) Travels to Wanaka, Christchurch, Dunedin, Greymouth and Invercargill.
Catch-a-Bus (☎ 03-479 9960) Heads to Dunedin.
Wanaka Connexions (☎ 03 443 9122; www.time2. co.nz) Offers regular services to Wanaka.

TRAMPERS' & SKIERS' TRANSPORT
Backpacker Express at the **Info & Track Centre** (Map p306; ☎ 03-442 9708; www.infotrack.co.nz; 37 Shotover St) arranges transport to and from the Routeburn, Greenstone, Caples and Rees-Dart Tracks, all via Glenorchy. The service costs $40 (Queenstown to trailhead), and lots of other transport options are available. **Kiwi Discovery** (Map p306; ☎ 0800 505 504, 03-442 7340; www. kiwidiscovery.com; 37 Camp St) can also arrange transport to the tracks.

Bus services between Queenstown and Milford Sound via Te Anau can be used for track transport. See p344 for information on the tramper-servicing company TrackNet.

For the ski slopes, if you pre-buy your lift ticket to the Remarkables, you are able to catch the ski shuttle for free from the Station (Map p306) – the shuttle to Coronet Peak will cost you $10. The bus to Cardrona is $38 and Treble Cone is $45. Most companies offer transport and lift deals and special rates for children:

Gravity Action (Map p306; ☎ 03-442 5277; 19 Shotover St)
Info & Track Centre (Map p306; ☎ 03-442 9708; www.infotrack.co.nz; 37 Shotover St) Travels to Cardrona only.
Kiwi Discovery (Map p306; ☎ 0800 505 504, 03-442 7340; www.kiwidiscovery.com; 37 Camp St)
Snowrental (Map p306; ☎ 03-442 4187; 39 Camp St)

Getting Around
TO/FROM THE AIRPORT
Queenstown Airport (Map p302; ☎ 03-450 9031; www. queenstownairport.co.nz; Frankton) is 8km east of town.
Super Shuttle (☎ 0800 748 885; www.supershuttle.co.nz) picks up and drops off in Queenstown (from $15). **Connectabus** (Map p306; ☎ 03-441 4471; www. connectabus.com; cnr Beach & Camp Sts) runs to the airport ($6) hourly from 6.30am to 10.20pm. **Alpine Taxis** (☎ 03-442 6666) or **Queenstown Taxis** (☎ 03-442 7788) charge around $25.

PUBLIC TRANSPORT
Connnectabus (☎ 03-441 4471; www.connectabus.com) has three colour-coded routes. Catch the blue route for accommodation in Fernhill ($6) and the red or green routes for accommodation in Frankton ($6). The green route continues on to Lake Hayes ($7) and Arrowtown ($8). A day pass ($19) allows travel on the entire network. Pick up a route map and timetable from the i-SITE. Buses leave from the corner of Beach and Camp Sts.

ARROWTOWN
pop 2400
Beloved by day-trippers from Queenstown, exceedingly quaint Arrowtown sprang up in the 1860s following the discovery of gold in the Arrow River. Today the town retains more than 60 of its original wooden and stone buildings, and has pretty, tree-lined avenues, excellent galleries and an expanding array of fashionable shopping opportunities.

The only gold being flaunted these days is on credit cards and, surrounded by a bonanza of daytime tourists, you might grow wary of the quaint historical ambience. Instead take advantage of improved public transport to the town, and use it as a base for exploring Queenstown and the wider region. That way you can enjoy Arrowtown's history, charm and excellent restaurants after dark when the tour buses have decamped back to Queenstown.

Sights & Activities

The **Arrowtown visitor information centre** (☎ 03-442 1824; www.arrowtown.com; 49 Buckingham St; ⏲ 8.30am-5pm) shares premises with the **Lake District Museum and Gallery** (www.museumqueenstown.com; adult/child $7/1; ⏲ 8.30am-5pm), which has exhibits on the gold-rush era. Younger travellers will enjoy the Museum Fun Pack ($5), which includes activity sheets, museum treasure hunts, stickers and a few flecks of gold.

Arrowtown has NZ's best example of a gold-era **Chinese settlement** (admission by gold coin donation; ⏲ 24hr). Interpretive signs explain the lives of Chinese 'diggers' during and after the gold rush, while restored huts and shops make the story more tangible. Subjected to significant racism, the Chinese often had little choice but to rework old tailings rather than seek new claims. The Chinese settlement is off Buckingham St.

Try your luck **gold panning** on the Arrow River. Rent pans from the visitor information centre ($3) and head to the northern edge of town. This is also a good spot for **walking**. Pick up *Arrowtown Area Walks* (free) from the visitor information centre; you'll find routes and history on walks to **Macetown** (14km, seven hours) and on **Tobins Track** (one hour).

Arrowtown Golf Course (☎ 03-442 1719; www.arrowtown.nzgolf.net; green fees $55, club hire $30) is picturesque and challenging. Flasher golfers should head to **Millbrook Golf Course** (☎ 03-441 7010; www.millbrook.co.nz; Malaghans Rd; green fees $165, club hire $55), and in January the **New Zealand Golf Open** (www.nzga.co.nz) is held at the private 'Hills' course of NZ retail magnate Michael Hill. Queenstown and Arrowtown are very busy on weekends. Book ahead.

Sleeping

Arrowtown has accommodation from budget to top end, but during summer rooms fill up fast.

Poplar Lodge (☎ 03-442 1466; www.poplarlodge.co.nz; 4 Merioneth St; dm/s/d $27/60/65; ☞) Budget accommodation options are limited in A-town, but this is your best bet. A converted house, Poplar has a cosy feel and is off the bus-bound tourist trail. A couple of self-contained units ($95 to $120) are also available.

Arrowtown Holiday Park (☎ 03-442 1876; www.arrowtownholidaypark.co.nz; 11 Suffolk St; sites $34, d $60-130) Mountain views come as standard, even if you're paying more for the flash new studio units. Amenities blocks are equally pristine.

Viking Lodge (☎ 03-442 1765; www.vikinglodge.co.nz; 21 Inverness Cres; d $95-150; ☒) These older A-frame units have a comfortable and family-friendly stamp. If the kids still have energy after a day's travelling, wear them out even more in the swimming pool or on the playground.

Shades (☎ 03-442 1613; www.shadesofarrowtown.co.nz; cnr Buckingham & Merioneth Sts; d $100-150) A garden setting gives these bungalow-style cottages a relaxed air. Family units ($175) are good value if you're travelling with the whole clan.

Old Villa Homestay B&B (☎ 03-442 1682; www.arrowtownoldvilla.co.nz; 13 Anglesea St; s/d $110/160) Freshly baked bread and homemade preserves welcome visitors to this heritage-style villa with a garden just made for summer barbecues. Two en-suite double rooms come trimmed with fresh sprigs of lavender. One of the rooms has an additional single bed if you've got an extra travelling companion.

Arrowtown Lodge (☎ 03-442 1101; www.arrowtownlodge.co.nz; 7 Anglesea St; d incl breakfast $200; ☐ ☞) From the outside, the guest rooms look like heritage cottages, but inside they're cosy and modern. The family owners are super-friendly and the breakfast is hearty.

Millbrook (☎ 0800 800 604, 03-441 7000; www.millbrook.co.nz; Malaghans Rd; d $435-715; ☐ ☞ ☒) Just outside Arrowtown, this enormous resort is a town unto itself. At the end of the day enjoy a massage in the spa, and take your pick from four restaurants.

Eating

For its size, Arrowtown has a good range of restaurants.

Arrowtown Bakery (☎ 03-442 1587; Buckingham St; gourmet pies $5; ⏲ 7am-7pm) Once the Arrowtown Bakery has lured you with yummy aromas, you'll be powerless. We can recommend the smoked fish or satay chicken pies. Don't blame us if you order a second.

Café Mondo (☎ 03-442 0227; Ballarat Arcade, Buckingham St; breakfast $7-15, lunch & dinner $12-25; ⏲ 8am-late; ☐) In a courtyard, this place is an excellent spot for a relaxed breakfast. Have coffee and a snack if you're in a hurry, or linger with a wine from a range of local tipples. There's a good kids' menu, too.

Stables (☎ 03-442 1818; 28 Buckingham St; mains $15-32; ⏲ 11am-9pm) With courtyard tables adjoining a grassy square, Stables is a good spot to share a tasting platter ($29.50) with your closest travelling companion. Have a local Brewski beer from Wanaka, or a glass of Central Otago wine. Later at night, step inside the 1860s stone building for a more intimate dining experience.

Pesto (☎ 03-442 0885; 18 Buckingham St; mains $17-30; ☷ 5pm-late) This candlelit restaurant serves Italian food with a contemporary spin. It's Saffron's slightly rowdier, younger, family-friendly sibling, and the culinary expectations are kept high with good pasta and gourmet pizzas.

Bonjour Cafe (☎ 03-409 8946; Ramshaw Lane; mains $18-30; ☷ 8.30am-late) Authentic French cuisine direct from the continent. Come for breakfast and tuck into one of the 17 different crepe options – you'll struggle to choose, that we guarantee. Come back for dinner to treat yourself to cheese fondue.

Saffron (☎ 03-442 0131; 18 Buckingham St; lunch $12-28, dinner $30-50; ☷ noon-late) One of the South Island's best restaurants, Saffron has grown-up food including duck cassoulet and a trio of curries featuring pork, duck and king prawns. The ambience is more sophisticated than Pesto's.

Drinking

Blue Door (☎ 03-442 0415; 18 Buckingham St; ☷ 3pm-late) Hidden away behind a tricky-to-find, yet perfectly appropriate, blue door. The low ceilings, low light and abundant candles make for an intimate quaffing location. Blue Door has a formidable wine list and enough rustic ambience to keep you entertained for the evening.

Tap (☎ 03-442 1860; 51 Buckingham St; ☷ 11am-late) The Tap dates back to the gold rush. Inside, there are wines, a pool table, pub grub and liquid gold on tap. Sit outside and slow down to Arrowtown's languid pace.

New Orleans Hotel (☎ 03-442 1860; 51 Buckingham St; ☷ 11am-late) With looks transplanted more from the Wild West than the Deep South, this heritage pub is a good escape from Arrowtown's growing array of expensive designer shops.

Entertainment

Dorothy Browns (☎ 03-442 1964; www.dorothybrowns.com; cnr Ballarat Arcade, Buckingham St; adult/child/student $18/6.50/12) This is what a cinema should be. Ultra-comfortable seating with the option to cuddle with your neighbour. Fine wine and

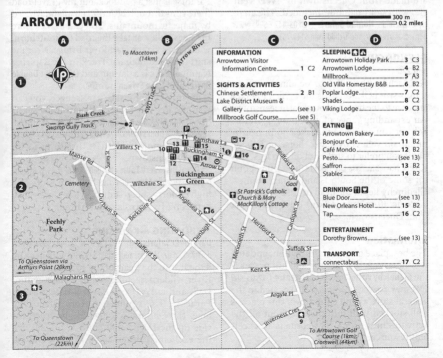

ARROWTOWN

0 _____ 300 m
0 _____ 0.2 miles

INFORMATION
Arrowtown Visitor
  Information Centre.................1 C2

SIGHTS & ACTIVITIES
Chinese Settlement..................2 B1
Lake District Museum &
  Gallery..........................(see 1)
Millbrook Golf Course............(see 5)

SLEEPING
Arrowtown Holiday Park..........3 C3
Arrowtown Lodge....................4 B2
Millbrook..............................5 A3
Old Villa Homestay B&B..........6 B2
Poplar Lodge.........................7 C2
Shades.................................8 C2
Viking Lodge.........................9 C3

EATING
Arrowtown Bakery.................10 B2
Bonjour Cafe.......................11 B2
Café Mondo.........................12 B2
Pesto.............................(see 13)
Saffron..............................13 B2
Stables..............................14 B2

DRINKING
Blue Door........................(see 13)
New Orleans Hotel................15 B2
Tap..................................16 C2

ENTERTAINMENT
Dorothy Browns..................(see 13)

TRANSPORT
connectabus.......................17 C2

To Macetown (14km)

Arrow River

Bush Creek

Swamp Gully Track

Villiers St

Buckingham St

Ramshaw La

Buckingham Green

Manse Rd

Wiltshire St

Cemetery

Berkshire St

Caernarvon St

Anglesea St

Denbigh St

Durham St

Feehly Park

St Patrick's Catholic Church & Mary MacKillop's Cottage

Old Gaol

Merioneth St

Hertford St

Cardigan St

Bedford St

Stafford St

Suffolk St

Kent St

To Queenstown via Arthurs Point (20km)

Malaghans Rd

To Queenstown (22km)

Argyle Pl

Inverness Cres

To Arrowtown Golf Course (1km); Cromwell (44km)

4WD Track

cheese boards are available to accompany the mostly art-house films on offer. Every screening has an intermission – a perfect opportunity to tuck into a tub of gourmet ice cream.

Getting There & Away

From Queenstown, **connectabus** (☎ 03-441 4471; www.connectabus.com) runs regular services (7.15am to 10pm) on its green route to Arrowtown (adult/child $8/5). If you're planning a day trip to Arrowtown, a day pass (adult/child $19/9.50) is a little cheaper. The bus also stops at Millbrook.

The **Double-Decker Bus Tour** (☎ 03-441 4421; $48) does a three-hour round-trip tour to Arrowtown twice daily. **Arrowtown Scenic Bus** (☎ 03-442 1900; www.arrowtownbus.co.nz) has three services daily (return $25).

AROUND ARROWTOWN

Fourteen kilometres north of Arrowtown lies **Macetown**, a ghost town reached via a rugged, flood-prone road (the original miners' wagon track), which crosses the Arrow River more than 25 times. Don't even think about taking the rental car here – instead four-hour trips are made from Queenstown by 4WD vehicle, with gold panning included. The main operator is **Nomad Safaris** (☎ 03-442 6699; www.nomadsafaris.co.nz; adult/child from $149/75).

GLENORCHY

pop 220

Set in achingly beautiful surroundings, postage-stamp-sized Glenorchy is the perfect low-key antidote to the hype and bustle of Queenstown. An expanding range of adventure operators will get you active on the lake and in nearby mountain valleys by kayak, horse or jetboat, but if you prefer to strike out on two legs, tiny Kinloch just across the lake is the starting point for some of the South Island's finest tramps. Glenorchy lies at the head of Lake Wakatipu, a scenic 40-minute (68km) drive northwest from Queenstown.

Information

The best place for local information, updated weather, track information and hut passes is the **Glenorchy visitor information centre** (☎ 03-409 2049; www.glenorchy-nz.co.nz; Oban St). Located in the general store as you enter town, this place is well stocked with information about all the activities in the area. Its website is an excellent resource.

Also check out the **Destination Glenorchy** (Map p306; ☎ 03-441 3003; 39 Camp St) booking office in Queenstown, and see www.glenorchy.com.

There is a petrol station in Glenorchy, but you'd be wise to fill up with cheaper fuel before you leave Queenstown.

Activities

Almost all organised activities offer shuttles to and from Queenstown for a small surcharge.

TRAMPING & SCENIC DRIVING

The DOC leaflet *Glenorchy Walkway* (free) details an easy waterside walk around the outskirts of town that's pretty but not thrilling. For something more demanding, pick up *Great Wilderness Walks* (free) from the visitor information centre. It's got tramps from two hours to two days, taking in Routeburn Valley, Lake Sylvan, Dart River and Lake Rere. For track snacks or meals, stock up on groceries in Queenstown.

Those with sturdy wheels can explore the superb valleys north of Glenorchy. **Paradise** lies 15km northwest of town, just before the start of the Dart Track. Keep your expectations low: Paradise is just a paddock, but the gravel road there runs through beautiful farmland fringed by majestic mountains. You can also explore the Rees Valley or take the road to Routeburn, which goes via the Dart River Bridge. Near the start of the Routeburn Track in Mt Aspiring National Park is a day hut and the short **Double Barrel** and **Lake Sylvan** tramps.

If you'd rather just be a passenger, you can visit the Rees Valley with **Mountainland Rovers** (☎ 03-441 1323; www.mountainlandrovers.co.nz; 37 Mull St; adult/child from $109/60), which runs 4WD tours into the remote wilderness. It also picks up from Queenstown.

Rural Discovery Tours (☎ 0800 738 687; www.rdtours.co.nz; adult/child $180/90) runs half-day tours of a high country sheep station in a remote valley between Mts Earnslaw and Alfred.

JETBOATING & KAYAKING

Dart River Safaris (☎ 0800 327 8538, 03-442 9992; www.dartriver.co.nz; Mull St; adult/child $199/99) journeys by jetboat into the heart of the spectacular Dart River wilderness, followed by a short nature walk and a 4WD trip down a back road to Paradise. The round trip from Glenorchy takes three hours. A longer 2½-hour jetboat ride up the Dart (adult/child $229/129) ups the excitement level, and you can combine a jetboat ride with a river descent in an inflatable three-seater 'funyak' (adult/child $279/179); from Glenorchy it's seven hours return. For all trips add a couple of hours if you're departing from Queenstown.

Kayak Kinloch (☎ 03-442 4900; www.kayakkinloch. co.nz; adult $40-80, child $35-50) runs excellent guided trips exploring the lake. Trips depart from Queenstown, Glenorchy or Kinloch.

OTHER ACTIVITIES

An extreme way to take in the scenery is with a 45-second free fall from 12,000ft. **NZSkydive** (☎ 0800 586 749, 03-409 0363; www.nzskydive.com; 9000ft/12,000ft/15,000ft $245/295/395) offers the heart-stopping chance to jump out of a plane above Glenorchy. Prices include free transport from Queenstown.

For horsey types, **Dart Stables** (☎ 0800 474 3464, 03-442 5688; www.dartstables.com; Coll St) offers a two-hour ride ($145), a full-day trot ($305) and a 1½-hour Ride of the Rings trip ($165) for Hobbitty types. If you're really keen, consider the overnight two-day trek with a sleepover in Paradise ($595).

High Country Horses (☎ 0508 595 959, 03-442 9915; www.high-country-horses.co.nz) also runs two-hour rides ($105) and full-day rides ($205).

For all horse-riding trips add a couple of hours if starting in Queenstown.

Sleeping & Eating

At the base of the Kinloch Lodge there's a DOC campsite ($7), which has basic lakeside facilities.

Glenorchy Holiday Park (☎ 03-441 0303; www. glenorchy-nz.co.nz; 2 Oban St; unpowered/powered sites $20/25, dm/cabins $20/45) Set up camp in a field surrounded by basic cabins and handy barbecues. Out front is a small shop and the handy Glenorchy Visitor Information Centre.

Glenorchy Hotel (☎ 03-442 9902; www.glenorchynz. com; Mull St; dm $30, d $90-105; 🖤) Attached to a pub, the rooms here are surprisingly comfy. The backpacker unit is bright and basic and a popular base for returning trampers.

our pick **Kinloch Lodge** (Map p302; ☎ 03-442 4900; www.kinlochlodge.co.nz; Kinloch Rd; dm $30-33, d $80-120, r $175-195; 🖳) Across Lake Wakatipu from Glenorchy, this excellent retreat is a great place to unwind or prepare for a tramp. Rooms in the bunkhouse are comfy and colourful, with an outdoor hot tub and an indoor DVD-packed lounge, both just right for putting your feet up after a long tramp. The

19th-century Heritage Rooms are small but plusher. A cafe, a bar and a good restaurant (mains $15 to $31, open 8am to 8pm) are on-site, and if you're eating outside, look forward to stunning lake views and the attention of maybe the South Island's friendliest dogs. Kinloch is a 26km drive from Glenorchy, or you can organise a five-minute boat ride ($15) across the lake. Kinloch Lodge can also arrange track transfers to various trailheads. Even if you're not a tramping type, it's worth staying at least a night to soak up the relaxed ambience.

Mt Earnslaw Motels (☎ 03-442 6993; mtearnslaw@ xtra.co.nz; Mull St; d $110; 🖤) This cute row of units is older from the outside but redone inside, creating cosy, well-priced rooms with big, comfy recliners, a small kitchen and an enormous bed.

Glenorchy Lodge (☎ 03-442 9968; wakatipu@xtra. co.nz; Mull St; d $120-140; 🖤) Tidy yet tiny rooms live upstairs from this central-as pub. Some rooms have loft-style ceilings and some have en suites – all have great views. Take in the serenity from private balconies before retiring downstairs to Foxy's Café for excellent coffee.

Glenorchy Lake House (☎ 03-442 7084; www. glenorchylakehouse.co.nz; Mull St; d $345-400) Newly opened in late 2007, the three rooms at this luxury lakefront B&B feature Egyptian cotton sheets, flat-screen TVs and luxury toiletries. Good luck tearing yourself away from the inner glories to get active out and about in the Wakatipu area. Once you return, recharge in the spa or with a massage.

Blanket Bay (Map p302; ☎ 03-442 9442; www.blanket bay.com; Glenorchy Rd; r $1450-2750; 🖳🖤🖳) An excessively discreet world-class resort that's a home away from home for the rich and famous. This alpine lodge is all native timber and local schist stone, and boasts stunning views. Blanket Bay is multi-award-winning and a firm favourite of the well heeled – whether they are Hollywood A-listers, development demi-gods or regular folk who aren't afraid to spend up large for the stay of their lives.

our pick **Glenorchy Café** (☎ 03-442 9958; Mull St; breakfast & lunch mains $10-15, pizza $20; 🕑 8am-late May-Oct, dinner Nov-Apr) With a reputation extending beyond little old GY, the Glenorchy Café is an institution oozing cool and natural style. The portions are as big as the surrounding peaks, and the coffee has powered many a mountain mission. Perennial favourites like pizza and breakfast stacks keep locals coming back time after time. Sit among the shadow of the peaks in the back garden – you'll struggle to leave.

Getting There & Away

With sweeping vistas and gem-coloured waters, the sealed Glenorchy to Queenstown Rd is wonderfully scenic. Its constant hills are a killer for cyclists. Pick up the *Queenstown to Glenorchy Road* leaflet from the Queenstown i-SITE for points of interest along the way.

Backpacker Express at the **Info & Track Centre** (Map p306; ☎ 03-442 9708; www.infotrack.co.nz; 37 Shotover St) provides transport to Glenorchy from Queenstown (adult/child $20/15). It will also drop you off (and pick you up) from the Routeburn and Greenstone Tracks.

LAKE WAKATIPU REGION

The mountainous region at the northern head of Lake Wakatipu has some gorgeous, remote scenery, best viewed while tramping along the famous Routeburn and lesser-known Greenstone, Caples and Rees-Dart Tracks. For shorter tracks, see the DOC brochure *Lake Wakatipu Walks and Trails* ($1). Glenorchy is a convenient base for all these tramps.

Ultimate Hikes (☎ 03-442 8200; www.ultimatehikes. co.nz) has a three-day guided tramp on the Routeburn ($1100/1240 low/high season); a six-day Grand Traverse ($1525/1725), combining walks on the Routeburn and Greenstone Tracks; and a one-day Routeburn Encounter ($165), which is available from mid-October to April. All prices include return transport, accommodation and all meals.

Track Information

For details of accommodation, transport to and from all trailheads and DOC visitor information centres, see Queenstown (p303) and Te Anau (p338).

DOC staff advise on maps and sell hut and Great Walks passes; before setting out, it's essential that you contact them for up-to-date track conditions. It's also advised that you book your intentions, and but be sure to let DOC know when you return. For more details on all these tracks see Lonely Planet's *Tramping in New Zealand*.

Routeburn Track

Passing through a huge variety of landscapes with fantastic views, the three- to four-day Routeburn Track is one of the most popular rainforest/subalpine tracks in NZ. Increased pressure on the track has necessitated the introduction of a booking system; reservations are required throughout the main season (October to April), either through DOC visitor information centres, or online via great walksbooking@doc.govt.nz or www.doc.govt. nz. The **Great Walks huts pass** (per night adult/child $45/free) allows you to stay at Routeburn Flats Hut, Routeburn Falls Hut, Mackenzie Hut and Howden Hut; various 'family' passes are also available. A **camping pass** (per night adult/child $15/free) allows you to pitch a tent only at Routeburn Flats and Lake Mackenzie.

Outside the main season, passes are still required; huts cost $15/free per adult/child per night. Camping is $5/free in the off season. Note that the Routeburn Track is often closed by snow in winter and stretches of the track are very exposed and dangerous in bad weather; always check conditions with DOC.

There are car parks at the Divide and Glenorchy ends of the Routeburn, but they're unattended, so don't leave any valuables in your car.

The track can be started from either end. Many people travelling from Queenstown try to reach the Divide in time to catch the bus to Milford and connect with a cruise on the sound. En route, you'll take in breathtaking views from Harris Saddle and the top of nearby Conical Hill, from where you can see waves breaking at Martins Bay. From Key Summit, there are panoramic views of the Hollyford Valley and the Eglinton and Greenstone River Valleys.

Estimated walking times:

Route	Time
Routeburn Shelter to Flats Hut	1½-2½hr
Flats Hut to Falls Hut	1-1½hr
Falls Hut to Mackenzie Hut	4½-6hr
Mackenzie Hut to Howden Hut	3-4hr
Howden Hut to the Divide	1-1½hr

Greenstone & Caples Tracks

Following meandering rivers through lush, peaceful valleys, these two tracks form a loop that many trampers stretch out into a moderate four- or five-day tramp. Basic huts en route are Mid Caples, Upper Caples, McKellar and Greenstone. All are $15/5 per adult/child (11 to 17 years) per night, and Backcountry Hut Passes must be purchased in advance.

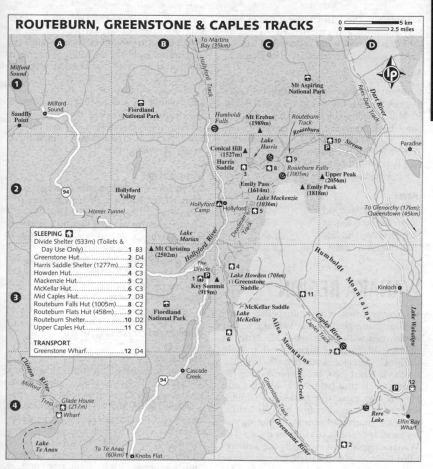

ROUTEBURN, GREENSTONE & CAPLES TRACKS

0 _____ 5 km
0 _____ 2.5 miles

SLEEPING

Divide Shelter (533m) (Toilets & Day Use Only)............1	B3
Greenstone Hut.........................2	D4
Harris Saddle Shelter (1277m)......3	C2
Howden Hut............................4	C3
Mackenzie Hut.........................5	C2
McKellar Hut...........................6	C3
Mid Caples Hut.........................7	D3
Routeburn Falls Hut (1005m)......8	C2
Routeburn Flats Hut (458m)......9	C2
Routeburn Shelter....................10	D2
Upper Caples Hut....................11	C3

TRANSPORT

Greenstone Wharf....................12	D4

You can camp (free) but not on private land; check with DOC for where not to pitch your tent. Both tracks meet up with the Routeburn Track; you can either follow its tail end to the Divide or (if you've prebooked) pursue it back to Glenorchy.

From McKellar Hut you can tramp two or three hours to Howden Hut on the Routeburn Track (you'll need to book this hut from October to April), which is an hour from the Divide.

Access to the Greenstone and Caples Tracks is from Greenstone Wharf; nearby you'll find unattended parking. The road from Kinloch to Greenstone Wharf is unsealed and rough; during the summer season **Backpacker Express** (☎ 03-442 9939) and Kinloch

Lodge (p323) usually run a boat across the lake from Glenorchy.

Estimated walking times:

Route	Time
Greenstone Wharf to Mid Caples Hut	3hr
Mid Caples Hut to Upper Caples Hut	2-3hr
Upper Caples Hut to McKellar Hut	5-8hr
McKellar Hut to Greenstone Hut	5-7hr
Greenstone Hut to Greenstone Wharf	4-6hr

Rees-Dart Track

This is a difficult, demanding four- to five-day circular route from the head of Lake Wakatipu, taking you through valleys and over an alpine pass, with the possibility of a side trip to the Dart Glacier if you're suitably equipped and experienced. Access by vehicle is possible as far as Muddy Creek on the Rees side, from where it's two hours to 25-Mile Hut.

Park your car at Muddy Creek or arrange transport with Queenstown's **Info & Track Centre** (Map p304; ☎ 03-442 9708; www.infotrack.co.nz; 37 Shotover St). Most people go up the Rees track first and come back down the Dart. The three basic DOC huts (Shelter Rock, Daleys Flat and the Dart) cost $10 per person and Backcountry Hut Passes must be purchased in advance.

Estimated walking times:

Route	Time
Muddy Creek to Shelter Rock Hut	6hr
Shelter Rock Hut to Dart Hut	5-7hr
Dart Hut to Daleys Flat Hut	6-8hr
Daleys Flat Hut to Paradise	6-8hr

WANAKA REGION

With overgrown valleys, unspoiled rivers and tumbling glaciers, the Wanaka region is crowned with the colossal Mt Aspiring (Tititea; 3035m), the highest peak outside the Mt Cook region. Enter this area from the north via Haast Pass, and you encounter the region's beautiful twin lakes, Wanaka and Hawea, two expansive freshwater siblings wedged between awesome hills and cliffs. From the south via Cardrona, stunning valley views and mountain vistas are on tap. The Wanaka region, and especially the activity-filled town of Wanaka itself, is seeing more and more travellers, but it's still a quieter alternative to pumpin' Queenstown. And once you've sampled a few closer-to-Wanaka action activities and told tall stories in the town's pubs and bars, get off the tourist trail by exploring the Mt Aspiring National Park or the forested wilderness around Makarora.

WANAKA
pop 5000

Beautiful scenery, tramping and skiing opportunities, and a huge roster of adrenaline-inducing activities have transformed the lakeside town of Wanaka into a year-round tourist destination. Travellers come here as an alternative to Queenstown, and while some locals worry their home is starting to resemble its hyped-up Central Otago sibling across the

Crown Range, Wanaka's lakefront area retains a laid-back, small-town feel. It's definitely not a sleepy hamlet anymore, though, and new restaurants and bars are adding a veneer of sophistication. Note that Wanaka wakes up in a big way for New Year's Eve.

Wanaka is located at the southern end of Lake Wanaka, just over 100km northeast of Queenstown via Cromwell. It's the gateway to Mt Aspiring National Park and to the Treble Cone, Cardrona, Harris Mountains and Pisa Range Ski Areas.

Information

DOC Wanaka visitor information centre (DOC; ☎ 03-443 7660; Ardmore St; ☺ 8am-4.30pm Mon-Fri, 9.30am-4pm Sat & Sun, closed noon-12.30pm) In an A-framed building on the edge of town, this is the place to inquire about tramps, and there's a small museum (admission free) on Wanaka geology, flora and fauna.

Lake Wanaka i-SITE (☎ 03-443 1233; www.lake wanaka.co.nz; ☺ 8.30am-5.30pm, to 7pm in summer) Off Ardmore St, on the waterfront.

Wanaka Medical Centre (☎ 03-443 7811; 21 Russell St; ☺ 9am-5pm Mon-Fri, clinics at 9am & 5pm Sat & Sun) Patches up adventure-sports mishaps.

Wanakaweb (1st fl, 3 Helwick St) Get online here.

Sights

With its emphasis on the stunning outdoors, Wanaka isn't brimming with conventional sights, but you can keep busy on a rainy day.

Puzzling World (☎ 03-443 7489; www.puzzlingworld. com; 188 Main Hwy 84; adult/child $12.50/9; ☺ 8.30am-5.30pm) has a 3-D Great Maze and lots of 'now-you-see-it, now-you-don't' visual tomfoolery to keep kids of all ages bemused, bothered and bewildered. It's en route to Cromwell, 2km from town.

The poignant and interesting **New Zealand Fighter Pilots Museum** (☎ 03-443 7010; www.nzfpm. co.nz; Wanaka Airport; adult/child/family $10/5/25; ☺ 9am-5pm) is dedicated to NZ combat pilots, the aircraft they flew and the sacrifices they made. There is a well-preserved collection of Hawker Hurricanes, de Havilland Vampires and vintage Soviet fighter planes, and at the time of writing plans were under way for a major expansion of the collection and facilities.

More light-hearted is the neighbouring **Wanaka Transport & Toy Museum** (☎ 03-443 8765; www.wanakatransportandtoymuseum.com; SH6; adult/child/family $10/4/20; ☺ 8.30am-5pm), the end result of one man's obsessive collecting. Among the 40,000 items, watch for a Cadillac Coupe de

Ville, a mysteriously acquired MiG jet fighter, and toys that you're guaranteed to remember with a wry smile from rainy childhood afternoons.

Afterwards, toast the past and the future at **Wanaka Beerworks** (☎ 03-443 1865; www.wanaka beerworks.co.nz; SH6; ◷ 9am-4pm, tours 2pm) with this small brewery's three award-winning products: a Vienna lager, a German-style black beer and our favourite, the hops-laden 'Brewski' Bohemian pilsener. Bookings are recommended for brewery tours.

Activities
Wide valleys, alpine meadows, more than 100 glaciers and sheer mountains make **Mt Aspiring National Park** an outdoor enthusiast's paradise. Protected as a national park in 1964, and later included in the Southwest New Zealand (Te Wahipounamu) World Heritage Area, the park now blankets more than 3500 sq km along the Southern Alps, from the Haast River in the north to its border with Fiordland National Park in the south.

TRAMPING
While the southern end of Mt Aspiring National Park is well trafficked by visitors and includes popular tramps such as the Routeburn Track (p324), there are great short walks and more demanding multiday tramps in the Matukituki Valley, close to Wanaka; see the DOC leaflet *Matukituki Valley Tracks* ($1). The dramatic **Rob Roy Valley Track** (three to four hours return) takes in glaciers, waterfalls and a swing bridge, yet is a fairly easy route. The **West Matukituki Valley** track goes on to Aspiring Hut (four to five hours return), a scenic, more difficult walk over mostly grassy flats. For overnight or multiday tramps, continue up the valley to **Liverpool Hut** for great views of Mt Aspiring, or over the very difficult **Cascade Saddle** to link up with the Rees-Dart Track (p325), north of Glenorchy.

Many of these tramps are subject to snow and avalanches and can be treacherous. Register your intentions and seek advice from DOC in Wanaka before heading off. Also purchase hut passes. Tracks are reached from Raspberry Creek at the end of Mt Aspiring Rd, 54km from Wanaka; for shuttle-service details, see p334.

For walks closer to town, pick up the DOC brochure *Wanaka Walks and Trails* ($1). This includes the easy lakeside stroll to **Eely Point** (20 minutes) and on to **Beacon Point** (30 minutes), as well as the **Waterfall Creek Walk** (one hour return) east along the lakeshore.

The fairly gentle climb to the top of **Mt Iron** (549m, 1½ hours return) reveals panoramic views. Fit folks after a view can undertake the taxing, winding 8km tramp up **Mt Roy** (1578m, five to six hours return), starting 6km from Wanaka on the Mt Aspiring Rd. The high track crosses private land and is closed from October to mid-November for lambing. From Mt Roy, continue along the **Skyline Track** (five to six hours) to Cardrona Rd, 10km south of Wanaka. Don't do this in winter; low cloud eliminates views and makes it treacherous.

To the north of Wanaka, the **Minaret Burn Track** (six to seven hours) in the Mt Alta Conservation Area is suitable for walking and mountain biking. You can pick up a map (50c) at DOC.

Many outfits offer guided walking tours around Wanaka, some into Mt Aspiring National Park:

Alpinism & Ski Wanaka (☎ 03-442 6593; www. alpinismski.co.nz; half-/full day $130/195) Day walks and overnight tramps.
Eco Wanaka Adventures (☎ 03-443 2869; www. ecowanaka.co.nz; half-/full day from $105/170) Day, half-day and multiday trips.
Wild Walks (☎ 03-442 4476; www.wildwalks.co.nz; 3 days from $720) Multiday tramps.

JETBOATING & RAFTING
Lakeland Adventures (☎ 03-443 7495; www.lakeland adventures.co.nz; adult/child $95/45), at the i-SITE, offers one-hour jetboat trips across the lake that include an exciting ride in the winding Clutha River. **Pioneer Rafting** (☎ 03-443 1246; www.ecoraft. co.nz; half-day rafts per adult/child $135/75, full-day $185/95) runs ecorafting on the high-volume Clutha, with Grade II to III rapids, gold panning and birdwatching.

CANYONING & KAYAKING
Adventurous souls will love canyoning, a summer activity staged by **Deep Canyon** (☎ 03-443 7922; www.deepcanyon.co.nz; from $225; ◷ mid-Nov–Apr) that involves climbing, swimming and waterfall-abseiling through confined, steep and wild gorges. Transport to the canyon, lunch, instruction and equipment are included. If you're a supremely confident adventure junkie, consider the Leaping Burn trip ($460).

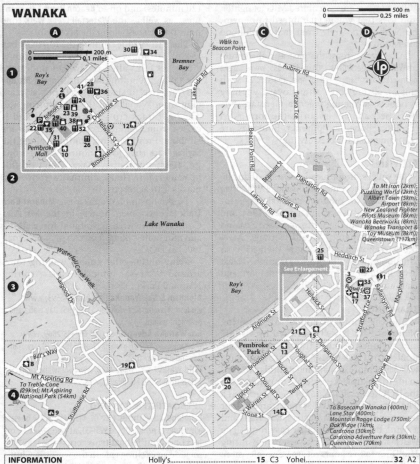

Alpine Kayak Guides (☎ 03-443 9023; www.alpine kayaks.co.nz; half-/full day $149/195; ☉ Nov-May) paddles down the Hawea, Clutha and Matukituki Rivers. Kids can join a more leisurely half-day Grandview trip (two adult and two kids $450), and if you really get a taste for paddling, sign up for a full-day kayaking basics course ($280).

Wanaka Kayaks (☎ 0800 926 925; www.wanaka kayaks.co.nz; ☉ summer only), opposite Subway on the beach, rents kayaks ($10 to $18) and offers guided lake tours (from $60 per person).

Hire kayaks from **Lakeland Adventures** (☎ 03-443 7495; www.lakelandadventures.co.nz), off Ardmore St, on the waterfront, for $15 per hour.

SKYDIVING & PARAGLIDING
Skydive Lake Wanaka (☎ 03-443 7207; www.sky divewanaka.com; adult $295-395) does jumps from 12,000ft and a scary 15,000ft; the latter lets you fall for 60 seconds. Count on another $130 or so for video evidence for the folks back home.

Wanaka Paragliding (☎ 0800 359 754; www.wanaka paragliding.co.nz; adult $180) will take you on tandem flights at 800m from Treble Cone. Count on around 20 minutes soaring on the Central Otago thermals.

ROCK CLIMBING & MOUNTAINEERING
Mt Aspiring National Park is a favourite playground of mountaineering and alpine climbing companies. **Aspiring Guides** (☎ 03-443 9422; www.aspiringguides.com; 5 days from $3350), **Adventure Consultants** (☎ 03-443 8711; www.adventure.co.nz; 5 days from $4100 with a 1:1 guide ratio) and **Alpinism & Ski** (☎ 03-443 6593; www.alpinismski.co.nz; 5 days from $3385) all offer beginners' courses and multiday guided ascents of Mts Aspiring, Tasman and Tutoko.

Excellent rock climbing can be found at **Hospital Flat** – 25km from Wanaka towards Mount Aspiring NP. Those not in the know can climb with **Wanaka Rock Climbing & Abseil Adventures** (☎ 03-443 6411; www.wanakarock.co.nz), which has an introductory rock-climbing course (half-/full day $120/190), a half-day abseiling intro ($120), and bouldering and multipitch climbs for the experienced.

Before you hit the mountains, learn the ropes on the indoor and outdoor climbing walls at **Basecamp Wanaka** (☎ 03-443 1110; www.basecampwanaka.co.nz; 50 Cardrona Valley Rd; adult/child $15/12; ☉ 10am-9pm, to 7pm Sat & Sun). Climbing gear can also be hired.

MOUNTAIN BIKING
Many tracks and trails in the region are open to cyclists. DOC produces *Mountain-Biking Around Wanaka* (50c), describing mountain-bike rides ranging from 2km (the steep Mt Iron track) to 20km (West Matukituki Valley).

For spectacular guided mountain biking, contact **Freeride NZ** (☎ 0800 743 369; www.freeridenz.com), which does full-day trips (from $185), including helibiking options. If you're happiest on two wheels, jump on a three-day ($1050) or eight-day ($2750) expedition.

Rent bikes from **Lakeland Adventures** (☎ 03-443 7495; www.lakelandadventures.co.nz; per hr/full day $10/40).

FISHING
Lakes Wanaka and Hawea (16km away) have excellent trout fishing, and the surrounding rivers are also popular angling spots. Numerous guides are based in Wanaka, including **Hatch** (☎ 03-443 8446; www.hatchfishing.co.nz; 2 adults half-/full day $390/650) and **Riversong** (☎ 03-443 8567; www.wanakaflyfishingguides.co.nz; half-/full day $400/600). Hatch also runs adventure fishing trips incorporating hiking ($650 per day), and for $75 per hour, the expert team at Riversong offer tuition in the dark art of fly-fishing.

Lakeland Adventures (☎ 03-443 7495; www.lakelandadventures.co.nz; up to 3 people $299) offers guided trout fishing on Lake Wanaka.

OTHER ACTIVITIES
For skiers after untouched powder and exclusive views, there are companies offering heliskiing (p83). More easily reached slopes include Treble Cone (p80), Cardrona (p80) and Snow Farm New Zealand (for cross-country skiing; p81).

Wanaka Golf Club (☎ 03-443 7888; www.wanakagolf.co.nz; Ballantyne Rd; green fees $55, club hire from $20) has a view-filled 18-hole course.

Outside Sports (☎ 03-443 7966; www.outsidesports.co.nz; 17 Dunmore St) offers a wide range of outdoor gear – for sale or rent, tramping, skiing, climbing, camping and just about anything else you might need to get into the outdoors.

Tours
AERIAL SIGHTSEEING
The following companies are all based at Wanaka Airport. Book trips through the i-SITE.

Aspiring Air (☎ 0800 100 943, 03-443 7943; www.aspiringair.com) A range of scenic flights, including a

50-minute flight over Mt Aspiring (adult/child $210/120), a Milford Sound fly-past and landing ($375/230) and a sprint around Mt Cook and the glaciers ($395/230).

Classic Flights (☎ 027 220 9277; www.classicflights. co.nz; from $225) Runs sightseeing flights in a vintage Tigermoth. 'Biggles' goggles provided, but BYO flowing silk scarf.

Wanaka Flightseeing (☎ 0800 105 105, 03-443 8787; www.flightseeing.co.nz) Offers similar flights to Aspiring Air at similar prices – it also throws in free admission to the adjacent Fighter Pilots Museum (p326) and discounts on first-thing-in-the-morning flights.

The following offer 20-minute flights around Wanaka for about $175, and 60-minute tours of Mt Aspiring and the glaciers for about $450.

Alpine Helicopters (☎ 03-443 4000; www.alpineheli. co.nz)

Aspiring Helicopters (☎ 03-443 7152; www.aspiring helicopters.co.nz)

Wanaka Helicopters (☎ 03-443 1085; www.heli flights.co.nz)

OTHER TOURS
Book at the i-SITE.

Clean Green Photo Tours (☎ 03-443 7951; www. cleangreen.co.nz; 3hr/half-day/full day $300/400/750) Gives you expert hints and tips as you capture Central Otago's stunning scenery.

Lake Wanaka Cruises (☎ 03-443 1230; www. wanakacruises.co.nz; from $60) Similar tours to Lakeland Adventures aboard a catamaran; with overnight options.

Lakeland Adventures (☎ 03-443 7495; www.lakeland adventures.co.nz) Has 2½-hour trips to Stevensons Island (adult/child $70/40) and a 3½-hour trip with a guided bushwalk on Mou Waho ($90/45). To explore the lake under your own steam, kayaks (from $10 per hour) and aqua bikes ($15 per 20 minutes) are also available.

Ridgeline (☎ 0800 234 000; www.ridgelinenz.com) Runs tours (3½ hours, $195) combining a 4WD farm safari and wine tasting at the beautiful Rippon Vineyard.

Wanaka Sightseeing (☎ 03-443 1855; www.wanaka sightseeing.co.nz; half-/full day $170/299) For any lingering *Lord of the Rings* fans, there are exhaustive tours of filming sights where you can dress up like a hobbit and sometimes hang out with Ian Brodie, author-cum-guru of *The Lord of the Rings: Location Guidebook*.

Festivals & Events

Rippon Festival (www.ripponfestival.co.nz) Music fans should diary this popular festival held every second year in early February at the lakeside Rippon Vineyard. Big-name Kiwi acts headline with a variety of styles represented – dance, reggae, rock and electronica to name a few. If the music doesn't relax you (highly unlikely), the wine certainly will. Rippon's Riesling is great for summer picnics.

Warbirds over Wanaka (☎ 0800 496 920, 03-443 8619; www.warbirdsoverwanaka.com; Wanaka Airport; 3-day adult/child $165/25, 1st day only $45/10, each of last 2 days $70/10) Every second Easter (even-numbered years), Wanaka hosts this huge and incredibly popular international airshow attracting 100,000 people.

Wanaka Fest (www.wanakafest.co.nz) Held mid-October, this festival is a four-day event with the feel of a small-town fair. Street parades, live music and wacky competitions get the locals saying gidday to the warmth of spring.

Sleeping

Like Queenstown, Wanaka is bursting with hostels and luxury accommodation, but good midrange options are harder to find. Across summer, and especially around New Year, prices and demand increase considerably. During winter, the town is hit with an influx of international snowboarders.

BUDGET

our pick **YHA Wanaka Purple Cow** (☎ 03-443 1880; www.yha.co.nz; 94 Brownston St; dm $24-31, d $90-96; 🖳 🛜) Warmed by a wood stove, the lounge at this ever-popular hostel holds commanding lake and mountain views; that's if you can tear yourself away from the regular movie nights. There are four- and six-bed dorms and a small array of nice doubles with en suites. Outdoor patios and bike hire will get you breathing in crisp mountain air.

Fern Lodge (☎ 0800 555 556; www.fernlodge.co.nz; 122 Brownston St; dm $25, d $80-120) Rooms at this sprawling reader-recommended spot run from straightforward doubles to flasher lodge rooms with Sky TV, spa baths and ritzy gas kitchens. The common theme throughout is excellent value for money.

Matterhorn South (☎ 03-443 1119; www.matter hornsouth.co.nz; 56 Brownston St; dm $25-30, s $65, d $65-90, tr & q $110-120; 🖳 🛜) Right at the edge of central Wanaka, this friendly spot has clean, good-value dorms and studios, and a sunny TV and games room. It has a shared country-style kitchen and a private garden to rest up in after a day's outdoor adventuring. The triple and quad en-suite rooms are excellent value.

Wanaka Bakpaka (☎ 03-443 7837; www.wanaka bakpaka.co.nz; 117 Lakeside Rd; dm $26-28, s $50, d $62-76; 🖳 🛜) An energetic brother-and-sister team are steadily upgrading this friendly hostel high above the lake with stunning views. Amenities are top-shelf and the staff is ready to throw down the red carpet for weary travellers. The colourful rooms are good value and the outlook from the lounge will inspire you to (finally) get your diary up to date.

Wanaka Lakeview Holiday Park (☎ 03-443 7883; www.wanakalakeview.kiwiholidayparks.com; 212 Brownston St; sites/cabins $32/46) Grassy sites set amid established pine trees with a kids' playground and lots of space to set up camp. Rooms range from basic cabins to en-suite flats.

Aspiring Campervan Park (☎ 0800 229 8439, 03-443 6603; www.campervanpark.co.nz; Studholme Rd; sites $45; 🖳 🛜) Trimmed grass sites, trees and pretty views add up to a relaxing spot. Great facilities include a barbecue area with gas heaters and a spa and sauna, all at no additional cost. Campervans only, please; no tents.

Altamont Lodge (☎ 03-443 8864; www.altamontlodge.co.nz; 121 Mt Aspiring Rd; d $65; 🖳 🛜) At the quieter end of town, natural wood gives this place a ski-lodge ambience. Tennis courts, a spa pool, and a lounge with a big fire provide plenty of off-piste action. It's often booked by big groups, so reserve ahead.

Also recommended:

Base Backpackers (☎ 03-443 4291; www.stayatbase. com; 73 Brownston St; dm $25-29, d $43; 🖳 🛜) This new hostel is a filing cabinet for backpacker-bus types. The facilities are sparkling and the on-site bar, Mint, is good fun too.

Mountain View Backpackers (☎ 03-443 9050; www.mtnview.co.nz; 7 Russell St; dm/d $25/68) A newly renovated characterful house with a big lawn and warm, comfortable rooms.

Holly's (☎ 03-443 8187; www.hollybackpacker.co.nz; 71 Upton St; dm $26-28, d $64; 🖳 🛜) A family-run low-key hostel that's a good antidote to busier places around town. Showing a bit of wear and tear, but a friendly spot. Bikes are for hire (half-/full day $10/20).

MIDRANGE

Harpers (☎ 03-443 8894; www.harpers.co.nz; 95 McDougall St; s/d incl breakfast $100/140) The garden (with pond and waterfall no less…) is a labour of love at this friendly B&B in a quiet location down a long driveway. Legendary breakfasts are served on a sunny deck with expansive views. You'd be wise to factor a leisurely second cup of breakfast coffee into your day's plans.

Aspiring Lodge (☎ 03-443 7816; www.aspiringlodge. co.nz; cnr Dunmore & Dungarvon Sts; d $135) Older but well-maintained motel units trimmed with

natural wood and with easy access to lakefront bars and restaurants. The following morning the motel's helpful team will have plenty of ideas for local activities.

Brook Vale (☎ 0800 438 333, 03-443 8333; www.brookvale.co.nz; 35 Brownston St; d $135; 🛜 🧺) Self-contained studio and family units with a few classy touches and patios that open onto a grassy lawn complete with a gently flowing creek. You'll also find a barbecue, a spa and a swimming pool for those sunny Central Otago days.

Bay View Motel (☎ 0800 229 843, 03-443 7766; www.bayviewwanaka.co.nz; Studholme Rd; r $135-155; 🖳 🛜) The original units date back 40 years, but the switched-on owners have modernised the interiors nicely with TVs and DVD players to keep up with the sterling views outside.

Riversong (☎ 03-443 8567; www.riversongwanaka. co.nz; 5 Wicklow Tce, Albert Town; d $150-170) On the banks of the Clutha River in the nearby hamlet of Albert Town, Riversong has two rooms in a lovely heritage B&B surrounded by established fruit trees. The well-travelled owners may well have the best nonfiction library in NZ, and if you can tear yourself away from the books, there's excellent trout fishing just metres away. Dinner including wine is available for $55 per person. Riversong is down a no-exit road, so it is very quiet.

TOP END

our pick **Mountain Range Lodge** (☎ 03-443 7400; www.mountainrange.co.nz; Heritage Park, Cardrona Valley Rd; r incl breakfast $280-390; 🖳 🛜) This stunning lodge is a vision of rustic luxury. Seven rooms named for nearby mountain ranges are home to comfy duvets, fluffy robes, and views that'll distract you from the nearby skiing and tramping options. Cool touches like a complimentary glass of wine – from the lodge's own label no less – and an on-site hot tub complete an already pretty picture.

Wanaka Homestead (☎ 03-443 5022; www.wanakahomestead.co.nz; 1 Homestead Close; d $295, cottages $410-525; 🖳 🛜) Warm wooden interiors, oriental rugs and local artwork punctuate this boutique lodge, which has won awards for its ecofriendly approach to sustainability. Despite the focus on green good deeds, it's still very luxurious, with underfloor heating and an under-the-stars hot tub. Choose from rooms in the main lodge or in self-contained cottages that sleep up to seven.

Eating

Wanaka has a surprising range of places to eat, drink and generally celebrate the fact that you're on holiday.

RESTAURANTS

White House Café & Bar (☎ 03-443 9595; 33 Dunmore St; mains $35-45; ☷ 6.30pm-late; Ⓥ) It looks like a Greek townhouse miraculously airlifted from Santorini, and inside this long-running local favourite you can linger over plates of Mediterranean and Middle Eastern cuisine with lots of vegetarian options. Polished wooden floors and Turkish rugs do nothing to break the delicious spell. In summer, relax under endless Central Otago blue skies seemingly also imported straight from the Med.

Relishes (☎ 03-443 9018; 99 Ardmore St; mains $15-30; ☷ 8am-9pm) A cafe by day, this place whips out the white tablecloths at night and becomes a classy restaurant with a good wine list. Try the antipasto platter ($26) with local salmon, and toast the lakefront setting.

Missy's Kitchen (☎ 03-443 5099; Level 1, 80 Ardmore St; mains $30-35; ☷ 4pm-late) A dramatic upstairs dining room with equally spectacular lake views serves up local beef, lamb and salmon in innovative and award-winning ways. Prolong the experience with a cocktail at the bar. The list of local beers and wine make returning for a second night worthwhile.

Botswana Butchery (☎ 03-443 6745; Post Office Lane; mains $30-45; ☷ 5pm-late) It's a humble name for Wanaka's classiest eatery. In a dining room trimmed with dark wood and leather, Asian-inspired dishes like seven-spiced big eye tuna go head to head with Botswana Butchery's signature aged beef steaks. Definitely food for grown-ups, as is the serious Central Otago–skewed wine list. Just come with a few imbibing partners, as surprisingly few wines are available by the glass. Downstairs in Post Office Lane there's a growing range of bars to explore after dinner. Let us know what you discover.

Lone Star (☎ 03-443 6901; 50 Cardrona Valley Rd; mains $25-33; ☷ 11am-late) The line 'everything's bigger in Texas' seems to fit the food here. Massive plates of grub are the calling card of Lone Star. Tex-Mex flavours and a festive atmosphere keep the mood light – though too many meals here and *you* won't be. Best to tuck into the Fred Flintstone–worthy ribs after going rock climbing at Basecamp Wanaka (p329), which is located in the same building.

CAFES & QUICK EATS

Soulfood Store & Cafe (☎ 03-443 7885; 74 Ardmore St; mains $7-15; ☷ 8am-5pm Mon-Fri, to 3pm Sat & Sun; Ⓥ) Park yourself in a rustic wooden booth and stay healthy with organic soups, pizza, pasta and muffins. Not everything's strictly vegetarian, and breakfast with free-range eggs breaks the spell in a tasty way. The attached organic food store, which has freshly baked bread, is a good spot for a pre-picnic stock-up.

Yohei (03-443 4222; Spencer House Mall, 23 Dunmore St; snacks $8-12; ☷ 7.30am-6pm; Ⓥ) Tucked away in a shopping arcade, this funky Japanese-inspired eatery does interesting local spins on sushi (how about venison or lamb?), and superlative juices and smoothies. Very cool music too, and a good range of vego options.

Kai Whakapai (☎ 03-443 7795; cnr Helwick & Ardmore Sts; meals $10-30; ☷ 7am-late) A Wanaka institution, Kai (the Maori word for food) is the place to be on a sunny day, with perhaps the best patio in all of Aotearoa. Massive sandwiches, great coffee and exceptionally slow service are all a part of the experience. They have the locally brewed Wanaka Beerworks beer on tap, and some local Central Otago wines as well.

Ardmore St Food Company (☎ 03-443 2230; The Waterfront, 155 Ardmore St; meals $12-18; ☷ 8am-4pm) This cosmopolitan lakefront cafe has everything from muffins the size of Mt Aspiring to quirkily dubbed breakfasts like Green Eggs and Ham (bacon, eggs and pesto if you're wondering…). There's a concise but considered list of local wines and boutique beers, and the attached deli is a good place to pick up gourmet goodies for a lakeside picnic.

Café Gusto (☎ 03-443 6639; 1 Lakeside Rd; mains $15-20; ☷ 8am-5pm) The most common answer to the question 'Who's got the best coffee in town?', Gusto provides robust meals like breakfast burrito with jalapeno peppers, or smoked salmon and scrambled eggs. Both will set you up for the most active of days, and after you've kayaked/mountain biked/rafted/hiked, come back in the afternoon and recount the experience over excellent cakes and Wanaka's best coffee.

Red Star (☎ 03-443 9322; 26 Ardmore St; burgers $9-15; ☷ 11am-late) Burgers are burgers, right? Wrong. Taking the idea that fast food doesn't have to be rubbish (or even that fast) and running with it, Red Star spoils diners with a menu featuring inventive ingredients and 17 different burgers. Everybody is catered for –

even vegetarians, who get a show-stopping three options.

Around the waterfront where Pembroke Mall meets Ardmore St, you'll find a small enclave of cheaper spots for takeaway food. Dubbed 'Curry in a Hurry' by locals, **Sagun** (☎ 03-443 9220; 139 Ardmore St) does good Indian food, and the **Doughbin Bakery** (☎ 03-443 7290; 123 Ardmore St) – motto: 'Baking at sparrow's fart since Adam was a cowboy' – specialises in McGregor's fine pies. With a motto like that, you just know they're going to be fresh.

The **New World supermarket** (Dunmore St; ☒ 8am-8pm) is well stocked for self-caterers.

Drinking

Barluga (☎ 03-442 5400; Post Office Lane; ☒ 4pm-late) In the up-and-coming Post Office Lane area, Barluga's leather armchairs and coolly retro wallpaper at first make you think of a refined gentlemen's club. Wicked cocktails and killer back-to-back beats soon break the illusion.

Uno (☎ 03-443 4911; 99 Ardmore St; ☒ 4pm-late) This slick and contemporary wine bar is the perfect place to watch the sun go down. It's a pretty good spot to head back to after dinner as well.

Red Rock (☎ 03-443 5545; Level 1, 68 Ardmore St; ☒ 5pm-late) With terracotta-red walls, decks to admire the moon from, and weekend DJs and occasional live gigs from around 10pm, this is a friendly place in which to get cosy in cowhide-covered booths. It's popular in winter with the snowboarder crowd, but in summer the lakefront bars get busier.

Trout (☎ 03-443 2600; 151 Ardmore St; ☒ 11am-late Wed-Sun, 3pm-late Mon & Tue) The best of the busier beer barns down on the lakefront, this place is more the new Trout than the old trout. It's a slick, designer Kiwi pub with the full range of Monteith's West Coast beers on tap.

Wanaka Ale House (☎ 03-443 2920; 155 Ardmore St; ☒ 11am-late) Next door to Trout, this place owns the coveted corner office. The rustic ambience morphs into a Southern Man wet dream of exposed beams, mountain views and an ample supply of Monteith's that flows like water.

Entertainment

our pick **Cinema Paradiso** (☎ 03-443 1505; www.paradiso.net.nz; 1 Ardmore St; adult/child $14/9; ☐) Playing first-run and classic movies, Cinema Paradiso has got to be the coolest movie theatre around. Forget boring, stiff cinema seats, this theatre is filled with vintage couches to snuggle up on. Extra cushions are available to stretch out on the floor and there's even an old Morris Minor to sit in for the true drive-in movie experience. At intermission they throw open the doors and the smell of freshly baked cookies wafts through the theatre and you just can't help yourself. There is a great cafe that can prepare a meal to be ready at the break. Then sit back and watch the second half of the film with a plate of fantastic grub. Now that's dinner and a movie! Try the homemade ice cream and don't forget to arrive early to get a good couch.

Shopping

For its size, Wanaka has a good number of interesting shops.

Originz (☎ 03-443 4488; Pembroke Mall) This gift shop is filled with local crafts, including cards, soaps, clocks, candles, paintings and pottery. You'll find unique, reasonably priced objects, and it's all proudly made in NZ. A good place for unusual gifts that are easy to transport home. It's off Ardmore St.

Gallery Thirty Three (☎ 03-443 4330; 33 Helwick St) Exhibitions of pottery, glass and jewellery. It's pricey, but even if you're not planning to buy, it's an interesting look at what local artists are up to.

Mainly Tramping (☎ 03-443 2888; Dunmore St) This shop is filled with clothes, boots, tents, skis and everything else you need to get out and about.

Outside Sports (☎ 03-443 7966; www.outsidesports. co.nz; Dunmore St) More of the same to rent or buy.

Getting There & Away

AIR

Air New Zealand (☎ 0800 737 000; www.airnz.co.nz) has daily flights between Wanaka and Christchurch (from $99). **Aspiring Air** (☎ 0800 100 943, 03-443 7943; www.aspiringair.com) has daily flights between Queenstown and Wanaka ($155, 20 minutes) in small, twin-engine planes.

BUS

The bus stop for **InterCity** (☎ 03-443 7885; www.inter city.co.nz) is outside the i-SITE on the lakefront. Wanaka receives daily buses from Queenstown ($17), which motor on to Franz Josef ($46) via Haast Pass ($23). For Christchurch ($79) you'll need to change at Tarras.

Naked Bus (www.nakedbus.com) will take you to Queenstown, Christchurch, Cromwell and the West Coast.

Wanaka is well serviced by door-to-door shuttles and buses, nearly all of which can be booked at the i-SITE. **Wanaka Connexions** (☎ 03-443 9122; www.time2.co.nz) and **Atomic Shuttles** (☎ 03-349 0697; www.atomictravel.co.nz) all service Christchurch ($50 to $60) and Queenstown ($20 to $30). Wanaka Connexions and **Catch-a-Bus** (☎ 03-479 9960; www.catchabus.co.nz) head to Dunedin ($50); Atomic Shuttles goes to Fox ($40) and Franz Josef ($45) Glaciers and on to Greymouth ($80). The majority pick up near the i-SITE; inquire when you book.

Getting Around
Alpine Coachlines (☎ 03-443 7966; www.alpinecoachlines.co.nz; Dunmore St) meets and greets flights at Wanaka Airport ($15), and in summer has twice-daily shuttles for trampers ($35) to Mt Aspiring National Park and Raspberry Creek. See it also for winter transport to Treble Cone. **Wanaka Taxis** (☎ 03-443 7999; www.wanakataxis.com) also looks after airport transfers, while **Adventure Rentals** (☎ 03-443 6050; adventurerentals@xtra.co.nz; 20 Ardmore St) hires cars and 4WDs.

MAKARORA
pop 40

At Makarora you've left the West Coast and entered Otago, but the township still has a West Coast frontier feel. Visit the **DOC visitor information centre** (DOC; ☎ 03-443 8365; www.makarora.co.nz; SH6; ☉ 8am-4.45pm daily Nov-Apr, 8am-4.45pm Mon-Fri May-Oct) at the Makarora Wilderness Resort for conditions and routes before undertaking any regional tramps.

Activities
TRAMPING
Short tramps in this secluded area include the **Bridal Track** (1½ hours one-way, 5km), from the top of Haast Pass to Davis Flat, and the **Blue Pools Walk** (30 minutes return), where you can see huge rainbow trout.

Longer tramps go through magnificent countryside but shouldn't be undertaken lightly. Alpine conditions, flooding and the possibility of avalanches mean you must be well prepared; consult with DOC before heading off. DOC's *Tramping Guide to the Makarora Region* ($2) is a worthwhile investment.

The three-day **Gillespie Pass** tramp goes via the Young, Siberia and Wilkin Rivers; this is a high pass with avalanche danger. With a jet-boat ride down the Wilkin to complete it, this rates alongside the Milford Track as one of the great tramps. The **Wilkin Valley Track** heads off from Kerin Forks Hut, at the top of the Wilkin River, and on to Top Forks Hut and the picturesque **Lakes Diana, Lucidus** and **Castalia** (one hour, 1½ hours and three to four hours respectively from Top Forks Hut).

Jetboats go to Kerin Forks, and a service goes across the Young River mouth when the Makarora floods; inquire at **Wilkin River Jets** (☎ 0800 538 945, 03-443 8351; www.wilkinriverjets.co.nz; Kerin Forks $75) or at DOC.

OTHER ACTIVITIES
The lush Siberia Valley provides one of NZ's great outdoor adventures. The **Siberia Experience** (☎ 0800 345 666, 03-443 8666; www.siberiaexperience.co.nz; adult $310) is a thrill-seeking extravaganza combining a half-hour scenic small-plane flight, a three-hour bush walk through a remote mountain valley and a half-hour jetboat trip down the Wilkin and Makarora Rivers in Mt Aspiring National Park. To avoid getting lost, keep your eye on the markers as you descend from Siberia Valley. It's also possible to join the trip in Wanaka.

Wilkin River Jets does a superb 50km, one-hour jetboating trip ($95) into Mt Aspiring National Park, following the Makarora and Wilkin Rivers. It's cheaper than Queenstown options, and also offers trips including helicopter rides or tramping.

Southern Alps Air (☎ 0800 345 666, 03-443 4385; www.southernalpsair.co.nz) does trips to Mt Cook and the glaciers (adult/child $395/230) and landings at Milford Sound ($350/210).

Sleeping & Eating
The nearest DOC camping grounds are on SH6 at Cameron Flat, 10km north of Makarora, and at Boundary Creek Reserve, 18km south of Makarora on the shores of Lake Wanaka; both charge $6/3 per adult/child.

Makarora Wilderness Resort (☎ 03-443 8372; www.makarora.co.nz; SH6; powered sites $28, dm $30, d $70-120; ☐ ☒) In scrubby bush are self-contained chalets, basic cabins and backpacker doubles and dorms. They've all got a snug, alpine feel, and you'll find a cafe, outdoor pool, grocery store and petrol station. Campervan travellers are also welcome, and later at night the cafe effortlessly assumes the role of Makarora's pub.

Larrivee Homestay (☎ 03-443 9177; www.larrivee homestay.co.nz; off SH6; d incl breakfast $120 -150) This rustic two-bedroom self-contained cottage sleeping up to four is situated down a side road between DOC and the tourist centre. Surrounded by native bush and with a library full of books, it's a good spot to take the foot off the travel accelerator for a few days.

Getting There & Away

InterCity (☎ 03-442 8238; www.intercity.co.nz) and **Atomic Shuttles** (☎ 03-349 0697; www.atomictravel. co.nz) both travel through Makarora en route to Haast and the West Coast.

HAWEA

pop 1600

The small town of Hawea, 15km north of Wanaka, is mostly a collection of holiday and retiree homes with spectacular lake and mountain views. From **Lake Hawea** look out at the indomitable Corner Peak on the western shore and out to the distant Barrier Range. Separated from Lake Wanaka by a narrow isthmus called the Neck, Lake Hawea is 35km long and 410m deep, and home to trout and landlocked salmon. The lake was raised 20m in 1958 to facilitate the power stations downriver.

Lake Hawea Motor Inn (☎ 0800 429 324, 03-443 1224; www.lakehawea.co.nz; 1 Capell Ave; dm $30, d $140-160) has unbeatable views across the lake and an on-site restaurant.

On the lakeshore is the spacious and relatively peaceful **Lake Hawea Holiday Park** (☎ 03-443 1767; www.haweaholidaypark.co.nz; SH6; sites $28, d $50-100), a favourite of fishing and boating enthusiasts.

CARDRONA

The sealed **Crown Range Road** from Wanaka to Queenstown via Cardrona is much shorter than the route via Cromwell, but it's a narrow, twisting-and-turning mountain road that needs to be tackled with care, especially in poor weather. In winter it is often snow covered, necessitating chaining up the wheels, and is often subject to closure because of snow – you've been warned.

With views of lush valleys, foothills and countless snowy peaks, this is one of the South Island's most scenic drives. The road passes through tall, swaying tussock grass in the **Pisa Conservation Area**, which has a number of short walking trails. There are plenty of **rest stops** to drink in the view; particularly good ones are at the Queenstown end of the road, as you switchback down towards Arrowtown.

The unpretentious-looking **Cardrona Hotel** (☎ 03-443 8153; www.cardronahotel.co.nz; Crown Range Rd; d $135-185) first opened its doors in 1863. Today you'll find lovingly restored, peaceful rooms with snug, country-style furnishings and patios opening onto a garden. You'll also find a deservedly popular pub with a good **restaurant** (mains $15-20; ☽ lunch & dinner), and a garden bar that just might be NZ's best.

The hotel is located near the turn-off for the **Waiorau Snow Farm** (☎ 03-443 7542; www.snow farmnz.com). In winter this is home to fantastic cross-country skiing. Lessons and ski hire are available ($80 for both).

Also situated nearby is **Backcountry Saddle Expeditions** (☎ 03-443 8151; Crown Range Rd; adult/child from $70/50), which runs horse treks through the Cardrona Valley on Appaloosa horses.

Alternatively, the altogether less placid **Cardrona Adventure Park** (☎ 0800 102 122; www.ad venturepark.co.nz; monster trucks from $140, quad-bikes from $75, go-karts from $60; ☽ 10am-5pm) is a rambunctious and noisy collection of monster trucks (including a self-drive option), quad-bikes and off-road go-karts.

Fiordland & Southland

The bottom end of the South Island has some of the country's most spectacular landscape. To the west is Fiordland National Park, with jagged misty peaks, glistening lakes and an air of forbidding remoteness. The park can be accessed via the world-famous Milford Track, one of the various trails that meander through dense forests and allow views of spectacular mountains and glacier-sculpted canyons. Fiordland is also home to Milford and Doubtful Sounds, with forested cliffs soaring almost vertically from the still, deep waters, and relatively easy to access by road, boat or kayak.

In Southland's east, a sharp left turn off the beaten track, the peaceful Catlins are an area of bird-rich native forest, luxuriantly green farmland and rugged, windswept coasts. In addition to the forest birds the area is home to penguins, seals, sea lions, dolphins and the occasional whale. Wonderful accommodation abounds along wild beaches, in the midst of forests and in tiny waterside settlements.

Southland has the kind of New Zealand scenery that travellers dream of and postcards fail to capture. More than once, you're likely to round a corner, stop in your tracks and just say 'oh, wow' before you reach for the camera.

HIGHLIGHTS

- Sea kayaking, dwarfed by the steep cliffs of **Milford Sound** (p347)

- Exploring side roads, forest waterfalls and lonely southern beaches in the peaceful, windswept **Catlins** (p360)

- Walking through forest and mountains on the stunning **Milford Track** (p345) and **Hollyford Track** (p345)

- Overnighting on the vast, remote **Doubtful Sound** (p350)

- Sharing a beach with dolphins, whales, sea lions and penguins at **Porpoise Bay** (p362) in the Catlins

- Admiring the art at Invercargill's **Anderson Park Art Gallery** (p354)

- Diverting from the **Te Anau–Milford Hwy** (p344) to explore forest walks and still mountain lakes

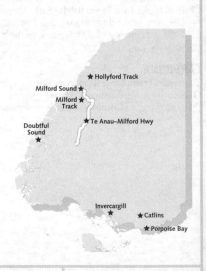

★ Hollyford Track

Milford Sound ★
Milford ★
Track

★ Te Anau–Milford Hwy

Doubtful
Sound
★

Invercargill
★

★ Catlins

★ Porpoise Bay

■ Telephone code: 03   ■ www.southland.org.nz   ■ www.fiordland.org.nz

Climate

Southland has a rather temperamental climate, and downpours can occur frequently in summer. Always prepare well for a cruise on the sounds (where the average annual rainfall is over 6000mm), a bush walk, road trip, or any other type of activity in the great outdoors.

Winter months can yield crisp, sunny days, and it's generally a few degrees cooler here than further north.

Getting There & Around

Air New Zealand connects Invercargill with Christchurch, while Stewart Island Flights connects Invercargill with Oban.

FIORDLAND & SOUTHLAND

FIORDLAND & SOUTHLAND FACTS

Eat Bluff oysters in Bluff (p359) or Tuatapere sausages in Tuatapere (p352)

Drink The fine beers crafted by the Invercargill Brewery (p355)

Read *The Gorse Blooms Pale* by Dan Davin, a collection of Southland short stories

Listen to The sound of silence while kayaking in Doubtful Sound (p350)

Watch *South* (2009), a TV series (available on DVD) hosted by quirky local media identity Marcus Lush.

Swim at Porpoise Bay (p362), where dolphins frolic and penguins waddle

Festival New Zealand Gold Guitar Awards (p360) in Gore

Tackiest tourist attraction The giant trout in Gore (p360)

Go green Take ecologically focused tours by boat on Doubtful Sound (p351) or by foot in the Catlins (p361)

Major bus operators shuttle to Te Anau and Invercargill from Queenstown or Dunedin, and some ply the Southern Scenic Route and take in Milford Sound. These include InterCity, Topline Tours, Atomic Shuttles, the Bottom Bus and Naked Bus. Companies confining themselves mostly to Southland include TrackNet and Scenic Shuttle.

FIORDLAND

Fiordland is NZ's rawest wilderness area, a jagged, mountainous, forested zone sliced by numerous deeply recessed sounds (which are technically fiords) reaching inland like crooked fingers from the Tasman Sea. Part of the Te Wahipounamu Southwest New Zealand World Heritage Area, it remains formidable and remote. Te Anau and Milford Sound see the bulk of the region's tourists, and small towns hold a small permanent population.

Of the region's wonderful bushwalks, Milford Track may be king, but Kepler and Hollyford are worthy knights, and the Routeburn, Greenstone and Caples Tracks all have one end here too, with the other at Queenstown.

TE ANAU
pop 3000

Peaceful, lakeside Te Anau township is a good base for trekkers and visitors to Milford Sound, and an ideal place to recharge your batteries. There are plenty of activities on offer, and on a sunny day it's also a beautiful place to just chill and step off the travel accelerator for a while.

Lake Te Anau defines the boundary of two very different countrysides. To the east are the relatively flat, pastoral areas of central Southland, while immediately west across the lake lie the rugged forested mountains of Fiordland. NZ's second-largest lake, Te Anau was gouged out by a huge glacier, and has several arms that penetrate into the mountainous forested western shore. The lake's deepest point is 417m, about twice the depth of Loch Ness.

Information

The road along Te Anau's main shopping strip is generally (and confusingly) referred to as 'Town Centre', or sometimes Milford Rd. ATMs are located near Te Anau Outside Sports (p341). Wi-fi is available at the Sandfly Café (p343) and the cafe in the Fiordland Cinema (p343).

Adventure Fiordland (☎ 03-249 8500; Town Centre; ⏱ 9am-5pm) An information kiosk that focuses mainly on adventure activities such as kayaking.

Department of Conservation visitor information centre (DOC; ☎ 03-249 0200; www.doc.govt.nz; fiordlandvc@doc.govt.nz; cnr Lakefront Dr & Manapouri Hwy; ⏱ 8.30am-6pm) An excellent resource centre for the area with interesting exhibits. Ask to see the DVD about Fiordland's flora and fauna. Includes the Great Walks counter (☎ 03-249 8514; greatwalksbooking@doc. govt.nz; ⏱ 8.30am-5pm) for bookings for the Milford, Routeburn and Kepler Tracks, track information and bookings. Computer terminals with NZ-wide DOC information are also available.

Discover NZ information centre (☎ 03-249 7516; Lakefront Dr; ⏱ 8am-7.30pm) For more information and activities.

Fiordland i-SITE (☎ 03-249 8900; fiordland-isite@ realjourneys.co.nz; 85 Lakefront Dr; ⏱ 8.30am-6pm summer, to 5pm winter) Brochures and info galore along with highway conditions, activities, accommodation and bus bookings.

Gateway Bookshop (64 Town Centre; ⏱ 9am-8pm Mon-Thu, to 9pm Fri & Sat, to 7pm Sun) A good place to trade in your post-tramp paperbacks.

Medical Centre (☎ 03-249 7007; Luxmore Dr; ⏱ 8am-6pm Mon-Fri, 9am-noon Sat)

Photocentre.com (☎ 03-249 7620; 62 Town Centre; 🖥 📶) Internet terminals and gear to print out your digital pics. Includes LAN access.

TE ANAU

INFORMATION
Adventure Fiordland	(see 35)
ATMs	**1** C2
Discover NZ Information Centre	**2** B3
DOC Visitor Information Centre	**3** C4
Fiordland i-SITE	**4** B3
Gateway Bookshop	**5** C2
Medical Centre	**6** C2
Photocentre.com	**7** C2
Post Office	**8** C2
Real Journeys	(see 4)
Wash'n'Surf	**9** C2

SIGHTS & ACTIVITIES
Bev's Tramping Gear	**10** D3
Southern Lakes Helicopters	**11** B3
Stardome	**12** C2
Te Anau Bike Hire	**13** B2
Te Anau Outside Sports	**14** C2
Te Anau Wildlife Centre	**15** C4
Wings & Water Te Anau	**16** B3

SLEEPING
Anchorage Motel	**17** C3
Cat's Whiskers B&B	**18** C3
Cosy Kiwi	**19** C2
Edgewater Motel	**20** C3
Keiko's B&B	**21** D2
Lakeside Motel	**22** C3
Rosies Backpacker Homestay	**23** D1
Te Anau Great Lakes Holiday Park	**24** C2
Te Anau Lakefront Backpackers	**25** C3
Te Anau Lakeview Holiday Park	**26** C4
Te Anau Lodge B&B	**27** D1
Te Anau Top 10 Holiday Park	**28** B2
Te Anau YHA	**29** B2

EATING
Fat Duck	**30** C2
Fresh Choice Supermarket	(see 37)
Glasshouse	**31** C2
La Dolce Vita	**32** C2
La Toscana	**33** C2
Miles Better Pies	**34** B2
Olive Tree Café & Restaurant	**35** C2
Redcliff Bar & Restaurant	**36** C2
Ruchee	(see 37)
Sandfly Café	**37** C2

DRINKING
Moose	**38** B2
Ranch Bar & Grill	**39** C2

ENTERTAINMENT
Fiordland Cinema	(see 37)

TRANSPORT
InterCity Departure	**40** C2
Kepler Water Taxi	**41** B2

Post office (102 Town Centre) Inside the Paper Plus newsagency.

Real Journeys (☎ 0800 656 501; www.realjourneys.co.nz) Shares a building with the i-SITE and offers a range of Fiordland-focused tours and activities.

Wash'n'Surf (122 Town Centre; per load $8; ☷ 9am-9pm) A combination laundry and internet cafe.

Sights
TE ANAU GLOWWORM CAVES
Once present only in Maori legends, these impressive caves on the lake's western shore were rediscovered in 1948. Accessible only by boat, the 200m-long system of caves is a magical place with sculpted rocks, waterfalls small and large, whirlpools and a glittering glowworm grotto in its inner reaches. Real

Journeys (left) runs 2¼-hour guided tours (per adult/child $63/20), reaching the heart of the caves by a walkway and a short underground boat ride.

TE ANAU WILDLIFE CENTRE
The DOC-run **Te Anau Wildlife Centre** (☎ 03-249 0200; Te Anau–Manapouri Rd; admission by donation; ☷ dawn-dusk) hosts native bird species – including the rare flightless takahe – NZ pigeons, tui, kaka, weka and various waterfowl.

Activities
TRAMPING
If you're planning on tramping, pick up information and register your intentions at the DOC office (opposite).

Kepler Track

This 60km circular Great Walk starts less than an hour's walk from Te Anau and heads west into the Kepler Mountains, taking in the lake, rivers, gorges, glacier-carved valleys and beech forest. The walk can be done in four days, or three if you exit at Rainbow Reach. On the first day you reach the tree line, giving panoramic views. The alpine stretch between Luxmore and Iris Burn Huts goes along a high ridge, well above the bush and offers fantastic views when it's clear; in poor weather it can be treacherous. It's recommended that the track be done in the Luxmore–Iris Burn–Moturau direction.

Like any Fiordland track, the weather has a major impact on the walk; you should expect at least one day of rain and be prepared for some wading. The alpine sections require a good level of fitness and may be closed in winter due to bad weather conditions. Other sections are considered moderate with climbs and descents of up to 1000m and unbridged stream crossings.

During the main walking season (October to April), advance bookings must be made by all trampers online at www.booking.doc.govt .nz or at any DOC visitor centre. Over this period, a **Great Walks hut pass** (per night adult/child $45/free) buys accommodation in the track's three well-maintained huts – Luxmore, Iris Burn and Moturau – each with heating and cooking facilities. A **camping pass** (per night adult/child $15/free) permits you to camp at the designated sites at Brod Bay and adjacent to Iris Burn

Hut. Outside this main season, a Backcountry Hut Pass still needs to be prepurchased (per night adult/child $15/free), but no heating or cooking is on offer. Off-season camping is free.

Estimated walking times:

Day	Route	Time
1	Te Anau DOC office to control gates	45min
1	Control gates to Brod Bay	1½hr
1	Brod Bay to Luxmore Hut	3½-4½hr
2	Luxmore Hut to Iris Burn Hut	5-6hr
3	Iris Burn Hut to Moturau Hut	5-6hr
4	Moturau Hut to Rainbow Reach	1½-2hr
4	Rainbow Reach to control gates	2½-3½hr

TrackNet (☎ 0800 483 262; www.tracknet.net) and **Topline Tours** (☎ 03-249 8059; www.toplinetours.co.nz) provide transport to and from the ends of the track for between $5 and $11.

Short Walks

You can set out along the Kepler Track on free day walks. **Kepler Water Taxi** (☎ 03-249 8364; stevsaunders@xtra.co.nz; one way/return $25/40) will scoot you over to Brod Bay from where you can walk to Mt Luxmore (seven to eight hours) or along the southern lakeshore back to Te Anau (two to three hours). Regular shuttles leave Te Anau lakefront at 8.30am and 9.30am during summer. There are also many short walks in the area (see p344).

During summer **Trips'n'Tramps** (☎ 03-249 7081; www.tripsandtramps.com; ⌚ Oct-Apr) takes trampers

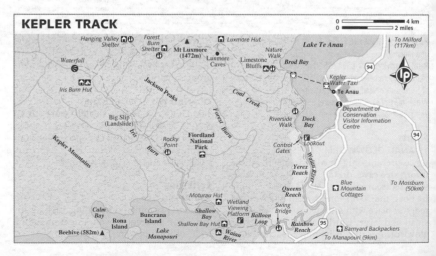

on small-group, half- to two-day guided hikes on sections of the Routeburn and Kepler and Hollyford Tracks. Some departures incorporate kayaking on Milford Sound. Real Journeys (p339) runs guided day hikes (adult/ child $190/123.50, November to mid-April) along an 11km stretch of the Milford Track.

Grab a copy of *Fiordland National Park Day Walks* ($1 from Fiordland i-SITE) for more options.

Equipment

Make sure you're well equipped and have good rain gear before commencing any tracks. **Bev's Tramping Gear** (☎ 03-249 7389; www.bevs-hire .co.nz; 16 Homer St; ☺ 9am-noon & 6.30-8pm, closed Sun morning) Topographical maps for sale and tramping and camping equipment for hire.

Te Anau Outside Sports (☎ 03-249 8195; 38 Town Centre) Equipment for sale or hire.

KAYAKING & JETBOATING

Kayaking in the pristine waterways of the World Heritage Area is unbeatable. **Fiordland Wilderness Experiences** (☎ 0800 200 434; www.fiord landseakayak.co.nz) runs one-day and multiday kayaking explorations of Lake Te Anau and Lake Manapouri. Prices start at $130 per day. See p348 for kayaking trips on Milford Sound and Doubtful Sound.

Luxmore Jet (☎ 0800 253 826, 03-249 6951; www. luxmorejet.com; per adult/child $95/45) does a one-hour ride on the stunningly beautiful Waiau River which links Lakes Te Anau and Manapouri, and includes *Lord of the Rings* locations.

OTHER ACTIVITIES

The i-SITE provides information on guided **trout fishing** (fly, trolling or spinning). River and stream fishing takes place roughly from October to May, while lake fishing occurs year-round. Pick up a licence from DOC.

Te Anau Bike Hire (☎ 03-249 7211; 7 Mokonui St; bike hire per hr/day from $10/25; ☺ from 10am Sep-Apr) hires mountain bikes, kids' bikes and tandems. **High Ride Adventures** (☎ 03-249 8591; www.highride.co.nz; quad-bike trips $145, horse trips $80) offers 3½-hour backcountry trips on quad-bikes and 3½-hour horseback trips along Whitestone River.

Fiordland Astronomy (☎ 0508 COSMOS; www.astro nomyfiordland.co.nz; per person $40; ☺ weather permitting) takes small groups (maximum eight) to view the night sky by binoculars and 30cm telescope on 'Night Sky Safaris'. The newly opened **Stardome** (Events Centre, Luxmore Dr; per person $30) is an interactive digital planetarium that's a good companion activity. Enquire at the Fiordland i-SITE about bookings and times.

Tours

With blue lakes, dark forests and steep snowy mountains visible the moment you get aloft, this is one of the greatest places in NZ to do some aerial sightseeing. **Wings & Water Te Anau** (☎ 03-249 7405; www.wingsandwater.co.nz; Lakefront Dr) has seaplane flights right off Lakefront Dr with a 10-minute zip around the local area (adult/child $95/55) and longer flights over the Kepler Track, and Doubtful and Milford Sounds (from $295). **Air Fiordland** (☎ 0800 107 505; www.airfiordland.co.nz) offers similar deals.

Southern Lakes Helicopters (☎ 03-249 7167; www.southernlakeshelicopters.co.nz; Lakefront Dr) buzzes over Te Anau for 25 minutes ($190) and does longer trips over Doubtful, Dusky and Milford Sounds (from $530) and a chopper/walk/boat option on a part of the Kepler Track ($180).

Sleeping

Although Te Anau has many hostels, cabins, motels and hotels, all the accommodation in town can still be booked out in the middle of the peak season (late December to February). It pays to book early if possible.

BUDGET

Te Anau Lakeview Holiday Park (☎ 03-249 7457; www. teanau.info; 77 Te Anau-Manapouri Rd; sites per person from $15.50, dm $27, s $35, d $60-89, cabins d $68-78, self-contained d $90-130; ☐ ☎) This huge lakeside complex, 1.5km out of town, combines the Te Anau Lakeview campsite (with tent/van sites and several types of cabins and self-contained motel units sleeping up to seven), West Arm singles accommodation (basic and institutional, but more private than dorms), and Steamers backpackers (characterless rooms but sharing a modern and comfortable communal kitchen and lounge space).

Te Anau Great Lakes Holiday Park (☎ 0800 249 555; www.greatlakes.co.nz; cnr Luxmore Dr & Milford Rd; sites per person $16.50, dm $25, cabins $58-65, units $95-195; ☐ ☎) A grassy holiday park with a big modern kitchen and a bunch of cabins and units.

Te Anau Lakefront Backpackers (☎ 03-249 7713; www.teanaubackpackers.co.nz; 48-50 Lakefront Dr; tent sites per person $18, dm $26-28, d $72-92; ☐ ☎) This sprawling collection of buildings has a huge variety of rooms, some sunny and spacious, others pokey and worn. Regardless, the staff

FIORDLAND & SOUTHLAND

are friendly and helpful, there's a nice communal vibe, lots of warm fires in the winter, a shady peaceful garden warbling with tui and a fantastic location right beside the lake. Backpackers are well loved, with lakeview dorms and a virtual encouragement to party, but there's everything through to quieter family options out the back. Bikes are available for hire.

Barnyard Backpackers (Map p340; ☎ 03-249 8006; www.barnyardbackpackers.com; 80 Mt York Rd, off SH95; dm $26-28, d $66; ☐) On a deer farm 9km south of town towards Manapouri, this charmingly rustic communal building and its collection of log cabins sit on a hillside with a view to the Kepler Mountains. Cabins are comfortable and en-suited, and the communal area is great for playing pool or sitting around the central fireplace. A good home base for the Kepler Track.

Te Anau YHA (☎ 03-249 7847; yha.teanau@yha.co.nz; www.yha.co.nz; 29 Mokonui St; dm/s/d from $28/51/74; ☐ 🛜) The most central of the backpackers in Te Anau. This bright and modern hostel has great facilities and comfortable, colourful rooms. Lounge in the hammock, barbecue in the grassy backyard, or get cosy by the wood fire.

our pick **Bob & Maxines** (☎ 03-9313161; bob.anderson@woosh.co.nz; 20 Paton Pl, off Oraka St; dm/tw $30/80; ☐) Only 2.5km out of town, off the Te Anau–Milford Hwy, but feeling a million miles away, this relaxed hostel gets rave reviews for the big mountain views from the communal lounge. Get toasty beside the woodburner, cook up a storm in the spacious modern kitchen, or just chill out a while. New additions include warming heat pumps and the whole place is wheelchair friendly. Bikes are available to get you back into town.

Rosie's Backpacker Homestay (☎ 03-249 8431; backpack@paradise.net.nz; 23 Tom Plato Dr; dm/d $31/74; ☐ 🛜) You're immediately made to feel part of the family in this small and intimate homestay. It's in the 'burbs a short walk north of the town centre. They're closed June and July.

Te Anau Top 10 Holiday Park (☎ 0800 249 746, 03-249 7462; www.teanautop10.co.nz; 128 Te Anau Tce; sites from $34, cabins $52-68, d $120-170; ☐ 🛜) This classic holiday park near the town and lake has excellent facilities with small but private sites, a playground, sauna, bike hire, barbecue area and modern kitchen. Cabins and units run from basic to fancy.

MIDRANGE & TOP END

If you're here in winter it's always worth asking the motels and B&Bs about a discount on their high-season rates.

Lakeside Motel (☎ 0800 452 537, 03-249 7435; www.lakesideteanau.com; 36 Lakefront Dr; d $130-220; ☐ 🛜) With most units directly facing across the grassy lawns to the lake, this motel has excellent views, particularly from the 1st floor. Inside, there's plenty of light from the large windows and good cooking facilities. It's also wheelchair friendly.

Cosy Kiwi (☎ 0800 249 700, 03-249 7475; www.cosykiwi.com; 186 Milford Rd; s $170-320, d $150-165; ☐ 🛜) The sign says B&B, but this friendly spot is actually more of a smart motel with modern, well-appointed rooms just a short stroll from bustling downtown Te Anau. Breakfast is included in the rates, and host Eleanor usually offers a couple of cooked options. You'll need a good start to the day if you're getting active in the great outdoors.

Te Anau Lodge B&B (☎ 03-249 7477; www.teanaulodge.com; 52 Howden St; s $170-320, d $200-350; ☐ 🛜) The former 1930s-built Sisters of Mercy Convent, relocated to a grand location just north of town, is a positively decadent accommodation option. Sip your drink in a Chesterfield in front of the fire, retire to your spa before collapsing on a king-size bed, then awaken to a fresh, delicious breakfast in the old chapel. Plans are afoot to hold concerts in the spacious lawns.

Cat's Whiskers B&B (☎ 03-249 8112; www.catswhiskers.co.nz; 2 Lakefront Dr; d $175-215; ☐ 🛜) This family home features four large recently redecorated en-suite rooms and great lake views just across the road. There's a sunny alfresco area to relax in at the back of the house, and the family room sleeps four.

Keiko's B&B (☎ 03-249 9248; www.keikos.co.nz; 228 Milford Rd; d $195; 🕙 closed Jun-Aug; 🛜) The private, self-contained cottages here are lovely, and the entirety is surrounded by an explosion of flowers and Japanese-style gardens. A Japanese breakfast in the morning and a bamboo-bordered hot tub in the evening are essential extras.

Blue Mountain Cottages (Map p340; ☎ 03-249 9030; www.bluemountaincottages.co.nz; Hwy 95; cabins $260) These two plush self-contained cabins surrounded by farmland 8km south of town can sleep up to six, so they're a good family option. Home-grown meat and produce is available to guests.

The following is a small selection of the local motels.

Anchorage Motel (☎ 03-249 7256; www.teanaumotel. co.nz; 47 Quintin Dr; d $85-175; 🖳 🛜) Good for kids and wheelchair friendly.

Edgewater Motel (☎ 0800 433 439, 03-249 7258; www.edgewater.net.nz; 52 Lakefront Dr; d $140-250; 🖳 🛜) Light, comfortable rooms with good cooking facilities. A stand-alone two-bedroom luxury villa is also available ($400).

Eating
RESTAURANTS & CAFES
Olive Tree Café & Restaurant (☎ 03-249 8496; 52 Town Centre; snacks & burgers from $7, mains $21-38; 😋 8am-9.30pm Sep-May, 9am-8pm Jun-Aug) Tucked away at the end of an unremarkable-looking arcade, Olive Tree is warm and funky inside, with excellent outdoor areas to sip coffee in the sun or enjoy a tasty Mediterranean-flavoured meal.

La Toscana (☎ 03-249 7756; 108 Town Centre; pasta $12-20, pizza $12-24; 😋 5.30pm-late) Buzzy, noisy and relaxed, with wooden booths and tables, this is a lively spot for a late-night snack, or a good dinner option. Pizzas and pastas are large and great value, and takeaways and deliveries are available.

Ruchee (☎ 03-249 9298; 5 The Lane; mains $16-22; 😋 5pm-late Mon, noon-3pm & 5pm-late Tue-Sun, closed May-Oct; Ⓥ) It's great to have a subcontinental alternative to Te Anau's plethora of Italian caterics, and this is a pleasant, mellow place for a curry. The cooking isn't going to change your life, but it's not bad for provincial NZ. Takeaways are available.

Glasshouse (Milford Cres; mains $20-33; 😋 9.30am-late) Come along for the ultimate pre-Milford Sound breakfast, and then return for dinner to sample innovative, well-priced variations on lamb, venison and chicken. The minimalist decor is slightly clinical, but the effusive and warm service easily compensates.

Fat Duck (☎ 03-249 8480; 124 Town Centre; dinner mains $22-38; 😋 noon-late Mon-Fri, from 10am Sat & Sun) Friendly service overcomes the slightly bland decor, and the Fat Duck gets top-notch reviews from most travellers. Dishes are tasty, and hearty in proportions, and variations on basics such as crispy duck, pork belly and salmon are imaginative. There's a bar almost as long as Doubtful Sound if you just want a drink before kicking on somewhere else. Closed Monday and Tuesday outside of the peak season.

La Dolce Vita (☎ 03-249 8895; 90 Town Centre; pasta & mains $28-32; 😋 3pm-late) Run by familia Lombardi, this very stylish, ultramodern-looking restaurant stretches beyond simple Italian fare to include Southland cuisine with fresh seafood, local lamb and big steaks. Fresh-made pasta dishes ($22) are also popular.

Redcliff Bar & Restaurant (☎ 03-249 7431; 12 Mokonui St; mains $30-39; 😋 5pm-late) Housed in a replica old settler's cottage, Redcliff specialises in a buzzy, convivial atmosphere and locally sourced produce. Try the wild Fiordland venison or tender herby hare. Wine is affordably priced, but a few more options by the glass wouldn't go amiss. They don't take bookings so kick off your night with a drink in the rustic front bar; it's also *the* place in town for a quiet after-dinner drink. There's occasional live music and a permanent friendly vibe with excellent service.

QUICK EATS & SELF-CATERING
Miles Better Pies (☎ 03-249 9044; cnr Town Centre & Mokonui St; pies $5; 😋 6am-4pm) The classic Kiwi pie has never looked better. Choose from freshly made gourmet venison, Thai curry or apricot pies. There are a few pavement tables, but sitting beside the lake is nicer, and the pies also make a good snack for the road.

Sandfly Café (☎ 03-249 9529; 9 The Lane; breakfast & lunch $6-15; 😋 7am-4.30pm; 🖳 🛜) With the best coffee in Te Anau, this is a lovely, chilled-out place to relax. Enjoy the music, the all-day breakfast and the yummy baking including excellent wraps. Sandfly is closed Mondays during winter.

Self-catering provisions can be found at **Fresh Choice Supermarket** (1 The Lane; 😋 7am-8pm).

Drinking & Entertainment
Redcliff Bar & Restaurant (above) has occasional live music and is the most atmospheric option for drinks. More raucous is the **Ranch Bar & Grill** (☎ 03-249 8801; Town Centre; 😋 noon-late), with Happy Hour from 8pm to 9pm and good value Sunday-night roast dinners ($13.50). The cavernous lakefront **Moose** (☎ 03-249 7100; 84 Lakefront Dr) has big-screen sports and a sunny patio. It also does meals and bar snacks.

In between back-to-back showings of the excellent *Ata Whenua* ($10), essentially a 32-minute advertisement for stunning Fiordland scenery, **Fiordland Cinema** (☎ 03-249 8812; www.fiordlandcinema.co.nz; 7 The Lane; $15; 🛜)

shows other flicks too. There's also a good bar with lots of South Island wines, beers and wi-fi access.

Getting There & Away

InterCity (☎ 03-249 7559; www.intercity.co.nz) has daily bus services between Te Anau and Queenstown ($38, 2½ hours), Invercargill ($48, 2½ hours) and Dunedin ($45, 4¾ hours). Look online for discounts. Buses depart outside Kiwi Country on Miro St.

Other bus services include:

Bottom Bus (☎ 03-477 9083; http://travelheadfirst. com/bottom-bus/) Hop-on, hop-off bus service linking Te Anau to Queenstown, Invercargill and Milford Sound.

Naked Bus (☎ 0900 625 33; www.nakedbus.com) Connects Te Anau with Queenstown ($29), Invercargill ($24) and Milford Sound ($24).

Scenic Shuttle (☎ 0800 277 483; www.scenicshuttle. co.nz) Via the Southern Scenic Route past Manapouri and Tuatapere to Invercargill ($49).

Topline Tours (☎ 03-249 8059; www.toplinetours. co.nz) Daily door-to-door between Te Anau and Queenstown ($38).

TrackNet (☎ 0800 483 262; www.tracknet.net) Connects Te Anau with Queenstown (adult $43), Milford ($47, 2½ hours), Invercargill ($45) and to and from several tramping tracks.

The following transport options are available for trampers. TrackNet (see above) has daily shuttles to the Kepler, Hollyford and Milford Tracks, and to the western end of the Routeburn, Greenstone and Caples Tracks at the Divide.

The **Kepler Water Taxi** (☎ 03-249 8364; stevsaun ders@xtra.co.nz) runs regularly across the lake to Brod Bay (one way $20, 10 minutes) on the Kepler Track in summer. **Wings & Water** (☎ 03-249 7405; www.wingsandwater.co.nz) provides transport to Supper Cove ($315 per person, minimum two passengers) for Dusky Sound trampers.

TE ANAU–MILFORD HWY

If you don't have the opportunity to hike into Fiordland's wilderness, the 119km road from Te Anau to Milford is the most easily accessible taste of its vastness and beauty. Even if you don't do a cruise at the other end, it's still a top road trip for sheer scenic wonder.

Head out from Te Anau early (8am) or later in the morning (11am) to avoid the tour buses heading for midday sound cruises. See p349 for important information about chains and

avalanches (in winter) and petrol (always). It's a tricky road, so take care.

The trip takes two to 2½ hours if you drive straight through, but take time to stop and experience the majestic landscape. Pull off the road and explore the many viewpoints and nature walks en route. A few are listed in the following section, but a *Fiordland National Park Day Walks* brochure ($1 from DOC or the i-SITE) will equip you for some self-discovery.

The first part of the road meanders through rolling farmland atop the lateral moraine of the glacier that once gouged out Lake Te Anau. The road passes **Te Anau Downs** (there's accommodation here at Fiordland National Park Lodge, see p347) after 29km and heads towards the entrance of Fiordland National Park, passing patches of beech (red, silver and mountain), alluvial flats and meadows.

Just past the **McKay Creek** campsite (at 51km) are great views over Eglinton Valley with sheer mountains either side and Pyramid Peak (2295m) and Ngatimamoe Peak (2164m) ahead. The boardwalk at **Mirror Lakes** (at 58km) takes you through beech forest and wetlands, and on a calm day the lakes reflect the mountains across the valley. **Knobs Flat** (at 63km) also has accommodation (p347).

At the 77km mark is the area referred to as O Tapara, or more commonly as **Cascade Creek**. O Tapara is the original name of nearby Lake Gunn, and was a stopover historically for Maori parties heading to Anita Bay in search of *pounamu* (greenstone). A walking track (45 minutes) passes through tall red beech forest ringing with bird calls. Side trails lead to quiet lakeside beaches.

At 84km the vegetation changes as you pass across the **Divide**, the lowest east–west pass in the Southern Alps. There's a large roadside shelter here for walkers either finishing or starting the Routeburn, Greenstone or Caples Tracks; it's also used as a terminal for trampers' bus services (above left). A walk from the shelter, initially through beech forest along the start of the Routeburn, then climbing up alpine tussockland to **Key Summit** (two hours return), offers spectacular views of the three valleys that radiate from this point.

From the Divide, the road falls into the beech forest of the **Hollyford Valley** (stop at Pop's View for a great view) and there's a worthwhile detour to **Gunn's Camp & Museum** (p347) 8km along an unsealed road. About 9km further, at the end of that road, is a walk to the high **Humboldt Falls** (30 minutes return) and the start of the Hollyford Track (below).

Back on the main road to Milford, the road climbs to the **Homer Tunnel**, 101km from Te Anau and framed by a spectacular, high-walled, ice-carved amphitheatre. The tunnel is one-way outside avalanche season, with the world's most alpine set of traffic lights to direct traffic. Kea, the delinquent teenagers of the parrot world, hang around the eastern end of the tunnel hoping tourists stopped at the lights will be stupid enough to feed them. (Resist the urge, because what we eat just isn't good for them.) Dark, magnificently rough-hewn and dripping with water, the 1207m-long tunnel emerges at the other end at the head of the spectacular **Cleddau Valley**.

About 10km before Milford, the **Chasm Walk** (20 minutes return and even accessible by wheelchair, though you might appreciate assistance on the steeper parts) is well worth a stop. The forest-cloaked Cleddau River plunges through eroded boulders in a narrow chasm, creating deep falls and a natural rock bridge. From here, watch for glimpses of **Mt Tutoko** (2746m), Fiordland's highest peak, above the beech forest just before Milford.

Hollyford Track

This dramatic track starts in the midst of lowland forest, crossing mountain streams and passing pretty waterfalls as it follows the broad Hollyford River valley all the way to the sea. The Tasman coast makes a satisfying end point, with dolphins, seals and penguins often greeting hikers on their arrival. However, it does mean backtracking another four days back to your start point unless you take one of the sneaky shortcut options.

The 56km track is graded as a moderate hike, but involves some creek crossings and suffers frequent flash floods that can leave trekkers waiting it out en-route for several days until the trail becomes passable. The trickiest part of the route is the ominously named Demon Trail (10km) alongside Lake McKerrow. It's imperative that you check with DOC in Te Anau for the latest track and weather conditions and for detailed maps.

TrackNet (☎ 0800 483 262; www.tracknet.net) has shuttles between the Hollyford Rd turn-off and Te Anau ($47, one hour) and Queenstown ($87, 3¾ hours).

Options for reducing the length of the there-and-back journey include hitching a jetboat

---

TE WAHIPOUNAMU SOUTHWEST NZ WORLD HERITAGE AREA

In the southwest corner of NZ, the combination of four huge national parks make up Te Wahipounamu Southwest New Zealand World Heritage Area. Te Wahipounamu (The Place of Greenstone) covers 2.6 million hectares and is recognised internationally for its cultural significance to the Ngai Tahu, as well as for the area's unique fauna and wildlife. Te Wahipounamu incorporates the following national parks:

- Fiordland National Park (p338)
- Aoraki/Mt Cook National Park (p260)
- Westland Tai Poutini National Park (p200)
- Mt Aspiring National Park (p327)

---

ride south with **Hollyford Track Guided Walks** (☎ 0800 832 226, 03-442 3000; www.hollyfordtrack.com; $110) for the length of Lake McKerrow; book in advance. A more-luxurious, three-day guided walk ($1655) includes fancy accommodation, jetboat trips in both directions along Lake McKerrow and a flight back to Milford Sound from the coastal finish line at Martins Bay.

You can also arrange a flight between Martins Bay and civilisation with **Air Fiordland** (☎ 03-249 6720; www.airfiordland.com; to Milford/Te Anau $580/1160) for up to four people (price is per flight, so you can share the cost). Hollyford Track Guided Walks sometimes has empty seats when it flies from Milford Sound to pick up its walkers at Martins Bay, and can drop you at Martins Bay by plane ($135) or helicopter ($185). Booking these services is essential.

Milford Track

The famous Milford Track is a 53.5km walk often described as one of the finest in the world. The number of walkers is limited in the Great Walks season (late October to late April), and during that period you must follow a one-way, four-day set itinerary. Accommodation is only in huts (camping isn't allowed).

Even in summer, expect *lots* of rain, in the wake of which water will cascade everywhere and small streams will become raging torrents within minutes. Remember to bring wet-weather gear and pack belongings in an extra plastic bag or two.

In the off-season, experienced trampers can walk the track in either direction without bookings (hut tickets must be purchased). At this time there's limited trail transport, the huts aren't staffed, some of the bridges are removed and, in the height of winter, snow and avalanches make it unwise. It's vitally important you first visit DOC (p338) to check avalanche risk, as the geography of the valley makes it impossible to judge for yourself.

BOOKINGS

You can walk the track independently or with a guided tour. For independent bookings, contact DOC in Te Anau (p338) or book online at http://booking.doc.govt.nz/. The track must be booked during the Great Walks season (October to April), and it certainly pays to book as far ahead as possible. Bookings open up to 12 months before the start of the following season. A Great Walks pass (adult/child $135/free) allows you three nights in the huts. During the Great Walks season the track can only be done in one direction (Lake Te Anau to Milford) and

you must begin on the date specified on your DOC permit.

Ultimate Hikes (☎ 0800 659 255, 03-442 8200; www.milfordtrack.co.nz; Dec–Mar adult/child $1900/1700, Apr & Nov adult/child $1740/1540) has five-day guided walks that include everything from packs to snacks to raincoats and stays at much flasher accommodation, ending with a celebratory dinner at their last stay, Mitre Peak Lodge at Milford Sound.

Real Journeys (☎ 0800 656 501; www.realjourneys.co.nz; adult/child $190/123.50; ☼ Nov–mid-Apr) runs guided day hikes along an 11km stretch of the Milford Track.

WALKING THE TRACK

The trail starts at Glade House, at the northern end of Lake Te Anau, accessed by boat from Te Anau Downs or Te Anau. The track follows the flat bottom of the Clinton River Valley up to its head at Lake Mintaro, passing through rainforest and crystal-clear streams. From Mintaro you cross the dramatic **Mackinnon Pass**, which on a clear day gives spectacular views back to yesterday's Clinton Valley and forward to tomorrow's Arthur Valley. (If the pass appears clear when you arrive at Mintaro Hut, make the effort to climb it, as it may not be clear the next day.) From the pass a long, wooden staircase leads you down to Arthur River, following alongside the rapids. The trail then continues down to Quintin and Dumpling Huts and through the valley rainforest to Milford Sound. You can leave your pack at the Quintin public shelter while you make the return walk to the graceful, 630m-high **Sutherland Falls**, NZ's tallest falls. Estimated walking times:

Day	Route	Time
1	Wharf to Glade House	20min
1	Glade House to Clinton Hut	1–1½hr
2	Clinton Hut to Mintaro Hut	6hr
3	Mintaro Hut to Dumpling Hut	6–7hr
3	Side trip to Sutherland Falls	1½hr return
4	Dumpling Hut to Sandfly Point	5½–6hr

TRANSPORT TO GLADE WHARF

During the Great Walks season, **TrackNet** (☎ 0800 483 262; www.tracknet.net; $22) drives up

MILFORD TRACK

from Te Anau to Te Anau Downs. TrackNet also offers the option of transport from Queenstown to Te Anau Downs ($65). **Real Journeys** (☎ 0800 656 501; www.realjourneys.co.nz; $65) will then run you by boat from Te Anau Downs to Glade Wharf near the start of the track. Both of these trips can be booked at DOC in Te Anau at the same time as you book your walk. Outside the Great Walks season, talk to TrackNet about transport the whole way to Glade Wharf.

TRANSPORT FROM SANDFLY POINT

There are ferries leaving Sandfly Point at 2pm and 3.15pm for the Milford Sound cruise wharf (adult/child $34/19.50). From there you can bus back to Te Anau with TrackNet ($47, 2½ hours). These can both be booked via DOC at Te Anau.

PACKAGES

Cruise Te Anau (☎ 03-249 7593; www.cruiseteanau.co.nz) does a bus-boat combination trip for around $150.

Sleeping

Along State Highway 94 (SH94) are many basic **DOC camping grounds** (sites $10), the majority of them situated between 45km and 81km from Te Anau. You'll find them in *Conservation Campsites – South Island* (free from DOC in Te Anau), or search www .doc.govt.nz for Te Anau area conservation campsites.

At Te Anau Downs (29km from Te Anau) at the head of the lake where boats depart for Milford Track, **Fiordland National Park Lodge** (☎ 0800 500 805, 03-249 7811; www.teanau-milfordsound. co.nz; SH94; d hotel $65-140, motel $130-160; 🖳 🛜) has slightly dated hotel-motel-type units. Views of the lake and mountains are spectacular from the hotel rooms. Motel units have a less spectacular view, but are still comfortable. It's popular with Milford Track walkers, but other travellers are also welcome.

In the grassy Eglinton Valley, 63km from Te Anau, **Knob's Flat** (☎ 03-249 9122; www.knobsflat. co.nz; studio/motel units $115/135) has comfortable units catering to walkers and fisherfolk. TV, mobile phones, email and stress have no place here.

Gunn's Camp (Hollyford Rd; gunnscamp@ruralinzone. net; sites per person $10, d/tw $20/48), also known as Hollyford Camp, is on Hollyford Rd about halfway between SH94 (8km) and the

start of the Hollyford Track (9km). The old public-works cabins are very basic (linen hire is $5 per bed), and heating is via a coal/ wood-fired stove (fuel provided). A generator supplies limited electricity, turning off at 10.30pm, and there's gas for cooking and for hot showers. There's also a small shop and a small, wonderfully eccentric **museum** (admission adult/child $1/30c, guests free) with pioneering memorabilia.

Milford Sound Lodge (☎ 03-249 8071; www.milford lodge.com; just off SH94; unpowered/powered sites per person $16/20, dm/d $30/80; 🖳 🛜) is spectacularly located; nestled in forest, surrounded by towering mountains and alongside the Cleddau River. This simple but comfortable lodge has an unhurried, ends-of-the-earth air. There's no TV, and travellers and trampers relax in the large lounges to discuss their travels. There's a tiny shop-cafe-bar and a free shuttle to Milford Sound, just 1.5km away. Brand-new and very comfortable chalets ($225) enjoy an absolute riverside location, and the entire lodge was undergoing a makeover when we dropped in.

MILFORD SOUND
pop 170

The first sight of Milford Sound is stunning: still, dark waters out of which rise sheer rocky cliffs, and forests clinging to the slopes sometimes relinquish their hold, causing a 'tree avalanche' into the waters. The spectacular, photogenic 1692m-high Mitre Peak rises dead ahead. A cruise on Milford Sound is Fiordland's most accessible experience, complete with seals, dolphins, and an average rainfall of 7m; more than enough to fuel cascading waterfalls and add a shimmering moody mist to the scene.

Milford Sound receives about half a million visitors each year, most of them crammed into the peak months (January and February). Some 14,000 arrive by foot, via the Milford Track which ends at the sound, many more drive from Te Anau, but most arrive via the multitude of buses that pull into the cruise wharf. But don't worry. Out on the water all of this humanity seems tiny compared to nature's vastness.

There's not much else to town apart from the cruise terminal and the car park, though if you take the turn off to Deep Water Basin about 1km out of town, you can explore the small fishing wharf area.

Activities

SEA KAYAKING

One of the best perspectives on Milford Sound is from a kayak at water level dwarfed by the vertically rising cliffs. **Rosco's Milford Sound Sea Kayaks** (☎ 03-249 8500; www.roscosmilfordkayaks.com; $115-169) has tours taking in the sound's most breathtaking sights. Recommended excursions include the 'Morning Glory', a challenging early morning kayak (around five hours in the boat) the full length of the fiord to Anita Bay, and the 'Stirling Sunrise', which includes kayaking under the 151m-high Stirling Falls. For that one, you can probably forego your morning shower. Another option includes a 20-minute paddle to Sandfly Point and a 3½-hour walk on the Milford Track ($89). In Te Anau you'll find Rosco's at Adventure Fiordland (p338).

Fiordland Wilderness Experiences (☎ 0800 200 434, 03-249-7700; www.fiordlandseakayak.co.nz) also runs guided day paddles on the sound; they cost with/without return transport to Te Anau $155/125.

UNDERWATER EXPLORATION

Unique environmental circumstances have allowed the sound to become home to some rarely glimpsed marine life. Heavy rainfall sluicing straight off the rocky slopes washes significant organic matter into the ocean, creating a 5m-deep permanent tannin-stained freshwater layer above the warmer sea water. This dark layer filters out much of the sunlight and, coupled with the sound's calm, protected waters, replicates deep-ocean conditions. The result is that deep-water species thrive not far below the surface. A similar situation exists at Doubtful Sound (p350).

Milford Deep Underwater Observatory (adult/child $29/15; ☯ 9am-3.45pm) is a five-storey mostly submerged building that dangles from a system of interlinked pontoons attached to a rock face. Four storeys below the surface are resident deep-water corals, tube anemones and bottom-dwelling sea perch. The observatory visits are informative, but the accompanying tour groups may dilute the experience. Various operators stop here (charging around $29/15 extra for adults/kids), but not the late-afternoon cruises.

Tawaki Adventures (☎ 0800 829 254; www.tawaki dive.co.nz) takes scuba-dive trips on the sound. Trips include a three-hour boat cruise and two guided dives of a total of 30 minutes

($159); it's an extra $99 for gear hire. If you don't dive you can join the boat trip anyway ($99 plus $45 to hire snorkelling gear).

Tours

MILFORD SOUND CRUISES

Each Milford Sound cruise company claims to be quieter, smaller, bigger, cheaper or in some way preferable to the rest. What really makes a difference is the timing of the cruise; most bus tours aim for 1pm sailings so if you avoid that time of day there'll be less people on the boat (and on the road!). With some companies you get a better price on cruises outside rush hour too. If you're particularly keen on wildlife, ask whether there'll be a nature guide on board. It's wise to book ahead regardless. You generally need to arrive 20 minutes before departure. Most companies offer coach transfers from Te Anau for an additional cost. Day trips from Queenstown make for a very long 13-hour day.

All the cruises visit the mouth of the sound, only 15km from the wharf, poking their prow into the choppy waves of the Tasman Sea. The shorter cruises visit less of the en route 'highlights', which include Bowen Falls, Mitre Peak, Anita Bay and Stirling Falls. You'll have a good chance of seeing dolphins, seals and penguins. All cruises leave from the huge **cruise terminal** (☯ 8am-5.15pm Oct-Apr, 9am-4.15pm May-Sep), a 10-minute walk from the cafe and car park.

Real Journeys (☎ 0800 656 501; www.realjourneys. co.nz) does 1¾-hour scenic cruises (adult $62 to $84, child $15). The company also does 2½-hour nature cruises (adult $68 to $88, child $15) with a nature guide for commentary and Q&A.

Mitre Peak Cruises (☎ 0800 744 633; www.mitrepeak. com) does two-hour tours (adult $64 to $74, child $15) in smallish boats with a maximum capacity of 75. The 4.30pm summer cruise is good because many larger boats are heading back at this time.

Red Boat Cruises (☎ 0800 264 536, 03-441 1137; www. redboats.co.nz) does 1¾-hour trips (adult/child $65/15). The noon cruise is $75, because that's when most passengers will be here. The 2¼-hour wildlife cruise (adult $74 to $90, child $15) is more intimate.

Cruising Milford Sound (☎ 0800 500 121; www. cruizemilford.co.nz) does 1½-hour trips (adult $55 to $70, child $15) on a smallish, comfortable boat with lots of deck space.

OVERNIGHT CRUISES

Real Journeys (☎ 0800 656 501, 03-249 7416; www.real journeys.co.nz) does overnight cruises on two of its boats. You can kayak and take nature tours in tender crafts en route. The cost includes all meals but transport from Te Anau is additional. All depart from the Milford terminal around 4.30pm and return around 9.30am the following day. Cheaper prices apply in April, May, September and October.

The *Milford Wanderer,* modelled on an old trading scow, accommodates 61 passengers in four-bunk cabins (with shared bathrooms) and costs $230/115 per adult/child. The *Milford Mariner* sleeps 60 in more up-market, en-suite, twin-share cabins ($470/235 per adult/child).

Sleeping & Eating

The excellent Milford Sound Lodge (p347) is just 1.5km back up the road towards Te Anau. A small cafe is attached.

The **Blue Duck Café & Bar** (☎ 03-249 7931; car park; 🕑 8.30am-late; 🖥️) serves sandwiches and buffet-type meals. At night the attached bar sees a mix of travellers, trampers and locals.

Getting There & Away

BUS

InterCity (☎ 03-249 7559; www.intercity.co.nz) runs daily bus services from Queenstown ($80) and Te Anau ($39). Trampers' buses also operate from Te Anau (p650) and Queenstown (p319) and will pick up at the Milford Sound Lodge. All these buses pass the Divide and the start/end of the Routeburn, Greenstone and Caples Tracks.

Many bus trips include a boat cruise on the sound; most are around $160 from Te Anau (or around $230 from Queenstown).

CAR

It's a magnificent drive from Te Anau to Milford (see p344). Fill up with petrol in Te Anau before setting off. Chains must be carried on avalanche-risk days from May to November (there will be signs on the road) and can be hired from most service stations in Te Anau.

MANAPOURI

pop 210

Manapouri is largely used as a jumping-off point for cruises to the sublime Doubtful Sound (p350), and as a base for walking expeditions.

In 1969, Manapouri was the site of NZ's first major environmental campaign. The original plan for the West Arm power station, built to provide cheap electricity for the aluminium smelter near Invercargill, included raising the level of the lake by 30m. A petition gathered a staggering 265,000 signatures (17% of voting-age New Zealanders at the time) and the issue contributed to the downfall of the government at the following election. The action was successful: the power station was built but the lake's level remains unchanged. It was a success that spawned increasing national environmental action through the '70s and '80s. West Arm power station is NZ's largest producer of electricity: a tunnel dug through the mountain from Lake Manapouri to Doubtful Sound drops a hefty 180m from lake to sound, driving the power station's turbines.

Fiordland Ecology Holidays (☎ 0800 249 660; www.fiordland.gen.nz; 5 Waiau St) has its office on the premises of 45 South, their secondhand/new/rare-books bookshop specialising in local history, exploration and wildlife. Ask about their Doubtful Sound tours for details on their ecology-focused options.

Activities

Adventure Kayak & Cruise (☎ 0800 324 966; www. fiordlandadventure.co.nz), beside the garage in Manapouri, rents kayaks from $50 per person per day for paddles on Lake Manapouri from October to April. They'll only rent to groups of two paddlers or more, and provide VHF radios free-of-charge for safety. See p351 for information on their kayaking trips on Doubtful Sound.

You can rent rowboats from **Manapouri Stores** (☎ 03-249 6619; per day $20). **Fish Fiordland** (☎ 03-249 6855; www.fishfiordland.co.nz; 2hr fishing $195) does scenic trips on Lake Manapouri, guided nature walks, fishing trips, and operates as a water taxi to local walking tracks. **Adventure Manapouri** (☎ 03-249 8070; www.adventuremanapouri. co.nz) is another option for rowboat hire ($20 per day), water taxis and fishing trips.

With some form of water transport (kayak, dinghy or water taxi), you can cross the Waiau River for some easy low-altitude day walks, detailed in the DOC brochure *Fiordland National Park Day Walks* ($1). A walk along the **Circle Track** (three hours return) can be extended to **Hope Arm** (five to six hours return), crossing the uninvitingly named Stinking

Creek. Although Te Anau is the usual access point for the Kepler Track (p340), the trail touches the northern end of Lake Manapouri and part of it can be done as a day walk from Manapouri; access is via the swing bridge at Rainbow Reach, 10km north of town. From Pearl Harbour there's also a walk that doesn't require crossing the river: to **Frasers Beach** (1½ hours return), from where you can gaze across the beautiful lake.

Manapouri is also a staging point for the remote 84km **Dusky Track**, a walk that takes eight days if you tramp between Lakes Manapouri and Hauroko, with an extra two-day detour possible from Loch Maree Hut to Supper Cove on Dusky Sound. With regular tree falls, deep mud, river crossings, delaying floods and 21 three-wire bridges, this is an extremely challenging wilderness walk, suitable only for well-equipped, very experienced trampers. Contact DOC, and read Lonely Planet's *Tramping in New Zealand*, for more details. For transport options from either Te Anau or Tuatapere to the Dusky Track, contact **Lake Hauroko Tours** (☎ 03-226 6681; www.duskytrack.co.nz).

Sleeping

Freestone Backpackers (☎ 03-249 6893; free stonebackpackers@vodafone.co.nz; Manapouri–Hillside Rd; dm/cabins $30/60) These clean, comfortable and rustic cabins nestle on a hillside with magnificent views about 3km east of town. Each cabin has a small kitchen, potbelly stove and veranda. Bathrooms and fridges are communal. Dorm beds are also available. More comfortable options include accommodation ($70) with a kitchen and private bathroom, and a deluxe bed and breakfast ($190) with a spa.

Manapouri Lakeview Chalets & Motor Park (☎ 03-249 6624; www.manapourimotels.co.nz; SH95; unpowered/powered sites $30/32, cabins d $52-62, motel units $95-120; 🔲 🛜) This camping ground features eclectic cabins, ranging from mock–Swiss Alpine to mock–shanty town. There's a fabulous fleet of old Morris Minors in various states of repair and a vintage pinball-machine collection to relive your youth. There's also a playground for the kids.

Possum Lodge (☎ 03-249 6623; www.possum lodge.co.nz; 13 Murrell Ave; sites $30, cabins d $42-50; 🗓 Oct-Easter; 🔲 🛜) A charming, shady little campsite only a few trees away from the lakeside, this property has old-school, relatively

basic cabins and more modern motel-style units ($95). Best bring some sandfly repellent, too.

Manapouri Lakeview Motor Inn (☎ 03-249 6652; www.manapouri.com; 68 Cathedral Dr; d $85-140; 🔲 🛜) All rooms face the lake and mountains, with the big windows from the budget rooms at the top having the best views. All rooms have en suites and some have cooking facilities, or there's a communal kitchen. Downstairs is a casual restaurant and pub.

Eating & Drinking

Café 23 (☎ 03-249 6988; 23 Waiau St; lunch from $8, meals $25-28; 🗓 7.30am-7.30pm; 🔲) This cafe in a charming old Presbyterian church has great coffees and tasty panini or gourmet sandwiches. If you're heading out on the water, grab your lunch here before you go.

Lakeside Café & Bar (☎ 03-249 6652; 68 Cathedral Dr; lunch $9-16, dinner $18-33; 🗓 11.30am-late; 🔲 🛜) Serves substantial meals with a generous side order of lake views. The public bar attached (open till late) is a large, cheery affair, with crazy silver helicopters providing the wacky ventilation.

Getting There & Away

Scenic Shuttle (☎ 0800 277 483; www.scenicshuttle.co.nz) stops at Manapouri en route from Invercargill to Te Anau. **Topline Tours** (☎ 03-249 8059; www.toplinetours.co.nz; $20) travels between Manapouri and Te Anau daily.

DOUBTFUL SOUND

Massive, magnificent Doubtful Sound is a wilderness area of rugged peaks, dense forest and thundering post-rain waterfalls. It's one of NZ's largest sounds: three times the length and 10 times the area of Milford Sound. Doubtful is also much, *much* less trafficked. If you have the time and the money, it's an essential experience. Fur seals, dolphins, Fiordland crested penguins and seals are all also occasional visitors.

Until relatively recently, only the most intrepid tramper or sailor ever explored Doubtful Sound. Even Captain Cook only observed it from off the coast in 1770, because he was 'doubtful' whether the winds in the sound would be sufficient to blow the ship back out to sea. The sound became more accessible when the road over Wilmot Pass opened in 1959 to facilitate construction of the West Arm power station.

Tours

Doubtful Sound is only accessible by tour. You'll cross Lake Manapouri by boat to the West Arm power station, drive by bus the winding 22km through dense rainforest to Deep Cove (permanent population: one), then head out on Doubtful on another boat. Many tours include the power station. The easiest place to base yourself is Manapouri, although many tours pick up in Te Anau and some in Queenstown.

Real Journeys (☎ 0800 656 502; www.realjourneys. co.nz; Pearl Harbour, Manapouri; day trip adult/child $275/60) has a Wilderness Cruise, beginning with a 45-minute boat ride across Lake Manapouri to West Arm power station, followed by a bus ride over Wilmot Pass to the sound, which you explore on a three-hour cruise. There's pick-up from Te Anau (adult/child $21/10.50) or from Queenstown (adult/child $82/41).

If you'd rather venture underground to admire the engineering marvels of the power station than continue over to the sound, do that on a separate Lake Manapouri cruise (adult/child $65/20, October to April).

From September to May, Real Journeys also runs a Doubtful Sound overnight cruise. The *Fiordland Navigator* sleeps 70 and has twin-share, en-suite cabins (per adult/child $675/348) and quad-share bunkrooms ($365/182.50). Transport to and from Te Anau or Queenstown is available. Prices include meals and kayaking or tender-craft trips.

Fiordland Ecology Holidays (☎ 0800 249 660, 03-249 6600; www.fiordland.gen.nz; 5 Waiau St, Manapouri) has boat tours (maximum 10 guests) of up to a week, led by people with a passion for the area's flora and fauna. The superbly equipped yacht sails into remote parts of the World Heritage Area along Doubtful and Dusky Sounds. Rates start at $745 for an overnight trip.

Adventure Kayak & Cruise (☎ 0800 324 966; www.fiordlandadventure.co.nz; ⊗ late Sep-May) does Doubtful Sound day trips; cruise and kayaking is $255 while overnight kayak camping trips on the shores of the sound are $235.

Fiordland Wilderness Experiences (☎ 0800 200 434; www.fiordlandseakayak.co.nz; ⊗ Oct-Apr) also does overnight ($380) and up to five-day ($750) guided kayak trips on the sound.

Other cruising options:

Deep Cove Charters (☎ 0800 249 682; www.doubtful -sound.com; overnight per person $380) Intimate overnight cruises with a maximum of 12 passengers. Includes meals, or you can fish for your own dinner.

Fiordland Cruises (☎ 0800 483 262; www.fiordland cruises.co.nz; overnight from $495) Overnight cruise including wildlife viewing and fishing. Maximum 12 passengers. Includes meals and transfers to/from Te Anau.

Fiordland Expeditions (☎ 0508 888 656; www. fiordlandexpeditions.co.nz; overnight cruises adult/child $499/350) Overnight cruise. Ten-passenger maximum. Kayaking, diving, fishing (dinner is whatever they catch that night).

Fiordland Explorer Charters (☎ 0800 434 673; www.doubtfulsoundcruise.com; day cruise adult/child $250/80) Day cruise with maximum of 20 people. Includes power-station tour and three hours on the sound. Free transfers to/from Te Anau.

Sleeping

If you'd like to spend the night on the sound, it generally means joining an overnight cruise

---

THE SOUND OF SILENCE *Brett Atkinson*

Just 90 minutes after leaving Manapouri township in morning sunshine, Doubtful Sound's Deep Cove is shrouded in misty, moody squall. But rain and mist doesn't equate to disappointment, and a chorus of Southern birdsong and the occasional passing raft of yellow-eyed penguins inspires me to keep paddling away.

Technically Doubtful Sound and Milford Sound are both fiords – narrow inlets with steep sides carved by glacial activity – but that's where any similarity ends. The almost-sheer granite cliffs of Milford Sound feel rugged and imposing, but Doubtful Sound is longer, deeper and gentler. The walls are shrouded with more vegetation and escalate upwards more slowly. Negotiating a series of mossy curtains along the banks, I feel like I'm cocooned by nature.

Adorned with a necklace of waterfalls, the spacious natural harbour of Hall Arm provides the opportunity for self-exploration. Amid pristine silence, I dig my paddle purposely into the obsidian-coloured water and catch a glimpse up Hall Arm to Mt Danae. The centuries roll back, and I realise one of New Zealand's most iconic views has been unchanged for millennia.

or kayak/camping trip. The only other option is **Deep Cove Hostel** (☎ 03-218 7655; www.deepcovehostel.co.nz; justinet@woosh.co.nz; per person $25-40; 🖳) with bunks, cooking facilities and dinghies, situated right on Doubtful Sound with a number of bush walks radiating from it. It's predominantly used by school groups, but casual guests are welcome. Booking ahead is essential.

SOUTHERN SCENIC ROUTE

The quiet, unhurried Southern Scenic Route begins in Te Anau and heads south to Tuatapere, Riverton and Invercargill. See www.southernscenicroute.co.nz or pick up *Southern Scenic Route* (free). Public transport is limited, but **Bottom Bus** (☎ 03-477 9083; www.travelheadfirst.com) and **Scenic Shuttle** (☎ 03-477 9083; www.scenicshuttle.co.nz) offer regular shuttles.

From Manapouri the road follows the Waiau River south between the forested Takitimu and Hunter Mountains. Near Clifden is the elegant **Clifden Suspension Bridge**, built in 1899 and one of the longest bridges in the South Island. **Clifden (Waiau) Caves** are signposted on Otautau Rd, 2km from the Clifden Rd corner. These caves offer a scramble through crawl spaces and up ladders. Bring a friend, a spare torch, and lots of caution. Visit Tuatapere visitor information centre (above right) for conditions and a map beforehand.

Just south of the suspension bridge is a turn-off to a walking track through **Dean Forest**, a reserve of ancient totara trees, 23km off the main road. From Clifden you can drive 30km of mostly unsealed road to **Lake Hauroko**, the deepest lake in NZ and surrounded by dark, brooding, steeply forested slopes. The area has many ancient *urupa* (burial sites) so be respectful and keep to trails. The Dusky Track (p350) also ends (or begins) here. **Lake Hauroko Tours** (☎ 03-226 6681; www.duskytrack.co.nz; tours incl lunch $100; 🕑 tours Nov-Apr) has day-trip return tours from Tuatapere, connecting with the Scenic Shuttle.

Tuatapere
pop 740
Formerly a timber-milling town, sleepy Tuatapere is now largely a farming centre. Those early woodcutters were very efficient, so only a remnant of a once large tract of native podocarp forest remains. Tuatapere is fondly referred to by Kiwis as NZ's 'sausage capital'; though it would rather be known as a base for the Hump Ridge Track. Grab some of the real deal from the butcher to cook up. The paua (abalone) flavour is particularly interesting.

Tuatapere visitor information centre (☎ 03-226 6739; www.humpridgetrack.co.nz; 31 Orawia Rd; 🕑 8.30am-5pm, limited hr in winter; 🖳) assists with visits to the Clifden Caves, Hump Ridge hut passes and transport. Adjacent is the **Bushmans Museum** (admission by donation).

For more information on Tuatapere and the Western Southland area, see www.westernsouthland.co.nz.

ACTIVITIES
Hump Ridge Track
The excellent 53km Hump Ridge Track climbs to craggy subalpine heights with views north to Fiordland and south to Stewart Island, and then descends through lush native forests of rimu and beech to the rugged coast. There's bird life aplenty, with the chance to see Hector's dolphins on the lonely windswept coast back to the start point. En route the path crosses a number of towering historic wooden viaducts, including NZ's highest. Beginning and ending at Bluecliffs Beach on Te Waewae Bay, 20km from Tuatapere, the track takes three fairly long days to complete.

Estimated walking times:

Route	Time
Bluecliffs Beach Car Park to Okaka Hut	6-8hr
Okaka Hut to Port Craig Village	7-9hr
Port Craig Village to Bluecliffs Beach Car Park	3-5hr

It's essential to book for this track, which is administered privately rather than by DOC. Contact **Tuatapere Hump Ridge Track** (☎ 03-226 6739; www.humpridgetrack.co.nz). Summer bookings cost from $90 for two nights; winter bookings (May to October) cost $45. There are also guided tour, jetboating and helihiking options.

Jetboating
Jetboat rides cross Lake Hauroko then zoom around up the rugged Wairahurahiri River, the breathtaking ride lasting two or three hours. Operators include **W-Jet** (☎ 0800 376 174; www.wjet.co.nz; adult/child $225/119) and **Humpridge Jet** (☎ 0800 270 556; www.wildernessjet.co.nz; from $150),

which also has a jetboat/helicopter option. **Waiau Jet Tours** (☎ 0800 009 993) can take you from Tuatapere Bridge to Clifden Bridge ($50, one hour) or Dean Forest ($100, 3½ hours). See them at Shooters Backpackers & Tuatapere Motel (below).

SLEEPING & EATING
Shooters Backpackers & Tuatapere Motel (☎ 03-226 6250; shooters.backpackers@xtra.co.nz; 73 Main St; un-powered/powered sites $12/30, dm $28, d $60-90, motel s/d $70/110; 🖳) Communal spaces are the high-light here; there's a modern kitchen with a wood stove, a big deck with a barbecue, plus a spa and sauna. Camping is on a stretch of green lawn, and diving and fishing trips can also be arranged.

   Waiau Hotel (☎ 03-226 6409; www.waiauhotel.co.nz; 47 Main St; s $35-55, d $70-110; 🖳) Has a number of standard pub-type rooms and en suites. The bistro (lunch $5 to $12, dinner $15 to $24) is renowned for their blue cod, but you can also tuck into world-famous Tuatapere sausages. For some sausages for the road, see **Tuatapere Butchery** (☎ 03-226 6596; 75 Main St).

   Alternatively, head to **Yesteryears Café** (☎ 03-226 6681; 3a Orawia Rd; light meals $8-12; ⏰ from 9am), which boasts a collection of quirky house-hold items from local families. Meals are deliciously home-cooked and the coffee is splendid. Rip into Aunt Daisy's sugar buns and a quintessentially Kiwi milkshake, and buy homemade jams and preserves for future on-the-road breakfasts.

Tuatapere to Riverton
On SH92, around 10km south of Tuatapere, stop at the spectacular lookout at McCracken's Rest. Cast your eye down the arcing sweep of **Te Waewae Bay** – where Hector's dolphins and southern right whales are sometimes seen – to the snowy peaks of Fiordland.

   Colac Bay is a popular holiday place and a good surfing spot. Southerlies provide the best swells here, but it's pretty consistent year-round and never crowded. **Dustez Bak Paka's & Camping Ground** (☎ 03-234 8399; www.dustezbakpakas.co.nz; 15 Colac Bay Rd; sites per person $13, dm $27, d $54-58) has basic rooms open-ing onto a covered courtyard and camp-sites in a grassy field. Guests can borrow surfboards. Get dinner next door at the Colac Bay Tavern. Down at the beach, the **Pavilion Tavern** (☎ 03-234 8445; 188 Colac Foreshore Rd; ⏰ 10am-late) gets visitors from as far as

Invercargill hungry for its fresh fish, organic lamb and garden-fresh herbs.

Riverton
pop 1850
Quiet little Riverton, only 38km short of Invercargill, is worth a lunch stop and, if near-Antarctic swimming takes your fancy, the **Riverton Rocks** area and **Taramea Bay** (don't venture past the point) are good for a dip. The town is a common overnight stop between the Catlins and Fiordland.

   Riverton visitor information centre (☎ 03-234 8260; www.riverton-aparima.co.nz; 127 Palmerston St; ⏰ 10am-5pm) has information about exploring the region's interesting geological heritage. Inside, **Te Hikoi Southern Journey** (☎ 03-234 8260; www.tehikoi.co.nz; adult/child $12/4; ⏰ 10am-4pm summer, 11am-3pm winter) tells the story of the area's early Maori and Pakeha history in video and inter-active displays. A number of galleries along Palmerston St are also worth a look.

   The Riverton visitor information centre can advise on camping, motel and B&B accom-modation. **Globe Backpackers** (☎ 03-234 8527; www.theglobe.co.nz; 144 Palmerston St; dm/d $25/65) is well set up for travellers, with basic, comfortable rooms. A couple of attached self-contained motel units cost $100 for two. The bar down-stairs does a roaring trade in pizzas (from $10) and other bar snacks.

   Beach House (☎ 03-234 8274; 126 Rocks Hwy; snacks from $10, dinner $25-35; ⏰ 10am-late; 🖳) is a stylish, comfortable cafe that is famous for its seafood, especially its takeaway chowder ($12). On a sunny day with a warm breeze wafting off Foveaux Strait, the outside tables are a must; the other 90% of the time, retire inside to ad-mire the sea view warm behind the windows. To find the cafe, follow signs along the coast to the lookout.

   The chic little **Mrs Clarks Café** (☎ 03-234 8600; 108 Palmerston St; meals $9-16; ⏰ 10am-4pm), with lots of reused timbers, chilled-out music and South Island beers and wines, occupies an insanely turquoise building that has been vari-ous forms of eatery since 1891. We doubt if its espressos were quite so delicious back then. Don't miss its tasty cheese rolls, amusingly dubbed 'Southland Sushi'.

   The **South Coast Environment Centre** (☎ 03-234 8717; www.sces.org.nz; 154 Palmerston St) has a good range of organic fruit, vegies and meats, is the local wwoof agent, and organises the Riverton farmers market (Friday afternoons).

CENTRAL SOUTHLAND

Although it's home to the majority of Southland's permanent population, for travellers the central area of the province serves mostly as a through station. It's a good jumping-off point for the Catlins and Fiordland, and the gateway to Stewart Island.

INVERCARGILL
pop 49,300

Flat and suburban, with endlessly treeless streets, Invercargill won't enthral you if you came here via the Catlins or Fiordland. Nevertheless, most travellers in Southland will find themselves here at some point – perhaps stocking up on supplies and equipment before setting off to the Catlins or Stewart Island. It's worth taking some time to investigate the town's arty bits, some good restaurants, and a great little microbrewery. Forward-thinking local mayor Tim Shadbolt – formerly a 1970s student radical – has put the city on the map with strong support of Invercargill's tertiary education institutions and sporting organisations, and if you're missing an urban buzz just a little, the city's got plenty of options to recharge your socialising skills.

Information
Automobile Association (AA; ☎ 03-218 9033; 47 Gala St; ☺ 8.30am-5pm Mon-Fri)
Comzone.net (45 Dee St; ☺ 10am-10pm; ☐ ☏) Get online. Wi-fi is also available at the Tuatara Café (p357).
DOC office (☎ 03-211 2400; 7th fl, Cue on Don, 33 Don St; ☺ 8.30am-4.30pm Mon-Fri) For info on tracks around Stewart Island and Southland.
Invercargill i-SITE (☎ 03-214 6243; www.invercargill.org.nz; Gala St, Queens Park; ☺ 8am-6pm Oct-Apr, to 5pm May-Sep; ☐) Handily located in the same building as the Southland Museum & Art Gallery. Bikes can be rented, and it's also a good place to get information on the Catlins and Stewart Island.
Post office (51 Don St)

Sights & Activities
SOUTHLAND MUSEUM & ART GALLERY
This **museum & gallery** (☎ 03-218 9753; www.southlandmuseum.com; Gala St, Queens Park; admission by gold-coin donation; ☺ 9am-5pm Mon-Fri, 10am-5pm Sat & Sun) is definitely worth a look after you've visited the adjacent i-SITE. The art gallery hosts visiting exhibitions from contemporary Maori and other local artists as well as occasional international shows.

If you're headed for Stewart Island, check out the museum's interesting 'Beyond the Roaring 40s' exhibition showcasing the natural history of New Zealand's rugged southern islands. Fans of Burt Munro and *The World's Fastest Indian* (2005) movie should race to the small theatrette in the 1st floor sports gallery for a screening of the original 1971 TV documentary *Burt Munro – Offerings to the God of Speed*.

The museum's rock stars are undoubtedly the tuatara, NZ's unique lizardlike reptiles, unchanged for 220 million years and thus proclaimed 'living fossils'. And if the slow-moving 100-years-old-and-counting patriarch Henry is any example, they're not planning to do much for the next 220 million years either.

However, Henry did surprise the reptile world in early 2009 when he finally became a Dad with the sprightly 80-year-old Mildred. You'll find Henry and his mates looking dignified in the tuatara enclosure at the back. Feeding time is 4pm on Fridays, and is your best opportunity to see the tuataras in (slow) motion. Outside opening hours, you can see the tuatara through the viewing windows at the rear of the pyramid.

ANDERSON PARK ART GALLERY
In a 1925 Georgian-style manor, this **gallery** (☎ 03-215 7432; McIvor Rd; admission by donation; ☺ gallery 10.30am-5pm, gardens 8am-dusk) contains works from many NZ artists. There are beautiful, original antique furnishings, block prints, pottery, sculptures, grand landscapes, Greek-mythic Maori village scenes, and portraits. Visit the tearoom to partake of a very civilised (free) cup of tea. Outside, 24 hectares of landscaped gardens are a lovely place to linger, with trees and trails, a children's playground and a *wharepuni* (sleeping house). The gallery is 7km north of the city centre; follow North Rd then turn right into McIvor Rd.

OTHER SIGHTS & ACTIVITIES
Wander around the half-wild, half-tamed **Queens Park**, with its trees, duck ponds, children's playground and Alice's castle.

In town, the **City Gallery** (☎ 03-214 1319; 28 Don St; admission free; ☺ 11am-4pm Tue-Fri, 10am-2pm Sat) showcases talent from NZ's south, including sculpture, photography and paintings (most of which are for sale). If you've been travelling in the South Island, you'll definitely recognise some scenes.

If you're a fan of motorcyclist Burt Munro's speedy achievements, captured in *The World's Fastest Indian* (2005), you can see his **famous motorbike** at E Hayes & Sons (172 Dee St). There are a few other retro two-wheelers on display and film merchandise for sale. Oreti Beach (site of Burt's race against the troupe of insolent young tearaways) is 10km to the southwest and a nice spot for a swim. The helpful folk at the Invercargill i-SITE will happily direct you to other locations relevant to Burt and the film. The Burt Munro Challenge (www.burtmunro challenge.com) is a hugely popular motorbike event held each November.

For a self-guided walk or drive, pick up the *Invercargill Heritage Trail* brochure (free) from the i-SITE. In **Thomson's Bush**, 1km north along Queen's Dr, you can follow a one-hour loop beneath the ancient kahikatea and matai trees that once covered the now-treeless plains of Invercargill.

The **Invercargill Brewery** (☎ 03-214 5070; www. invercargillbrewery.co.nz; 8 Wood St; ⏰ 11am-5.30pm Mon-Thu, to 6.30pm Fri, to 4pm Sat) promotes itself as NZ's southernmost microbrewery, but in reality, its beers are good enough for anywhere in the country. Tastings of the range are free of charge, and if you're a real beer buff, the staff may be able to show you around the brewery (but only if they're not busy). Our favourites are the crisp Biman Pilsner and

FIORDLAND & SOUTHLAND

INVERCARGILL

0 — 800 m
0 — 0.5 miles

INFORMATION
Automobile Association (AA)................1 B3
Comzone.net...2 C4
DOC Office..3 D4
Invercargill i-SITE....................................4 B3
Post Office..5 D4
Tuatara Café...(see 11)

SIGHTS & ACTIVITIES
City Gallery...6 D4
E Hayes & Sons...7 A3
Invercargill Brewery...............................8 C4
Southland Museum & Art Gallery......(see 4)

SLEEPING
Kackling Kea Backpackers.....................9 B4
Living Space.......................................(see 33)
Southern Comfort Backpackers........10 A3
Tuatara Lodge..11 C4
Victoria Railway Hotel.........................12 C4

EATING
Buster Crabb..13 A2
Countdown...14 B4
Devil Burger...15 C4
Duo...16 D4
EuropaNZ...17 D4
Rocks & Shop 5.......................................18 C3

Seriously Good Chocolate
Company...19 D3
Sopranos Pizzeria..........................(see 31)
Three Bean Café.....................................20 C4
Tuatara Café.......................................(see 11)
Turkish Kebabs..21 C4
Zookeepers Cafe.....................................22 D4

DRINKING
Kiln..23 C4
Louie's Café...24 A3
One Blue Dog...25 C4
Saints & Sinners.....................................26 C4
Speights Ale House................................27 C4
Tillermans Music Lounge..............(see 15)
Waxy O'Shea's...28 C3

ENTERTAINMENT
Reading Cinemas....................................29 C4
Stadium Southland.................................30 D3

SHOPPING
H&J's Outdoor World.......................(see 31)
Southern Adventure..............................31 D4

TRANSPORT
Air New Zealand......................................32 D4
Cycle Surgery..33 C4

To Invercargill Top 10 Holiday Park (2.5km); Anderson Park Art Gallery (2.8km); Te Anau (152km); Queenstown (278km)

To Bushy Point Fernbirds (8km); Invercargill Airport (1.5km); Ziff's Café & Bar (5.5km); Cabbage Tree (6.2km); Oreti Beach (9km)

To Gore (66km); Dunedin (217km)

To Bluff (27km)

See Enlargement

0 — 400 m
0 — 0.2 miles

the hoppy Stanley Green Pale Ale. Regular seasonal brews are also concocted, including Smokin' Bishop, a German-style *rauchbier* made with smoked malt.

Sleeping

Many places will store luggage for guests heading to Stewart Island. You'll find countless midrange motels along Hwy 1 East (Tay St) and Hwy 6 North (North Rd).

Invercargill Top 10 Holiday Park (☎ 0800 486 873, 03-215 9032; www.invercargilltop10.co.nz; 77 McIvor Rd; sites per person $18, cabins $75, motel units $96-110; 🖳) Near parkland, with trees for shade and surrounded by macrocarpa hedge, this quiet little place 6.5km drive north of town has private sites and good communal facilities. Modern, comfortable studios and self-contained cabins have en suites.

Tuatara Lodge (☎ 03-214 0954; www.tuataralodge. co.nz; 30-32 Dee St; dm $25, d $60-80; 🖳 🛜) Rooms here are fairly basic, but they're clean and comfortable enough. Communal facilities are good too, with cosy TV lounges and a large modern kitchen. Staff are friendly, it's the most central of all the budget accommodation, and downstairs is a nice little traveller-focused cafe-bar. Transport to/from Bluff for Stewart Island stops just outside.

Kackling Kea Backpackers (☎ 03-214 7950; www. kacklingkea.co.nz; 25 Tweed St; dm $26-28, d $62; 🖳) This family-run house south of town is light and spacious, and the relaxed communal areas and rooms have recently been redecorated. Look forward to a huge, well-equipped kitchen and a friendly welcome from the owners' children. A good place to recover after walking the Hump Ridge Track or Stewart Island's Rakiura Track.

Southern Comfort Backpackers (☎ 03-218 3838; 30 Thomson St; dm/d $27/66; 🖳) Mellow, comfortable house with a Zen lounge (hooray, no TV! Watch the fireplace instead), colourful rooms and a modern, well-equipped kitchen. Doubles are spacious, though some prefer the basic playhouse. Lovely gardens provide fresh herbs for cooking. Cash only.

Living Space (☎ 03-211 3800; www.livingspace.net; 15 Tay St; d $89-119; 🖳 🛜) Colourful, modern decor, ergonomically savvy design, and relaxed service are showcased at this transformed 1907 warehouse. The studios – especially the bathrooms – are not huge, but self-contained kitchenettes, speedy internet access, and lots of Sky channels all come as standard.

Bushy Point Fernbirds (☎ 03-213 1302; www.fern birds.co.nz; 197 Grant Rd, Otatara; s/d incl breakfast $100/120) Two friendly corgis are among the hosts at this very comfortable, eco-aware homestay set on the edge of 4.5 hectares of private forest reserve and wetlands. Some of the trees are over 400 years old and on a clear day you can see across to Stewart Island. Fernbirds is very popular with birding types, so booking ahead is recommended. It's five minutes' drive from central Invercargill, but Ziff's and the Cabbage Tree restaurant (opposite) are both nearby. Rates include a guided walk in the forest reserve.

Victoria Railway Hotel (☎ 0800 777 557, 03-218 1281; www.vrhotel.info; cnr Leven & Esk Sts; d $130-180; 🖳 🛜) For a spot of 19th-century luxury, the plush rooms and swanky guests' areas in this grand old refurbished hotel fit the bill. The guests' dining room is elegant and the opulent house bar is crammed with South Island wines and local beers. This spot is a quietly unique gem underpinned by genuinely personal service.

Eating

Invercargill has a surprisingly diverse restaurant scene, with a few gems worth seeking out.

RESTAURANTS

Rocks & Shop 5 (☎ 03-218 7597; Courtville Pl, 101 Dee St; lunch $13-20, dinner $17-32; 🕑 11am-2pm & 5pm-late Tue-Sat) Tucked away in a shopping arcade, this stylish candlelit bar with a couple of dining areas is a laid-back choice for a tasty meal. Lunch highlights are decent burgers, pasta and salad, and later at night the focus shifts to pork belly, Moroccan chicken and Stewart Island salmon.

Duo (☎ 03-218 8322; 16 Kelvin St; lunch $15, dinner $30; 🕑 10.30am-late) Just off Invercargill's main drag, the elegant Duo has good-value lunch specials (all $15) and a more expensive evening menu. Standout menu items include smoked salmon, herb-and-feta-crusted pork steaks, and oven-baked blue cod. The wine list travels mainly to nearby Central Otago for some hard-to-find boutique tipples.

Buster Crabb (☎ 03-214 4214; 326 Dee St; meals $25-34; 🕑 10.30am-late) Inexplicably named after a British navy frogman who went missing in 1956, Buster Crabb overcomes a silly name to transform a spacious heritage-listed villa into a cosmopolitan dining experience. Local farming types – doing very well thank you –

FIORDLAND & SOUTHLAND

crowd in for scallops, pork belly, venison and blue cod. A tiny deck is a late afternoon suntrap, and it's one of the only places in town that serves the Invercargill Brewery's excellent Pitch Black stout on tap.

On the main road to the Oreti Beach at Otatara you'll find two restaurants, both specialising in *big* meals, and therefore both local favourites.

Ziff's Café & Bar (☎ 03-213 0501; 143 Dunns Rd, Otatara; mains $18-34; ☽ 10.30am-late) Fun atmosphere and a stylish interior. Transfers from town are $2.

Cabbage Tree (☎ 03-213 1443; 379 Dunns Rd, Otatara; mains $20-40; ☽ 11am-late; Ⓥ) Huge menu, huge dishes, huge wine list, and a free courtesy bus.

CAFES & QUICK EATS

Seriously Good Chocolate Company (☎ 03-218 8060; 147 Spey St; chocolates around $1.20 each; ☽ 8.30am-5pm Mon-Fri) This sunny spot a short walk from central Invercargill specialises in individual homemade chocolates. Order a coffee and then abandon yourself to the difficult task of choosing flavours. The chilli and peanut cluster variations were both good enough for us to return a second day. Like it says on the tin…seriously good.

EuropaNZ (☎ 03-214 6371; 82 Tay St; meals $5-10; ☽ 8am-5pm Mon-Fri, 10am-3pm Sat) Great-value Bavarian-style breakfasts – look forward to an $8 feast of egg, potato and sausage – and Invercargill's best baked cheesecake feature at this German-owned deli-bakery. The daily soup and sourdough special ($5) is almost too affordable. There's a play area for the kids, too.

Tuatara Café (☎ 03-214 0954; 30-32 Dee St; meals $7-20; ☽ 7am-late; 🖳 🗟) The cafe attached to this backpackers' hotel (opposite) is cool in a traveller-focused, dreadlocks-and-Kiwi dub kinda way. Eggs on toast ($7.50) make a hearty good-value start to the day and burgers ($15) are tasty and interesting. Team one with a Biman lager.

Devil Burger (☎ 03-218 9666; 16 Don St; burgers $10-14, wraps $12-14; ☽ 11am-9pm Sun-Wed, to 1am Thu, to 4am Fri & Sat; Ⓥ) Only open a couple of weeks when we dropped by, and already doing great business with tasty gourmet burgers and healthy wraps. Their own beer is on tap, there's loads of vegie options on offer, and even the phone number is a sly in-joke. On weekends, expect crowds of hungry burger fans from upstairs at Tillermans Music Lounge (right).

ourpick Three Bean Café (☎ 03-214 1914; 73 Dee St; meals $10-15; ☽ 7am-5pm Mon-Fri, 8.30am-2pm Sat)

Believe us, we've done the hard yards for the discerning caffeine hound, and hands-down Invercargill's best coffee is at this cosmopolitan main drag cafe. There are switched-on staff that remember you from the day before, and a tasty array of food – kick your day off with a salmon bagel ($11). Leave room for a baked slice of something sweet.

Turkish Kebabs (☎ 03-218 3399; 29 Esk St; kebabs from $11; ☽ 8am-late; Ⓥ) With assorted Turkish paraphernalia, this is an atmospheric spot for a sit-down meal, but it's equally popular for takeaways, with tasty hummusy felafels and the namesake kebabs. For the indecisive diner, there is pretty good Japanese and Indian food a few doors either side.

Zookeepers Cafe (☎ 03-218 3373; 50 Tay St; meals $12-28; ☽ 10am-late Mon-Sat, 11am-late Sun) Easily spotted by the giant corrugated-iron elephant on the ceiling. The zoo-keeping staff are laid-back and friendly, and the meals are good value and tasty. Tuck into a warm balsamic beef salad or sip an Invercargill Brewery beer. Try the Wasp lager, a southern honey-infused spin on a traditional Pilsner.

Sopranos Pizzeria (☎ 03-218 3464; 33 Tay St; pizzas $17-28, pasta $17-24; ☽ 5pm-late Tue-Thu, 11am-late Fri & Sat, 4-9pm Sun) Trying just a little *too* hard to cash in on the mafia shtick, this cafe certainly does good pizzas, and its pasta and gourmet burgers ($21.50) are delicious, too.

SELF CATERING
Countdown (cnr Doon & Tay Sts; ☽ 8am-midnight)

Drinking & Entertainment
One Blue Dog (☎ 03-214 6970; 34 Esk St; ☽ 9pm-late Thu-Sat) Advertising four Jäger and Red Bulls for 30 bucks when we dropped by, this compact upstairs bar has free pool tables and a raucous devil-may-care, don't-waste-the-weekend atmosphere. DJs and occasional bands kick in later at night. It's definitely not sophisticated, but after four Jägerbombs, will you really care?

ourpick Tillermans Music Lounge (☎ 03-218 9240; 16 Don St; cover charge $5; ☽ 9pm-late) Upstairs from Don St, Tillerman's is an alternative live music/DJ venue, with live music ranging from local thrash bands to visiting rock or reggae talents, and DJs doing mostly dub and house. Decrepit black couches and a battered old dance floor prove its credentials. Free entry Thursdays.

Saints & Sinners (☎ 03-214 3366; 25 Tay St; cover charge varies; ☽ 11am-late) This is the nightclub that ate Invercargill – an intricate collage of bars, pool halls, dance floors and flashing lights. Maybe take a GPS with you. While entrapped, you'll discover Saints & Sinners, the preferred live music venue for touring Kiwi bands, and the equally raucous Players Entertainment Venue.

Louie's Café (☎ 03-214 2913; 142 Dee St; tapas $10, mains $19-28; ⏲ 5.30pm-late Sat) This cosy, mellow little cafe-bar specialises in delicious tapas-style snacks, and there's a concise blackboard menu, too. It's a great spot for a late-night wine or an organic beer. Relax fireside, tuck yourself away in various nooks and crannies, or spread out on a comfy padded sofa and enjoy the chilled-out music. There are occasional live gigs.

Kiln (☎ 03-218 2258; 7 Don St) Stylish Monteiths bar with hanging lampshades, underlit bar and Great Aunt Edith's wallpaper. Easily the most civilised drinking option in town and surprisingly good food, too. Try the parmesan-crusted blue cod with a honey- and spice-infused Summer Ale.

Speight's Ale House (☎ 03-214 5333; 38 Dee St) Innumerable TV screens in case someone somewhere takes a wicket or the All Blacks score another try. A good selection of Speight's brews south from Dunedin, and outside tables to watch Invercargill's after dark cavalcade of annoying boy racers in their hotted-up Mazdas. What would Burt Munro think?

Waxy O'Sheas (☎ 03-214 0313; 90 Dee St) Noisy drinking den of the clan O'Bogan. Reputedly the planet's southernmost Irish pub.

Reading Cinemas (☎ 03-211 1555; www.reading cinemas.co.nz; 29 Dee St; adult/child $15/10) shows recent blockbusters. Tuesday nights offer a discount.

Stadium Southland (☎ 03-217 1200; www.stadiumsouth. co.nz; Surrey Park, Isabella St) is home to Invercargill's extremely successful and popular Southern Steel women's netball team (www.southern steel.co.nz; season April to July). You can try out rock climbing here from $5 (7pm Tuesdays and Thursdays) and there's also New Zealand's only indoor velodrome. Come along Tuesday at 5.30pm for the opportunity (per hour $10) to get high on the wall on two wheels. Coaching is provided.

Shopping

Check out **Southern Adventure** (☎ 03-218 3239; 31 Tay St) and **H&J's Outdoor World** (☎ 03-214 2052; 32 Tay St) next door for everything from maps and boots to sleeping bags and dried food.

Getting There & Away

AIR

Flights link Invercargill to Christchurch (from $79, one hour) several times a day via **Air New Zealand** (☎ 0800 737 000; www.airnewzealand.co.nz; 46 Esk St; ⏲ 9am-5pm Mon-Fri, to 12.30pm Sat). **Stewart Island Flights** (☎ 03-218 9129; www.stewartislandflights. com) flies to Oban from Invercargill (adult/ child one-way $105/65, return $185/105, 30 minutes) three times a day.

BUS

Buses leave from the Invercargill i-SITE, where you can also book your tickets. **InterCity** (☎ 03-214 6243; www.intercity.co.nz) connects Invercargill with Dunedin ($43, four hours), Te Anau ($48, three hours) and Christchurch ($70, 10 hours). Look online for significant discounts.

Other bus services include:

Atomic Shuttles (☎ 03-214 6243; www.atomictravel. co.nz) Dunedin ($35) and Christchurch ($70).

Knightrider (☎ 0800 317 057; www.knightrider.co.nz) Overnight to Dunedin ($41) and Christchurch ($76).

Naked Bus (☎ 0900 625 33; www.nakedbus.com) Te Anau ($35), Queenstown ($39) and Dunedin ($34). Look online for discounts.

Scenic Shuttle (☎ 0800 277 483; www.scenicshuttle. co.nz) Via the Southern Scenic Route past Tuatapere ($39) to Te Anau ($49).

TrackNet (☎ 0800 483 262; www.tracknet.net) Te Anau ($45) and Queenstown ($45).

Catlins Coaster and Bottom Bus pass through Invercargill; see p361. See opposite for buses to Bluff and p374 for full details on Stewart Island ferries.

Getting Around

Invercargill Airport (☎ 03-218 6920; 106 Airport Ave) is 3km west of central Invercargill. The door-to-door **Airport Shuttle** (☎ 03-214 3434) costs $12 from the city centre to the airport; more for residential pick-up. By taxi it's around $18; try **Blue Star Taxis** (☎ 03-218 6079) or **City Cabs** (☎ 03-214 4444).

Cycle Surgery (☎ 03-218 8055; www.cyclesurgery. co.nz; 21 Tay St; ⏲ 8.30am-6pm Mon-Thu, to 7pm Fri, 9.30am-4pm Sat, 10am-3pm Sun) rents mountain bikes for $35 per day.

Invercargill's **Freebie bus** (☎ 03-218 7108; www. icc.govt.nz; ⏲ 10am-2.30pm Mon-Sat) is a free bus service around the town centre, departing every 15 minutes. Grab a map of the route from the i-SITE. Other **city buses** (single trip adult/

child $2/1, day pass adult/child $4.50/2.50; 7am-6pm Mon-Fri, 9am-3pm Sat) run to the suburbs; these buses are free from 9am to 2.30pm.

BLUFF

pop 2100

Bluff (www.bluff.co.nz) is Invercargill's port, 27km south of the city. The main reasons to come here are to catch the ferry to Stewart Island, pose for photos beside the **Stirling Point signpost** or buy famous Bluff oysters straight from the wharf. Also at Stirling Point is a huge chain link sculpture by NZ artist Russell Beck. It symbolises the Maori legend where the South Island is the canoe of Maui and Stewart Island is the boat's anchor. At Stirling Point, the chain disappears into the ocean, and a companion sculpture on Stewart Island represents the other end of the anchor chain.

While Bluff isn't the South Island's southernmost point (that claim to fame belongs to Slope Point in the Catlins), and even though Stewart Island and other dots of rock lie even further south, the phrase 'from Cape Reinga to Bluff' is oft-quoted to signify the entire length of NZ. NZ's main highway, SH1, terminates south of Bluff at Stirling Point, so it really does feel like the end of the country.

Kids will enjoy the small **Bluff Maritime Museum** (03-212 7534; 241 Foreshore Rd; adult/child $2/free; 10am-4.30pm Mon-Fri, 1-5pm Sat & Sun) and clambering over a century-old oyster boat, while steam nerds will love the big old 600hp steam engine. Interesting displays on Bluff's history complete the exhibition.

The **Foveaux Walk** (2½ hours return, 6.6km) begins from the signpost around the rugged coast to Ocean Beach. Alternatively, follow that track for 1km and return through rimu and rata forest via the 1.5km **Glory Track**. Drive or walk the 3km to the observation point on top of 265m-high **Bluff Hill** (accessed off Lee St) for a great view of Stewart Island. Pick up *Bluff Walking Tracks* (free) and a Bluff town map from the Invercargill i-SITE.

The **Bluff Oyster & Southland Seafood Festival** (www.bluffoysterfest.co.nz) celebrates Bluff's most famous exports, and is held annually, usually in May. The oysters are in season from late March to late August.

Sleeping & Eating

Bluff Camping Ground (027-626 2018; 11 Gregory St; unpowered/powered sites $25/34, cabins $44) Basic cabins sit on a wide grassy area with sites for vans and

tents. The communal facilities are fine, though they cost $6 a pop ($6 for a shower, $6 to use the kitchen, $6 for the laundry). BYO linen.

Foveaux Hotel (03-212 7196; www.foveauxhotel. com; 40 Gore St; s $60-75, d $90-110) This funky art-deco building has a number of clean, spacious rooms and a comfy guests' lounge/bar downstairs (with big comfy red sofas and a big comfy cat). Rooms are good value, and this is a nice spot to relax and catch your breath. Grab fish and chips next door and bring them back for dinner.

Land's End (03-212 7575; www.landsend.net. nz; Stirling Point; s/d incl breakfast $120/165) Opposite the Stirling Point signpost, this prominent house has luxurious if quaint rooms, most with good views of the sea. There's also a restaurant downstairs (lunch from $13, dinner from $27), specialising in fresh seafood and open around 9.30am; closing around 8pm (earlier in winter).

Drunken Sailor Cafe & Bar (03-212 8855; Stirling Point; mains $18-32; 11.30am-4pm Sun-Fri, to late Sat) Up on the hill above the signpost at Stirling Point, this seafood restaurant's huge curve of windows offers magnificent views of the ocean, the islands beyond, and the forested curve of the bluff itself.

Next door to Foveaux Hotel, **Gallery Takeaway** (03-312 7391; 42 Gore St; 11.30am-8pm Sun-Thu, to 9pm Fri & Sat) does arguably the planet's finest fish and chips, and has a small tribute to the sadly lamented Bluff paua-shell house. If fresh oysters aren't in season, try a Blue Cod meal ($13). To buy fresh Bluff oysters, visit **Fowlers Oysters** (03-212 8523; Ocean Beach Rd; 9am-5pm Mar-Aug) on the way into town on the left.

Near the 4 Square supermarket, **Stella's** (03-212 8856; 64 Gore St; 6.30am-2pm) is your best bet for a coffee before braving the ferry crossing to Stewart Island. The seafood chowder and pies are pretty good, too.

Getting There & Away

Stewart Island Experience (0800 000 511, 03-212 7660; www.stewartislandexperience.co.nz) runs a shuttle between Bluff and Invercargill (adult/child $18/9) connecting with the Stewart Island ferry. It also offers secure vehicle storage by the ferry terminal ($5 per day).

INVERCARGILL TO DUNEDIN

Following SH1 across interior farmland is the most direct route between Invercargill and Dunedin. While the scenery is pretty in a pastoral way, it's certainly not as dramatic as the route via the Catlins. If you have the time, opt for the latter.

Gore
pop 8500

Gore is the proud 'home of country music' in New Zealand, with the annual **Gold Guitar Week** (www.goldguitars.co.nz; late May/early Jun) ensuring all the town's accommodation is booked out for at least 10 days per year. For the other 355 days, good reasons to stop include a surprisingly cool art gallery, and whisky tasting at the Hokonui Moonshine Museum. Don't leave town without a picture of Gore's Giant Trout; the surrounding region offers excellent trout fishing.

The **Gore i-SITE** (☎ 03-203 9288; www.gorenz.com; 16 Hokonui Dr; 8.30am-5pm Mon-Fri, 9.30am-4pm Sat & Sun) has information on accommodation, transport, and fishing or bushwalking distractions. The interesting **Hokonui Moonshine Museum** (admission $5; 9am-4.30pm Mon-Fri, 10am-3.30pm Sat & Sun) and the **Gore Historical Museum** (admission by donation; hours as above) share the same building, celebrating Gore's proud history of fishing, farming and illegal distilleries. Admission to the Moonshine Museum includes a wee dram of the local product.

Across the car park the **public library** (9.30am-6pm Mon-Fri, 10.15am-1pm Sat) has internet access.

Across the road, the outstanding **Eastern Southland Gallery** (☎ 03-208 9907; 14 Hokonui Dr; admission by donation; 10am-4.30pm Mon-Fri, 1-4pm Sat & Sun), in Gore's gorgeous century-old former public library, houses a hefty collection of NZ art including a large Ralph Hotere collection. The amazing John Money Collection combines indigenous folk art from West Africa and Australia with works by iconic New Zealand artist Rita Angus. Nicknamed the 'Goreggenheim', this excellent gallery would be an asset to any city, and is well worth a stop.

Croydon Aircraft Company (☎ 03-208 9755; www.croydonaircraft.com; SH94, Mandeville), 16km down the road to Queenstown, restores vintage aircraft and, for wannabe WWI flying aces, offers flights in a two-seater 1930s Tiger Moth biplane ($85/200 for 10/30 minutes), or other wee aircraft. There's a restaurant attached.

Old Fire Station Backpackers (☎ 03-208 1925; www.thefirestation.co.nz; 19 Hokonui Dr; dm/d $25/60;) is a small hostel opposite the i-SITE. There's a good kitchen, laundry and a pleasant patio with a barbecue. Linen costs $2 extra.

There are also plenty of motels in town; the modern **Riverlea Motel** (☎ 03-208 3130; www.riverleamotel.co.nz; 46 Hokonui Dr; s $98-110, d $113-135) is a nice option. Gore i-SITE can hook you up with lots of others, plus local B&Bs or farmstays.

Green Room Café (☎ 03-208 1005; 59 Irk St; mains $8-10; 7.30am-5pm Mon-Sat;) is a sunlight-dappled cafe with wooden floors, old-fashioned-movie seats and welcoming, relaxed service. The cakes are yummy, coffees are legendary and it is exceptionally child-friendly.

With decor that's faux-Texan and barnlike, **Howl at the Moon** (☎ 03-208 3851; 2 Main St; dinner mains $17-28; noon-2pm & 6-9pm;) serves up predictably large, but surprisingly tasty, dinners.

THE CATLINS

If you veer off SH1 and head for the coastal route between Invercargill and Dunedin (via SH92), you wind through the enchanting Catlins, a region that combines lush farmland, native forests and rugged bays. With bushwalks, wildlife-spotting opportunities and lonely beaches to explore, the Catlins is well worth a couple of days. You won't find much in the way of facilities but there is plenty of wonderful accommodation.

On a clear summer's day, surrounded by forest greens and ocean blues, there's nothing more beautiful than the Catlins coast, and everyone wants to stay an extra day or two. In the face of a grey, sleety Antarctic southerly, however, travellers tend to leave in droves. This route has many twists, turns and narrow sections; it's similar in distance but slower going than the inland route along SH1.

Flora & Fauna

The Catlins is a wonderful place for independent wildlife-watching. Fur seals and sea lions laze along the coast, while elephant seals breed at Nugget Point (p364). In spring, keep your eyes peeled for southern right whales, which are occasionally spotted offshore. Dolphins are also frequent visitors.

Unlike much of Southland, tall kahikatea, totara and rimu forests still exist in the Catlins. Prolific bird life includes the wonderfully noisy tui, and you'll see more kereru (wood pigeons) here in a day than in a month

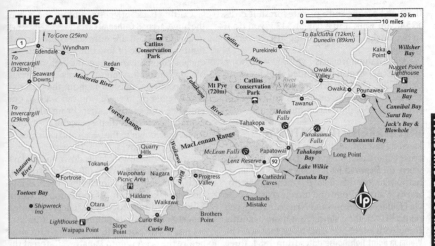

THE CATLINS

in the rest of NZ. There are also many other sea, estuary and forest birds, including the endangered yellow-eyed penguin and the rare mohua (yellowhead).

Information

Contact the main **Catlins information centre** (☎ 03-415 8371; catlinsinfo@cluthadc.govt.nz; 20 Ryley St, Owaka; ☻ 9.30am-1pm & 1.30-4.30pm Mon-Fri, 10am-4pm Sat & Sun; 💻) in Owaka (p365), or the smaller **Waikawa visitors centre** (☎ 03-246 8464; waikawa museum@hyper.net.nz; Main Rd, Waikawa; ☻ 10am-5pm; 💻). The Invercargill i-Site (p354) also has lots of Catlins information.

All centres stock the free two-sided *Catlins Highway Guide* map, with comprehensive accommodation phone numbers. Both www.catlins.org.nz and www.catlins-nz.com are well-maintained websites on the region.

The Catlins has no banks and limited options for eating out or grocery shopping (except Owaka). There's an ATM at the 4 Square supermarket in Owaka, and petrol stations (hours can be irregular) in Fortrose, Papatowai and Owaka. Stock up and fill up before you arrive.

Activities

The rugged Catlins coastline is good for surfing. Located in Porpoise Bay near Curio Bay, the **Catlins Surf School** (☎ 03-246 8552; www.catlins -surf.co.nz) runs 90-minute surfing lessons for $50. The occasional group of dolphin spectators is free of charge. You'll usually find local surf guru Nick at his caravan in the Curio Bay

Camping Ground (p363). If you're already confident on the waves, hire a board and wetsuit (very necessary) for three hours ($40).

Explore the idiosyncratic coastline and landscapes on four legs with **Catlins Horse Riding** (☎ 03-415 8368; www.catlinshorseriding.co.nz; 41 Newhaven Rd, RD1 Owaka; 1-/2-/3-hr rides $40/60/80). Full-day rides including lunch are $140.

Tours

Bottom Bus (☎ 03-477 9083; www.bottombus.co.nz) does a regular loop from Queenstown to Dunedin, south through the Catlins to Invercargill, along the Southern Scenic Route to Te Anau, then back to Queenstown. It stops at all main points of interest, and you can always hop off and catch the next bus coming through. There are lots of pass options; the Southlander pass ($425) lets you start anywhere on the loop and includes a Milford Sound cruise.

Catlins Coaster (☎ 03-477 9083; www.catlinscoaster. co.nz), run by Bottom Bus, offers day tours and trips through the Catlins from Dunedin and Invercargill. Ring them or check the website for details. Departures are more limited in winter.

Papatowai-based **Catlins Wildlife Trackers** (☎ 0800 228 5467; www.catlins-ecotours.co.nz) offers ecocentric guided walks and tours (three nights $600, one week $1500) with food, accommodation and transport (from Balclutha if necessary). These conservation gurus have been running tours here since 1990 and also manage **Top Track**, a 26km self-guided walk through beaches and a private forest. It costs $25 if you walk it in a day or $45 if you do it in two, including overnighting in a converted trolley bus.

Catlins Natural Wonders (☎ 0800 304 333; www.catlinsnatural.co.nz) also has guided trips focusing on wildlife. One-day trips cost $130/85 out of Dunedin/Balclutha, or there's an overnight trip ($200/150, plus accommodation).

INVERCARGILL TO PAPATOWAI

Heading east and south from Invercargill, SH92 enters the Catlins region at Fortrose, from where the **Shipwreck Ino** is visible across the sandy harbour at low tide. Take the turn-off here towards Waipapa Point and use the coastal route via Haldane, Waikawa and Niagara (where you rejoin SH92). It's a slower, but more beautiful route, with lots to check out along the way. The **Waipapa Point lighthouse** dates from 1884, three years after a terrible maritime disaster when SS *Tararua* sank and 131 people drowned.

Turn off at Tokanui and drive 13km to **Slope Point**, the South Island's most-southerly point. A 20-minute walk across farmland leads to a stubby beacon and stubbier signpost (photograph compulsory) atop a windswept spur of rock with views up and down the coast. The track is closed in September and October for lambing.

Further east at **Curio Bay**, fossilised Jurassic-age trees are visible for four hours either side of low tide. It's a fun spot to explore among the rock pools down at sea level where the texture of the petrified wood is more easily made out. The lookout is the place to be an hour or so before sunset, when you'll see yellow-eyed penguins waddling ashore. Just before Curio Bay, neighbouring **Porpoise Bay** has excellent accommodation (see Curio Bay sleeping options, opposite) and a gorgeously sandy, windswept beach that's safe for swimming. Blue penguins nest in the dunes and in summer Hector's dolphins come here to rear their young. It's also a good place to learn to surf (p361). Whales are occasional visitors, and fur seals and sea lions are often lounging on the rocks.

A 4km drive past the McLean Falls Holiday Park, the walk to **McLean Falls** (40 minutes return) passes through tree ferns and rimu. Don't stop at the first falls – the real thing is a bit further on. If you're relatively nimble you can clamber up to a cool pool (take care on the climb down).

Cutting back into cliffs right on the beach, the huge, arched **Cathedral Caves** (www.cathedralcaves.co.nz; adult/child $5/1) are only accessible for two hours either side of low tide (tide timetables are posted on the website, at the highway turn-off, at visitor information centres, and myriad other roadside signs throughout the Catlins). If you're happy to wade, you can walk in one entrance and out the other. From SH92 it's 2km to the car park, then a peaceful 15-minute forest walk down to the beach and a further 25 minutes to the caves.

An easy forest walk leads down to the dark peaty waters of **Lake Wilkie** (30 minutes return) and a cool, and educational, boardwalk alongside the lake. A turn-off soon after is worth following down to the beach at secluded **Tahakopa Bay**. In late summer the slopes are smeared crimson with flowering rata. Just before the descent into Papatowai, stop at the Florence Hill lookout for spectacular views of the sweeping arc of **Tautuku Bay**.

Further east is the cute forested village of **Papatowai**, a base for forays into the nearby forests. There's a handful of accommodation, and a general store selling petrol. There's good picnicking here down at the mouth of the Tahakopa River.

Lost Gypsy Gallery (☎ 03-415 8908; SH92, Papatowai; ☽ 11am-5pm, closed Wed) occupies a roadside house bus at Papatowai, and is almost worth a trip to the Catlins on its own. Based on found objects and specialising on self-wound automata and things that go whirrr, this place is guaranteed to make you both laugh and think. A newly opened gallery (admission $5, young children not allowed sorry…) showcases some of artist Blair Sommerville's larger one-off pieces. We especially like the TV that runs on bicycle power. Blair's always up for a good chat, and at the time of writing, future plans included a coffee caravan. Don't miss this place.

Sleeping

SLOPE POINT

Slope Point Backpackers (☎ 03-246 8420; www.slopepoint.co.nz; Slope Point Rd; powered sites $25, dm $21-26, d $46) Surrounded by trees and farmland, this property has rooms ranging from basic to modern, along with a new well-equipped self-contained unit ($85). There's plenty of grass to park a tent ($11 per person), and the owners' young children are always keen to show visitors what's new on the working farm.

Nadir Outpost (☎ 03-246 8544; www.catlins-slope point.com; 174 Slope Point Rd; d $90) Next door to Slope Point, Nadir offers double rooms inside the owners' house, and a cosy, stand-alone cabin with kitchen facilities. There's a shop selling basic supplies and a forested area to pitch a tent ($12 per person) or park a van ($25 for two people). Meals are also available (breakfast $7 to $14 and dinner $20). Don't make our mistake of calling the owners 'Scottish'. They're actually a very friendly Welsh couple.

CURIO BAY

Curio Bay Camping Ground (☎ 03-246 8897; 601 Curio Bay Rd; unpowered/powered sites $15/25) Very private campsites lost in a sea of tall flax make this a really beautiful spot to camp. The camping ground nestles up to the small outcrop between Curio and Porpoise Bays, within easy walking distance to both. Guided nature walks are available, and it's also where you will usually find Nick from the Catlins Surf School (p361).

Dolphin Lodge (☎ 03-246 8579; dolphin.lodge@ yahoo.co.nz; 529 Curio Bay Rd; dm/d $23/56) There's a focus on surfing here. The rooms are looking slightly tired, but the view from the big lounge and deck towards the Porpoise Bay breakers is just fine. It's $3 more for a duvet in dorm rooms.

Catlins Beach House (☎ 03-246 8340; www.catlins beachhouse.co.nz; 499 Curio Bay Rd; dm $25, d $75-95) This extremely comfortable house has a cosy woodburner for heating, good kitchen and a deck that opens onto a grassy lawn sloping down to the beach. Blue penguins nest hereabouts and can be heard waddling past making cute penguin sounds at night.

Curio Bay Backpackers (☎ 03-246 8897; accommoda tion@curiobay.com; Curio Bay Rd; dm $30, d $70) Right on the sand dunes above the beach, this characterful cottage has a lovely laid-back, communal atmosphere.

Curio Bay Boutique Studios (☎ 03-246 8897; accom modation@curiobay.com; 501 Curio Bay Rd; d $180) With big windows and an even bigger deck, these two plush beachside units are open to awesome sea views. Recline on your giant, rustic, timber-framed bed to feel like a king.

A range of self-contained cottages and houses around Curio Bay can also be rented from **Catlins Surf** (☎ 03-246 8552; www.catlins-surf. co.nz; houses $100-190). One-night rentals are fine, and it's a good option for travelling families or groups of three or four.

WAIKAWA

Penguin Paradise Holiday Lodge (☎ 03-246 8552; www.catlins-surf.co.nz; 1612 Niagara–Waikawa Rd; dm/d/tw $25/50/54) Laid-back backpackers in a heritage cottage in Waikawa village near the estuary. Special combo deals ($65) of one night's accommodation and a 90-minute surf lesson are also available.

Anchorage (☎ 03-205 8006, 03-246 8464; www.anchor age.co.nz; 52 Antrim St; units $90-180) Has a number of roomy units sleeping up to six.

Waikava Harbourview (☎ 03-246 8866; www.south catlins.co.nz; 14 Larne St; d $110-150) A four-bedroom house that's a good option for families or a group. The newly opened one- and two-bedroom Harakeke and Toi Tois units are also good value.

MCLEAN FALLS

Just off the main road, **McLean Falls Holiday Park** (☎ 03-415 8338; www.catlinsnz.com; SH92; sites per person $20, d $65-195; 🖳 🛜) has a number of Kiwiana-style cabins, newer motel units, and sites for vans and tents. The amenities blocks are spacious and very well maintained. The attached **Whistling Frog Café & Bar** (meals $10-30; ⏲ 8.30am-9pm) does breakfast, lunch and dinner with a surprisingly cosmopolitan spin, and there's a good selection of South Island beer and wine.

PAPATOWAI

Hilltop (☎ 03-415 8028; www.hilltopcatlins.co.nz; 77 Tahakopa Valley Rd; dm $28, d $75-90) High on a hill 1.5km out of town, with native forest at the back door and surrounded by sheep farm, this lovely old renovated pair of houses has the most spectacular view of hills and ocean. The en-suite double makes for a luxurious mini-splurge.

The tour company **Catlins Wildlife Trackers** (☎ 0800 228 5467; www.catlins-ecotours.co.nz) rents two houses in Papatowai: a charmin' old-school crib (two people $70) complete with portaloo, and another larger, modern, very ecofriendly house (two people $145).

Other options in Papatowai:

Kauri Glen (☎ 03-415 8044; 13 Tahakopa Rd; d $50) Wee cabin with sunny deck.

Papatowai Scenic Highway Motel & Store (☎ 03-415 8147; b.bevin@paradise.net.nz; Main Rd; d $90; Ⓟ) Modern motel units behind the store.

Southern Secrets Motel (☎ 03-415 8777; southern secret@xtra.co.nz; Main Rd; d $99) A simple weatherboard house conceals very comfortable rooms with a quirky

FIORDLAND & SOUTHLAND

nautical theme. The owner's got 900 videos if the weather turns to custard. Also manages Erehwon (double $135), a three-bedroom holiday home that's a good option for families.

Eating

our pick **Niagara Falls Café** (☎ 03-246 8577; Main Rd, Niagara; meals $13-24; ☻ 8am-10pm) Housed in a lovely old schoolhouse, half of which is given over to local arts, this is a warm, friendly spot for a meal. Gaze out the window at the gardens and farm, or tuck into delicious, good-value meals. Home-cooked cakes and muffins, and good coffees, make it a good spot to stop for morning or afternoon play lunch too. The beer and wine list is impressive, and the mighty falls themselves are nearby, only marginally less spectacular than their North American cousins.

You'll also find roadside takeaways in Waikawa and Papatowai. The Papatowai **store** (☻ 9am-6pm Mon-Sat, from 10am Sun) has a limited range of groceries.

PAPATOWAI TO BALCLUTHA

From Papatowai, follow the highway north to **Matai Falls** (a 30-minute return walk) on the Maclennan River, then head southeast on the signposted road to the tiered **Purakaunui Falls** (20 minutes). Both falls are reached via cool, dark forest walks through totara and tree ferns, and both falls are much more impressive after heavy rain.

You can continue along the gravel road from Purakaunui Falls to the 55m-deep **Jack's Blowhole** (☻ closed for lambing Sep & Oct). In the middle of a sheep paddock 200m from the sea but connected by a subterranean cavern, this huge cauldron was named after Chief Tuhawaiki, nicknamed Bloody Jack for his cussin'. It's a fairly brisk 30-minute walk each way.

Owaka is the Catlins' main town (population a hefty 395), with a good information centre, a 4 Square grocery store – including an ATM – and petrol station. An excellent new **museum** (adult/child $5/free; ☻ 9.30am-1pm & 1.30-4.30pm Mon-Fri, 10am-4pm Sat & Sun), attached to the information centre, has displays on local history. An attached theatrette shows interesting videos on the Catlins' deserved reputation as a shipwreck coast. There's accommodation in town, but once you're stocked up and perhaps stopped for a meal (opposite), it's worth venturing off to more remote, more attractive parts of the Catlins.

Pounawea, 4km away, is a beautiful little riverside town with some lovely places to stay (opposite); across the inlet, **Surat Bay** is even quieter and also has accommodation. Sea lions are often seen on the beach between here and **Cannibal Bay**, a 30-minute beach walk away.

Heading north from Owaka, detour off SH92 to **Nugget Point**, stopping for the short walk out to the lighthouse at the end – the last 100m or so, with drops to the ocean on either side, is breathtaking, and the view of wave-thrashed vertical rock formations from the end is great too. A spacious new DOC viewing platform huddles around the lighthouse. Fur seals, sea lions and elephant seals occasionally bask together on the rocks down to your left, a rare and noisy coexistence. Yellow-eyed and blue penguins, shags and sooty shearwaters all breed here. Ten minutes' walk down from a car park is **Roaring Bay**, where a well-placed hide allows you to see yellow-eyed penguins coming ashore (best two hours before sunset). The best viewing is from a newly constructed hide. You should not use a flash when photographing the penguins. If you don't have your own transport, nightly **twilight tours** (☎ 0800 525 278; www.catlins.co.nz; per person $20) are run by the Nugget View & Kaka Point Motels (opposite).

From Nugget Point the road loops back through the little township of **Kaka Point**, which has a sandy, quiet beach, accommodation and a nice spot for a meal. The road continues north from here to Balclutha (p291).

Sleeping

OWAKA & PURAKAUNUI

There are **DOC camping grounds** (campsites $6) at Purakaunui Bay and inland at Tawanui.

Walking distance from Purakaunui Falls, **Falls Backpackers** (☎ 03-415 8724; rmsbkerr@ispnz. co.nz; Purakaunui Falls Rd; dm/d $27/60) is a comfortable old farmhouse with views from some of the windows and the deck of rolling, sheep-dotted hills.

The beautifully renovated **Catlins Backpackers** (☎ 03-454 5635; www.catlinsbackpackers.co.nz; 24 Main Rd; dm/d $30/66; ▣) is a handsome pair of houses sporting warm colours, characterful, comfortable rooms and spacious shared kitchens. This is probably the nicest place to stay in Owaka. Cash only.

Also in Owaka:

Thomas Catlins Lodge & Holiday Park (☎ 03-415 8333; www.thomascatlins.co.nz; cnr Ryley & Clark Sts; unpowered/powered sites per person $10/16, dm $28, d $60-95; 🖥️) Old hospital grounds converted to campsites and other accommodation. Unsurprisingly, it's all a bit institutional.

Split Level Backpackers (☎ 03-415 8304; bookings@ thesplitlevel.co.nz; 9 Waikawa Rd; dm $28, d $64-72)

Catlins Area Motel (☎ 03-415 8821; catlinsareamotel @hotmail.com; cnr Ryley & Clark Sts; d $95-110) Modern, spacious self-contained units with individual decks.

POUNAWEA

our pick **Pounawea Motor Camp** (☎ 03-415 8483; www.catlins-nz.com/pounawea-motor-camp/; Park Lane; unpowered/powered sites $22/26, cabins per person $22-60) Sitting right on the estuary (some cabins' decks face right onto the water) and surrounded by native bush ringing with birdsong, this is a gem of a place to park your tent. Others think so too, and in the frenzied post-Christmas season you'll be sharing this beautiful spot with many Kiwi and international holidaymakers.

Kiwi Crib (☎ 03-415 8411; galan@farmside.co.nz; 19 Ocean Grove; d $110) Three-bedroom house up a quiet road surrounded by native bush and just a short walk to the water.

SURAT BAY

Newhaven Holiday Park (☎ 03-415 8834; www.new havenholiday.com; Newhaven Rd; unpowered/powered sites $26/30, cabin d $62, flat d $90-100; 🖥️ 🛜) Only a few minutes' walk from the beach is this sweet little camping area with modern cabins and facilities and three new self-contained flats. Kayaks and bikes can be rented next door at Surat Bay Lodge.

Surat Bay Lodge (☎ 03-415 8099; www.suratbay. co.nz; Surat Bay Rd; dm/d $28/66; 🖥️) Right beside the start of the track down to the beach, and next-door neighbours with the sea lions, this superbly located hostel has cosy, brightly decorated rooms and a friendly vibe. Rent a kayak ($12 to $40) or bike ($30 per day) and get exploring.

NUGGET & KAKA POINTS

Kaka Point Camping Ground (☎ 03-412 8801; kaka point@hotmail.com; 39 Tarata St, Kaka Point; unpowered/powered sites per adult $12/12.50, cabins per adult $22) Cabins here are fairly basic but functional, but there is a lovely grassy, hedged area to pitch tents. There are bushwalks into the surrounding forest and it's a short, though steep, stroll downhill to the beach and town.

Fernlea Backpackers (☎ 03-412 8834, 03-418 0117; Moana St, Kaka Point; dm/d $20/50) Perched atop a hill, and a leafy, zigzag path above the street below, this tiny, basic bungalow is ultrasnug, with lovely sea views and basic facilities.

Nugget View & Kaka Point Motels (☎ 0800 525 278; www.catlins.co.nz; 11 Rata St, Kaka Point; d $85-160) A veritable mini-village of motel options ranging from excellent-value older units through to more modern accommodation with private spa baths and verandas. The friendly owners also operate one- and two-day tours of the Catlins, and twilight tours to view Nugget Point and the penguin colony at Roaring Bay.

Nugget Lodge (☎ 03-412 8783; www.nuggetlodge. co.nz; Nugget Rd, Nugget Point; d $160) Perched above the sea on the road south to the lighthouse, this pair of self-contained units is supercomfortable and has spectacular views up and down the coast. It's worth including their huge breakfast ($12.50 per person) with freshly baked bread and homemade muesli. Wonderfully secluded and a worthwhile splurge. And if you're lucky, you might spy a couple of resident sea lions lolling on the beach below you.

Eating
OWAKA

Things close pretty early in Owaka, so head out for dinner early, or stock up for self-catering at the local 4 Square supermarket. A good eating and drinking option is the cosy **Ryley's Café & Bar** (☎ 03-415 8350; 21 Ryley St; 🕙 11am-9pm Thu-Mon) at the Catlin's Inn Hotel. It's the locals' favourite, and you can also get meals at the **Lumberjack Bar & Café** (☎ 03-415 8747; 3 Saunders St; mains $15-30; 🕙 11.30am-9pm Tue-Sun). Park yourself at the wooden bar made from one 6m-long slab of golden-hued timber, and peruse robust options including chicken, steak and venison.

KAKA POINT

Point Café & Bar (☎ 03-412 8800; 58 Esplanade; bar menu $5-15, mains $27-30; 🕙 11am-late) An interesting beach-themed bar serving up bar meals and more substantial dinners. Prop yourself at the driftwood bar for a cool beer, or grab a window seat for a sea view. Takeaways are also available at the attached store; grab a burger ($5) for the road.

Stewart Island

Travellers who undertake the short jaunt to Stewart Island will be rewarded with a warm welcome from both the local kiwi and the local Kiwis. New Zealand's 'third' island is a good place to spy the country's shy, feathered icon in the wild, and the close-knit community of Stewart Islanders (population 420) are relaxed hosts. If you're staying on the island for just a few days, don't be too surprised if most people quickly know who you are and where you came from – especially if you mix and mingle over a beer at NZ's southernmost pub.

Once you've said g'day to the locals, there's plenty of active adventure on offer including kayaking and setting off on a rewarding tramp in Stewart Island's Rakiura National Park. With a worthwhile injection of effort, relative newcomers to tramping can easily complete one of NZ's Great Walks, and be surprised and entertained with an uninterrupted aria from native birds. And if a multiday tramp still sounds too intense, spying a kiwi in the wild can also be achieved with the straightforward combination of a short boat ride and an even shorter bush and beach walk.

All this exercise is bound to make you hungry, so refuel with the freshest NZ seafood before resurrecting your 'Mainland' journey back on the South Island.

STEWART ISLAND

HIGHLIGHTS

- Discovering perfect coves and secluded bays around the **Rakiura Track** (p370)
- Listening to the chorus of birdsong on tiny protected **Ulva Island** (p369)
- Dining on blue cod, mussels and crayfish – all fresh from the southern ocean – in **Oban** (p373)
- Kayaking languidly around the natural harbour of **Paterson Inlet** (p370)
- Heading off in the southern twilight to get up close and personal with a Stewart Island kiwi at **Mason Bay** (p370)

- Telephone code: 03
- www.stewartisland.co.nz

CLIMATE

Stewart Island's changeable weather can bring four seasons in one day. Frequent downpours create a misty, mysterious air and lots of mud, making boots and waterproof clothing mandatory. Nevertheless, the temperature is milder than you'd expect, with winter averaging around 10°C and summer 16.5°C.

HISTORY

Stewart Island's Maori name is Rakiura (Glowing Skies), and catch a glimpse of a spectacular blood-red sunset or the aurora australis and you'll quickly know why. According to myth, NZ was hauled up from the ocean by Maui (p51), who said, 'Let us go out of sight of land, far out in the open sea, and when we have quite lost sight of land, then let the anchor be dropped'. The North Island was the fish that Maui caught, the South Island his canoe and Rakiura was the anchor – Te Punga o te Waka o Maui.

There is evidence that parts of Rakiura were occupied by moa hunters as early as the 13th century. The titi (muttonbird or sooty shearwater) on adjacent islands were an important seasonal food source for the southern Maori.

The first European visitor was Captain Cook, who sailed around the eastern, southern and western coasts in 1770 but couldn't figure out if it was an island or a peninsula. Deciding it was attached to the South Island, he called it South Cape. In 1809 the sealing vessel *Pegasus* circumnavigated Rakiura and named it after its first officer, William Stewart.

In June 1864 Stewart and the adjacent islets were bought from the Maori for £6000. Early industries were sealing, timber-milling, fish-curing and shipbuilding, with a short-lived gold rush towards the end of the 19th century. Today the island's economy is dependent on tourism and fishing, including crayfish (lobster), paua (abalone), salmon, mussels and cod.

FLORA & FAUNA

You don't even have to step off your balcony to experience the island's lush flora and fauna, but the more you explore, the more you'll encounter. Nature has cranked the birdsong up to 11 here; you can't miss the tui, parakeets,

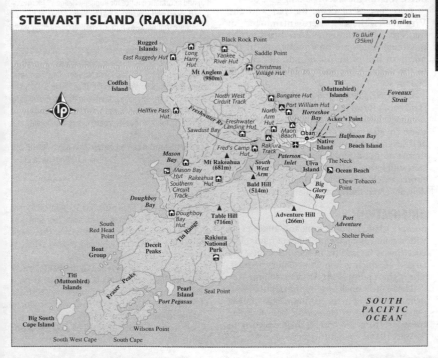

STEWART ISLAND (RAKIURA)

STEWART ISLAND FACTS

Eat Fresh blue cod at Stewart Island's Kai Kart (p373)

Drink Healthy juices and smoothies at Justcafé (p373), NZ's southernmost cafe

Read Stewart Island – A Rakiura Ramble by Neville Peat

Listen to The questions very carefully during NZ's southernmost pub quiz at the South Sea Hotel (p373)

Watch Foveaux Strait's wild southern swell rise and fall from the Stewart Island ferry

Swim at Remote Mason Bay where the water's cold but the sand is frequented by kiwi

Go green Explore the predator-free bird sanctuary of Ulva Island (opposite)

---

kaka, bellbirds, fernbirds, robins and dotterels that constantly flap overhead and serenade you from gardens. You can also see kiwi and Fiordland crested, yellow-eyed and blue penguins. Ask at the i-SITE about the evening parade of penguins on a small beach near the wharf. Resist the temptation to feed any of the birds; you run the risk of passing on diseases.

Two species of deer, the red and the Virginia (whitetail), were introduced in the early 20th century, as were brush-tailed possums, which are now numerous in the northern half of the island and destructive to the native bush. Stewart Island also has NZ fur seals.

Unlike NZ's North and South Islands, there is no beech forest on Stewart Island. The predominant lowland vegetation is hardwood but there are also lots of tree ferns, ground ferns and several types of orchid. Along the coast there's muttonbird scrub, grass tree, tree daisies, supplejack and leatherwood. Around the shores are clusters of bull kelp, fine red weeds, delicate green thallus and bladder ferns.

ORIENTATION

Stewart Island is 65km long and 40km at its widest point, and only has 20km of roads. The coastline is incised by numerous inlets, the largest of which is known as Paterson Inlet. The highest point is Mt Anglem (980m).

The island's small, easy-going population is primarily settled in the fishing village of **Oban** (Map opposite) in Halfmoon Bay. Regular transport from Invercargill makes getting to Stewart Island straightforward.

INFORMATION

Stop off at the Invercargill i-Site (p354) for a wider range of information than what is available on the ferry from Bluff.

There are no banks on Stewart Island. Credit cards are accepted for most activities but it's wise to bring enough cash for your stay. There's internet access at Justcafé (including wi-fi), the South Sea Hotel, and most accommodation.

Online see www.stewartisland.co.nz.

DOC Rakiura National Park visitor centre (Department of Conservation; Map p369; ☎ 03-219 0009; rakiuravc@doc.govt.nz; Main Rd, Oban; ☺ 8.30am-7.30pm Mon-Fri, 9am-4pm Sat & Sun) The free exhibition is an essential stop to understand Stewart Island's flora and fauna before heading off on your tramp. Backcountry Hut Passes and detailed maps of local tracks are also available.

Post office (Map p369; Elgin Tce, Oban) At Stewart Island Flights.

Ruggedy Range Birds & Forest Booking Office (Map p369; ☎ 0508 484 337, 03-219 1066; www.ruggedyrange.com; cnr Main Rd & Dundee St, Oban; ☺ 7.30am-8pm Mon-Sun Sep-May, 8.30am-5.30pm Mon-Fri, 9.30am-2pm Sat & Sun Jun-Aug) Dedicated booking and information office for Ruggedy Range Wilderness Experience with birdwatching, tramping and water taxis on offer. Note that Ruggedy Range is not represented by other information centres on the island.

Stewart Island Experience (Map p369; ☎ 0800 000 511, 03-212 7660; www.stewartislandexperience.co.nz; 12 Elgin Tce, Oban; ☺ 8am-7pm Mon-Fri, 9am-7pm Sat & Sun summer, 8am-5pm Mon-Fri, 10am-noon Sat & Sun winter) The ferry company is housed in the big red building and books accommodation and activities. Also handles sightseeing tours, and rents scooters, cars, fishing rods, dive gear and golf clubs.

Stewart Island Health Centre (Map p369; ☎ 03-219 1098; Argyle St, Oban; ☺ 10.30am-12.30pm) Has a 24-hour on-call service.

SIGHTS

Rakiura Museum (Map p369; Ayr St, Oban; adult/child $2/50c; ☺ 10am-1.30pm Mon-Sat, noon-2pm Sun) has models of various ferries from over the years, a sobering exhibit on whaling, Maori artefacts and early European settlement.

The wooden **Presbyterian Church Hall** (Map p369; Kamahi Rd, Oban) was relocated to Oban from a whaling base in Paterson Inlet in 1937. At Harrold Bay, 2.5km southwest of town, is a **stone house** (off Map p369) built by Lewis Acker around 1835, one of NZ's oldest stone buildings.

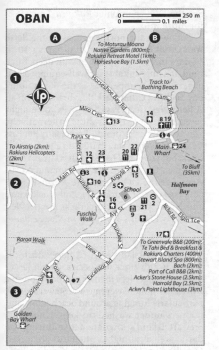

Stop in and learn about the work done at the **Halfmoon Bay Habitat Rehabilitation Project** (Map p369), which is striving to restore the native bird life around Halfmoon Bay.

Ulva Island

Ulva Island (Map p367) is a tiny paradise covering only 250 hectares. An early naturalist, Charles Traill, was honorary postmaster here. He would hoist a flag to signal that mail had arrived and hopefuls would paddle in from surrounding islands. His postal service was replaced by one at Oban in 1921, and in 1922 Ulva Island was declared a bird sanctuary.

With an absence of predators, the air is alive with the song of tui and bellbirds, and you'll also see kaka, weka, kakariki and kereru (NZ pigeon).

Good walking tracks in the island's northwest are detailed in *Ulva: Self-Guided Tour* ($2), available from the Department of Conservation (DOC). Popular routes include **Flagstaff Point Lookout** (20 minutes return) and **Boulder Beach** (1½ hours return). Many paths intersect amid beautiful stands of rimu, miro,

totara and rata. During summer, a ferry (return adult/child $20/10) departs from Golden Bay wharf to Ulva Island at 9am, noon and 4pm, and water taxis can take you to Ulva independently (return $25; p374).

To get the most out of Ulva Island, consider going with a guide from Ruggedy Range Wilderness Experience (p370) or Ulva's Guided Walks (p371).

ACTIVITIES

NZ's third-largest island features unspoilt wilderness and is a haven for a symphony of birdsong. Rakiura National Park protects 85% of the island, making it a mecca for trampers and birdwatchers, and there are countless sandy, isolated coves that are good for swimming if you're brave/mad enough to venture into the cool water.

STEWART ISLAND

Tramping

Even if you're not a gung-ho tramper, Stewart Island is great to stretch your legs and immerse yourself in wilderness on a short tramp. For more serious trampers, there are excellent, multiday, DOC-maintained trails. The DOC Rakiura National Park visitor centre (p368) sells Backcountry Hut Passes and has detailed pamphlets on local tramps. Store gear here in small/large lockers for $5/10 per day. Storage bins are $10 per day.

In the north, there's a good network of tracks with huts occupied on a first-come, first-served basis. Each hut has foam mattresses, wood stoves for heating, running water and toilets. You'll need to carry a stove, food, sleeping bags, utensils and first-aid equipment. A tent can be useful over the busy summer holidays and Easter period. The southern part of the island is undeveloped and desolate, and you shouldn't tramp on your own or go off the established tracks.

DAY TRAMPS

There are a number of short tramps, ranging from half an hour to seven hours; the majority are easily accessed from Halfmoon Bay. Pick up *Day Walks* ($1) from DOC Rakiura National Park visitor centre. The walk to **Observation Rock** (Map p369; 30 minutes return) has good views past Paterson Inlet. Continue past the old stone house at Harrold Bay to **Acker's Point Lighthouse** (three hours return), for good views of Foveaux Strait and the chance to see blue penguins and a colony of titi.

MULTIDAY TRAMPS

The 29km, three-day **Rakiura Track** is one of NZ's Great Walks and is a well-defined, easy circuit starting and ending at Oban with copious bird life, beaches and lush bush en route. Huts along this scenic, extensively boardwalked track get quite crowded, particularly those at Port William and North Arm, both of which have room for 30 trampers. There are also camping grounds at Sawdust Bay, Maori Beach and Port William. A rerouting and upgrade of the track was planned to be completed by June 2011, so it's vital to check with DOC for the latest information. Overnight trampers need to buy from DOC either a date-stamped **Great Walks huts pass** (per night adult/child $15/free) or **camping pass** (per night adult/child $5/2.50); there's a limit of two consecutive nights in any one hut.

See the DOC pamphlet *Rakiura Track* ($1) for more info.

Following the northern coast is the **North West Circuit Track**, a 125km trail taking 10 to 12 days that is often plagued with deep, thick mud. It's only suitable for well-equipped and experienced trampers, as is the 56km, four-day **Southern Circuit Track** that branches off it. A **North West Circuit Pass** ($45) gives you a night in each of these tracks' huts. Alternatively, you can buy a 12-month **Backcountry Hut Pass** (adult/child $90/45) to stay in huts on either circuit track, but you'll still have to buy a Great Walks huts pass for use at Port William and North Arm. See the DOC brochure *North West & Southern Circuit Tracks* ($1). Both the Rakiura and North West Circuit Tracks are detailed in Lonely Planet's *Tramping in New Zealand*.

Kiwi-Spotting

The Stewart Island kiwi *(Apteryx australis lawryi)* is a distinct subspecies, with a larger beak and longer legs than its northern cousins. Kiwi are common over much of Stewart Island, particularly foraging around beaches for sand hoppers under washed-up kelp. Unusually, Stewart Island's kiwi are active during the day as well as at night – the birds are forced to forage for longer to attain breeding condition. Many trampers on the North West Circuit Track spot them. For a helping hand with sightings, see Tours (opposite). Because of Stewart Island's often-fickle weather, tours are sometimes cancelled, and you may need to spend a few nights on the island to finally see a kiwi.

Other Activities

Paterson Inlet consists of 100 sq km of sheltered, kayak-friendly waterways, with 20 islands, DOC huts and two navigable rivers. A popular trip is a paddle to **Freshwater Landing** (7km upriver from the inlet) followed by a three- to four-hour walk to Mason Bay to see kiwi in the wild. **Rakiura Kayaks** (☎ 03-219 1160; www.rakiura.co.nz) rents kayaks from $45 a day and also runs half-/full-day guided trips around the inlet ($60/85). You'll find Liz from Rakiura Kayaks at Bunkers Backpackers (p372).

Ruggedy Range Wilderness Experience (Map p369; ☎ 0508 484 337, 03-219 1066; www.ruggedyrange.com; cnr Main Rd & Dundee St, Oban) runs guided walks on Ulva Island and has guided trips from half a day to 3½ days including camping and tramping. Prices range from $100 to $2500.

Stewart Island Experience (Map p369; ☎ 0800 000 511, 03-212 7660; www.stewartislandexperience.co.nz; 12 Elgin Tce, Oban; ☺ 8am-7pm Mon-Fri, 9am-7pm Sat & Sun summer, 8am-5pm Mon-Fri, 10am-noon Sat & Sun winter) rents mountain bikes (half-/full day $25/35) and motor scooters (half-/full day $55/65). The island's **Community Centre** (Map p369; ☎ 03-219 1477; 10 Ayr St, Oban; nonmembers $5) houses a gym, sauna, netball and squash courts, all of which are open to visitors. It's also home to a **library** (☺ 6.30-7.30pm Mon, 2-3pm Wed, 11am-noon Fri & Sat) open to visitors.

Stewart Island Spa (off Map p369; ☎ 03-219 1422; www.stewartislandspa.co.nz; ☺ Dec-Mar) is in a refurbished hilltop cottage. Options include crystal healing, a rainforest bath, and a sauna and massage. Premium organic beauty products are used for all treatments. See Britt at Justcafé (p373).

TOURS

Ulva's Guided Walks (☎ 03-219 1216; www.ulva.co.nz) offers Maori history and conservation included in excellent three- to five-hour tours costing from $95 to $150 (transport included). Options include Ulva Island and Port William, a historic Maori and sealing site.

Coast to Coast (Map p369; ☎ 03-218 9129; www.stewartislandflights.com; Elgin Tce, Oban; adult/child from $185/135) offers adventure-packed days with a flight from Oban and beach landing at Mason Bay, a four-hour tramp and a one-hour boat ride through Paterson Inlet to Golden Bay.

Stewart Island Experience (Map p369; ☎ 0800 000 511, 03-212 7660; www.stewartislandexperience.co.nz; 12 Elgin Tce, Oban; ☺ 8am-7pm Mon-Fri, 9am-7pm Sat & Sun summer, 8am-5pm Mon-Fri, 10am-noon Sat & Sun winter) runs 2½-hour Paterson Inlet cruises (adult/child $80/20, daily at 12.45pm October to April) via

Ulva Island; daily 1½-hour minibus tours of Oban and the surrounding bays (adult/child $42/20); and daily, 45-minute semisubmersible cruises (adult/child $35/120).

To see a kiwi in the wild, **Bravo Adventure Cruises** (☎ 03-219 1144; philldismith@xtra.co.nz) runs twilight tours ($120). In order to protect the kiwi, numbers are limited so make sure you book *well* ahead. Kiwi-spotting is also available with Ruggedy Range.

Ruggedy Range Wilderness Experience (Map p369; ☎ 0508 484 337, 03-219 1066; www.ruggedyrange.com; cnr Main Rd & Dundee St, Oban) takes small groups on guided walks with an ecofriendly, conservation angle. It also specialises in the viewing of pelagic seabirds. Excursions range from a half-day trip to Ulva Island ($100) to a 3½-day wilderness experience ($2500). One- and two-night expeditions to see kiwi in the wild ($425 to $835) are also available.

Charter companies offer various fishing trips and wildlife cruises. Options include the following:

Bravo Adventure Cruises (☎ 03-219 1144; philldismith@xtra.co.nz)

Rakiura Charters (off Map p369; ☎ 0800 725 487, 03-219 1487; www.rakiuracharters.co.nz) Sightseeing and fishing outings on the very comfortable *Rakiura Suzy*. Most popular is the half-day fishing cruise (adult/child $125/80) including a stop at a historic Whalers' Base. Multiday diving, fishing and hunting charters and overnight trips are also available.

Rawhiti Excursions (☎ 03 219 1023; per half-/full day $70/90) Traditional hand fishing with a lunch option of 'catch and cook' your own blue cod.

To see Stewart Island from the air on a scenic flight, see Rakiura Helicopters (p374).

STEWART ISLAND

SPOTTING A KIWI: A BRUSH WITH THE GODS

Considered the king of the forest by Maori, the kiwi has been around for 70 million years and is related to the now extinct moa. Brown feathers camouflage the kiwi against its bush surroundings and a nocturnal lifestyle means spying a kiwi in the wild is a challenge. They're a smart wee bird – they even build their burrows a few months before moving in so newly grown vegetation can further increase their privacy.

Stewart Island is one of the few places on earth where you can spot a kiwi in the wild. As big as a barnyard chicken and numbering 20,000, the tokoeka, or Stewart Island brown kiwi, is larger in size and population than other subspecies. They are also the only kiwi active during daylight hours. About two hours after sunrise and an hour before sunset, tokoeka forage for food in grassed areas, particularly on Mason Bay. Watch for white kiwi poo and telltale holes made by their long hunting beaks. When you spot one, keep silent, and stay still and well away. The birds' poor eyesight and single-mindedness in searching for food will often lead them to bump right into you.

SLEEPING

Despite Oban's surprisingly high number of motels, hostels, holiday homes and B&Bs, finding accommodation can be difficult, even in the low season when many places shut down. It's wise to book ahead. Self-contained holiday homes offer good value, especially for families and groups.

See www.stewartisland.co.nz for the widest range of accommodation options.

Budget

Stewart Island Backpackers (Map p369; ☎ 03-219 1114; www.stewart-island.co.nz/backpackers; cnr Dundee & Ayr Sts, Oban; dm/s/d $25/40/55; 🖳) Rooms are basic but brightly painted, and many open onto a courtyard. There are only three beds per dorm, and a spacious lounge, common kitchen, table tennis table and barbecue keep things nicely social. Tenting is $15 per person.

our pick Bunkers Backpackers (Map p369; ☎ 03-219 1160; www.bunkersbackpackers.co.nz; 13 Argyle St, Oban; dm/s/d $28/48/76; 🖳 🛜) A recently renovated wooden villa houses Stewart Island's newest and friendliest hostel. Shared areas are modern and sunny, and the rooms are spacious and spotless. Owners Liz and Heath can arrange kayaking and seafood barbecues, while friendly canine assistant Pip is always up for a cuddle or a sausage.

Jo & Andy's B&B (Map p369; ☎ 03-219 1230; jariksem@clear.net.nz; cnr Morris St & Main Rd, Oban; s $45-60, d $74; 🖳 🛜) An excellent option for budget travellers, this cosy blue home squeezes in twin, double and single rooms. A big breakfast of muesli, fruit and homemade bread prepares you for tramping and dinner is available for $20. After a long tramp, dissolve into the skilful hands of the on-site massage therapist.

Midrange

South Sea Hotel (Map p369; ☎ 03-219 1059; www.stewart-island.co.nz; 26 Elgin Tce, Oban; s $65-100, d $85-110, units $155; 🖳 🛜) Built in 1890, this harbourside hotel has floral rooms and a big sunny deck. The downstairs pub often overpowers the ocean sounds on weekends while out the back sunny motel units manage a South Pacific look with high ceilings, kitchenettes and verandas.

Pilgrim Cottage (Map p369; ☎ 03-219 1144; philldismith@xtra.co.nz; 8 Horseshoe Bay Rd, Oban; d $120) This quaint, weatherboard cottage in a leafy oasis near town has wooden furnishings, a potbelly stove and a well-equipped kitchen. Expect lots of bird life.

Rakiura Retreat Motel (off Map p369; ☎ 03-219 1096; www.rakiuraretreat.co.nz; Horseshoe Bay Rd; units $140-160; 🖳) Surrounded by native bush, this row of motel units has comfortable and peaceful rooms. It's a pleasant 20-minute walk from town and there's a winding walking track from the motel down to secluded Bragg's Bay. Mountain bikes are complimentary.

Top End

Bay Motel (Map p369; ☎ 03-219 1119; www.baymotel.co.nz; 9 Dundee St, Oban; d $160-200) Modern, comfortable units with lots of light and views over the harbour. Some units have big spa tubs, all rooms have full kitchens and two are wheelchair-accessible. When you've exhausted the island's bustling after-dark scene, Sky TV's on hand for on-tap entertainment.

Te Tahi Bed & Breakfast (off Map p369; ☎ 0800 725 487, 03-219 1487; www.rakiuracharters.co.nz; 14 Kaka Ridge Rd; d $200) A sunny conservatory immersed in verdant bush, ocean views and colourfully decorated bedrooms are the standouts at this friendly B&B just five minutes' walk from the bustling hub of Oban and Halfmoon Bay.

Kaka Retreat (Map p369; ☎ 03-219 1252; www.stewartisland.net; 7 & 9 Miro Cres, Oban; d $320; 🖳 🛜) These self-contained studio units have luxury interiors and cosy veranda. With crisply modern decor and flash bathrooms, the newly redecorated superior units are among the island's best. Most mornings you'll be greeted by kaka. Just don't feed them, OK? An older-style family unit ($299) is good value for up to six people.

Greenvale B&B (off Map p369; ☎ 03-219 1357; www.greenvalestewartisland.co.nz; Elgin Tce; s/d $300/375; 🛜) Just 50m from the sea, this modern home has stunning views over Foveaux Strait. Both rooms have quality cotton bed linen and contemporary furnishings. It's a five-minute walk to Halfmoon Bay, and a two-second transition to the sunny deck. The owner's family has been resident on Stewart Island for several generations.

Stewart Island Lodge (Map p369; ☎ 03-219 1085; www.stewartislandlodge.co.nz; Nichol Rd, Oban; d incl breakfast $390) This upmarket retreat with six features king-size beds, a shared deck, and a garden teeming with bird life. On a hill at the edge of town, the lodge commands magnificent views. Look forward to complimentary drinks and nibbles at 5pm every night.

It's the little things that make a difference at **Port of Call B&B** (off Map p369; ☎ 03-219 1394;

www.portofcall.co.nz; Leask Bay Rd; s/d incl breakfast $345/385), such as a welcome fruit basket and 20 hectares of surrounding bush. Take in ocean views, get cosy before an open fire or explore an isolated beach. Nearby is a modern self-contained studio unit called the **Bach** (off Map p369; unit $250). You'll find both 1.5km south-west of Oban on the way to Acker's Point. In the heart of Halfmoon Bay, the self-contained **Turner Cottage** (Map p369; Golden Bay Rd; cottage $180) is perfect for romantic island escapees. All three properties have a two-night minimum stay, and guided walks and water taxi trips can also be arranged.

EATING & DRINKING

our pick **Kai Kart** (Map p369; ☎ 03-219 1225; Ayr St, Oban; meals $5-20; ☼ 11.30am-2.30pm & 5-9pm, closed Mon-Tue May-Nov) Owned by a mussel farmer, the seafood at this tiny caravan of cuisine is exceptionally fresh. The sweet-as-sweet blue cod could be the best fish you'll ever have, and the mussels with spicy satay sauce aren't far behind. Park yourself in an interior booth, grab an outside table, or eat your goodies on the beach. Don't blame us if you've finished them before you get there.

Justcafé (Map p369; ☎ 03-219 1422; Main Rd, Oban; meals $10-14; ☼ 8am-8pm; 🖳 🛜) This warm lit-tle place has wooden-bench tables and lots of magazines. Fill up on soups, tasty sandwiches and baking. Nurse a good coffee or an even better smoothie or raw juice. There's wi-fi available, and owner Britt also sells wholesale gemstone jewellery and designs made from paua shells.

South Sea Hotel (Map p369; ☎ 03-219 1059; 26 Elgin Tce, Oban; mains $15-30; ☼ 11am-late) With old

B&W photos, this cafe-style spot does su-perb fish, and robust seafood chowder. It's listed under 'Starters' but it's a meal in itself. The attached pub is the town's main drinking hole, enlivened by occasional weekend bands and a loads-of-fun pub quiz that kicks off at 6.30pm on Sunday nights. Say hi to Vicky, quiz-mistress extraordinaire. Friday's also a good night to meet the locals, when Happy Hour kicks off at 5.30pm.

Church Hill Cafe, Bar & Restaurant (Map p369; ☎ 03-219 1323; 36 Kamahi Rd, Oban; mains $25-35; ☼ 5.30-9pm) Look beyond the gimmicky 'Stone Grill' menu to local flavours such as blue cod and mutton-bird (in season). In summer the sunny, spa-cious deck and lawn provide hilltop views, and in cooler months you'll need to beat out the friendly cat for a cosy spot by the fire. It's essen-tial to book for dinner, and by 5pm at the latest.

our pick **Perfect Dinner** (☎ 027 444 1802; annett_ei selt@web.de; 3-course menu per person $70; ☼ Oct-May) Relocated from Germany to the southern ocean, Annett Eiselt specialises in 'moveable feasts'. That means she's available to provide three-course menus or gourmet platters wher-ever you desire on the island; at your accom-modation, on a beach, or somewhere else with equally terrific views. Produce is always sea-sonal, and ideally organic and sourced locally. Annett can also recommend on lodge-style accommodation.

Self-caterers can get groceries and beer and wine from Oban's general store, **Ship to Shore** (Map p369; ☎ 03-219 1069; Elgin Tce, Oban; ☼ 7.30am-7pm). Also available are sandwiches and baked goodies ($3 to $6), and staff can prepare a packed lunch if you're going for a day tramp. It's also the kind of friendly place that an-nounces locals' birthdays on a blackboard outside.

The Fishermen's Co-op on the main wharf often sells fresh fish and crayfish.

SHOPPING

Opposite the DOC office, the **Fernery** (Map p369; ☎ 03-219 1216; Main Rd, Oban; ☼ 11am-5pm) sells crafts, paintings and island-themed books, especially titles for kids. Pick up a CD of bird calls, so you'll know your kiwi from your kaka.

Glowing Sky (Map p369; ☎ 03-219 1528; www.glow ingsky.co.nz; Elgin Tce, Oban; ☼ 11am-3pm) sells hand-printed T-shirts.

Ruggedy Range Wilderness Experience can set you up with tramping and camping gear at its Birds & Forest Booking Office (p368).

YOU CAUGHT IT. NOW COOK IT.

You're (literally) surrounded by fishing op-portunities on Stewart Island, but if you're not staying in self-contained accommoda-tion, you'll need to explore other avenues to prepare your freshly caught *kai moana* (seafood).

For a small fee, the good people at the Kai Kart (above) will perform kitchen duties on your behalf, and if you're an alfresco kind of chef, fire up the public barbecues (buy charcoal at Ship to Shore, right) in the pleas-ant **Moturau Moana Native Gardens** on the eastern edge of Halfmoon Bay.

GETTING THERE & AWAY
Air
Rakiura Helicopters (off Map p369; ☎ 03-219 1155; www.rakiurahelicopters.co.nz; 151 Main Rd) is the only helicopter company based on Stewart Island. It's available for transfers from Bluff (per person $250), scenic flights (per person $50 to $560), and charter flights for hunters and trampers.

Stewart Island Flights (Map p369; ☎ 03-218 9129; www.stewartislandflights.co.nz; Elgin Tce, Oban) flies between the island and Invercargill (adult/child one way $105/65, return $185/105). Flights depart three times daily year-round. Phone ahead for occasional discount and standby fares. The bus trip from the island's airstrip to Oban is included in the fare.

Boat
The passenger-only **Stewart Island Experience Ferry** (Map p369; ☎ 0800 000 511, 03-212 7660; www.stewartislandexperience.co.nz; Main Wharf) runs between Bluff and Oban (adult/child $63/31.50) around three times daily. Book a few days ahead in summer. The crossing takes one hour and can be a rough ride. The company also runs a shuttle between Bluff and Invercargill (adult/child $20/10) with pick-up and drop-off in Invercargill at the i-SITE, Tuatara Backpackers and Invercargill Airport. Cars and campervans can be stored in a secure car park at Bluff for an additional cost.

A shuttle also runs between Bluff and Queenstown (adult/child $65/32.50), and Bluff and Te Anau (adult/child $65/32.50) with pick-up and drop-off at the Real Journeys Visitor Centres.

GETTING AROUND
Water taxis offer pick-ups and drop-offs to remote parts of the island – a handy service for trampers. The taxis also service Ulva Island (return $25). Try **Stewart Island Water Taxi & Eco Guiding** (☎ 03-219 1394), **Aihe Eco Charters & Water Taxi** (☎ 03-219 1066; www.aihe.co.nz), **Sea View Water Taxi** (☎ 03-219 1014; www.seaviewwatertaxi.co.nz) or **Rakiura Adventure** (☎ 03-219 1013).

Rent a scooter (per half-/full day $55/65) or a car (per half-/full day $65/105) from Stewart Island Experience (p368).

Directory

CONTENTS

ACCOMMODATION

Across the South Island, you can bed down at night in guest houses that creak with history, facility-laden hotels, comfortably uniform motel units, beautifully situated campsites, and hostels that range in character from clean-living and relaxed to tirelessly party-prone.

Accommodation listings in this guidebook are ordered by budget from cheapest to most expensive. We generally designate a place as budget accommodation if it charges up to $100 per double. Accommodation qualifies as midrange if it costs roughly $100 to $160 per double, while we've given the top-end tag to double rooms costing over $160. Price ranges generally increase by 20% to 25% in Christchurch. Here you can still find budget accommodation at up to $100 per double, but

BOOK YOUR STAY ONLINE

For more accommodation reviews and recommendations by Lonely Planet authors, check out the online booking service at www.lonelyplanet.com/hotels. You'll find the true, insider low-down on the best places to stay. Reviews are thorough and independent. Best of all, you can book online.

midrange stretches from $100 to $200, with top-end rooms more than $200.

If you're travelling during peak tourist seasons, book your bed well in advance. Accommodation is most in demand (and at its priciest) during the summer holidays from Christmas to late January, at Easter, and during winter in snowy resort towns like Queenstown. At other times, weekday rates may be cheaper than weekend rates (except in business-style hotels in larger cities, where the reverse applies), and you'll certainly discover that low-season rates abound. When they're not run off their feet, accommodation operators often offer walk-in rates that are significantly below advertised rates – ask late in the day. Also see the big-name global accommodation websites (www.wotif.co.nz, www.lastminute.co.nz, www.hotels.co.nz etc) for last-minute deals.

Visitor information centres provide reams of local accommodation information, often in the form of folders detailing facilities and up-to-date prices; many can also make bookings on your behalf. Alternatively, flick through one of NZ's free, widely available accommodation directories, including the annual *New Zealand Accommodation Guide* published by the **Automobile Association** (AA; www.aatravel.co.nz), as well as the *Holiday Parks & Campgrounds* and *Motels, Motor Lodges & Apartments* directories produced by **Jasons** (www.jasons.com).

B&Bs & Guest houses

Bed and breakfast (B&B) accommodation in private homes is a growth industry in NZ, popping up in the middle of cities, in rural hamlets and on stretches of isolated coastline, with rooms on offer in everything from sub-

DIRECTORY

urban bungalows to stately manors owned by one family for generations.

Guest houses are usually spartan, cheap, 'private' (unlicensed) hotels, mostly low-key places patronised by people who eschew the impersonal atmosphere of many motels. Some guest houses are reasonably fancy and offer self-contained rooms.

Although breakfast is included at genuine B&Bs, it may or may not feature at guest houses. Your morning meal may be 'continental' (cereal, toast and tea or coffee), 'hearty continental' (add yoghurt, fruit, home-baked bread or muffins), or a stomach-loading cooked meal including eggs, bacon and sausages. Some B&B hosts, especially in isolated locations or within the smaller towns where restaurants are limited, may cook dinner for guests and advertise dinner, bed and breakfast (DB&B) packages.

Tariffs are typically in the $120 to $180 bracket (per double), though some places charge upwards of $300 per double. Some hosts continue to be cheeky-as-a-Kea, charging hefty prices for what is, in essence, a bedroom in their home. Many upmarket B&Bs demand bookings and deposits at least a month in advance, and enforce strict and expensive cancellation policies – ie cancel within a week of your arrival date and you'll forfeit your deposit plus the balance of the room rate. Check conditions before you book.

New Zealand's *Bed and Breakfast Directory* (www.bed-and-breakfast.co.nz) and *Bed & Breakfast Book* (www.bnb.co.nz) are available online, and at bookshops and visitor information centres.

Camping & Campervan Parks

Campers and campervan drivers alike converge upon NZ's hugely popular 'holiday parks', slumbering peacefully in powered and unpowered sites, cheap bunk rooms (dorm rooms), cabins and self-contained units that are often called motels or tourist flats. Well-equipped communal kitchens, dining areas and games and TV rooms often feature. In cities, holiday parks are usually a fair way from the action, but in smaller towns they can be impressively central or near lakes, beaches, rivers and forests.

The nightly cost of holiday-park camping is usually between $15 and $18 per adult, with children charged half-price; powered sites are a couple of dollars more. Cabin/unit accommodation normally ranges from $60 to $120 per double. Unless noted otherwise, the prices we've listed for campsites, campervan sites, huts and cabins are for two people.

If you'll gladly swap facilities for wilder, less-developed locations such as national parks, head for one of the 250-plus, vehicle-accessible camping grounds managed by the **Department of Conservation** (DOC; www.doc.govt.nz). DOC also looks after hundreds of backcountry huts, most of which can only be reached on foot. For more information, see Tramping (p76), and go to DOC's website www.camping.org.nz for more tips on freedom camping around NZ.

Farmstays

Farmstays open the door on the agricultural side of NZ life, with visitors encouraged to get some dirt beneath their fingernails at

---

PRACTICALITIES

- For weights and measures, NZ uses the metric system.

- DVDs and videos viewed in NZ are based on the PAL system – the same system used in Australia, the UK and most of Europe.

- Use a three-pin adaptor (the same as in Australia; different to British three-pin adaptors) to plug yourself into the electricity supply (230V AC, 50Hz).

- For news, leaf through Wellington's *Dominion Post* or Christchurch's *The Press* newspapers, or check out www.stuff.co.nz.

- Tune in to Radio National for current affairs and Concert FM for classical and jazz (see www.radionz.co.nz for frequencies). Kiwi FM (www.kiwifm.co.nz) plays 100% NZ music; Radio Hauraki (www.hauraki.co.nz) cranks out classic rock (too much Split Enz is barely enough…).

- Watch one of the national government-owned TV stations (TV One, TV2, TVNZ 6, TVNZ 7, Maori TV and the 100% Maori language Te Reo) or the subscriber-only Sky TV (www.skytv.co.nz).

WWOOFING

If you don't mind getting your hands dirty, an economical way of travelling around NZ involves doing some voluntary work as a member of **Willing Workers on Organic Farms** (WWOOF; ☎ 03-544 9890; www.wwoof.co.nz). Membership of this popular, well-established international organisation (which has representatives in Africa, Asia, North America, Europe and Australia) scores you access to many hundreds of organic and permaculture farms, market gardens and other environmentally sound cottage industries across the country. Down on the farm, in exchange for a hard day's work, owners provide food, accommodation and some hands-on organic farming experience. Contact farm owners a week or two beforehand to arrange your stay, as you would for a hotel or hostel – don't turn up unannounced!

A one-year online membership costs $40 (for one person, or two people travelling together); or $50 for online membership and to have a farm-listing book mailed to you. You should be part of a Working Holiday Scheme (p391) when you visit NZ, as the immigration department considers WWOOFers to be working.

One word of caution: it seems that some hostels have started employing travellers under the name of WWOOFing, without requiring membership or providing any of the benefits (not to mention the lack of an organic farm). It's a vague kind of exploitation, and probably harmless, but it's a definite misnomer.

orchards, and dairy, sheep and cattle farms. Costs can vary widely, with B&B generally ranging from $80 to $120. Some farms have separate cottages where you can fix your own food, while others offer low-cost, shared, backpacker-style accommodation.

Farm Helpers in NZ (FHINZ; www.fhinz.co.nz) produces a booklet ($25) that lists around 190 farms throughout NZ providing lodging in exchange for four- to six-hours work per day. **Rural Holidays NZ** (☎ 03-355 6218; www.ruralholidays.co.nz) lists farmstays and homestays throughout the country on its website. See also the WWOOFing boxed text on p377.

Hostels

The South Island is packed to the rafters with backpacker hostels, ranging from small, homestay-style affairs with a handful of beds to refurbished hotels with scuffed facades and the towering modern structures you'll find in the big cities. Hostel bed prices listed throughout this book are the non-membership rates.

If you're a Kiwi travelling in your own country, be warned that some hostels only admit overseas travellers, typically inner-city places. If you encounter such discrimination, either try another hostel or insist that you're a genuine traveller and not a bedless neighbour.

HOSTEL ORGANISATIONS

NZ's biggest hostel group is **Budget Backpacker Hostels** (BBH; ☎ 03-379 3014; www.bbh.co.nz), which has around 320 hostels on its books, including homestays and farmstays. Membership costs $45, including a $20 phonecard, and entitles you to stay at member hostels at a cost no greater than the rates advertised in the annual (free) *BBH Backpacker Accommodation* booklet. Non-members pay an extra $3 per night, though not all hostel owners charge the difference. Pick up a membership card from any member hostel, or have one mailed to you overseas for $50 (including postage; see the website for details). BBH rates each hostel according to traveller feedback, using a percentage figure that supposedly tells you how good (or at least how popular) each hostel is.

NZ's **Youth Hostels Association** (YHA; ☎ 0800 278 299, 03-379 9970; www.yha.co.nz) has been around for more than 75 years and has hostels in 54 prime NZ locations. The YHA is part of the **Hostelling International** (HI; www.hihostels.com) network. If you're already an HI member in your own country, your membership entitles you to use NZ hostels. If you don't already have a membership card from home, you can buy one at major NZ YHA hostels for $40 for 12 months, or book online and have your card mailed to you overseas for $50. Nightly charges are usually between $20 and $40 per person for members; hostels also take non-YHA members for an extra $3 per night.

YHA hostels provide reliable, basic accommodation for individuals, families and groups in dorms (bunk rooms, usually with four to six beds) and most also have a supply of single, twin and double rooms, sometimes

DIRECTORY

with bathrooms. They have 24-hour access, cooking facilities, a communal area with a TV, laundry facilities and, in larger hostels, travel offices. There's often a maximum-stay period (usually five to seven days). NZ YHA hostels supply all bed linen so you don't need to bring a sleeping bag. The annual *YHA New Zealand Hostel & Discount Guide* booklet details all Kiwi hostels and member discounts (transport, activities etc). Stuff their *Backpacker Map* in your pocket for on-the-road reference.

VIP Backpackers (www.vip.co.nz) run around 70 NZ hostels, mainly in the cities and major tourist spots. VIP is an international organisation with a large network of hostels in nearby Fiji, Australia, southern Africa, Europe and America. For around $52 ($60 including postage) you'll receive a 12-month membership entitling you to a $1 discount on accommodation. You can join online (www.vipbackpackers.com), at VIP hostels or at larger agencies dealing in backpacker travel.

Base Backpackers (www.stayatbase.com) have South Island hostels in Queenstown, Wanaka and Christchurch. Expect clean dorms, girls-only areas and party opportunities aplenty.

INDEPENDENT HOSTELS
NZ is an incubator for independent hostels, hatching them across both islands at an impressive rate. Owners try hard to differentiate their properties from their clubby competitors: some promote low-key ambience, lazy gardens, personable management and avoidance of noisy bus groups of backpackers while others bury you in extras such as free breakfasts, free DVDs, spa pools, use of bikes and kayaks, shuttle buses, theme nights and tour bookings. This is usually a successful formula, but with individuality comes risk: if possible, check out your accommodation before handing over the cash to ensure the atmosphere and facilities correspond with your expectations. If travelling with your family, note that a number of hostels designate themselves 'unsuitable for children'.

Independent backpacker establishments typically charge $20 to $30 for a dorm bed, $40 to $50 for a single and $50 to $80 for a twin or double room (usually with shared bathroom facilities). Some also have space for a few tents.

Hotels & Motels
The least expensive form of South Island hotel accommodation is the humble pub. As is often the case elsewhere, some old pubs are full of character and local characters, while others are grotty, ramshackle places that are best avoided, especially by women travelling solo. If you're renting a room above a pub towards the end of the week, check whether there's a band cranking out the tunes that night – you could be in for some sleeplessness. In the cheapest pubs, singles/doubles might cost as little as $30/50 (with a shared bathroom down the hall), though $50/70 is more common.

At the other end of the hotel scale are five-star international chains, resort complexes and architecturally splendorous boutique hotels, all of which charge a hefty premium for their mod cons, snappy service and/or historic opulence. We quote 'rack rates' (official advertised rates) for such places throughout this book, but discounts and special deals often mean you won't have to pay these.

The South Island's towns have a glut of nondescript, low-rise motels and 'motor lodges', charging between $80 and $160 for double rooms. These tend to be squat structures congregating just outside CBDs, or skulking by highways on the edge of towns. Most are modernish (though decor is often mired in the '80s) and have similar facilities (tea- and coffee-making, fridge, TV). Prices vary with standard. Some Kiwis refer to the actual room as a 'motel', rather than the collective complex of rooms – so you might hear, 'Sorry, our motels are full tonight', as opposed to, 'Sorry, our motel is full tonight'.

Rental Accommodation
The basic Kiwi holiday home is called a 'bach' (short for 'bachelor' as they were often used by single men as hunting and fishing hideouts); in Otago and Southland they're known as 'cribs'. These are simple self-contained cottages that can be rented in rural and coastal areas, often in isolated locations. They can be handy for longer stays in a region, although some are only available for one or two nights at a time. Prices are typically $80 to $130 per night, which isn't bad for a whole house or self-contained bungalow.

For more upmarket holiday houses, the current trend is to throw rusticity to the wind and erect luxurious cottages on beautiful nature-surrounded plots. Expect to pay anything from $120 to $400 a double.

Good websites to help you find a bach or holiday house include www.holidayhomes. co.nz and the AA's www.bookabach.co.nz; for swanky self-contained apartments try www. newzealand-apartments.co.nz. If it's a longer stay you're thinking about, check out www. nzflats.co.nz.

ACTIVITIES

See the Active South Island chapter (p72) for more info on NZ's outdoor-activity smorgasbord.

Aerial Sightseeing

Small planes and helicopters circle the skies on sightseeing trips (called 'flightseeing' by the locals) all over NZ, operating from local aerodromes. It's a great (but not particularly environmentally friendly) way to absorb the country's contrasting landscapes, soaring mountains and seldom-viewed terrain deep within national parks. Some of the most photo-worthy trips take place over Mt Cook (p263), the West Coast glaciers (p204) and Fiordland (from Te Anau; p341).

A far more sedate approach is to jump in a hot-air balloon. A float above Methven (p248) grants you spectacular views of the Southern Alps and contrasting Canterbury Plains, and there are also balloon trips from Queenstown.

Fishing

Thanks to the introduction of trout, salmon, perch and char (among other species), NZ has become one of the world's great recreational fisheries. South Island rivers and lakes also fare well on the trout index, most notably the Mataura River (Southland) and Lake Brunner and the Arnold River (the West Coast). The rivers of Otago and Southland have some of the best salmon fishing in the world.

The South Island's colder waters, especially around the Marlborough Sound, are great for snapper, hake, hapuku, trumpeter, butterfish, ling, barracouta and blue cod. Kaikoura Peninsula offers good surfcasting. Catch and cook your own blue cod off Stewart Island; Kurow, in the Waitaki Valley, North Otago, is good for salmon and trout.

You can hire fishing gear at sports stores in larger towns. If you bring your own rods and tackle they may have to be treated by NZ quarantine officials, especially if they're made with natural materials such as cane or feathers.

A fishing permit is required to fish in inland waters. Sold at sport shops, permits cover particular regions and are valid for a day, month or season. Consult local visitor information centres or DOC offices (p390) for details. Other fishy business is covered at www.fishing.net.nz, a huge website covering recreational fishing in NZ. If you're interested in guided fishing trips, see the **New Zealand Professional Fishing Guides' Association** (www.nzpfga. com) website.

Golf

NZ has more golf courses per capita than any other country, and among over 400 courses there are some magnificently situated fairways and greens.

Popular courses include Clearwater, outside Christchurch; Terrace Downs, in the high country near Methven; and Millbrook, near Queenstown. The Hills course in Arrowtown proclaims itself 'Home to the NZ Golf Open'. The only catch is that you can't play there – it's strictly millionaire members-only.

The average green fee for an 18-hole course usually ranges from $30 to $50, though private resorts can charge a substantial amount more.

For more information check out www. nzgolf.org.nz.

Sailing

Surrounded by sea, NZ has a habit of producing some of the world's best mariners. If you're keen on yacht racing, try visiting the country's various sailing clubs and ask if you can help crew in local competitions. Otherwise, there are plenty of sailing operators who allow you to just laze around on deck or play a more hands-on role. The southern lakes (Te Anau and Wakatipu) and Nelson are good places to get some wind in your sails. Go to www.yachtingnz.org.nz for more details.

BUSINESS HOURS

Most shops and businesses open their doors at 9am and close at 5.30pm Monday to Friday, and either 12.30pm or 5pm on Saturday. Late-night shopping (until 9pm) happens in the larger cities on Thursday and/or Friday nights; Sunday trading is the norm in most big towns and cities. Supermarkets are usually open from 8am until at least 7pm, often until 9pm or later in cities. Dairies (corner

DIRECTORY

stores) and superettes (small supermarkets) close later than most shops.

Banks normally open from 9.30am to 4.30pm Monday to Friday (some city branches also open on Saturday mornings). Post offices are open 8.30am to 5pm Monday to Friday, with main branches also open 9.30am to 1pm Saturday; postal desks in newsagencies (Take Note, Paperplus) often open later.

Restaurants typically take orders until at least 9pm, but often serve food until 11pm or later on Friday and Saturday nights; the main restaurant strips in large cities keep longer hours throughout the week. Cafes sometimes open as early as 7am and close around 5pm, though cafe-bar hybrids push the envelope well into the night. Pubs usually serve food from noon to 2pm and from 6pm to 8pm. Pubs and bars generally start pouring drinks at noon and stay open until late, particularly from Thursday to Saturday.

Don't count on many attractions being open on Christmas Dayor Good Friday.

CHILDREN

For helpful general tips, see Lonely Planet's *Travel with Children.* All cities and most major towns have centrally located public rooms where mothers (and sometimes fathers) can go to nurse a baby or change a nappy (diaper); check with the local visitor information centre or city council, or ask a local – Kiwis are a friendly bunch!

Practicalities

Many motels and holiday parks have playgrounds, games and DVD players, and occasionally fenced swimming pools and trampolines. Cots, highchairs and baby baths aren't always easy to find at budget and midrange accommodation, but top-end hotels are usually able to supply them and the plushest places have child-minding services. B&Bs are not usually amenable to families – many of these businesses promote themselves as grown-up getaways where peace and quiet are valued above all else. Hostels focussing on the young backpacker demographic don't welcome kids either, but there are plenty of other hostels (including YHA hostels) that do.

There are plenty of so-called family restaurants in NZ, where toddlers' highchairs are provided and kids can choose from their own menu. Pubs often serve kids' meals and

most cafes and restaurants (with the exception of upmarket eateries) can handle the idea of child-sized portions.

For specialised childcare, look under 'baby-sitters' and 'child care centres' in the *Yellow Pages* directory or contact the local council.

Child concessions (and family rates) are often available for accommodation, tours, attraction entry fees, and air, bus and train transport, with discounts of as much as 50% off the adult rate. Do note, however, that the definition of 'child' can vary from under 12 to under 18 years; toddlers (under four years old) usually get free admission and transport.

NZ's medical services and facilities are world-class, with goods like formula and disposable nappies widely available in urban centres. Some smaller car-hire companies struggle with the concept of baby seats – double-check that the company you choose can supply the right size of seat for your child, and that the seat will be properly fitted. Some companies may legally require you to fit the seat yourself.

Sights & Activities

Fabulous kids' playgrounds (with slides, swings, see-saws etc) proliferate across NZ. Some regions produce free information booklets geared towards sights and activities for kids; one example is *Kidz Go!* (www.kidzgo. co.nz), which details child-friendly activities and restaurants in the larger urban centres. Ask at local visitor information centres. Other handy websites for families include www.kids pot.co.nz, with lots of kid-centric info from pregnancy through to school-age, and www. kidsnewzealand.com, which has plenty of activity suggestions. Finally, www.kidsfriendly nz.com has extensive links to various facets of kiddy-culture.

CLIMATE CHARTS

NZ sits smack-bang in the Roaring Forties, which means it gets 'freshened' (some say blasted) by cool, damp winds blowing in from the Tasman Sea and is consistently slapped by the winds howling through Cook Strait.

On the South Island, the Southern Alps act as a barrier for these moisture-laden easterlies, creating a wet climate on the western side of the mountains (around 7500mm of rain annually!), and a dry climate on the eastern

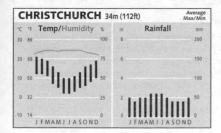

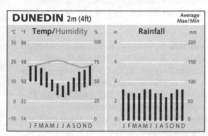

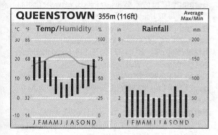

side (about 330mm). After dumping their moisture, the winds continue east, gathering heat and speed as they blow downhill and cross the Canterbury Plains; in summer this katabatic or föhn wind can be hot and fierce.

See p18 for further seasonal instruction.

CUSTOMS REGULATIONS

For the low-down on what you can and can't bring into NZ, see the **New Zealand Customs Service** (www.customs.govt.nz) website.

When entering NZ you can bring most articles in free of duty provided customs is satisfied they're for personal use and that you'll be taking them with you when you leave. There's a per person duty-free allowance of 1125mL of spirits or liqueur, 4.5L of wine or beer, 200 cigarettes (or 50 cigars or 250g of tobacco) and dutiable goods up to the value of $700. Customs officers are obviously fussy about drugs, so declare all medicines. Bio-security

is another customs buzzword – authorities are serious about keeping out any diseases that may harm NZ's agricultural industry. Tramping gear such as boots and tents will be checked and may need to be cleaned before being allowed in; ditto golf clubs and bicycles. You must declare any plant or animal products (including anything made of wood), and food of any kind. You'll also come under greater scrutiny if you've arrived via Africa, southeast Asia or South America. Weapons and firearms are either prohibited or require a permit and safety testing.

DANGERS & ANNOYANCES

Although it's no more dangerous than other developed countries, violent crime does happen in NZ, so it's worth taking sensible precautions on the streets at night or if staying in remote areas. Gang culture permeates some parts of the country; give any black-jacketed, insignia-wearing groups a wide berth.

Theft, primarily from cars, is a *major* problem around NZ, and travellers are viewed as easy marks. Avoid leaving valuables in vehicles, no matter where it's parked; the worst places to tempt fate are tourist parking areas and the car parks at trailheads. If the crown jewels simply must be left behind, pack them out of sight in the boot (trunk) of the car – but carry your passport with you, just in case.

Don't underestimate the dangers posed by NZ's unpredictable, ever-changing climate, especially in high-altitude areas.

NZ has thankfully been spared from the proliferation of venomous creatures found in neighbouring Australia (spiders, snakes, jellyfish etc). Sharks hang out in NZ waters, but are well fed by the abundant marine life and rarely nibble on humans; that said, attacks on humans do occasionally occur. Much greater hazards in the ocean, however, are the rips and undertows that plague some beaches and can quickly drag swimmers out to sea. Take notice of local warnings when swimming, surfing or diving.

The South Island's roads are often made hazardous by speeding locals, wide-cornering campervans and traffic-ignorant sheep. Set yourself a reasonable itinerary instead of careening around the country at top speed and keep your eyes on the road no matter how photogenic the scenery may be. If you're cycling, take care – motorists can't always overtake easily on skinny roads.

SANDFLIES *Sir Ian McKellen*

As an unpaid but enthusiastic proselytiser on behalf of all things Kiwi, including the New Zealand tourist industry, I hesitate to mention the well-kept secret of sandflies. I first met them en masse at the glorious Milford Sound, where visitors (after the most beautiful drive in the world) are met, at least during the summer, by crowds of the little buggers. There are patent unctions that cope, and tobacco repels them too, but I would hope that travellers find them an insignificant pest compared with the glory of their habitat.

Oddly, when actually filming scenes for *Lord of the Rings*, I don't recall being bothered by sandflies at all. Honestly. Had there been, we would have set the orcs on them.

Sir Ian McKellen is a UK-based actor who spent several years in NZ filming and has become something of an unofficial ambassador for NZ tourism.

In the annoyances category, NZ's sandflies are a royal pain (see the boxed text above). Lather yourself with insect repellent in coastal areas.

DISCOUNT CARDS

The **International Student Travel Confederation** (ISTC; www.istc.org) is an international collective of specialist student travel organisations and the body behind the internationally recognised International Student Identity Card (ISIC). The card is issued to full-time students aged 12 years and over and provides red-hot discounts on accommodation, transport and admission to attractions. The ISTC also produces the International Youth Travel Card (IYTC), available to folks between 12 and 26 who are not full-time students, and gives equivalent benefits to the ISIC. A similar ISTC brainchild is the International Teacher Identity Card (ITIC), available to teaching professionals. All three cards (NZ$25 each) are available online at www.isiccard.co.nz, or from student travel companies like **STA Travel** (www.statravel.co.nz).

Another option is the **New Zealand Card** (www.newzealandcard.com), a $35 discount pass that'll score you between 5% and 50% off a range of accommodation, tours, sights and activities.

Senior and disabled travellers who live overseas will find that the cards issued by their respective countries are not always 'officially' recognised in NZ, but that many places still acknowledge such cards and grant concessions where applicable.

EMBASSIES & CONSULATES

Most principal diplomatic representations to NZ are in Wellington, with a few in Auckland. Embassies, consulates and high commissions include:

Australia (Map p90; ☎ 04-473 6411; www.australia.org.nz; 72-76 Hobson St, Thorndon, Wellington)

Canada (Map p90; ☎ 04-473 9577; www.newzealand.gc.ca; L11, 125 The Terrace, Wellington)

Fiji (Map p90; ☎ 04-473 5401; www.fiji.org.nz; 31 Pipitea St, Thorndon, Wellington)

France (Map p94; ☎ 04-384 2555; www.ambafrance-nz.org; 34-42 Manners St, Wellington)

Germany (Map p90; ☎ 04-473 6063; www.wellington.diplo.de; 90-92 Hobson St, Thorndon, Wellington)

Ireland (☎ 09-977 2252; www.ireland.co.nz; L7, Citigroup Bldg, 23 Customs St E, Auckland)

Israel (Map p90; ☎ 04-471 0079; L13, Greenock House, 102 Lambton Quay, Wellington)

Japan (Map p94; ☎ 04-473 1540; www.nz.emb-japan.go.jp; L18 & L19, The Majestic Centre, 100 Willis St, Wellington)

Netherlands (Map p90; ☎ 04-471 6390; www.netherlandsembassy.co.nz; L10, Investment House, cnr Featherston & Ballance Sts, Wellington)

UK (Map p90; ☎ 04-924 2888; www.britain.org.nz; 44 Hill St, Thorndon, Wellington)

USA (Map p90; ☎ 04-462 6000; http://wellington.usembassy.gov; 29 Fitzherbert Tce, Thorndon, Wellington)

It's important to know what your national embassy can and can't do to help you if you get into trouble. Generally speaking, embassies won't be much help in emergencies if the fix you're in is self-induced. While in NZ you're bound by NZ laws – your embassy will not be sympathetic if you end up in jail after committing a crime locally, even if such actions are legal in your own country.

In genuine emergencies you might get some assistance, but only if other channels have been exhausted. For example, if you need to get home urgently, a free ticket is exceedingly unlikely – the embassy would expect you to have insurance. If you have all your money and documents stolen, your embassy may assist with getting a new passport, but a loan for onward travel is out of the question.

FESTIVALS & EVENTS

Want to plan your travels around the various food and wine, sporting or arts festivals staged throughout the South Island? Check out the **Tourism New Zealand** (www.newzealand.com/travel) website – click on Sights, Activities & Events, then Events Calendar. See also www.nzlive.com and www.eventfinder.co.nz.

Details of South Island festivals and events are provided throughout destination chapters in this book. A handful of highlights:

Goldrush Multisport Event (www.goldrush.co.nz) 376km of kayaking, cycling and running along old gold-mining trails in Central Otago during March.

Marlborough Wine Festival (www.wine-marlborough-festival.co.nz) Features wine from over 50 Marlborough wineries, fine food and entertainment. Over-indulgence aplenty. Held in February.

New Zealand Cup & Show Week (www.nzcupand show.co.nz) Have a flutter on the nags or inspect some prize bulls in Christchurch in November.

New Zealand International Comedy Festival (www.comedyfestival.co.nz) Three-week laugh-fest in May with venues across various regional centres.

New Zealand International Film Festivals (www. enzedff.co.nz) After separate film festivals in Dunedin and Christchurch, a selection of flicks hits the road for screenings in regional towns from July to November.

Rugby World Cup (www.rugbyworldcup.com) NZ hosts the greatest rugby show on Earth in September/October 2011 (go All Blacks!).

Wildfoods Festival (www.wildfoods.co.nz) Eat some worms, hare testicles or crabs at Hokitika's comfort-zone-challenging food fest in March.

FOOD

The NZ foodie scene once slavishly reflected Anglo-Saxon stodge, but nowadays the country's restaurants and cafes are adept at throwing together trad staples (lamb, beef, venison, green-lipped mussels) with Asian, European and pan-Pacific flair.

Eateries themselves range from fry-'em-up fish-and-chip shops and pub bistros; to cafes drowned in faux-European, grungy or retro stylings; restaurant-bars with full à la carte service; and fine-dining establishments with linen is so crisp you're afraid to prop your elbows on it. For online listings, see www.dineout.co.nz and www.menus.co.nz.

Most large urban centres have at least one dedicated vegetarian cafe or restaurant. See the **New Zealand Vegetarian Society** (www.vegsoc.org.nz) restaurant guide for listings.

On the liquid front, NZ wine is world class, and you'll be hard-pressed to find a South Island town of any size without decent espresso. NZ microbrewed beers have also become mainstream.

Eating recommendations in this book are in budget order, from cheapest to most expensive. Cafes are often the best value, with bang-up meals in casual surrounds for under $20. Some city pubs label themselves 'gastropubs', offering classy restaurant-style fare, but most pubs serve standard bistro meals, usually under $20. Midrange restaurants can charge as much as $30 for a main course, but don't be surprised to see mains priced from $35 to $45 at trendy top-end restaurants.

Smoking is banned in all restaurants, pubs and bars. Tipping in restaurants and cafes is not expected.

For more info, see the Food & Drink chapter (p57).

GAY & LESBIAN TRAVELLERS

The G&L tourism industry in NZ isn't as high-profile as in neighbouring Australia, but homosexual communities are prominent, with myriad support organisations. NZ has relatively progressive laws protecting the rights of gays and lesbians; the legal minimum age for sex between consenting persons is 16. Generally speaking Kiwis are fairly relaxed and accepting about homosexuality, but that's not to say that homophobia doesn't exist.

There are loads of websites dedicated to gay and lesbian travellers. **Gay Tourism New Zealand** (www.gaytourismnewzealand.com) is a good starting point, with links to various sites. Other worthwhile queer websites include www.gaynz.com, www.gaynz.net.nz and www.lesbian.net.nz. For accommodation listings see www.gaystay.co.nz. Queenstown visitors should check out www.gayqueenstown.com.

Check out nationwide magazines like *express* (www.gayexpress.co.nz) every second Wednesday and *Out!* (www.out.co.nz) published every two months for the latest happenings, reviews and listings on the NZ gay scene.

Out Takes (www.outtakes.org.nz) is a G&L film festival staged in Christchurch in June, while Queenstown stages the annual **Gay Ski Week** (www.gayskiweeknz.com) in August/September.

DIRECTORY

HOLIDAYS
Public Holidays
NZ's main public holidays:
New Year 1 & 2 January
Waitangi Day 6 February
Easter Good Friday & Easter Monday; March/April
Anzac Day 25 April
Queen's Birthday 1st Monday in June
Labour Day 4th Monday in October
Christmas Day 25 December
Boxing Day 26 December

In addition, each NZ province has its own anniversary-day holiday. The dates of these provincial holidays vary – when these holidays fall between Friday and Sunday, they're usually observed the following Monday; if they fall between Tuesday and Thursday, they're held on the preceding Monday – the great Kiwi tradition of the 'long weekend' continues.

South Island provincial anniversary holidays:
Southland 17 January
Nelson 1 February
Otago 23 March
South Canterbury 25 September
Marlborough 1 November
Westland 1 December
Canterbury 16 December

School Holidays
The Christmas holiday season, from mid-December to late January, is part of the summer school vacation. It's the time you'll most likely find transport and accommodation booked out, and long, grumpy queues at tourist attractions. There are three shorter school-holiday periods during the year: from mid- to late April, early to mid-July, and mid-September to early October. For exact dates see the **Ministry of Education** (www.minedu.govt.nz) website.

INSURANCE
A watertight travel insurance policy covering theft, loss and medical problems is essential; nothing will ruin your holiday more quickly than an accident or having your duty-free digital camera pilfered. There are plenty of policies to choose from – compare the fine print and shop around.

Some policies specifically exclude designated 'dangerous activities' such as scuba diving, parasailing, bungy jumping, white-water rafting, motorcycling, skiing, and even bushwalking. If you plan on doing any of these things (a distinct possibility on the South Island), make sure the policy you choose covers you fully.

You may prefer a policy that pays doctors or hospitals directly rather than you having to pay on the spot and claim later. If you have to claim later make sure you keep all documentation. Some policies ask you to call back (reverse charges) to a centre in your home country where an immediate assessment of your problem is made. Check that the policy covers ambulances and emergency medical evacuations by air.

It's worth mentioning that under NZ law, you cannot sue for personal injury (other than exemplary damages). Instead, the country's **Accident Compensation Corporation** (ACC; www.acc.co.nz) administers an accident compensation scheme that provides accident insurance for NZ residents and visitors to the country, regardless of fault.

While some people cry foul of this arrangement, others point to the hugely expensive litigation 'industries' in other countries and raise a cheer. This scheme, however, does not cancel out the necessity for your own comprehensive travel insurance policy, as it doesn't cover you for such things as loss of income or treatment in your home country or ongoing illness.

See also p405 for notes on medical insurance. For car insurance information see p402.

Worldwide cover for travellers from over 44 countries is available online at www.lonelyplanet.com/bookings/insurance.do.

INTERNET ACCESS
Getting online in NZ is easy in all but the most remote locales. If you don't already have one, it's worth setting up a travelling address with one of the many free email services (www.yahoo.com, www.hotmail.com, www.gmail.com etc).

The internet icon (🖳) in accommodation, eating and drinking listings in this book indicates internet access is available (a kiosk or dedicated guest computer); the wi-fi icon (🛜) denotes wireless access.

For a list of useful NZ websites, see p21.

Internet Cafes
Internet cafes in the bigger urban centres or tourist areas are usually brimming with high-

speed terminals. Obnoxious teens often swamp the machines in the after-school hours – time your visit anytime other than 4pm to 6pm! Facilities are a lot more haphazard in small, out-of-the-way towns, where a so-called internet cafe could turn out to be a single terminal in the corner of a video store.

Most hostels make an effort to hook you up, with internet access sometimes free for guests. Many public libraries have free internet access too, but there can be a limited number of terminals – head for an internet cafe first.

Internet access at cafes ranges anywhere from $4 to $6 per hour – the lowest rates can be found in cities where competition and traveller numbers generate dirt-cheap prices. There's often a minimum period of access, usually 10 or 15 minutes.

Wireless Access & Internet Service Providers

Increasingly, you'll be able to find wi-fi access around the South Island, from hotel rooms to pub beer gardens to hostel dining rooms. Usually you have to be a guest or customer to access the internet at these locations – you'll be issued with a code, a wink and a secret handshake to enable you to get on-line. Sometimes it's free; sometimes there's a charge.

The country's main telecommunications company is **Telecom New Zealand** (www.telecom. co.nz), which has wireless hotspots around the country. If you have a wi-fi-enabled device, you can purchase a Telecom wireless prepaid card from participating hotspots. Alternatively, you can purchase a prepaid number from the login page and any wireless hotspot using your credit card. See the website for hotspot listings.

If you've brought your palmtop or note-book computer and want to get connected to a local internet service provider (ISP), there are plenty of options, though some limit their dial-up areas to major cities or particular regions. Major ISPs:

Clearnet (☎ 0508 888 800; www.clearnet.co.nz)
Earthlight (☎ 03-479 0303; www.earthlight.co.nz) Has a page on its website detailing prepaid internet access for travellers to NZ.
Slingshot (☎ 0800 892 000; www.slingshot.co.nz)
Xtra (☎ 0800 003 040; www.xtra.co.nz/products)

Wireless is more common, but if you're planning on manually plugging in, NZ uses British BT431A and RJ-11 jacks, but neither are universal; local electronics shops should be able to help. A lot of midrange accommodation and nearly all top-end hotels have wall sockets, but you'll be hit with expensive call charges. In most cheaper places you'll probably find that phones are hardwired into the wall.

Keep in mind that your PC-card modem may not work in NZ. The safest option is to buy a reputable 'global' modem before you leave home or buy a local PC-card modem once you get to NZ.

LEGAL MATTERS

Marijuana (aka 'New Zealand Green', 'electric puha' or 'dac') is widely indulged in but illegal, and anyone caught carrying this or other illicit drugs will have the book thrown at them. Even if the amount of drugs is small and the fine minimal, a conviction will still be recorded against you, which may affect your visa status.

Always carry your licence when driving; for more info, see p400. Drink-driving is a serious offence and remains a significant problem in NZ despite widespread campaigns and severe penalties. The legal blood alcohol limit is 0.08% for drivers over 20, and 0.03% for those under 20.

If you are arrested, it's your right to consult a lawyer before any formal questioning begins.

MAPS

Top-notch maps are widely available throughout NZ – from detailed street maps and atlases to topographic masterpieces.

The **Automobile Association** (AA; www.aa.co.nz) produces excellent city, town, regional, island and highway maps, available from their local offices; members of affiliated overseas automobile associations can obtain free maps and discounts on presentation of a membership card. The AA also produces a detailed *New Zealand Road Atlas*. Other reliable country-wide atlases, available from visitor information centres and bookshops, are published by Hema, KiwiMaps and Wises.

Land Information New Zealand (www.linz.govt. nz) publishes several exhaustive map series, including street, country and holiday maps, national and forest park maps, and topographical trampers' maps. Scan the larger bookshops, or try the nearest DOC office or visitor information centre for topo maps.

Online, log onto **AA SmartMap** (www.aamaps.co.nz) or the **Yellow Maps** (maps.yellowpages.co.nz) to pinpoint exact addresses in NZ cities and towns.

MONEY

See the Quick Reference section on the inside front cover for a list of exchange rates.

ATMs & Eftpos

Branches of the country's major banks, including the Bank of New Zealand, ANZ, Westpac and ASB, have 24-hour ATMs that accept cards from other banks and provide access to overseas accounts. You won't find ATMs everywhere, but they're widespread across both islands.

Many NZ businesses use electronic funds transfer at point of sale (Eftpos), a convenient service that allows you to use your bank card (credit or debit) to pay directly for services or purchases, and often withdraw cash as well. Eftpos is available practically everywhere, even in places where it's a long way between banks. Just like an ATM, you need to know your personal identification number (PIN) to use it.

Bank Accounts

We've heard mixed reports on how easy it is for nonresidents to open a bank account in NZ. Some sources say it's as simple as flashing a few pieces of ID, providing a temporary postal address (or your permanent address) and then waiting a few days while your request is processed. Other sources say that many banks won't allow visitors to open an account with them unless they're planning to stay in NZ for at least six months, or unless the application is accompanied by some proof of employment. Bank websites are also rather vague on the services offered to short-term visitors. If you think you'll need to open an account, do your homework before you arrive in the country and be prepared to shop around to get the best deal.

Credit & Debit Cards

Perhaps the safest place to keep your NZ travelling money is inside a plastic card! The most flexible option is to carry both a credit and a debit card.

Credit cards (Visa, MasterCard etc) are widely accepted for everything from a hostel bed to a bungy jump. Credit cards are pretty much essential if you want to hire a car. They can also be used for over-the-counter cash advances at banks and from ATMs, depending on the card, but be aware that such transactions incur charges. Charge cards such as Diners Club and Amex are not as widely accepted.

Apart from losing them, the obvious danger with credit cards is maxing out your limit and going home to a steaming pile of debt. A safer option is a debit card with which you can draw money directly from your home bank account using ATMs, banks or Eftpos machines. Any card connected to the international banking network (Cirrus, Maestro, Visa Plus and Eurocard) should work, provided you know your PIN. Fees for using your card at a foreign bank or ATM vary depending on your home bank; ask before you leave. Companies such as Travelex offer debit cards (Travelex calls them Cash Passport cards) with set withdrawal fees and a balance you can top-up from your personal bank account whilst on the road – nice one!

Currency

NZ's currency is the NZ dollar, comprising 100 cents. There are 10c, 20c, 50c, $1 and $2 coins, and $5, $10, $20, $50 and $100 notes. Prices are often still marked in single cents and then rounded to the nearest 10c when you hand over your money.

Unless otherwise noted, all prices quoted in this book are in NZ dollars. For an idea of the costs associated with travelling around the country, see p19.

There are no notable restrictions on importing or exporting travellers cheques. Though not prohibited, cash amounts equal to or in excess of the equivalent of NZ$10,000 (in any currency) must be declared on arrival or departure – you'll need to fill out a Border Cash Report.

Money changers

Changing foreign currency or travellers cheques is usually no problem at banks throughout the South Island or at licensed money changers such as Travelex (formerly Thomas Cook) in the major cities. Money changers can be found in all major tourist areas, cities and airports, and conveniently tend to stay open beyond normal business hours during the week (often open until 9pm).

Taxes & Refunds

The Goods and Services Tax (GST) is a flat 12.5% tax on all domestic goods and services. Prices in this book include GST, but look out for any small print announcing that the price is GST-exclusive. There's no GST refund available when you leave NZ.

Tipping

Tipping is completely optional in NZ, and staff do not depend on tips for income – the total at the bottom of a restaurant bill is all you need to pay (note that sometimes there's an additional service charge). That said, it's totally acceptable to reward good service and the tip you leave depends entirely on your satisfaction – between 5% and 10% of the bill is the norm.

Travellers Cheques

The ubiquity of debit- and credit-card access in NZ can make travellers cheques seem rather old-hat. Nevertheless, Amex, Travelex and other international brands of travellers cheques are easily exchanged. You need to present your passport for identification when cashing them. Fees per transaction for changing foreign-currency travellers cheques vary from bank to bank, while Amex or Travelex perform the task commission-free if you use their cheques. Private moneychangers found in the larger cities are sometimes commission free, but shop around for the best rates.

POST

The services offered by **New Zealand Post** (☎ 0800 501 501; www.nzpost.co.nz) are reliable and reasonably inexpensive. Within NZ standard post costs 50c for standard letters and postcards, and $1 for larger letters.

International destinations are divided into two zones: Australia and the South Pacific, and the rest of the world. Standard rates (express services also available):

Item	Aust & South Pacific	Rest of World
Postcard	$1.80	$1.80
Letter	$1.80	$2.30
Large letter	$2.30	$2.80
Oversize letter	$3.50	$5
Approx delivery (work days)	3-10	6-10

International parcel zones are the same as for letters; pricing depends on weight and whether you send the parcel 'economy' (three to five weeks), 'air' (one to two weeks) or 'express' (within a matter of days). To send parcels by 'air' is roughly 20% more expensive; by 'express' at least 50% more. Check out the incredibly precise calculator on the website.

Many NZ post offices are called 'PostShops' these days, as most have been removed from their traditional old buildings and set up in modern shop-style premises, but we still stubbornly refer to them as post offices throughout this guidebook. For standard post office opening hours, see p379. Stamps can usually also be purchased at supermarkets and bookshops.

You can have mail addressed to you care of 'Poste Restante, Main PostShop' in whichever town you require. Mail is usually held for 30 days and you need to provide some form of identification (such as a passport) to collect it.

SHOPPING

NZ isn't one of those countries where it's necessary to buy a T-shirt to help you remember your visit; the spectacular landscapes are mementoes in themselves, to be plucked later from the depths of memory or the innards of your camera. But there are numerous locally crafted items you can purchase for their own unique qualities.

Clothing

Christchurch (p232) boasts fashion-conscious boutiques ablaze with the sartorial flair of young and well-established NZ designers. Pick up new threads on Colombo St, High or Cashel Sts, then hit the bars and restaurants of SOL Sqaure and the Lichfield Lanes area.

Check out www.fashionz.co.nz for up-to-date information on the hottest designers and labels and where to find them. Keep an eye out for labels such as Zambesi, Kate Sylvester, Karen Walker, Trelise Cooper, NOM D and Little Brother.

To see just how far New Zealanders are prepared to push the boundaries of fashionable creativity, visit the amazing World of WearableArt & Classic Cars Museum (p154) in Nelson, or attend the namesake festival in Wellington (p101).

From the backs of NZ sheep come sheepskin products such as footwear (including the much-loved ugg boot) and beautiful woollen jumpers (jerseys or sweaters) made from hand-spun, hand-dyed wool. Other knitted knick-knacks include hats, gloves and scarves. Look for garments made from a lovely soft yarn that's a combination of merino wool and possum fur.

Long woollen Swanndri jackets, shirts and pullovers are so ridiculously practical, they're practically the national garment in country areas. Most common are the red-and-black or blue-and-black plaid ones; pick up 'Swannies' in outdoor-gear shops.

Crafts

Fine NZ craft products can be purchased in most sizable towns. Few (if any) places in the country are devoid of someone who's been inspired to hand-shape items for sale to passing visitors. In Christchurch, the Arts Centre (p219) offers dozens of shops and galleries selling locally designed and crafted jewellery, ceramics, glassware and accessories. The Nelson region (p149) is another very crafty place, heavily populated by galleries and the occasional market. Ditto Arrowtown (p319), an artsy enclave near Queenstown.

Maori Arts

Keep an eye out for intricate examples of Maori *whakairo rakau* (woodcarving). You'll pay a premium for high-quality work; avoid buying poor examples of the craft that lines the souvenir shops in Christchurch and Queenstown. Instead, visit the Visually Maori and Te Toi Mana galleries at the Arts Centre (p219).

Maori bone carvings are undergoing something of a renaissance around NZ. Maori artisans have always made bone carvings in the shape of humans and animals, but nowadays they cater to the tourist industry. Bone fish-hook pendants, carved in traditional Maori and modernised styles, are most common, worn on a leather string around the neck. To make your own bone carving, visit the Bone Dude (p222), or Bonz 'N' Stonz (p196), in Hokitika.

To confirm the authenticity of any Maori-made piece, see if it's accompanied by the trademark **toi iho** (www.toiiho.com), a symbol created by a Maori arts board to identify the output of individual artists or groups of artists of Maori descent. There are also modified versions of the trademark, identifying items produced by groups of 'mainly Maori' artists and via 'co-productions' between Maori and non-Maori artists. Do note that not all Maori artists are registered with this scheme.

Paua

Abalone shell, called paua in NZ, is carved into some beautiful ornaments and jewellery and is often used as an inlay in Maori carvings. Lovers of kitsch and general tackiness will find that it's also incorporated into generic souvenirs, often in delightfully unattractive ways. Shells are used as ashtrays in places where paua is plentiful. Be aware that it's illegal to take natural paua shells out of the country – only processed ornaments can be taken with you.

Pounamu

Maoris consider *pounamu* (greenstone, or jade or nephrite) to be a culturally invaluable raw material. It's found predominantly on the west coast of the South Island – Maoris called the island Te Wahi Pounamu (The Place of Greenstone) or Te Wai Pounamu (The Water of Greenstone).

You're unlikely to come across any *mere* (war clubs) in *pounamu* studios or souvenir shops, but you will find lots of stony green incarnations of Maori motifs. One of the most popular is the *hei tiki,* the name of which literally means 'hanging human form' – in Maori legend, Tiki was the first man created and *hei* is 'to hang'. They are tiny, stylised Maori figures, usually depicted with their tongue stuck out in warlike repose, worn on a leather string or chain around the neck. They've got great *mana* (power), but they also serve as fertility symbols. Other popular motifs are the *taniwha* (monster) and the *marakihau* (sea monster).

The best place to buy *pounamu* is Hokitika (p197), which is strewn with jade workshops and gift shops. To see impressive collections both ancient and modern, visit the Otago Museum (p269) in Dunedin and Canterbury Museum (p219) in Christchurch.

Traditionally, *pounamu* is bought as a gift for another person, not for yourself. Ask a few questions to ensure you're buying from a local operator who crafts local stone, not an offshore company selling imported (usually Chinese or European) jade.

TELEPHONE

Telecom New Zealand (www.telecom.co.nz) is the country's key domestic player and also has a stake in the local mobile (cell) market. Another mobile network option is **Vodafone** (www.vodafone.co.nz).

Local & International Calls

INFORMATION & TOLL-FREE CALLS

Numbers starting with ☎ 0900 are usually recorded information services, charging upwards of $1 per minute (more from mobiles); these numbers cannot be dialled from payphones.

Toll-free numbers in NZ have the prefix ☎ 0800 or ☎ 0508 and can be called free of charge from anywhere in the country, though they may not be accessible from certain areas or from mobile phones. Telephone numbers beginning with ☎ 0508, ☎ 0800 or ☎ 0900 cannot be dialled from outside NZ.

INTERNATIONAL CALLS

Payphones allow international calls but the cost and international dialling code for calls will vary depending on which provider you're using. International calls from NZ are relatively inexpensive and subject to specials that reduce the rates even more, so it's worth shopping around – consult the *Yellow Pages* for a list of providers.

The toll-free Country Direct service connects callers in NZ with overseas operators to make reverse-charge (collect) or credit-card calls. Country Direct numbers and other details are listed in the front of telephone directories or are available from the NZ international operator. The access number varies, depending on the number of phone companies in the country you call, but is usually ☎ 000-9 (followed by the country code).

To make international calls from NZ you need to dial the international access code (☎ 00), the country code, and the area code (without the initial 0). So for a London number you'd dial ☎ 00-44-20, then the number. Certain operators will have you dial a special code to access their service.

If dialling NZ from overseas, the country code is ☎ 64, followed by the appropriate area code minus the initial zero.

LOCAL CALLS

Local calls from private phones are free! Local calls from payphones cost 50c, though coin-operated payphones are scarce – you'll need a phonecard (see p389). Both involve unlimited talk time. Calls to mobile phones attract higher rates and are timed.

LONG-DISTANCE CALLS & AREA CODES

NZ uses regional area codes for long-distance calls, which can be made from any payphone.

If you're making a local call (ie to someone else in the same town), you don't need to dial the area code. But if you're dialling within a region (even if it's to a nearby town) you do have to dial the area code, regardless of the fact that the place you're calling has the same code as the place you're dialling from. All the numbers in this book are listed with their relevant area codes.

Mobile Phones

Local mobile phone numbers are preceded by the prefix ☎ 021, ☎ 025 or ☎ 027. Mobile phone coverage can be patchy away from urban centres on the South Island.

If you want to bring your own phone and use a prepaid service with a local SIM card, **Vodafone** (www.vodafone.co.nz) is a practical option. Any Vodafone shop (found in most major towns) will set you up with a SIM card and phone number (about $35, including $10 worth of calls); top-ups can be purchased at newsagencies, post offices and shops practically anywhere.

Alternatively, if you don't bring your own phone from home, you can rent one from **Vodafone Rental** (www.vodarent.co.nz) priced from $6/25 per day/week, with pick-up and drop-off outlets at NZ's major airports. You can also rent a SIM card for $2.50 per day (minimum charge $10) or $40 per month. You can arrange this in advance via the website. We've also had some positive feedback on **Phone Hire New Zealand** (www. phonehirenz.com), who hire out mobile phones, SIM cards, modems and GPS systems.

Phonecards

NZ has a wide range of phonecards available, which can be bought at hostels, newsagencies and post offices for a fixed dollar value (usually $5, $10, $20 and $50). These can be used with any public or private phone by dialling a toll-free access number and then the PIN number on the card. It's worth shopping around – call rates vary from company to company.

TIME

Being close to the international date line, NZ is one of the first places in the world to start the new day (Pitt Island in the Chatham Islands sees the first sunrise each new year). NZ is 12 hours ahead of GMT/UTC and two hours ahead of Australian Eastern Standard Time.

In summer, NZ observes daylight-saving time, where clocks are wound forward by one hour on the last Sunday in September; clocks are wound back on the first Sunday of the following April.

So (excluding the duration of daylight saving), when it's noon in NZ it's 10am in Sydney, 8am in Singapore, midnight in London and 5pm the previous day in San Francisco. The Chathams are 45 minutes ahead of NZ's main islands.

TOURIST INFORMATION

Even before the success of recent international marketing campaigns and the country's cult status as a pseudo-Middle-earth, NZ had a highly developed tourism infrastructure that busily generated mountains of brochures and booklets, plus information-packed internet pages.

Local Tourist Offices

Almost every Kiwi city or town – whether it has any worthwhile attractions or not – seems to have a visitor information centre. The bigger centres stand united within the outstanding i-SITE (www.newzealand.com/travel/i-sites) network, which is affiliated with Tourism New Zealand (the official national tourism body), and have trained staff, abundant information on local activities and attractions, and free brochures and maps. Staff also act as travel agents, booking activities, transport and accommodation. Not to be outdone, staff at smaller centres are often overwhelmingly helpful.

Bear in mind that many information centres only promote accommodation and tour operators who are paying members of the local tourist association, while others are ironically hamstrung by the demands of local operators that they be represented equally. In other words, sometimes information centre staff aren't supposed to recommend one activity or accommodation provider over another, a curious situation that exists in highly competitive environments.

There's also a network of Department Of Conservation (DOC; www.doc.govt.nz) visitor centres to help you plan your recreation activities and make bookings. Visitor centres usually have displays and info on local lore, and NZ's unique flora and fauna and biodiversity challenges. DOC visitor centres are found in national parks, major regional centres and in each of the major cities. It's important to check local weather conditions at the nearest visitor centre before you set out. Collect the DOC visitor centres brochure from the website or at visitor centres.

In this book, contact details for local visitor information centres or offices are listed under Information headings in relevant city and town sections.

Tourist Offices Abroad

Tourism New Zealand (☎ 04-917 5400; www.new zealand.com) has representatives in various countries around the world. A good place for pretrip research is the official website (emblazoned with the hugely successful 100% Pure New Zealand branding), which has information in several languages (including German and Japanese). Overseas offices:

Australia (☎ 02-8299 4800; L12, 61 York St, Sydney)
UK & Europe (☎ 020-7930 1662; New Zealand House, 80 Haymarket, London, UK)
USA & Canada (☎ 310-395 7480; 501 Santa Monica Blvd, Santa Monica, USA)

TRAVELLERS WITH DISABILITIES

Kiwi accommodation generally caters fairly well for travellers with disabilities, with a significant number of hostels, hotels, motels and B&Bs equipped with wheelchair-accessible rooms. Many tourist attractions similarly provide wheelchair access, with wheelchairs often available at key attractions with advance notice.

Tour operators with accessible vehicles operate from most major centres. Key cities are also serviced by kneeling buses(buses that hydraulically stoop down to kerb level to allow easy access); taxi companies offer wheelchair-accessible vans. Large car-hire firms (Avis, Hertz etc) provide cars with hand controls at no extra charge; advance notice is required. Mobility parking permits are available from branches of **CCS Disability Action** (☎ 0800 227 200, 04-384 5677; www.ccsdisabilityaction.org.nz) in the main centres.

For good general information, see NZ's **disability information website** (www.weka.net. nz). Click on Living with a Disability, then categories including Transport, Holiday Accommodation, and Travel and Tourism. The latter lists NZ tour operators catering specifically to travellers with disabilities.

Travellers with disabilities need not miss out on NZ's great outdoors. If you'd like to tackle a wilderness pathway, pick up a copy of *Accessible Walks* by Anna and Andrew Jameson ($26), which offers first-hand descriptions of more than 100 South Island walks. It's available online at www.acces siblewalks.co.nz. If cold-weather activity is more your thing, see the **Disabled Snowsports New Zealand** (www.disabledsnowsports.org.nz) website.

VISAS

Visa application forms are available from NZ diplomatic missions overseas, travel agents or through **Immigration New Zealand** (☎ 0508 558 855, 09-914 4100; www.immigration.govt.nz). Immigration New Zealand has over a dozen offices overseas; consult the website.

Visitor's Visa

Citizens of Australia don't need a visa to visit NZ and can stay indefinitely (provided they have no criminal convictions). UK citizens don't need a visa either and can stay in the country for up to six months.

Citizens of another 56 countries that have visa-waiver agreements with NZ don't need a visa for stays of up to three months, provided they have an onward ticket, sufficient funds to support their stay (NZ$1000 per month, or NZ$400 per month if accommodation has been prepaid) and a passport valid for three months beyond the date of their planned departure from NZ. Nations in this group include Canada, France, Germany, Ireland, Japan, the Netherlands and the USA.

Citizens of other countries must obtain a visa before entering NZ. Visas come with three months' standard validity and cost NZ$100 if processed in Australia or certain South Pacific countries (eg Samoa, Fiji), or NZ$130 if processed elsewhere in the world.

Visitors' visas can be extended for stays of up to nine months within one 18-month period, or to a maximum of 12 months in the country. Applications are assessed on a case-by-case basis; visitors will need to meet criteria such as proof of ongoing financial self-support. Apply for extensions at any Immigration New Zealand office – see the website for locations.

Work Visa & Working Holiday Scheme

It's illegal for foreign nationals to work in NZ on a visitor's visa, except for Australians who can legally gain work without a visa or permit. If you're visiting NZ to find work, or you already have an employment offer, you'll need to apply for a work visa, which translates into a work permit once you arrive and is valid for up to three years. You can apply for a work permit after you're in NZ, but it's validity will be backdated to when you entered the country. The fee for a work visa ranges from NZ$180 to NZ$280 depending on where it's processed and the type of application.

Eligible travellers who are only interested in short-term employment to supplement their travels can take part in one of NZ's working holiday schemes (WHS). Under these schemes citizens aged 18 to 30 years from 31 countries – including Canada, France, Germany, Ireland, Japan, Malaysia, the Netherlands, Scandinavian countries, the UK and the USA – can apply for a visa. For most nationalities the visa is valid for 12 months. It's only issued to those seeking a genuine working holiday, not permanent work, so you're not supposed to work for one employer for more than three months.

Most WHS-eligible nationals must apply for this visa from within their own country; residents of some countries can apply online. Applicants must have an onward ticket, a passport valid for at least three months from the date they will leave NZ and evidence of at least NZ$4200 in accessible funds. The application fee is NZ$120 regardless of where you apply, and isn't refunded if your application is declined.

The rules vary for different nationalities, so make sure you read up on the specifics of your country's agreement with NZ at www. immigration.govt.nz/migrant/stream/work/ workingholiday. See also p392.

WOMEN TRAVELLERS

NZ is generally a very safe place for women travellers, although the usual sensible precautions apply. It's best to avoid walking alone late at night in any of the major cities and towns, and never hitchhike alone. If you're out on the town, always keep enough money aside for a taxi back to your accommodation. The same applies in rural towns where there may be a lot of unlit, semideserted streets between you and your bed. Lone women should also be wary of staying in basic pub accommodation unless it looks safe and well managed.

Sexual harassment is not a widely reported problem in NZ, but of course it does happen.

See www.womentravel.co.nz for more information.

DIRECTORY

WORK

If you arrive in NZ on a visitor's visa you're not allowed to work for pay. If you're caught breaching this (or any other) visa condition, you could be booted back to where you came from.

If you have been approved for a WHS visa (see p391), look into the possibilities for temporary employment. There's plenty of casual work around, mainly in agriculture (fruit picking, farming), hospitality or ski resorts. Office-based work can be found in IT, banking, finance and telemarketing. Register with a local office-work agency to get started.

Seasonal fruit picking, pruning and harvesting is prime short-term work for visitors. More than 30,000 hectares of apples, kiwi fruit and other fruit and veg are harvested from summer to early autumn. As an optimist once said, 'The pay is bad, but the work is difficult'. Rates are around $10 to $15 an hour for physically taxing toil – turnover of workers is high. You're usually paid by how much you pick (per bin, bucket or kilogram). The picking season is from December to May. Prime South Island picking locations include Nelson (Tapawera and Golden Bay), Marlborough (around Blenheim) and Central Otago (Alexandra and Roxburgh). Approach prospective employers directly, otherwise local hostels or holiday parks often help travellers to find work. Other agricultural work is available year-round.

Winter work at ski resorts and their service towns includes bartending, waiting, cleaning, ski-tow operation and, if you're properly qualified, ski or snowboard instructing. Check resort websites for opportunities.

Information

Backpacker publications, hostel managers and other travellers are the best sources of info on local work possibilities.

Kiwi Careers (www.kiwicareers.govt.nz) lists opportunities in various fields (agriculture, creative, health, teaching, volunteer work and recruitment agencies), while **Seek** (www.seek.co.nz) is one of the biggest NZ job-search networks with thousands of jobs listed.

Seasonal Work NZ (www.seasonalwork.co.nz) has a database of thousands of casual jobs, including region-specific 'Harvest Trail' jobs in fruit-picking and agriculture. It gives the contact details of employers looking for workers, rates of pay and nearby accommodation. **Pick NZ** (www.picknz.co.nz) provides a similar service, focusing on seasonal horticultural work.

Base Backpackers (www.stayatbase.com/work) runs an employment service via its website, while the Networking link on **Budget Backpacker Hostels** (BBH; www.bbh.co.nz) lists job vacancies in BBH hostels and a few other possibilities.

Income Tax

There is no escaping it! For the vast majority of travellers, any Kiwi dollars earned in NZ will be subject to income tax, deducted from payments by employers – a process called Pay As You Earn (PAYE). Standard NZ income tax rates are 12.5% for annual salaries up to $17,500, then 21% up to $40,000, 33% up to $75,000, then 39% for higher incomes. A NZ Accident Compensation Corporation (ACC) scheme levy (1.7%) will also be deducted from your pay packet. At the time of writing, these rates were set to change slightly from April 2011.

If you visit NZ and work for a short time (eg on a working holiday scheme), you may qualify for a tax refund when you leave. Complete a Refund Application – People Leaving New Zealand (document no IR50) form and submit it with your tax return, along with proof of departure (eg air ticket copies) to the Inland Revenue Department (IRD). For more info see the IRD website, or contact the **Inland Revenue Non-Resident Centre** (☎ 03-467 7020; nonres@ird.govt.nz; Private Bag 1932, Dunedin).

IRD Number

Travellers undertaking paid work in NZ must obtain an IRD number. Download the application form from the **Inland Revenue Department** (www.ird.govt.nz) website – use the search function to find document no IR595. An IRD number normally takes eight to 10 working days to be issued.

Transport

CONTENTS

New Zealand's peaceably isolated location in a distant patch of the South Pacific is a major drawcard, but it also means that unless you travel from Australia, you have to contend with a long-haul flight to get there. As NZ is serviced by good airline and bus networks, travelling around the country is a much less taxing endeavour.

Flights, tours and rail tickets can be booked online at www.lonelyplanet.com/bookings.

GETTING THERE & AWAY

ENTERING THE COUNTRY

Disembarkation in NZ is generally a straightforward affair, with only the usual customs declarations to endure (see Customs, p381) and the uncool scramble to get to the luggage carousel first. Recent global instability has resulted in increased security in NZ airports, in both domestic and international terminals, and you may find customs procedures more time-consuming. One procedure has the Orwellian title Advance Passenger Screening, a system whereby documents that used to be checked after you touched down in NZ (passport, visa etc) are now checked before you board your flight – make sure all your documentation is in order so your check-in is stress-free.

Passport
There are no restrictions when it comes to foreign citizens entering NZ. If you have a current passport and visa (or don't require one; see p391), you should be fine.

AIR
There is a number of competing airlines servicing New Zealand and a wide variety of fares to choose from if you are flying in from Asia, Europe or North America, though ultimately you'll still pay a lot for a flight unless you jet in from Australia. NZ's inordinate popularity and abundance of year-round activities mean that almost any time of year airports can be swarming with inbound tourists – if you want to fly at a particularly popular time of year (eg Christmas), book well in advance.

The high season for flights into NZ is during summer (December to February), with slightly less of a premium on fares over the shoulder months (October/November and March/April). The low season generally tallies with the winter months (June to August), though this is still a busy time for airlines ferrying ski bunnies and powder hounds.

Airports & Airlines
On the South Island, the following airports handle international flights:

Christchurch (CHC; ☎ 03-358 5029; www.christchurch airport.co.nz)

Dunedin (DUD; ☎ 03-486 2879; www.dnairport.co.nz)

Queenstown (ZQN; ☎ 03-450 9031; www.queens townairport.co.nz)

THINGS CHANGE...

The information in this chapter is particularly vulnerable to change. Check directly with the airline or a travel agent to make sure you understand how a fare (and ticket you may buy) works and be aware of the security requirements for international travel. Shop carefully. The details given in this chapter should be regarded as pointers and are not a substitute for your own careful, up-to-date research.

TRANSPORT

AIRLINES FLYING TO & FROM NEW ZEALAND

NZ's own overseas carrier is Air New Zealand, which flies to runways across Europe, North America, eastern Asia and the Pacific. Airlines that connect NZ with international destinations include the following (note that 0800 and 0508 phone numbers mentioned here are for dialling from within NZ only):

Aerolineas Argentinas (airline code AR; ☎ 09-379 3675; www.aerolineas.com.ar)
Air New Zealand (NZ; ☎ 0800 737 000, 09-357 3000; www.airnewzealand.co.nz)
Air Pacific (FJ; ☎ 0800 800 178, 09-379 2404; www.airpacific.com)
Air Vanuatu (NF; ☎ 09-373 3435; www.airvanuatu.com)
Cathay Pacific (CX; ☎ 0800 800 454, 09-379 0861; www.cathaypacific.com)
Emirates (EK; ☎ 0508 364 728, 09-968 2208; www.emirates.com)
Garuda Indonesia (GA; ☎ 09-366 1862; www.garuda-indonesia.com)
Jetstar (JQ; ☎ 0800 800 995; www.jetstar.com)
Korean Air (KE; ☎ 09-914 2000; www.koreanair.com)
Malaysia Airlines (MH; ☎ 0800 777 747, 09-379 3743; www.malaysiaairlines.com)
Pacific Blue (☎ 0800 670 000; www.flypacificblue.com)
Polynesian Blue (DJ; ☎ 0800 670 000; www.polynesianblue.com)
Qantas (QF; ☎ 0800 808 767, 09-357 8900; www.qantas.com.au)
Royal Brunei Airlines (BI; ☎ 09-977 2209; www.bruneiair.com)
Singapore Airlines (SQ; ☎ 0800 808 909, 09-379 3209; www.singaporeair.com)
Thai Airways International (TG; ☎ 09-256 8518; www.thaiairways.com)
Virgin Blue (DJ; ☎ 0800 670 000; www.virginblue.com)

Tickets

Automated online ticket sales work well if you're doing a simple one-way or return trip on specified dates, but are no substitute for a travel agent with the low-down on special deals, strategies for avoiding layovers and other useful advice.

INTERCONTINENTAL (RTW) TICKETS

If you're flying to NZ from the other side of the world, round-the-world (RTW) tickets can be real bargains. They're generally put together by the three biggest airline alliances, **Star Alliance** (www.staralliance.com), **Oneworld** (www.oneworldalliance.com) and **Skyteam** (www.skyteam.com), and give you a limited period (usually a year) in which to loop the planet. You can go anywhere the participating airlines go, as long as you stay within the prescribed kilometre extents or number of stops and don't backtrack when flying between continents. Backtracking is generally permitted within a single continent, though with certain restrictions; see the websites for details.

An alternative type of RTW ticket is one put together by a travel agent or RTW–specialist websites (see p394). These are often more expensive than airline RTW fares but allow you to devise your own itinerary.

Bargain RTW tickets start from around UK£600 ex-UK, US$1500 ex-USA.

CIRCLE PACIFIC TICKETS

A Circle Pacific ticket is similar to a RTW ticket but covers a more limited region, using a combination of airlines to connect Australia, NZ, North America and Asia, with stopover options in the Pacific islands. As with RTW tickets, there are restrictions on how many stopovers you can take.

ONLINE TICKET SITES

For online ticket bookings, including RTW fares, start with the following websites:

Air Brokers (www.airbrokers.com) This US company specialises in cheaper tickets. To fly LA-Tahiti-Auckland-Sydney-Bangkok-Hong Kong-LA costs around US$2200 (excluding taxes).
Cheap Flights (www.cheapflights.com) Informative site with specials, destination information and flight searches from the USA.
Cheapest Flights (www.cheapestflights.co.uk) Cheap worldwide flights from the UK; get in early for the bargains.
Expedia (www.expedia.com) Microsoft's travel site; good for USA-related flights.
Flight Centre International (www.flightcentre.com) Respected operator handling direct flights, with sites for NZ, Australia, the UK, the USA, Canada and South Africa.

DEPARTURE TAX

An international departure tax of NZ$25 applies when leaving NZ at all airports except Auckland, payable by anyone aged 12 and over (NZ$10 for children aged two to 11, free for those under two years of age). The tax is not included in the price of airline tickets, but must be paid separately at the airport before you board your flight. Pay via credit card or cash.

TRANSPORT

CLIMATE CHANGE & TRAVEL

Climate change is a serious threat to the ecosystems that humans rely upon, and air travel is the fastest-growing contributor to the problem. Lonely Planet regards travel, overall, as a global benefit, but believes we all have a responsibility to limit our personal impact on global warming.

Flying & Climate Change

Pretty much every form of motor travel generates CO_2 (the main cause of human-induced climate change) but planes are far and away the worst offenders, not just because of the sheer distances they allow us to travel, but because they release greenhouse gases high into the atmosphere. The statistics are frightening: two people taking a return flight between Europe and the US will contribute as much to climate change as an average household's gas and electricity consumption over a whole year.

Carbon Offset Schemes

Climatecare.org and other websites use 'carbon calculators' that allow jetsetters to offset the greenhouse gases they are responsible for with contributions to energy-saving projects and other climate-friendly initiatives in the developing world – including projects in India, Honduras, Kazakhstan and Uganda.

Lonely Planet, together with Rough Guides and other concerned partners in the travel industry, supports the carbon offset scheme run by climatecare.org. Lonely Planet offsets all of its staff and author travel.

For more information check out our website: lonelyplanet.com.

Flights.com (www.flights.com) International site for flights; cheap fares and an easy-to-search database.

Roundtheworldflights.com (www.roundtheworld flights.com) This excellent site allows you to build your own trip from the UK with up to six stops. A six-stop trip including Asia, Australia, NZ and the USA costs from UK£550 in the NZ winter.

STA Travel (www.statravel.com) Prominent in international student travel (but you don't have to be a student). Linked to worldwide STA sites.

Travel Online (www.travelonline.co.nz) Good place to check worldwide flights from NZ.

Travel.com.au (www.travel.com.au) Good Australian site; look up fares and flights to/from the country.

Travelocity (www.travelocity.com) US site that allows you to search fares (in US dollars) from/to practically anywhere.

Asia

Most Asian countries offer fairly competitive air-fare deals, with Bangkok, Singapore and Hong Kong being the best places to shop around for discount tickets. Hong Kong's travel market can be unpredictable, but excellent bargains are sometimes available. **Phoenix Services** (☎ 2722 7378) is recommended.

STA Travel (Bangkok ☎ 02-236 0262; www.statravel. co.th; Singapore ☎ 6737 7188; www.statravel.com.sg; Tokyo ☎ 03-5391 2922; www.statravel.co.jp) has offices in major Asian cities.

Australia

Air New Zealand and Qantas operate a network of flights linking key NZ cities with most major Australian gateway cities, while quite a few other international airlines include NZ and Australia on their Asia-Pacific routes.

Cohorts Pacific Blue, Virgin Blue and Polynesian Blue offer direct flights between Christchurch and east-coast capitals, with connections on the domestic Virgin Blue network to many other Australian cities. Pacific Blue also link Dunedin and Brisbane.

Qantas' budget subsidiary, Jetstar, flies between Auckland and Sydney, Cairns and the Gold Coast; and between Christchurch and Sydney, Melbourne, Hobart, Brisbane, Cairns and the Gold Coast.

If you book early, shop around and have the gods smiling upon you, you may pay under AU$180 for a one-way fare on a budget carrier from either Sydney or Melbourne to Christchurch or Wellington. More common prices are from AU$200 to AU$250 one-way. If you are travelling around both islands, you can fly into Auckland and out of Christchurch to save backtracking, but you may not get the cheapest fares with this itinerary.

From key NZ cities, you'll pay between NZ$240 and NZ$280 for a one-way ticket to an Australian east-coast city. There's usually

TRANSPORT

not a significant difference in price between seasons, as this is a popular route year-round. The intense competition, however, inevitably results in some tasty discounting.

For some reasonably priced fares, try an Australian capital-city branch of **STA Travel** (☎ 134 782; www.statravel.com.au). Another good option, also with dozens of offices strewn around the country, is **Flight Centre** (☎ 133 133; www.flightcentre.com.au).

Canada

The air routes flown from Canada are similar to those from mainland USA, with most Toronto and Vancouver flights stopping in a US city such as Los Angeles or Honolulu before continuing to NZ. Air New Zealand has direct flights between Auckland and Vancouver year-round.

The air fares sold by Canadian discount air-ticket sellers (consolidators) tend to be about 10% higher than those sold in the USA. **Travel CUTS** (☎ 866 246 9762; www.travelcuts.com) is Canada's national student travel agency and has offices in all major cities.

Return fares from Vancouver to Auckland cost between C$1800 and C$2100 via the US west coast. From Toronto, fares cost around C$2000. One-way fares from NZ start at around NZ$1800 to Toronto and NZ$1500 to Vancouver.

Continental Europe

Frankfurt and London are the major arrival and departure points for flights to and from NZ, both with extensive connections to other European cities. From these two launching pads, most flights to NZ travel via one of the Asian capitals. Return air fares from NZ to key European hubs such as Paris and Frankfurt usually cost between NZ$2100 and NZ$2600.

An option in the Dutch travel industry is **Holland International** (www.hollandinternational.nl). From Amsterdam, return fares start at €1400.

In Germany, good travel agencies include the Berlin branch of **STA Travel** (☎ 069-7430 3292; www.statravel.de). Return fares from Frankfurt start at around €1400.

In France, return fares from Paris start from €1200. Recommended companies:
Nouvelles Frontières (☎ 0149 206 400; www.nouvelles-frontieres.fr/nf)
Odysia (☎ 0825 082 525; www.odysia.fr)
Voyageurs du Monde (☎ 0892 235 656; www.vdm.com/vdm)

UK & Ireland

Depending on which airline you travel with from the UK, flights to NZ go via Asia or the USA. If you fly via Asia you can often make stopovers in countries such as India, Thailand, Singapore and Australia; in the other direction, stopover possibilities include New York, Los Angeles, Honolulu and sundry Pacific islands.

Discount air travel is big business in London. Advertisements for many travel agencies appear in the travel pages of the weekend broadsheet newspapers, in *Time Out*, in the *Evening Standard* and in the free magazine *TNT*.

Typical one-way/return fares from London to Auckland start at around £550/750; note that June, July and mid-December fares can go up by as much as 30%. From NZ you can expect to pay between NZ$2500 and NZ$3000 for return fares to London.

Popular agencies in the UK:
Flight Centre (☎ 0800 587 0058; www.flightcentre.co.uk)
STA Travel (☎ 0871 230 0040; www.statravel.co.uk)
Trailfinders (☎ 0845 058 5858; www.trailfinders.co.uk)

USA

Most flights between the North American mainland and NZ are to/from west-coast USA, with the bulk routed through Los Angeles but some going through San Francisco. Some airlines offer flights via various Pacific islands (Hawaii, Tahiti, Cook Islands).

San Francisco is the ticket consolidator capital of America, although some good deals can be found in Los Angeles, New York and other big cities. **STA Travel** (☎ 800 781 4040; www.statravel.com) has offices all over the USA.

Return tickets to NZ from the US west coast start at US$1100/1350 in the NZ winter/summer; fares from the east coast start at US$1850 in both seasons. Return fares from NZ to the US west coast are around NZ$2200; to New York NZ$2800.

SEA

It's possible (though by no means easy or safe) to make your way between NZ and Australia, and some smaller Pacific islands, by hitching rides or crewing on yachts. Try asking around at harbours, marinas, and yacht and sailing clubs. Popular yachting harbours in NZ include the Bay of Islands and Whangarei (both located in Northland), Auckland and Wellington. March and April are the best months to look for boats heading to Australia. From Fiji, October to November is a peak departure season as cyclones are starting to spin in that neck of the woods.

There are no passenger liners operating to/from NZ and finding a berth on a cargo ship (much less enjoying the experience) is no easy task.

GETTING AROUND

AIR
Those who have limited time to get between NZ's attractions can make the most of a widespread network of intra- and inter-island flights.

Airlines in New Zealand
The country's major domestic carrier, Air New Zealand, has an aerial network covering most of the country. Australia-based Jetstar also flies between main urban areas.

Several small-scale regional operators provide essential transport services to the small outlying islands such as Great Barrier Island in the Hauraki Gulf, Stewart Island and the Chathams. Regional operators include the following:

Air Chathams (☎ 0508 247 248, 03-305 0209; www.airchathams.co.nz) Services to the remote Chatham Islands from Wellington, Christchurch and Auckland, and occasionally Napier.

Air Fiordland (☎ 0800 107 505, 03-249 6720; www.airfiordland.com) Services around Milford Sound, Te Anau and Queenstown.

Air New Zealand (☎ 0800 737 000, 09-357 3000; www.airnewzealand.co.nz) Offers flights between 26 domestic destinations.

Air West Coast (☎ 0800 247 937, 03-738 0524; www.airwestcoast.co.nz) Flies between Greymouth and Christchurch and runs charter flights.

Air2there.com (☎ 0800 777 000, 04-904 5130; www.air2there.com) Connects destinations across Cook Strait, including Blenheim, Napier, Nelson and Wellington.

Golden Bay Air (☎ 0800 588 885, 03-525 8725; www.capitalair.co.nz) Flies regularly between Wellington and Takaka in Golden Bay.

Jetstar (☎ 0800 800 995; www.jetstar.com) Joins the dots between key tourism centres: Auckland, Wellington, Christchurch and Queenstown.

Soundsair (☎ 0800 505 005, 03-520 3080 www.soundsair.co.nz) Hops across Cook Strait between Wellington and Picton up to 16 times per day. Also links Wellington with Blenheim and Nelson.

Stewart Island Flights (☎ 03-218 9129; www.stewartislandflights.com) Flies between Invercargill and Stewart Island.

Air Passes
With discounting being the norm these days, and a number of budget airlines now serving the trans-Tasman route as well as the Pacific islands, the value of air passes isn't as red-hot as in the past.

Air New Zealand offers the **South Pacific Airpass** (☎ 1800 262 1241; www.airnewzealand.com), valid for selected journeys within NZ, and between NZ, Australia and a number of Pacific islands. The pass is only available to nonresidents of these countries, and must be issued outside NZ. Passes are issued in conjunction with an international ticket (with any airline) and are valid for the life of that ticket.

The pass involves purchasing coupons for domestic flights (one-way from NZ$99 to NZ$378, depending on distance), or flights to/from major Australian cities or Pacific islands including Fiji, New Caledonia and Tonga, and as far afield as the Cook Islands and Samoa (one-way from NZ$231 to NZ$855).

BICYCLE
Touring cyclists proliferate in NZ, particularly over summer – the roads and trails run thick with fluoro-clad creatures with aerodynamic heads. The country is popular with cyclists because it's clean, green and relatively uncrowded, and has lots of cheap accommodation (including camping) and easily accessible freshwater. The roads are generally in good nick, and the climate generally not too hot or too cold (except on the South Island's rain-soaked West Coast). The many hills make for hard going at times, but there are expansive flats and lows to accompany the highs. As in any country, road traffic is the biggest danger, and you'll hear numerous cyclists' tales about inconsiderate or unsafe behaviour from drivers. Trucks overtaking too close to the cyclist are a particular threat. Take care! Bikes and cycling gear (to rent or buy) are readily available in the main centres, as are bicycle repair shops.

The choice of itineraries is limited only by your imagination. Cycling some of the coastline will be a highlight, but inland routes have their share of devotees. One increasingly popular expedition is to follow an upgraded path along an old railway line into the former

TRANSPORT

gold-mining heartland of Otago – for details, see the boxed text, p286.

A major nationwide project has been in motion since late 2009, expanding and improving NZ's network of bike trails. See the Ministry of Tourism's website for updates (www.tourism.govt.nz).

By law all cyclists must wear an approved safety helmet (or risk a fine); it's also vital to have good reflective gear, so that you can be easily seen by cars or trucks overtaking from behind. Cyclists who use public transport will find that major bus lines and trains only take bicycles on a 'space available' basis (meaning bikes may not be allowed on) and charge up to $10. Some of the smaller shuttle bus companies, on the other hand, make sure they have storage space for bikes, which they carry for a surcharge.

If importing your own bike or transporting it by plane within NZ, check with the relevant airline for costs and the degree of dismantling and packing required.

Hire

Rates offered by most outfits for renting road or mountain bikes – not including the discounted fees or freebies offered by accommodation places to their guests – are anywhere from $10 to $20 per hour and $30 to $50 per day.

Purchase

Bicycles can be readily bought in the South Island's cities and larger towns, but prices for newer models are high. For a decent hybrid bike or rigid mountain bike you'll pay anywhere from $700 to $1600, though you can get a cheap one for around $400 to $500 – however, then you still need to get panniers, a helmet and other essential touring gear, and the cost quickly climbs. Arguably you're better off buying a used bike (assuming you can't bring your own over), but finding something that's in good enough shape for a long road trip isn't always as easy as it sounds. Other options include the post-Christmas sales and midyear stocktakes, when newish cycles can be heavily discounted.

BOAT

NZ may be an island nation but there's virtually no long-distance water transport around the country. The South Island exceptions are the inter-island ferries that chug across Cook Strait

between Wellington and Picton (see p110 and p129), and the passenger ferry that negotiates the width of Foveaux Strait between Bluff and the town of Oban on Stewart Island (see p374).

BUS

Bus travel in NZ is relatively easy and well organised, with services transporting you to the far reaches of both islands (including the start/end of various walking tracks), but it can be expensive, tedious and time-consuming. The bus 'terminals' in smaller places usually comprise a parking spot outside a prominent local business.

The dominant bus company is **InterCity** (☎ Auckland 09-583 5780, Wellington 04-385 0520, Christchurch 03-365 1113, Dunedin 03-471 7143; www.intercity.co.nz), which also has an extra-comfort travel and sightseeing arm called **Newmans Coach Lines** (☎ 09-623 1504; www.newmanscoach.co.nz). InterCity can drive you to just about anywhere on the South Island.

South Island shuttle-bus companies:
Abel Tasman Coachlines (☎ 03-548 0285; www.abeltasmantravel.co.nz) Traverses the tarmac between Nelson, Motueka, Golden Bay, and Kahurangi and Abel Tasman National Parks.
Atomic Shuttles (☎ 03-349 0697; www.atomictravel.co.nz) Has services throughout the South Island, including to Christchurch, Dunedin, Invercargill, Picton, Nelson, Greymouth/Hokitika, Te Anau and Queenstown/Wanaka.
Cook Connection (☎ 0800 266 526; www.cookconnect.co.nz) Triangulates between Mt Cook, Twizel and Lake Tekapo.
East West Coaches (☎ 0800 142 622, 03-789 6251) Offers a service between Christchurch and Westport, running via the Hanmer Springs turn-off, Maruia Springs and Reefton.
Hanmer Connection (☎ 0800 242 663; www.atsnz.com) Provides services between Hanmer Springs and Christchurch, and three services weekly between Hanmer and Kaikoura.
Knightrider (☎ 03-342 8055; www.knightrider.co.nz) Runs a nocturnal service from Christchurch to Invercargill via Dunedin. David Hasselhoff nowhere to be seen…
Naked Bus (☎ 0900 625 33; www.nakedbus.com) Low-cost routes across the South (and North) Island, from Nelson to Invercargill and most places in between.
Scenic Shuttle (☎ 0800 304 333, 03-477 9083; www.scenicshuttle.co.nz) Drives between Te Anau and Invercargill via Manapouri.
Southern Link Travel (☎ 0508 458 835; www.southernlinkkbus.co.nz) Roams across most of the South Island, taking in Christchurch, Nelson, Picton, Greymouth, Queenstown and Dunedin, among others.

Topline Tours (☎ 03-249 8059; www.toplinetours.
co.nz) Connects Te Anau and Queenstown.

Tracknet (☎ 0800 483 262, 03-249 7777; www.
tracknet.net) Daily track transport (Milford, Routeburn,
Hollyford, Kepler etc) between Queenstown, Te Anau,
Milford Sound, Invercargill, Fiordland and the West Coast.

West Coast Shuttle (☎ 03-768 0028; www.west
coastshuttle.co.nz) Daily bus from Greymouth to Christchurch and back.

InterCity Bus Passes

InterCity (☎ Christchurch 03-365 1113, Dunedin 03-471 7143;
www.intercity.co.nz) offers bus passes, covering
either the whole country, or the North and
South Islands separately. If you're covering
a lot of ground, passes can be cheaper than
paying as you go, but they lock you into using
InterCity buses (rather than, say, the convenient shuttle buses that cover much of the
country). There's a 15% discount for YHA,
BBH and VIP backpacker members; there
may be an additional reservation charge ($3
per sector, depending on the agent).

SOUTH ISLAND PASSES
There are 10 InterCity South Island passes:
Kaikoura Discovery ($40; 1-day minimum travel)
Christchurch to Kaikoura and back.
West Coast Passport ex-Greymouth ($135; 2-day
minimum travel) Greymouth to Queenstown via Franz
Josef Glacier, Fox Glacier and Wanaka. Available in both
directions.
West Coast Passport ex-Nelson ($155; 2-day
minimum travel) Nelson to Queenstown via Greymouth,
Franz Josef Glacier, Fox Glacier and Wanaka. Available in
both directions.
West Coast Passport ex-Picton ($180; 3-day mini-
mum travel) Picton to Queenstown via Nelson, Greymouth,
Franz Josef Glacier, Fox Glacier and Wanaka. Available in
both directions.
Southern Trail ($188; 3-day minimum travel) Grey-
mouth to Christchurch via Franz Josef Glacier, Fox Glacier,
Wanaka, Queenstown and Tekapo. Available in both
directions.
Greenstone Encounter ($189; 2-day minimum travel)
Christchurch to Milford Sound via Tekapo, Queenstown and
Te Anau. Available in both directions.
Goldminers Trail ($221; 2-day minimum travel)
Christchurch to Milford Sound via Dunedin, Queenstown
and Te Anau. Available in both directions.
Te Hamo's Adventure ($259; 2-day minimum travel)
Christchurch to Milford Sound via Aoraki/Mt Cook, Queens-
town and Te Anau. Available in both directions.
Maui's Canoe ($442; 5-day minimum travel) South
Island circuit starting/ending in Christchurch via Queen-

stown, Milford Sound, Fox Glacier, Franz Josef Glacier,
Nelson and Kaikoura. Available in both directions.
Alpine Discovery ($539; 5-day minimum travel) South
Island circuit starting/ending in Christchurch via Aoraki/
Mt Cook, Queenstown, Te Anau, Milford Sound, Fox Glacier,
Franz Josef Glacier, Greymouth, Nelson and Kaikoura. Avail-
able in both directions.

NATIONWIDE PASSES
If you're considering moving beyond the
South Island, InterCity's pan-NZ **Travelpass**
(☎ 0800 339 966; www.travelpass.co.nz) combines
bus travel with a Cook Strait ferry crossing.
There are three hop-on/hop-off passes avail-
able, each valid for a year. Adult and child
prices are the same:
Kia Ora New Zealand ($579; 7-day minimum travel)
A one-way trip between Auckland and Christchurch via
Rotorua, Wellington, Dunedin, Queenstown and Milford
Sound. Available in both directions.
Kiwi Explorer ($623; 9-day minimum travel) A one-way
trip between Auckland and Christchurch via Rotorua,
Napier, Wellington, the West Coast, Milford Sound and
Queenstown. Available in both directions.
Aotearoa Adventurer ($1283; 14-day minimum travel)
A monster loop from Auckland to Milford Sound and back,
via Northland, Rotorua, Wellington, Christchurch, Queens-
town, the West Coast and Napier.

The appropriately named **Flexi-Pass** (☎ 0800 222
146; www.flexipass.co.nz) is valid for one year and
allows you to travel pretty much anywhere
(and in any direction) on the InterCity network; you can get on and off wherever you
like and can change bookings up to two hours
before departure without penalty. The pass is
purchased in five-hour blocks of travel time,
from a minimum of 15 hours ($169) up to a
maximum of 60 hours ($605) – the average
cost of each block becomes cheaper the more
hours you buy. You can top up the pass if you
need more time.

Seat Classes
There are no allocated economy or luxury
classes on NZ buses; smoking is a no-no.

Reservations
Over summer, school holidays and public
holidays, book well ahead on more popular
routes. At other times you should have few
problems accessing your preferred service, but
if your long-term travel plans rely on catching
a particular bus, book at least a day or two
ahead just to be safe.

TRANSPORT

TRANSPORT

BACKPACKER VAN RENTALS

There are several budget players in the campervan industry, offering slick deals and funky, well-kitted-out vehicles to attract young, independent travellers (the kind who would shun the larger, more traditional box-on-wheels). All companies offer living, sleeping and cooking equipment, 24-hour roadside assistance, and maps and travel tips. Rates are competitive (from $35 per day May to September; from $70 per day December to February). Check out the following:

- **Backpacker Sleeper Vans** (☎ 0800 325 939, 03-359 4731; www.sleepervans.co.nz) Low-cost family-run business.
- **Escape Rentals** (☎ 0800 216 171; www.escaperentals.co.nz) 'The freedom to sleep around' – loud, original artwork on van exteriors, pitched squarely at young travellers after something different. DVDs, TVs and outdoor barbecues available for rent.
- **Jucy** (☎ 0800 399 736, 09-374 4360; www.jucy.co.nz) The flashpacker's vehicle of choice.
- **Spaceships** (☎ 0800 772 237, 09-526 2130; www.spaceshipsrentals.co.nz) The customised 'Swiss Army Knife of campervans', with extras including DVD and CD players, roof racks and solar showers.
- **Wicked Campers** (☎ 0800 246 870; www.wicked-campers.co.nz) Spray-painted vans bedecked with everything/everyone from Mr Spock to Sly Stone.

InterCity fares vary widely depending on availability and how the tickets are booked (online or via an agent). The best prices are generally available online, booked a few weeks in advance.

CAR & MOTORCYCLE

The best way to explore NZ in depth is to have your own transport, which allows you to create your own leisurely, flexible itinerary. Good-value car- and campervan-hire rates are not hard to track down; alternatively, consider buying your own set of wheels.

Automobile Association (AA)

NZ's **Automobile Association** (AA; ☎ 24hr road service 0800 500 222; www.aa.co.nz) provides emergency breakdown services, excellent touring maps and detailed guides to accommodation (from holiday parks to motels and B&Bs).

Members of foreign automobile associations should bring their membership cards – many of these bodies have reciprocal agreements with NZ's AA.

Driving Licence

International visitors to NZ can use their home country's driving licence – if your licence isn't in English, it's a good idea to carry a certified translation with you. Alternatively, use an International Driving Permit (IDP), which will usually be issued on the spot (valid for 12 months) by your home country's automobile association.

Fuel

Fuel is available from service stations with the well-known international brand names. LPG (gas) is not always stocked by rural suppliers; if you're on gas it's safer to have dual fuel capability. Prices vary from place to place, but basically petrol (gasoline) isn't pumped cheaply in NZ, with per-litre costs at the time of research averaging around $1.65. More remote destinations may charge a small fortune to fill your tank and you're better off getting fuel before you reach them – places in this category include Milford Sound (fill up at Te Anau) and Mt Cook (buy fuel at Twizel or Lake Tekapo). Fuel is also difficult to find on the Otago Peninsula; fill up before you leave Dunedin.

Hire
CAMPERVAN

Check your rear-view mirror on any far-flung NZ road and you'll likely see a shiny white campervan (aka mobile home, motor home, RV) packed with liberated travellers, mountain bikes and portable barbecues cruising along behind you.

Campervanning around NZ is big business. It's flexible and affordable, and you can leave the trampled tourist trails behind and crank up the AC/DC as loud as hell! Most towns of any size have a camping ground or campervan park with powered sites for around $35 per night. There are also places where 'freedom camping' is permitted, but you should never just *assume* it's OK to camp somewhere. Always ask a local first. Check at the local i-SITE or DOC office, or even with local commercial camping grounds. If you are freedom camping, please treat the area with respect – if your van doesn't have toilet facilities, find a public loo. See www.camping.org.nz for more tips on freedom camping.

You can hire campervans from assorted companies, prices varying with time of year, how big you want your home-on-wheels to be, and length of rental. Major operators:

Britz (☎ 0800 831 900, 09-255 3910; www.britz.co.nz)
Kea Campers (☎ 0800 520 052, 09-441 7833; www.keacampers.com)
Maui (☎ 0800 651 080, 09-255 3910; www.maui.co.nz)

A small van for two people typically has a mini-kitchen and fold-out dining table, the latter transforming into a double bed when dinner is done 'n' dusted. Larger 'superior' two-berth vans include shower and toilet. Four- to six-berth campervans are the size of trucks (and similarly sluggish) and, besides the extra space, usually contain a toilet and shower.

Over summer, rates offered by the main rental firms for two-/four-/six-berth vans start at around $160/290/320 per day, dropping to as low as $50/80/95 in winter for month-long rentals; industry infighting often sees even lower rates.

CAR

Competition between car-rental companies in NZ is torrid – rates tend to be variable and lots of special deals come and go (we've heard of discounted rates as low as $15 per day, so shop around). On the South Island, car rental is most competitive in Christchurch and Picton. The main thing to remember when assessing your options is distance – if you want to travel far, you need unlimited kilometres. Some (but not all) companies require drivers to be at least 21 years old – ask around.

Sizable multinational companies, with offices or agents in most major cities, towns and larger airports:

Avis (☎ 0800 655 111, 09-526-2847; www.avis.co.nz)
Budget (☎ 0800 283 438, 09-529 7784; www.budget.co.nz)

SOUTH ISLAND ROAD DISTANCES (km)

Distances are approximate only

	Aoraki/Mt Cook	Arthur's Pass	Blenheim	Christchurch	Dunedin	Franz Josef Glacier	Greymouth	Hanmer Springs	Hokitika	Invercargill	Kaikoura	Milford Sound	Nelson	Oamaru	Picton	Queenstown	Te Anau	Timaru	Wanaka
Arthur's Pass	410																		
Blenheim	635	420																	
Christchurch	330	150	310																
Dunedin	325	455	665	360															
Franz Josef Glacier	485	230	500	390	560														
Greymouth	510	95	330	250	550	180													
Hanmer Springs	460	265	260	140	490	395	215												
Hokitika	510	100	370	250	550	135	40	255											
Invercargill	440	660	870	570	210	530	710	700	665										
Kaikoura	505	290	130	185	535	540	330	135	390	745									
Milford Sound	540	840	1060	760	410	630	805	890	770	275	930								
Nelson	745	370	115	425	775	470	290	310	335	990	245	1100							
Oamaru	210	340	550	250	115	510	430	375	435	325	420	525	660						
Picton	660	450	30	340	690	530	355	290	400	900	160	1090	120	580					
Queenstown	260	565	785	480	285	355	530	610	490	190	660	290	820	290	815				
Te Anau	420	725	945	640	295	515	690	770	650	160	815	120	980	410	975	170			
Timaru	210	260	465	165	200	490	350	295	360	410	340	605	580	85	495	330	490		
Wanaka	210	510	730	430	280	285	465	555	420	245	600	345	755	230	760	70	230	275	
Westport	610	195	260	340	650	280	100	220	145	810	330	905	230	535	290	630	790	455	565

TRANSPORT

Europcar (☎ 0800 800 115, 03-357 0920; www.europcar.co.nz)
Hertz (☎ 0800 654 321, 03-520 3044; www.hertz.co.nz)
Thrifty (☎ 0800 737 070, 03-359 2720; www.thrifty.co.nz)

Local rental firms and firms with limited locations can be found in the *Yellow Pages* – see the regional chapters in this guide. These are almost always cheaper than the big boys – sometimes half the price – but the cheap rates may come with serious restrictions, vehicles are often older, and with less formality sometimes comes less protective legal structure for renters.

Affordable, independent operators with national networks:

Ace Rental Cars (☎ 0800 502 277, 09-303 3112; www.acerentalcars.co.nz)
Apex Rentals (☎ 0800 939 597, 03-379 6897; www.apexrentals.co.nz)
Ezy Rentals (☎ 0800 399 736, 09-374 4360; www.ezy.co.nz)
Go Rentals (☎ 0800 467 368, 09-525 7321; www.gorentals.co.nz)
Omega Rental Cars (☎ 0800 525 210, 09-377 5573; www.omegarentalcars.com)
Pegasus Rental Cars (☎ 0800 803 580, 03-548 2852; www.rentalcars.co.nz)

The big firms sometimes offer one-way rentals (eg collect a car in Dunedin, leave it in Picton), but there are a variety of restrictions, and a one-way drop-off fee may apply. Fees are often waived for rentals of a month or more. If you're lucky, an operator in Queenstown may need to get a vehicle back to Christchurch (for example) and will offer an amazing one-way deal.

If you are travelling to the North Island, most car-hire firms suggest (or insist) that you don't take their vehicles between islands on the Cook Strait ferries. Instead, you leave your car at either Wellington or Picton terminal and pick up another car once you've crossed the strait. This saves you paying to transport a vehicle on the ferries, and is a pain-free exercise.

The major companies offer a choice of either unlimited kilometres, or 100km (or so) per day free plus so many cents per subsequent kilometre. Daily rates in main cities typically start at around $40 per day for a compact, late-model, Japanese car, and around $75 for medium-sized cars (including GST, unlimited kilometres and insurance). Local firms start

at around $30 per day for the smallest option. It's obviously cheaper if you rent for a week or more and there are often low-season and weekend discounts. Credit cards are the usual payment method.

MOTORCYCLE
Born to be wild? NZ has great terrain for motorcycle touring, despite the fickle weather in some regions. If you're tempted to bring your own motorcycle into NZ, be aware that this will entail an expensive shipping exercise, valid registration in the country of origin and a *Carnet de Passages en Douanes* (a customs document that identifies your motor vehicle).

Most of the South Island's motorcycle-hire shops are in Christchurch, where you can hire anything from a little 50cc moped (aka nifty-fifty) for zipping around town, to a throbbing 750cc touring motorcycle. Recommended operators:

New Zealand Motorcycle Rentals & Tours (☎ 09-634 9118; www.nzbike.com) Yamahas, BMWs, Hondas and Harleys from $120 to $395 per day. Rates vary with size of bike, length of rental and season. Guided tours also available.
Te Waipounamu Motorcycle Tours (☎ 03-372 3537 www.motorcycle-hire.co.nz) Yamahas, Ducatis, Kawasakis, BMWs, Hondas and Suzukis from $115 to $300 per day. Guided tours also available.

Insurance
When it comes to renting a vehicle, know exactly what your liability is in the event of an accident. Rather than risk paying out a large amount of cash if you do have an accident (minor collisions are common in NZ), you can take out your own comprehensive insurance policy, or (the usual option) pay an additional daily amount to the rental company for an 'insurance excess reduction' policy. This brings the amount of excess you must pay in the event of an accident down from around $1500 or $2000 to around $150 or $200. Smaller operators offering cheap rates often have a compulsory insurance excess, taken as a credit-card bond, of around $900.

Most insurance agreements won't cover the cost of damage to glass (including the windscreen) or tyres, and insurance coverage is often invalidated on beaches and certain unsealed roads – always read the fine print.

For information on the country's no-fault Accident Compensation Corporation scheme, see p384.

Purchase

For longer stays and/or for groups, buying a car then selling it at the end of your travels can be one of the cheapest and best ways to see NZ. You can often pick up a car as cheap as (or cheaper than) a one- or two-month rental, and you should be able to get back most of your money when you sell it. The danger, of course, is that you'll buy a lemon that breaks down every five minutes.

On the South Island, Christchurch is the easiest place for travellers to buy a car. An easy option for a cheap car is to scour the notice boards of backpacker places, where other travellers sell their cars before moving on; you can pick up an old car for just a few hundred dollars. Some backpackers specials are so cheap it may be worth taking the risk that they may expire on you. Besides, these vehicles often come complete with water containers, tools, road maps and even camping gear.

Car markets and car auctions are also worth investigating – check out information on car markets in the Christchurch (p234) section. At auctions you can pick up cheap cars from around $1000 to $6000 – **Turners Auctions** (☎ 09-580 9360; www.turners.co.nz) is the country's largest such outfit, with 10 locations.

Make sure any car you buy has a Warrant of Fitness (WoF) and that the registration lasts for a reasonable period. A WoF certificate, proving that the car is roadworthy, is valid for six months but must be less than 28 days old when you buy a car. To transfer registration, both you and the seller are legally required to independently notify **Land Transport New Zealand** (www.landtransport.govt.nz) of the change of ownership within seven days. To do so, fill out a *Notice of Change of Ownership of Motor Vehicle* form (MR 13 or MR 13B), which can be filed at any AA office or post office. Papers are sent to you by mail within 10 days (you'll need an address!). If needed, registration can be purchased for six months ($268) or a year ($388).

Car buyers should also take out third-party insurance, covering the cost of repairs to another vehicle in an accident that is your fault: try the **Automobile Association** (AA; ☎ 0800 500 231; www.aainsurance.co.nz). The no-fault Accident Compensation Corporation scheme (p384) covers personal injury, but make sure you have travel insurance as well (p384).

Car inspections are highly recommended as they'll protect you against any dodgy WoFs (such scams have been reported in the past)

and may save you a lot of grief and repair bills later on. Various car-inspection companies will check a car you intend to buy for less than $150; you'll find them at car auctions for on-the-spot inspections, or they will come to you. Try **Vehicle Inspection New Zealand** (VINZ; ☎ 0800 468 469; www.vinz.co.nz). The AA also offers a mobile inspection service – it is slightly cheaper if you bring the car to an AA-approved mechanic. AA checks are thorough, but most garages will inspect a car for less.

Before you buy it's wise to confirm the ownership of the vehicle, and find out if there's anything dodgy about the car in question (eg any outstanding debts on it). A number of companies offer this service, including the AA's **LemonCheck** (☎ 04-233 8590; www.lemoncheck.co.nz). A search costs $25 and is done using the Vehicle Identification Number (VIN; found on a plate near the engine block) or licence-plate number.

BUY-BACK DEALS

One way of getting around the hassles of buying and selling a vehicle privately is to enter into a buy-back arrangement with a car or motorcycle dealer. However, dealers may find ways of knocking down the price when you return the vehicle (even if it was agreed to in writing), often by pointing out expensive repairs that allegedly will be required to gain the WoF certificate needed to transfer the registration. The buy-back amount varies, but may be 50% less than the purchase price – in a strictly financial sense, hiring or buying and selling the vehicle yourself (if you have the time) is usually a much better idea.

Road Hazards

The full spectrum of drivers and driving habits occurs on NZ roads, from the no-fuss motorist who doesn't mind pulling over to let you past, to back-road tailgaters who believe they know a particular stretch of bitumen so well they can go as fast as they like, despite narrow, twisting roads. Traffic is usually pretty light, but it's easy to get stuck behind a slow-moving truck or campervan on uphill climbs – pack plenty of patience. There are also lots of gravel or dirt roads to explore, which require a more cautious driving approach than for sealed roads. And watch out for sheep!

Road Rules

Kiwis drive on the left-hand side of the road and all cars are right-hand drive. A 'give way to the right' rule applies and is interpreted to a rather strange extreme here – if you're turning left and an oncoming vehicle is turning right into the same street, you have to give way to it.

Speed limits on the open road are generally 100km/h; in built-up areas the limit is usually 50km/h. An 'LSZ' (Limited Speed Zone) sign on the open road means that the speed limit is reduced from 100km/h to 50km/h in certain conditions – this applies when conditions are unsafe due to bad weather, limited visibility, pedestrians, cyclists or animals on the road, excessive traffic, or lousy road conditions. Speed cameras and radars are used extensively.

At single-lane bridges (of which there are a surprisingly large number), a smaller red arrow pointing in your direction of travel means that *you* give way, so slow down as you approach and pull a little to the side if you see a car approaching the other end of the bridge.

All new cars in NZ have seat belts back and front and it's the law to wear them – you're risking a fine if you don't. Small children must be belted into an approved safety seat.

Drivers might want to buy a copy of the *New Zealand Road Code*, which will tell you all you need to know about life on the road. Versions applicable to both cars and motorcycles are available at AA offices and bookshops, or you can check the online rundown of road rules on the **Land Transport New Zealand** (www.landtransport.govt.nz/roadcode) website.

HITCHING

Until quite recently it was quite fair and logical to think, 'If there's anywhere in the world where I can still hitch a ride, NZ is it.' However, a few unsavoury incidents in recent years suggest that NZ is no longer immune from the perils of solo hitching (especially for women). Those who decide to hitch should understand that they are taking a small but potentially serious risk. Prospective hitchers will be safer if they travel in pairs and let someone know where they are planning to go. That said, it's not unusual to see hitchhikers by the side of country roads (signalling with a thumbs-up or a downward-pointed finger), although extensive bus networks and cheap car-rental rates mean that hitching a ride isn't as common among travellers as it once was.

People looking for travelling companions for car journeys often leave notices on boards in backpacker accommodation. The website www.carshare.co.nz is an excellent resource for people seeking or offering a lift.

LOCAL TRANSPORT
Bus, Train & Tram

Most of NZ's urban buses have been privatised. Larger cities have fairly extensive bus services but, with a few honourable exceptions, they are mainly daytime, weekday operations; on weekends, particularly on Sunday, bus services can be hard to find or may cease altogether. Negotiating the inner-city area in Christchurch is made easier by the Shuttle Bus service and the historic tramway. The bigger South Island centres have a late-night bus service roaming central entertainment districts on boozy, end-of-week nights.

Taxi

The main cities have plenty of taxis and even small towns may have a local service. Taxis cruise the busy areas in Christchurch, but elsewhere you usually have to either phone for one or find a taxi rank.

TRAIN

NZ train travel is about the journey, not about getting anywhere in a hurry. **Tranz Scenic** (☎ 0800 872 467, 04-495 0775; www.tranzscenic.co.nz) operates several visually stunning routes, such as the *TranzCoastal* between Christchurch and Picton, and the *TranzAlpine*, which rattles over the Southern Alps between Christchurch and Greymouth. These routes run in both directions daily.

Reservations can be made through Tranz Scenic directly, or at most train stations, travel agents and visitor information centres, where you can also pick up booklets detailing timetables. Ask about discount fares – reductions apply for children (50% off standard fares), seniors and students (30% off), and holders of backpackers cards (20% off).

Train Passes

Given the South Island's limited rail network, buying a train pass isn't particularly good value.

Tranz Scenic's **Scenic Rail Pass** (www.tranzscenic.co.nz) allows unlimited travel on all of its rail services (with the exception of the *Capital Connection*), with the option of including passage on the Interislander ferry between Wellington and Picton. A pass (with ferry trip) lasting two weeks costs $517/394 per adult/child.

Health Dr David Millar

New Zealand is one of the healthiest countries in the world in which to travel. The risk of diseases such as malaria and typhoid is unheard of, and thanks to NZ's quarantine standards, even some animal diseases such as rabies have yet to be recorded. The absence of poisonous snakes or other dangerous animals makes this a very safe region to get off the beaten track and out into the beautiful countryside.

BEFORE YOU GO

Since most vaccines don't produce immunity until at least two weeks after they're given, visit a physician four to eight weeks before departure. Ask your doctor for an International Certificate of Vaccination (or 'the yellow booklet'), which will list all the vaccinations you've received. This is mandatory for countries that require proof of yellow-fever vaccination upon entry, but it's a good idea to carry it wherever you travel.

Bring medications in their original, clearly labelled containers. A signed and dated letter from your physician describing your medical conditions and medications, including generic names, is also a good idea. If carrying syringes or needles, be sure to have a physician's letter documenting their medical necessity.

INSURANCE

If your current health insurance doesn't cover you for medical expenses incurred overseas, you should think about getting extra insurance – check out www.lonelyplanet.com for more information. Find out in advance if your insurance plan will make payments directly to providers or reimburse you at a later date for overseas health expenditures. (In many countries doctors expect payment in cash.)

RECOMMENDED VACCINATIONS

NZ has no vaccination requirements for any traveller. The World Health Organization recommends that all travellers should be covered for diphtheria, tetanus, measles, mumps, rubella, chickenpox and polio, as well as hepatitis B, regardless of their destination. Planning to travel abroad is an ideal time to

ensure that all routine vaccination cover is complete. The consequences of these diseases can be severe and while NZ has high levels of childhood vaccination coverage, outbreaks of these diseases do occur.

INTERNET RESOURCES

You'll find that there's a wealth of travel health advice available on the internet. For further information on health, **Lonely Planet** (www.lonely planet.com) is a good place to start. The **World Health Organization** (www.who.int/ith/) publishes an excellent book called *International Travel and Health,* which is revised annually and is available online at no cost. Another good website of general interest is **MD Travel Health** (www.mdtravelhealth.com), which provides complete travel health recommendations for every country and is updated daily.

IN TRANSIT

DEEP VEIN THROMBOSIS (DVT)

Blood clots may form in the legs during plane flights, chiefly because of a prolonged period of immobility. The longer the flight, the greater the risk. The chief symptom of deep vein thrombosis (DVT) is swelling or pain of the foot, ankle or calf, usually – but not always – on just one side. When a blood clot travels to the lungs, it may result in chest pain and difficulty breathing. Travellers with any of these symptoms should seek medical attention immediately.

To prevent the development of DVT on long flights, you should walk about the cabin, perform compressions of the leg muscles (ie flex the leg muscles while sitting), drink plenty of fluids and avoid alcohol and tobacco.

JET LAG & MOTION SICKNESS

Jet lag is common when crossing more than five time zones, resulting in insomnia, fatigue, malaise and/or nausea. To avoid the effects of jet lag, try drinking plenty of nonalcoholic fluids and eating light meals. Upon arrival at your destination, get exposure to natural sunlight and readjust your schedule (for meals, sleep etc) as soon as possible.

Antihistamines such as dimenhydrinate (Dramamine) and meclizine (Antivert, Bonine) are usually the preferred choice for treating motion sickness. Their main side effect is drowsiness. A herbal alternative is ginger, which works like a charm for some people.

IN NEW ZEALAND

AVAILABILITY & COST OF HEALTH CARE

Health insurance is essential for all travellers. While health care in NZ is of a high standard and not overly expensive by international standards, considerable costs can be built up and repatriation can be extremely expensive. See p405 for insurance information.

Health Care in New Zealand

NZ does not have a government-funded system of public hospitals. All travellers are, however, covered for medical care resulting from accidents that occur while in NZ (eg motor-vehicle accidents, adventure-activity accidents) by the Accident Compensation Corporation (ACC). Costs incurred by treatment of a medical illness that occurs while in NZ will only be covered by travel insurance. For more details see www.moh.govt.nz and www.acc.co.nz.

NZ has excellent specialised public health facilities for women and children in the major centres. No specific health concerns exist for women but greater care for children is recommended to avoid environmental hazards such as heat, sunburn, cold and marine hazards.

The 24-hour, free-call **Healthline** (☎ 0800 611 116) offers health advice throughout NZ.

Self-care in New Zealand

In NZ it is possible to find yourself in a remote location where, in the event of a serious accident or illness, there may well be a significant delay in emergency services getting to you. This is usually the result of weather and rugged terrain, particularly on the South Island. Therefore, an increased level of self-reliance and preparation is essential. Consider taking a wilderness first-aid course (such as the one from the Wilderness Medicine Institute). In addition, you should carry a comprehensive first-aid kit that is appropriate for the activities planned. To be really safe, ensure that you

have adequate means of communication – NZ has extensive mobile-phone coverage, but additional radio communication equipment is important for remote areas, and can usually be hired from Department of Conservation visitor centres in popular tramping areas.

Pharmaceutical Supplies

Over-the-counter medications are widely available in NZ through private chemists. These include painkillers, antihistamines for allergies, and skin care products.

Some medications that are available over the counter in other countries are only available by a prescription obtained from a general practitioner. These include the oral contraceptive pill, most medications for asthma and all antibiotics. If you take a medication on a regular basis, bring an adequate supply and ensure you have details of the generic name, as brand names differ between countries. The majority of medications in use outside of the region are available.

INFECTIOUS DISEASES
Amoebic Meningitis

There is a small risk of developing amoebic meningitis as a result of bathing or swimming in geothermal pools in NZ – mostly in regions such as Rotorua and Taupo. In such pools, keeping the head above water to prevent movement of the organism up the nasal passage reduces the risk (which is pretty low to start with). Symptoms usually start three to seven days after swimming in a geothermal pool and early symptoms of this serious disease include headache, fever and vomiting. Urgent medical care is essential to differentiate the disease from other causes of meningitis and for appropriate treatment.

Giardiasis

The giardia parasite is widespread in the waterways of NZ. Drinking untreated water from streams and lakes is not recommended. Using water filters and boiling or treating water with iodine are effective ways of preventing the disease. Symptoms consist of intermittent bad-smelling diarrhoea, abdominal bloating and wind. Effective treatment is available (tinidazole or metronidazole).

Hepatitis C

This disease is a growing problem among intravenous drug users. Blood-transfusion services fully screen all blood before use.

HIV
The country's HIV rates have stabilised after major media campaigns, and levels are similar to other Western countries. Clean needles and syringes are widely available.

Meningococcal Disease
This occurs worldwide and is a risk with prolonged dormitory-style accommodation. A vaccine exists for some types of the disease (meningococcal A, C, Y and W).

Sexually Transmitted Diseases (STDs)
In NZ, STDs (including herpes, gonorrhoea and chlamydia) occur at rates similar to most Western countries. The most common symptoms are pain on passing urine and a discharge. Infection can be present without symptoms, so seek medical screening after any unprotected sex with a new partner. Sexual health clinics are run as part of major hospitals.

TRAVELLER'S DIARRHOEA
If you develop diarrhoea, be sure to drink plenty of fluids, preferably an oral rehydration solution containing lots of salt and sugar. A few loose stools don't require treatment but if you start having more than four or five stools a day, you should start taking an antibiotic (usually a quinolone drug) and an antidiarrhoeal agent (such as loperamide). If diarrhoea is bloody, persists for more than 72 hours and/or is accompanied by fever, shaking chills or severe abdominal pain you should seek medical attention.

ENVIRONMENTAL HAZARDS
Hypothermia
This is a significant risk, especially during the winter months or year-round in the mountains of the North Island and all of the South Island. Mountain ranges and/or strong winds produce a high chill factor which can result in hypothermia, even in moderately cool temperatures. Early signs include the inability to perform fine movements (such as doing up buttons), shivering and a bad case of the 'umbles' (fumbles, mumbles, grumbles, stumbles). The key elements of treatment are changing the environment to one where heat loss is minimised, changing out of any wet clothing, adding dry clothes with wind- and waterproof layers, adding insulation and providing fuel (water and carbohydrate) to

allow shivering to build the internal temperature. In severe hypothermia, shivering actually stops; this is a medical emergency requiring rapid evacuation in addition to the above measures.

Spider Bites
NZ has two poisonous spiders, the native katipo (not very poisonous and uncommon to the point of being endangered) and the introduced (thanks, Australia) white-tailed spider (also uncommon). White-tailed spider bites have been known to cause ulcers that are very difficult to heal. Clean the wound thoroughly and seek medical assistance if an ulcer develops.

Surf Beaches & Drowning
NZ has exceptional surf beaches, particularly on the western, southern and eastern coasts. The power of the surf can fluctuate as a result of the varying slope of the seabed at many beaches. Check with local surf life-saving organisations before entering the surf and be aware of your own limitations and expertise.

Ultraviolet Light Exposure
NZ has one of the highest rates of skin cancer in the world, so you should monitor UV exposure closely. UV exposure is greatest between 10am and 4pm – avoid skin exposure during these times. Always use SPF30+ sunscreen, making sure you apply it 30 minutes before exposure and that you reapply regularly to minimise sun damage.

Water
Tap water is universally safe in NZ. Increasing numbers of streams, rivers and lakes, however, are being contaminated by bugs that cause diarrhoea, making water purification when tramping essential. The simplest way of purifying water is to boil it thoroughly. You should also consider purchasing a water filter. It's very important when buying a filter to read the specifications so that you know exactly what it removes from the water and what it doesn't. Simple filtering will not remove all dangerous organisms, so if you cannot boil water it should be treated chemically. Chlorine tablets will kill many pathogens, but not parasites such as giardia or amoebic cysts. Iodine is more effective in purifying water. Follow the directions carefully and remember that too much iodine can be harmful.

HEALTH

Language

New Zealand has two official languages: English and Maori. English is what you'll usually hear, but Maori has been making a comeback. You can use English to speak to anyone in NZ, but there are some occasions when knowing a small amount of Maori is useful, such as when visiting a *marae*, where often only Maori is spoken. Maori is also useful to know since many places in NZ have Maori names.

KIWI ENGLISH

Like the people of other English-speaking countries in the world, New Zealanders have a unique way of speaking the language. The flattening of vowels is the most distinctive feature of Kiwi pronunciation. The NZ treatment of 'fish and chips' – 'fush and chups' – is an endless source of delight for Australians in particular. On the North Island sentences often have 'eh!' attached to the end. In the far south a rolled 'r' is common, a holdover from that region's Scottish heritage – it's especially noticeable in Southland. See the Glossary on p411 for an explanation of some Kiwi English words and expressions.

A Personal Kiwi-Yankee Dictionary by Louis S Leland Jr is an often hilarious book of translations, and explains some of the quirks that distinguish Kiwi and American ways of speaking English.

MAORI

The Maori have a vividly chronicled history, recorded in songs and chants that dramatically recall the migration to NZ from Polynesian Hawaiki as well as other important events. Early missionaries were the first to record the language in a written form, and achieved this with only 15 letters of the English alphabet.

Maori is closely related to other Polynesian languages such as Hawaiian, Tahitian and Cook Islands Maori. In fact, NZ Maori and Hawaiian are quite similar, even though over 7000km separates Honolulu and Auckland.

The Maori language was never dead – it was always used in Maori ceremonies – but over time familiarity with it was definitely on the decline. Fortunately, recent years have seen a revival of interest in it, and this forms an integral part of the renaissance of *Maoritanga* (Maori culture). Many Maori people who had heard the language spoken on the *marae* for years but had not used it in their day-to-day lives, are now studying it and speaking it fluently. Maori is taught in schools throughout NZ, some TV programs and news reports are broadcast in it, and many English place names are being renamed in Maori. Even government departments have been given Maori names: for example the Inland Revenue Department is also known as Te Tari Taake (the last word is actually *take*, which means 'levy', but the department has chosen to stress the long 'a' by spelling it 'aa').

In many places, Maori have come together to provide instruction in their language and culture to young children; the idea is for them to grow up speaking both Maori and English, and to develop a familiarity with Maori tradition. It's a matter of some pride to have fluency in the language. On some *marae* only Maori can be spoken.

PRONUNCIATION

Maori is a fluid, poetic language and surprisingly easy to pronounce once you remember to split each word (some can be amazingly long) into separate syllables.

Most consonants in Maori – **h**, **k**, **m**, **n**, **p**, **t** and **w** – are pronounced much the same as in English. The Maori **r** is a flapped sound (not rolled) with the tongue near the front of the mouth. It's closer to the English 'l' in pronunciation.

The **ng** is pronounced as in the English words 'singing' or 'running', and can be used at the beginning of words as well as at the end. To practise, just say 'ing' over and over, then isolate the 'ng' part of it.

The **wh** is generally pronounced as a soft English 'f'. This pronunciation is used in

MAORI GEOGRAPHICAL TERMS

The following words form part of many place names in NZ:

a – of
ana – cave
ara – way, path or road
awa – river or valley
heke – descend
hiku – end; tail
hine – girl; daughter
ika – fish
iti – small
kahurangi – treasured possession; special greenstone
kai – food
kainga – village
kaka – parrot
kare – rippling
kati – shut or close
koura – crayfish
makariri – cold
manga – stream or tributary
manu – bird
maunga – mountain
moana – sea or lake
moko – tattoo
motu – island
mutu – finished; ended; over
nga – the (plural)
noa – ordinary; not *tapu*
nui – big or great
nuku – distance
o – of, place of...
one – beach, sand or mud
pa – fortified village
papa – large blue-grey mudstone
pipi – common edible bivalve
pohatu – stone
poto – short

pouri – sad; dark; gloomy
puke – hill
puna – spring; hole; fountain
rangi – sky; heavens
raro – north
rei – cherished possession
roa – long
roto – lake
rua – hole in the ground; two
runga – above
tahuna – beach; sandbank
tane – man
tangata – people
tapu – sacred, forbidden or taboo
tata – close to; dash against; twin islands
tawaha – entrance or opening
tawahi – the other side (of a river or lake)
te – the (singular)
tonga – south
ure – male genitals
uru – west
waha – broken
wahine – woman
wai – water
waingaro – lost; waters that disappear in certain seasons
waka – canoe
wera – burnt or warm; floating
wero – challenge
whaka... – to act as ...
whanau – family
whanga – harbour, bay or inlet
where – house
whenua – land or country
whiti – east

Knowledge of just a few such words can help you make sense of many Maori place names. For example: Waikaremoana is the Sea *(moana)* of Rippling *(kare)* Waters *(wai)*; Rotorua means the Second *(rua)* Lake *(roto)*; and Taumatawhakatangihangakoauauotamateaturipukakapikimaunga-horonukupokaiwhenuakitanatahu means... well, perhaps you'd better see p392 for that translation. Some easier place names composed of words in this list:

Aramoana – Sea *(moana)* Path *(ara)*
Awaroa – Long *(roa)* River *(awa)*
Kaitangata – Eat *(kai)* People *(tangata)*
Maunganui – Great *(nui)* Mountain *(maunga)*
Opouri – Place of *(o)* Sadness *(pouri)*
Te Araroa – The *(te)* Long *(roa)* Path *(ara)*

Te Puke – The *(te)* Hill *(puke)*
Urewera – Burnt *(wera)* Penis *(ure)*
Waimakariri – Cold *(makariri)* Water *(wai)*
Wainui – Great *(nui)* Waters *(wai)*
Whakatane – To Act *(whaka)* as a Man *(tane)*
Whangarei – Cherished *(rei)* Harbour *(whanga)*

(Note that the adjective comes after the noun in Maori constructions. Thus 'cold water' is *wai makariri* not *makariri wai*.)

many place names in NZ, such as Whakatane, Whangaroa and Whakapapa (all pronounced as if they begin with a soft 'f'). There is some local variation: in the region around the Whanganui River, for example, the **wh** is pronounced as in the English words 'when' and 'why'.

The correct pronunciation of the vowels is very important. The examples below are a rough guideline – it helps to listen carefully to someone who speaks the language well. Each vowel has both a long and a short sound with long vowels often denoted by a macron (a line over the letter) or a double vowel. We have not indicated long/short vowel forms in this book.

VOWELS

a	as in 'large', with no 'r' sound
e	as in 'get'
i	as in 'marine'
o	as in 'pork'
u	as the 'oo' in 'moon'

VOWEL COMBINATIONS

ae, ai	as the 'y' in 'sky'
ao, au	as the 'ow' in 'how'
ea	as in 'bear'
ei	as in 'vein'
eo	as 'eh-oh'
eu	as 'eh-oo'
ia	as in the name 'Ian'
ie	as the 'ye' in 'yet'
io	as the 'ye o' in 'ye old'
iu	as the 'ue' in 'cue'
oa	as in 'roar'
oe	as in 'toe'
oi	as in 'toil'
ou	as the 'ow' in 'how'
ua	as the 'ewe' in 'fewer'

Each syllable ends in a vowel and there is never more than one vowel in a syllable. There are no silent letters.

There are many Maori phrasebooks, grammar books and Maori–English dictionaries if you want to take a closer look at the language. The *Collins Maori Phrase Book* by Patricia Tauroa is an ideal book for starting to speak the language, with sections on every-day conversation and using the language in a cultural context. Lonely Planet's *South Pacific Phrasebook* has a section on the Maori language and several other Pacific languages that you may hear spoken around Wellington or South Auckland.

Other good references include the *English–Maori Maori–English Dictionary* by Bruce Biggs, and the *Reed Dictionary of Modern Maori* by PM Ryan, which is one of the most authoritative.

Learning a few basic greetings will enrich your travels, especially if you plan to go onto a *marae*.

GREETINGS & SMALL TALK

Maori greetings are finding increased popularity; don't be surprised if you're greeted with *Kia ora*.

Haere mai!	Welcome!
Kia ora.	Hello./Good luck./Good health.
Tena koe.	Hello. (to one person)
Tena korua.	Hello. (to two people)
Tena koutou.	Hello. (to three or more people)
E noho ra.	Goodbye. (to person staying)
Haere ra.	Goodbye. (to person leaving)

Kei te pehea koe?
　How are you? (to one person)
Kei te pehea korua?
　How are you? (to two people)
Kei te pehea koutou?
　How are you? (to three or more)
Kei te pai.
　Very well, thanks./That's fine.

Glossary

This glossary is a list of abbreviations, 'Kiwi English', Maori, and slang terms and phrases you may come across in New Zealand. Also see the Maori Geographical Terms boxed text (p409) in the Language chapter for Maori words that pop up again and again in NZ place names.

AA – New Zealand's Automobile Association; provides road information and roadside assistance
across the ditch – referring to Australia, across the Tasman Sea
afghan – popular homemade chocolate biscuit (origin of recipe unknown, but unlikely to be Afghanistan)
All Blacks – NZ's revered national rugby union team (the name comes from 'All Backs', which is what the press called the NZ rugby team on an early visit to England); this moniker has started a trend for many national sporting teams to be similarly nicknamed (including the Tall Blacks for the basketball team, the Black Caps for the cricket team and, briefly before being dropped, the Black Cocks for the badminton team!)
ANZAC – Australia and New Zealand Army Corps
Aoraki – Maori name for Mt Cook, meaning 'Cloud Piercer'
Aotearoa – Maori name for NZ, most often translated as 'Land of the Long White Cloud'
ariki – chief
aroha – love
atua – spirits or gods
awa – river

B&B – 'bed and breakfast' accommodation
bach – holiday home, usually a wooden cottage (pronounced 'batch'); see also *crib*
BBH – Budget Backpacker Hostels; a popular hostelry affiliation
Beehive – Parliament House in Wellington, so-called because of its distinctive shape
black-water rafting – rafting or tubing underground in a cave or *tomo*
blokarting – sand sailing
bogan – rough-edged fellow, probably wearing a black T-shirt, drinking beer and listening to AC/DC
boozer – public bar
bro – literally 'brother'; usually meaning mate, as in 'just off to see the *bros*'
BYO – 'bring your own' (usually applies to alcohol at a restaurant or cafe)
BYOW – 'bring your own wine', implying you can't bring beer or any other alcoholic beverages

cervena – farmed deer
chardy – chardonnay
chillie bin – cooler; esky; large insulated box for keeping food and drinks cold
choice/chur – fantastic; great
ciggies – cigarettes
crib – the name for a *bach* in Otago and Southland
cuzzie, cuz – cousin; relative or mate, most often used by Maori to refer to fellow Maori; see also *bro*
cuzzie bro – an emphasised version of both *cuzzie* and *bro*

dairy – small corner store that sells milk, bread, newspapers, ice cream and pretty much everything else
daggy – uncool; from the dags that hang off sheep's bottoms
DB&B – 'dinner, bed and breakfast' accommodation
DOC – Department of Conservation (or *Te Papa Atawhai*); government department that administers national parks and thus all tracks and huts
domain – open grassed area in a town or city, often the focus of recreational activities or civic amenities such as gardens, picnic areas and bowling clubs (and sometimes camping grounds)
Dorkland – derogatory reference to the big city
dropkick – a certain method of kicking a rugby ball; a personal insult

eh – roughly translates as 'don't you agree?' and is commonly added to the end of many *Kiwi* sentences, usually followed by *bro* (as in 'Choice jandals, eh bro?')

farmstay – accommodation on a *Kiwi* farm where you're encouraged to join in the typical day-to-day activities
football – rugby, either union or league; occasionally soccer
freezing works – slaughterhouse or abattoir for sheep and/or cattle

Godzone – New Zealand (from Richard Seddon who referred to NZ as 'God's own country')
good as gold, good as – very good; no problem
Great Walks – a set of nine popular tramping tracks within NZ
greenstone – jade; *pounamu*
gumboots – rubber boots or Wellingtons; originated from diggers on the gum-fields
haka – any dance, but usually refers to the traditional challenge; war dance
hakari – feast

handle – beer glass with a handle

hangi – oven made by digging a hole and steaming food in baskets over embers in the hole; a feast of Maori food

hapu – subtribe or smaller tribal grouping

hard case – hilarious, unusual or strong-willed character

Hawaiki – Polynesian homeland from where the Maori tribes migrated by canoe (probably Ra'iatea in the Society Islands); also a name for the Afterworld

hei tiki – carved, stylised human figure worn around the neck representing the first human and supposed to bring good luck; also called a *tiki*

hikoi – march, walk, sometimes a protest march or pilgrimage

hoa – friend; usually pronounced 'e hoa'

hokey pokey – delicious variety of vanilla ice cream with butterscotch chips

hoki – type of fish common in fish and chip shops

homestay – accommodation in a family house where you're treated as one of the family

hongi – Maori greeting; the pressing of foreheads and noses, and sharing of life breath

hui – gathering; meeting

Interislander – large ferries crossing Cook Strait between Wellington and Picton

i-SITE – information centre

'Is it what!' – strong affirmation or agreement; 'Yes, isn't it!'

Islander – Pacific Islander; see also *'Nesian, PI* and *Poly*

iwi – large tribal grouping with common lineage back to the original migration from *Hawaiki*; people; tribe

jandals – a contraction of Japanese sandals; flip-flops; thongs; usually rubber footwear

jersey – jumper, usually woollen; the shirt worn by rugby players

jiff – short measurement of time (as in 'I'll be back in a *jiff*'); see also *two ticks*

judder bars – bumps in the road to make you drive slowly; speed humps

ka kite (ano) – see you again; goodbye

ka pai – good; excellent

kai – food; almost any word with *kai* in it has a connection with food

kainga – village; pre-European unfortified Maori village

kapa haka – traditional Maori group singing and dancing

karakia – prayer, incantation

kaumatua – highly respected members of a tribe; the people you would ask for permission to enter a *marae*

kauri – native pine

kina – sea urchins, a Maori delicacy

Kiwi – A New Zealander; an adjective to mean anything relating to NZ

kiwi – the flightless, nocturnal brown bird with a long beak that is the national symbol

Kiwiana – the collective term for anything uniquely connected to NZ life and culture, especially from years gone by, and likely to bring on waves of nostalgia in any expat *Kiwi* (examples include *hokey pokey, jandals* and *pavlova*)

kiwifruit – small, succulent fruit with fuzzy brown skin and juicy green flesh; a Chinese gooseberry; never called a *kiwi*

koha – donation

kohanga reo – schools where Maori language and culture are at the forefront of the education process; also called language nest schools

korero – to talk

kumara – Polynesian sweet potato, a Maori staple food

kunekune – type of wild pig introduced by Chinese gold diggers in the 19th century

Kupe – early Polynesian navigator from *Hawaiki,* credited with the discovery of the islands that are now NZ

L&P – Lemon & Paeroa; lemon-flavoured fizzy drink

laters – 'see you later'

league – rugby league football

lounge bar – more upmarket bar than a public bar; called a 'ladies bar' in some countries

Mainlander – self-referential term for South Islander

mana – spiritual quality of a person or object; prestige; authority of a chief or priest

manaia – traditional carving design; literally means 'bird-headed man'

manuhiri – visitor; guest

Maori – indigenous people of NZ

Maoritanga – Maori culture

marae – literally refers to the sacred ground in front of the Maori meeting house, more commonly used to refer to the entire complex of buildings

marakihau – sea monster

Maui – a figure in Maori (Polynesian) mythology

maunga – mountain

mauri – life force/principle

mere – a *patu* made of *greenstone*

metal/metalled road – gravel (unsealed) road

MMP – Mixed Member Proportional; the electoral system used in NZ and Germany; a form of proportional voting

moa – large, extinct flightless bird

moe – sleep

moko – tattoo; usually refers to facial tattoos

Moriori – isolated Polynesian group, inhabitants of the Chatham Islands

motorway – freeway or expressway

marnis – something or someone shameful

munted – damaged, destroyed

munter – see *bogan*

naiad – rigid-hull inflatable boat (used for dolphin swimming, whale watching etc)

'Nesian – Pacific Islander; see also *Islander*, *PI* and *Poly*

nga – the (plural); see also *te*

ngai/ngati – literally, 'the people of' or 'the descendants of'; tribe (on the South Island it's pronounced 'kai')

NZ – the universal term for New Zealand; pronounced 'en zed'

OE – Overseas Experience; a working holiday abroad, traditionally to the UK (the young *Kiwi's* near-mandatory 'tour of duty')

pa – fortified Maori village, usually on a hilltop

Pacific Rim – term used to describe modern NZ cuisine; cuisine with an innovative use of local produce, especially seafood, with imported styles

Pakeha – Maori for a white or European person

pakihi – unproductive and often swampy land on the South Island's west coast; pronounced 'par-kee'

papa – large blue-grey mudstones; the word comes from the Maori for Earth Mother

parapenting – paragliding

Pasifika – Pacific Island culture

patch – gang logo worn on clothing

patu – flat war club made of wood, bone or greenstone

paua – abalone; tough shellfish pounded, minced, then made into patties (fritters), which are available in almost every NZ fish-and-chip shop; the beautiful, iridescent *paua* shell is often used in decoration and jewellery

pavlova – meringue cake, usually topped with cream and *kiwifruit;* the quintessential *Kiwi* dessert

PI – Pacific Islander; see also *Islander*, *Poly* and *'Nesian*

pig islander – derogatory term used by a person from one island for someone from the other island

pillocking – 'surfing' across mud flats on a rubbish-bin lid

plpi – common edible bivalve

piss – urine; urinate; alcohol, as in 'get on the piss'

poi – ball of woven flax

poi dance – women's formation dance that involves singing and manipulating a *poi*

polly – politician

Poly – Pacific Islander; see also *Islander*, *PI* and *'Nesian*

pou – wooden post, sometimes carved

ponga – the *silver fern;* called a bungy (pronounced 'bungee', with a soft 'g', in parts of the South Island)

pounamu – Maori name for *greenstone*

powhiri – traditional Maori welcome onto a *marae*

quad bikes – four-wheel farm bikes

Rakiura – literally 'Land of Glowing Skies'; Maori name for Stewart Island, which is important in Maori mythology as the anchor of *Maui's* canoe

rap jump – face-down abseil

'rattle your dags' – move quickly; from the dags that hang off sheep's bottoms

raupo – bulrush

Remuera tractor – 4WD, after wealthy suburbanites pointlessly driving them

Rheiny – affectionate term for Rheineck beer

rigger – a refillable half-gallon plastic bottle for holding draught beer

rip – dangerously strong current running away from the shore at a beach

Roaring Forties – the ocean between 40° and 50° south, known for very strong winds

rumble – see *scrap*

sav – sauvignon blanc

scrap – a fight

section – small block of land

silver fern – the symbol worn by the *All Blacks* and other national sportsfolk on their jerseys, representative of the underside of a *ponga* leaf; the national netball team is called the Silver Ferns

Steinie – affectionate term for Steinlager beer

superette – grocery store or small supermarket

sweet, sweet as – all-purpose term like *choice;* fantastic, great

taiaha – spear

tall poppy syndrome – NZ tradition of diminishing successful people, as in 'tall poppies get their heads chopped off'

tane – man

tangata – people

tangata whenua – people of the land; local people

taniwha – awe-inspiring water spirit

taonga – something of great value; a treasure

tapu – a strong force in Maori life, with numerous meanings; in its simplest form it means sacred, forbidden, taboo

tatts – tattoos, often of a gang nature; as opposed to *moko*

tauihu – canoe prow

te – the (singular); see also *nga*

Te Papa – literally 'our place', the national museum in Wellington

Te Papa Atawhai – Maori name for *DOC*

te reo – literally 'the language'; the Maori language

tiki – short for *hei tiki*

tiki tour – scenic tour; roundabout way

toheroa – large clam

tohunga – priest; wizard; general expert

toi toi – tall native grass

tomo – hole; entrance to a cave

tramp – bushwalk; trek; hike

tua tua – type of shellfish

tuatara – prehistoric reptile dating back to the age of dinosaurs
tui – native parson bird
tukutuku – Maori wall panels in *marae* and churches
tuna – eel
two ticks – short measurement of time (as in 'I'll be there in *two ticks*'); see also *jiff*

umu – earth oven
urupa – burial site

varsity – university

wahine – woman
wai – water
waiata – song
Waikikamukau – mythical NZ town, far from anywhere (and pronounced along the lines of 'Why-kick-a-moo-cow')
wairua – spirit
Waitangi – short way of referring to the Treaty of Waitangi
waka – canoe

Warriors – NZ's popular rugby league club, affiliated with Australia's NRL
Watties – the NZ food and canning giant; NZ's answer to Heinz (until Heinz took over the company)
Wellywood – Wellington, because of its thriving film industry
whakairo rakau – Maori woodcarving
whakapapa – genealogy
whanau – family
whare – house
wharepuni – sleeping house
whare runanga – meeting house
whare whakairo – carved meeting house
whenua – land
whitebait – tiny translucent fish that is scooped up in nets and eaten whole (head, eyes and all!) or made into patties
wopwops – remote; 'out in the *wopwops*' is out in the middle of nowhere

zorbing – rolling down a hill inside an inflatable plastic ball

The Authors

BRETT ATKINSON   Coordinating Author, Christchurch & Canterbury, Dunedin & Otago, Fiordland & Southland, Stewart Island

Although he's lived in Auckland for four decades, Brett never misses a chance to explore the rugged mountains, lakes, and coastline of New Zealand's South Island. On his second extended research trip to the 'Mainland', he kayaked Doubtful Sound, shared the audacious scenery of Banks Peninsula and the Catlins with his family, and unearthed more than a few places to drink NZ's excellent microbrewed beers. Brett has contributed to guidebooks covering four of the planet's continents, and covered more than 40 countries as a freelance travel writer. See www.brett-atkinson.net for his latest work.

SARAH BENNETT   Wellington Region, Marlborough & Nelson

Raised among the cherry trees of Marlborough, Sarah migrated to Wellington at 16 and has lived there ever since, except for various travels and a stint in London working in Lonely Planet's UK office. An arguably flawed guidebook writer due to eternal optimism and irrepressible nationalism ('New Zealand... what's not to like?'), she has done her best to find fault wherever she can, especially in regard to ill-chosen garnish and inadequate beer selection. Sarah's other books are *The Best of Wellington*, *Let's Go Camping* and *The New Zealand Tramper's Handbook*, all of which she co-authored with her husband, Lee Slater.

SCOTT KENNEDY   The West Coast, Queenstown & Wanaka

Scott grew up in the mountains of Western Canada and has always been drawn to wild places. When he first set foot in New Zealand a decade ago he knew he'd found the place he was looking for. For the last eight years he's called Queenstown home and jumped at the chance to pass on the inside story to Lonely Planet readers. A passionate fan of the outdoors, Scott is an avid skier, mountain biker, rock climber, tramper, runner and surfer. When Scott isn't travelling the world penning guidebooks for Lonely Planet he works as a freelance writer, photographer and filmmaker – with a focus on adventure of course. Visit Scott's website at www.adventureskope.com.

LONELY PLANET AUTHORS

Why is our travel information the best in the world? It's simple: our authors are passionate, dedicated travellers. They don't take freebies in exchange for positive coverage so you can be sure the advice you're given is impartial. They travel widely to all the popular spots, and off the beaten track. They don't research using just the internet or phone. They discover new places not included in any other guidebook. They personally visit thousands of hotels, restaurants, palaces, trails, galleries, temples and more. They speak with dozens of locals every day to make sure you get the kind of insider knowledge only a local could tell you. They take pride in getting all the details right, and in telling it how it is. Think you can do it? Find out how at **lonelyplanet.com**.

THE AUTHORS

CONTRIBUTING AUTHORS

Professor James Belich wrote the History chapter (p26). James is one of NZ's pre-eminent historians and the award-winning author of *The New Zealand Wars, Making Peoples* and *Paradise Reforged*. He has also worked in TV – *New Zealand Wars* was screened in NZ in 1998.

Peter Dragicevich wrote the majority of the Culture chapter (p35). As managing editor of Auckland-based *Express* newspaper he spent much of the 90s writing about the local arts, club and bar scene. He has co-authored more than 17 books for Lonely Planet.

Tony Horwitz wrote the Captain James Cook boxed text (p29) in the History chapter. Tony is a Pulitzer-winning reporter and nonfiction author. His fascination with James Cook, and with travel, took him around NZ, Australia and the Pacific while researching *Blue Latitudes* (alternatively titled *Into the Blue*), part biography of Cook and part travelogue.

John Huria (Ngai Tahu, Muaupoko) wrote the Maori Culture chapter (p50). John has an editorial, research and writing background with a focus on Maori culture. He was senior editor for Maori publishing company Huia (NZ) and now runs an editorial and publishing services company, Ahi Text Solutions Ltd (www.ahitextsolutions.co.nz).

Lauraine Jacobs wrote the Food & Drink chapter (p57). Lauraine is an award-winning food writer, and food editor of *Cuisine* magazine. Passionate about NZ's wine and food, she travels the country extensively in her quest to seek out the best culinary experiences.

Josh Kronfeld wrote the Surfing in New Zealand boxed text (p85) in the Active New Zealand chapter. Josh is an ex–All Black flanker, whose passion for surfing NZ's beaches is legendary and who found travelling for rugby a way to surf other great breaks around the world.

Dr David Millar wrote the Health chapter (p405). David is a travel-medicine specialist, diving doctor and lecturer in wilderness medicine.

Gareth Shute wrote the Music section of the Culture chapter (p46). Gareth is the author of four books, including *Hip Hop Music in Aotearoa* and *NZ Rock 1987-2007*. He is also a musician and has toured the UK, Europe and Australia as a member of The Ruby Suns. He now plays in The Conjurors, The Investigations and The Cosbys.

Nandor Tanczos wrote the Environmental Issues in Aotearoa New Zealand boxed text (p66). NZ's first Rastafarian Member of Parliament (NZ Greens Party), and the first to enter parliament in dreadlocks and a hemp suit, he was also the Greens' spokesperson on constitutional issues and the environment from 1999 to 2008.

Vaughan Yarwood wrote the Environment chapter (p64). Vaughan is an Auckland-based writer whose most recent book is *The History Makers: Adventures in New Zealand Biography*. Earlier work includes *The Best of New Zealand, a Collection of Essays on NZ Life and Culture by Prominent Kiwis,* which he edited, and the regional history *Between Coasts: from Kaipara to Kawau*. He has written widely for NZ and international publications and is the former associate editor of *New Zealand Geographic,* for which he continues to write.

Thanks to: Sir Ian McKellen (Sandflies boxed text, p382); Grace Hoet for her contribution to the Maori Culture chapter; and all the New Zealand regional tourism organisations, for their help with pre-research briefings.

Behind the Scenes

THIS BOOK

Lonely Planet's first New Zealand guide came out way back in 1977, when Tony Wheeler, clad in corduroy flares and wide-collared shirt, trawled the length of the island nation to research the book. Over thirty years later, our first South Island guide was coordinated by Charles Rawlings-Way. This second-edition guide to the South was re-searched and written anew by Brett Atkinson, Sarah Bennett and Scott Kennedy. Contributing authors include historian Professor James Belich, journo Tony Horwitz, Maori publisher John Huria, food-award judge Lauraine Jacobs, surfer Josh Kronfeld, health expert Dr David Millar, musician/author Gareth Shute, environmental activist Nandor Tanczos, and author Vaughan Yarwood. The guidebook was commissioned in Lonely Planet's Melbourne office, and produced by the following:

Commissioning Editor Errol Hunt
Coordinating Editor Chris Girdler
Coordinating Cartographer Hunor Csutoros
Coordinating Layout Designer Kerrianne Southway
Managing Editor Liz Heynes
Managing Cartographers David Connolly, Corey Hutchison
Managing Layout Designer Indra Kilfoyle
Assisting Editors Elisa Arduca, Jackey Coyle, Kate Evans, Anne Mulvaney, Alison Ridgway, Dianne Schallmeiner, Elizabeth Swan, Angela Tinson, Simon Williamson

Assisting Cartographer Alex Leung
Cover Naomi Parker, lonelyplanetimages.com
Internal Image Research Jane Hart, lonelyplanet images.com
Language Content Laura Crawford
Thanks to Imogen Bannister, Sarah Ewing, James Hardy, Lisa Knights, Daniel Moore, Susan Paterson, Averil Robertson, Suzannah Shwer, Jane Thompson, Saralinda Turner, Chris Zeiher

THANKS
BRETT ATKINSON

Firstly thanks to my mother and father, and wife Carol, for sharing parts of this research trip with me. Now you know what I really get up to when I disappear for six weeks at a time. Thanks also to the thoroughly professional staff at all the i-SITEs, DOC offices, and visitor information centres I tapped for vital facts before, during, and after my research trip. It's always great to work with commissioning editor Errol Hunt, and the rest of the Kiwi-as author team.

SARAH BENNETT

First up, thanks to helpful pals Betzy Iannuzzi, Bonita Marshall, Jenny Allan, Reece Miller, Trecia Smith, Marla Grau, Fritz Kuckuck, Tricia and Stewart Macpherson, the Wellington posse, and

THE LONELY PLANET STORY

Fresh from an epic journey across Europe, Asia and Australia in 1972, Tony and Maureen Wheeler sat at their kitchen table stapling together notes. The first Lonely Planet guidebook, *Across Asia on the Cheap*, was born.

Travellers snapped up the guides. Inspired by their success, the Wheelers began publishing books to Southeast Asia, India and beyond. Demand was prodigious, and the Wheelers expanded the business rapidly to keep up. Over the years, Lonely Planet extended its coverage to every country and into the virtual world via lonelyplanet.com and the Thorn Tree message board.

As Lonely Planet became a globally loved brand, Tony and Maureen received several offers for the company. But it wasn't until 2007 that they found a partner whom they trusted to remain true to the company's principles of travelling widely, treading lightly and giving sustainably. In October of that year, BBC Worldwide acquired a 75% share in the company, pledging to uphold Lonely Planet's commitment to independent travel, trustworthy advice and editorial independence.

Today, Lonely Planet has offices in Melbourne, London and Oakland, with over 500 staff members and 300 authors. Tony and Maureen are still actively involved with Lonely Planet. They're traveling more often than ever, and they're devoting their spare time to charitable projects. And the company is still driven by the philosophy of *Across Asia on the Cheap*: 'All you've got to do is decide to go and the hardest part is over. So go!'

the Bennett clan. Thanks, too, to the many i-SITE and RTO people who shared their time and insight, especially Tina Narsey, Rebecca Mitchell, Chris Barber, Gaylene Sanderson, Astrid Fisher, Amy Chandler, Rachael Brown, Tracy Johnston, Brent Matthews, Vicky Roebuck, Barbara Hyde, and winery experts Lucy Chambers and Julia Hill. I wish to acknowledge the contribution of all the friendly folks who helped me out on the road, and my fellow authors and editors who supported me through the ether. As ever, my deepest gratitude to Lee – you make every day a flight in a microlight.

SCOTT KENNEDY

Thanks to my fellow authors Brett and Sarah – it's a pleasure to share a title page with this fine lot. Big thanks to our fabulous and fearless editor Errol Hunt who always kept it fun. To all of the fellow travellers I met along the way who offered advice, shared your experiences and helped me out, I owe you all a huge thanks. All of the hoteliers, restaurateurs, activity operators and tireless visitor centre staff who answered all my questions – cheers guys. Big thanks to the all-star team – Christian Martin, Alice Hill, Brett Black, Adrian Nankivell, Ned Myopus, Mark Banham, Steve Wilson, 'GC' Mike, Katy Shorthouse, Debbie Nelson, Andy

---

SEND US YOUR FEEDBACK

We love to hear from travellers – your comments keep us on our toes and help make our books better. Our well-travelled team reads every word on what you loved or loathed about this book. Although we cannot reply individually to postal submissions, we always guarantee that your feedback goes straight to the appropriate authors, in time for the next edition. Each person who sends us information is thanked in the next edition and the most useful submissions are rewarded with a free book.

To send us your updates – and find out about Lonely Planet events, newsletters and travelnews–visitouraward-winningwebsite: **lonelyplanet.com/contact**.

Note: we may edit, reproduce and incorporate your comments in Lonely Planet products such as guidebooks, websites and digital products, so let us know if you don't want your comments reproduced or your name acknowledged. For a copy of our privacy policy visit lonelyplanet.com/privacy.

McDonald, Jan & Steve, Di Liddell, Shaun, Becs & Tannin. To mom and dad thanks for all your support over the years and to my wonderful wife Sophie – for everything.

OUR READERS

Many thanks to the travellers who used the last edition and wrote to us with helpful hints, useful advice and interesting anecdotes:

A Elisabeth Nordeng Aanes, John Adam, Nikki Annand **B** Heike Baars, Selina Barlet, Rebecca Barnshaw, Bridget Beal, Neil Beaumont, Chris Beek, Nicolas Berger, Insa Beuse, Ben Blee, Jason Borthwick, Judy Bounds, Euan Brown, Catherine Bruckner, Anna Bucholz, Wilco Burghout, Lee Burrows **C** Geoff Caflisch, Sue Cebulko, Laura Claassen, Tiere Clynich, Brendan Connolly, Nicola Coombe, Georgie Curtis, Jonathan Cutler **D** Matthew Dalton, Stuart & Pamela Davis, Annelies De Bruijne, Jan Dependahl, Jo Drew, Tarne Duffield, Angela Dunlop, Alison Dye **E** Alec Edwards, Bernadette Ekberg, Rowan Enright, Jo Evans **F** Robin Falvey, Mutiara Förster, Nick Fowler **G** Franck Gally, Juliane Gansert, Eleanor Gee, Tanya Genthe, Bob Gilchrist, Katherine Golding, Sharine Gordon, Ed Groves, Peter Gush, Stuart Guy **H** Steven Hankey, Bernie Healy, Glenda Heywood, Jo Hibbert, Dave Hill, Leah Holloway, Libby Howard-Blood, Barbara Huijgen **I** Jaki Ilbery, **K** Robert Kennedy, Huia Kirk, Rolf Knütter **L** Barry Landesman, Steve Lavezzo, Carol Lee, Robert Levy, Ann Lewis, Brian & Lorna Lewis, Beate Lippold **M** Michael MacBroom, Jerome Magisson, John Mandeville, Hanna Manski, Jane Manson, Stephen Marais, Lou McCarthy, Gail McConnell, Gillian McIlroy, Jan McVerry, Lisa Moeller, Chris Monson, Melanie Morcom, Bruce Morris, Hugh & Eileen Morton, Alastair Moulton **N** Patrick Näf, Greg Napp, Surasak Netraprajag, Nick Newman, David Nicola, Alexandra Nisbeck, Ronald Noordstrand, Graeme Nye **O** Andrea O'Connor, Michael Ortiz, Jenny Owen, Maurice Owen **P** Benoît Panizzon, Natasha Parker-Coughlin, Marie Parton, Lindsay Petrie, Daniela Petroni, Rochelle Pincini, Katerina Poddana, Neville Pulver, Kerrie Purrington **R** Barbara Rausch, Jim Revell, John Rieley, Christine Rikihana, Valentina Baez Rizzi, Jeffrey Robinson, Louise Rothols, Alba Rull, Jenna Russell **S** Kane Salanoa, Nathan Sandland-Jones, Miriam Schaefer, Miriam Scherpenzeel, Sybil Schlesinger, Lukas Schomann, Armand Schumer, Jonathan Sims, Frank Sinclair, Ray Sinniger, Maren Skrinjar, Afke Smolders, Raina Reva Snyder, Julie Stapleton, Sue Stone, Mona Strandberg, Anne Street **T** David Taylor, Sarah Taylor, Steve Taylor,

Monique Teggelove, Britta Thiel, Cathelijne Thiel, Petra Joho Thomma, Kay Toon, Steve Tritt **W** Amanda Watson, Arthur Watts, Kim Whitty, Jackie Whyte, Sven Wiechert, Hanneke Wijkamp, Lynda Willow, Carol Wilson, Tim Wilson, David Wilson-Howarth **Y** Holly Yelf, Kit Yoon **Z** Cosetta Zanobetti-Lawlor

ACKNOWLEDGMENTS
Many thanks to the following for the use of their content:

Globe on title page ©Mountain High Maps 1993 Digital Wisdom, Inc.

On the Road: photograph of Scott Kennedy courtesy of Shotover Canyon Swing.

Auto Parts
379-9851

Index

INDEX

INDEX

INDEX

INDEX

GreenDex

GOING GREEN

As Kermit the Frog asserts, it's not easy being green, but in tourism these days everyone wants to be 'eco'. But how can you know which businesses are legitimately ecofriendly and which are just jumping on the sustainable bandwagon?

The following listings have been selected by Lonely Planet authors because they demonstrate active sustainable-tourism policies. Some are involved in conservation or environmental education; many are owned and operated by local and indigenous operators, thus preserving local identity and culture. Some are also accredited by **Qualmark Green** (www.qualmark.co.nz) or listed by **Organic Explorer** (www.organicexplorer.co.nz).

All national parks and reserves (see the main index) and DOC–controlled areas (marked on maps) preserve native bush and fauna, and are by their very nature 'green'.

If you think we've omitted someone or you disagree with our choices, email us at talk2us@ lonelyplanet.com.au and set us straight. For more information about sustainable tourism and Lonely Planet, see www.lonelyplanet.com/responsibletravel.

GREENDEX

MAP LEGEND

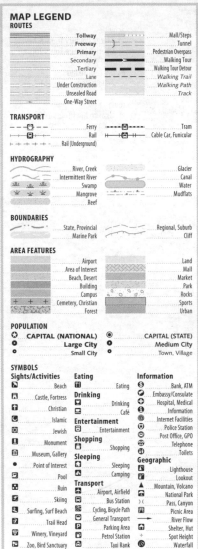

ROUTES

Tollway
Freeway
Primary
Secondary
Tertiary
Lane
Under Construction
Unsealed Road
One-Way Street

Mall/Steps
Tunnel
Pedestrian Overpass
Walking Tour
Walking Tour Detour
Walking Trail
Walking Path
Track

TRANSPORT

Ferry
Rail
Rail (Underground)

Tram
Cable Car, Funicular

HYDROGRAPHY

River, Creek
Intermittent River
Swamp
Mangrove
Reef

Glacier
Canal
Water
Mudflats

BOUNDARIES

State, Provincial
Marine Park

Regional, Suburb
Cliff

AREA FEATURES

Airport
Area of Interest
Beach, Desert
Building
Campus
Cemetery, Christian
Forest

Land
Mall
Market
Park
Rocks
Sports
Urban

POPULATION

⊛ **CAPITAL (NATIONAL)**
● **Large City**
● Small City

◉ **CAPITAL (STATE)**
● **Medium City**
° Town, Village

SYMBOLS

Sights/Activities
🐾 Beach
🏰 Castle, Fortress
✝ Christian
☪ Islamic
✡ Jewish
🗽 Monument
🏛 Museum, Gallery
● Point of Interest
🏊 Pool
🏛 Ruin
⛷ Skiing
🏄 Surfing, Surf Beach
🥾 Trail Head
🍇 Winery, Vineyard
🐦 Zoo, Bird Sanctuary

Eating
🍴 Eating

Drinking
☕ Drinking
☕ Café

Entertainment
🎭 Entertainment

Shopping
🛍 Shopping

Sleeping
🛏 Sleeping
⛺ Camping

Transport
✈ Airport, Airfield
🚌 Bus Station
🚲 Cycling, Bicycle Path
🚍 General Transport
🅿 Parking Area
⛽ Petrol Station
🚕 Taxi Rank

Information
🏧 Bank, ATM
🛂 Embassy/Consulate
➕ Hospital, Medical
ℹ Information
@ Internet Facilities
👮 Police Station
📮 Post Office, GPO
📞 Telephone
🚻 Toilets

Geographic
🗼 Lighthouse
👁 Lookout
▲ Mountain, Volcano
🏞 National Park
)(Pass, Canyon
🏕 Picnic Area
River Flow
🏠 Shelter, Hut
+ Spot Height
🌊 Waterfall

LONELY PLANET OFFICES

Australia (Head Office)
Locked Bag 1, Footscray, Victoria 3011
☎ 03 8379 8000, fax 03 8379 8111
talk2us@lonelyplanet.com.au

USA
150 Linden St, Oakland, CA 94607
☎ 510 250 6400, toll free 800 275 8555
fax 510 893 8572
info@lonelyplanet.com

UK
2nd fl, 186 City Rd,
London EC1V 2NT
☎ 020 7106 2100, fax 020 7106 2101
go@lonelyplanet.co.uk

Published by Lonely Planet Publications Pty Ltd
ABN 36 005 607 983

© Lonely Planet 2010

© photographers as indicated 2010

Cover photograph: Mt Cook National Park, Canterbury, Gareth McCormack/Lonely Planet Images. Many of the images in this guide are available for licensing from Lonely Planet Images: lonelyplanetimages.com.

Printed by Toppan Security Printing Pte. Ltd.
Printed in Singapore

Mixed Sources
Product group from well-managed forests and other controlled sources
www.fsc.org Cert no. SGS-COC-005002
© 1996 Forest Stewardship Council